PAYING THE LAND

ALSO BY JOE SACCO

War Junkie

Safe Area Goražde: The War in Eastern Bosnia, 1992–1995

Palestine

The Fixer: A Story from Sarajevo

Notes from a Defeatist

War's End: Profiles from Bosnia, 1995–1996

Footnotes in Gaza

Days of Destruction, Days of Revolt
(with Chris Hedges)

Journalism

The Great War: July 1, 1916, The First Day of the Battle of the Somme

PAYING THE LAND

JOE SACCO

METROPOLITAN BOOKS

HENRY HOLT AND COMPANY   NEW YORK

Metropolitan Books
Henry Holt and Company
Publishers since 1866
120 Broadway
New York, New York 10271

Metropolitan Books® and m® are registered trademarks of
Macmillan Publishing Group, LLC.

Copyright © 2020 by Joe Sacco
All rights reserved.
Distributed in Canada by Raincoast Book Distribution Limited

Library of Congress Cataloging-in-Publication Data

Names: Sacco, Joe, author, artist.
Title: Paying the land / Joe Sacco.
Description: New York : Metropolitan Books, Henry Holt and Company, [2020] | Chiefly illustrated.
Identifiers: LCCN 2019053376 (print) | LCCN 2019053377 (ebook) | ISBN 9781627799034 (hardcover) | ISBN 9781627799027 (ebook)
Subjects: LCSH: Chipewyan Indians—Northwest Territories—Mackenzie River Valley—Social conditions—Comic books, strips, etc. | Indians, Treatment of—Northwest Territories—Mackenzie River Valley—Comic books, strips, etc. | LCGFT: Social issue comics. | Nonfiction comics.
Classification: LCC E99.C59 S23 2020 (print) | LCC E99.C59 (ebook) | DDC 971.2004/972—dc23
LC record available at https://lccn.loc.gov/2019053376
LC ebook record available at https://lccn.loc.gov/2019053377

Our books may be purchased in bulk for promotional, educational, or business use. Please contact your local bookseller or the Macmillan Corporate and Premium Sales Department at (800) 221-7945, extension 5442, or by e-mail at MacmillanSpecialMarkets@macmillan.com.

First Edition 2020

Designed by Kelly S. Too

Printed in the United States of America

1 3 5 7 9 10 8 6 4 2

To the people of the land

I

YOU FIND YOURSELF IN THE CIRCLE

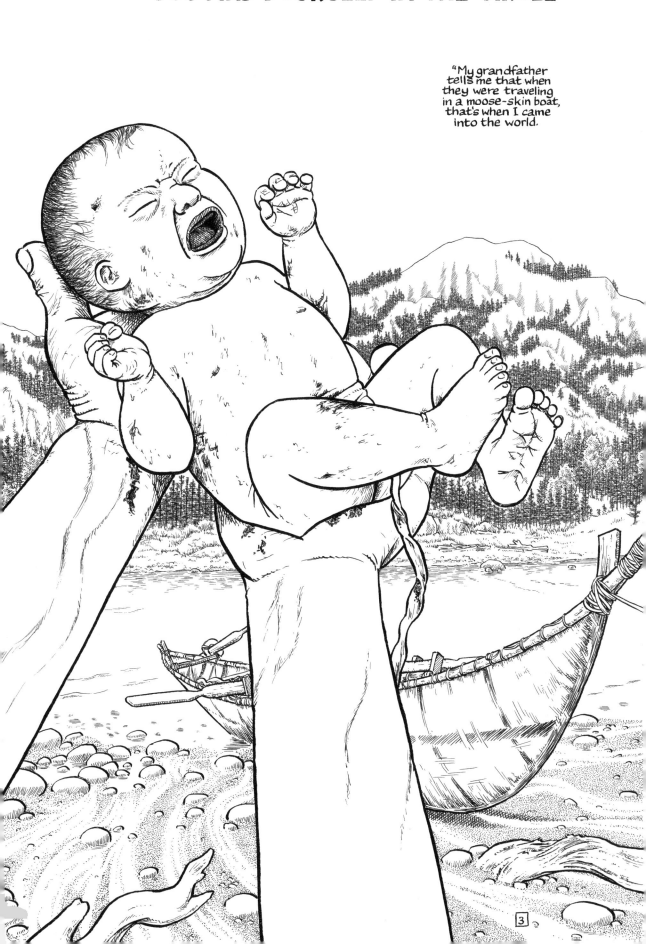

"My grandfather tells me that when they were traveling in a moose-skin boat, that's when I came into the world.

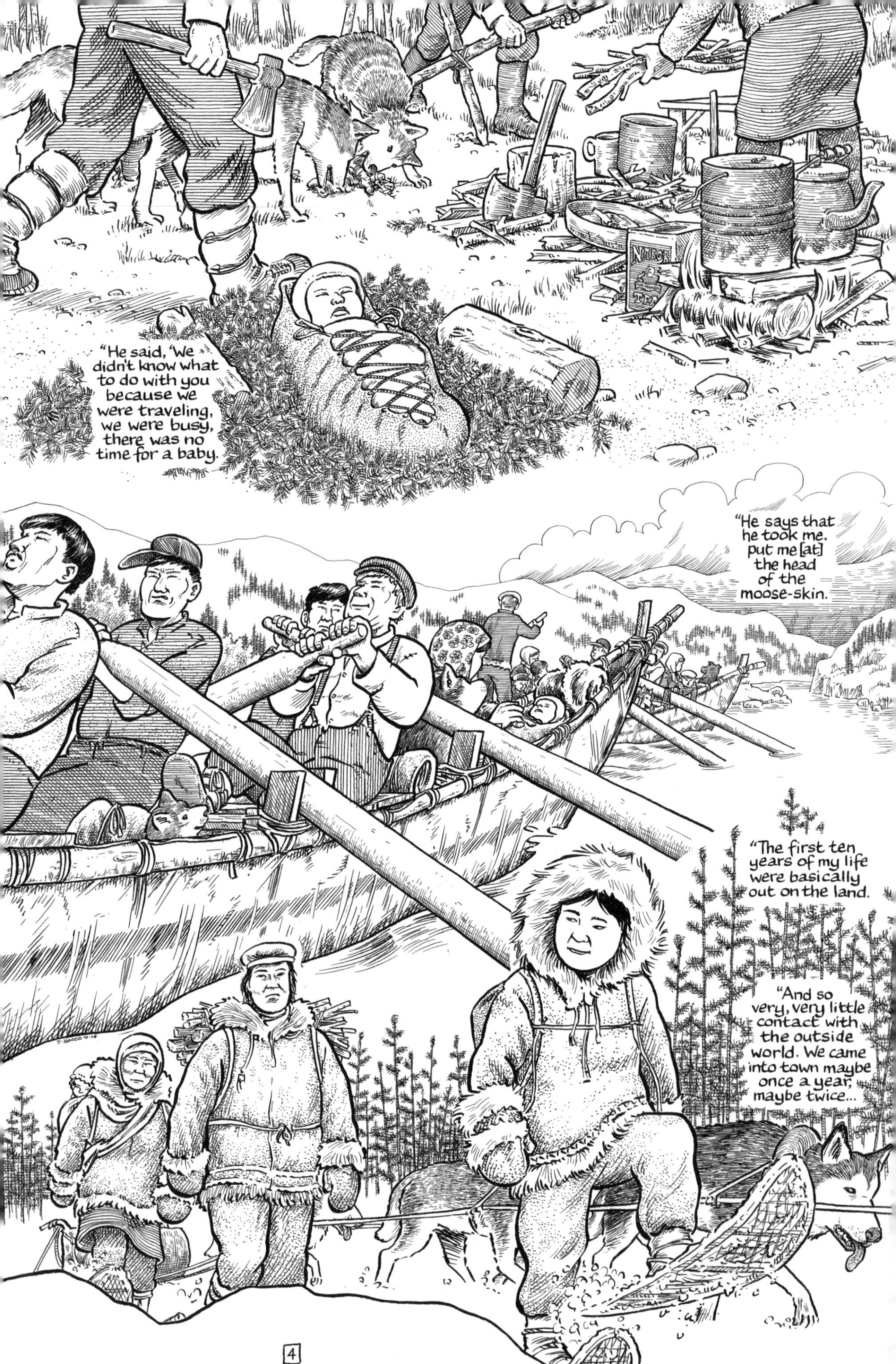
"He said, 'We didn't know what to do with you because we were traveling, we were busy, there was no time for a baby.
"He says that he took me, put me [at] the head of the moose-skin.
"The first ten years of my life were basically out on the land.
"And so very, very little contact with the outside world. We came into town maybe once a year, maybe twice...

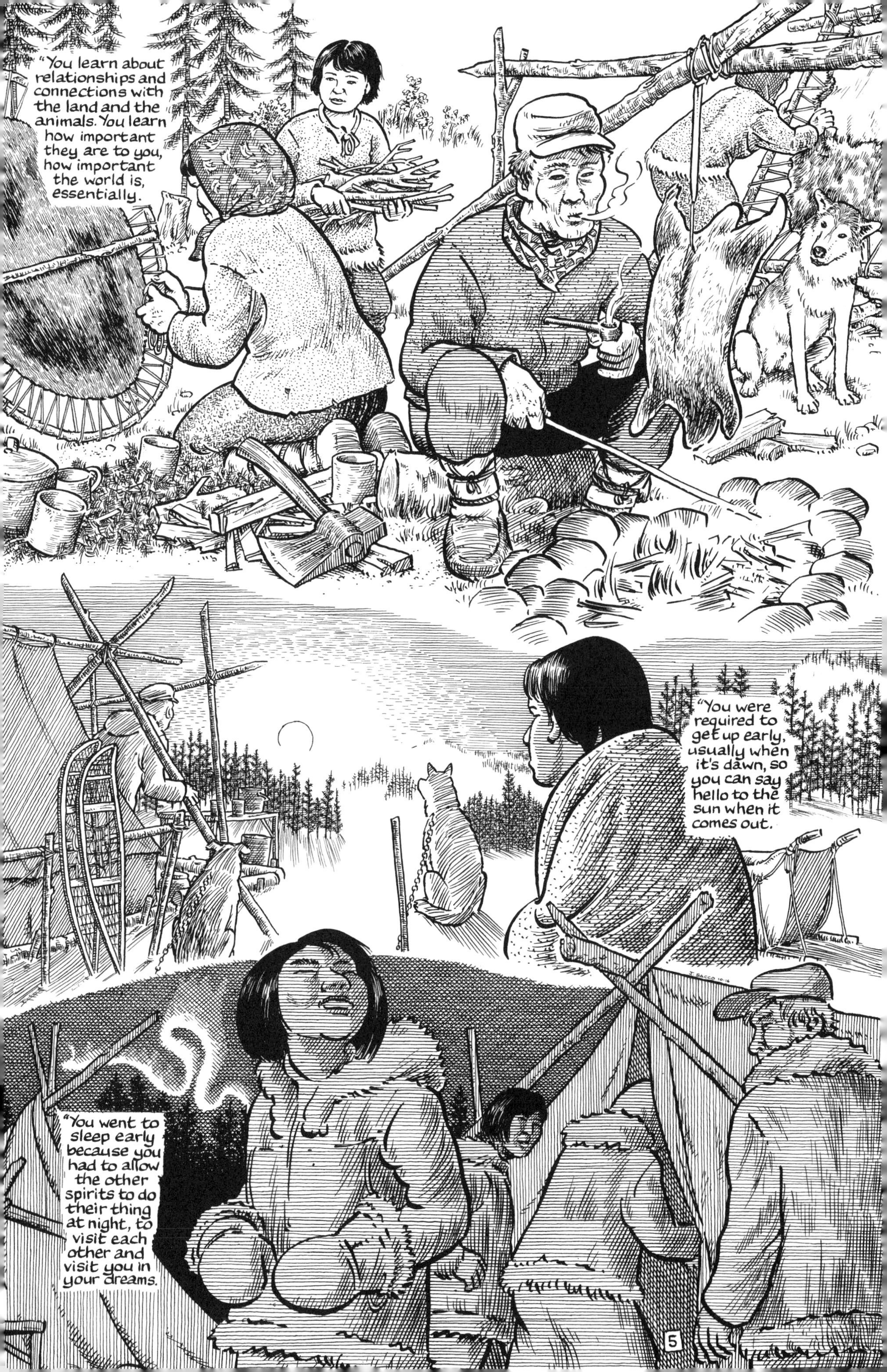
"You learn about relationships and connections with the land and the animals. You learn how important they are to you, how important the world is, essentially.
"You were required to get up early, usually when it's dawn, so you can say hello to the sun when it comes out.
"You went to sleep early because you had to allow the other spirits to do their thing at night, to visit each other and visit you in your dreams.
J. Sacco 10.16
5

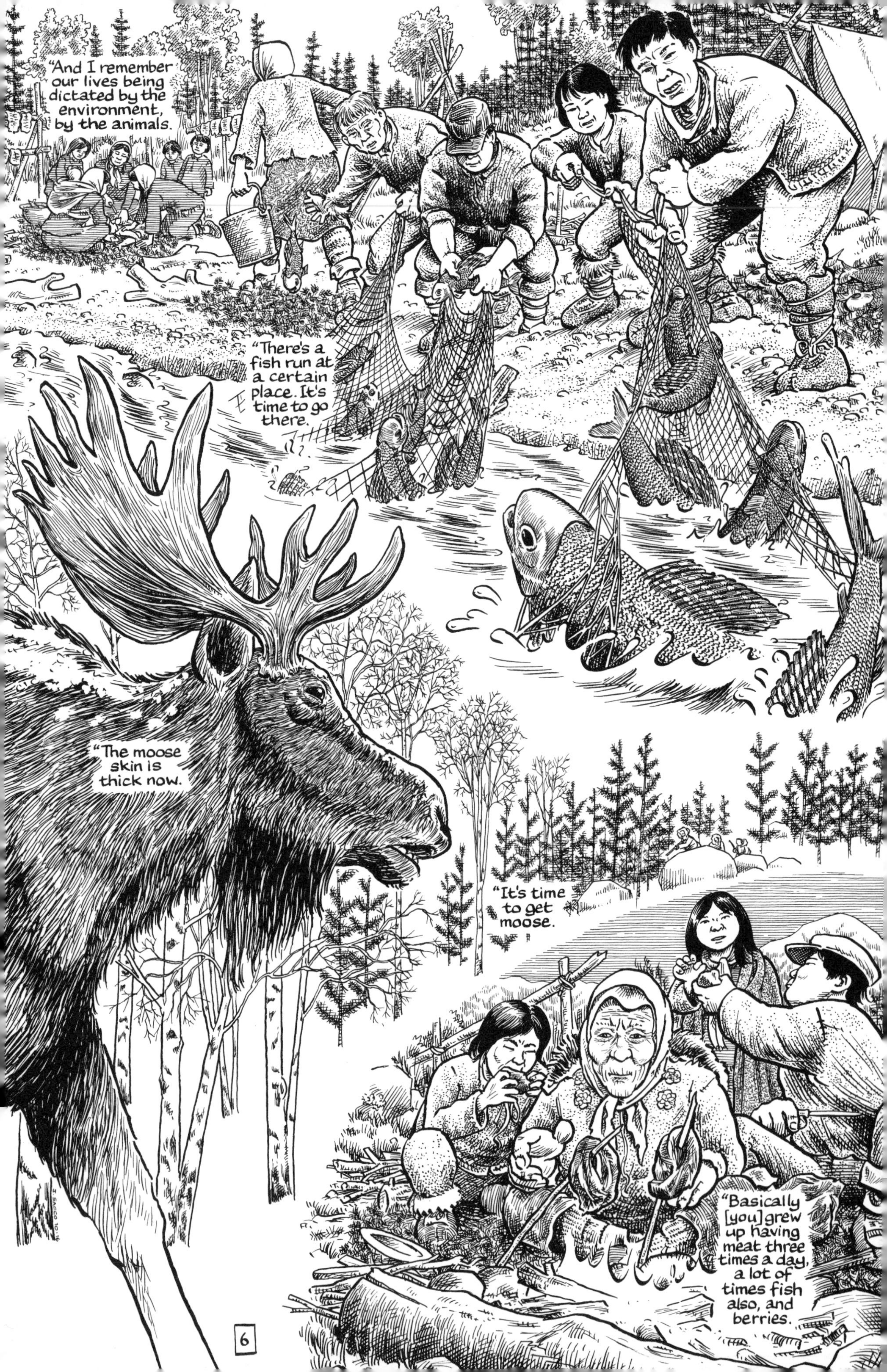

"And I remember our lives being dictated by the environment, by the animals.
"There's a fish run at a certain place. It's time to go there.
"The moose skin is thick now.
"It's time to get moose.
"Basically [you] grew up having meat three times a day, a lot of times fish also, and berries.

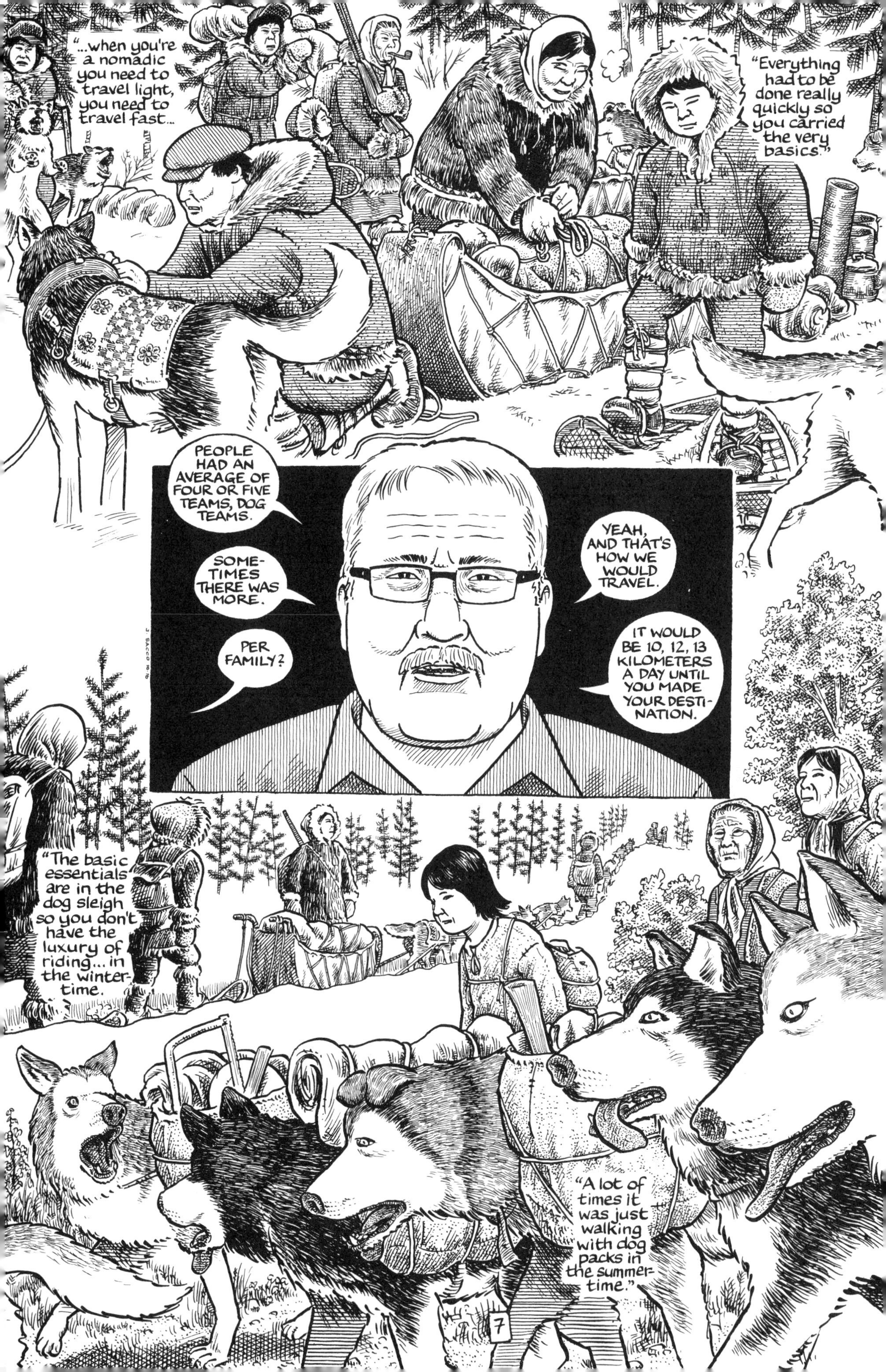

"...when you're a nomadic you need to travel light, you need to travel fast...
"Everything had to be done really quickly so you carried the very basics."
PEOPLE HAD AN AVERAGE OF FOUR OR FIVE TEAMS, DOG TEAMS.
SOME-TIMES THERE WAS MORE.
PER FAMILY?
YEAH, AND THAT'S HOW WE WOULD TRAVEL.
IT WOULD BE 10, 12, 13 KILOMETERS A DAY UNTIL YOU MADE YOUR DESTI-NATION.
"The basic essentials are in the dog sleigh so you don't have the luxury of riding... in the winter-time.
"A lot of times it was just walking with dog packs in the summer-time."

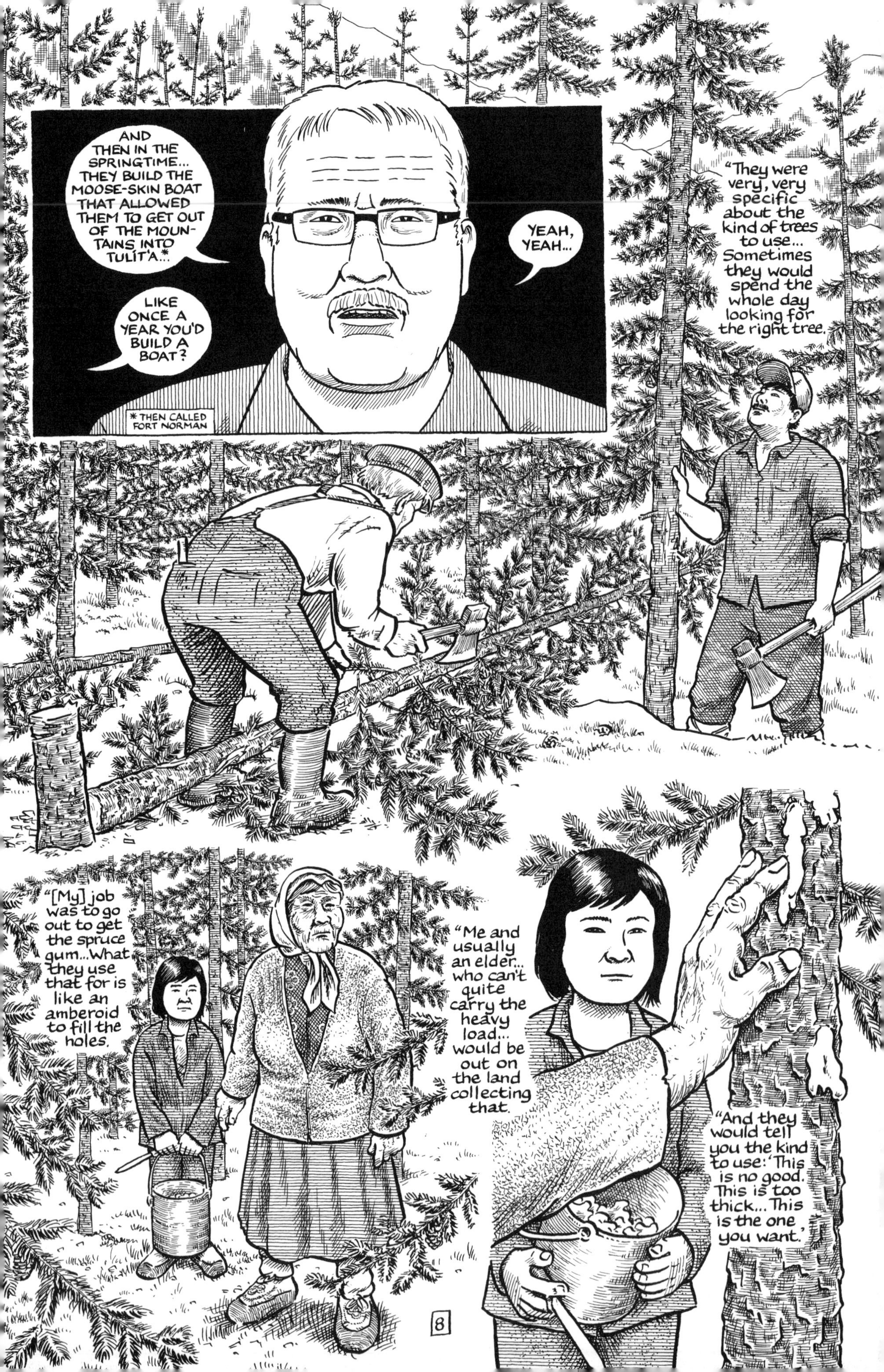
AND THEN IN THE SPRINGTIME... THEY BUILD THE MOOSE-SKIN BOAT THAT ALLOWED THEM TO GET OUT OF THE MOUNTAINS INTO TULIT'A...*
LIKE ONCE A YEAR YOU'D BUILD A BOAT?
YEAH, YEAH...
*THEN CALLED FORT NORMAN
"They were very, very specific about the kind of trees to use... Sometimes they would spend the whole day looking for the right tree.
"[My] job was to go out to get the spruce gum... What they use that for is like an amberoid to fill the holes.
"Me and usually an elder... who can't quite carry the heavy load... would be out on the land collecting that.
"And they would tell you the kind to use: 'This is no good. This is too thick... This is the one you want.'

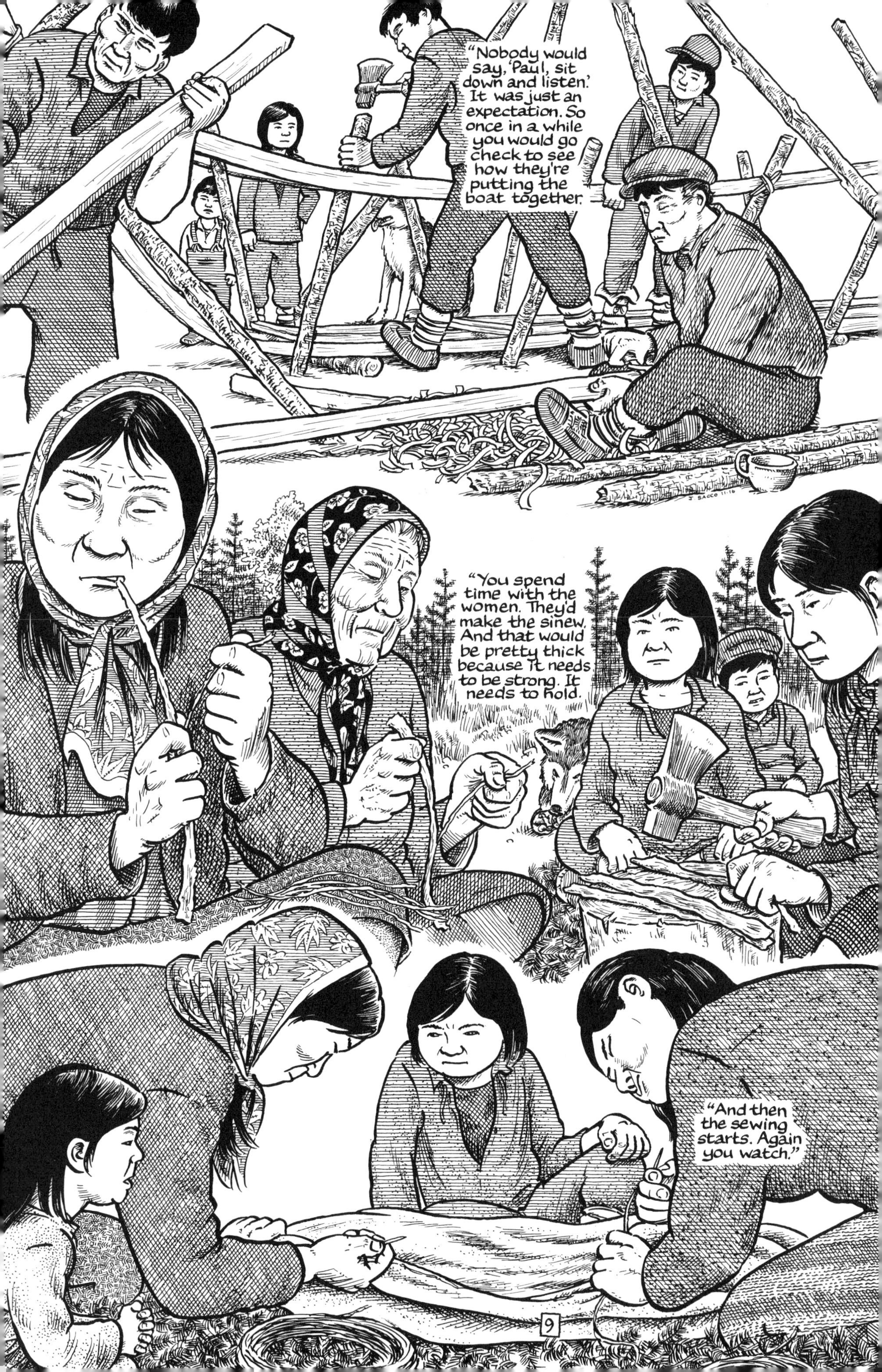
"Nobody would say, 'Paul, sit down and listen.' It was just an expectation. So once in a while you would go check to see how they're putting the boat together.
J. SACCO 11-16
"You spend time with the women. They'd make the sinew. And that would be pretty thick because it needs to be strong. It needs to hold.
"And then the sewing starts. Again you watch."

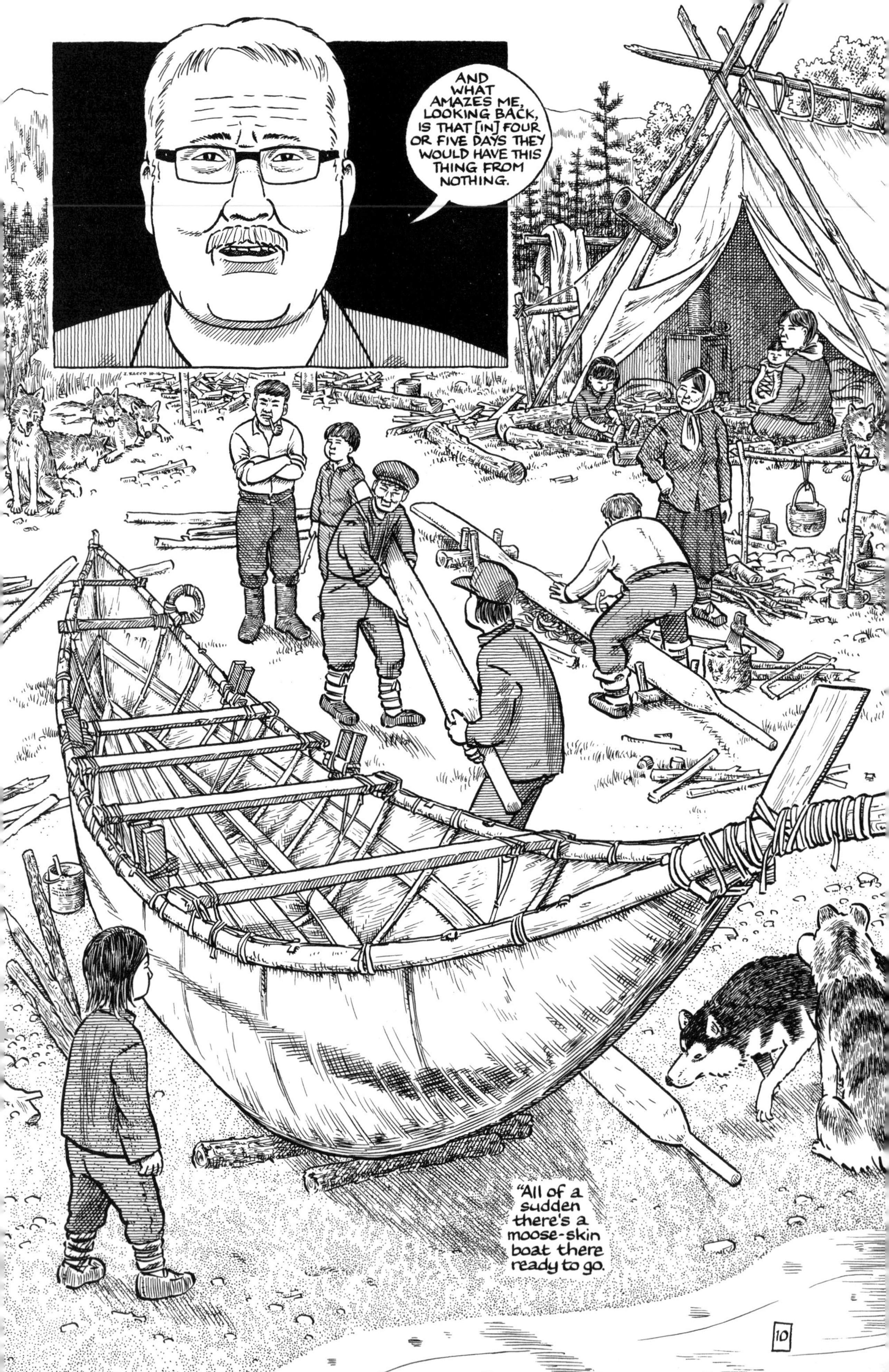
AND WHAT AMAZES ME, LOOKING BACK, IS THAT [IN] FOUR OR FIVE DAYS THEY WOULD HAVE THIS THING FROM NOTHING.
"All of a sudden there's a moose-skin boat there ready to go.

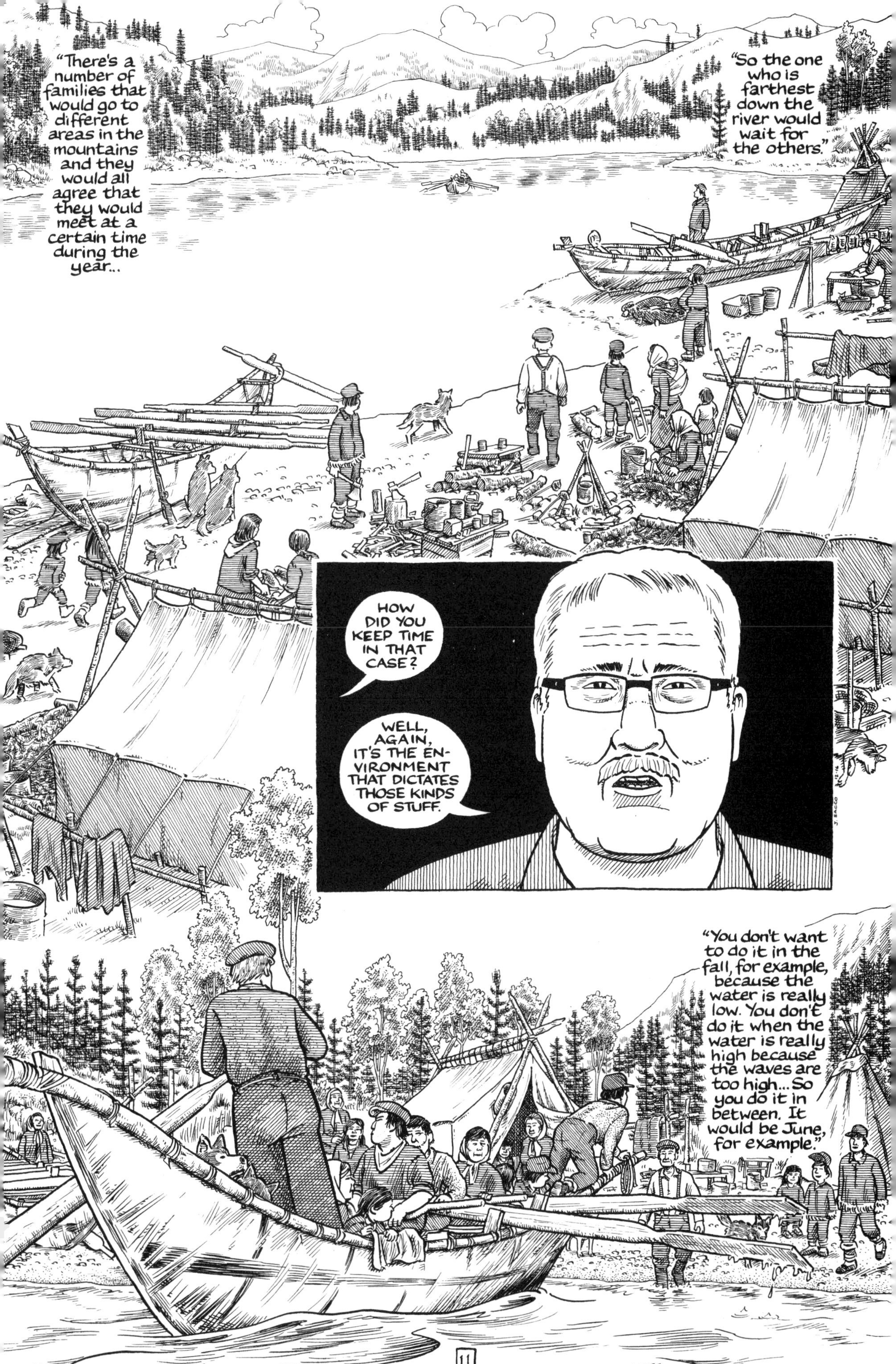
"There's a number of families that would go to different areas in the mountains and they would all agree that they would meet at a certain time during the year...
"So the one who is farthest down the river would wait for the others."
HOW DID YOU KEEP TIME IN THAT CASE?
WELL, AGAIN, IT'S THE EN-VIRONMENT THAT DICTATES THOSE KINDS OF STUFF.
"You don't want to do it in the fall, for example, because the water is really low. You don't do it when the water is really high because the waves are too high... So you do it in between. It would be June, for example."

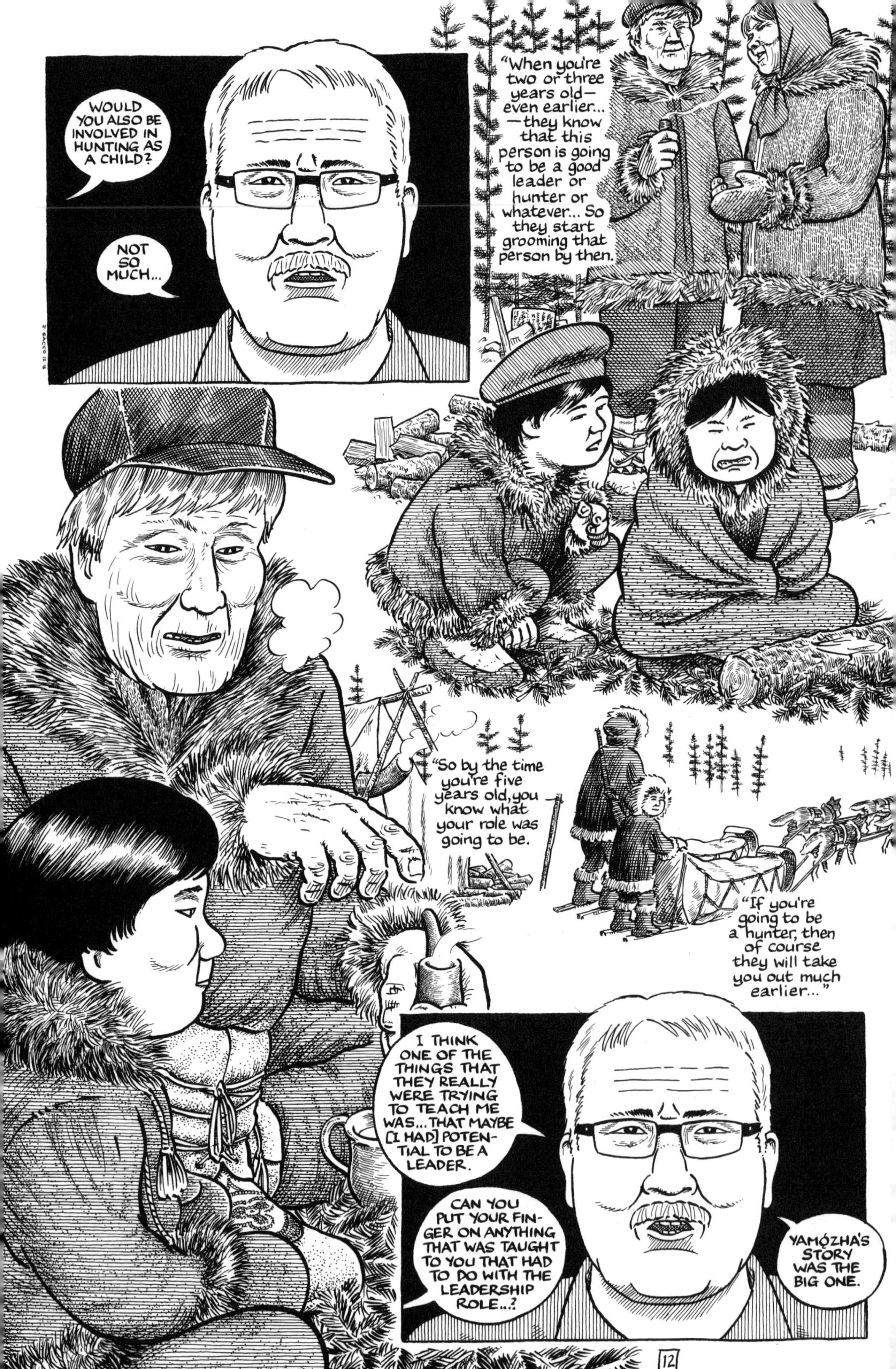

WOULD YOU ALSO BE INVOLVED IN HUNTING AS A CHILD?
NOT SO MUCH...
"When you're two or three years old— even earlier... —they know that this person is going to be a good leader or hunter or whatever... So they start grooming that person by then.
"So by the time you're five years old, you know what your role was going to be.
"If you're going to be a hunter, then of course they will take you out much earlier..."
I THINK ONE OF THE THINGS THAT THEY REALLY WERE TRYING TO TEACH ME WAS... THAT MAYBE [I HAD] POTEN-TIAL TO BE A LEADER.
CAN YOU PUT YOUR FIN-GER ON ANYTHING THAT WAS TAUGHT TO YOU THAT HAD TO DO WITH THE LEADERSHIP ROLE...?
YAMÓZHA'S STORY WAS THE BIG ONE.

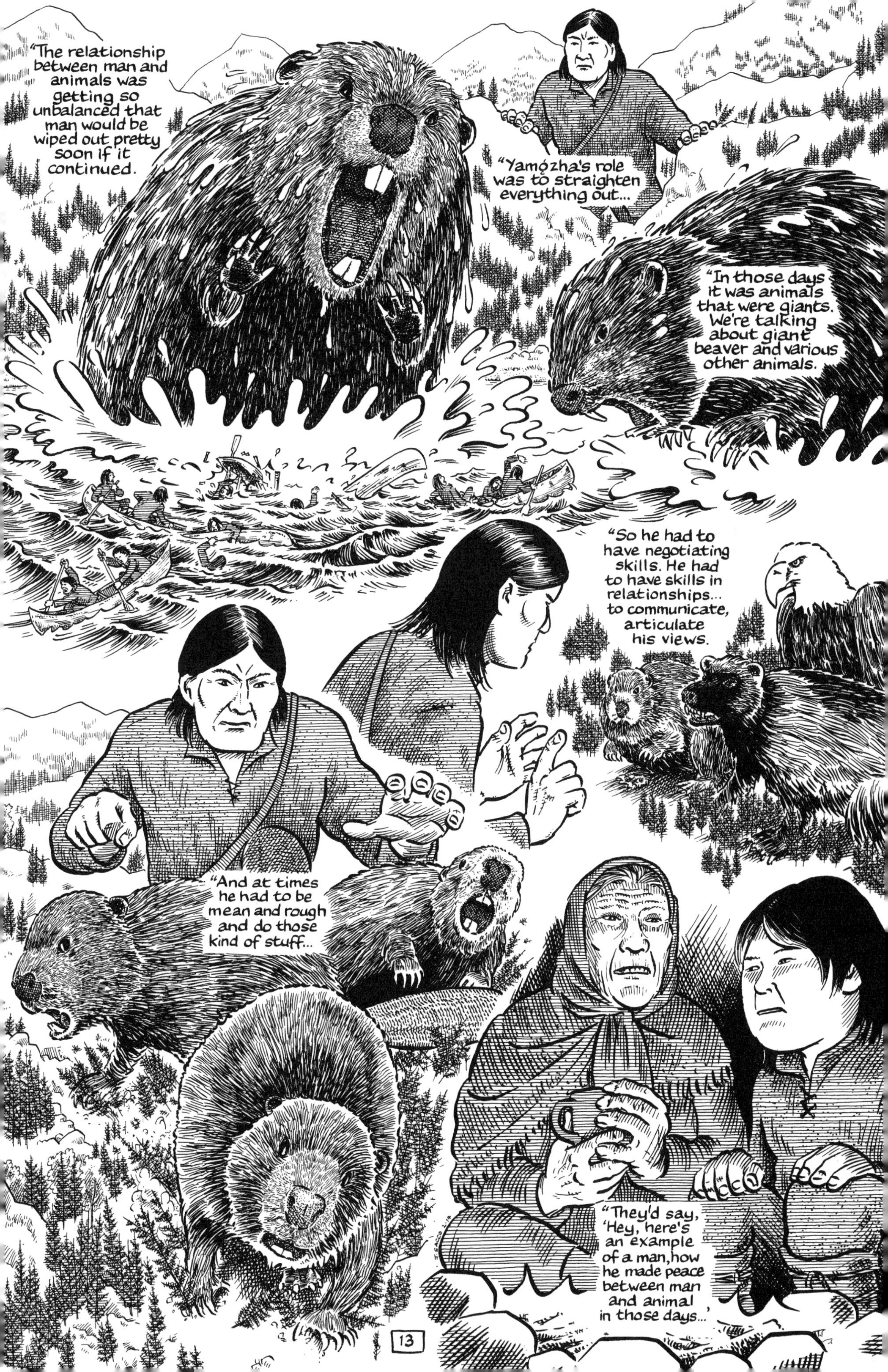
"The relationship between man and animals was getting so unbalanced that man would be wiped out pretty soon if it continued.
"In those days it was animals that were giants. We're talking about giant beaver and various other animals.
"Yamózha's role was to straighten everything out...
"So he had to have negotiating skills. He had to have skills in relationships... to communicate, articulate his views.
"And at times he had to be mean and rough and do those kind of stuff...
"They'd say, 'Hey, here's an example of a man, how he made peace between man and animal in those days...'

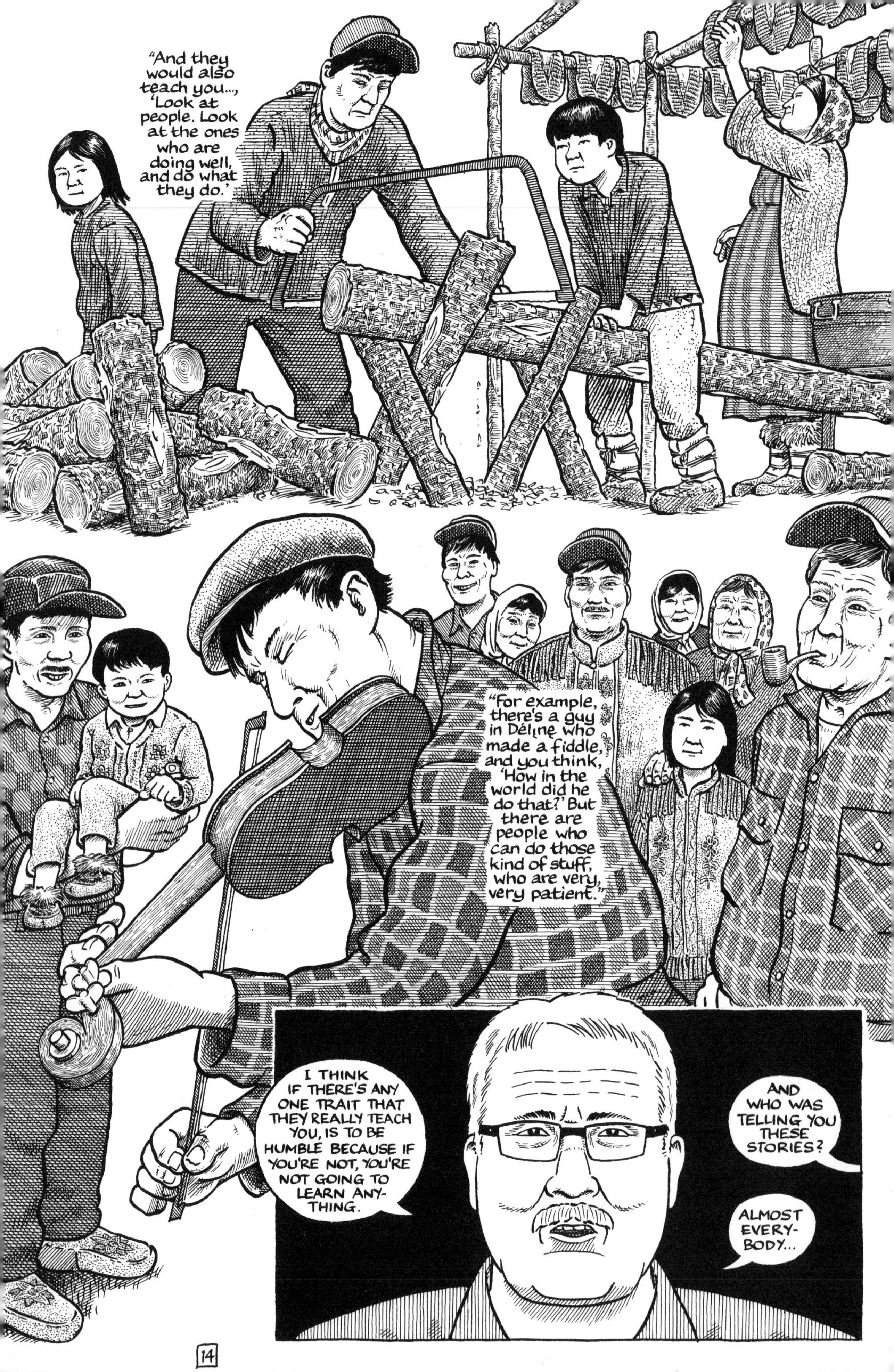
"And they would also teach you..., 'Look at people. Look at the ones who are doing well, and do what they do.'
J.SACCO 12-16
"For example, there's a guy in Délı̨nę who made a fiddle, and you think, 'How in the world did he do that?' But there are people who can do those kind of stuff, who are very, very patient."
I THINK IF THERE'S ANY ONE TRAIT THAT THEY REALLY TEACH YOU, IS TO BE HUMBLE BECAUSE IF YOU'RE NOT, YOU'RE NOT GOING TO LEARN ANY-THING.
AND WHO WAS TELLING YOU THESE STORIES?
ALMOST EVERY-BODY...

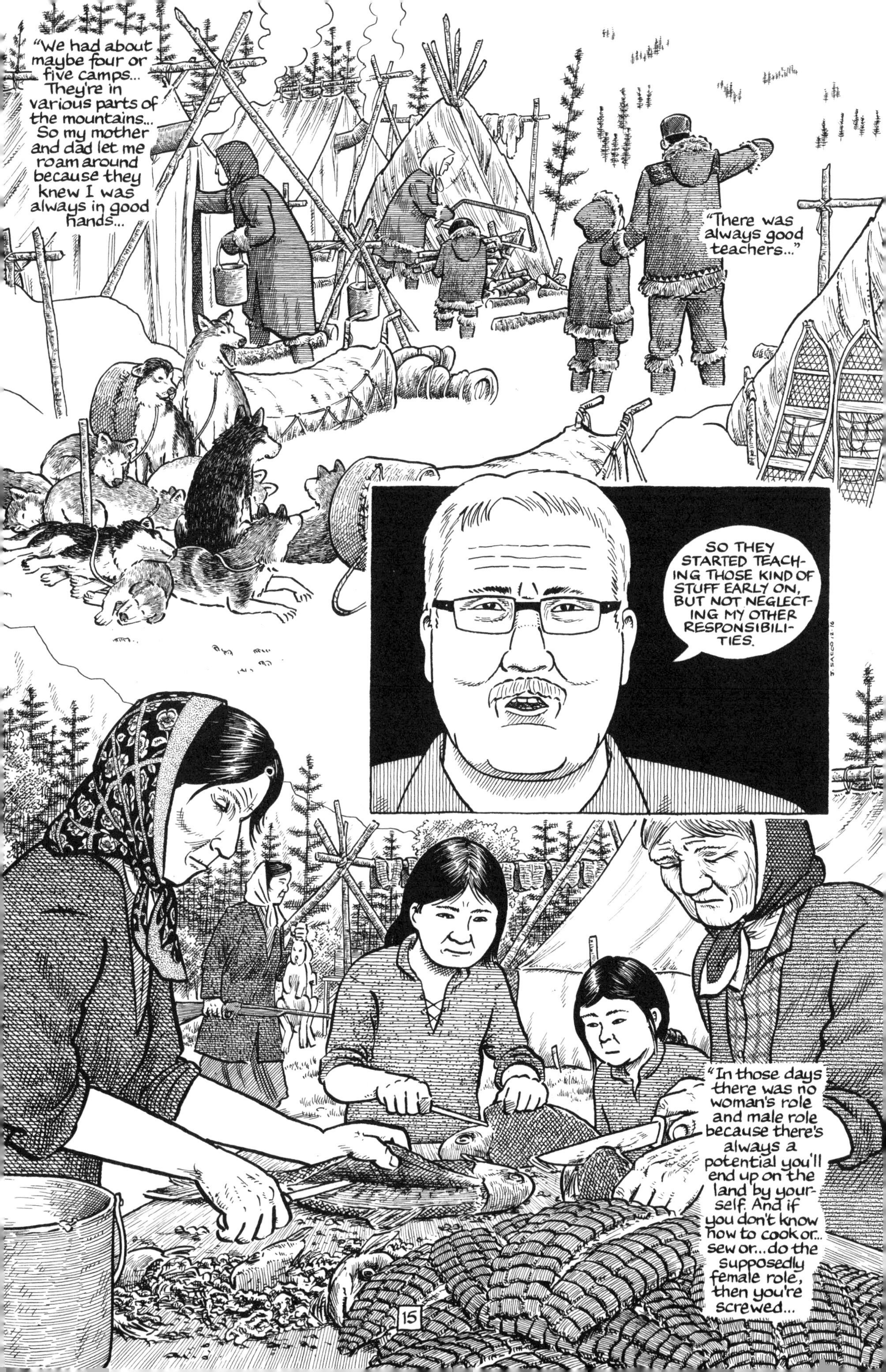
"We had about maybe four or five camps... They're in various parts of the mountains... So my mother and dad let me roam around because they knew I was always in good hands...
"There was always good teachers..."
SO THEY STARTED TEACHING THOSE KIND OF STUFF EARLY ON, BUT NOT NEGLECTING MY OTHER RESPONSIBILITIES.
J. SACCO 12.16
"In those days there was no woman's role and male role because there's always a potential you'll end up on the land by yourself. And if you don't know how to cook or... sew or... do the supposedly female role, then you're screwed...
15

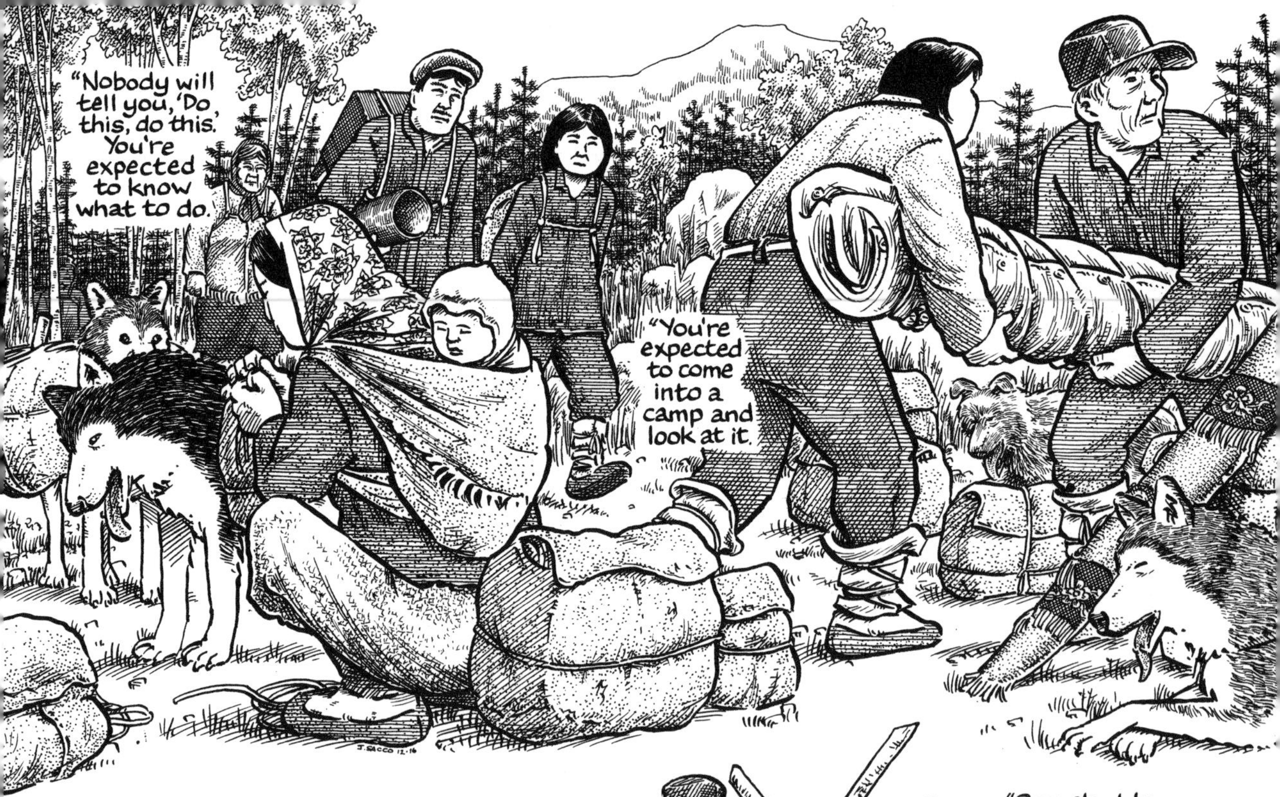
"Nobody will tell you, 'Do this, do this.' You're expected to know what to do.
"You're expected to come into a camp and look at it.
J. SACCO 12.16

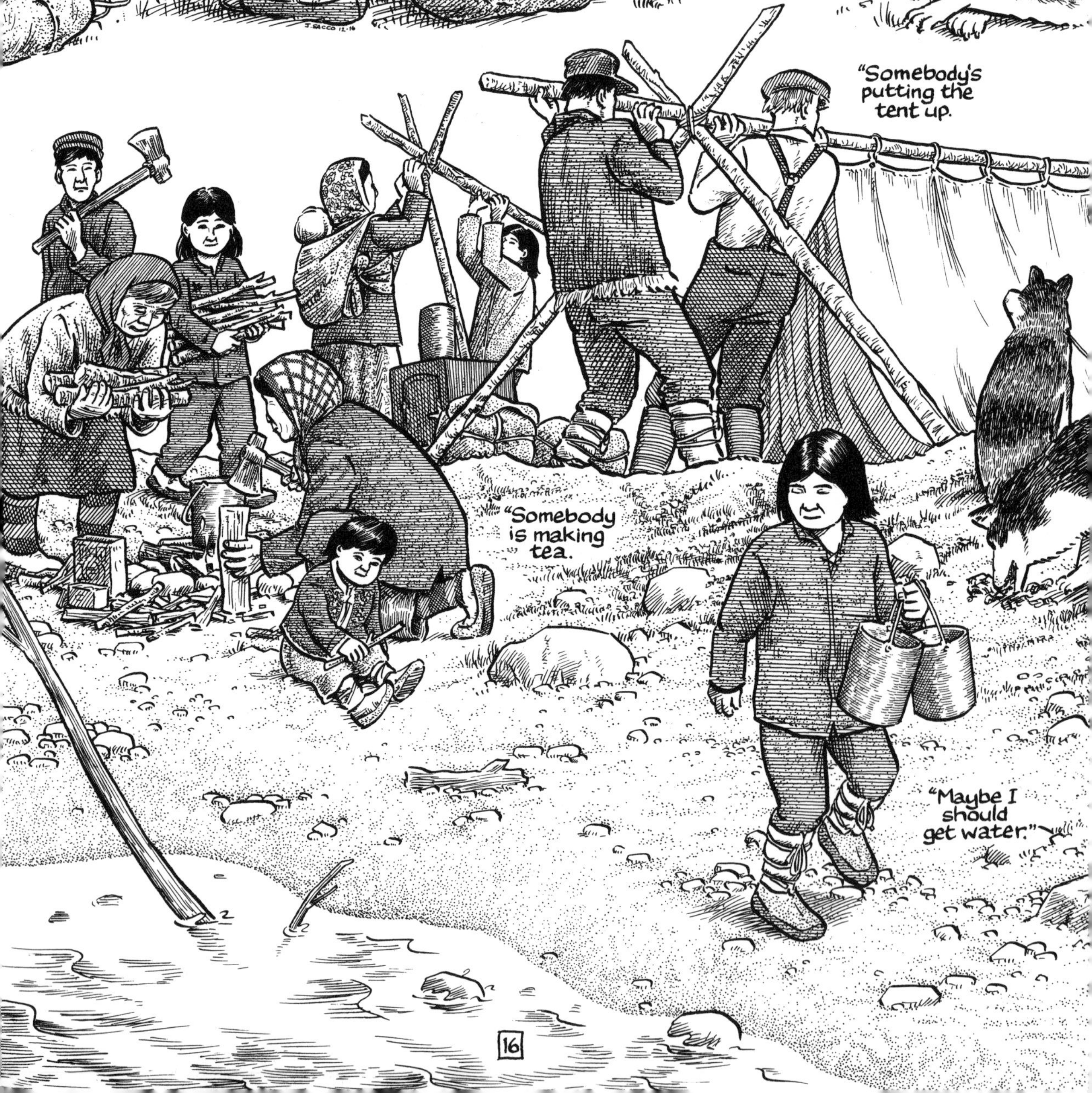
"Somebody's putting the tent up.
"Somebody is making tea.
"Maybe I should get water."

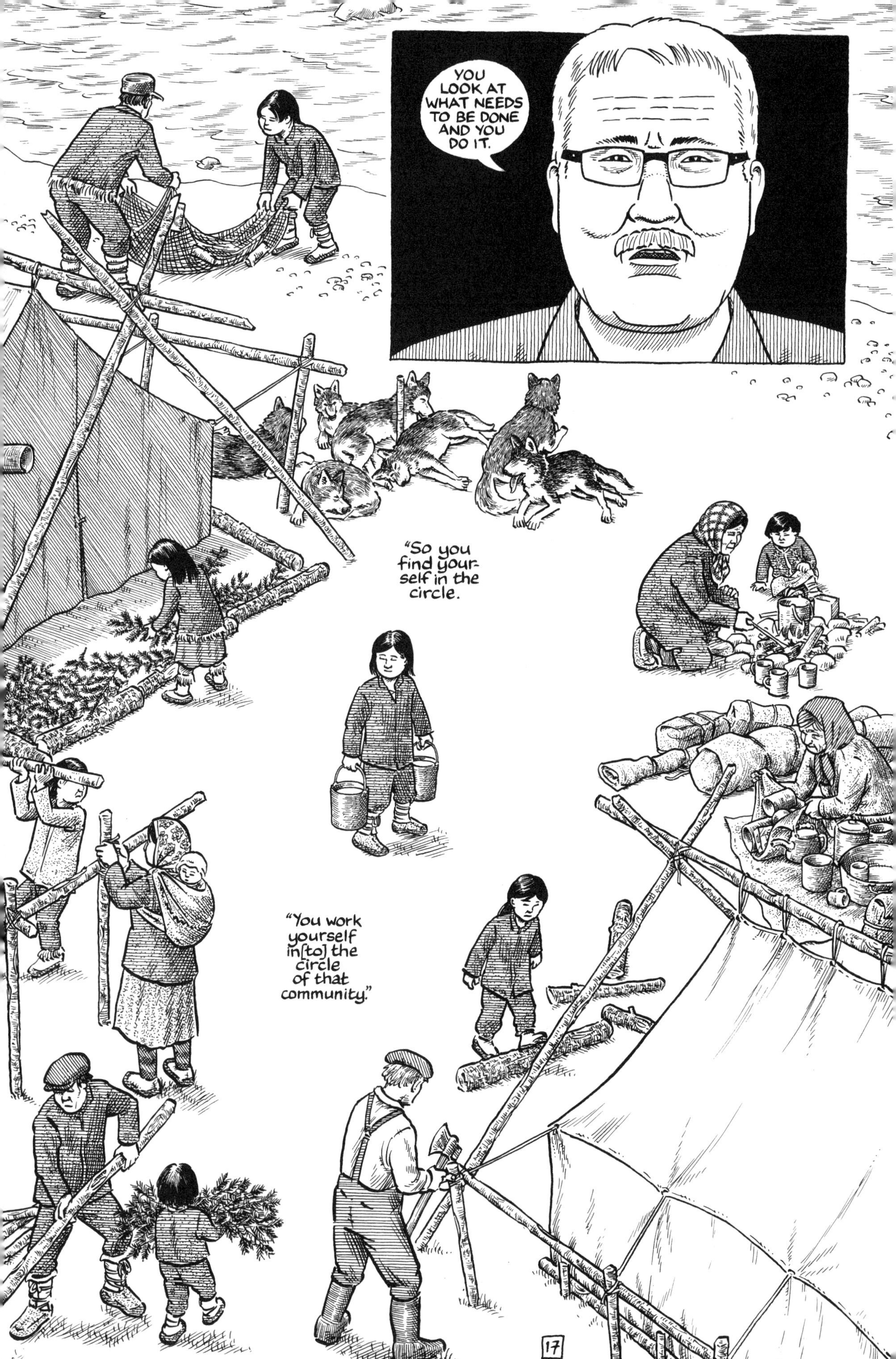
YOU LOOK AT WHAT NEEDS TO BE DONE AND YOU DO IT.
"So you find your-self in the circle.
"You work yourself in[to] the circle of that community."

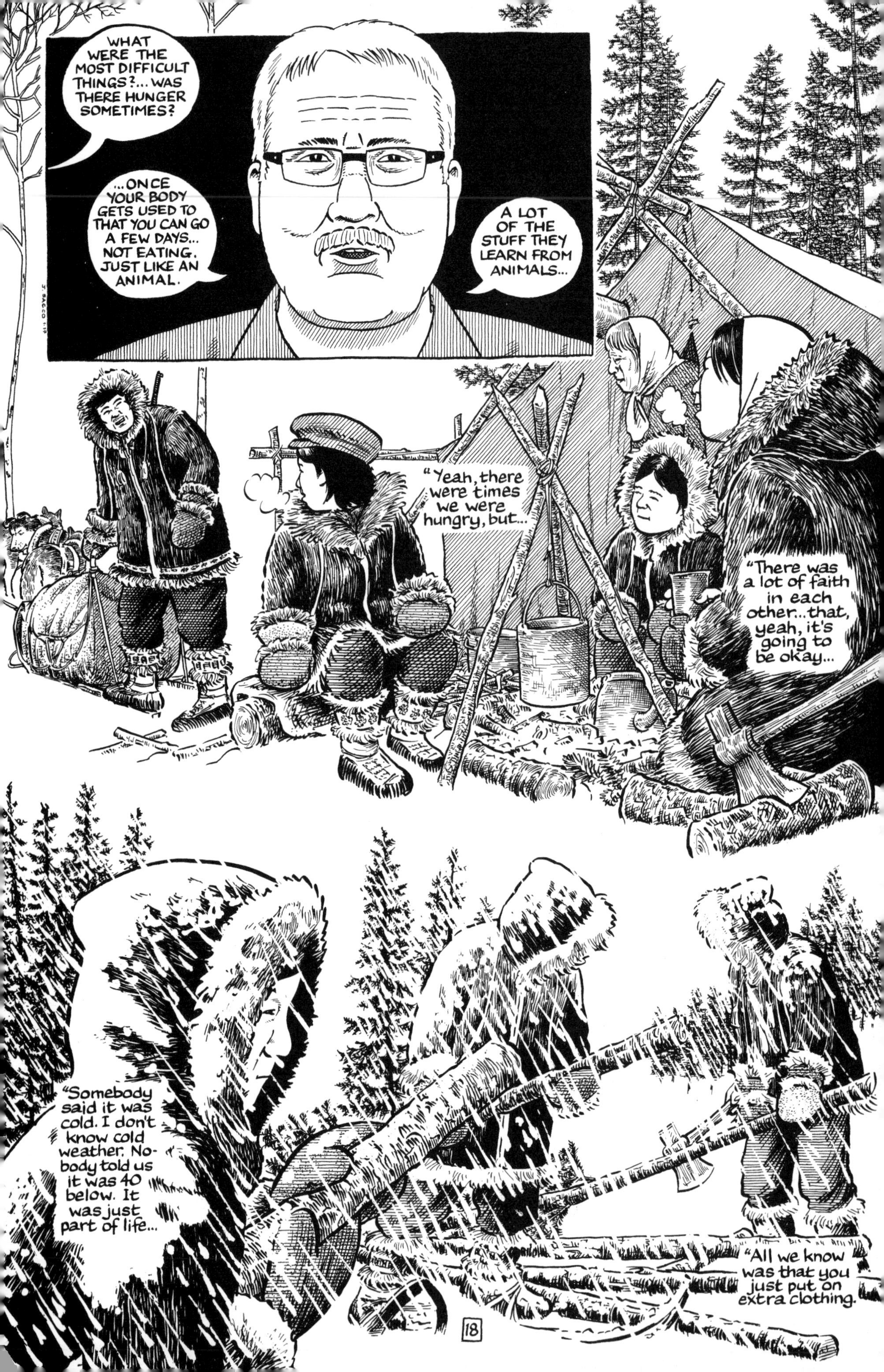
WHAT WERE THE MOST DIFFICULT THINGS?... WAS THERE HUNGER SOMETIMES?
...ONCE YOUR BODY GETS USED TO THAT YOU CAN GO A FEW DAYS... NOT EATING. JUST LIKE AN ANIMAL.
A LOT OF THE STUFF THEY LEARN FROM ANIMALS...
"Yeah, there were times we were hungry, but...
"There was a lot of faith in each other...that, yeah, it's going to be okay...
"Somebody said it was cold. I don't know cold weather. Nobody told us it was 40 below. It was just part of life...
"All we know was that you just put on extra clothing.

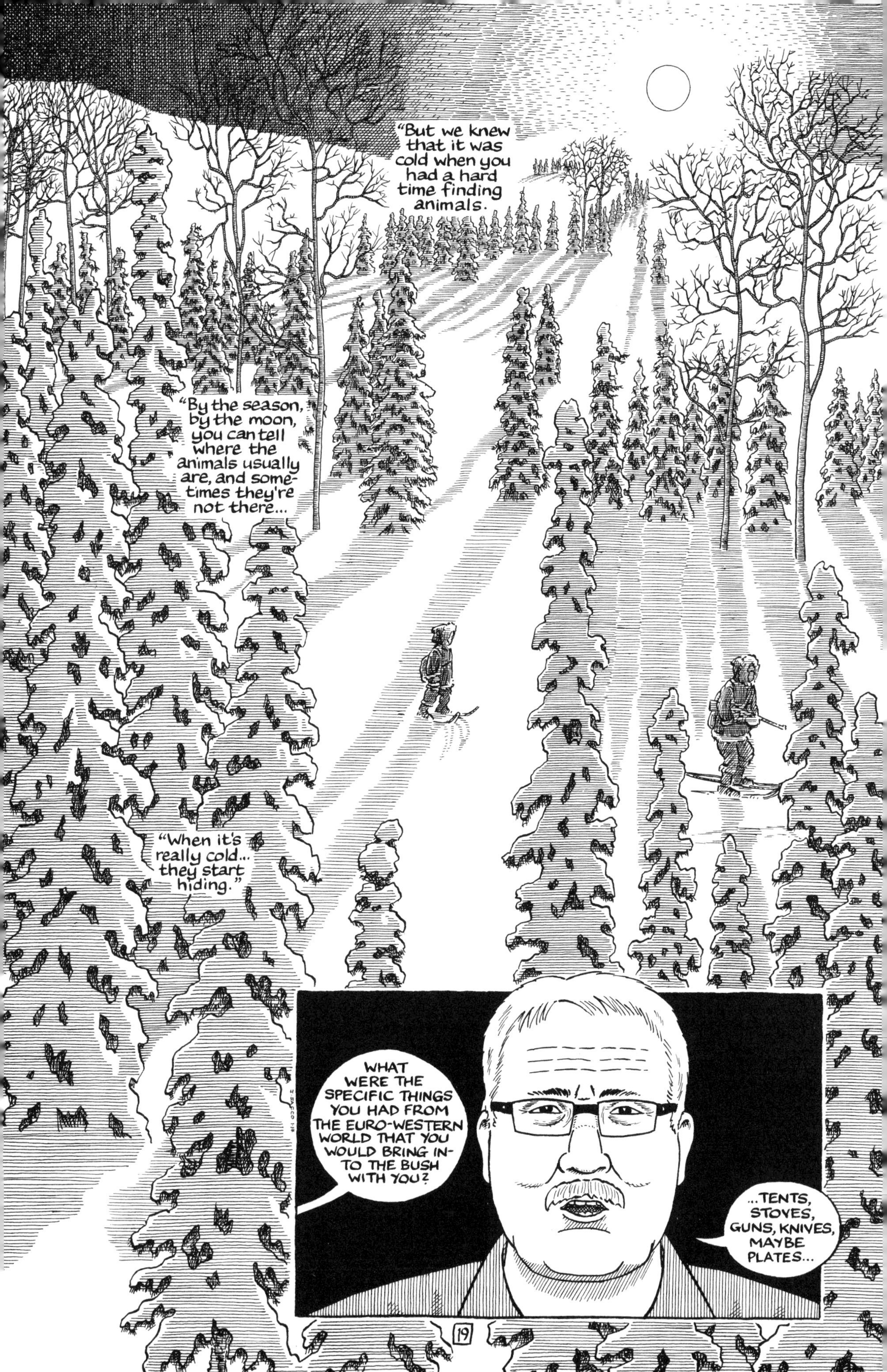
"But we knew that it was cold when you had a hard time finding animals.
"By the season, by the moon, you can tell where the animals usually are, and sometimes they're not there...
"When it's really cold... they start hiding."
WHAT WERE THE SPECIFIC THINGS YOU HAD FROM THE EURO-WESTERN WORLD THAT YOU WOULD BRING INTO THE BUSH WITH YOU?
...TENTS, STOVES, GUNS, KNIVES, MAYBE PLATES...

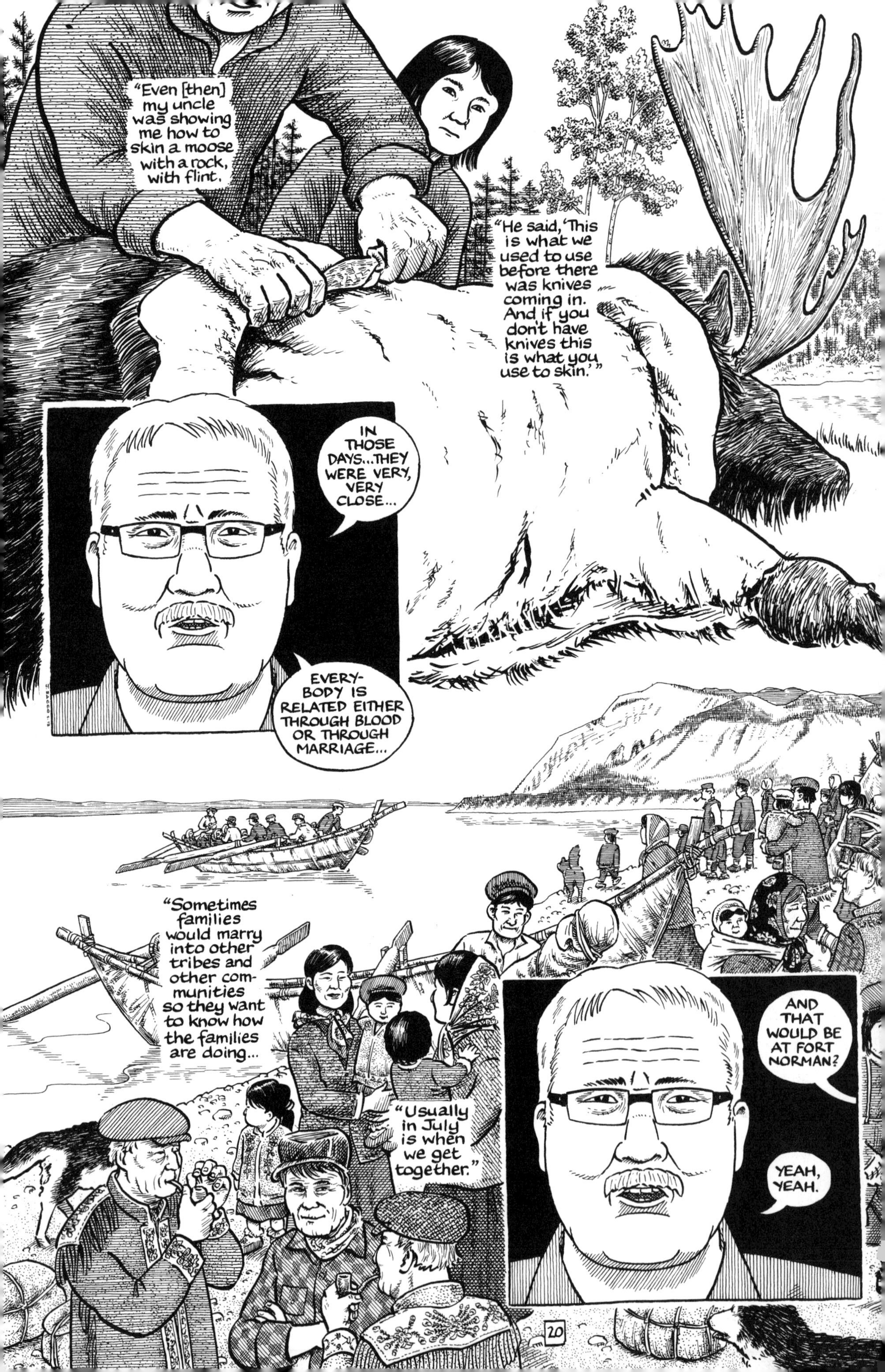

"Even [then] my uncle was showing me how to skin a moose with a rock, with flint.
"He said, 'This is what we used to use before there was knives coming in. And if you don't have knives this is what you use to skin.'"
IN THOSE DAYS...THEY WERE VERY, VERY CLOSE...
EVERYBODY IS RELATED EITHER THROUGH BLOOD OR THROUGH MARRIAGE...
"Sometimes families would marry into other tribes and other communities so they want to know how the families are doing...
"Usually in July is when we get together."
AND THAT WOULD BE AT FORT NORMAN?
YEAH, YEAH.

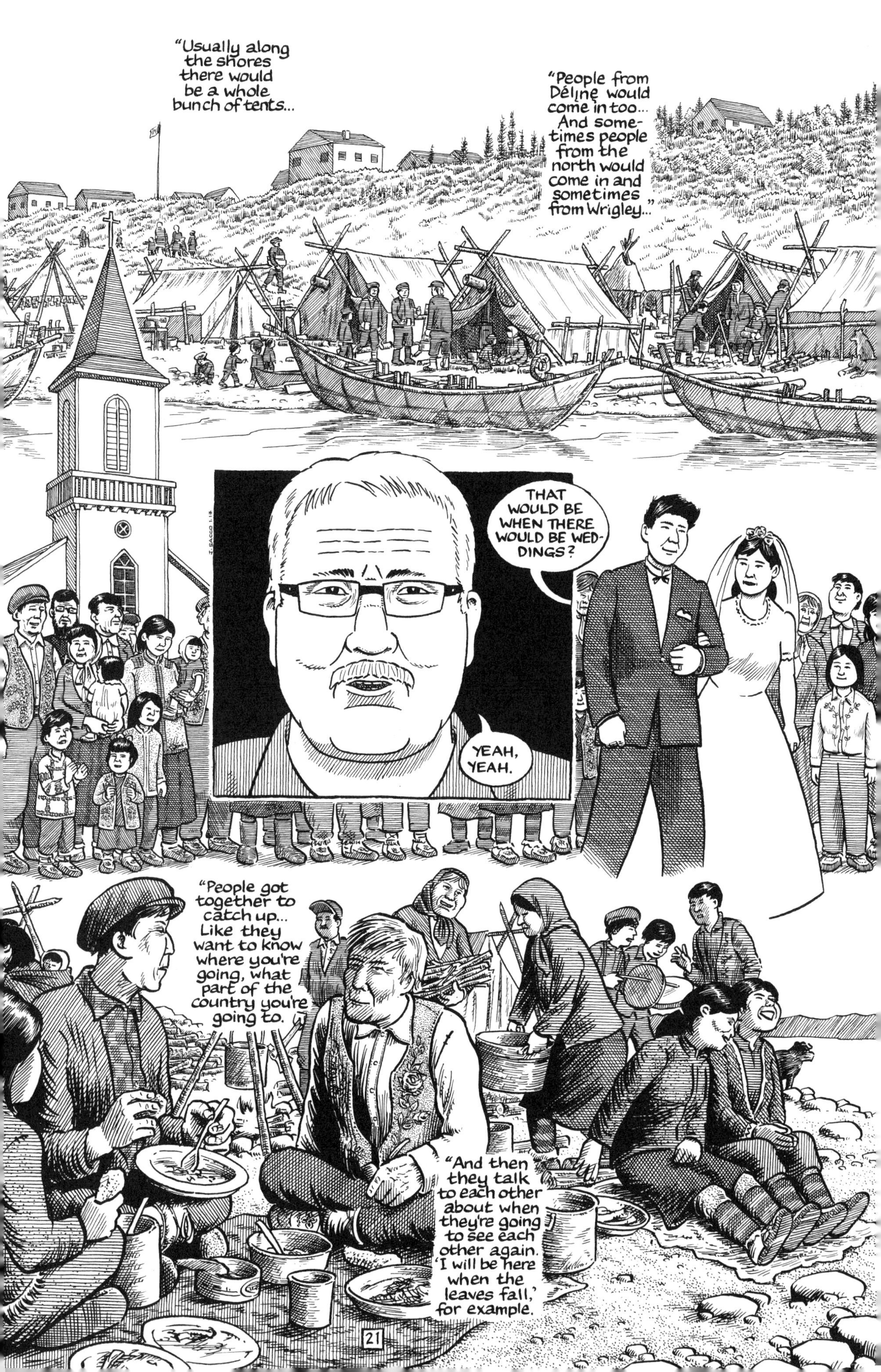
"Usually along the shores there would be a whole bunch of tents...
"People from Délı̨nę would come in too... And sometimes people from the north would come in and sometimes from Wrigley..."
THAT WOULD BE WHEN THERE WOULD BE WEDDINGS?
YEAH, YEAH.
"People got together to catch up... Like they want to know where you're going, what part of the country you're going to.
"And then they talk to each other about when they're going to see each other again. 'I will be here when the leaves fall,' for example.

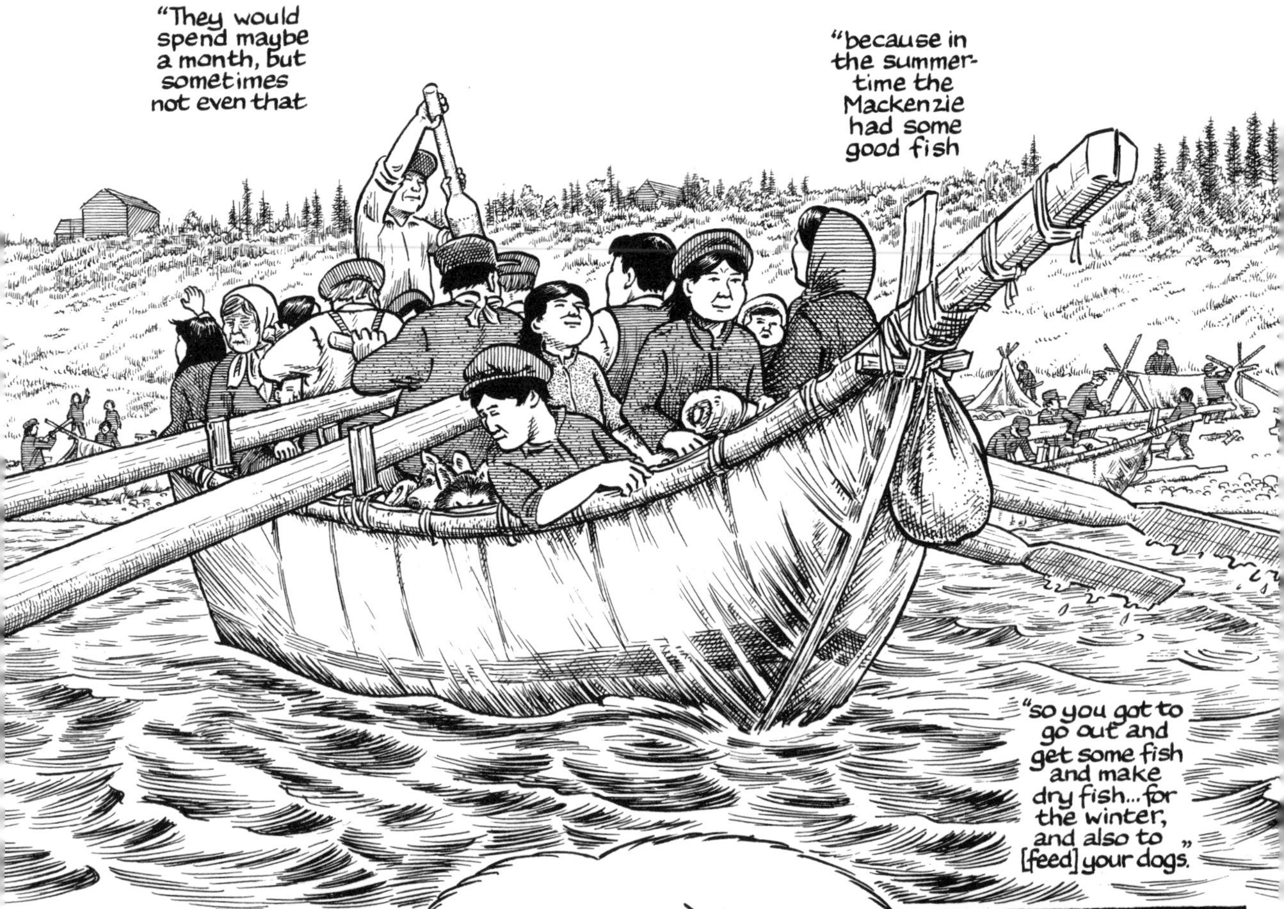
"They would spend maybe a month, but sometimes not even that
"because in the summer-time the Mackenzie had some good fish
"so you got to go out and get some fish and make dry fish... for the winter, and also to [feed] your dogs."

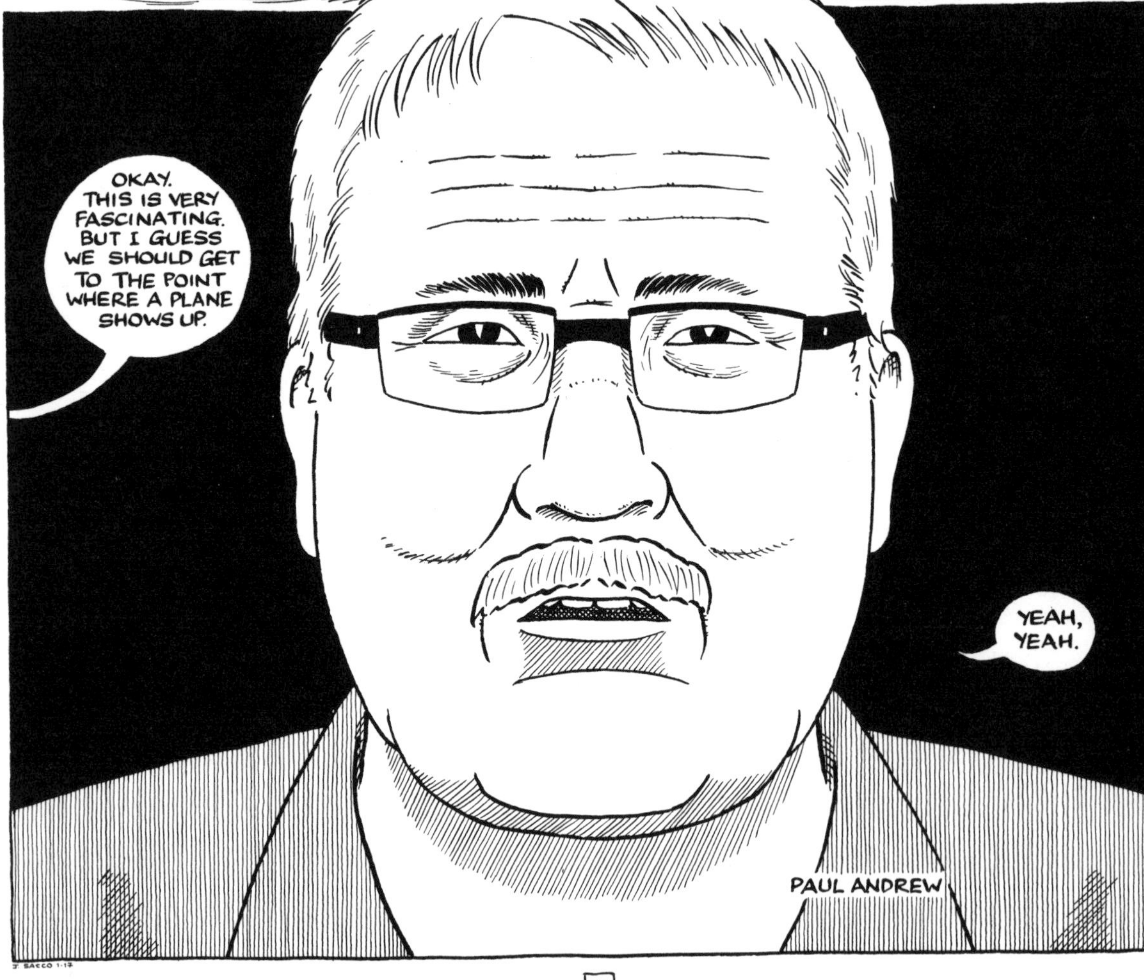
OKAY. THIS IS VERY FASCINATING. BUT I GUESS WE SHOULD GET TO THE POINT WHERE A PLANE SHOWS UP.
YEAH, YEAH.
PAUL ANDREW
J. SACCO 1-17

II

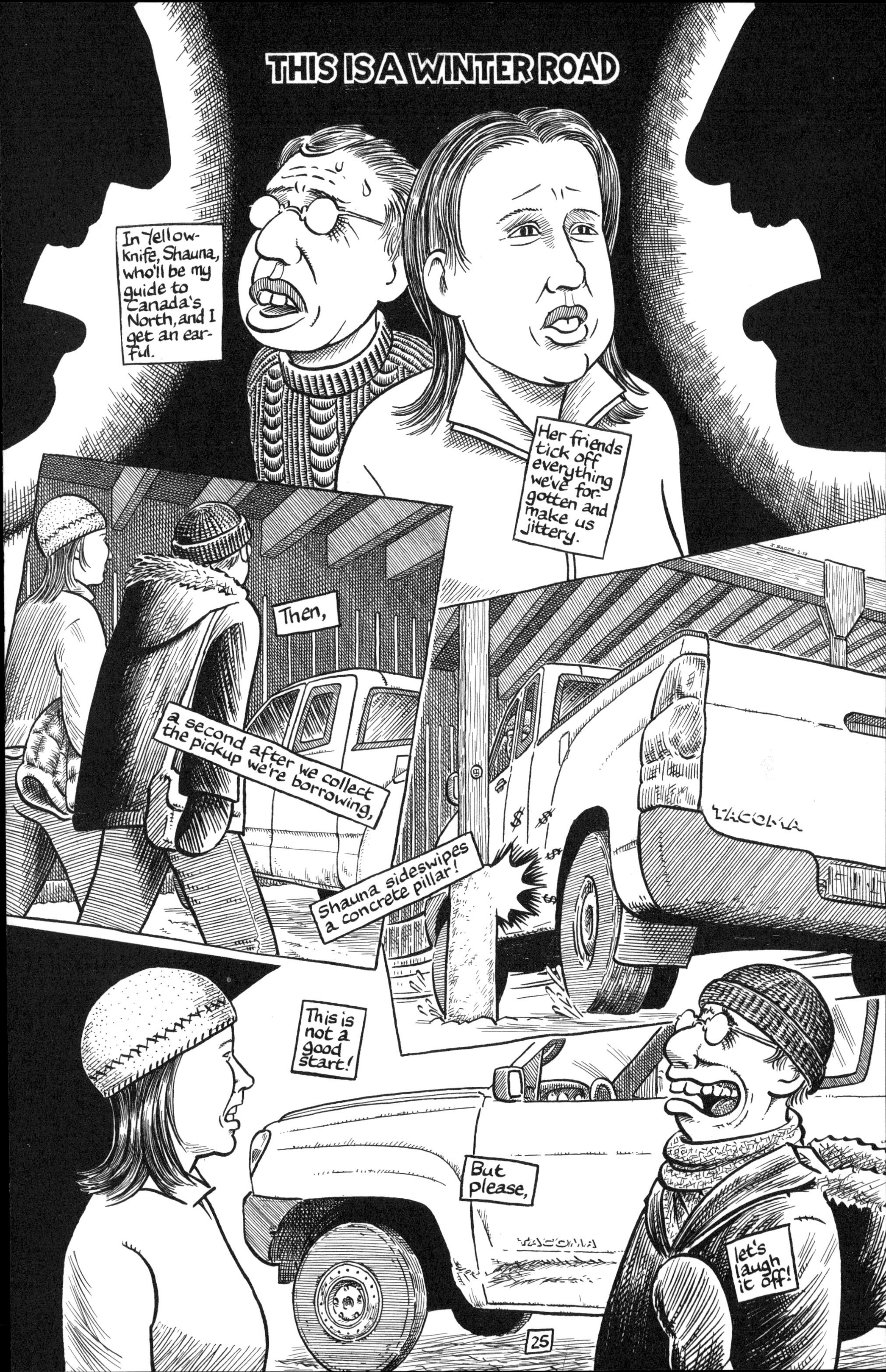
THIS IS A WINTER ROAD
In Yellowknife, Shauna, who'll be my guide to Canada's North, and I get an earful.
Her friends tick off everything we've forgotten and make us jittery.
Then,
a second after we collect the pickup we're borrowing,
Shauna sideswipes a concrete pillar!
TACOMA
This is not a good start!
But please,
let's laugh it off!
TACOMA

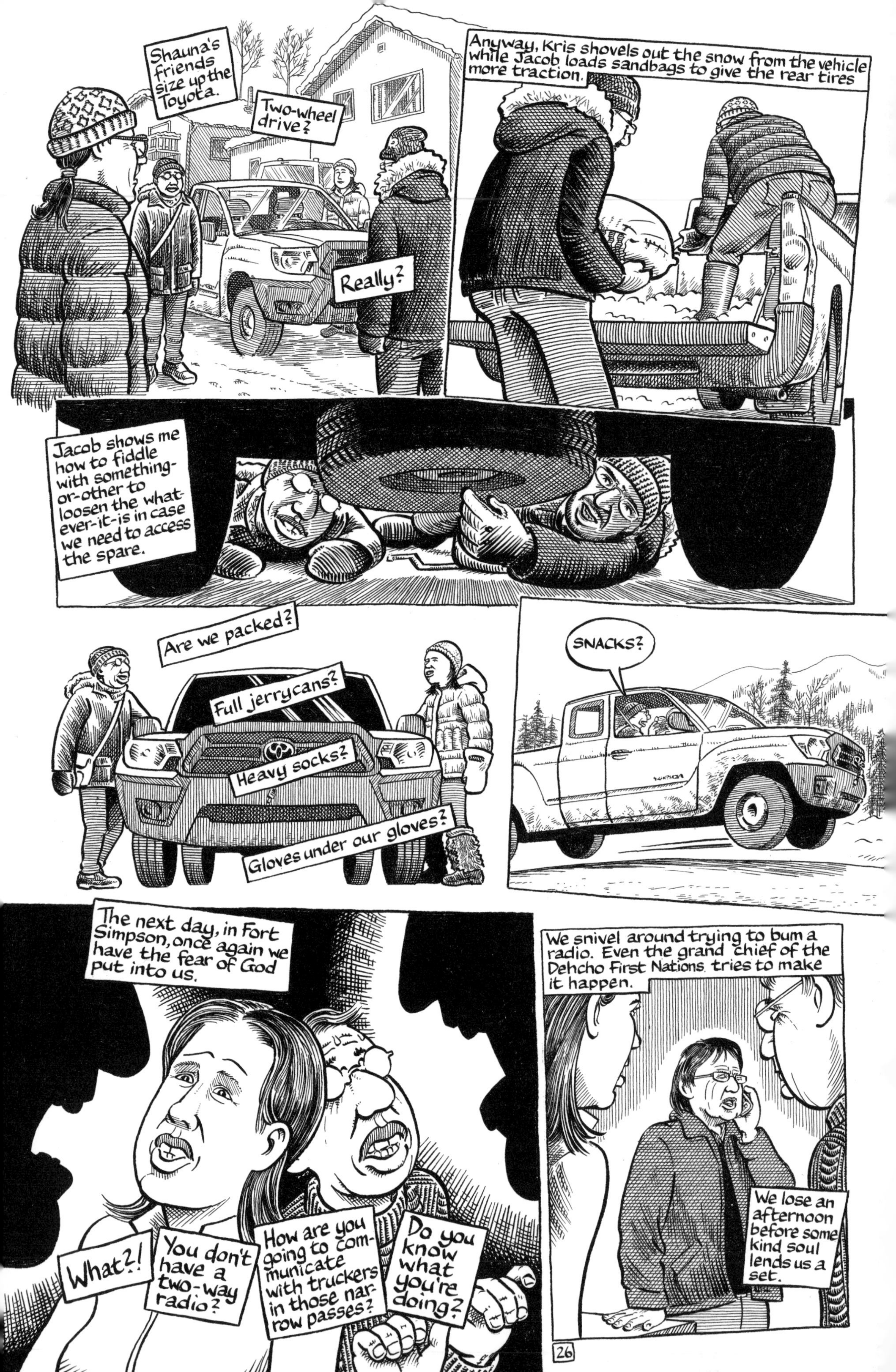

Shauna's friends size up the Toyota.
Two-wheel drive?
Really?
Anyway, Kris shovels out the snow from the vehicle while Jacob loads sandbags to give the rear tires more traction.
Jacob shows me how to fiddle with something-or-other to loosen the what-ever-it-is in case we need to access the spare.
Are we packed?
Full jerrycans?
Heavy socks?
Gloves under our gloves?
SNACKS?
The next day, in Fort Simpson, once again we have the fear of God put into us.
What?!
You don't have a two-way radio?
How are you going to communicate with truckers in those narrow passes?
Do you know what you're doing?
We snivel around trying to bum a radio. Even the grand chief of the Dehcho First Nations tries to make it happen.
We lose an afternoon before some kind soul lends us a set.

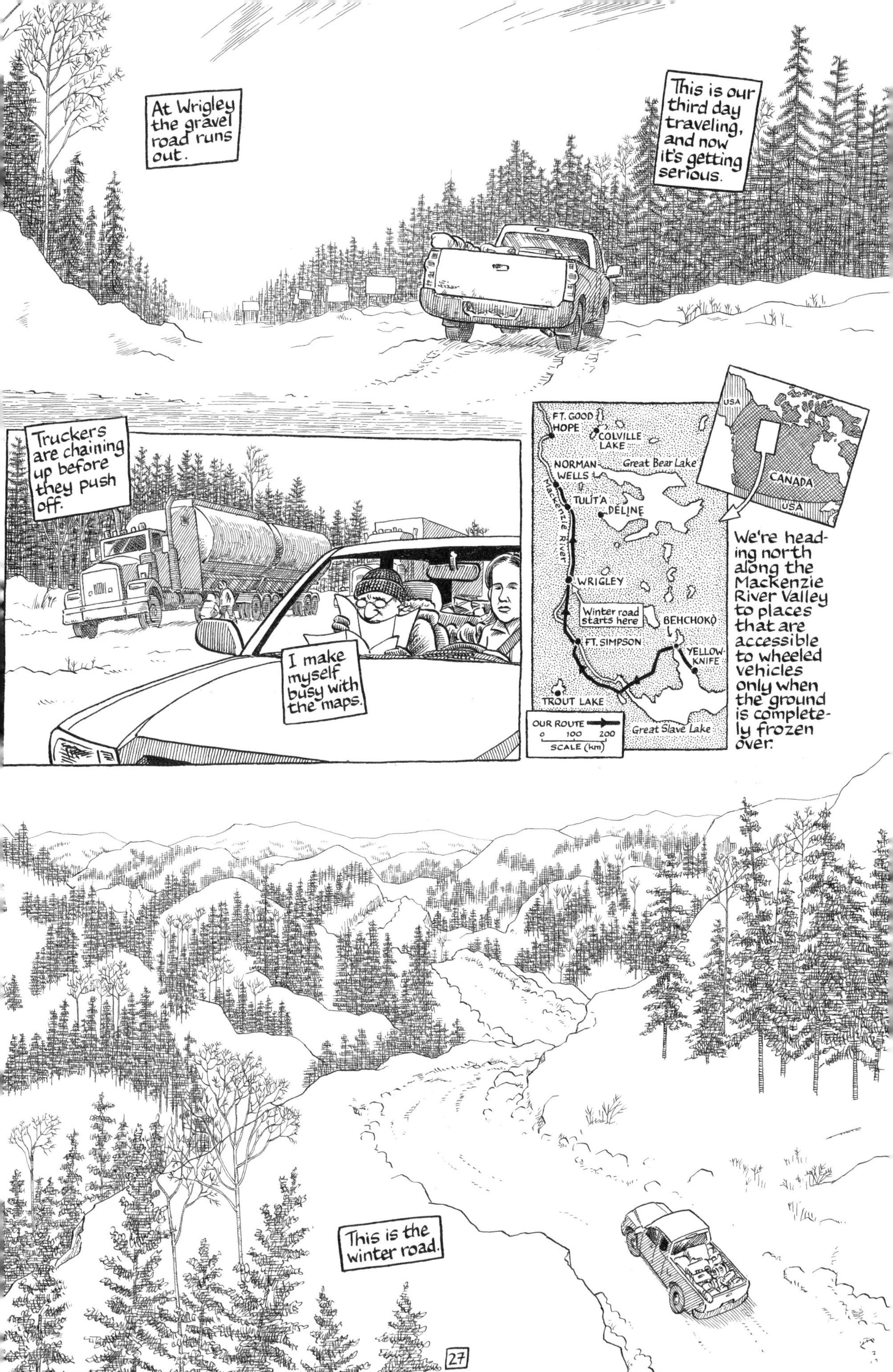

At Wrigley the gravel road runs out.
This is our third day traveling, and now it's getting serious.
Truckers are chaining up before they push off.
I make myself busy with the maps.
FT. GOOD HOPE
COLVILLE LAKE
NORMAN WELLS
Great Bear Lake
TULIT'A
DÉLINE
Mackenzie River
WRIGLEY
Winter road starts here
BEHCHOKÒ
FT. SIMPSON
YELLOWKNIFE
TROUT LAKE
Great Slave Lake
OUR ROUTE
0 100 200
SCALE (km)
USA
CANADA
USA
We're heading north along the Mackenzie River Valley to places that are accessible to wheeled vehicles only when the ground is completely frozen over.
This is the winter road.

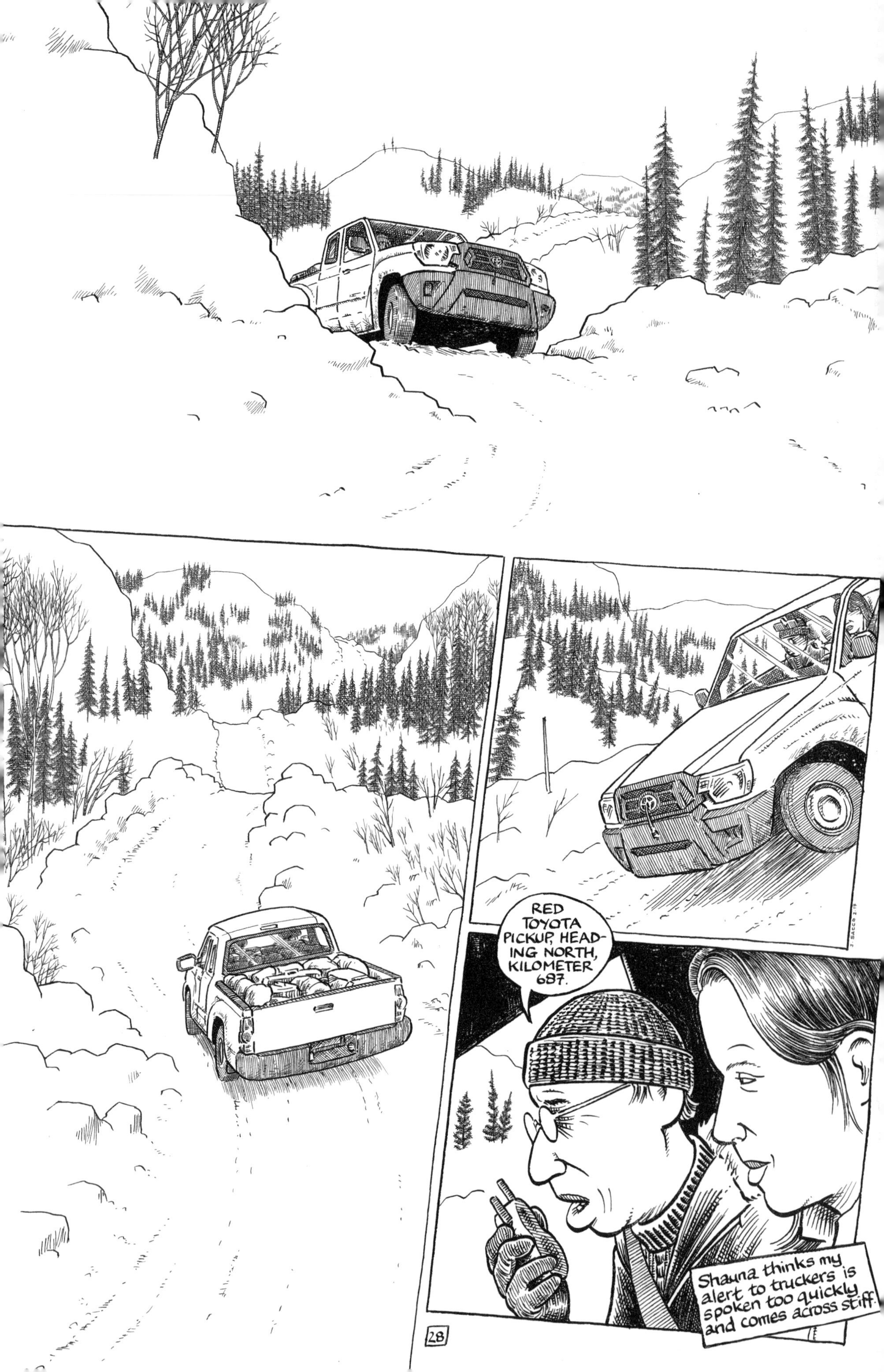
RED TOYOTA PICKUP, HEADING NORTH, KILOMETER 687.
Shauna thinks my alert to truckers is spoken too quickly and comes across stiff.

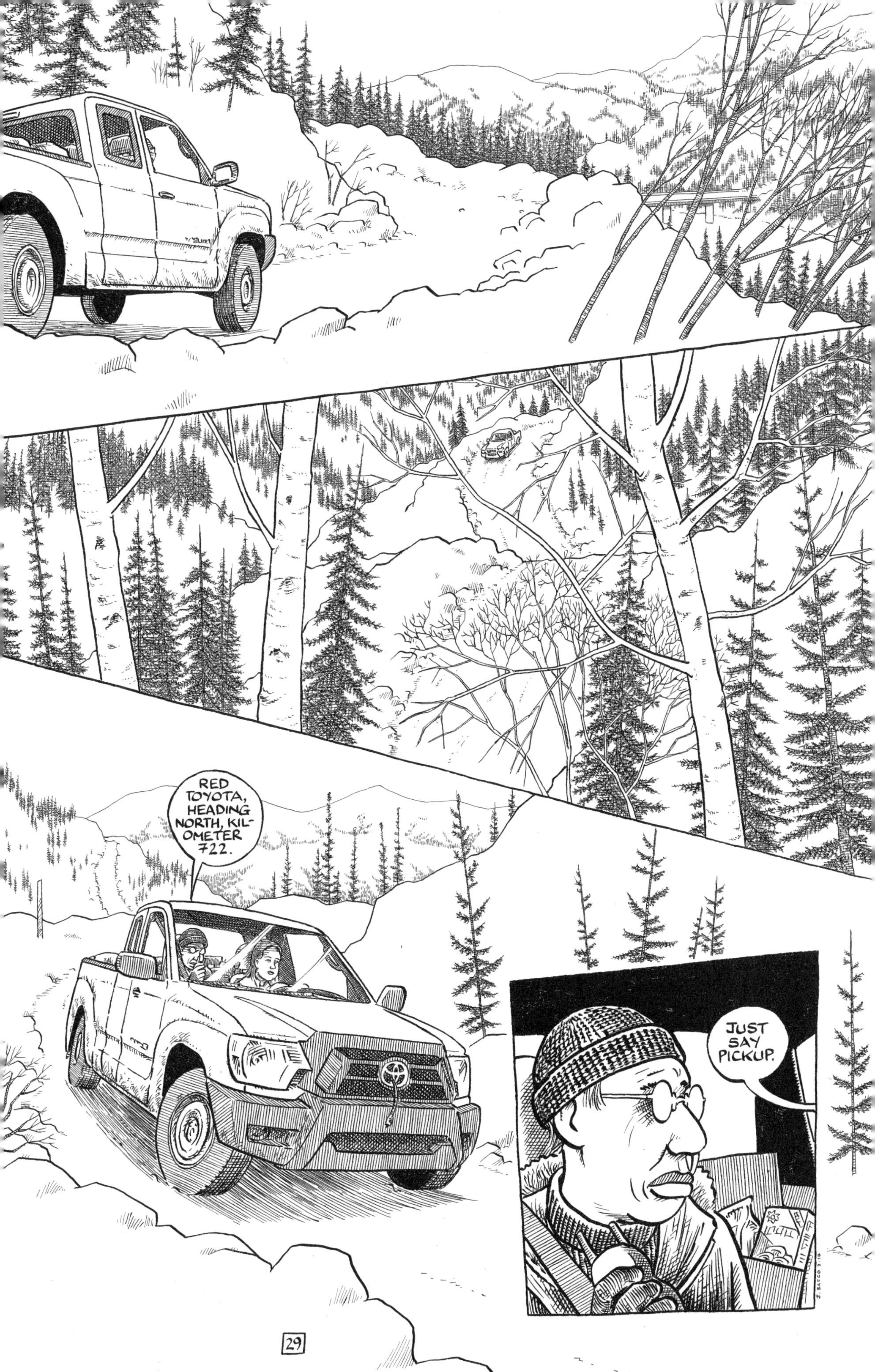
RED TOYOTA, HEADING NORTH, KILOMETER 722.
JUST SAY PICKUP.

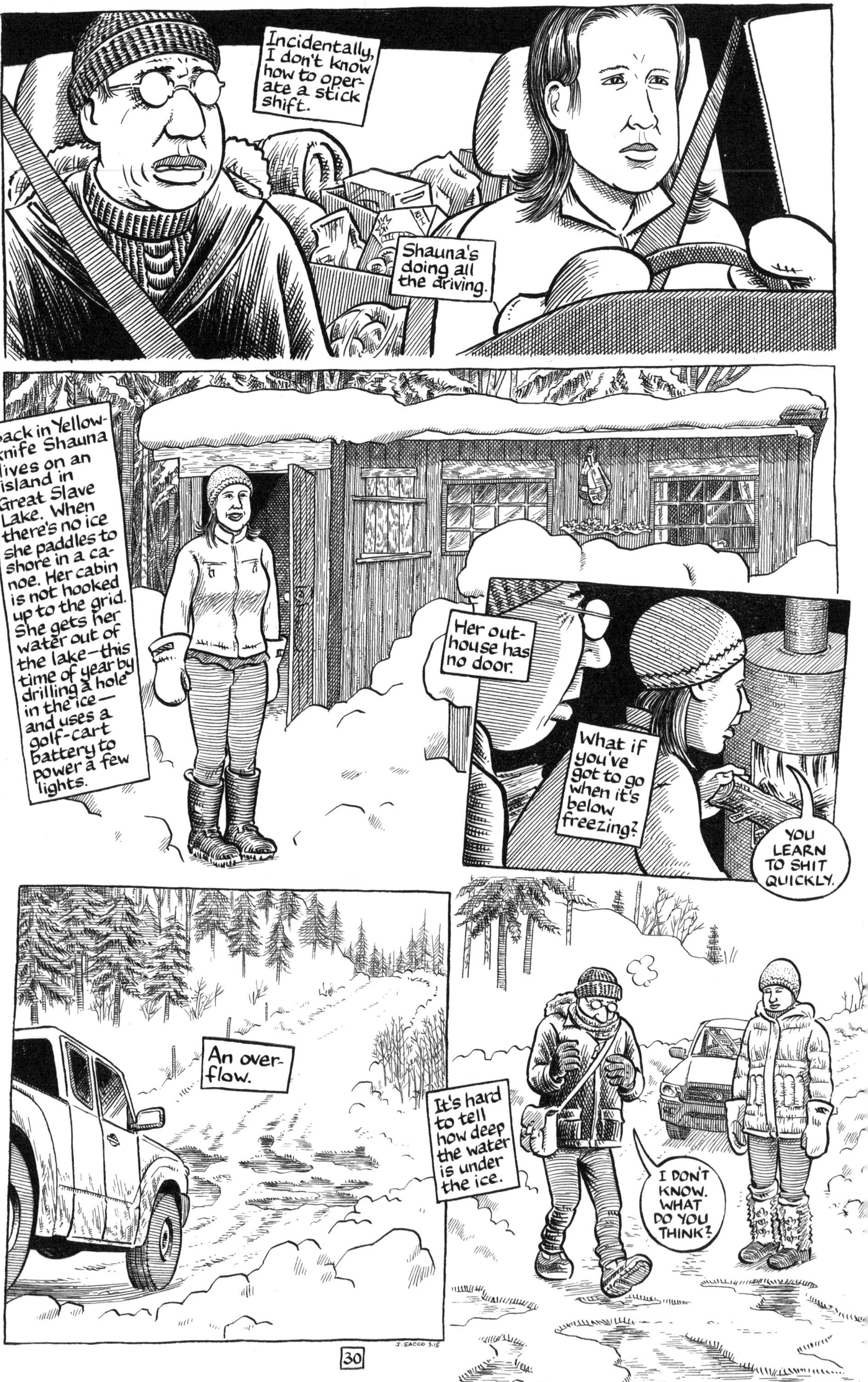
Incidentally, I don't know how to oper-ate a stick shift.
Shauna's doing all the driving.
Back in Yellow-knife Shauna lives on an island in Great Slave Lake. When there's no ice she paddles to shore in a ca-noe. Her cabin is not hooked up to the grid. She gets her water out of the lake—this time of year by drilling a hole in the ice—and uses a golf-cart battery to power a few lights.
Her out-house has no door.
What if you've got to go when it's below freezing?
YOU LEARN TO SHIT QUICKLY.
An over-flow.
It's hard to tell how deep the water is under the ice.
I DON'T KNOW. WHAT DO YOU THINK?
J. SACCO 9.15

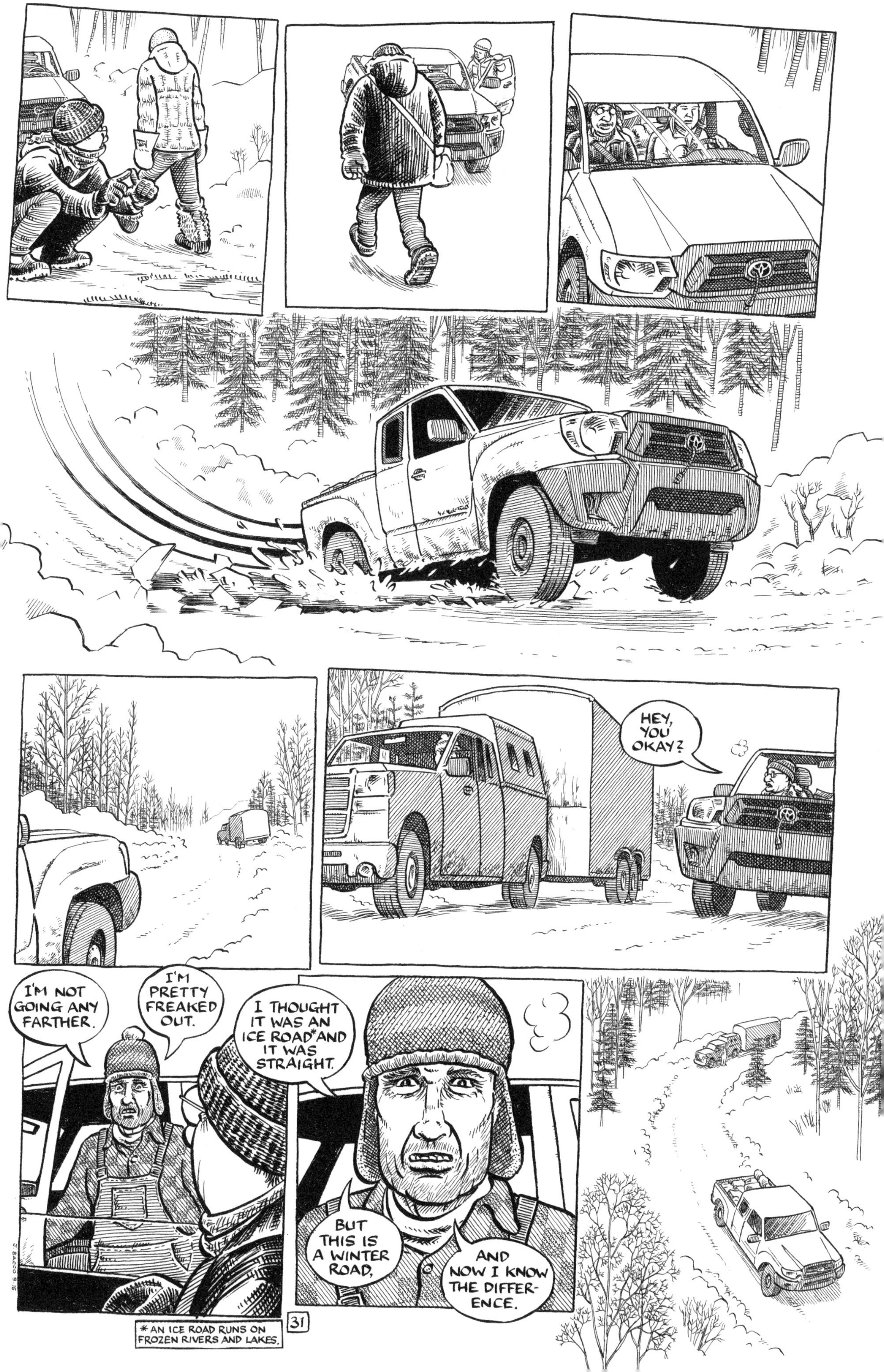
HEY, YOU OKAY?
I'M NOT GOING ANY FARTHER.
I'M PRETTY FREAKED OUT.
I THOUGHT IT WAS AN ICE ROAD* AND IT WAS STRAIGHT.
BUT THIS IS A WINTER ROAD,
AND NOW I KNOW THE DIFFERENCE.

*AN ICE ROAD RUNS ON FROZEN RIVERS AND LAKES.

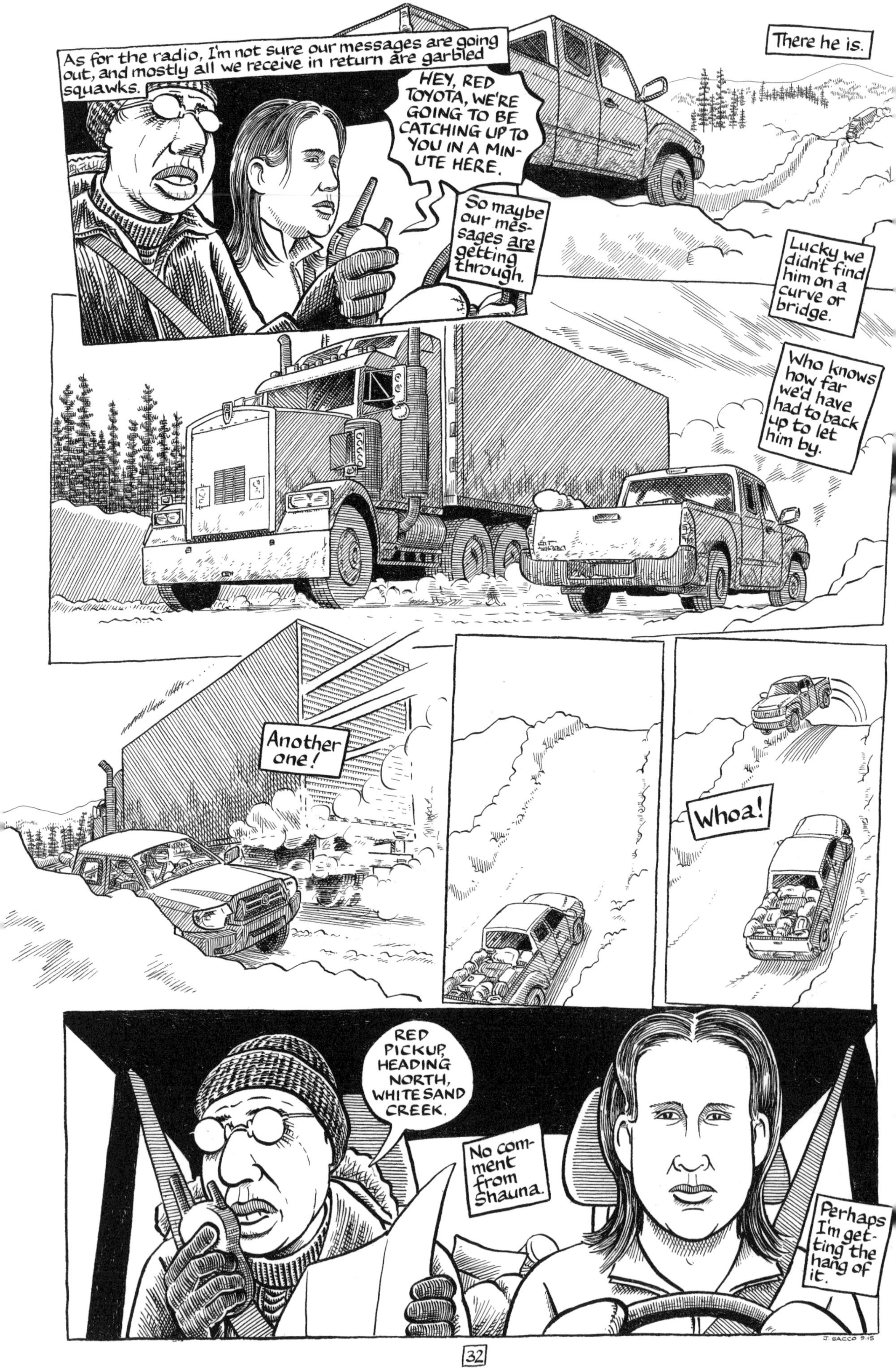
As for the radio, I'm not sure our messages are going out, and mostly all we receive in return are garbled squawks.
HEY, RED TOYOTA, WE'RE GOING TO BE CATCHING UP TO YOU IN A MINUTE HERE.
So maybe our messages are getting through.
There he is.
Lucky we didn't find him on a curve or bridge.
Who knows how far we'd have had to back up to let him by.
Another one!
Whoa!
RED PICKUP, HEADING NORTH, WHITESAND CREEK.
No comment from Shauna.
Perhaps I'm getting the hang of it.
J. SACCO 9.15

WHO WE ARE

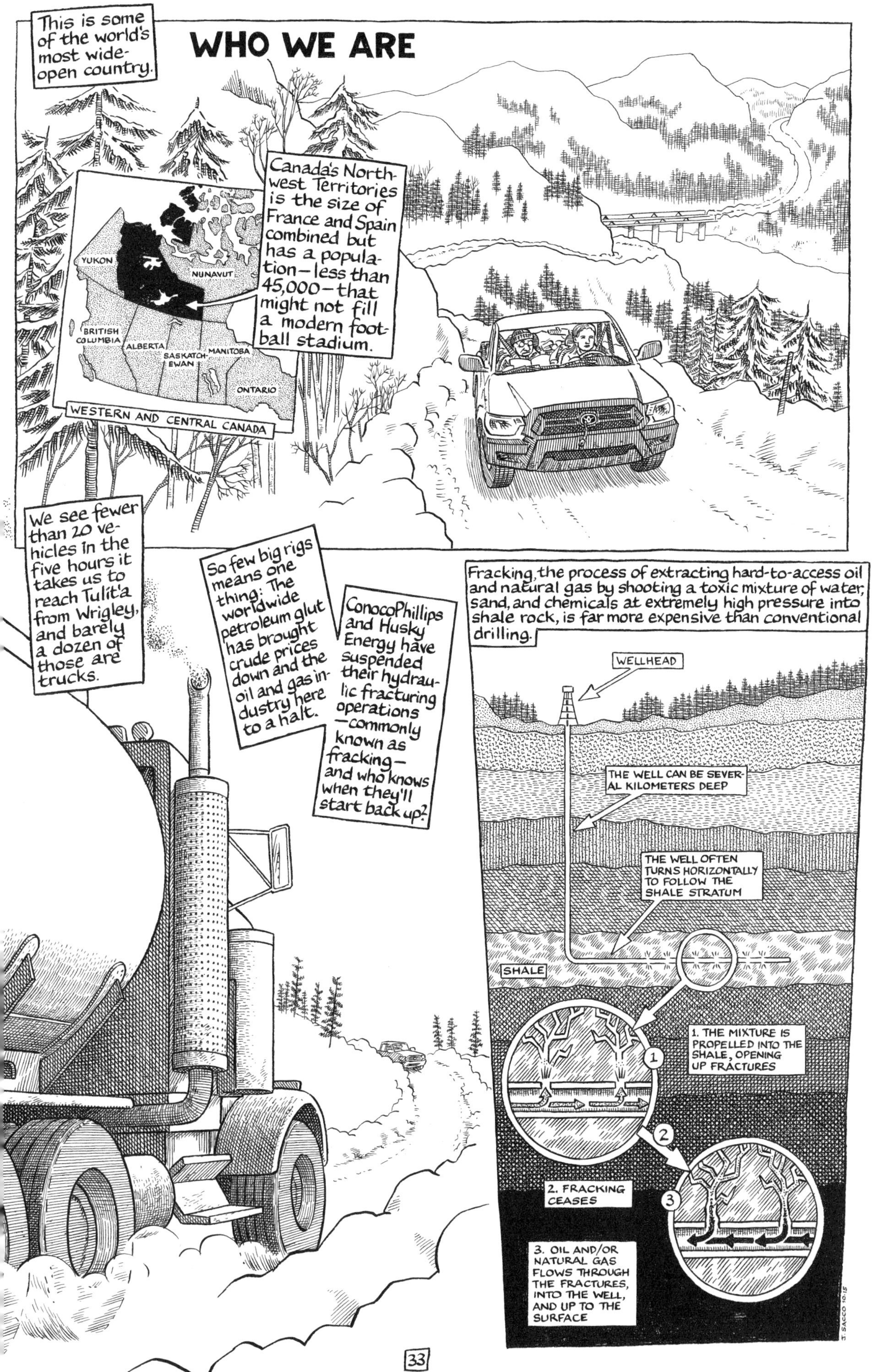
This is some of the world's most wide-open country.
Canada's Northwest Territories is the size of France and Spain combined but has a population—less than 45,000—that might not fill a modern football stadium.
YUKON
NUNAVUT
BRITISH COLUMBIA
ALBERTA
SASKATCHEWAN
MANITOBA
ONTARIO
WESTERN AND CENTRAL CANADA
We see fewer than 20 vehicles in the five hours it takes us to reach Tulit'a from Wrigley, and barely a dozen of those are trucks.
So few big rigs means one thing: The worldwide petroleum glut has brought crude prices down and the oil and gas industry here to a halt.
ConocoPhillips and Husky Energy have suspended their hydraulic fracturing operations—commonly known as fracking—and who knows when they'll start back up?
Fracking, the process of extracting hard-to-access oil and natural gas by shooting a toxic mixture of water, sand, and chemicals at extremely high pressure into shale rock, is far more expensive than conventional drilling.
WELLHEAD
THE WELL CAN BE SEVERAL KILOMETERS DEEP
THE WELL OFTEN TURNS HORIZONTALLY TO FOLLOW THE SHALE STRATUM
SHALE
1. THE MIXTURE IS PROPELLED INTO THE SHALE, OPENING UP FRACTURES
2. FRACKING CEASES
3. OIL AND/OR NATURAL GAS FLOWS THROUGH THE FRACTURES, INTO THE WELL, AND UP TO THE SURFACE
J. SACCO 10.15

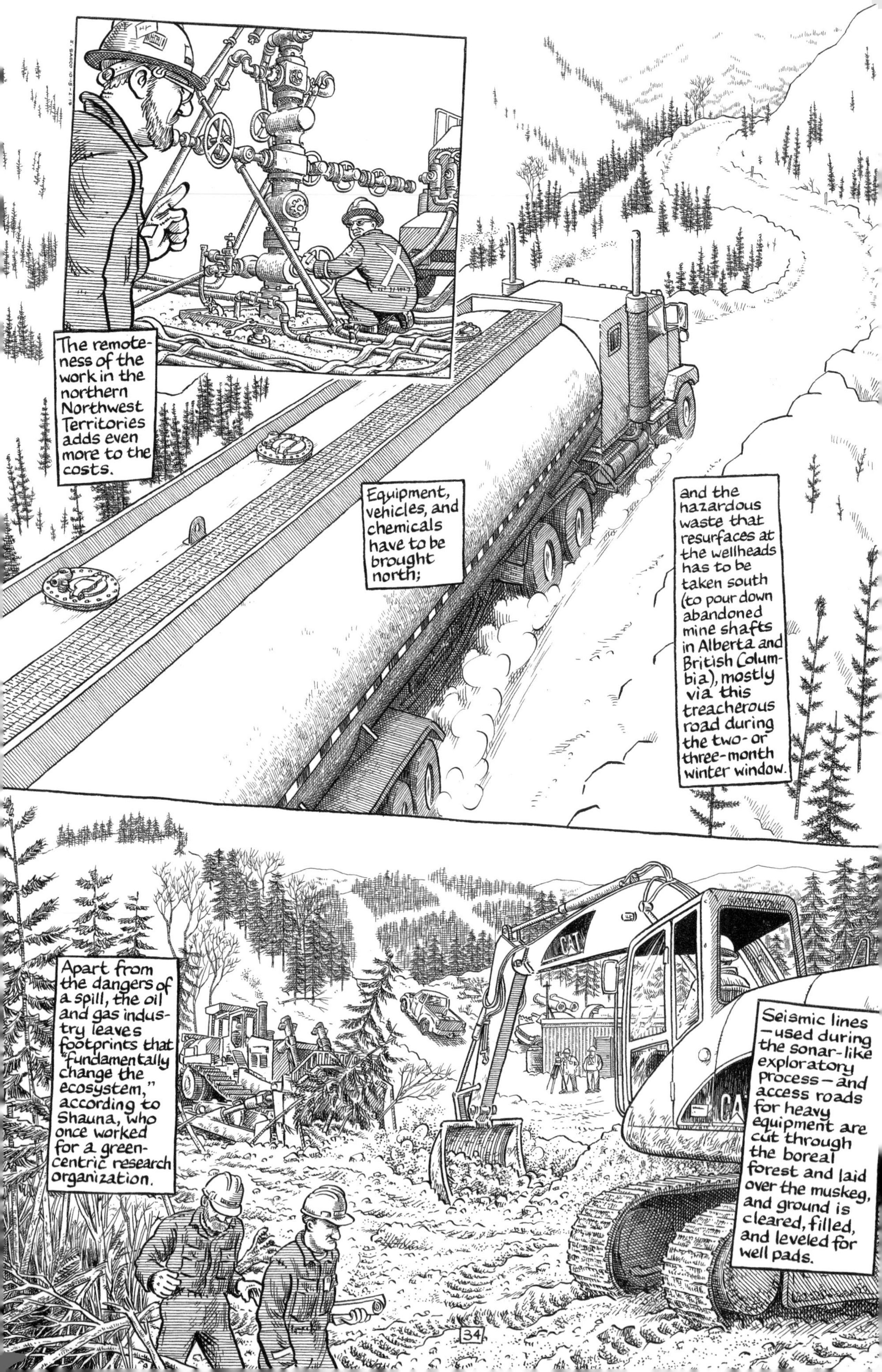
The remoteness of the work in the northern Northwest Territories adds even more to the costs.
Equipment, vehicles, and chemicals have to be brought north;
and the hazardous waste that resurfaces at the wellheads has to be taken south (to pour down abandoned mine shafts in Alberta and British Columbia), mostly via this treacherous road during the two- or three-month winter window.
Apart from the dangers of a spill, the oil and gas industry leaves footprints that "fundamentally change the ecosystem," according to Shauna, who once worked for a green-centric research organization.
Seismic lines—used during the sonar-like exploratory process—and access roads for heavy equipment are cut through the boreal forest and laid over the muskeg, and ground is cleared, filled, and leveled for well pads.

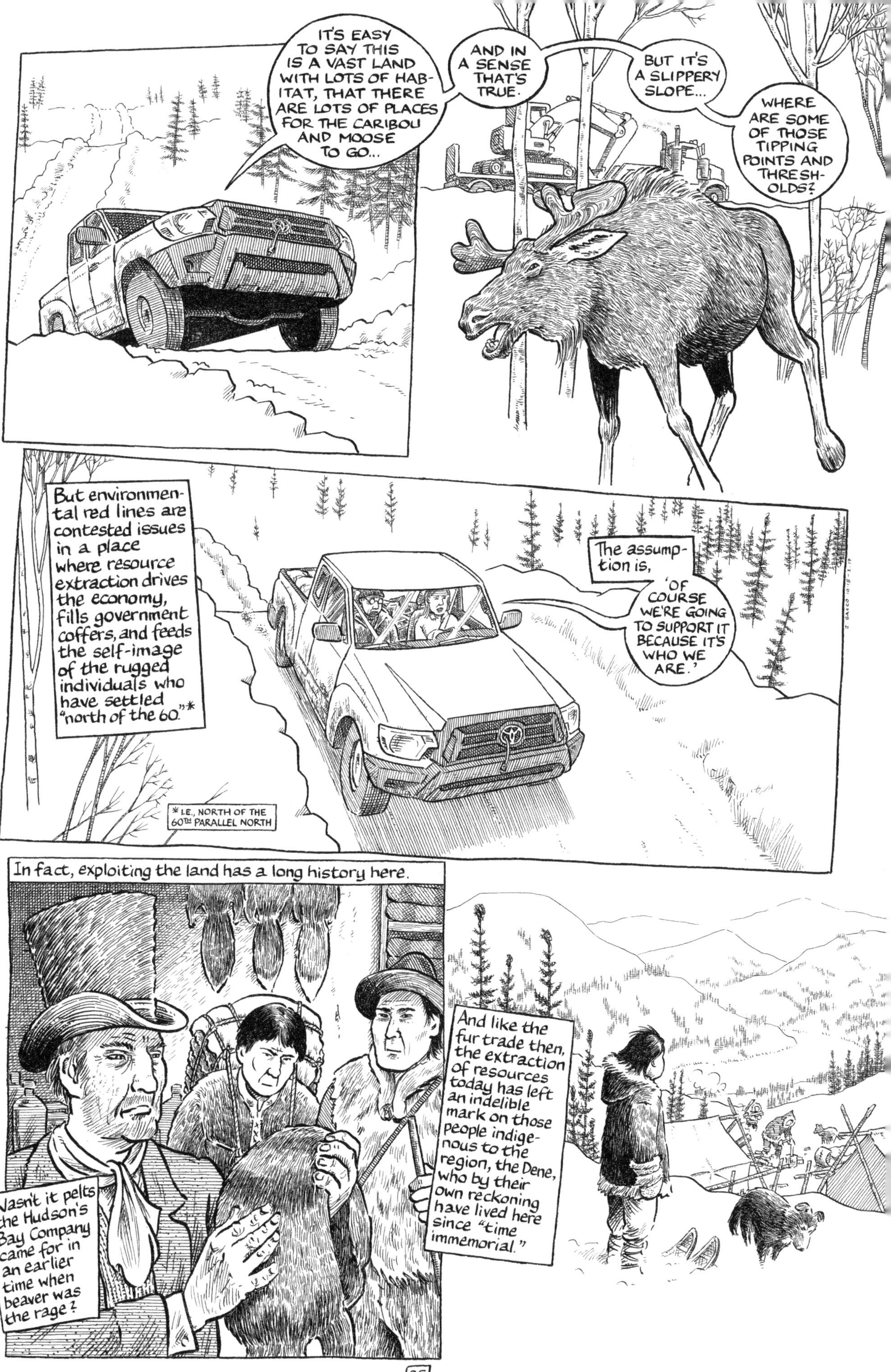
IT'S EASY TO SAY THIS IS A VAST LAND WITH LOTS OF HAB-ITAT, THAT THERE ARE LOTS OF PLACES FOR THE CARIBOU AND MOOSE TO GO...
AND IN A SENSE THAT'S TRUE.
BUT IT'S A SLIPPERY SLOPE...
WHERE ARE SOME OF THOSE TIPPING POINTS AND THRESH-OLDS?
But environmen-tal red lines are contested issues in a place where resource extraction drives the economy, fills government coffers, and feeds the self-image of the rugged individuals who have settled "north of the 60."*
The assump-tion is,
'OF COURSE WE'RE GOING TO SUPPORT IT BECAUSE IT'S WHO WE ARE.'
*I.E., NORTH OF THE 60TH PARALLEL NORTH
In fact, exploiting the land has a long history here.
Wasn't it pelts the Hudson's Bay Company came for in an earlier time when beaver was the rage?
And like the fur trade then, the extraction of resources today has left an indelible mark on those people indige-nous to the region, the Dene, who by their own reckoning have lived here since "time immemorial."

WE WON'T LET IT CONTROL US

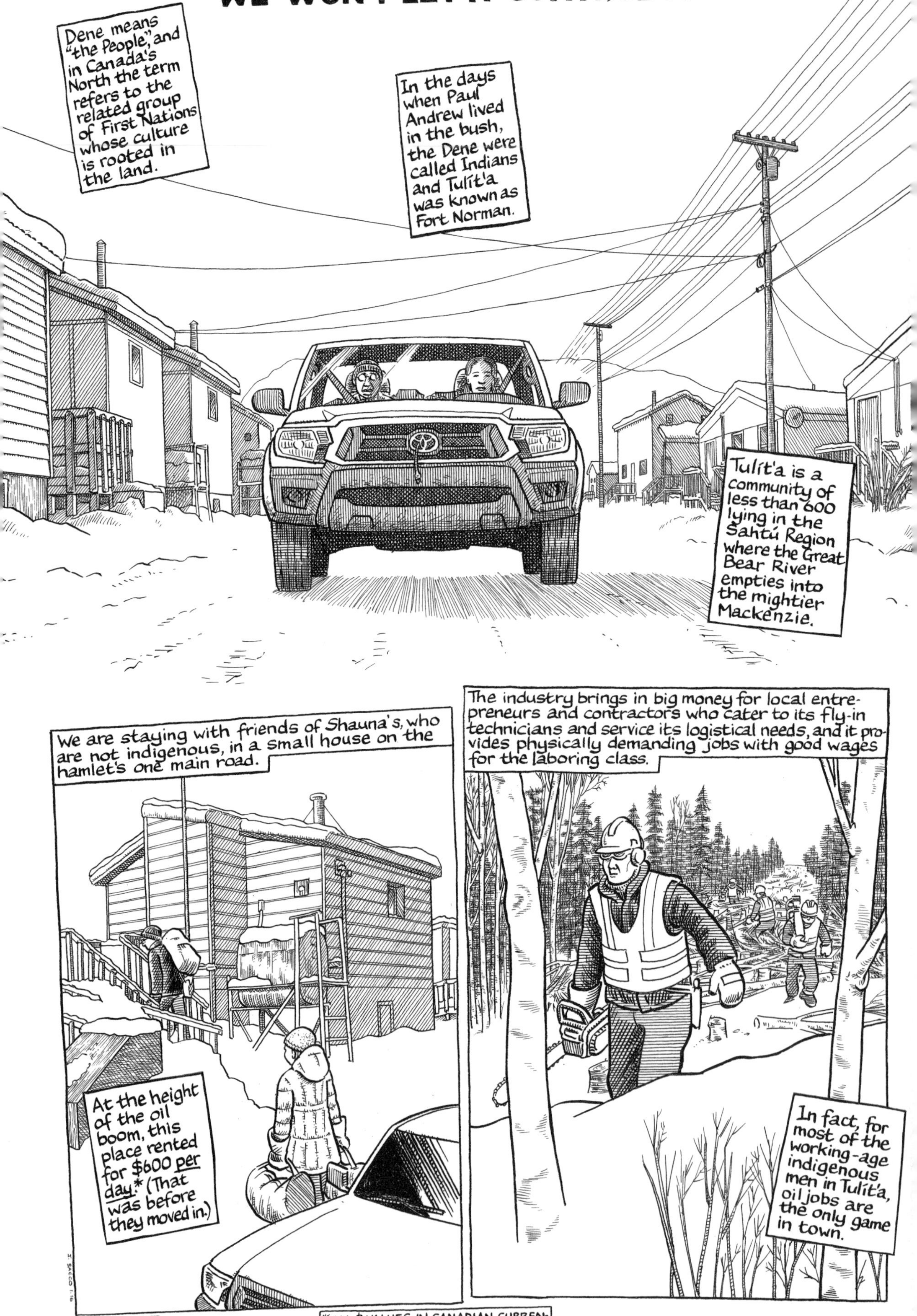

Dene means "the People," and in Canada's North the term refers to the related group of First Nations whose culture is rooted in the land.
In the days when Paul Andrew lived in the bush, the Dene were called Indians and Tulít'a was known as Fort Norman.
Tulít'a is a community of less than 600 lying in the Sahtú Region where the Great Bear River empties into the mightier Mackenzie.
We are staying with friends of Shauna's, who are not indigenous, in a small house on the hamlet's one main road.
At the height of the oil boom, this place rented for $600 per day.* (That was before they moved in.)
The industry brings in big money for local entrepreneurs and contractors who cater to its fly-in technicians and service its logistical needs, and it provides physically demanding jobs with good wages for the laboring class.
In fact, for most of the working-age indigenous men in Tulít'a, oil jobs are the only game in town.

*ALL $ VALUES IN CANADIAN CURRENCY. AT THIS TIME, $1 CAD ≈ $.80 USD.

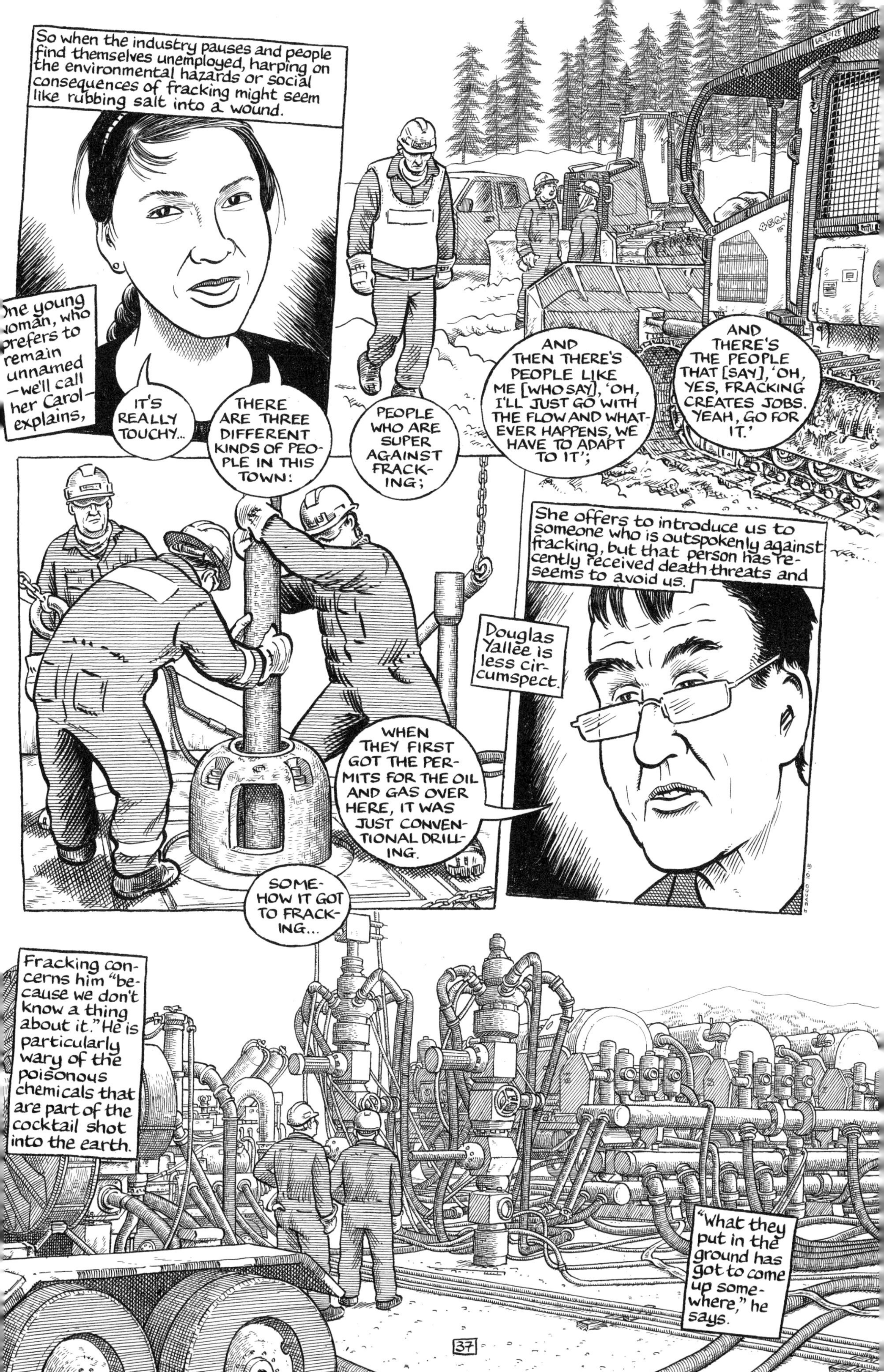
So when the industry pauses and people find themselves unemployed, harping on the environmental hazards or social consequences of fracking might seem like rubbing salt into a wound.
One young woman, who prefers to remain unnamed—we'll call her Carol—explains,
IT'S REALLY TOUCHY...
THERE ARE THREE DIFFERENT KINDS OF PEOPLE IN THIS TOWN:
PEOPLE WHO ARE SUPER AGAINST FRACKING;
AND THEN THERE'S PEOPLE LIKE ME [WHO SAY], 'OH, I'LL JUST GO WITH THE FLOW AND WHATEVER HAPPENS, WE HAVE TO ADAPT TO IT';
AND THERE'S THE PEOPLE THAT [SAY], 'OH, YES, FRACKING CREATES JOBS. YEAH, GO FOR IT.'
She offers to introduce us to someone who is outspokenly against fracking, but that person has recently received death threats and seems to avoid us.
Douglas Yallee is less circumspect.
WHEN THEY FIRST GOT THE PERMITS FOR THE OIL AND GAS OVER HERE, IT WAS JUST CONVENTIONAL DRILLING.
SOMEHOW IT GOT TO FRACKING...
Fracking concerns him "because we don't know a thing about it." He is particularly wary of the poisonous chemicals that are part of the cocktail shot into the earth.
"What they put in the ground has got to come up somewhere," he says.

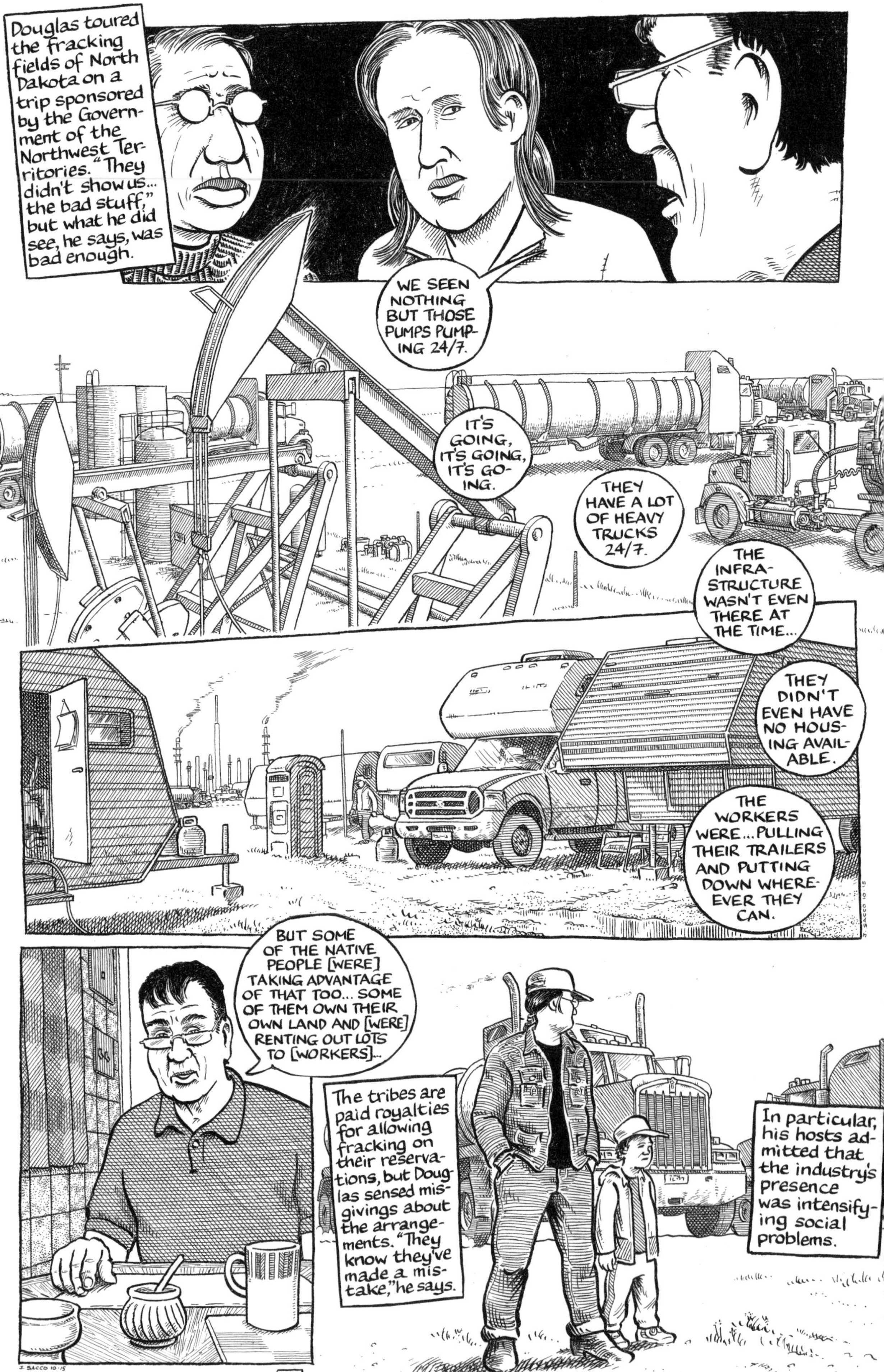

Douglas toured the fracking fields of North Dakota on a trip sponsored by the Government of the Northwest Territories. "They didn't show us... the bad stuff," but what he did see, he says, was bad enough.
WE SEEN NOTHING BUT THOSE PUMPS PUMPING 24/7.
IT'S GOING, IT'S GOING, IT'S GOING.
THEY HAVE A LOT OF HEAVY TRUCKS 24/7.
THE INFRASTRUCTURE WASN'T EVEN THERE AT THE TIME...
THEY DIDN'T EVEN HAVE NO HOUSING AVAILABLE.
THE WORKERS WERE... PULLING THEIR TRAILERS AND PUTTING DOWN WHEREEVER THEY CAN.
J. SACCO 10-15
BUT SOME OF THE NATIVE PEOPLE [WERE] TAKING ADVANTAGE OF THAT TOO... SOME OF THEM OWN THEIR OWN LAND AND [WERE] RENTING OUT LOTS TO [WORKERS]...
The tribes are paid royalties for allowing fracking on their reservations, but Douglas sensed misgivings about the arrangements. "They know they've made a mistake," he says.
In particular, his hosts admitted that the industry's presence was intensifying social problems.
J. SACCO 10-15

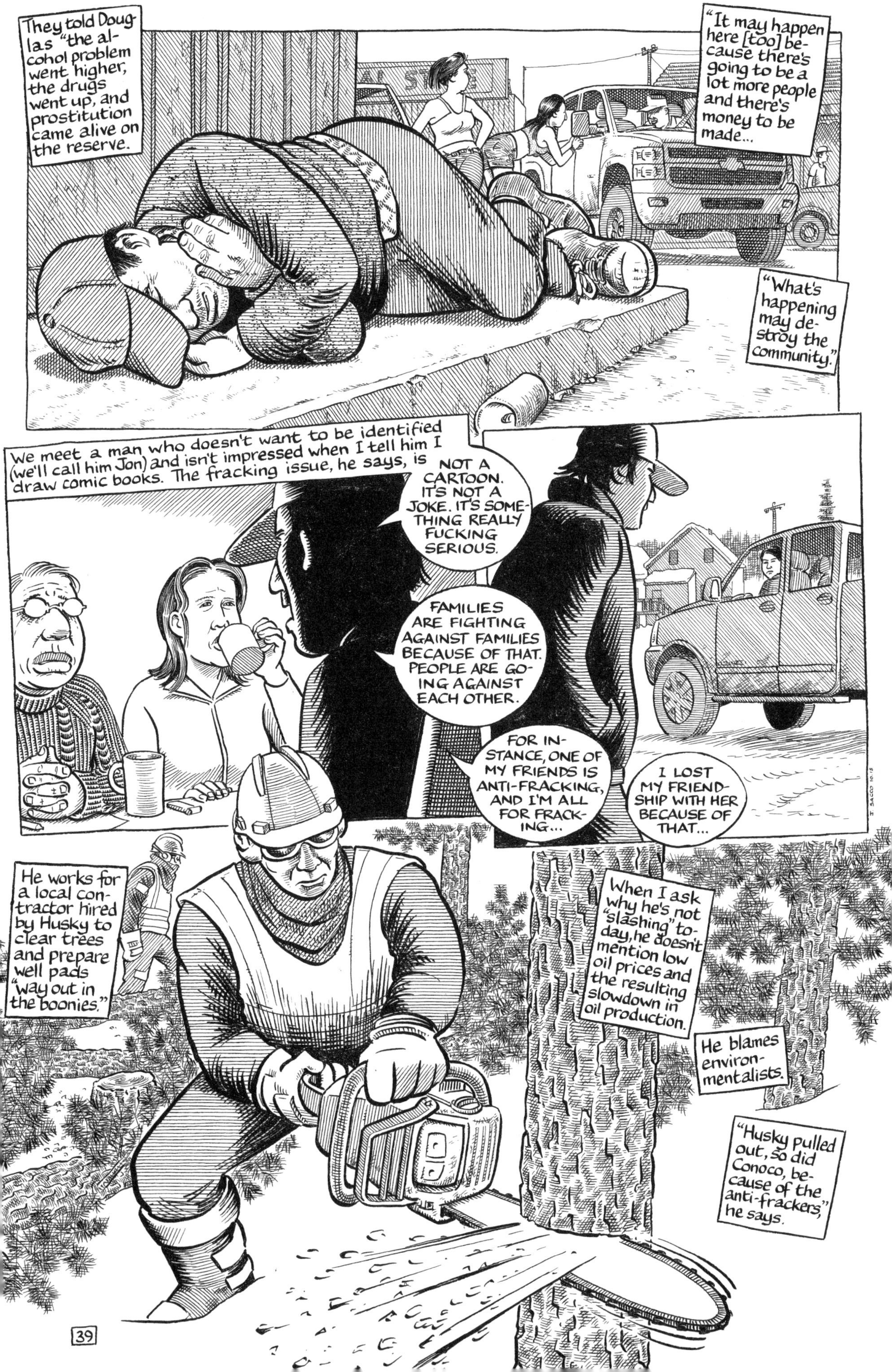

They told Douglas "the alcohol problem went higher, the drugs went up, and prostitution came alive on the reserve.
"It may happen here [too] because there's going to be a lot more people and there's money to be made...
"What's happening may destroy the community."
We meet a man who doesn't want to be identified (we'll call him Jon) and isn't impressed when I tell him I draw comic books. The fracking issue, he says, is
NOT A CARTOON. IT'S NOT A JOKE. IT'S SOMETHING REALLY FUCKING SERIOUS.
FAMILIES ARE FIGHTING AGAINST FAMILIES BECAUSE OF THAT. PEOPLE ARE GOING AGAINST EACH OTHER.
FOR INSTANCE, ONE OF MY FRIENDS IS ANTI-FRACKING, AND I'M ALL FOR FRACKING...
I LOST MY FRIENDSHIP WITH HER BECAUSE OF THAT...
He works for a local contractor hired by Husky to clear trees and prepare well pads "way out in the boonies."
When I ask why he's not "slashing" today, he doesn't mention low oil prices and the resulting slowdown in oil production.
He blames environmentalists.
"Husky pulled out, so did Conoco, because of the anti-frackers," he says.

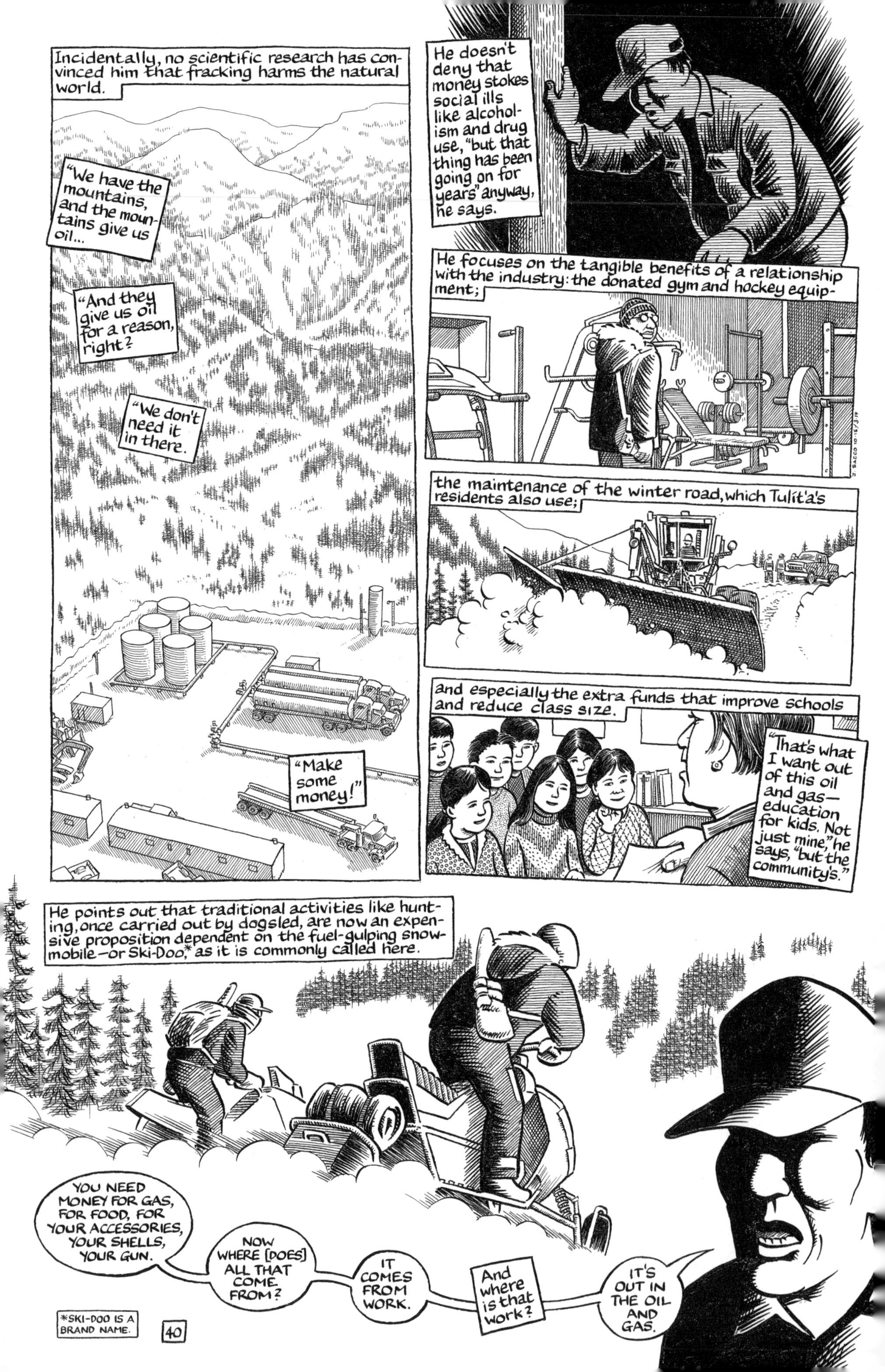

Incidentally, no scientific research has convinced him that fracking harms the natural world.
"We have the mountains, and the mountains give us oil...
"And they give us oil for a reason, right?
"We don't need it in there.
"Make some money!"
He doesn't deny that money stokes social ills like alcoholism and drug use, "but that thing has been going on for years" anyway, he says.
He focuses on the tangible benefits of a relationship with the industry: the donated gym and hockey equipment;
J. SACCO 10-15/3-14
the maintenance of the winter road, which Tulít'a's residents also use;
and especially the extra funds that improve schools and reduce class size.
"That's what I want out of this oil and gas— education for kids. Not just mine," he says, "but the community's."
He points out that traditional activities like hunting, once carried out by dogsled, are now an expensive proposition dependent on the fuel-gulping snowmobile—or Ski-Doo,* as it is commonly called here.
YOU NEED MONEY FOR GAS, FOR FOOD, FOR YOUR ACCESSORIES, YOUR SHELLS, YOUR GUN.
NOW WHERE [DOES] ALL THAT COME FROM?
IT COMES FROM WORK.
And where is that work?
IT'S OUT IN THE OIL AND GAS.

*SKI-DOO IS A BRAND NAME.

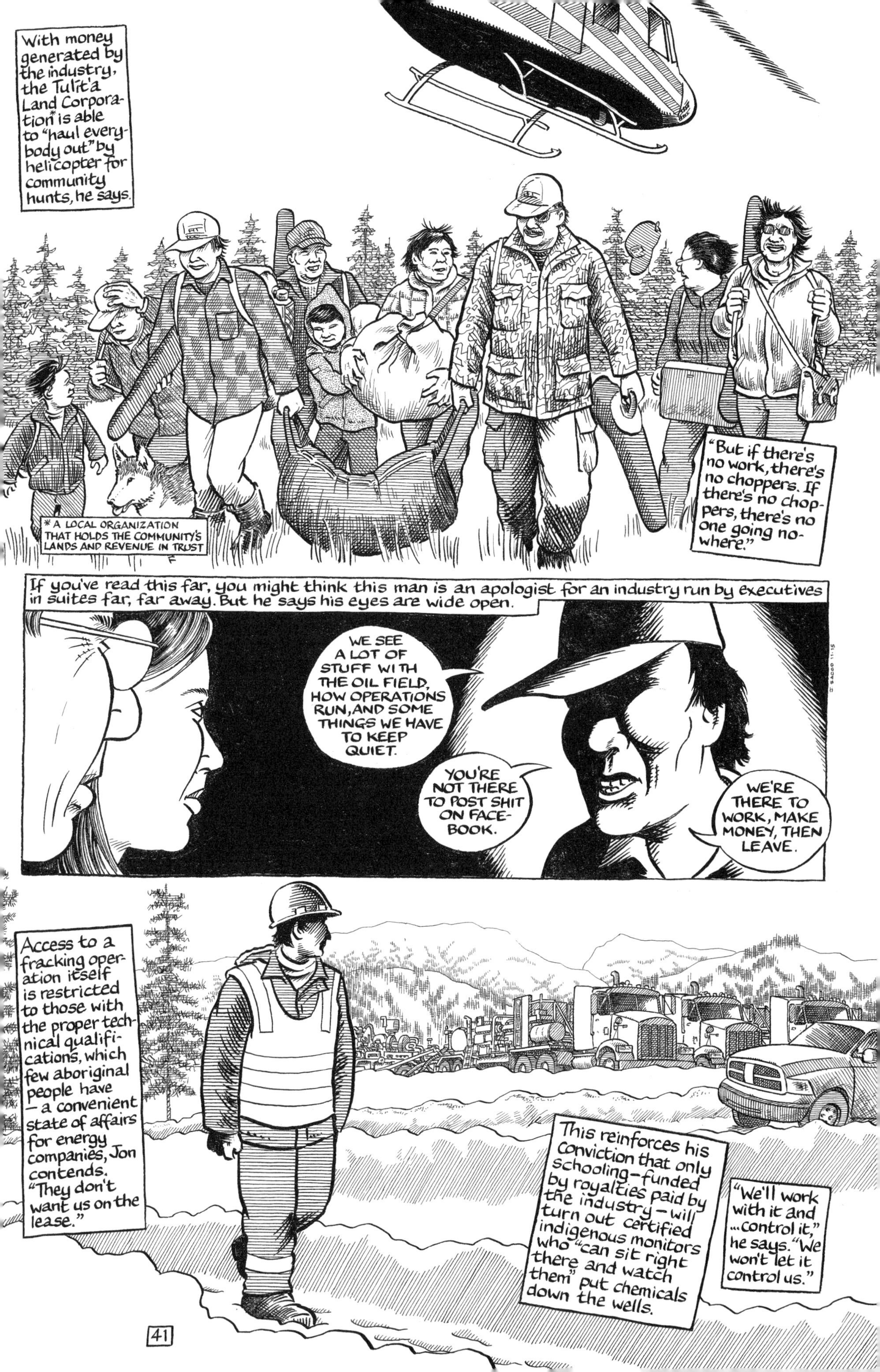
With money generated by the industry, the Tulít'a Land Corporation* is able to "haul everybody out" by helicopter for community hunts, he says.
* A LOCAL ORGANIZATION THAT HOLDS THE COMMUNITY'S LANDS AND REVENUE IN TRUST
"But if there's no work, there's no choppers. If there's no choppers, there's no one going nowhere."
If you've read this far, you might think this man is an apologist for an industry run by executives in suites far, far away. But he says his eyes are wide open.
WE SEE A LOT OF STUFF WITH THE OIL FIELD, HOW OPERATIONS RUN, AND SOME THINGS WE HAVE TO KEEP QUIET.
YOU'RE NOT THERE TO POST SHIT ON FACEBOOK.
WE'RE THERE TO WORK, MAKE MONEY, THEN LEAVE.
Access to a fracking operation itself is restricted to those with the proper technical qualifications, which few aboriginal people have — a convenient state of affairs for energy companies, Jon contends. "They don't want us on the lease."
This reinforces his conviction that only schooling — funded by royalties paid by the industry — will turn out certified indigenous monitors who "can sit right there and watch them" put chemicals down the wells.
"We'll work with it and ...control it," he says. "We won't let it control us."

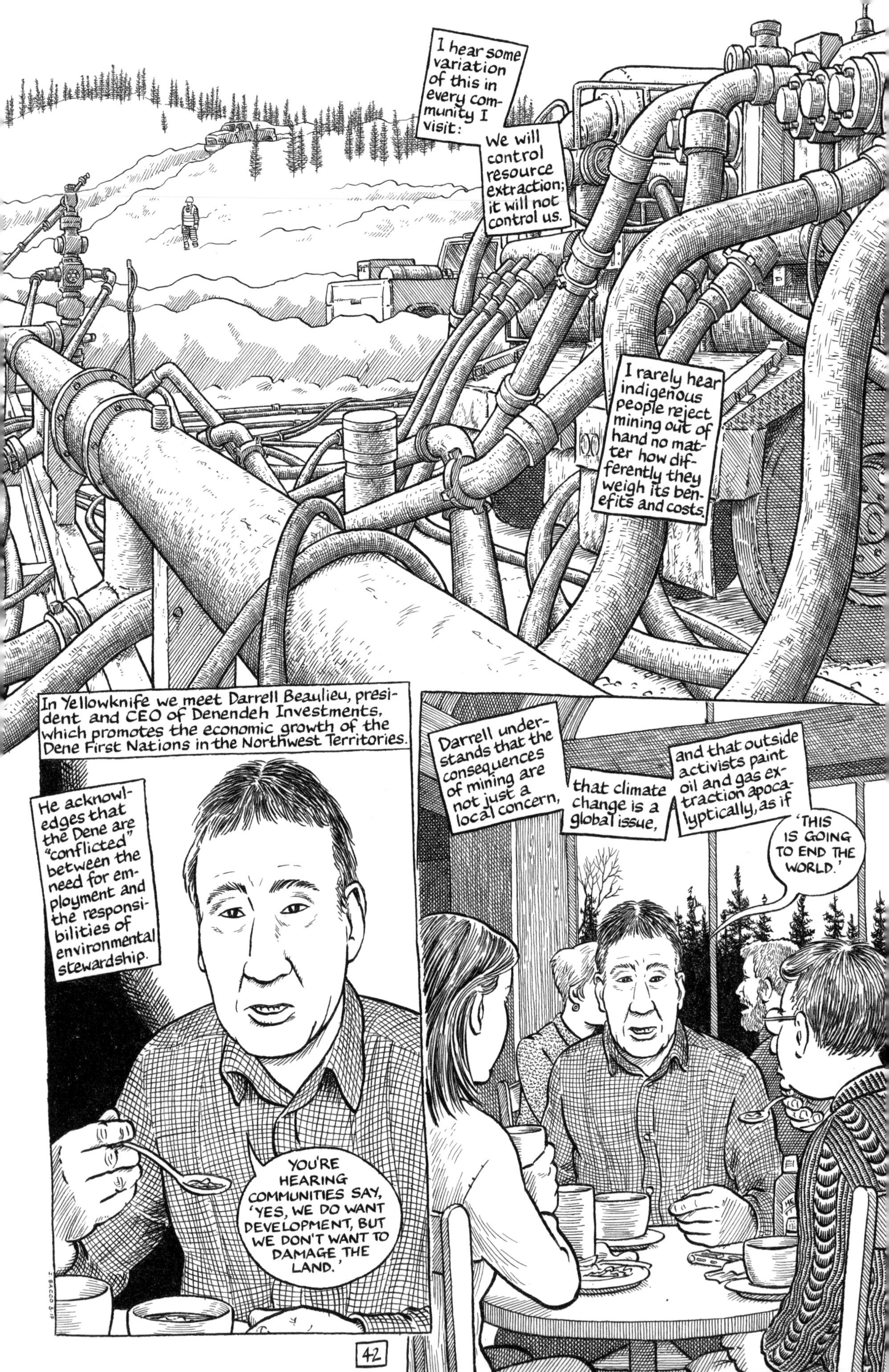

I hear some variation of this in every community I visit:
We will control resource extraction; it will not control us.
I rarely hear indigenous people reject mining out of hand no matter how differently they weigh its benefits and costs.
In Yellowknife we meet Darrell Beaulieu, president and CEO of Denendeh Investments, which promotes the economic growth of the Dene First Nations in the Northwest Territories.
He acknowledges that the Dene are "conflicted" between the need for employment and the responsibilities of environmental stewardship.
YOU'RE HEARING COMMUNITIES SAY, 'YES, WE DO WANT DEVELOPMENT, BUT WE DON'T WANT TO DAMAGE THE LAND.'
Darrell understands that the consequences of mining are not just a local concern,
that climate change is a global issue,
and that outside activists paint oil and gas extraction apocalyptically, as if
'THIS IS GOING TO END THE WORLD.'

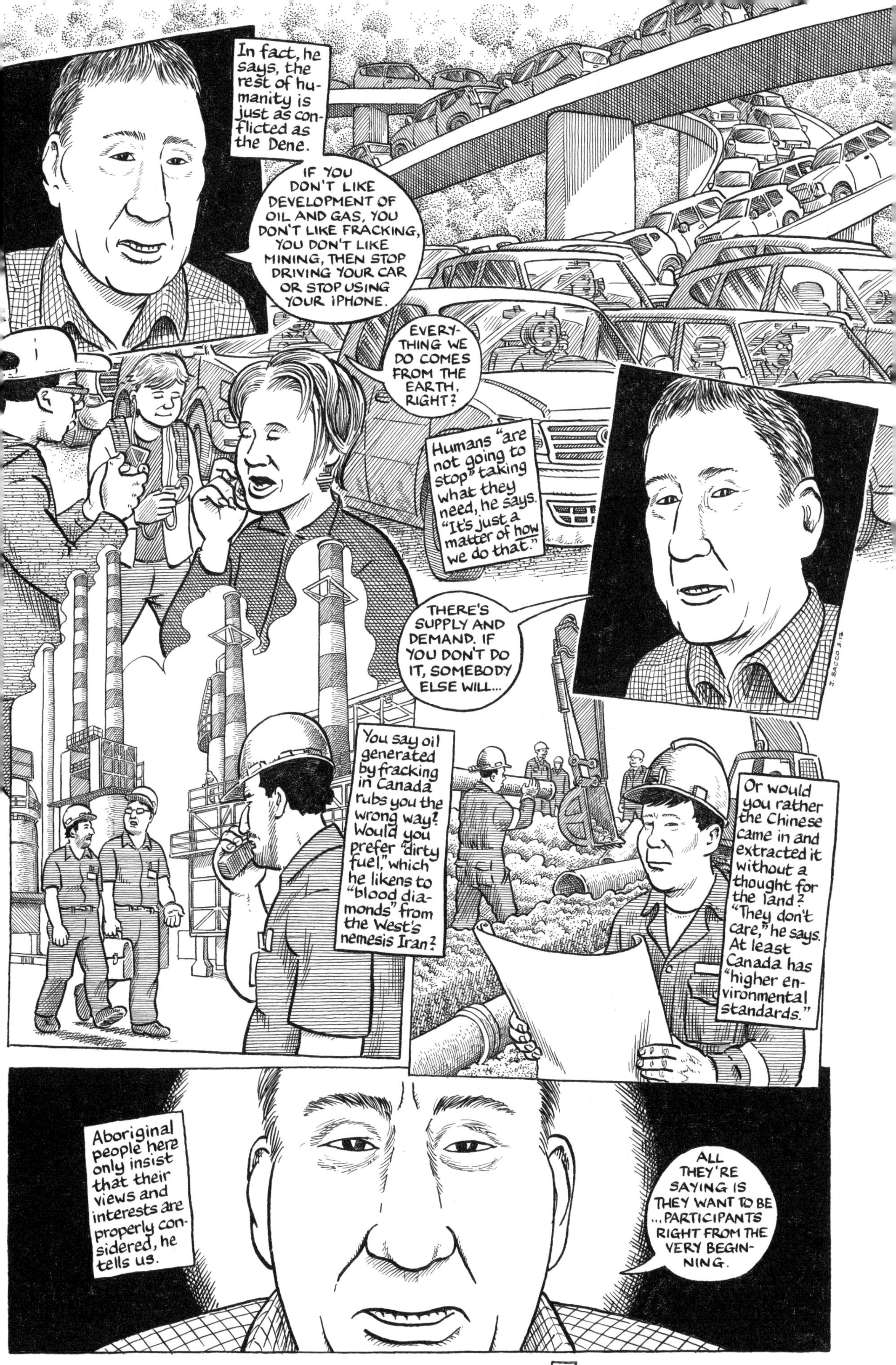
In fact, he says, the rest of humanity is just as conflicted as the Dene.
IF YOU DON'T LIKE DEVELOPMENT OF OIL AND GAS, YOU DON'T LIKE FRACKING, YOU DON'T LIKE MINING, THEN STOP DRIVING YOUR CAR OR STOP USING YOUR iPHONE.
EVERYTHING WE DO COMES FROM THE EARTH, RIGHT?
Humans "are not going to stop" taking what they need, he says. "It's just a matter of how we do that."
THERE'S SUPPLY AND DEMAND. IF YOU DON'T DO IT, SOMEBODY ELSE WILL...
J. SACCO 3.14
You say oil generated by fracking in Canada rubs you the wrong way? Would you prefer "dirty fuel," which he likens to "blood diamonds" from the West's nemesis Iran?
Or would you rather the Chinese came in and extracted it without a thought for the land? "They don't care," he says. At least Canada has "higher environmental standards."
Aboriginal people here only insist that their views and interests are properly considered, he tells us.
ALL THEY'RE SAYING IS THEY WANT TO BE ...PARTICIPANTS RIGHT FROM THE VERY BEGINNING.

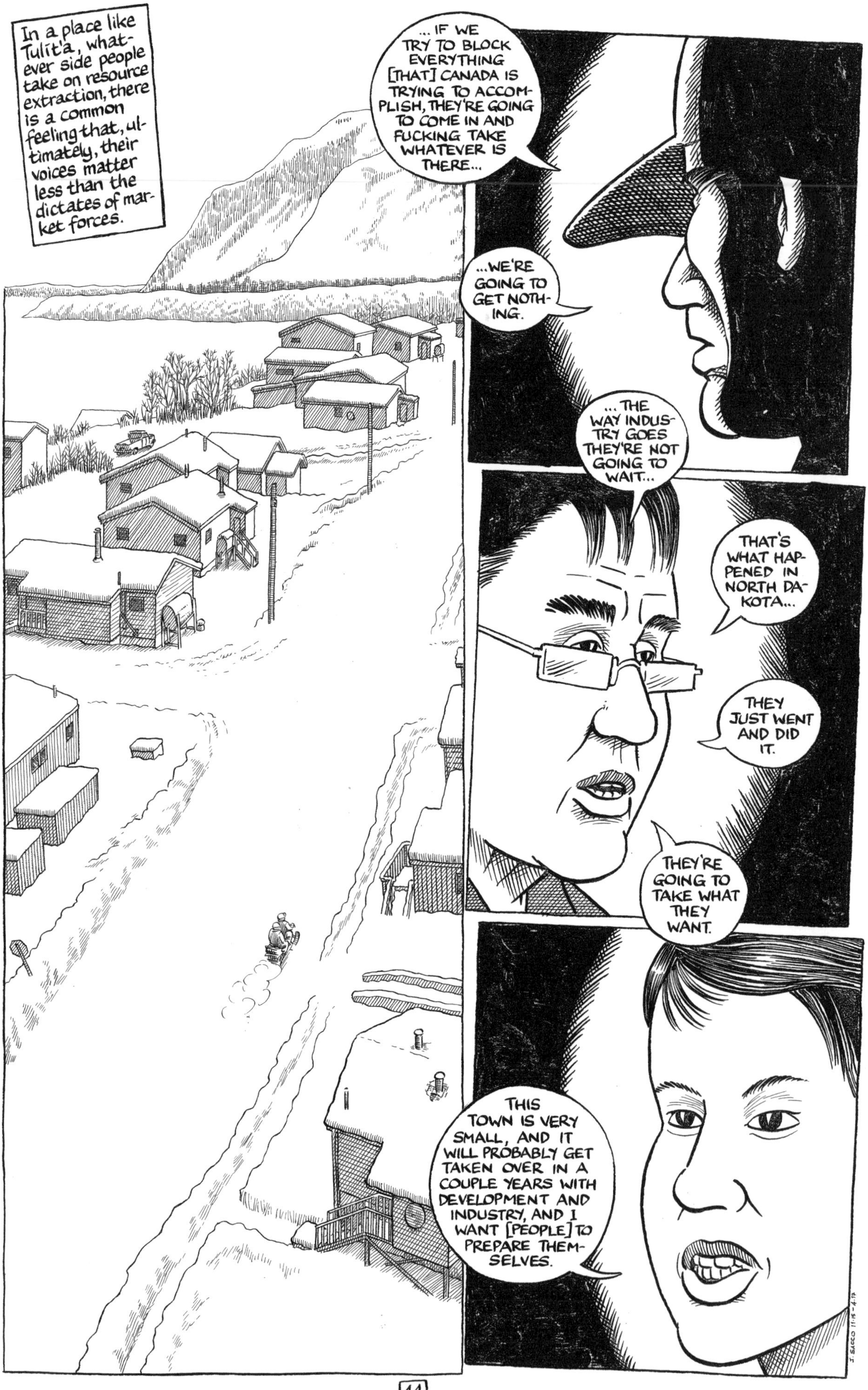
In a place like Tulít'a, whatever side people take on resource extraction, there is a common feeling that, ultimately, their voices matter less than the dictates of market forces.
...IF WE TRY TO BLOCK EVERYTHING [THAT] CANADA IS TRYING TO ACCOMPLISH, THEY'RE GOING TO COME IN AND FUCKING TAKE WHATEVER IS THERE...
...WE'RE GOING TO GET NOTHING.
...THE WAY INDUSTRY GOES THEY'RE NOT GOING TO WAIT...
THAT'S WHAT HAPPENED IN NORTH DAKOTA...
THEY JUST WENT AND DID IT.
THEY'RE GOING TO TAKE WHAT THEY WANT.
THIS TOWN IS VERY SMALL, AND IT WILL PROBABLY GET TAKEN OVER IN A COUPLE YEARS WITH DEVELOPMENT AND INDUSTRY, AND I WANT [PEOPLE] TO PREPARE THEMSELVES.

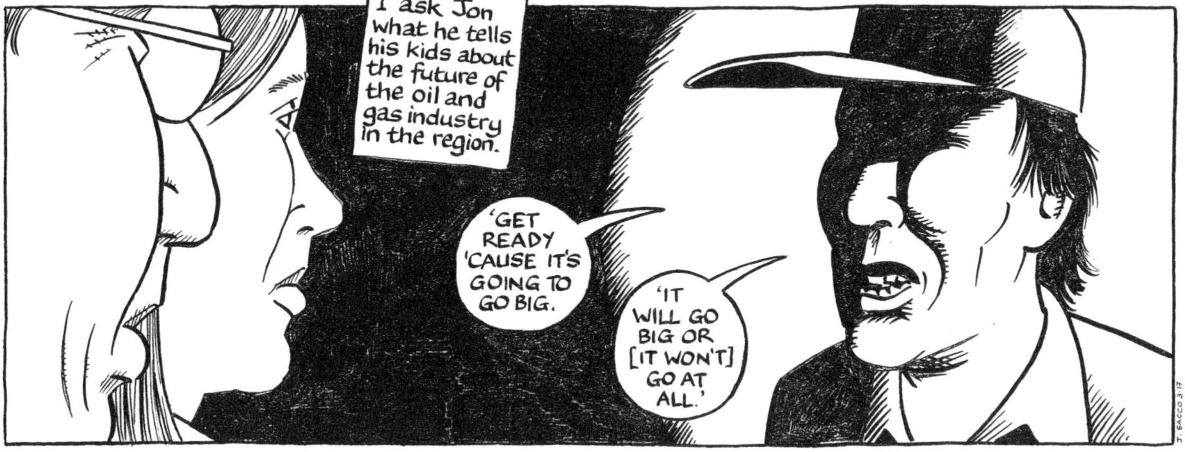
I ask Jon what he tells his kids about the future of the oil and gas industry in the region.
'GET READY 'CAUSE IT'S GOING TO GO BIG.
'IT WILL GO BIG OR [IT WON'T] GO AT ALL.'
J. SACCO 3.17

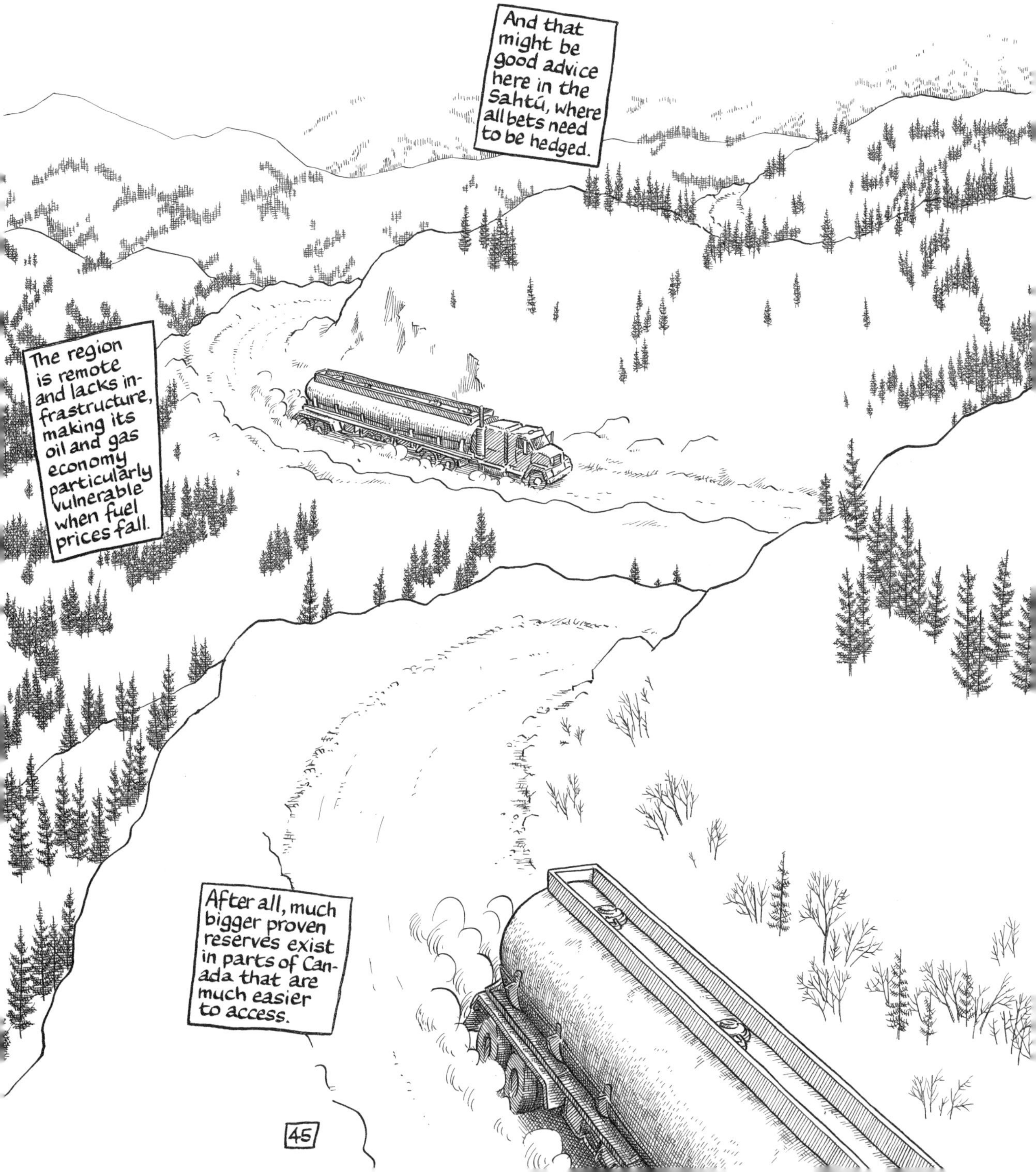
And that might be good advice here in the Sahtú, where all bets need to be hedged.
The region is remote and lacks in-frastructure, making its oil and gas economy particularly vulnerable when fuel prices fall.
After all, much bigger proven reserves exist in parts of Can-ada that are much easier to access.

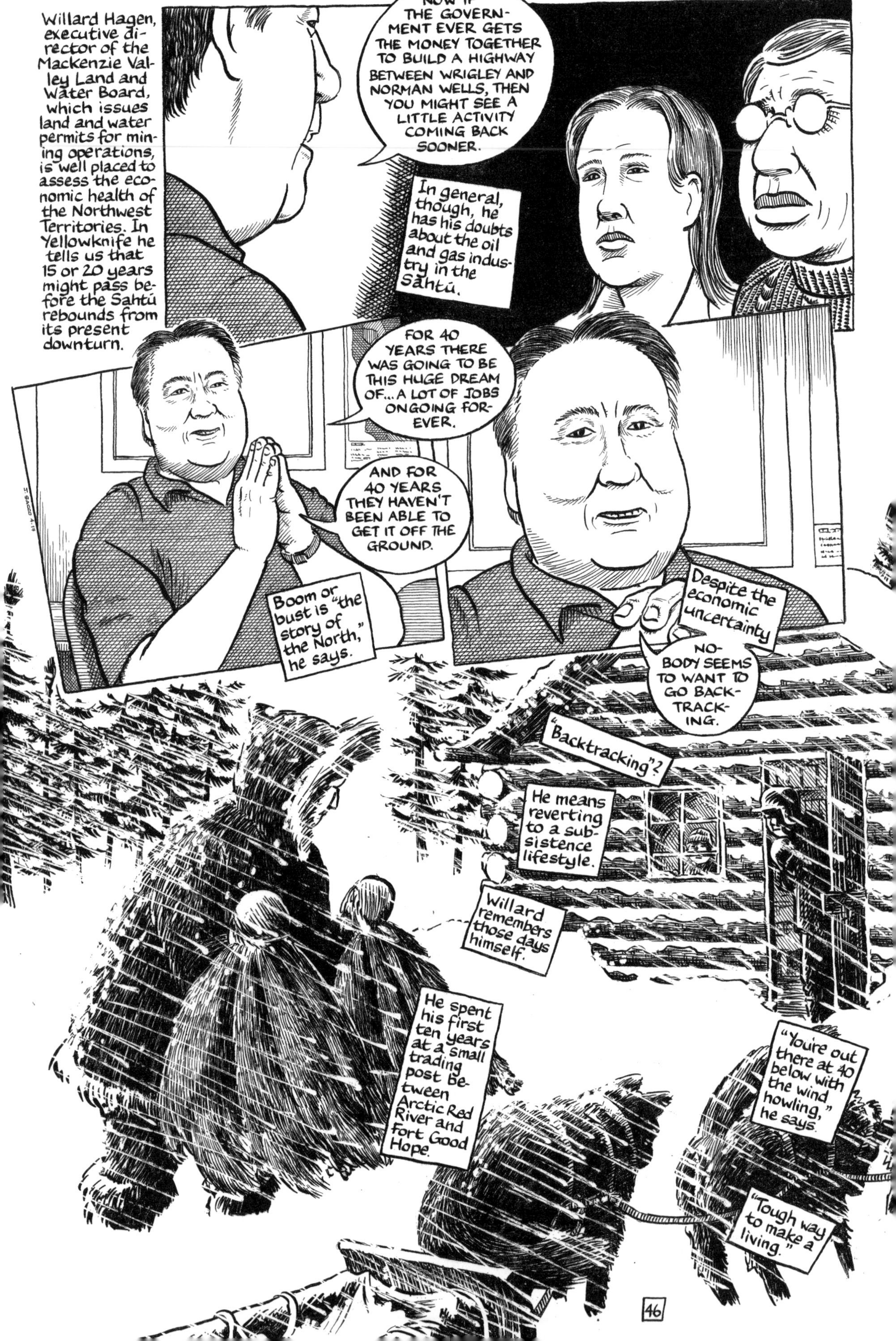
Willard Hagen, executive director of the Mackenzie Valley Land and Water Board, which issues land and water permits for mining operations, is well placed to assess the economic health of the Northwest Territories. In Yellowknife he tells us that 15 or 20 years might pass before the Sahtú rebounds from its present downturn.
NOW IF THE GOVERNMENT EVER GETS THE MONEY TOGETHER TO BUILD A HIGHWAY BETWEEN WRIGLEY AND NORMAN WELLS, THEN YOU MIGHT SEE A LITTLE ACTIVITY COMING BACK SOONER.
In general, though, he has his doubts about the oil and gas industry in the Sahtú.
FOR 40 YEARS THERE WAS GOING TO BE THIS HUGE DREAM OF... A LOT OF JOBS ONGOING FOREVER.
AND FOR 40 YEARS THEY HAVEN'T BEEN ABLE TO GET IT OFF THE GROUND.
Boom or bust is "the story of the North," he says.
Despite the economic uncertainty
NOBODY SEEMS TO WANT TO GO BACKTRACKING.
"Backtracking"?
He means reverting to a subsistence lifestyle.
Willard remembers those days himself.
He spent his first ten years at a small trading post between Arctic Red River and Fort Good Hope.
"You're out there at 40 below with the wind howling," he says.
"Tough way to make a living."

III

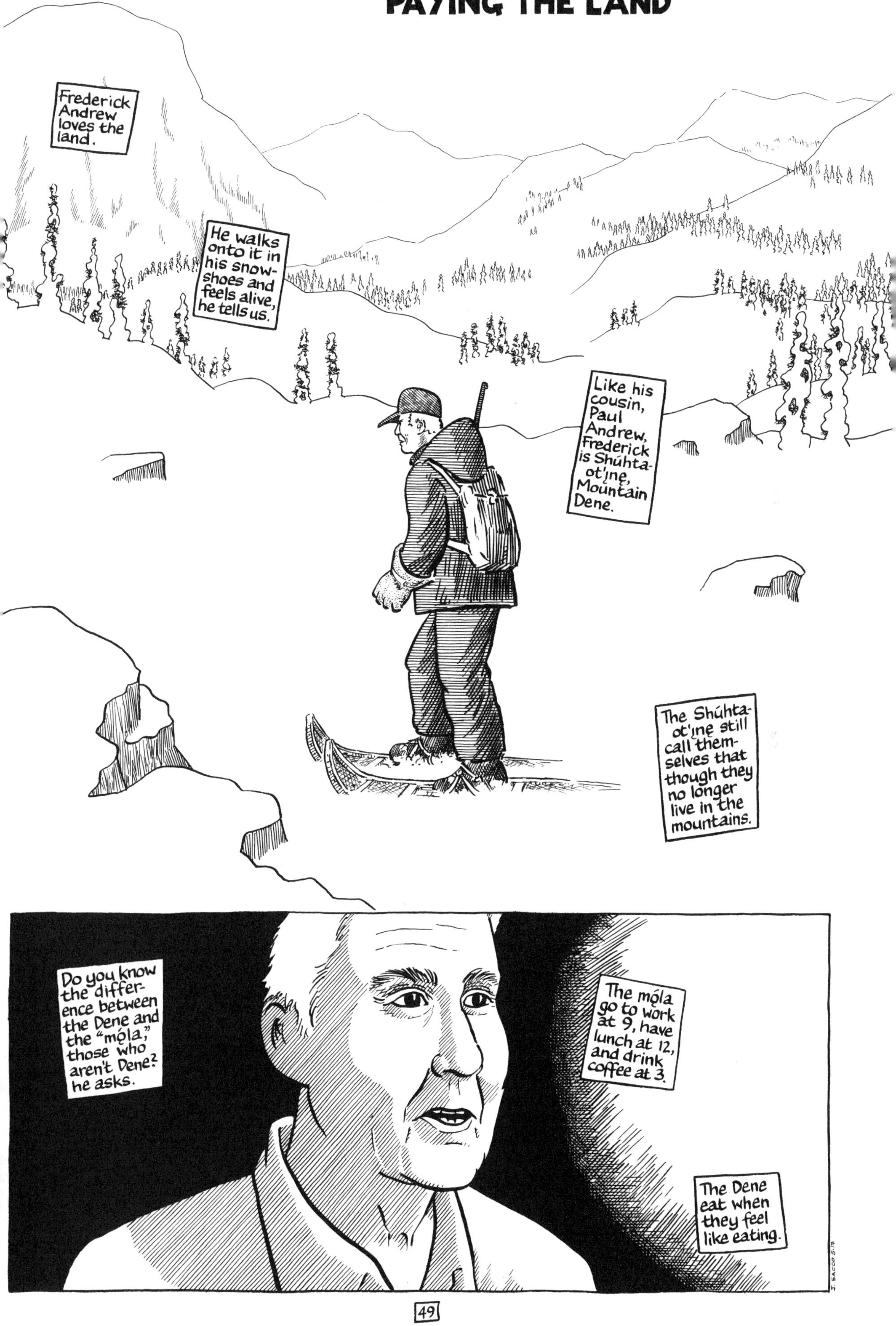
Frederick Andrew loves the land.
He walks onto it in his snow-shoes and feels alive, he tells us.
Like his cousin, Paul Andrew, Frederick is Shúhta-ot'ı̨nę, Mountain Dene.
The Shúhta-ot'ı̨nę still call them-selves that though they no longer live in the mountains.
Do you know the differ-ence between the Dene and the "mǫ́la," those who aren't Dene? he asks.
The mǫ́la go to work at 9, have lunch at 12, and drink coffee at 3.
The Dene eat when they feel like eating.

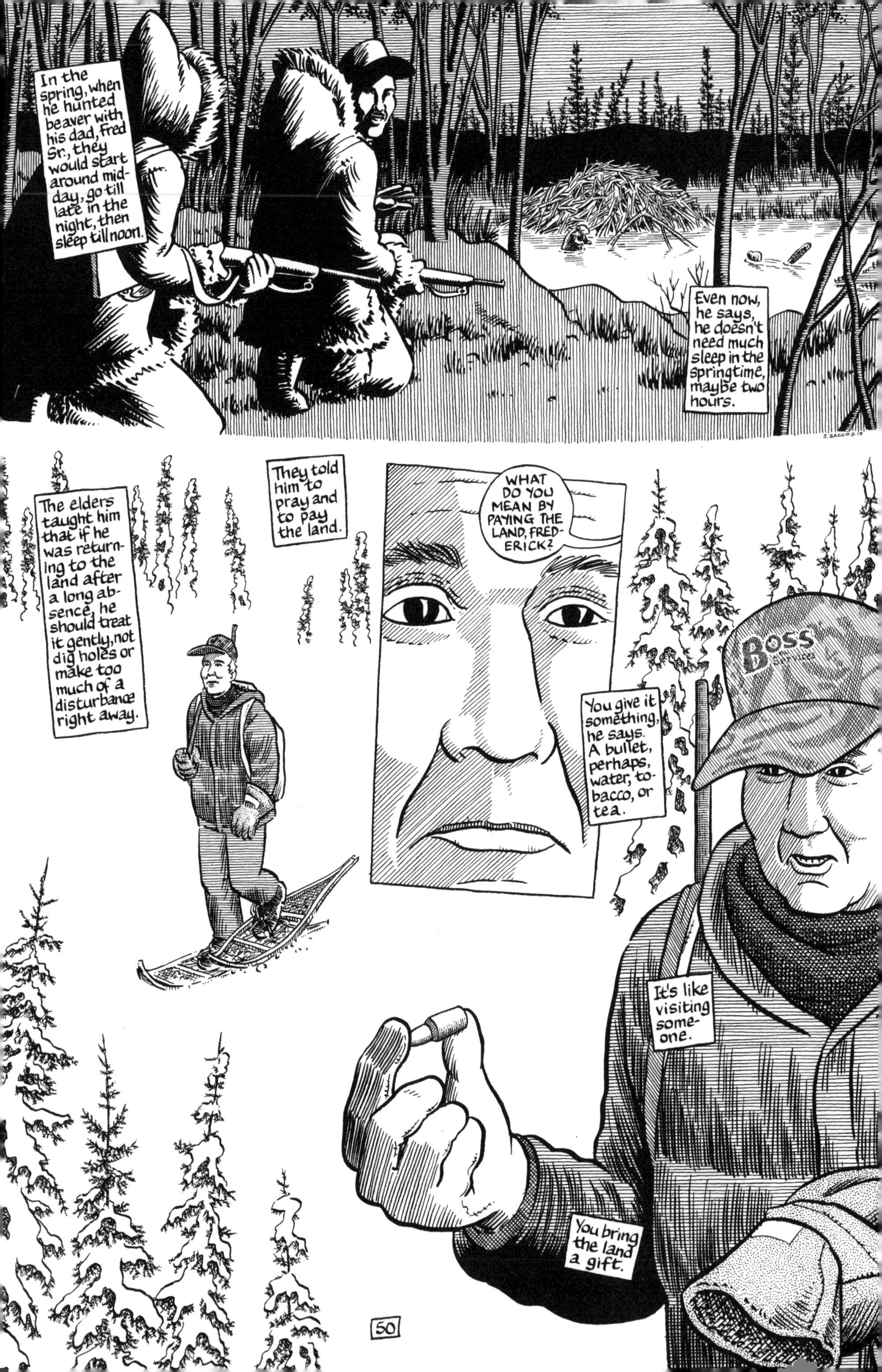
In the spring, when he hunted beaver with his dad, Fred Sr., they would start around midday, go till late in the night, then sleep till noon.
Even now, he says, he doesn't need much sleep in the springtime, maybe two hours.
J. SACCO 5.17
The elders taught him that if he was returning to the land after a long absence, he should treat it gently, not dig holes or make too much of a disturbance right away.
They told him to pray and to pay the land.
WHAT DO YOU MEAN BY PAYING THE LAND, FREDERICK?
You give it something, he says. A bullet, perhaps, water, tobacco, or tea.
BOSS
It's like visiting someone.
You bring the land a gift.

NO QUESTION OF POLITICS, OWNERSHIP, OR ANYTHING LIKE THIS

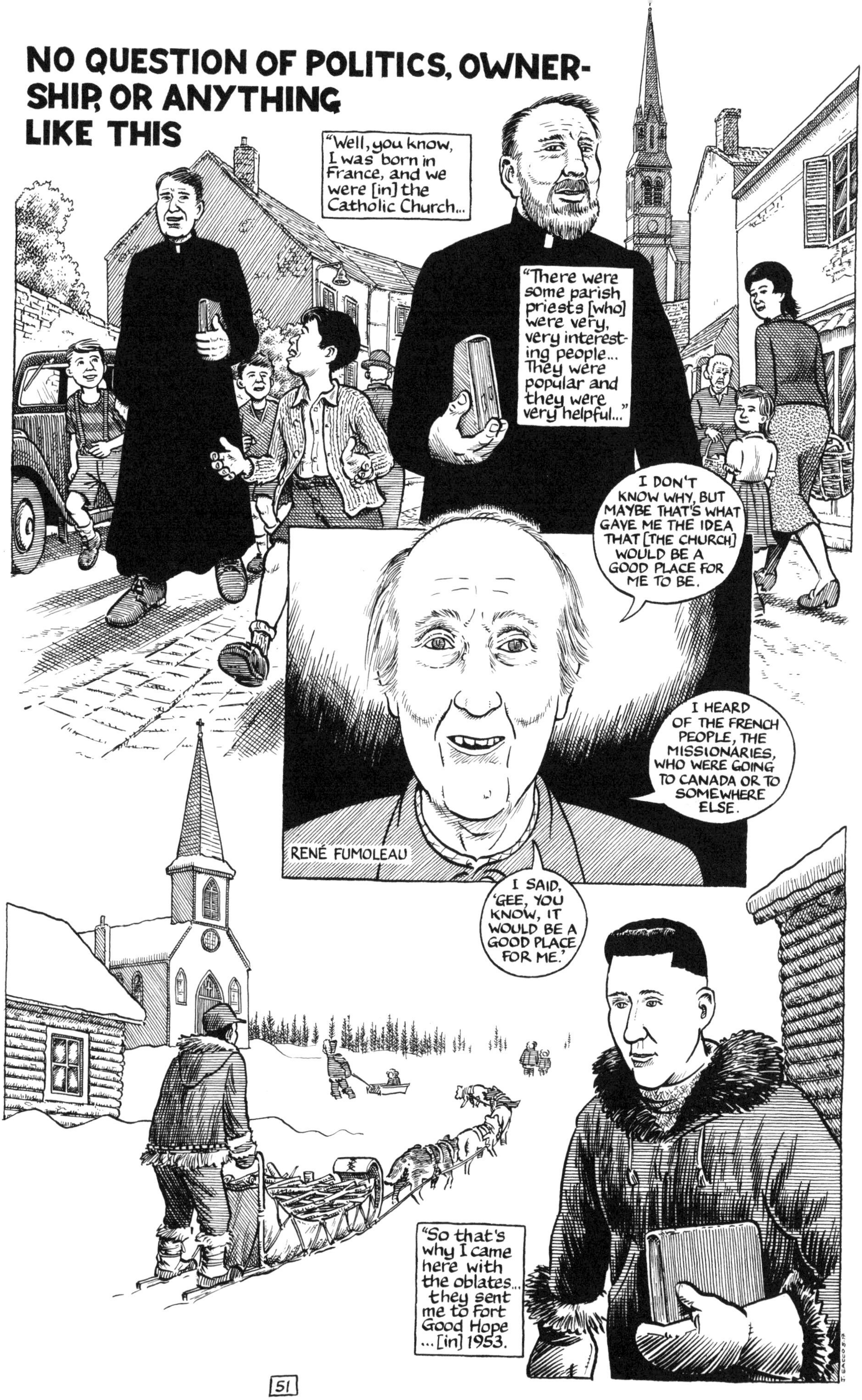
"Well, you know, I was born in France, and we were [in] the Catholic Church...
"There were some parish priests [who] were very, very interesting people... They were popular and they were very helpful..."
I DON'T KNOW WHY, BUT MAYBE THAT'S WHAT GAVE ME THE IDEA THAT [THE CHURCH] WOULD BE A GOOD PLACE FOR ME TO BE.
I HEARD OF THE FRENCH PEOPLE, THE MISSIONARIES, WHO WERE GOING TO CANADA OR TO SOMEWHERE ELSE.
RENÉ FUMOLEAU
I SAID, 'GEE, YOU KNOW, IT WOULD BE A GOOD PLACE FOR ME.'
"So that's why I came here with the oblates... they sent me to Fort Good Hope ...[in] 1953.

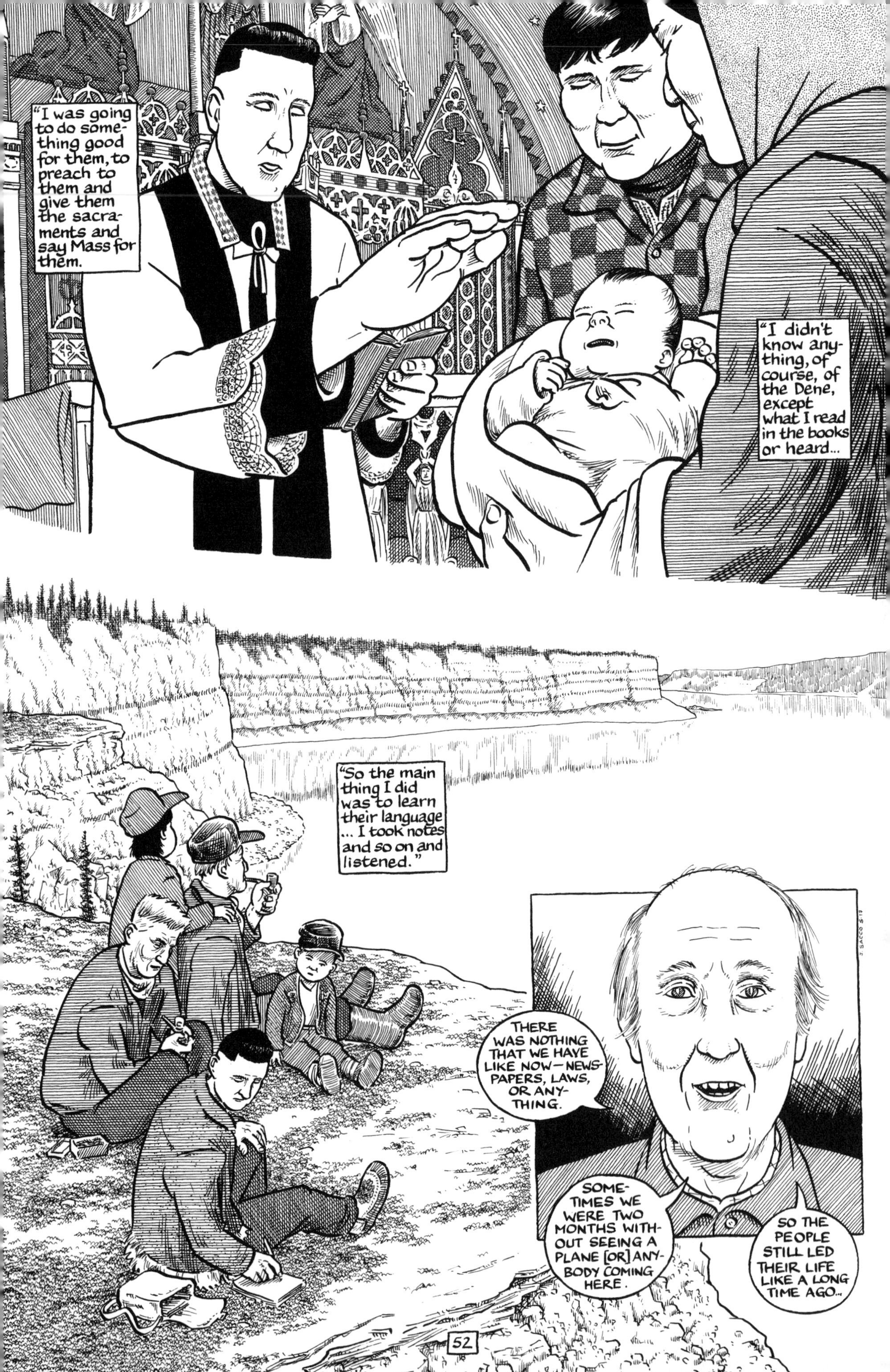
"I was going to do something good for them, to preach to them and give them the sacraments and say Mass for them.
"I didn't know anything, of course, of the Dene, except what I read in the books or heard...
"So the main thing I did was to learn their language ... I took notes and so on and listened."
THERE WAS NOTHING THAT WE HAVE LIKE NOW—NEWSPAPERS, LAWS, OR ANYTHING.
SOMETIMES WE WERE TWO MONTHS WITHOUT SEEING A PLANE [OR] ANYBODY COMING HERE.
SO THE PEOPLE STILL LED THEIR LIFE LIKE A LONG TIME AGO...

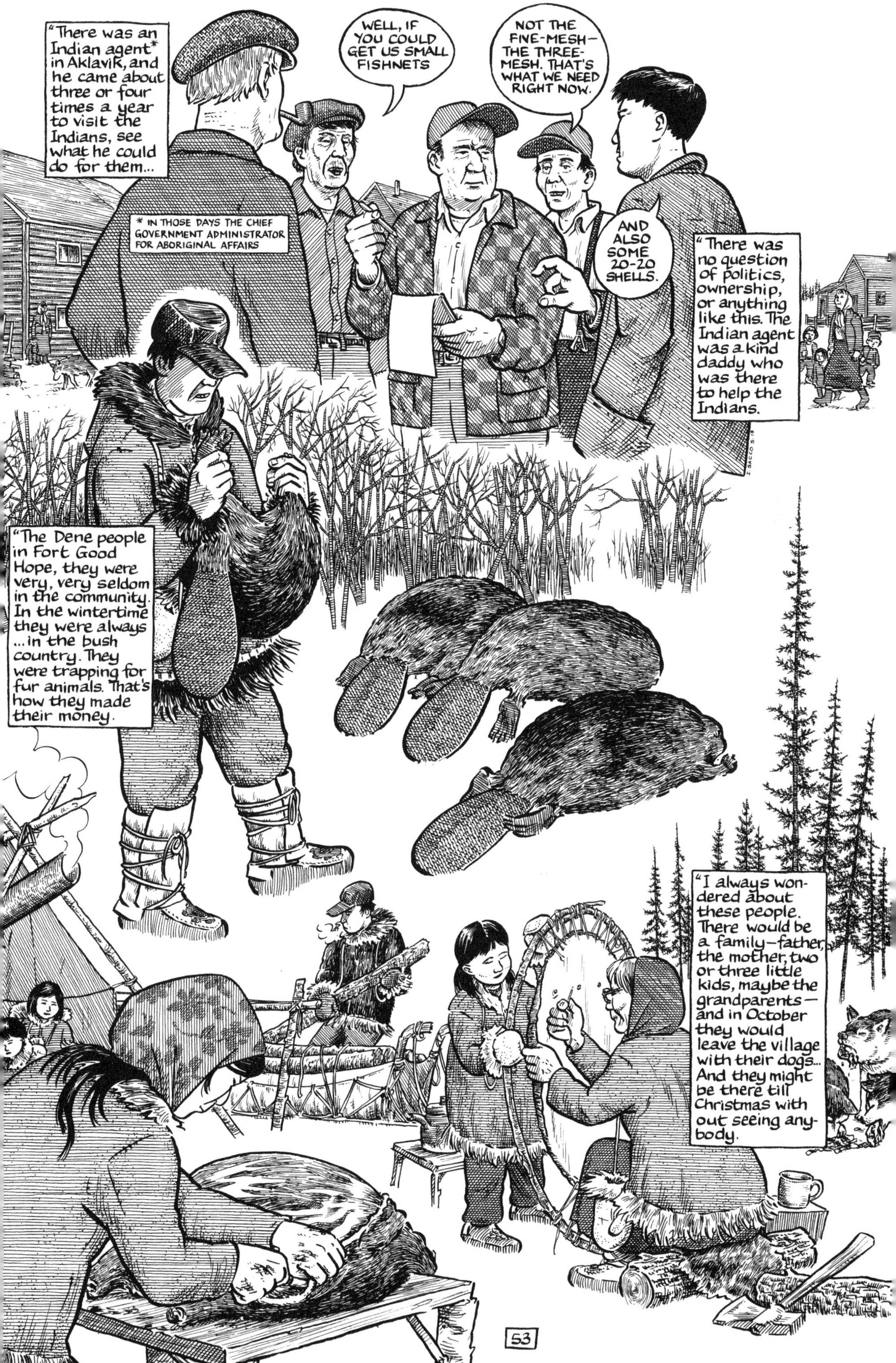
"There was an Indian agent* in Aklavik, and he came about three or four times a year to visit the Indians, see what he could do for them...
* IN THOSE DAYS THE CHIEF GOVERNMENT ADMINISTRATOR FOR ABORIGINAL AFFAIRS
WELL, IF YOU COULD GET US SMALL FISHNETS
NOT THE FINE-MESH— THE THREE-MESH. THAT'S WHAT WE NEED RIGHT NOW.
AND ALSO SOME 20-20 SHELLS.
"There was no question of politics, ownership, or anything like this. The Indian agent was a kind daddy who was there to help the Indians.
"The Dene people in Fort Good Hope, they were very, very seldom in the community. In the wintertime they were always ...in the bush country. They were trapping for fur animals. That's how they made their money.
"I always wondered about these people. There would be a family—father, the mother, two or three little kids, maybe the grandparents— and in October they would leave the village with their dogs... And they might be there till Christmas with out seeing anybody.

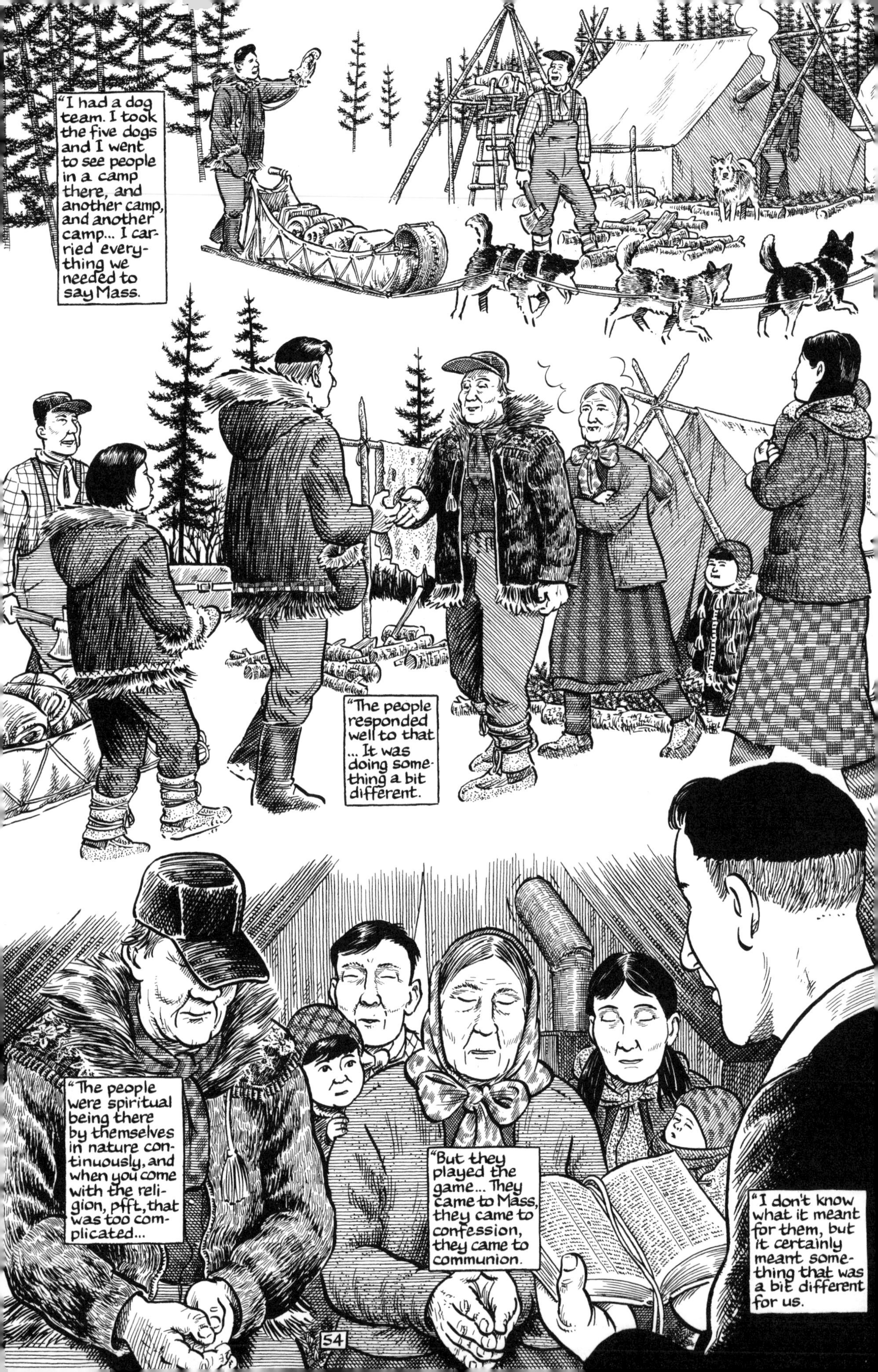
"I had a dog team. I took the five dogs and I went to see people in a camp there, and another camp, and another camp... I carried everything we needed to say Mass.
"The people responded well to that ... It was doing something a bit different.
"The people were spiritual being there by themselves in nature continuously, and when you come with the religion, pfft, that was too complicated...
"But they played the game... They came to Mass, they came to confession, they came to communion.
"I don't know what it meant for them, but it certainly meant something that was a bit different for us.

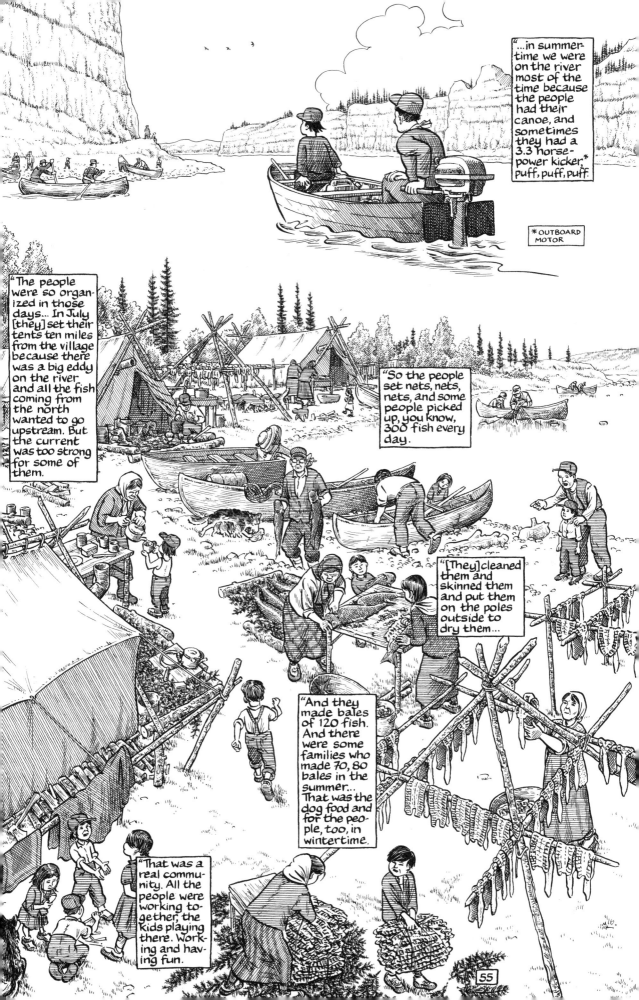

"...in summertime we were on the river most of the time because the people had their canoe, and sometimes they had a 3.3 horse-power kicker,* puff, puff, puff.

*OUTBOARD MOTOR

"The people were so organized in those days... In July [they] set their tents ten miles from the village because there was a big eddy on the river and all the fish coming from the north wanted to go upstream. But the current was too strong for some of them.

"So the people set nets, nets, nets, and some people picked up, you know, 300 fish every day.

"[They] cleaned them and skinned them and put them on the poles outside to dry them...

"And they made bales of 120 fish. And there were some families who made 70, 80 bales in the summer... That was the dog food and for the people, too, in wintertime.

"That was a real community. All the people were working together, the kids playing there. Working and having fun.

55

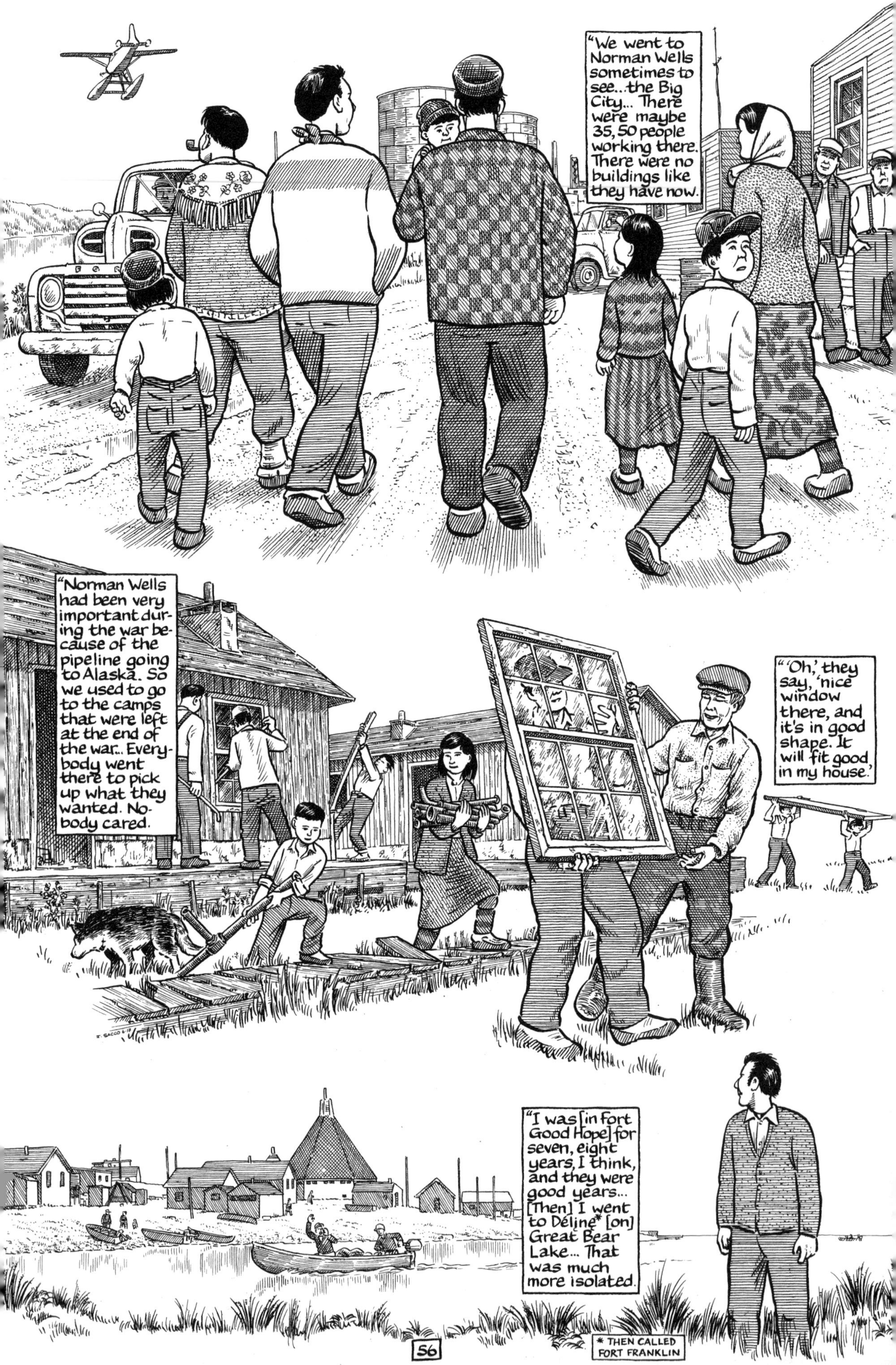
"We went to Norman Wells sometimes to see...the Big City... There were maybe 35, 50 people working there. There were no buildings like they have now.
"Norman Wells had been very important during the war because of the pipeline going to Alaska. So we used to go to the camps that were left at the end of the war... Everybody went there to pick up what they wanted. Nobody cared.
"'Oh,' they say, 'nice window there, and it's in good shape. It will fit good in my house.'
"I was [in Fort Good Hope] for seven, eight years, I think, and they were good years... [Then] I went to Déline* [on] Great Bear Lake... That was much more isolated.

* THEN CALLED FORT FRANKLIN

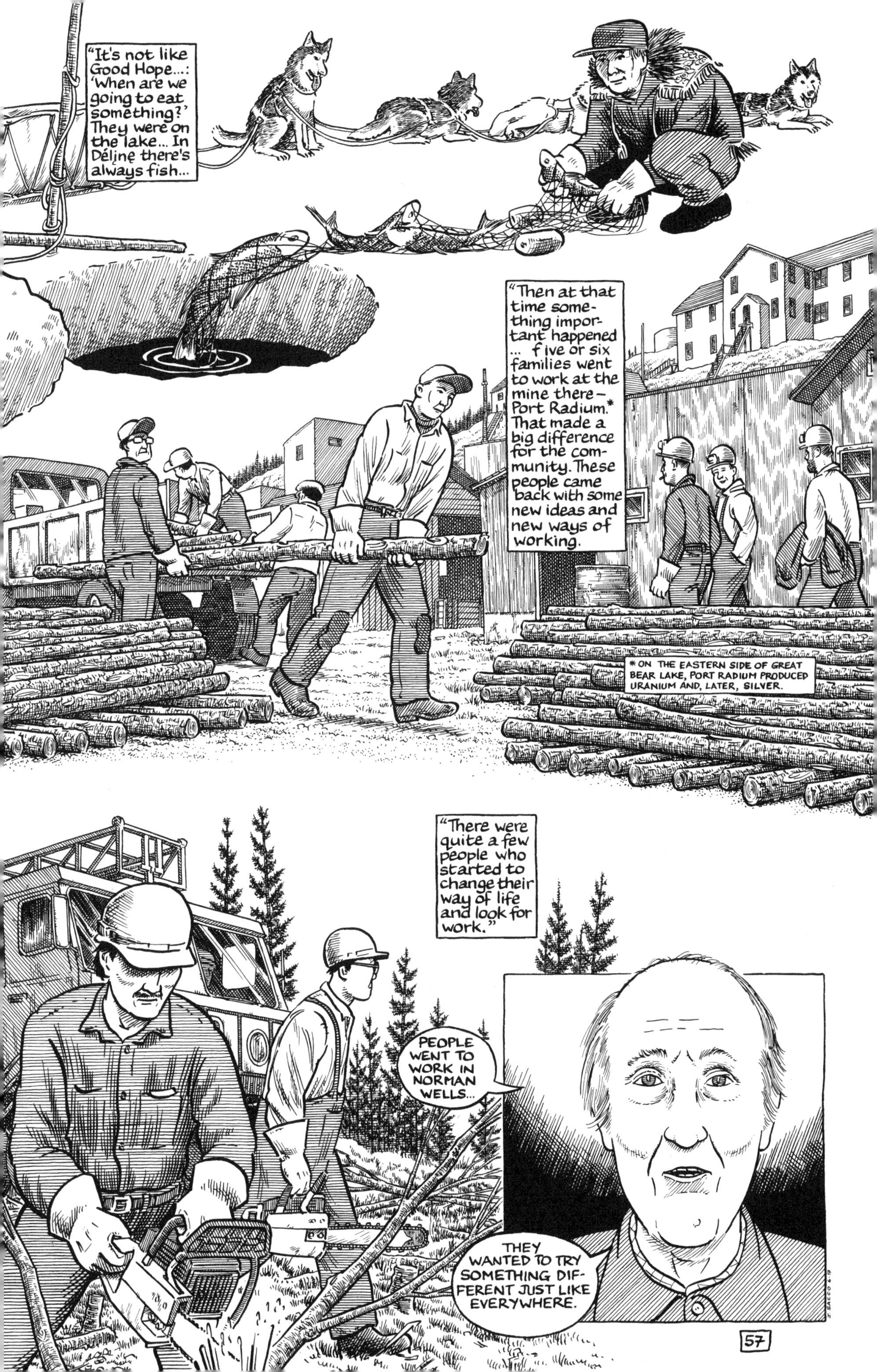

"It's not like Good Hope...: 'When are we going to eat something?' They were on the lake... In Délįnę there's always fish...
"Then at that time something important happened ... five or six families went to work at the mine there—Port Radium.* That made a big difference for the community. These people came back with some new ideas and new ways of working.
* ON THE EASTERN SIDE OF GREAT BEAR LAKE, PORT RADIUM PRODUCED URANIUM AND, LATER, SILVER.
"There were quite a few people who started to change their way of life and look for work."
PEOPLE WENT TO WORK IN NORMAN WELLS...
THEY WANTED TO TRY SOMETHING DIFFERENT JUST LIKE EVERYWHERE.

MEN WOULD COME WITH MACHINES

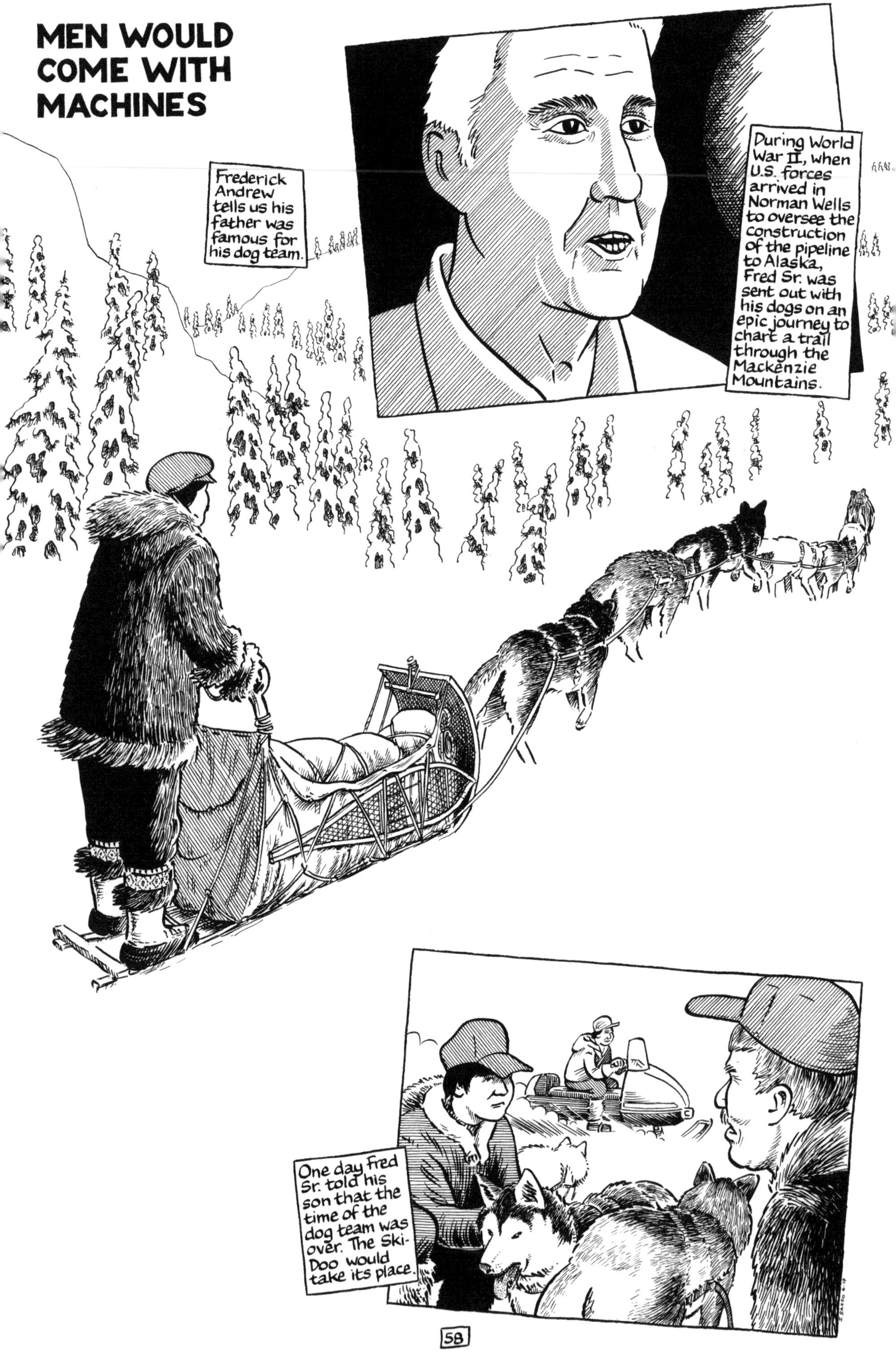

Frederick Andrew tells us his father was famous for his dog team.
During World War II, when U.S. forces arrived in Norman Wells to oversee the construction of the pipeline to Alaska, Fred Sr. was sent out with his dogs on an epic journey to chart a trail through the Mackenzie Mountains.
One day Fred Sr. told his son that the time of the dog team was over. The Ski-Doo would take its place.

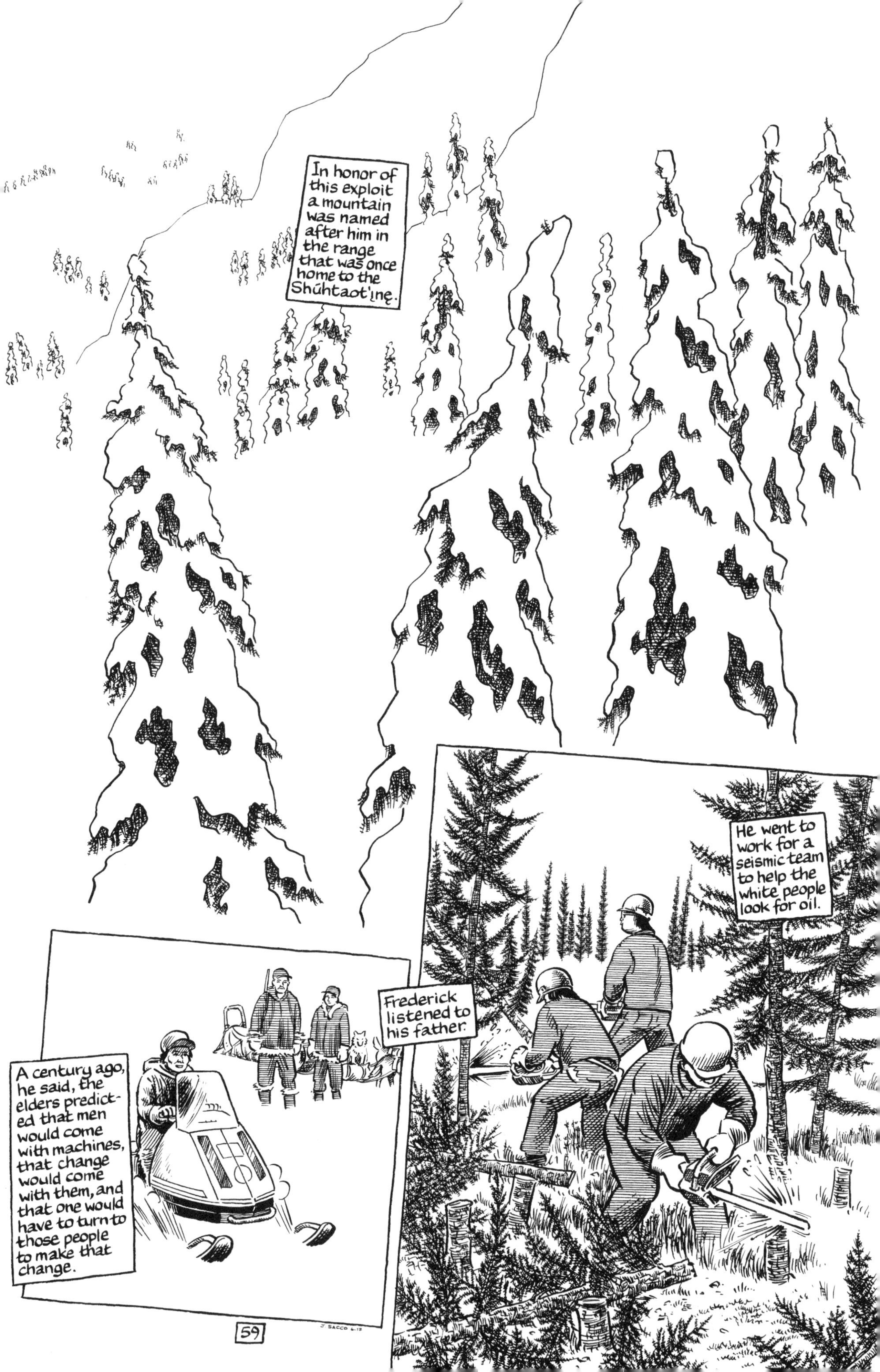
In honor of this exploit a mountain was named after him in the range that was once home to the Shúhtaot'ı̨nę.
A century ago, he said, the elders predicted that men would come with machines, that change would come with them, and that one would have to turn to those people to make that change.
Frederick listened to his father.
He went to work for a seismic team to help the white people look for oil.
J. SACCO 6.13

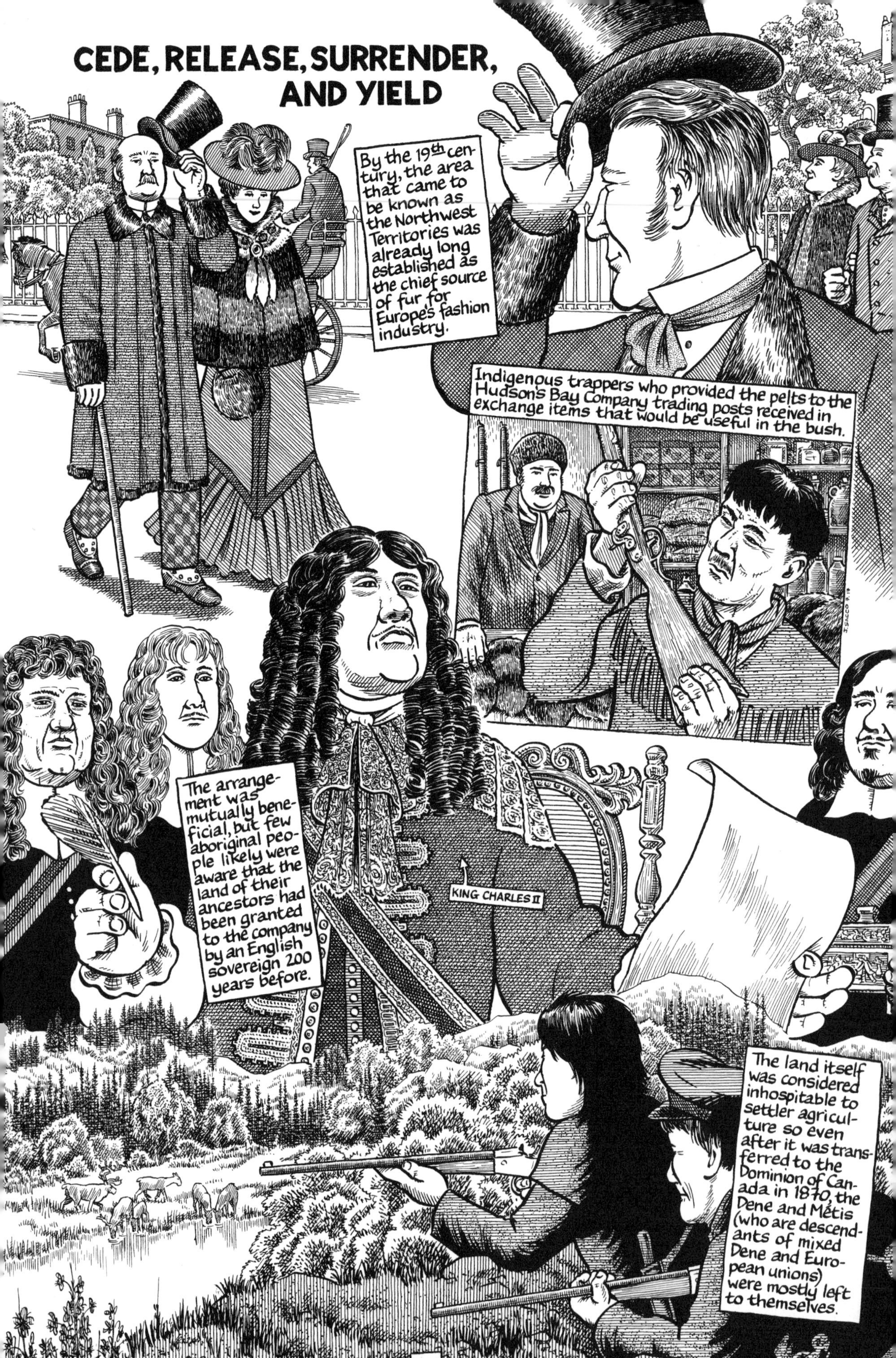
CEDE, RELEASE, SURRENDER, AND YIELD
By the 19th century, the area that came to be known as the Northwest Territories was already long established as the chief source of fur for Europe's fashion industry.
Indigenous trappers who provided the pelts to the Hudson's Bay Company trading posts received in exchange items that would be useful in the bush.
The arrangement was mutually beneficial, but few aboriginal people likely were aware that the land of their ancestors had been granted to the company by an English sovereign 200 years before.
KING CHARLES II
The land itself was considered inhospitable to settler agriculture so even after it was transferred to the Dominion of Canada in 1870, the Dene and Métis (who are descendants of mixed Dene and European unions) were mostly left to themselves.

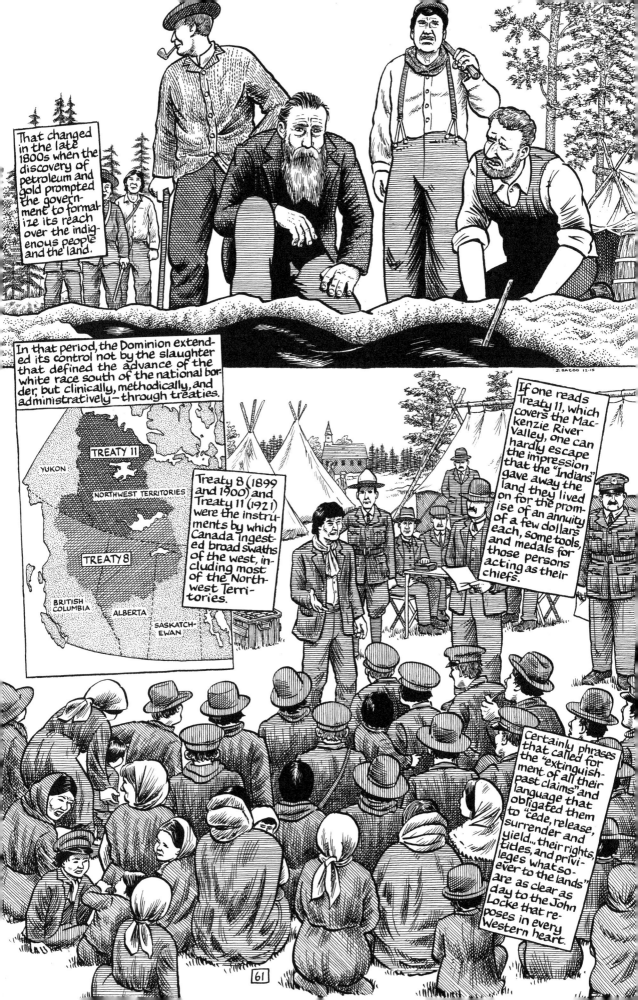

That changed in the late 1800s when the discovery of petroleum and gold prompted the government to formalize its reach over the indigenous people and the land.

In that period, the Dominion extended its control not by the slaughter that defined the advance of the white race south of the national border, but clinically, methodically, and administratively — through treaties.

J. SACCO 12-15

TREATY 11

YUKON

NORTHWEST TERRITORIES

TREATY 8

BRITISH COLUMBIA   ALBERTA   SASKATCHEWAN

Treaty 8 (1899 and 1900) and Treaty 11 (1921) were the instruments by which Canada ingested broad swaths of the west, including most of the Northwest Territories.

If one reads Treaty 11, which covers the Mackenzie River Valley, one can hardly escape the impression that the "Indians" gave away the land they lived on for the promise of an annuity of a few dollars each, some tools, and medals for those persons acting as their chiefs.

Certainly phrases that called for the "extinguishment of all their past claims" and language that obligated them to "cede, release, surrender and yield..." their rights, titles, and privileges whatsoever to the lands" are as clear as day to the John Locke that reposes in every Western heart.

61

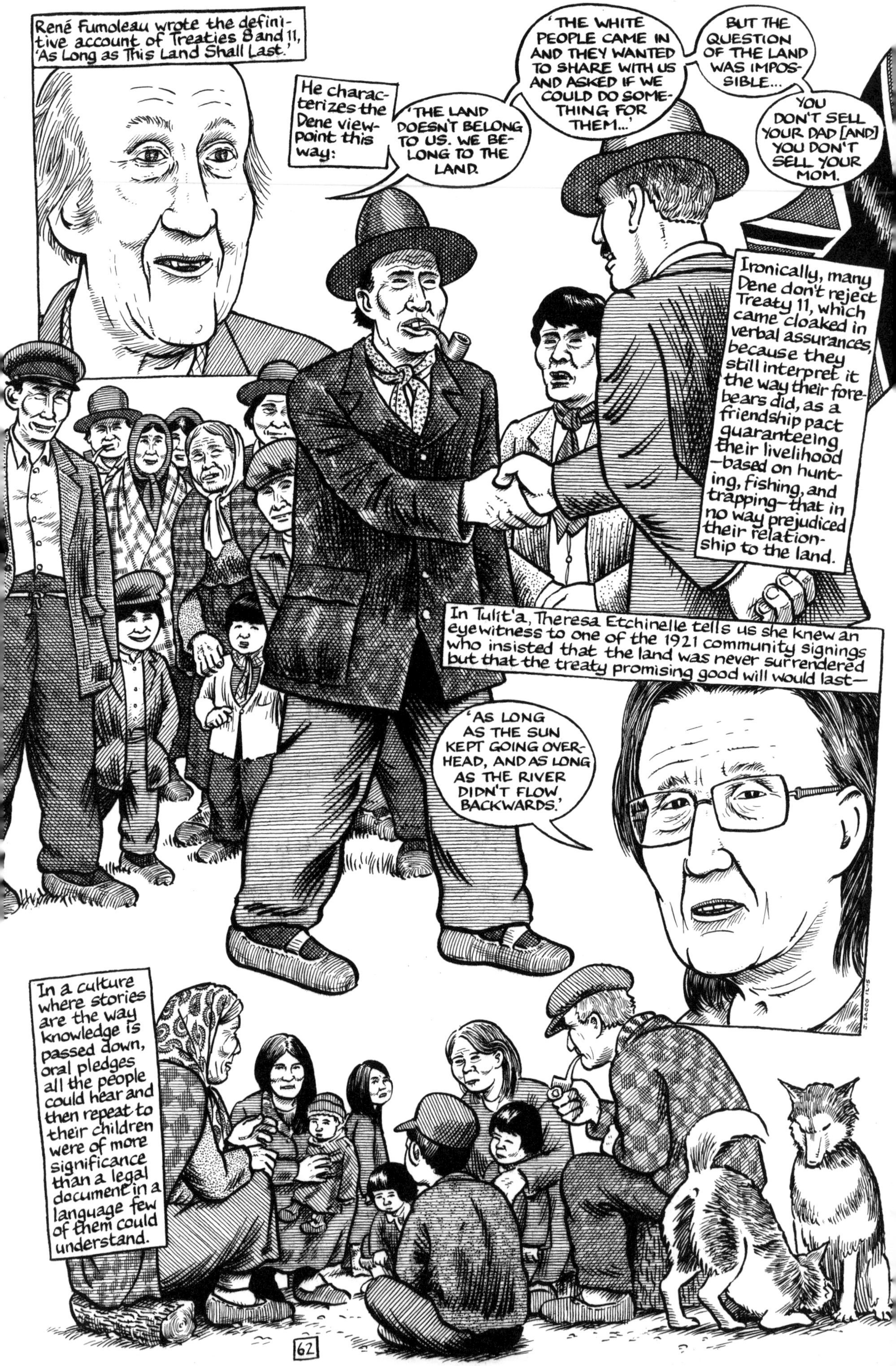
René Fumoleau wrote the definitive account of Treaties 8 and 11, 'As Long as This Land Shall Last.'
He characterizes the Dene viewpoint this way:
'THE LAND DOESN'T BELONG TO US. WE BELONG TO THE LAND.
'THE WHITE PEOPLE CAME IN AND THEY WANTED TO SHARE WITH US AND ASKED IF WE COULD DO SOMETHING FOR THEM...'
BUT THE QUESTION OF THE LAND WAS IMPOSSIBLE...
YOU DON'T SELL YOUR DAD [AND] YOU DON'T SELL YOUR MOM.
Ironically, many Dene don't reject Treaty 11, which came cloaked in verbal assurances, because they still interpret it the way their forebears did, as a friendship pact guaranteeing their livelihood—based on hunting, fishing, and trapping—that in no way prejudiced their relationship to the land.
In Tulit'a, Theresa Etchinelle tells us she knew an eyewitness to one of the 1921 community signings who insisted that the land was never surrendered but that the treaty promising good will would last—
'AS LONG AS THE SUN KEPT GOING OVERHEAD, AND AS LONG AS THE RIVER DIDN'T FLOW BACKWARDS.'
In a culture where stories are the way knowledge is passed down, oral pledges all the people could hear and then repeat to their children were of more significance than a legal document in a language few of them could understand.

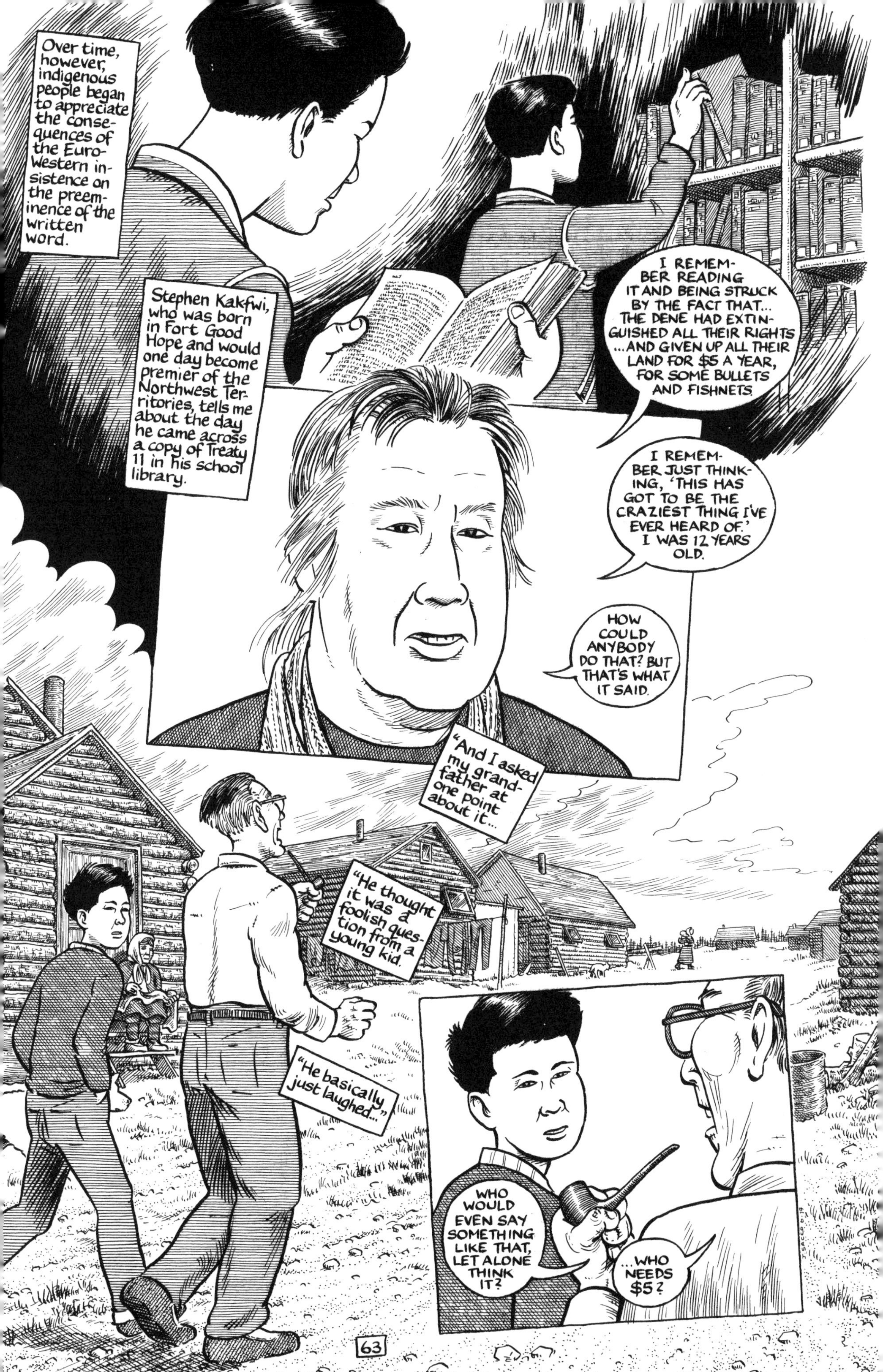
Over time, however, indigenous people began to appreciate the consequences of the Euro-Western insistence on the preeminence of the written word.
Stephen Kakfwi, who was born in Fort Good Hope and would one day become premier of the Northwest Territories, tells me about the day he came across a copy of Treaty 11 in his school library.
I REMEMBER READING IT AND BEING STRUCK BY THE FACT THAT... THE DENE HAD EXTINGUISHED ALL THEIR RIGHTS ...AND GIVEN UP ALL THEIR LAND FOR $5 A YEAR, FOR SOME BULLETS AND FISHNETS.
I REMEMBER JUST THINKING, 'THIS HAS GOT TO BE THE CRAZIEST THING I'VE EVER HEARD OF.' I WAS 12 YEARS OLD.
HOW COULD ANYBODY DO THAT? BUT THAT'S WHAT IT SAID.
"And I asked my grandfather at one point about it...
"He thought it was a foolish question from a young kid.
"He basically just laughed..."
WHO WOULD EVEN SAY SOMETHING LIKE THAT, LET ALONE THINK IT?
...WHO NEEDS $5?

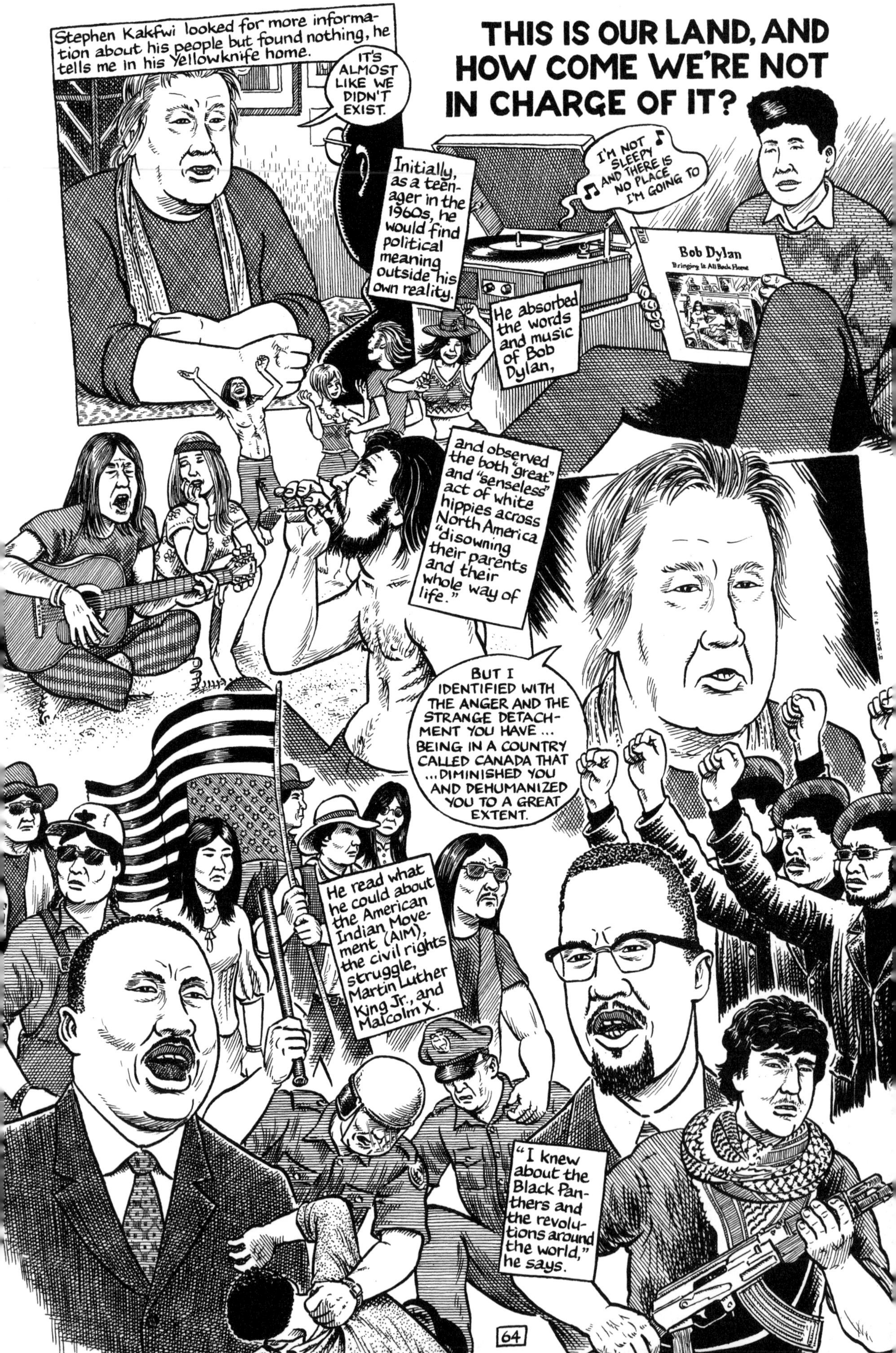

Stephen Kakfwi looked for more information about his people but found nothing, he tells me in his Yellowknife home.
IT'S ALMOST LIKE WE DIDN'T EXIST.
THIS IS OUR LAND, AND HOW COME WE'RE NOT IN CHARGE OF IT?
Initially, as a teenager in the 1960s, he would find political meaning outside his own reality.
I'M NOT SLEEPY AND THERE IS NO PLACE I'M GOING TO
Bob Dylan
Bringing It All Back Home
He absorbed the words and music of Bob Dylan,
and observed the both "great" and "senseless" act of white hippies across North America "disowning their parents and their whole way of life."
BUT I IDENTIFIED WITH THE ANGER AND THE STRANGE DETACHMENT YOU HAVE ... BEING IN A COUNTRY CALLED CANADA THAT ... DIMINISHED YOU AND DEHUMANIZED YOU TO A GREAT EXTENT.
He read what he could about the American Indian Movement (AIM), the civil rights struggle, Martin Luther King Jr., and Malcolm X.
"I knew about the Black Panthers and the revolutions around the world," he says.

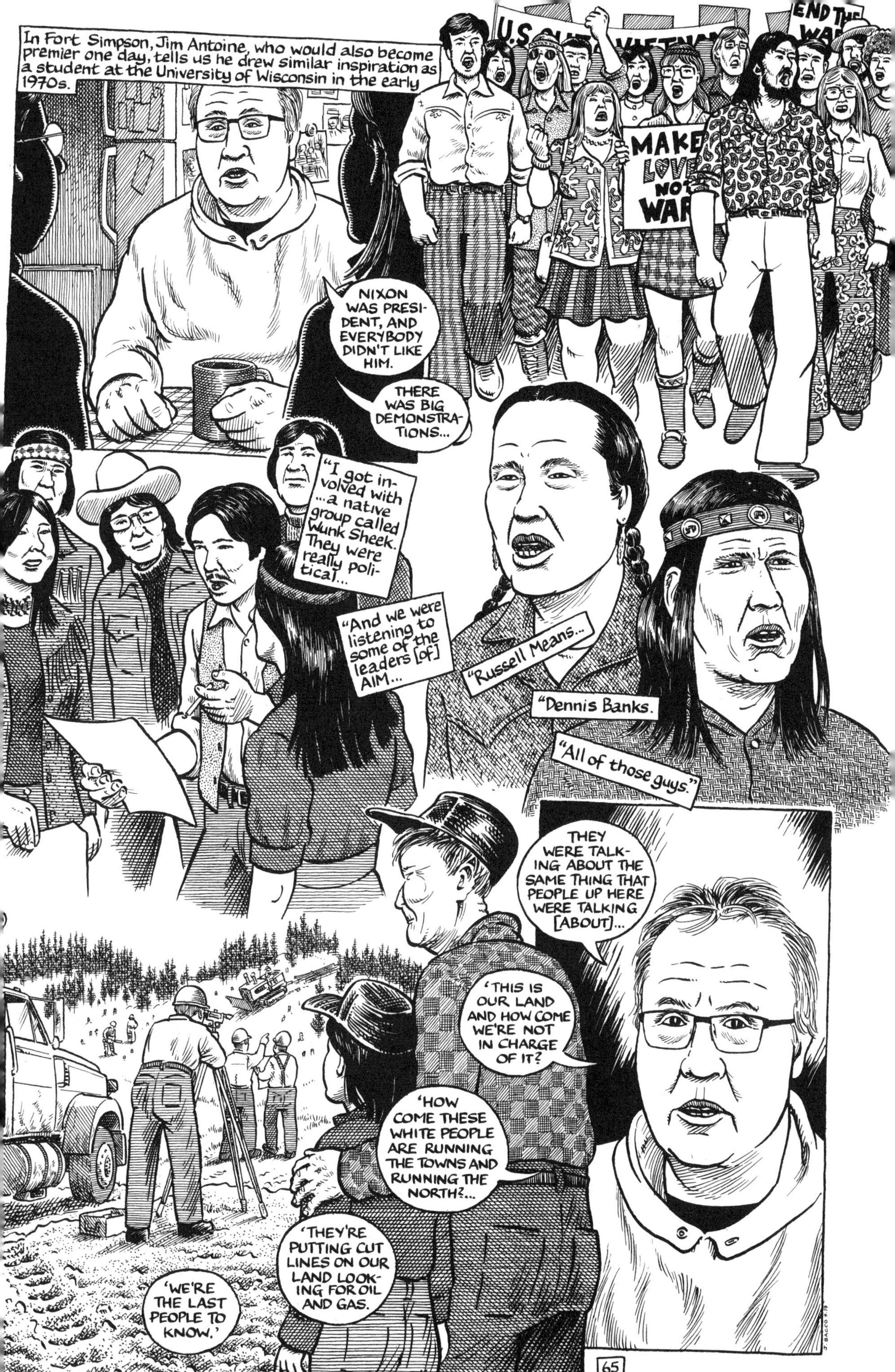
In Fort Simpson, Jim Antoine, who would also become premier one day, tells us he drew similar inspiration as a student at the University of Wisconsin in the early 1970s.
U.S. OUT OF VIETNAM
END THE WAR
MAKE LOVE NOT WAR
NIXON WAS PRESIDENT, AND EVERYBODY DIDN'T LIKE HIM.
THERE WAS BIG DEMONSTRATIONS...
"I got involved with ...a native group called Wunk Sheek. They were really political...
"And we were listening to some of the leaders [of] AIM...
"Russell Means...
"Dennis Banks.
"All of those guys."
THEY WERE TALKING ABOUT THE SAME THING THAT PEOPLE UP HERE WERE TALKING [ABOUT]...
'THIS IS OUR LAND AND HOW COME WE'RE NOT IN CHARGE OF IT?
'HOW COME THESE WHITE PEOPLE ARE RUNNING THE TOWNS AND RUNNING THE NORTH?...
'THEY'RE PUTTING CUT LINES ON OUR LAND LOOKING FOR OIL AND GAS.
'WE'RE THE LAST PEOPLE TO KNOW.'

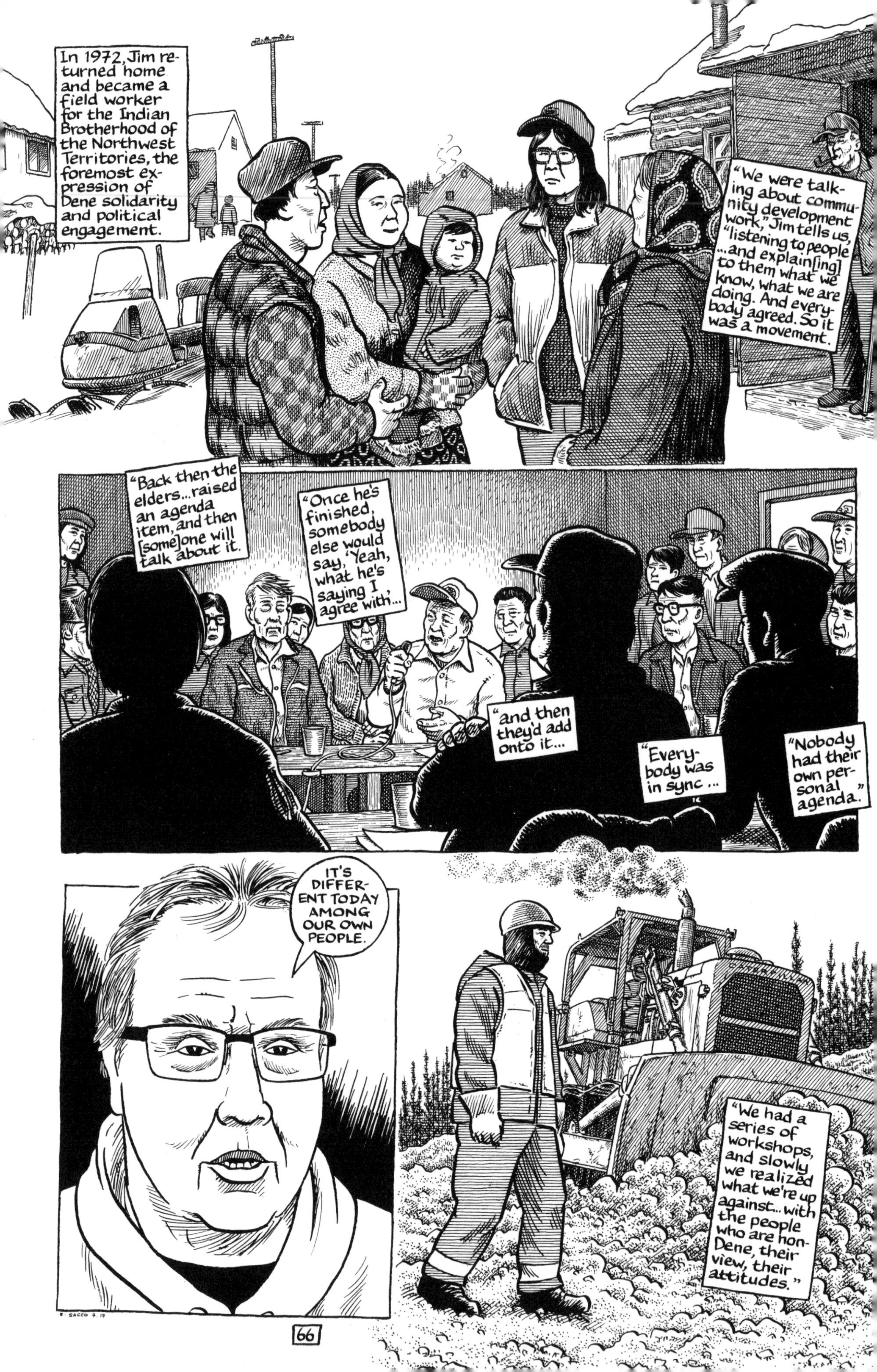

In 1972, Jim returned home and became a field worker for the Indian Brotherhood of the Northwest Territories, the foremost expression of Dene solidarity and political engagement.
"We were talking about community development work," Jim tells us, "listening to people ...and explain[ing] to them what we know, what we are doing. And everybody agreed. So it was a movement.
"Back then the elders...raised an agenda item, and then [some]one will talk about it.
"Once he's finished, somebody else would say, 'Yeah, what he's saying I agree with'...
"and then they'd add onto it...
"Everybody was in sync ...
"Nobody had their own personal agenda."
IT'S DIFFERENT TODAY AMONG OUR OWN PEOPLE.
"We had a series of workshops, and slowly we realized what we're up against... with the people who are non-Dene, their view, their attitudes."

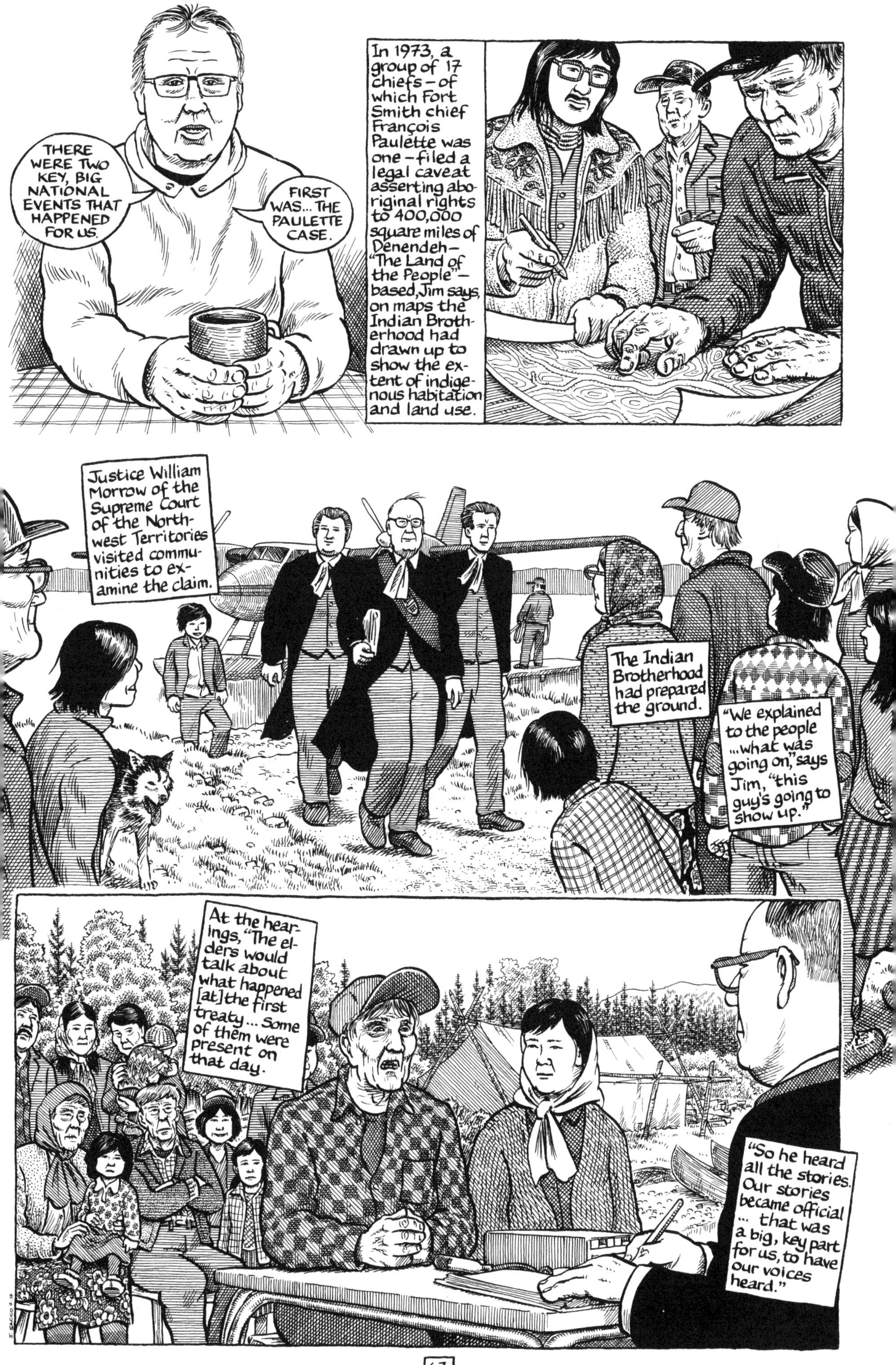
THERE WERE TWO KEY, BIG NATIONAL EVENTS THAT HAPPENED FOR US.
FIRST WAS... THE PAULETTE CASE.
In 1973, a group of 17 chiefs – of which Fort Smith chief François Paulette was one – filed a legal caveat asserting aboriginal rights to 400,000 square miles of Denendeh – "The Land of the People" – based, Jim says, on maps the Indian Brotherhood had drawn up to show the extent of indigenous habitation and land use.
Justice William Morrow of the Supreme Court of the Northwest Territories visited communities to examine the claim.
The Indian Brotherhood had prepared the ground.
"We explained to the people ...what was going on," says Jim, "this guy's going to show up."
At the hearings, "The elders would talk about what happened [at] the first treaty... Some of them were present on that day.
"So he heard all the stories. Our stories became official ... that was a big, key part for us, to have our voices heard."

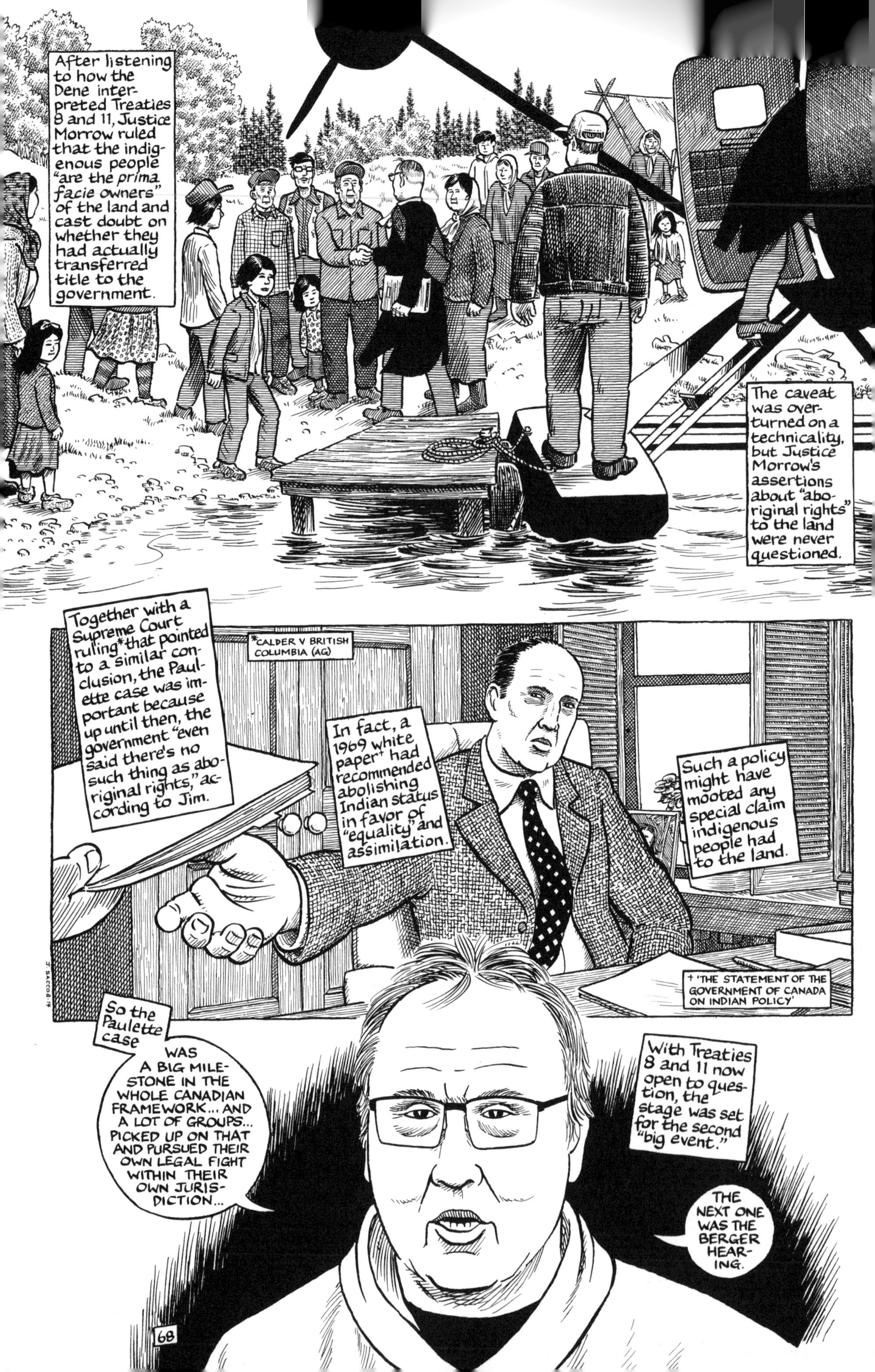
After listening to how the Dene interpreted Treaties 8 and 11, Justice Morrow ruled that the indigenous people "are the *prima facie* owners" of the land and cast doubt on whether they had actually transferred title to the government.
The caveat was overturned on a technicality, but Justice Morrow's assertions about "aboriginal rights" to the land were never questioned.
Together with a Supreme Court ruling* that pointed to a similar conclusion, the Paulette case was important because up until then, the government "even said there's no such thing as aboriginal rights," according to Jim.
*CALDER V BRITISH COLUMBIA (AG)
In fact, a 1969 white paper+ had recommended abolishing Indian status in favor of "equality" and assimilation.
Such a policy might have mooted any special claim indigenous people had to the land.
+ 'THE STATEMENT OF THE GOVERNMENT OF CANADA ON INDIAN POLICY'
So the Paulette case
WAS A BIG MILESTONE IN THE WHOLE CANADIAN FRAMEWORK... AND A LOT OF GROUPS... PICKED UP ON THAT AND PURSUED THEIR OWN LEGAL FIGHT WITHIN THEIR OWN JURISDICTION...
With Treaties 8 and 11 now open to question, the stage was set for the second "big event."
THE NEXT ONE WAS THE BERGER HEARING.

OUR OWN PLANS

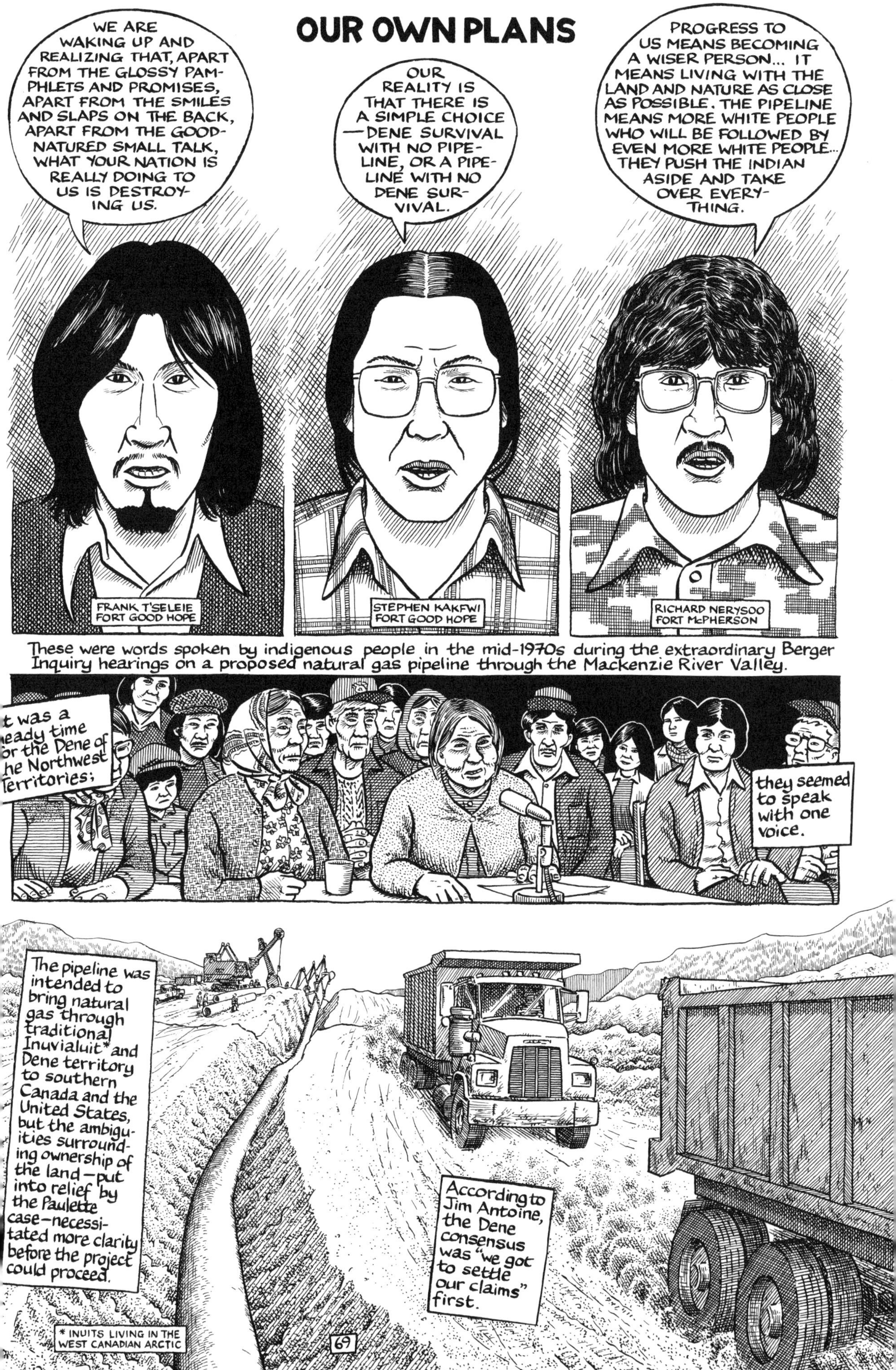

WE ARE WAKING UP AND REALIZING THAT, APART FROM THE GLOSSY PAMPHLETS AND PROMISES, APART FROM THE SMILES AND SLAPS ON THE BACK, APART FROM THE GOOD-NATURED SMALL TALK, WHAT YOUR NATION IS REALLY DOING TO US IS DESTROYING US.
OUR REALITY IS THAT THERE IS A SIMPLE CHOICE —DENE SURVIVAL WITH NO PIPELINE, OR A PIPELINE WITH NO DENE SURVIVAL.
PROGRESS TO US MEANS BECOMING A WISER PERSON... IT MEANS LIVING WITH THE LAND AND NATURE AS CLOSE AS POSSIBLE. THE PIPELINE MEANS MORE WHITE PEOPLE WHO WILL BE FOLLOWED BY EVEN MORE WHITE PEOPLE... THEY PUSH THE INDIAN ASIDE AND TAKE OVER EVERYTHING.
FRANK T'SELEIE FORT GOOD HOPE
STEPHEN KAKFWI FORT GOOD HOPE
RICHARD NERYSOO FORT McPHERSON
These were words spoken by indigenous people in the mid-1970s during the extraordinary Berger Inquiry hearings on a proposed natural gas pipeline through the Mackenzie River Valley.
t was a eady time or the Dene of he Northwest Territories;
they seemed to speak with one voice.
The pipeline was intended to bring natural gas through traditional Inuvialuit* and Dene territory to southern Canada and the United States, but the ambiguities surrounding ownership of the land—put into relief by the Paulette case—necessitated more clarity before the project could proceed.
According to Jim Antoine, the Dene consensus was "we got to settle our claims" first.
* INUITS LIVING IN THE WEST CANADIAN ARCTIC

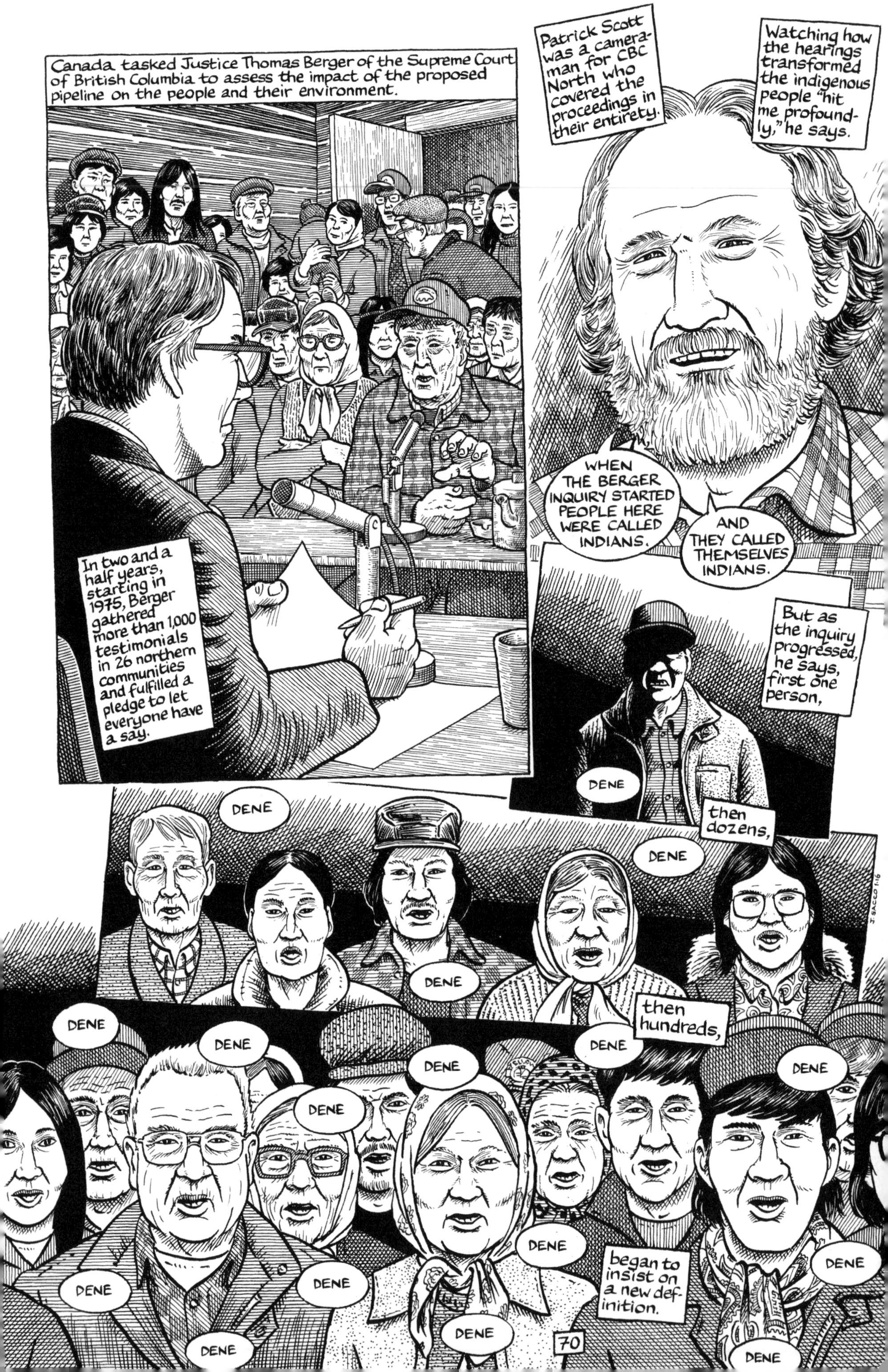
Canada tasked Justice Thomas Berger of the Supreme Court of British Columbia to assess the impact of the proposed pipeline on the people and their environment.
In two and a half years, starting in 1975, Berger gathered more than 1,000 testimonials in 26 northern communities and fulfilled a pledge to let everyone have a say.
Patrick Scott was a cameraman for CBC North who covered the proceedings in their entirety.
Watching how the hearings transformed the indigenous people "hit me profoundly," he says.
WHEN THE BERGER INQUIRY STARTED PEOPLE HERE WERE CALLED INDIANS.
AND THEY CALLED THEMSELVES INDIANS.
But as the inquiry progressed, he says, first one person,
DENE
then dozens,
DENE
DENE
DENE
J. SACCO 1-16
then hundreds,
DENE
DENE
DENE
DENE
DENE
DENE
DENE
DENE
DENE
DENE
began to insist on a new definition.
DENE
DENE

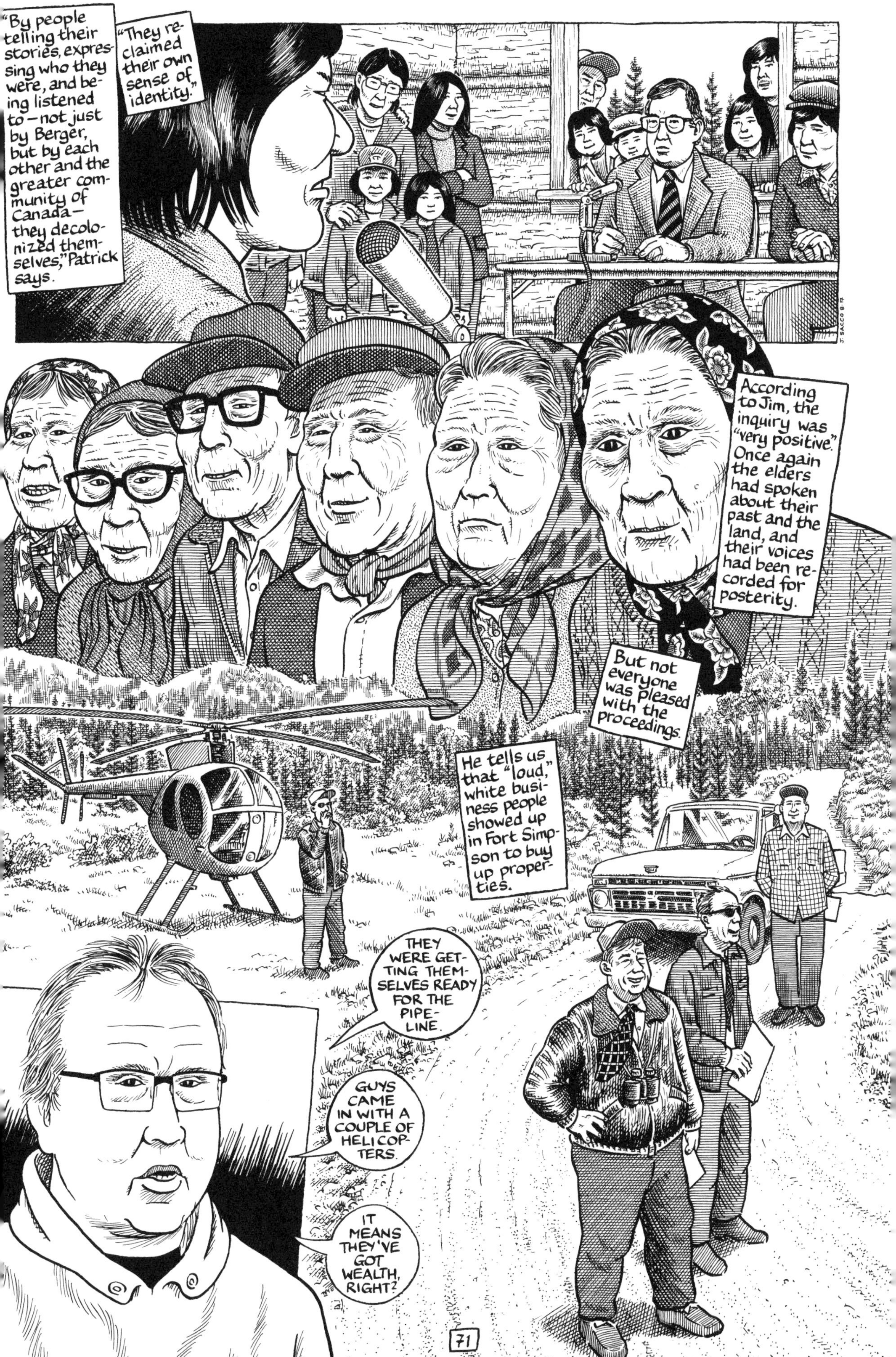
"By people telling their stories, expressing who they were, and being listened to—not just by Berger, but by each other and the greater community of Canada—they decolonized themselves," Patrick says.
"They reclaimed their own sense of identity."
J. SACCO 8.17
According to Jim, the inquiry was "very positive." Once again the elders had spoken about their past and the land, and their voices had been recorded for posterity.
But not everyone was pleased with the proceedings.
He tells us that "loud," white business people showed up in Fort Simpson to buy up properties.
THEY WERE GETTING THEMSELVES READY FOR THE PIPELINE.
GUYS CAME IN WITH A COUPLE OF HELICOPTERS.
IT MEANS THEY'VE GOT WEALTH, RIGHT?

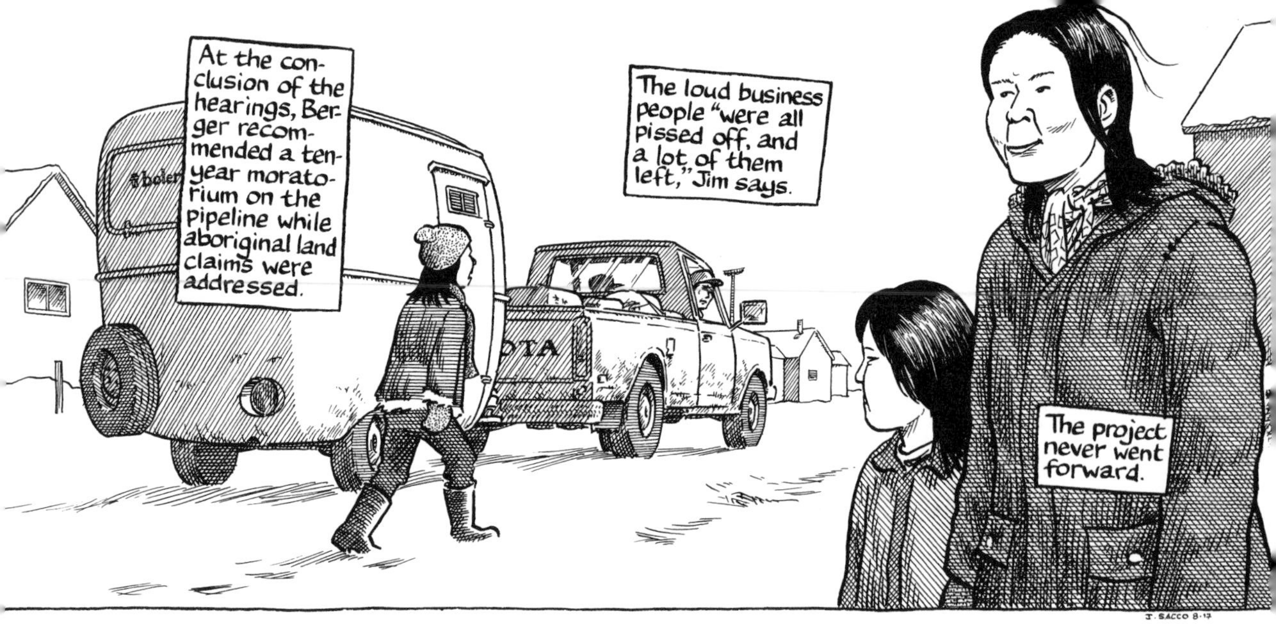
At the conclusion of the hearings, Berger recommended a ten-year moratorium on the pipeline while aboriginal land claims were addressed.
The loud business people "were all pissed off, and a lot of them left," Jim says.
The project never went forward.
J. SACCO 8·17

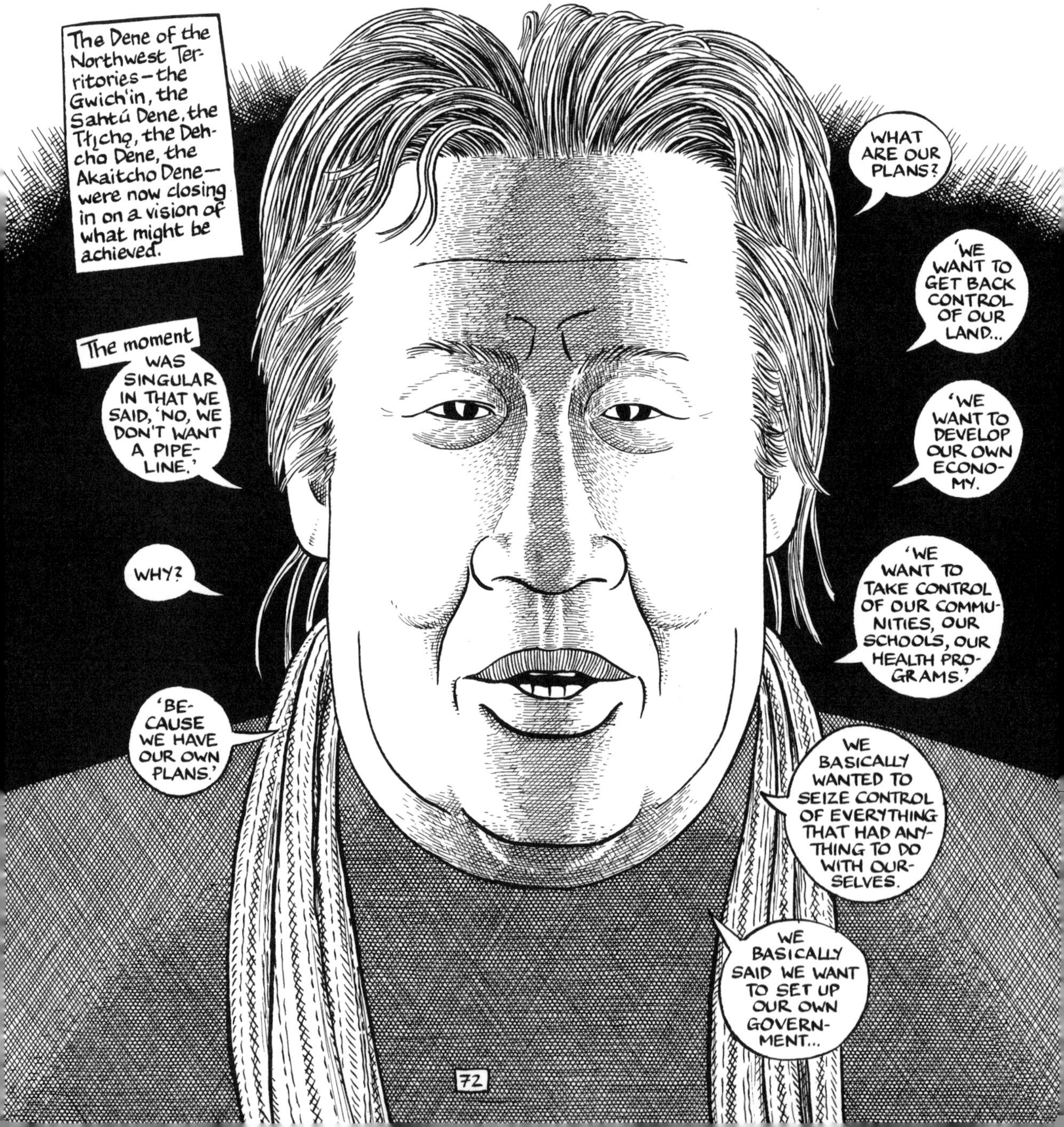
The Dene of the Northwest Territories—the Gwich'in, the Sahtú Dene, the Tłı̨chǫ, the Dehcho Dene, the Akaitcho Dene—were now closing in on a vision of what might be achieved.
The moment WAS SINGULAR IN THAT WE SAID, 'NO, WE DON'T WANT A PIPELINE.'
WHY?
'BECAUSE WE HAVE OUR OWN PLANS.'
WHAT ARE OUR PLANS?
'WE WANT TO GET BACK CONTROL OF OUR LAND...
'WE WANT TO DEVELOP OUR OWN ECONOMY.
'WE WANT TO TAKE CONTROL OF OUR COMMUNITIES, OUR SCHOOLS, OUR HEALTH PROGRAMS.'
WE BASICALLY WANTED TO SEIZE CONTROL OF EVERYTHING THAT HAD ANYTHING TO DO WITH OURSELVES.
WE BASICALLY SAID WE WANT TO SET UP OUR OWN GOVERNMENT...

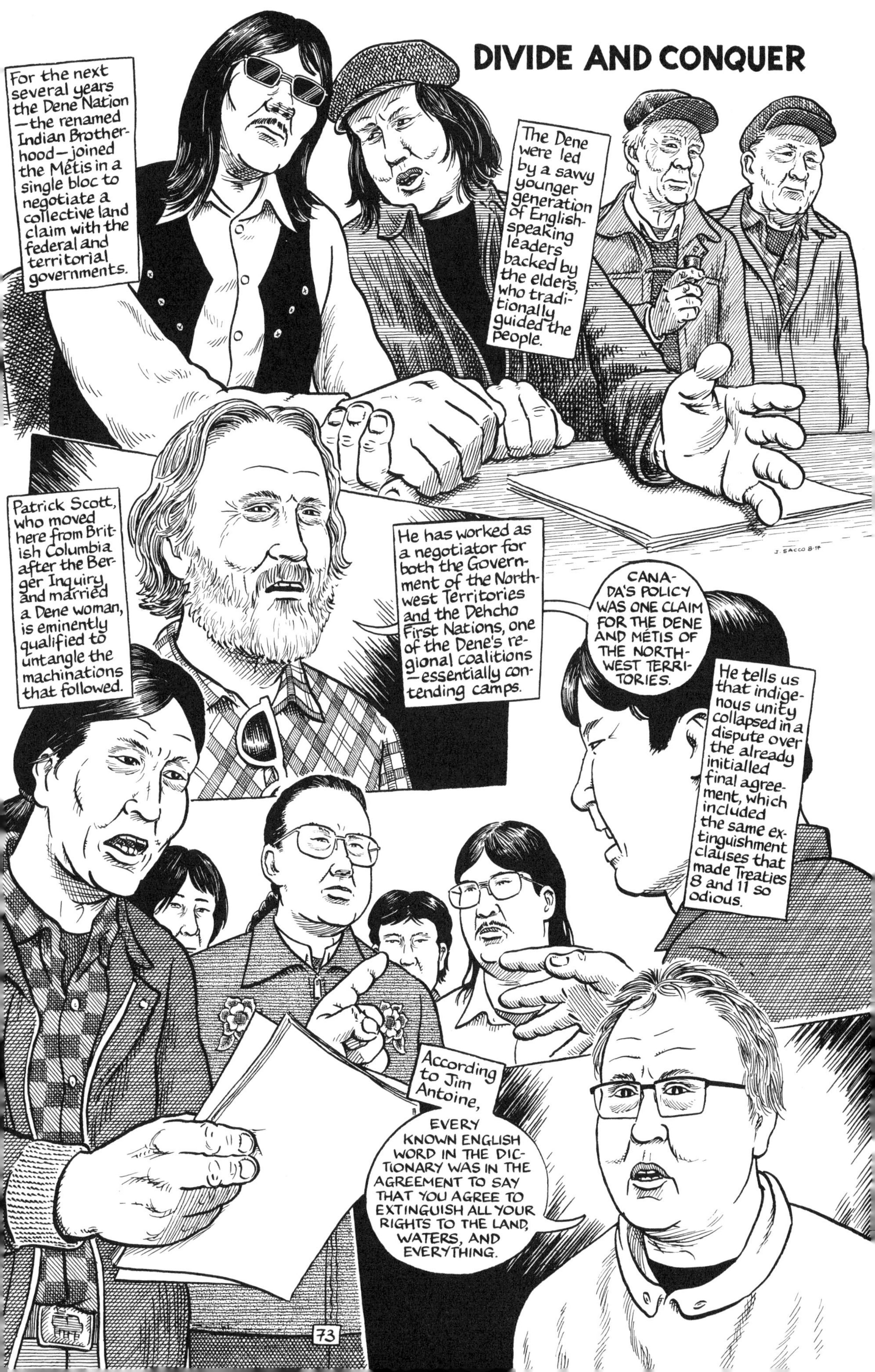

DIVIDE AND CONQUER
For the next several years the Dene Nation—the renamed Indian Brotherhood—joined the Métis in a single bloc to negotiate a collective land claim with the federal and territorial governments.
The Dene were led by a savvy younger generation of English-speaking leaders backed by the elders, who traditionally guided the people.
J. SACCO 8-17
Patrick Scott, who moved here from British Columbia after the Berger Inquiry and married a Dene woman, is eminently qualified to untangle the machinations that followed.
He has worked as a negotiator for both the Government of the Northwest Territories and the Dehcho First Nations, one of the Dene's regional coalitions—essentially contending camps.
CANADA'S POLICY WAS ONE CLAIM FOR THE DENE AND MÉTIS OF THE NORTHWEST TERRITORIES.
He tells us that indigenous unity collapsed in a dispute over the already initialled final agreement, which included the same extinguishment clauses that made Treaties 8 and 11 so odious.
According to Jim Antoine,
EVERY KNOWN ENGLISH WORD IN THE DICTIONARY WAS IN THE AGREEMENT TO SAY THAT YOU AGREE TO EXTINGUISH ALL YOUR RIGHTS TO THE LAND, WATERS, AND EVERYTHING.

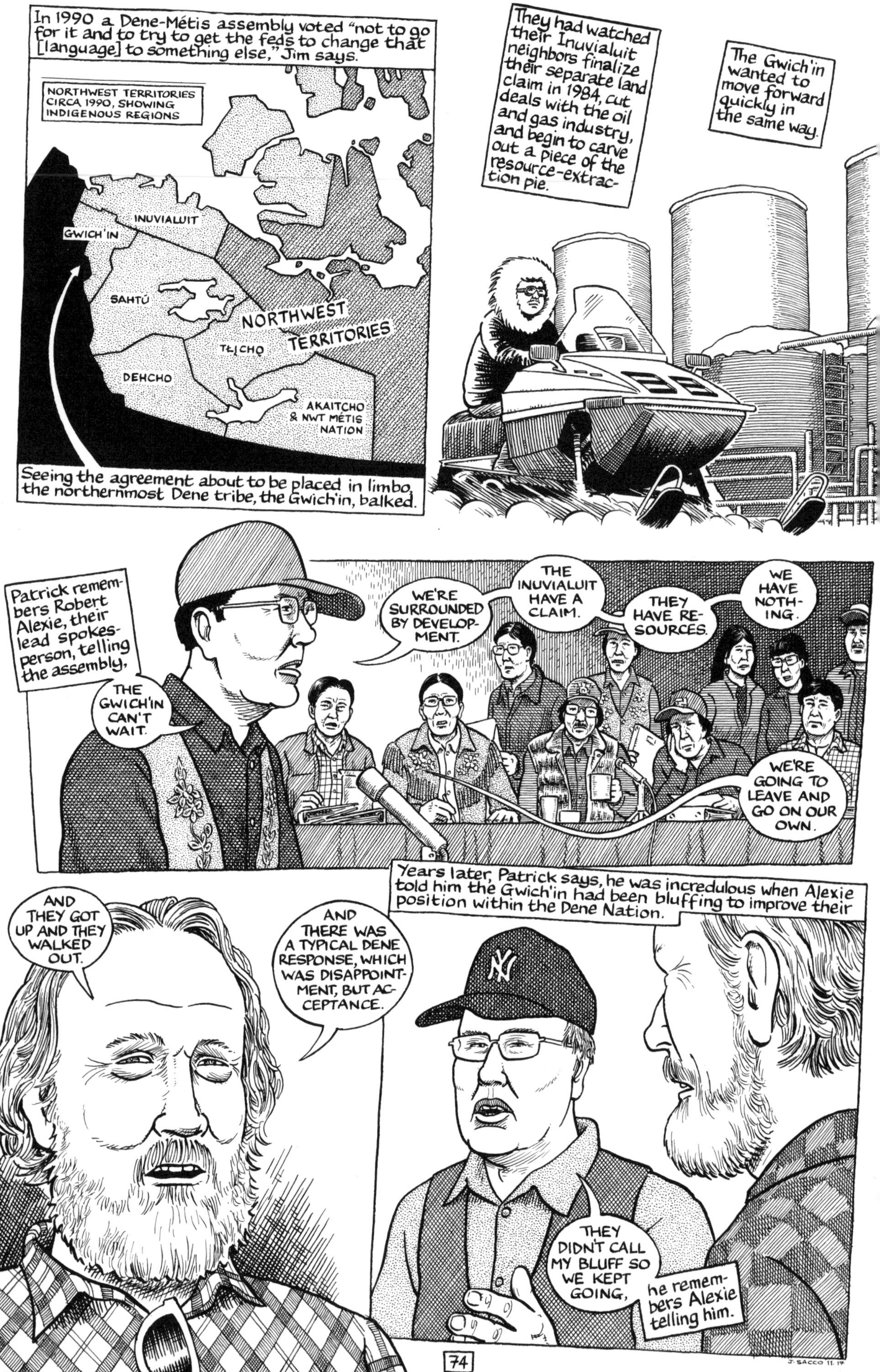

In 1990 a Dene-Métis assembly voted "not to go for it and to try to get the feds to change that [language] to something else," Jim says.
NORTHWEST TERRITORIES CIRCA 1990, SHOWING INDIGENOUS REGIONS
GWICH'IN
INUVIALUIT
SAHTÚ
NORTHWEST TERRITORIES
TŁĮCHǪ
DEHCHO
AKAITCHO & NWT MÉTIS NATION
Seeing the agreement about to be placed in limbo, the northernmost Dene tribe, the Gwich'in, balked.
They had watched their Inuvialuit neighbors finalize their separate land claim in 1984, cut deals with the oil and gas industry, and begin to carve out a piece of the resource-extraction pie.
The Gwich'in wanted to move forward quickly in the same way.
Patrick remembers Robert Alexie, their lead spokesperson, telling the assembly,
THE GWICH'IN CAN'T WAIT.
WE'RE SURROUNDED BY DEVELOPMENT.
THE INUVIALUIT HAVE A CLAIM.
THEY HAVE RESOURCES.
WE HAVE NOTHING.
WE'RE GOING TO LEAVE AND GO ON OUR OWN.
AND THEY GOT UP AND THEY WALKED OUT.
AND THERE WAS A TYPICAL DENE RESPONSE, WHICH WAS DISAPPOINTMENT, BUT ACCEPTANCE.
Years later, Patrick says, he was incredulous when Alexie told him the Gwich'in had been bluffing to improve their position within the Dene Nation.
THEY DIDN'T CALL MY BLUFF SO WE KEPT GOING,
he remembers Alexie telling him.
J. SACCO 11.17

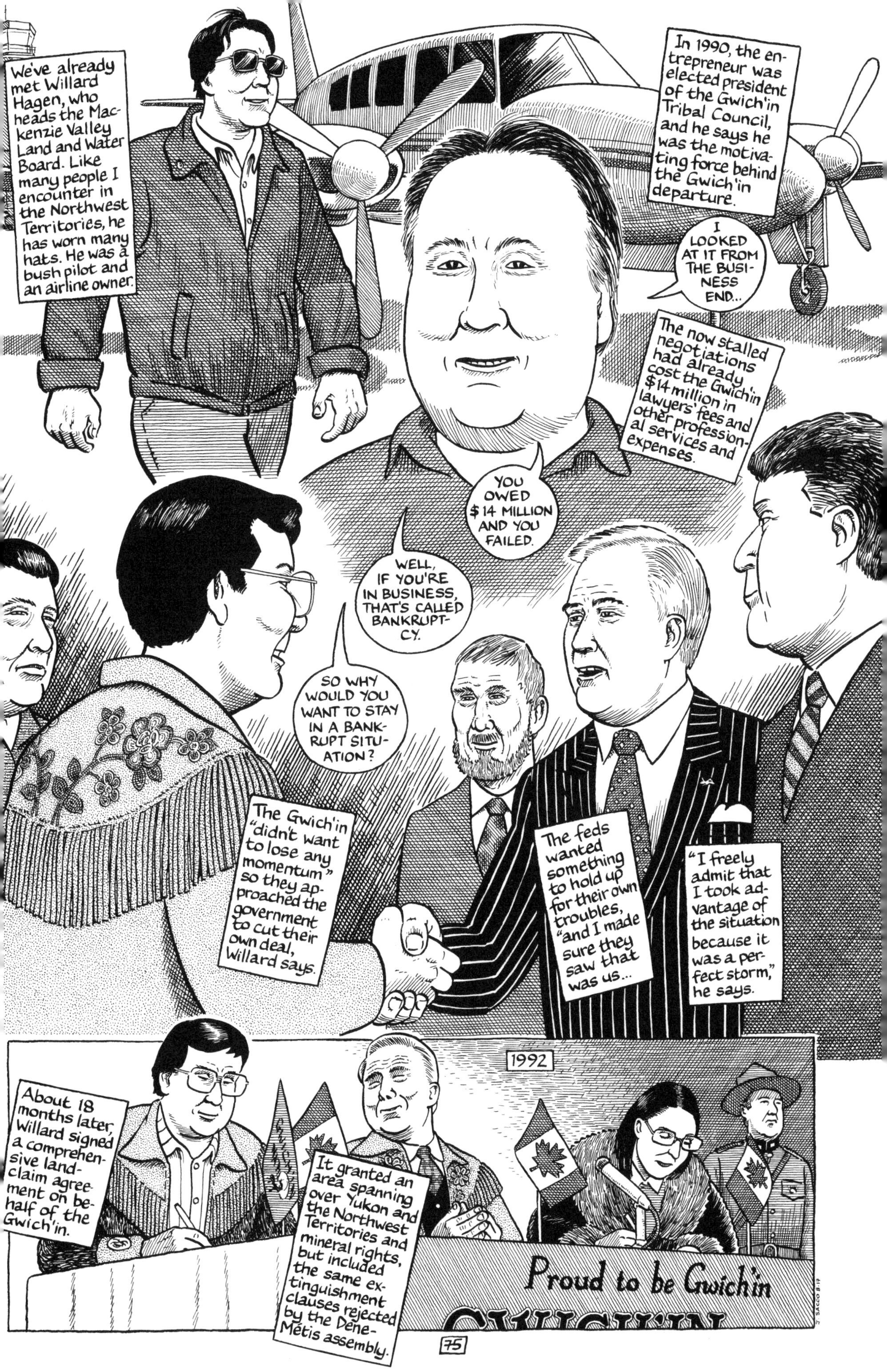
We've already met Willard Hagen, who heads the Mackenzie Valley Land and Water Board. Like many people I encounter in the Northwest Territories, he has worn many hats. He was a bush pilot and an airline owner.
In 1990, the entrepreneur was elected president of the Gwich'in Tribal Council, and he says he was the motivating force behind the Gwich'in departure.
I LOOKED AT IT FROM THE BUSINESS END...
The now stalled negotiations had already cost the Gwich'in $14 million in lawyers' fees and other professional services and expenses.
YOU OWED $14 MILLION AND YOU FAILED.
WELL, IF YOU'RE IN BUSINESS, THAT'S CALLED BANKRUPTCY.
SO WHY WOULD YOU WANT TO STAY IN A BANKRUPT SITUATION?
The Gwich'in "didn't want to lose any momentum" so they approached the government to cut their own deal, Willard says.
The feds wanted something to hold up for their own troubles, "and I made sure they saw that was us...
"I freely admit that I took advantage of the situation because it was a perfect storm," he says.
1992
About 18 months later, Willard signed a comprehensive land-claim agreement on behalf of the Gwich'in.
It granted an area spanning over Yukon and the Northwest Territories and mineral rights, but included the same extinguishment clauses rejected by the Dene-Métis assembly.
Proud to be Gwich'in
J. SACCO 8.17

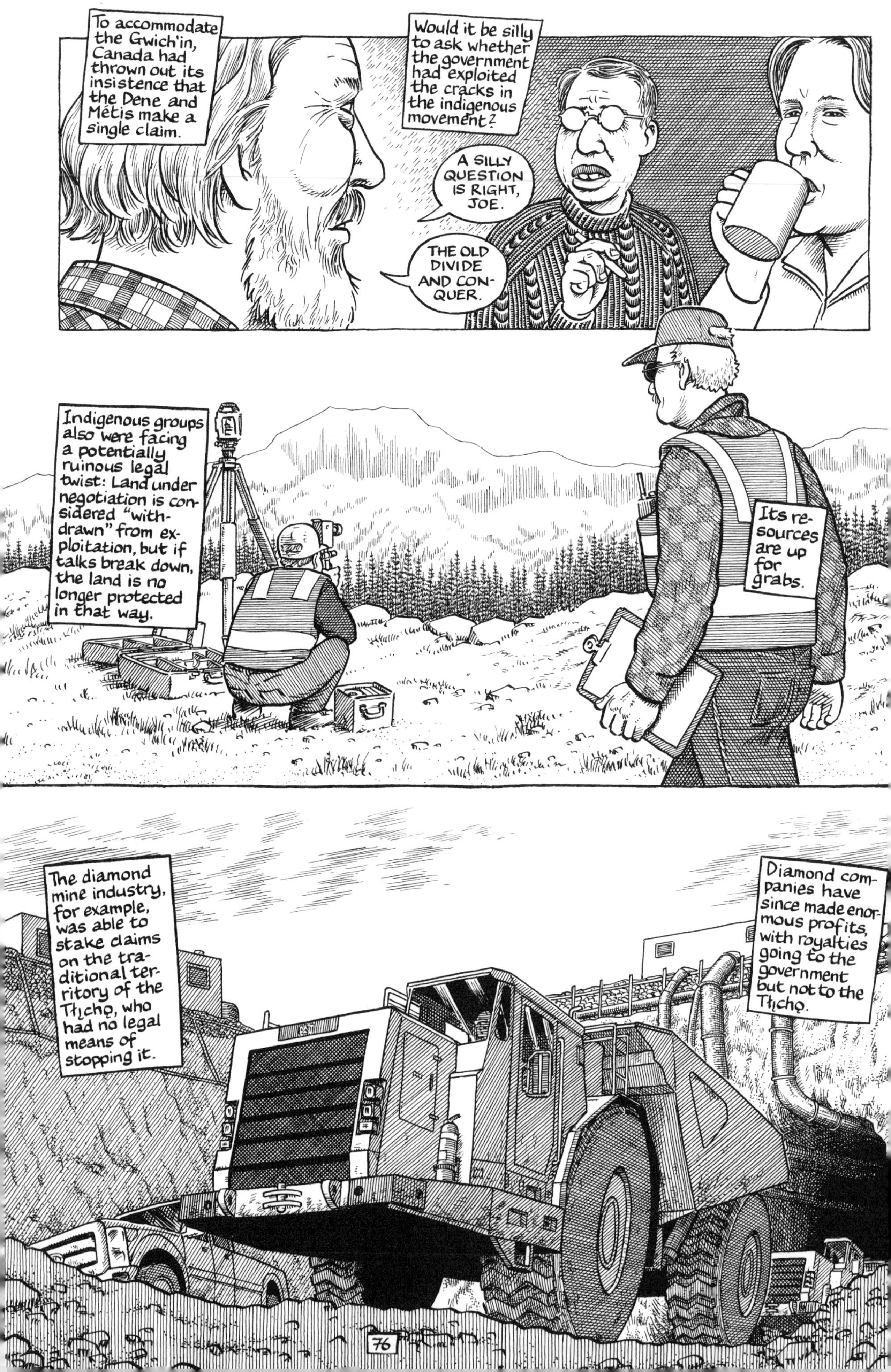

To accommodate the Gwich'in, Canada had thrown out its insistence that the Dene and Métis make a single claim.
Would it be silly to ask whether the government had exploited the cracks in the indigenous movement?
A SILLY QUESTION IS RIGHT, JOE.
THE OLD DIVIDE AND CONQUER.
Indigenous groups also were facing a potentially ruinous legal twist: Land under negotiation is considered "withdrawn" from exploitation, but if talks break down, the land is no longer protected in that way.
Its resources are up for grabs.
The diamond mine industry, for example, was able to stake claims on the traditional territory of the Tłįchǫ, who had no legal means of stopping it.
Diamond companies have since made enormous profits, with royalties going to the government but not to the Tłįchǫ.

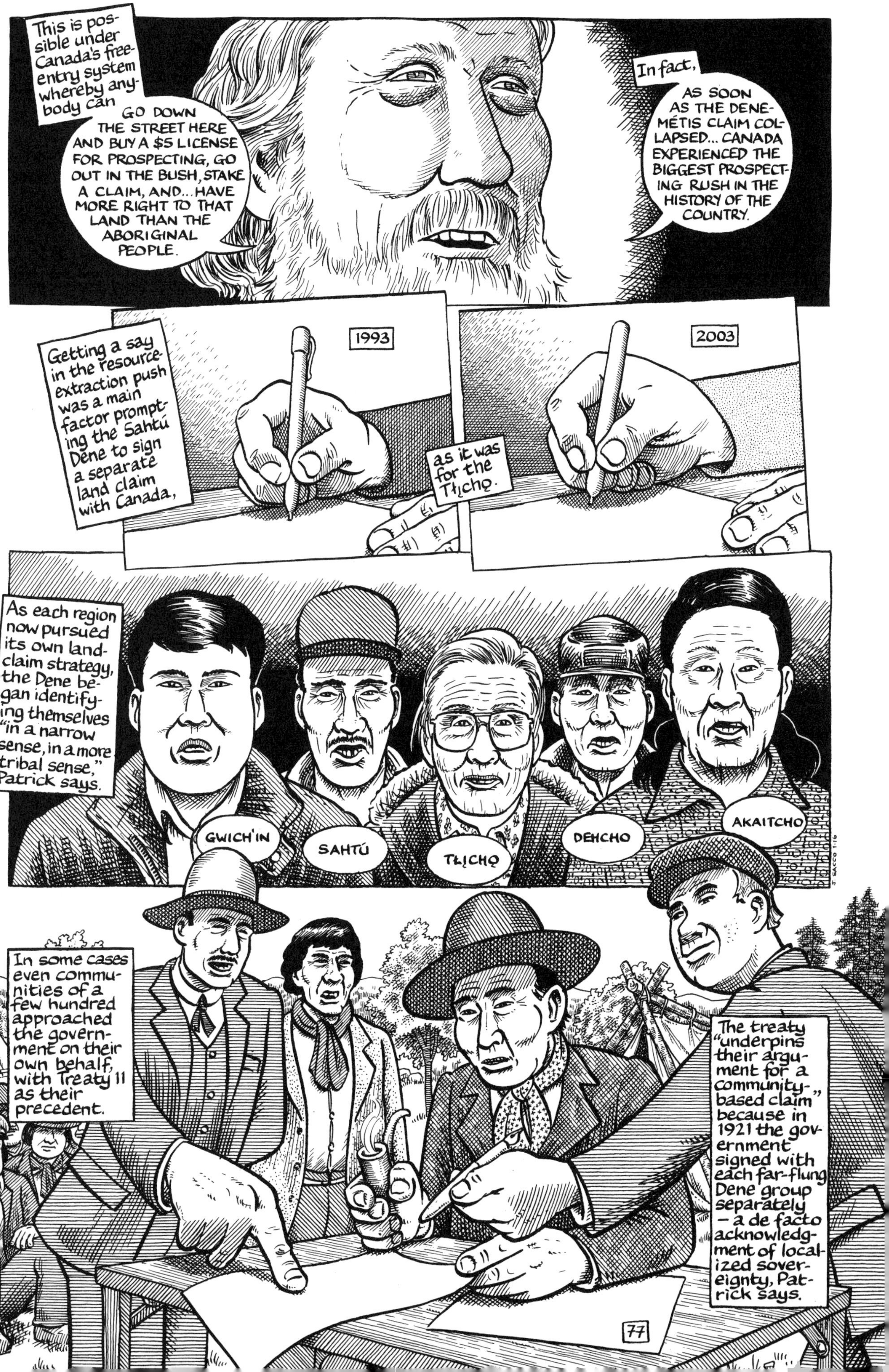

This is possible under Canada's free-entry system whereby anybody can
GO DOWN THE STREET HERE AND BUY A $5 LICENSE FOR PROSPECTING, GO OUT IN THE BUSH, STAKE A CLAIM, AND... HAVE MORE RIGHT TO THAT LAND THAN THE ABORIGINAL PEOPLE.
In fact,
AS SOON AS THE DENE-MÉTIS CLAIM COLLAPSED... CANADA EXPERIENCED THE BIGGEST PROSPECTING RUSH IN THE HISTORY OF THE COUNTRY.
Getting a say in the resource-extraction push was a main factor prompting the Sahtú Dene to sign a separate land claim with Canada,
1993
as it was for the Tłı̨chǫ.
2003
As each region now pursued its own land-claim strategy, the Dene began identifying themselves "in a narrow sense, in a more tribal sense," Patrick says.
GWICH'IN
SAHTÚ
TŁĮCHǪ
DEHCHO
AKAITCHO
In some cases even communities of a few hundred approached the government on their own behalf, with Treaty 11 as their precedent.
The treaty "underpins their argument for a community-based claim" because in 1921 the government signed with each far-flung Dene group separately — a de facto acknowledgment of localized sovereignty, Patrick says.

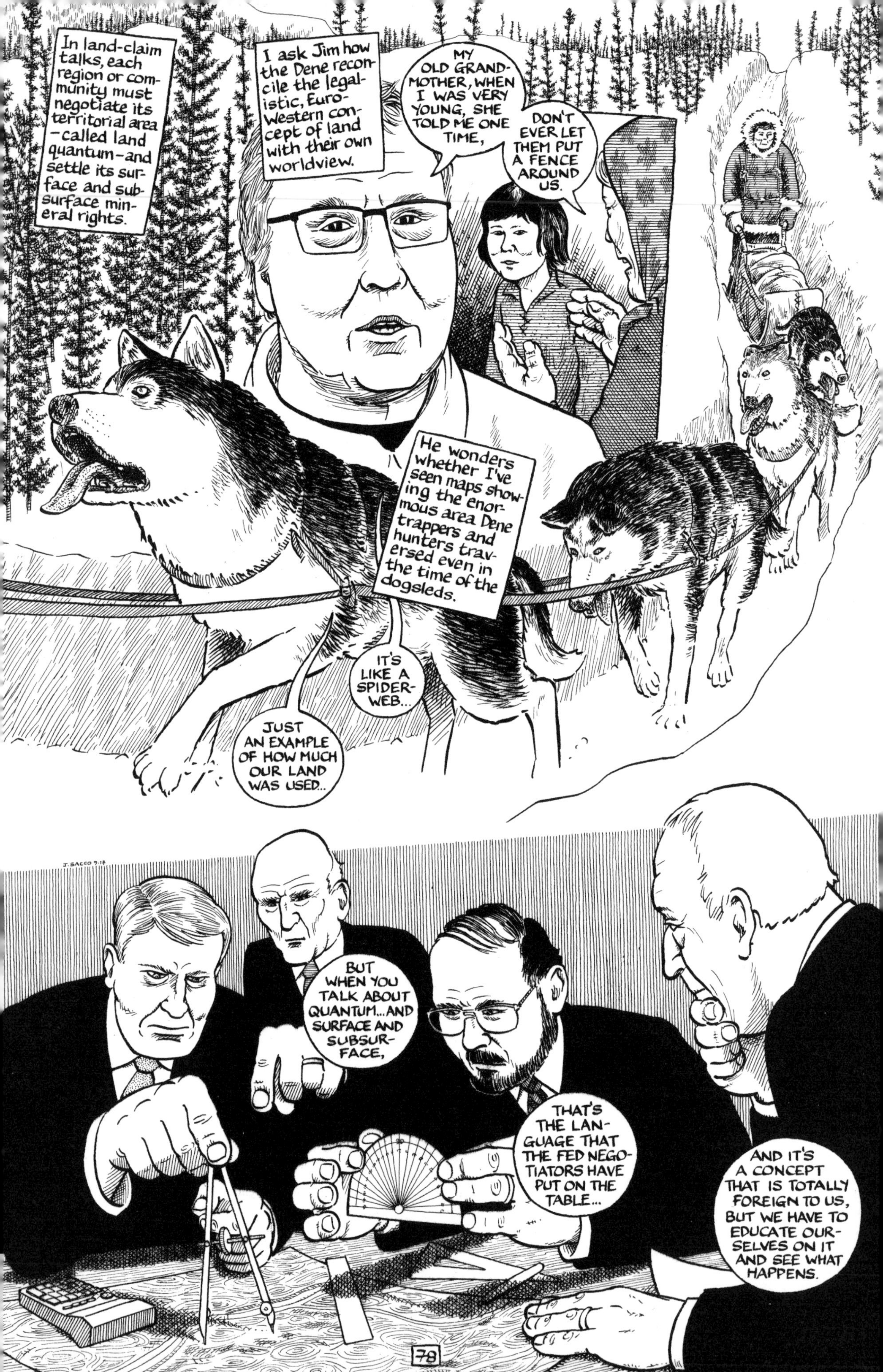
In land-claim talks, each region or community must negotiate its territorial area—called land quantum—and settle its surface and subsurface mineral rights.
I ask Jim how the Dene reconcile the legalistic, Euro-Western concept of land with their own worldview.
MY OLD GRANDMOTHER, WHEN I WAS VERY YOUNG, SHE TOLD ME ONE TIME,
DON'T EVER LET THEM PUT A FENCE AROUND US.
He wonders whether I've seen maps showing the enormous area Dene trappers and hunters traversed even in the time of the dogsleds.
IT'S LIKE A SPIDER-WEB...
JUST AN EXAMPLE OF HOW MUCH OUR LAND WAS USED...
J. SACCO 9.17
BUT WHEN YOU TALK ABOUT QUANTUM...AND SURFACE AND SUBSURFACE,
THAT'S THE LANGUAGE THAT THE FED NEGOTIATORS HAVE PUT ON THE TABLE...
AND IT'S A CONCEPT THAT IS TOTALLY FOREIGN TO US, BUT WE HAVE TO EDUCATE OURSELVES ON IT AND SEE WHAT HAPPENS.

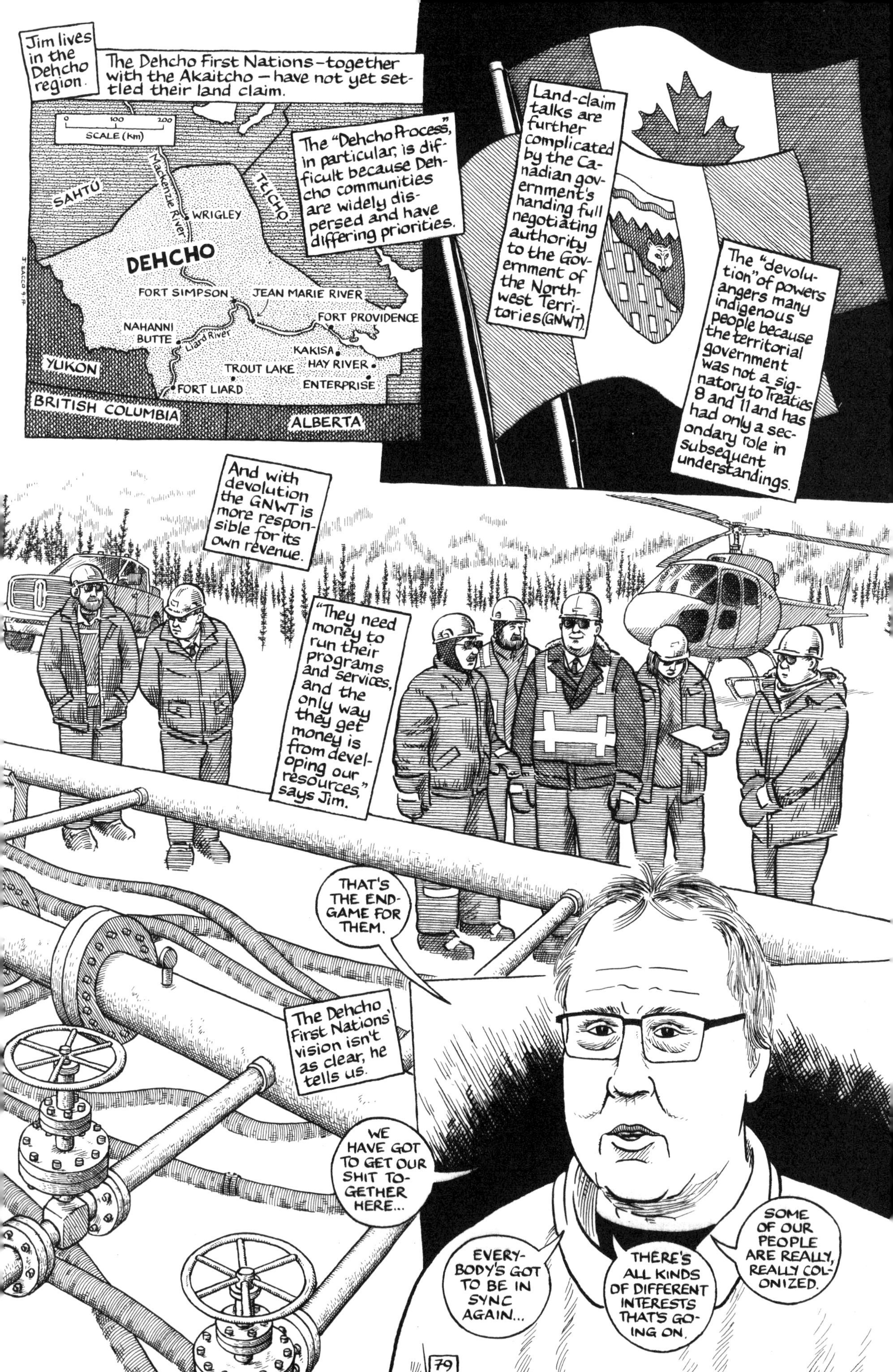

Jim lives in the Dehcho region.
The Dehcho First Nations—together with the Akaitcho—have not yet settled their land claim.
0 100 200
SCALE (km)
SAHTÚ
TŁICHO
Mackenzie River
WRIGLEY
DEHCHO
FORT SIMPSON
JEAN MARIE RIVER
FORT PROVIDENCE
NAHANNI BUTTE
Liard River
KAKISA
HAY RIVER
TROUT LAKE
ENTERPRISE
FORT LIARD
YUKON
BRITISH COLUMBIA
ALBERTA
The "Dehcho Process," in particular, is difficult because Dehcho communities are widely dispersed and have differing priorities.
Land-claim talks are further complicated by the Canadian government's handing full negotiating authority to the Government of the Northwest Territories (GNWT).
The "devolution" of powers angers many indigenous people because the territorial government was not a signatory to Treaties 8 and 11 and has had only a secondary role in subsequent understandings.
And with devolution the GNWT is more responsible for its own revenue.
"They need money to run their programs and services, and the only way they get money is from developing our resources," says Jim.
THAT'S THE END-GAME FOR THEM.
The Dehcho First Nations' vision isn't as clear, he tells us.
WE HAVE GOT TO GET OUR SHIT TOGETHER HERE...
EVERYBODY'S GOT TO BE IN SYNC AGAIN...
THERE'S ALL KINDS OF DIFFERENT INTERESTS THAT'S GOING ON.
SOME OF OUR PEOPLE ARE REALLY, REALLY COLONIZED.

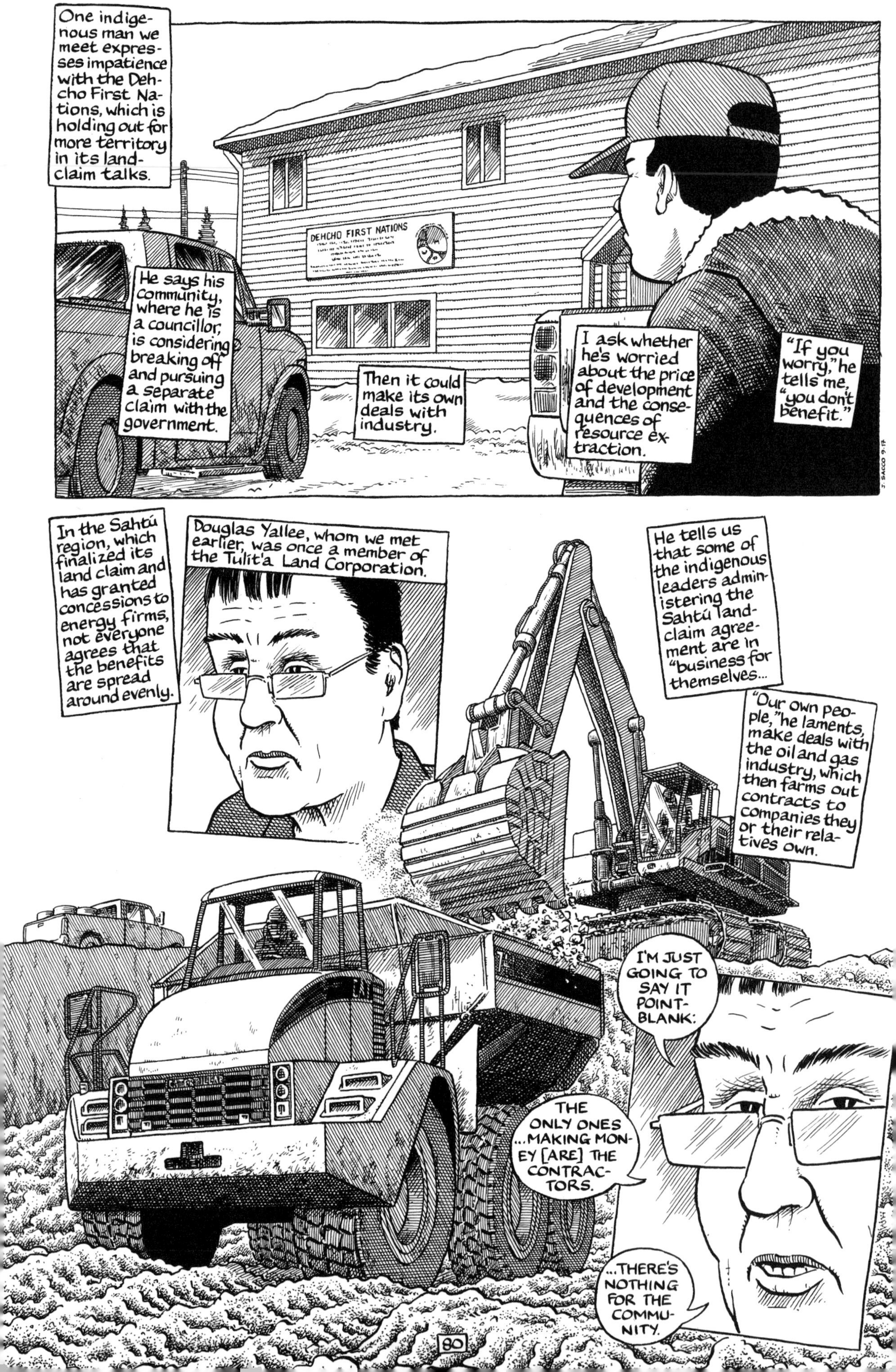
One indigenous man we meet expresses impatience with the Dehcho First Nations, which is holding out for more territory in its land-claim talks.
DEHCHO FIRST NATIONS
He says his community, where he is a councillor, is considering breaking off and pursuing a separate claim with the government.
Then it could make its own deals with industry.
I ask whether he's worried about the price of development and the consequences of resource extraction.
"If you worry," he tells me, "you don't benefit."
J. SACCO 9.17
In the Sahtú region, which finalized its land claim and has granted concessions to energy firms, not everyone agrees that the benefits are spread around evenly.
Douglas Yallee, whom we met earlier, was once a member of the Tulít'a Land Corporation.
He tells us that some of the indigenous leaders administering the Sahtú land-claim agreement are in "business for themselves...
"Our own people," he laments, make deals with the oil and gas industry, which then farms out contracts to companies they or their relatives own.
I'M JUST GOING TO SAY IT POINT-BLANK:
THE ONLY ONES ...MAKING MONEY [ARE] THE CONTRACTORS.
...THERE'S NOTHING FOR THE COMMUNITY.

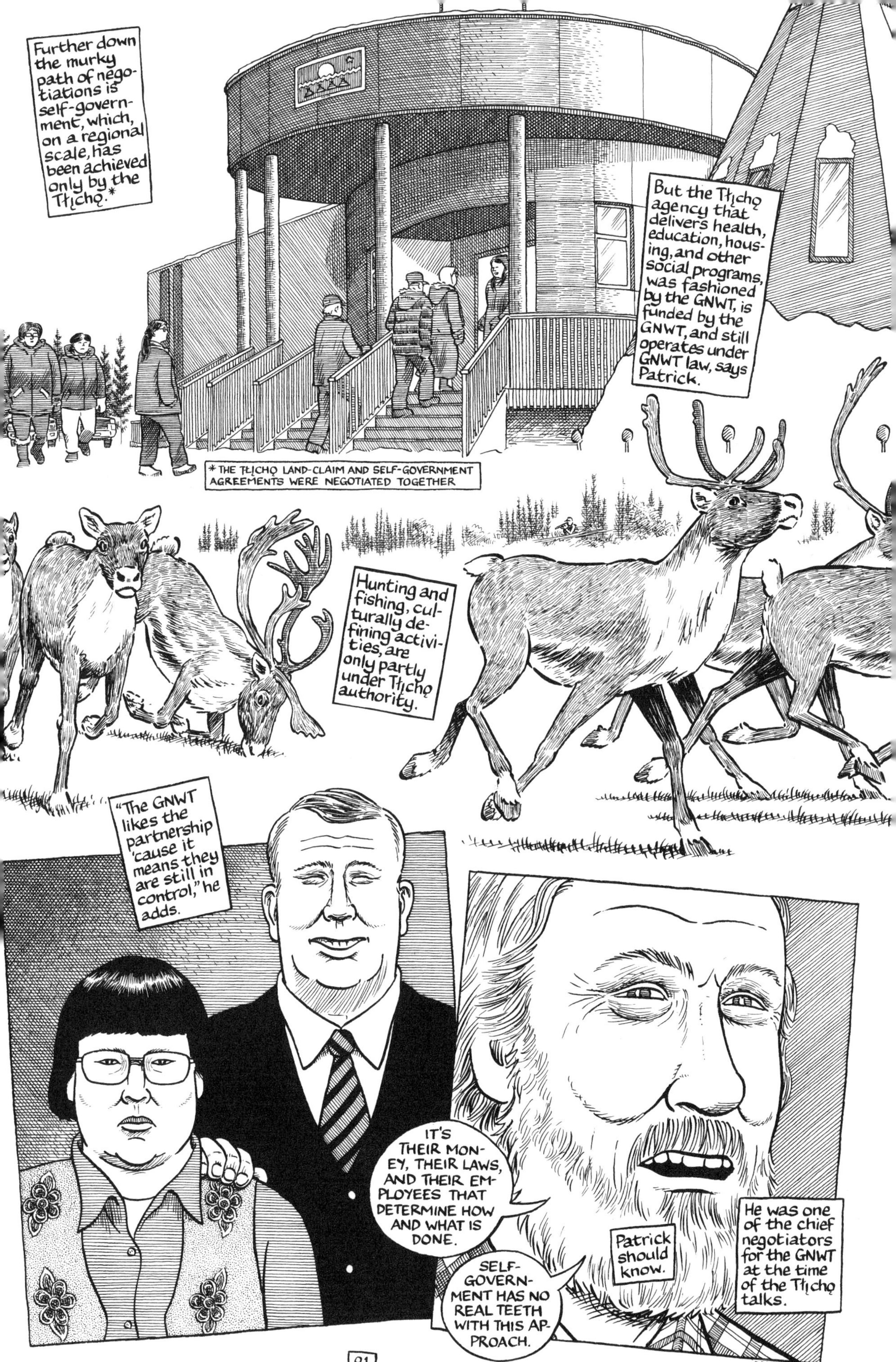

Further down the murky path of negotiations is self-government, which, on a regional scale, has been achieved only by the Tłı̨chǫ.*
But the Tłı̨chǫ agency that delivers health, education, housing, and other social programs, was fashioned by the GNWT, is funded by the GNWT, and still operates under GNWT law, says Patrick.
* THE TŁĮCHǪ LAND-CLAIM AND SELF-GOVERNMENT AGREEMENTS WERE NEGOTIATED TOGETHER
Hunting and fishing, culturally defining activities, are only partly under Tłı̨chǫ authority.
"The GNWT likes the partnership 'cause it means they are still in control," he adds.
IT'S THEIR MONEY, THEIR LAWS, AND THEIR EMPLOYEES THAT DETERMINE HOW AND WHAT IS DONE.
SELF-GOVERNMENT HAS NO REAL TEETH WITH THIS APPROACH.
Patrick should know.
He was one of the chief negotiators for the GNWT at the time of the Tłı̨chǫ talks.

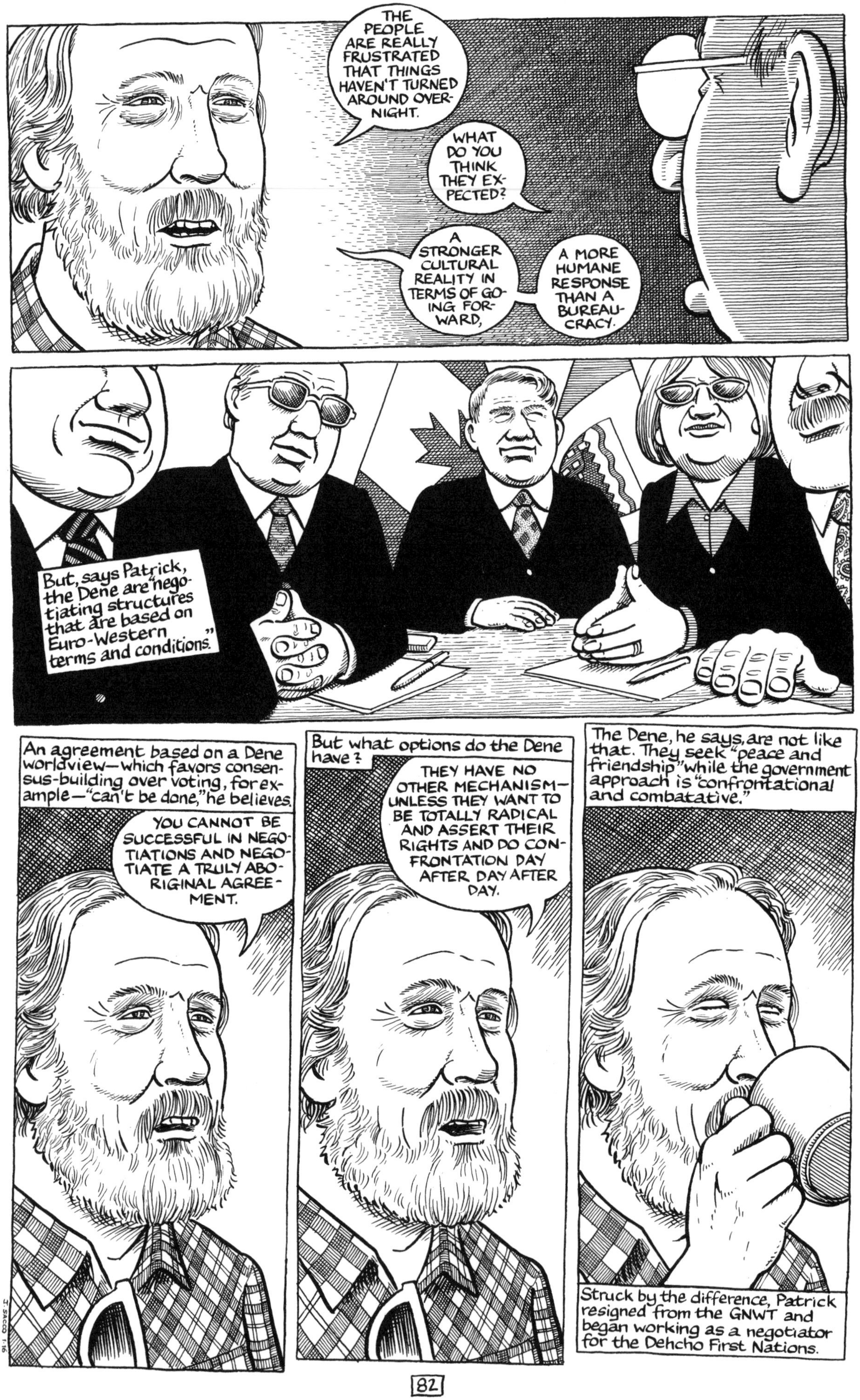
THE PEOPLE ARE REALLY FRUSTRATED THAT THINGS HAVEN'T TURNED AROUND OVER-NIGHT.
WHAT DO YOU THINK THEY EX-PECTED?
A STRONGER CULTURAL REALITY IN TERMS OF GO-ING FOR-WARD,
A MORE HUMANE RESPONSE THAN A BUREAU-CRACY.
But, says Patrick, the Dene are "nego-tiating structures that are based on Euro-Western terms and conditions."
An agreement based on a Dene worldview—which favors consen-sus-building over voting, for ex-ample—"can't be done," he believes.
YOU CANNOT BE SUCCESSFUL IN NEGO-TIATIONS AND NEGO-TIATE A TRULY ABO-RIGINAL AGREE-MENT.
But what options do the Dene have?
THEY HAVE NO OTHER MECHANISM—UNLESS THEY WANT TO BE TOTALLY RADICAL AND ASSERT THEIR RIGHTS AND DO CON-FRONTATION DAY AFTER DAY AFTER DAY.
The Dene, he says, are not like that. They seek "peace and friendship" while the government approach is "confrontational and combatative."
Struck by the difference, Patrick resigned from the GNWT and began working as a negotiator for the Dehcho First Nations.

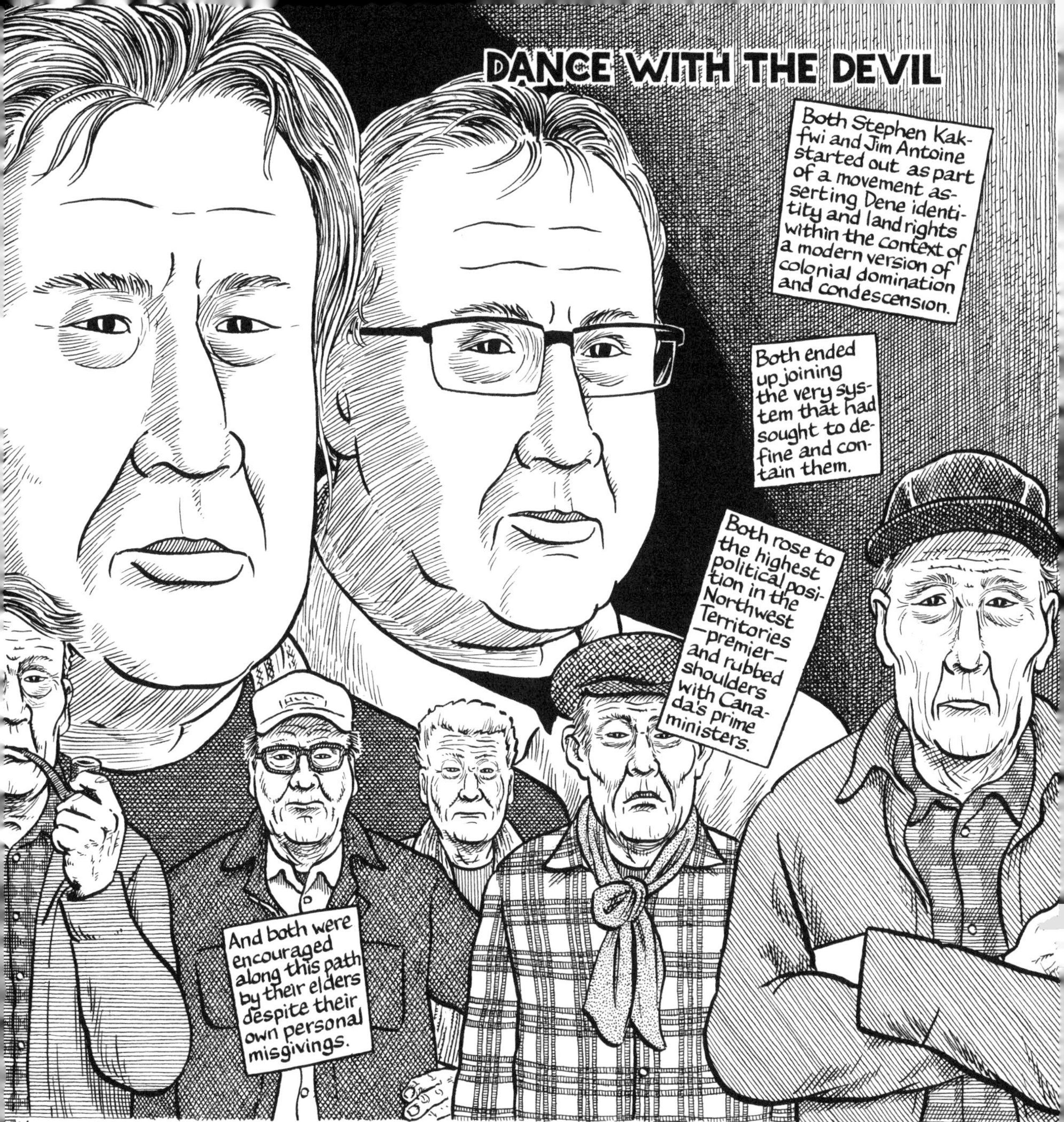
DANCE WITH THE DEVIL
Both Stephen Kakfwi and Jim Antoine started out as part of a movement asserting Dene identity and land rights within the context of a modern version of colonial domination and condescension.
Both ended up joining the very system that had sought to define and contain them.
Both rose to the highest political position in the Northwest Territories —premier— and rubbed shoulders with Canada's prime ministers.
And both were encouraged along this path by their elders despite their own personal misgivings.

Here we take up their stories to understand how and why the Dene entered Canada's political mainstream.

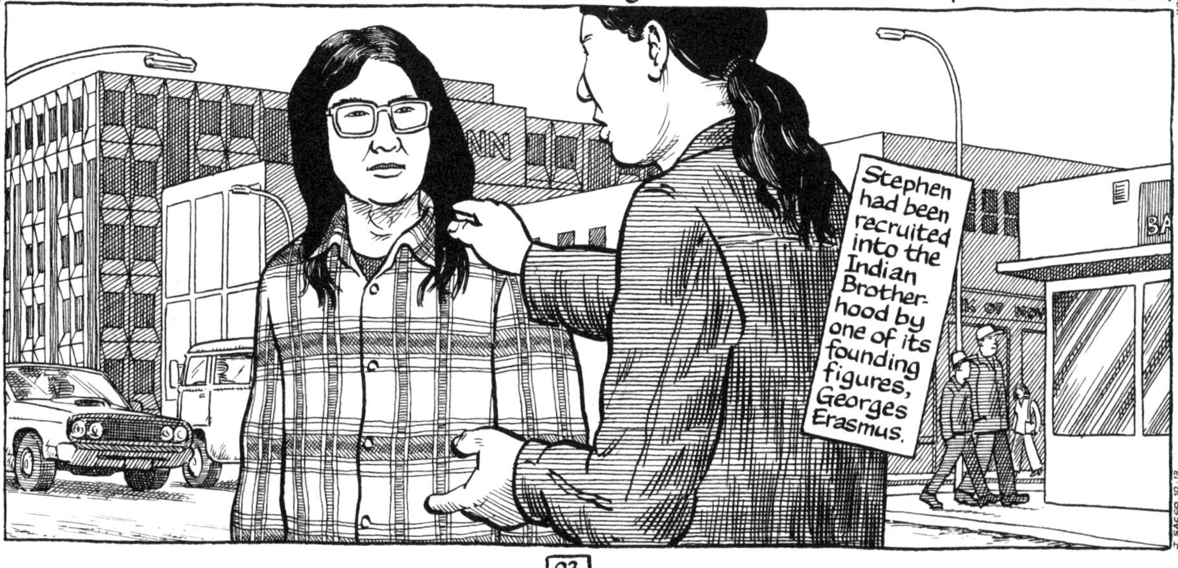
Stephen had been recruited into the Indian Brotherhood by one of its founding figures, Georges Erasmus.

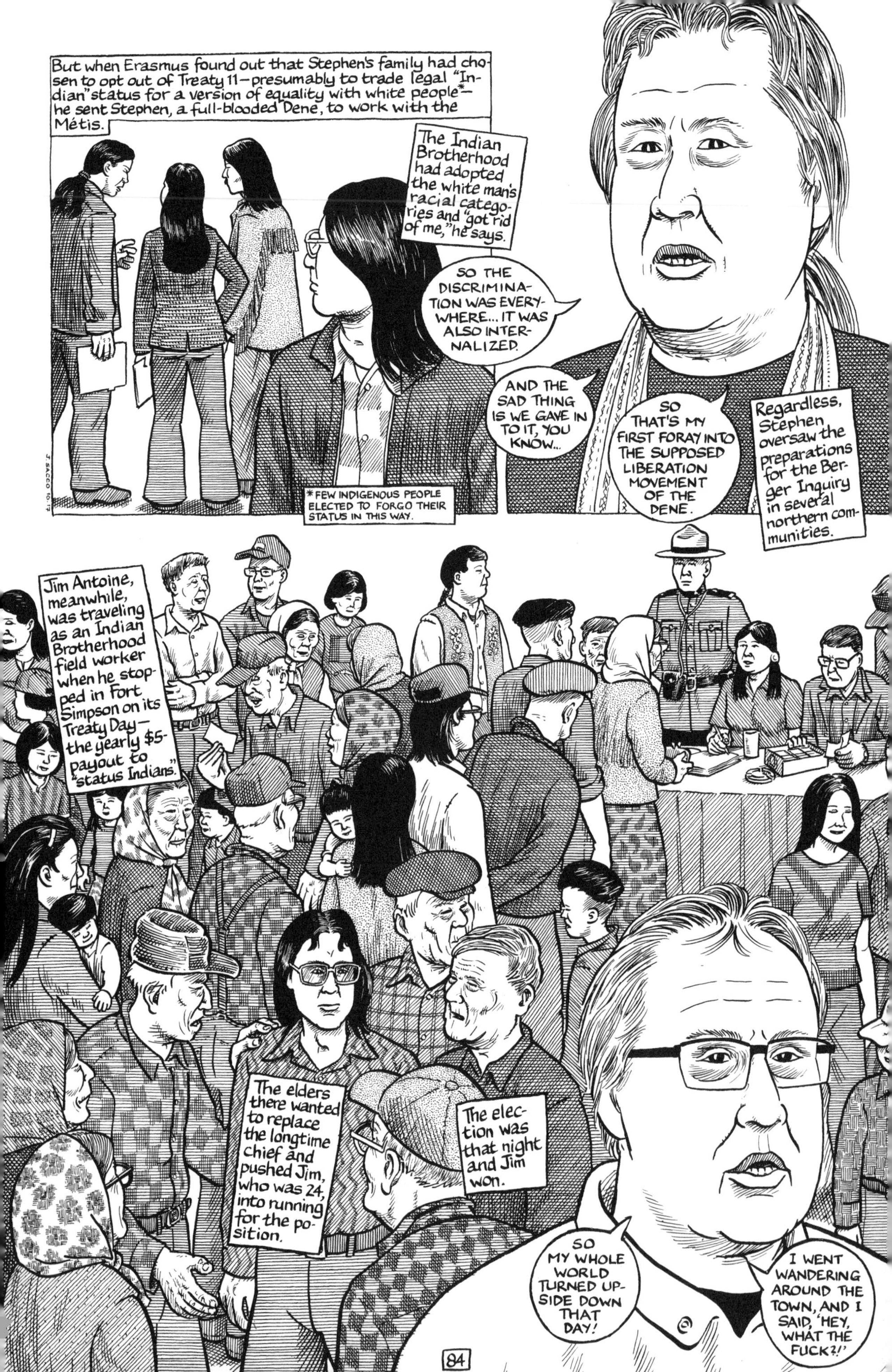

But when Erasmus found out that Stephen's family had chosen to opt out of Treaty 11—presumably to trade legal "Indian" status for a version of equality with white people*—he sent Stephen, a full-blooded Dene, to work with the Métis.
The Indian Brotherhood had adopted the white man's racial categories and "got rid of me," he says.
SO THE DISCRIMINATION WAS EVERYWHERE... IT WAS ALSO INTERNALIZED.
AND THE SAD THING IS WE GAVE IN TO IT, YOU KNOW...
SO THAT'S MY FIRST FORAY INTO THE SUPPOSED LIBERATION MOVEMENT OF THE DENE.
Regardless, Stephen oversaw the preparations for the Berger Inquiry in several northern communities.
*FEW INDIGENOUS PEOPLE ELECTED TO FORGO THEIR STATUS IN THIS WAY.
Jim Antoine, meanwhile, was traveling as an Indian Brotherhood field worker when he stopped in Fort Simpson on its Treaty Day—the yearly $5-payout to "status Indians."
The elders there wanted to replace the longtime chief and pushed Jim, who was 24, into running for the position.
The election was that night and Jim won.
SO MY WHOLE WORLD TURNED UPSIDE DOWN THAT DAY!
I WENT WANDERING AROUND THE TOWN, AND I SAID, 'HEY, WHAT THE FUCK?!'

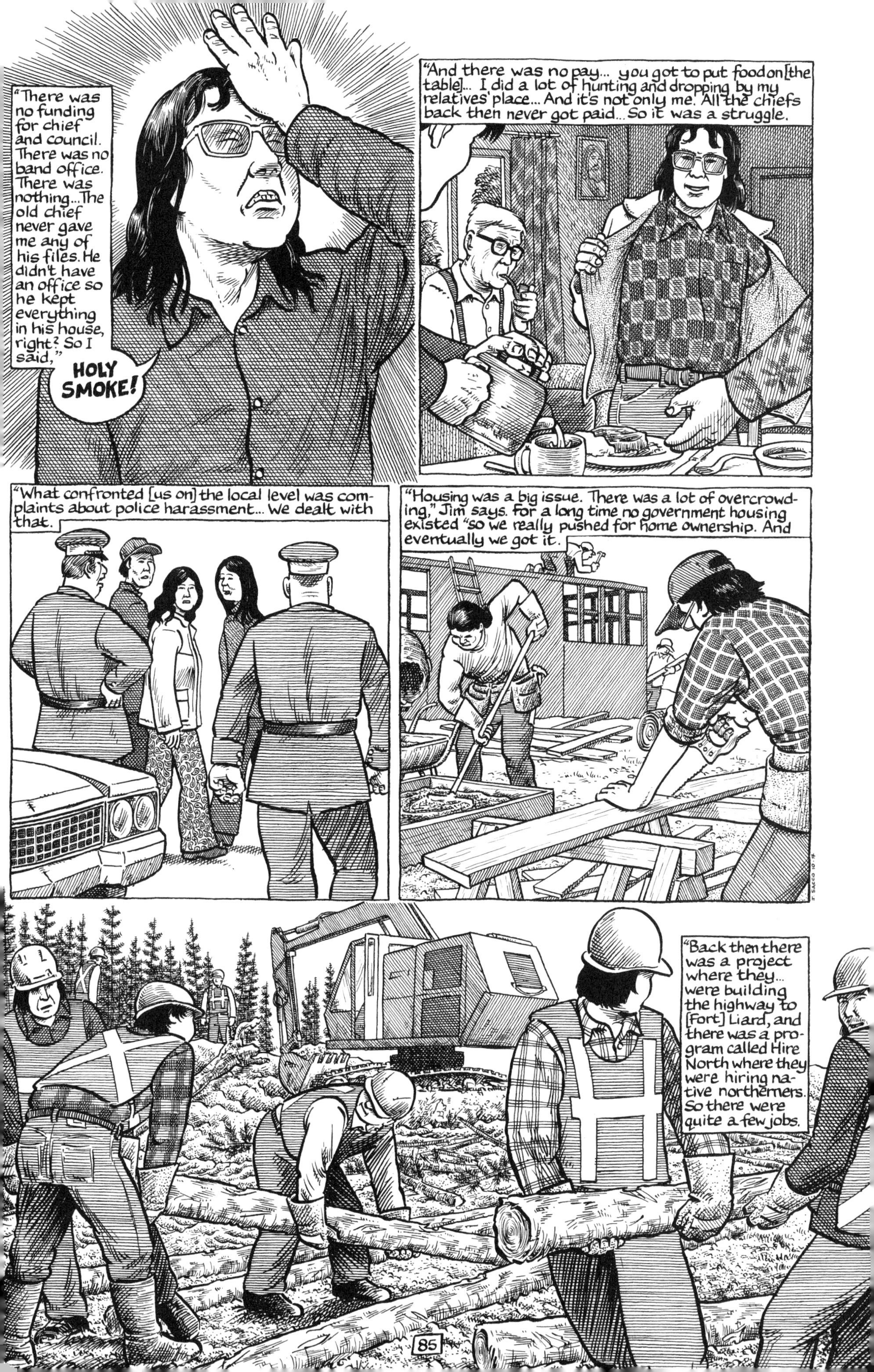
"There was no funding for chief and council. There was no band office. There was nothing... The old chief never gave me any of his files. He didn't have an office so he kept everything in his house, right? So I said,"
HOLY SMOKE!
"And there was no pay... you got to put food on [the table]... I did a lot of hunting and dropping by my relatives' place... And it's not only me. All the chiefs back then never got paid... So it was a struggle.
"What confronted [us on] the local level was complaints about police harassment... We dealt with that.
"Housing was a big issue. There was a lot of overcrowding," Jim says. For a long time no government housing existed "so we really pushed for home ownership. And eventually we got it.
"Back then there was a project where they... were building the highway to [Fort] Liard, and there was a program called Hire North where they were hiring native northerners. So there were quite a few jobs.

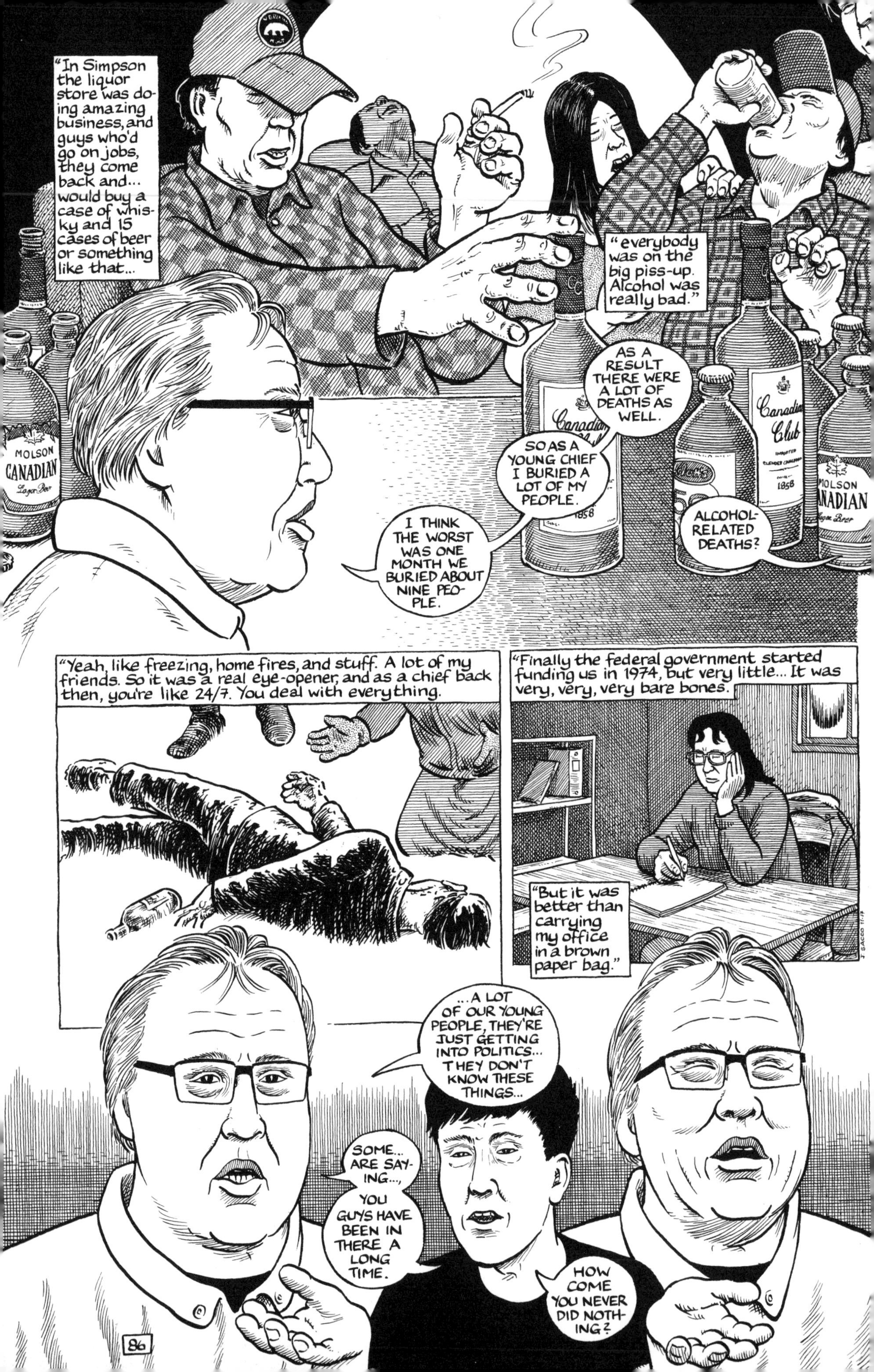
"In Simpson the liquor store was doing amazing business, and guys who'd go on jobs, they come back and... would buy a case of whisky and 15 cases of beer or something like that...
"everybody was on the big piss-up. Alcohol was really bad."
AS A RESULT THERE WERE A LOT OF DEATHS AS WELL.
SO AS A YOUNG CHIEF I BURIED A LOT OF MY PEOPLE.
I THINK THE WORST WAS ONE MONTH WE BURIED ABOUT NINE PEOPLE.
ALCOHOL-RELATED DEATHS?
MOLSON CANADIAN Lager Beer
Canadian Club
1858
"Yeah, like freezing, home fires, and stuff. A lot of my friends. So it was a real eye-opener, and as a chief back then, you're like 24/7. You deal with everything.
"Finally the federal government started funding us in 1974, but very little... It was very, very, very bare bones.
"But it was better than carrying my office in a brown paper bag."
...A LOT OF OUR YOUNG PEOPLE, THEY'RE JUST GETTING INTO POLITICS... THEY DON'T KNOW THESE THINGS...
SOME... ARE SAYING...,
YOU GUYS HAVE BEEN IN THERE A LONG TIME.
HOW COME YOU NEVER DID NOTHING?

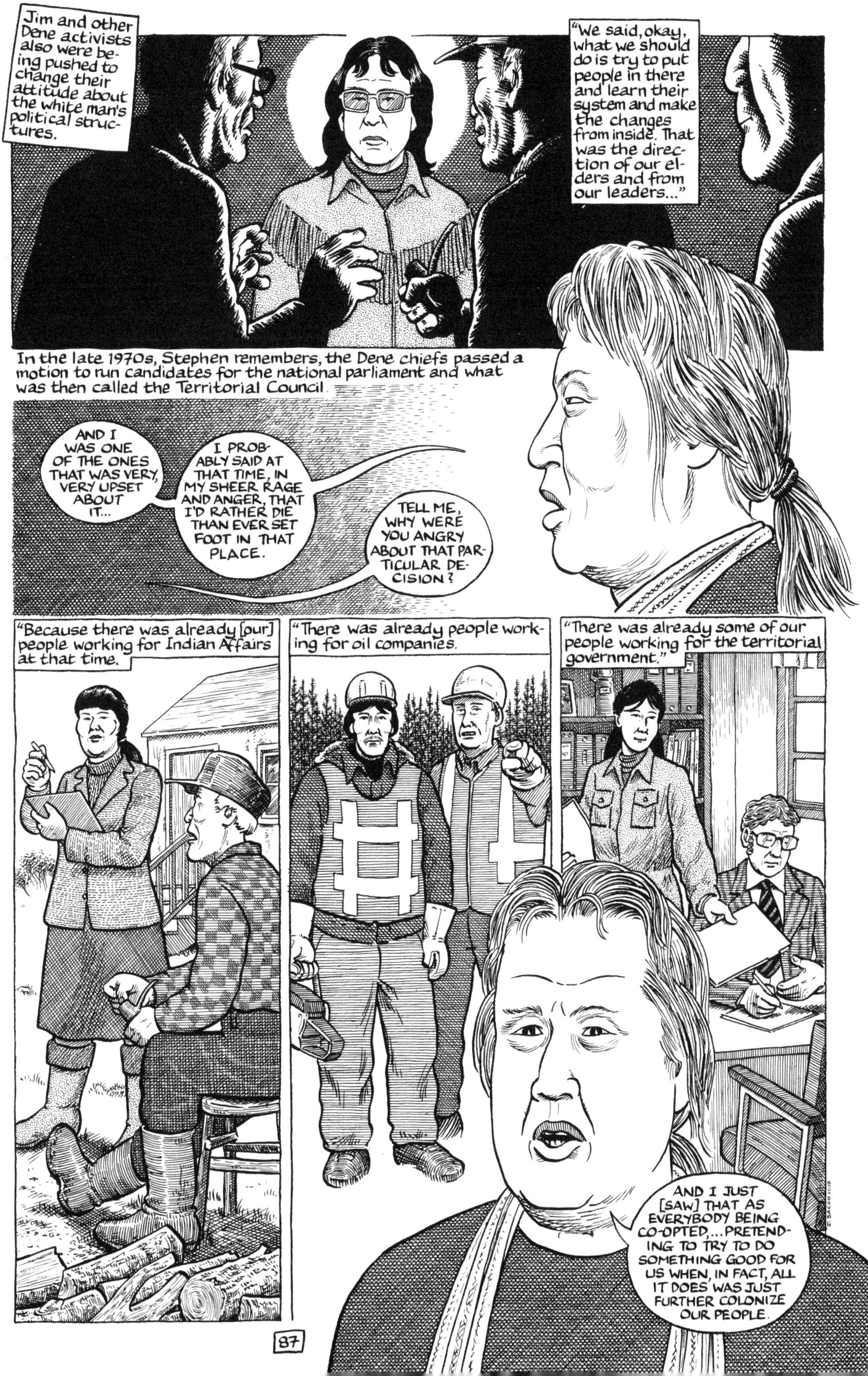

Jim and other Dene activists also were being pushed to change their attitude about the white man's political structures.
"We said, okay, what we should do is try to put people in there and learn their system and make the changes from inside. That was the direction of our elders and from our leaders..."
In the late 1970s, Stephen remembers, the Dene chiefs passed a motion to run candidates for the national parliament and what was then called the Territorial Council.
AND I WAS ONE OF THE ONES THAT WAS VERY, VERY UPSET ABOUT IT...
I PROBABLY SAID AT THAT TIME, IN MY SHEER RAGE AND ANGER, THAT I'D RATHER DIE THAN EVER SET FOOT IN THAT PLACE.
TELL ME, WHY WERE YOU ANGRY ABOUT THAT PARTICULAR DECISION?
"Because there was already [our] people working for Indian Affairs at that time.
"There was already people working for oil companies.
"There was already some of our people working for the territorial government."
AND I JUST [SAW] THAT AS EVERYBODY BEING CO-OPTED,... PRETENDING TO TRY TO DO SOMETHING GOOD FOR US WHEN, IN FACT, ALL IT DOES WAS JUST FURTHER COLONIZE OUR PEOPLE.

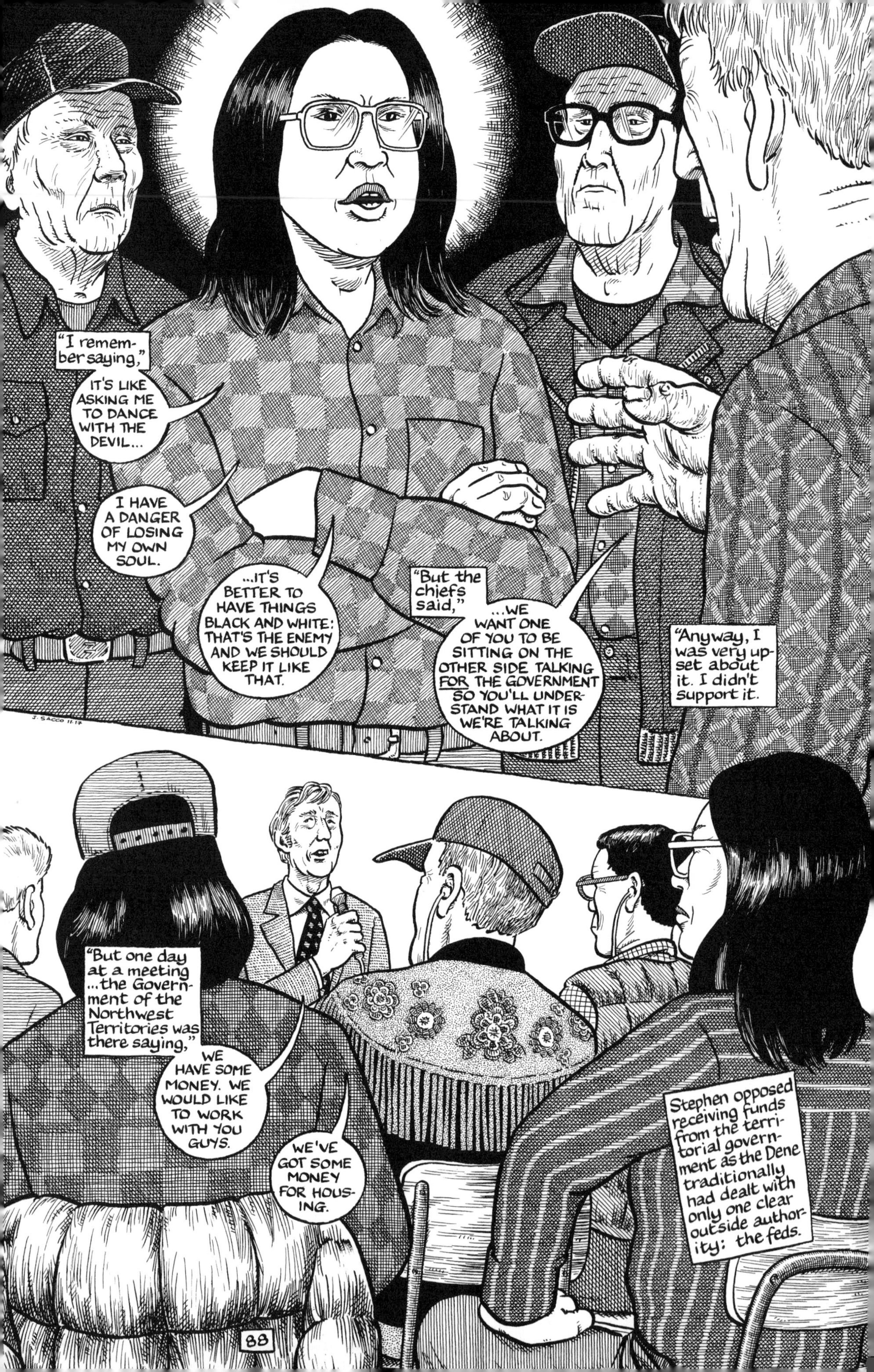

"I remember saying,"
IT'S LIKE ASKING ME TO DANCE WITH THE DEVIL...
I HAVE A DANGER OF LOSING MY OWN SOUL.
...IT'S BETTER TO HAVE THINGS BLACK AND WHITE: THAT'S THE ENEMY AND WE SHOULD KEEP IT LIKE THAT.
"But the chiefs said,"
...WE WANT ONE OF YOU TO BE SITTING ON THE OTHER SIDE TALKING FOR THE GOVERNMENT SO YOU'LL UNDERSTAND WHAT IT IS WE'RE TALKING ABOUT.
"Anyway, I was very upset about it. I didn't support it.
J. SACCO 11.17
"But one day at a meeting ...the Government of the Northwest Territories was there saying,"
WE HAVE SOME MONEY. WE WOULD LIKE TO WORK WITH YOU GUYS.
WE'VE GOT SOME MONEY FOR HOUSING.
Stephen opposed receiving funds from the territorial government as the Dene traditionally had dealt with only one clear outside authority: the feds.

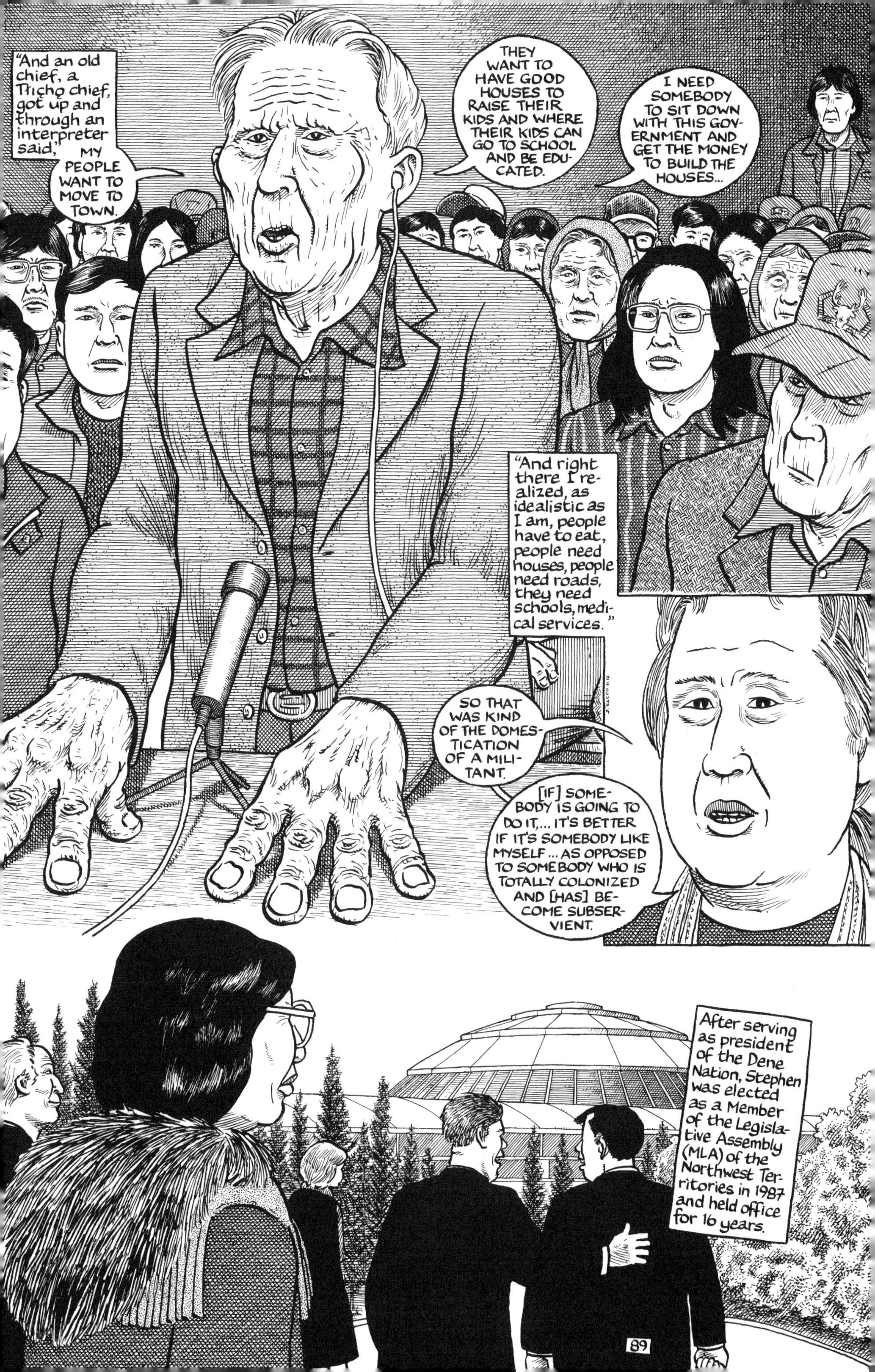
"And an old chief, a Tłı̨chǫ chief, got up and through an interpreter said,"
MY PEOPLE WANT TO MOVE TO TOWN.
THEY WANT TO HAVE GOOD HOUSES TO RAISE THEIR KIDS AND WHERE THEIR KIDS CAN GO TO SCHOOL AND BE EDUCATED.
I NEED SOMEBODY TO SIT DOWN WITH THIS GOVERNMENT AND GET THE MONEY TO BUILD THE HOUSES...
"And right there I realized, as idealistic as I am, people have to eat, people need houses, people need roads, they need schools, medical services."
SO THAT WAS KIND OF THE DOMESTICATION OF A MILITANT.
[IF] SOMEBODY IS GOING TO DO IT,... IT'S BETTER IF IT'S SOMEBODY LIKE MYSELF... AS OPPOSED TO SOMEBODY WHO IS TOTALLY COLONIZED AND [HAS] BECOME SUBSERVIENT.
After serving as president of the Dene Nation, Stephen was elected as a Member of the Legislative Assembly (MLA) of the Northwest Territories in 1987 and held office for 16 years.

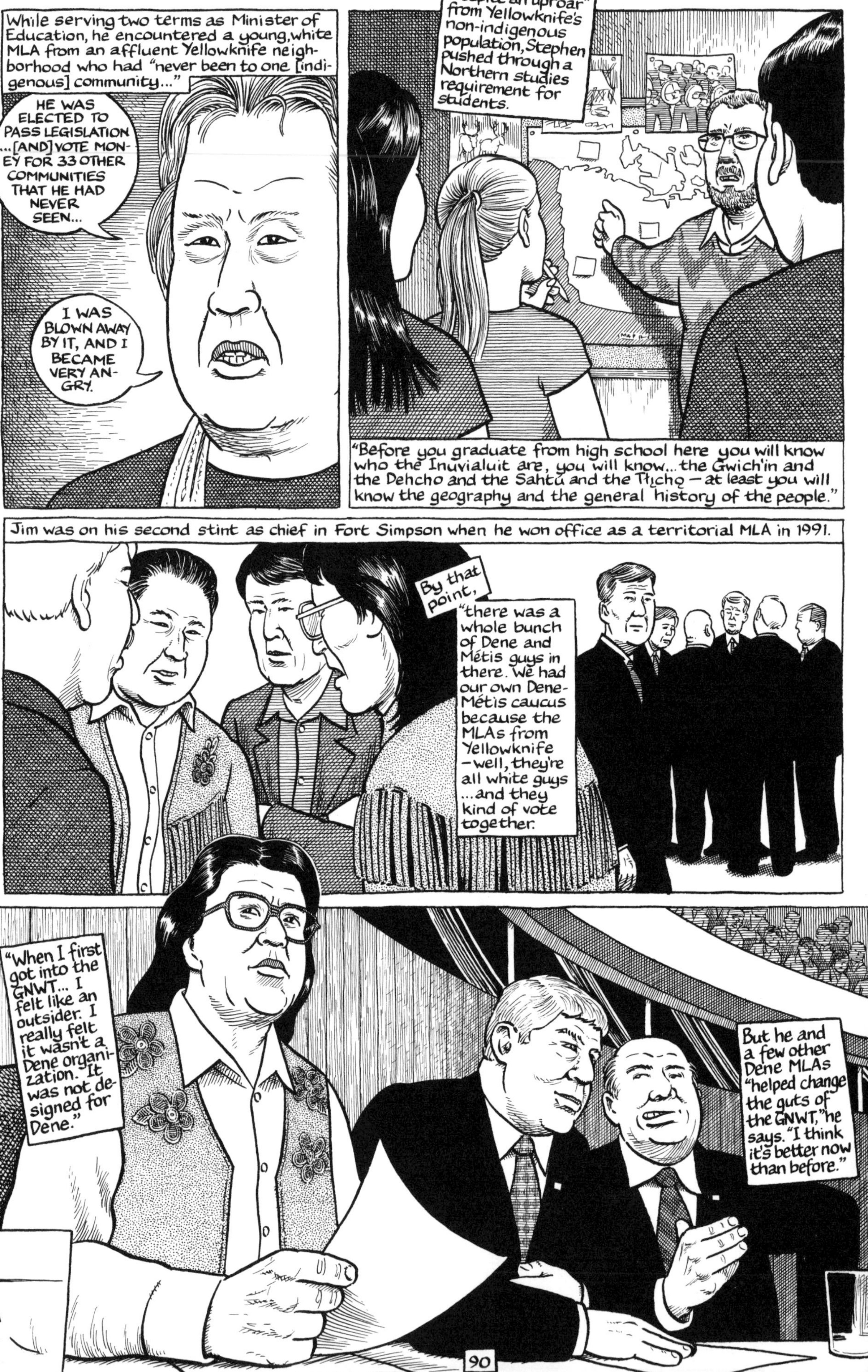
While serving two terms as Minister of Education, he encountered a young, white MLA from an affluent Yellowknife neighborhood who had "never been to one [indigenous] community..."
HE WAS ELECTED TO PASS LEGISLATION ...[AND] VOTE MONEY FOR 33 OTHER COMMUNITIES THAT HE HAD NEVER SEEN...
I WAS BLOWN AWAY BY IT, AND I BECAME VERY ANGRY.
Despite an "uproar" from Yellowknife's non-indigenous population, Stephen pushed through a Northern studies requirement for students.
"Before you graduate from high school here you will know who the Inuvialuit are, you will know... the Gwich'in and the Dehcho and the Sahtú and the Tłı̨chǫ — at least you will know the geography and the general history of the people."
Jim was on his second stint as chief in Fort Simpson when he won office as a territorial MLA in 1991.
By that point,
"there was a whole bunch of Dene and Métis guys in there. We had our own Dene-Métis caucus because the MLAs from Yellowknife — well, they're all white guys ...and they kind of vote together.
"When I first got into the GNWT... I felt like an outsider. I really felt it wasn't a Dene organization. It was not designed for Dene."
But he and a few other Dene MLAs "helped change the guts of the GNWT," he says. "I think it's better now than before."

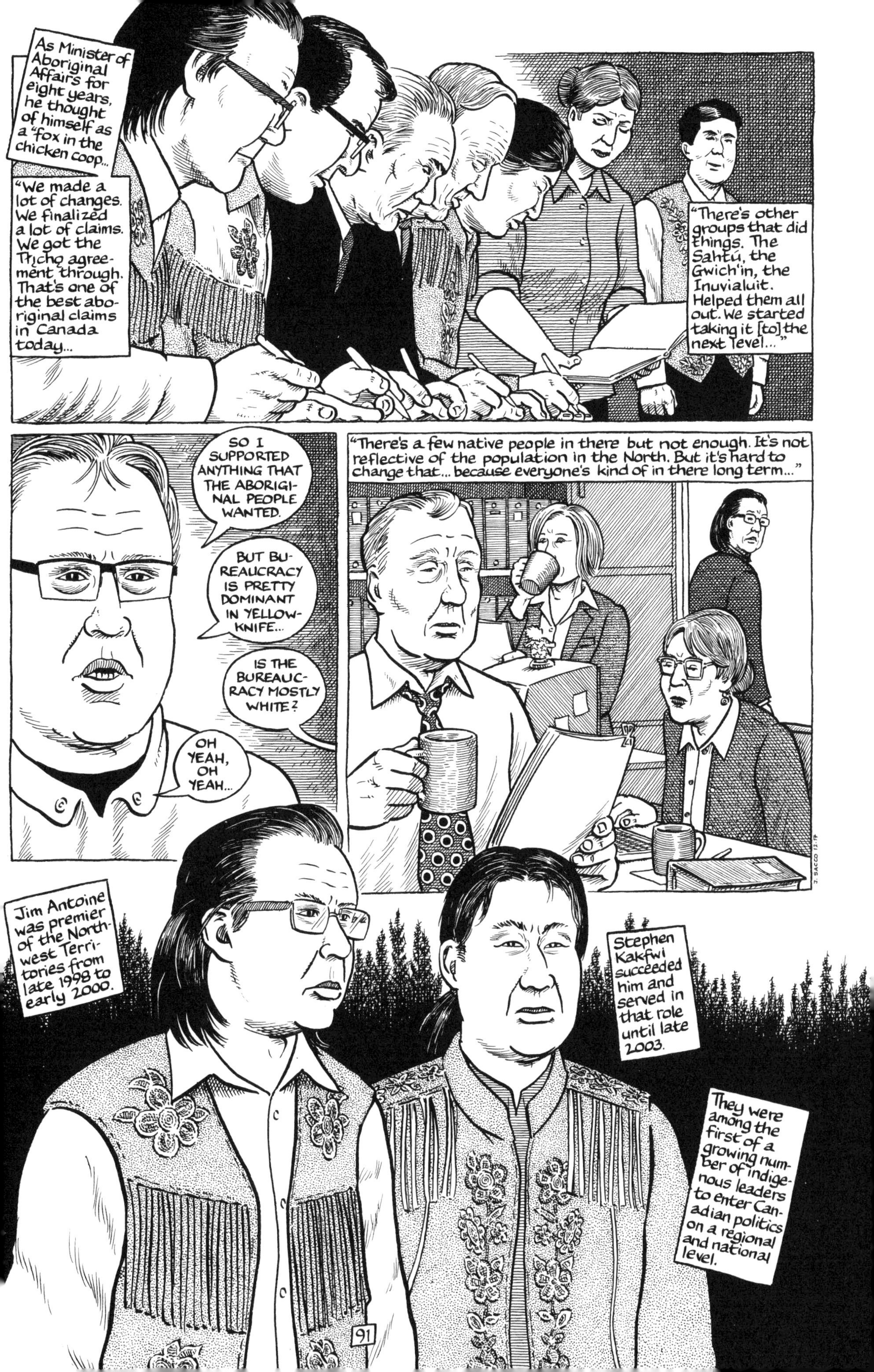

As Minister of Aboriginal Affairs for eight years, he thought of himself as a "fox in the chicken coop...
"We made a lot of changes. We finalized a lot of claims. We got the Tłı̨chǫ agreement through. That's one of the best aboriginal claims in Canada today...
"There's other groups that did things. The Sahtú, the Gwich'in, the Inuvialuit. Helped them all out. We started taking it [to] the next level..."
SO I SUPPORTED ANYTHING THAT THE ABORIGINAL PEOPLE WANTED.
BUT BUREAUCRACY IS PRETTY DOMINANT IN YELLOWKNIFE...
IS THE BUREAUCRACY MOSTLY WHITE?
OH YEAH, OH YEAH...
"There's a few native people in there but not enough. It's not reflective of the population in the North. But it's hard to change that... because everyone's kind of in there long term..."
J. SACCO 12.17
Jim Antoine was premier of the Northwest Territories from late 1998 to early 2000.
Stephen Kakfwi succeeded him and served in that role until late 2003.
They were among the first of a growing number of indigenous leaders to enter Canadian politics on a regional and national level.

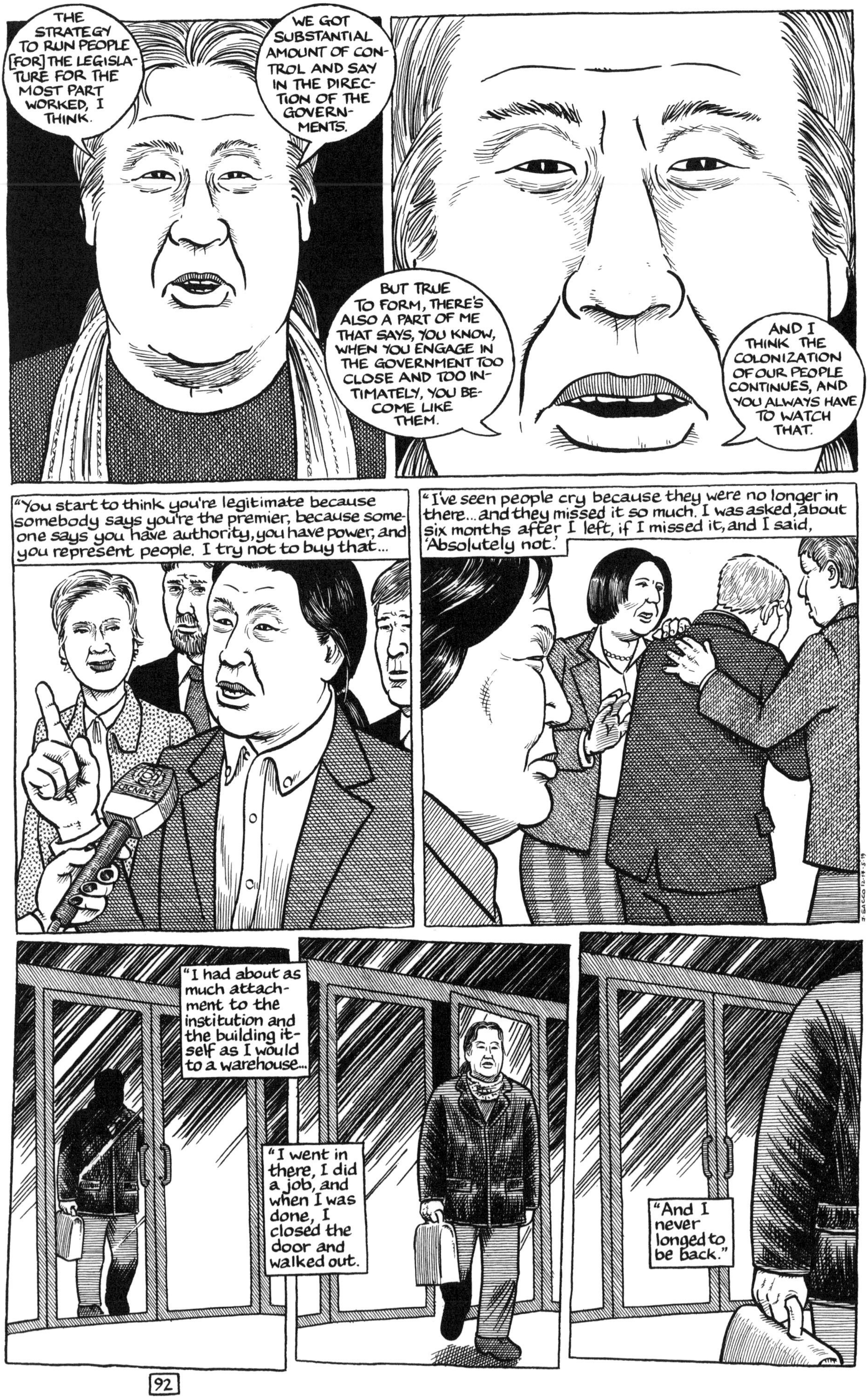
THE STRATEGY TO RUN PEOPLE [FOR] THE LEGISLATURE FOR THE MOST PART WORKED, I THINK.
WE GOT SUBSTANTIAL AMOUNT OF CONTROL AND SAY IN THE DIRECTION OF THE GOVERNMENTS.
BUT TRUE TO FORM, THERE'S ALSO A PART OF ME THAT SAYS, YOU KNOW, WHEN YOU ENGAGE IN THE GOVERNMENT TOO CLOSE AND TOO INTIMATELY, YOU BECOME LIKE THEM.
AND I THINK THE COLONIZATION OF OUR PEOPLE CONTINUES, AND YOU ALWAYS HAVE TO WATCH THAT.
"You start to think you're legitimate because somebody says you're the premier, because someone says you have authority, you have power, and you represent people. I try not to buy that...
CBC NEWS
"I've seen people cry because they were no longer in there... and they missed it so much. I was asked, about six months after I left, if I missed it, and I said, 'Absolutely not.'
"I had about as much attachment to the institution and the building itself as I would to a warehouse...
"I went in there, I did a job, and when I was done, I closed the door and walked out.
"And I never longed to be back."

IV

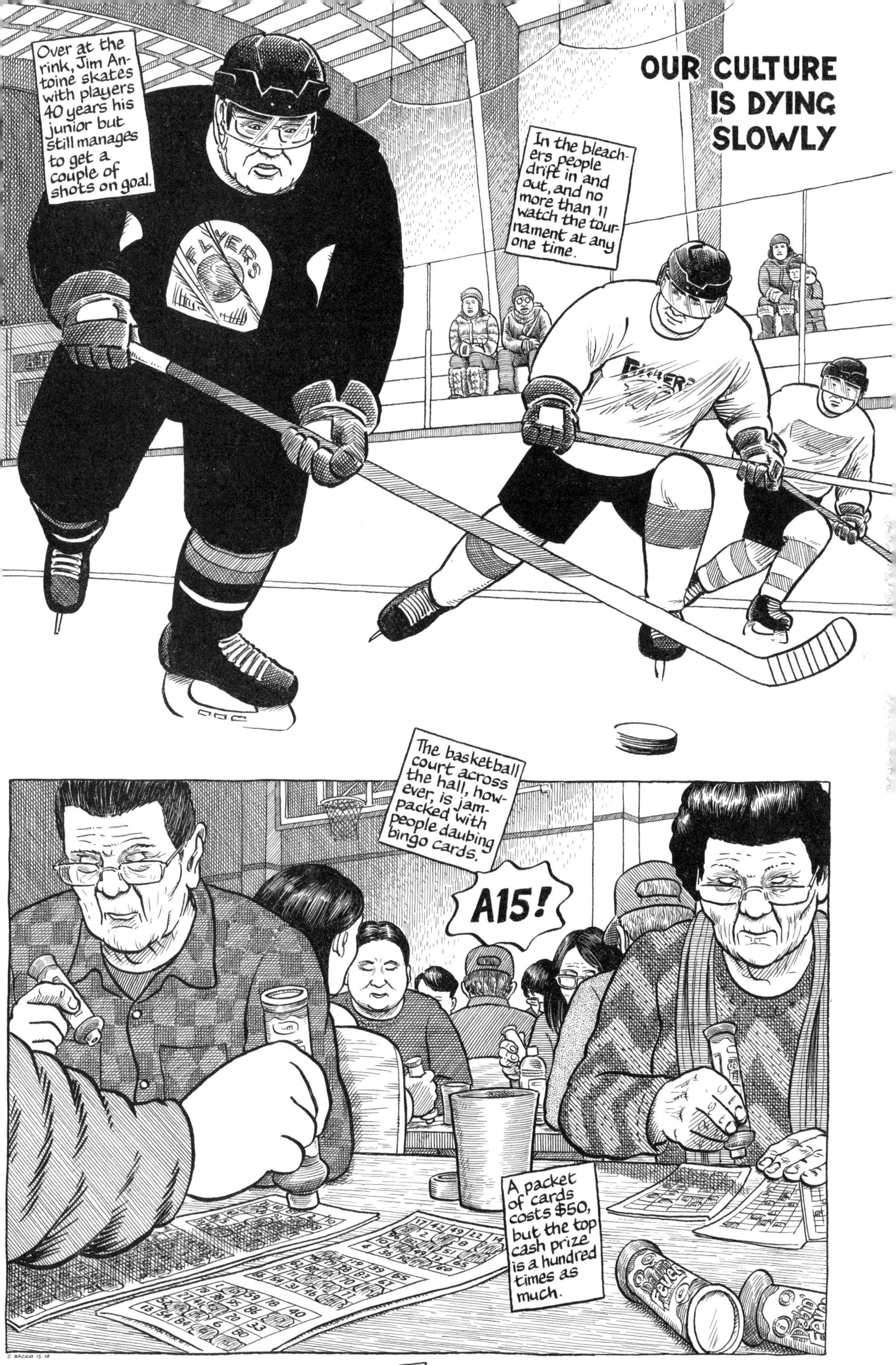
OUR CULTURE IS DYING SLOWLY
Over at the rink, Jim Antoine skates with players 40 years his junior but still manages to get a couple of shots on goal.
In the bleachers people drift in and out, and no more than 11 watch the tournament at any one time.
FLYERS
The basketball court across the hall, however, is jam-packed with people daubing bingo cards.
A15!
A packet of cards costs $50, but the top cash prize is a hundred times as much.
J. SACCO 12-17

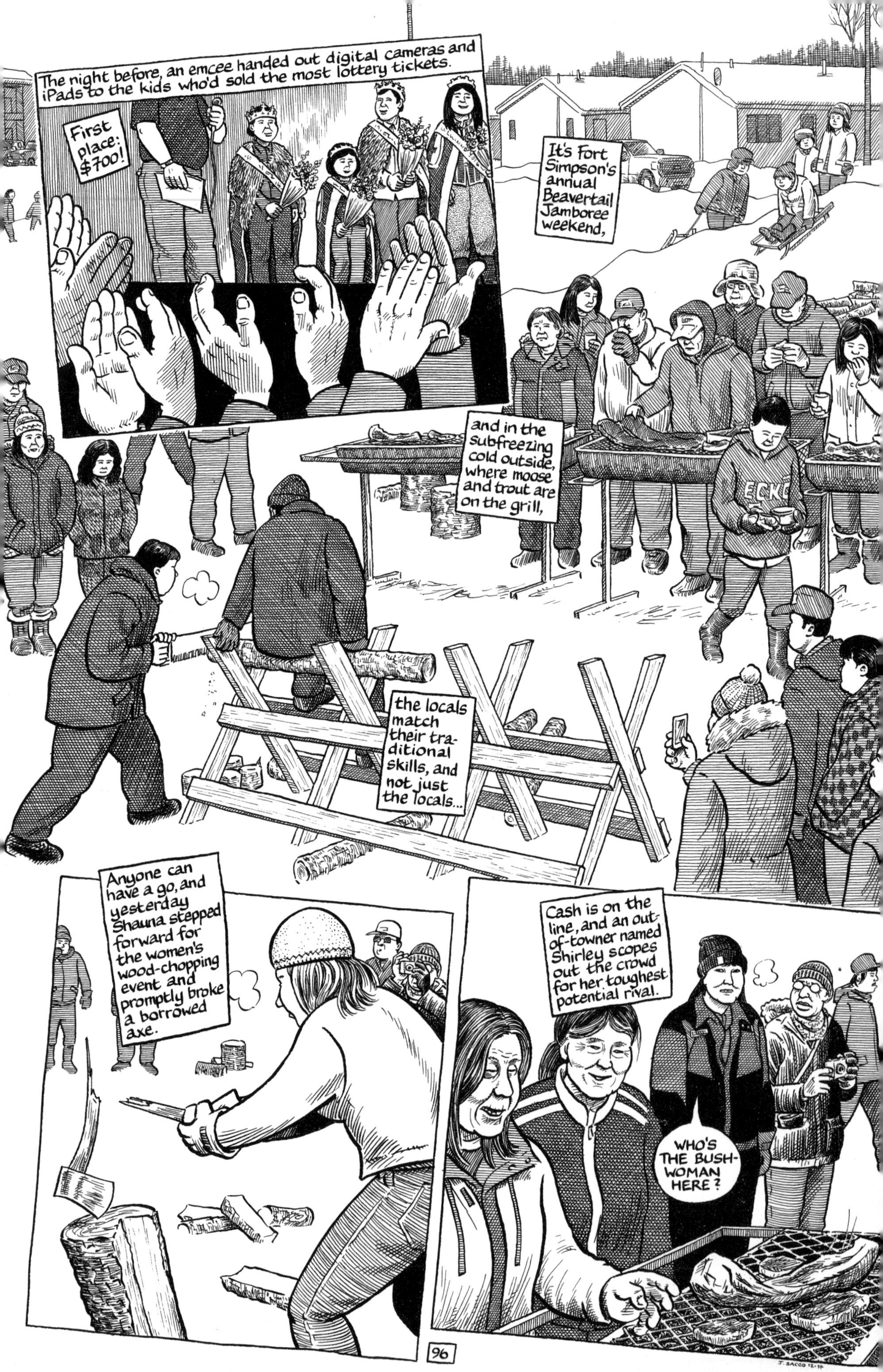

The night before, an emcee handed out digital cameras and iPads to the kids who'd sold the most lottery tickets.
First place: $700!
It's Fort Simpson's annual Beavertail Jamboree weekend,
and in the subfreezing cold outside, where moose and trout are on the grill,
the locals match their traditional skills, and not just the locals...
Anyone can have a go, and yesterday Shauna stepped forward for the women's wood-chopping event and promptly broke a borrowed axe.
Cash is on the line, and an out-of-towner named Shirley scopes out the crowd for her toughest potential rival.
WHO'S THE BUSH-WOMAN HERE?

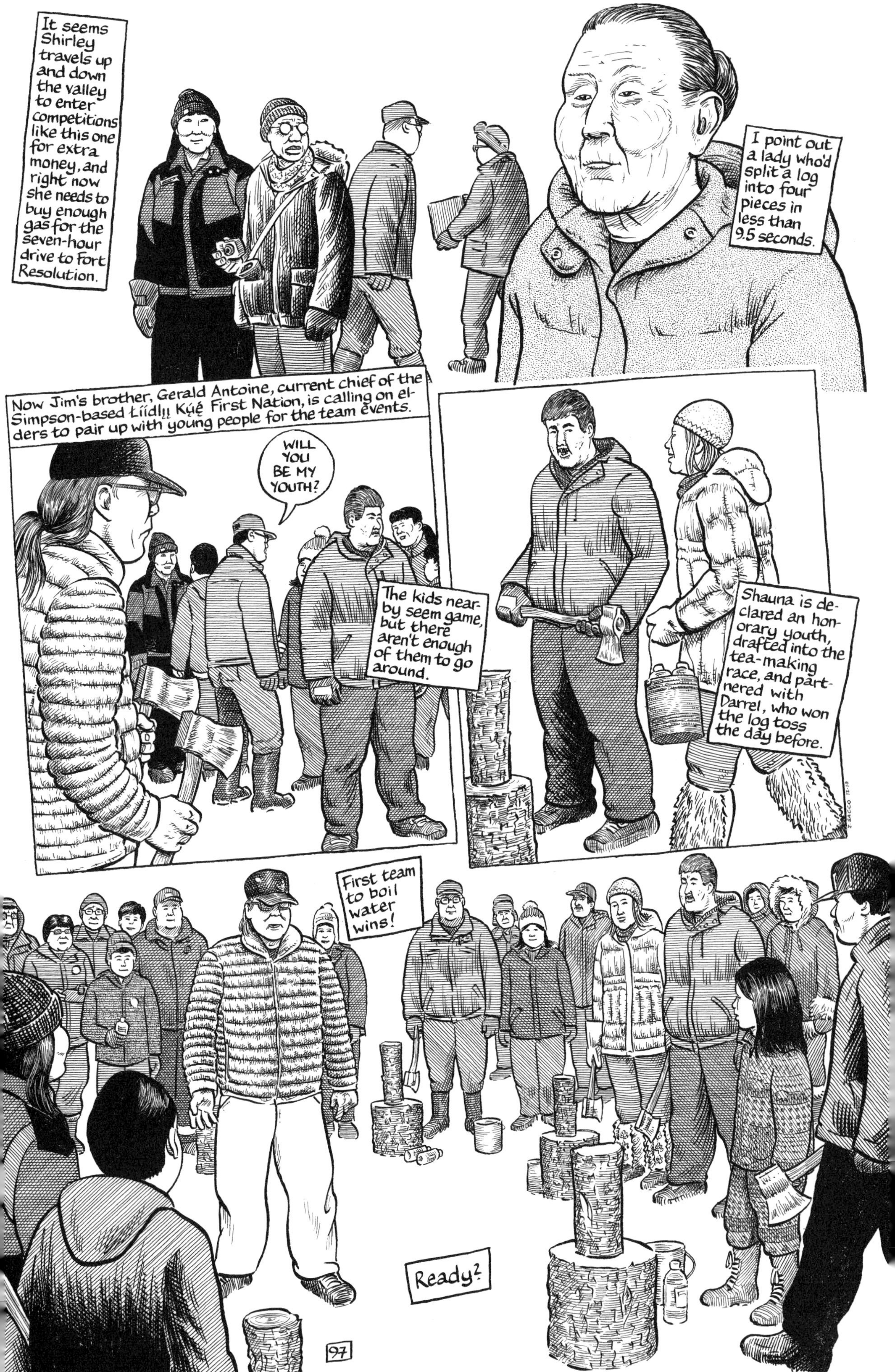
It seems Shirley travels up and down the valley to enter competitions like this one for extra money, and right now she needs to buy enough gas for the seven-hour drive to Fort Resolution.
I point out a lady who'd split a log into four pieces in less than 9.5 seconds.
Now Jim's brother, Gerald Antoine, current chief of the Simpson-based Łíídlįį Kų́ę́ First Nation, is calling on elders to pair up with young people for the team events.
WILL YOU BE MY YOUTH?
The kids nearby seem game, but there aren't enough of them to go around.
Shauna is declared an honorary youth, drafted into the tea-making race, and partnered with Darrel, who won the log toss the day before.
First team to boil water wins!
Ready?

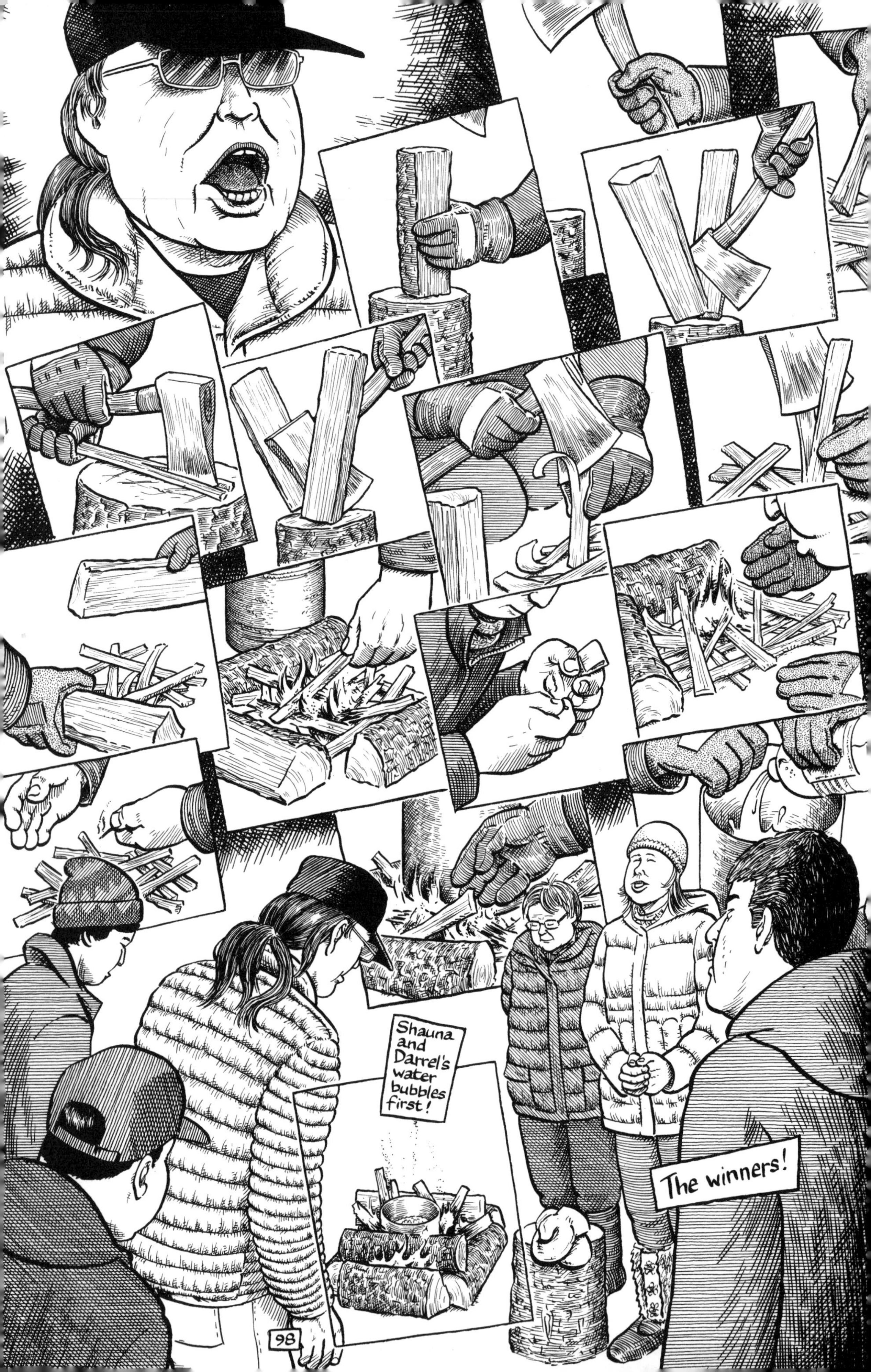
Shauna and Darrel's water bubbles first!
The winners!

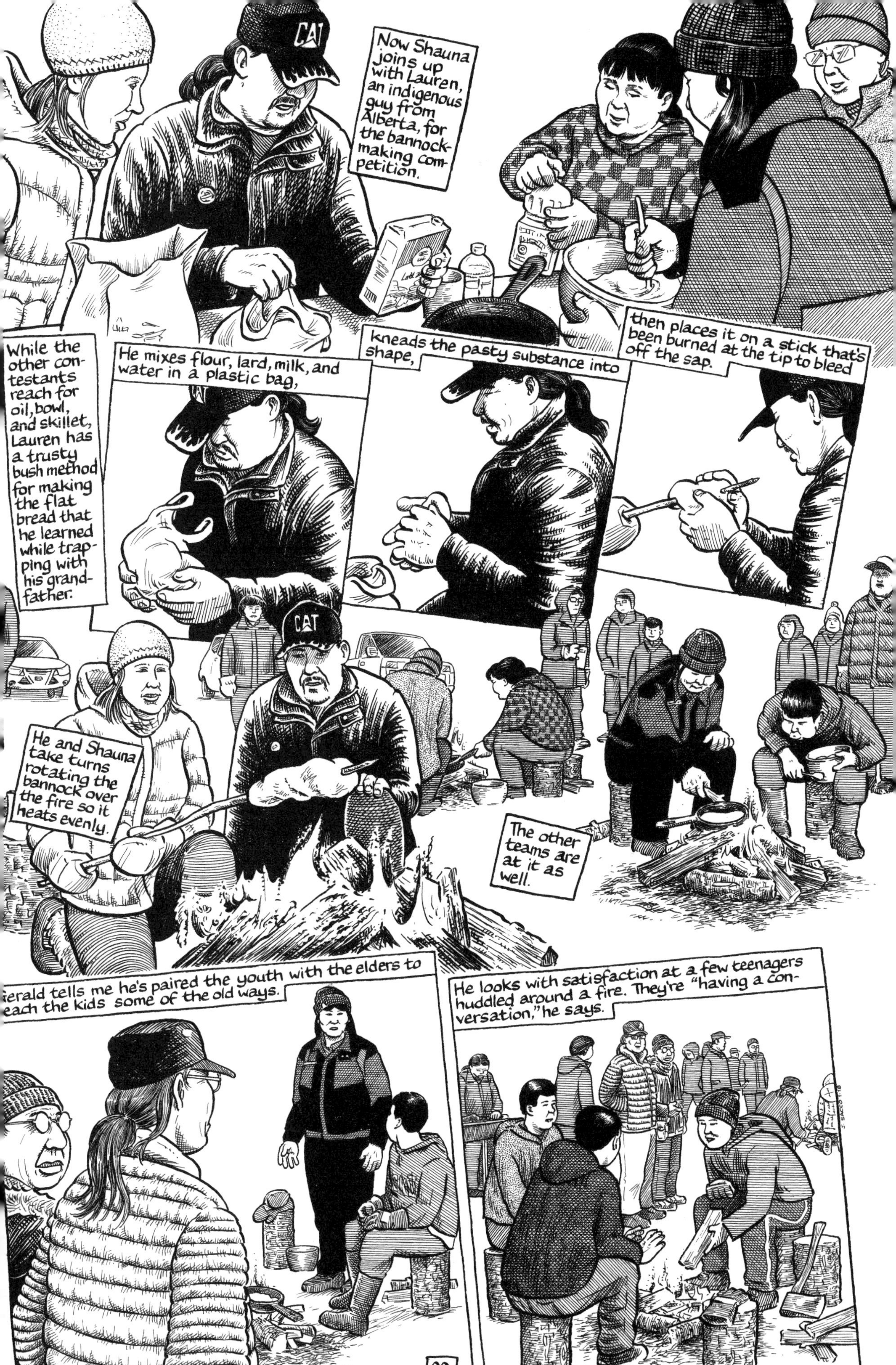

Now Shauna joins up with Lauren, an indigenous guy from Alberta, for the bannock-making competition.
While the other contestants reach for oil, bowl, and skillet, Lauren has a trusty bush method for making the flat bread that he learned while trapping with his grandfather.
He mixes flour, lard, milk, and water in a plastic bag,
kneads the pasty substance into shape,
then places it on a stick that's been burned at the tip to bleed off the sap.
CAT
He and Shauna take turns rotating the bannock over the fire so it heats evenly.
The other teams are at it as well.
Gerald tells me he's paired the youth with the elders to teach the kids some of the old ways.
He looks with satisfaction at a few teenagers huddled around a fire. They're "having a conversation," he says.

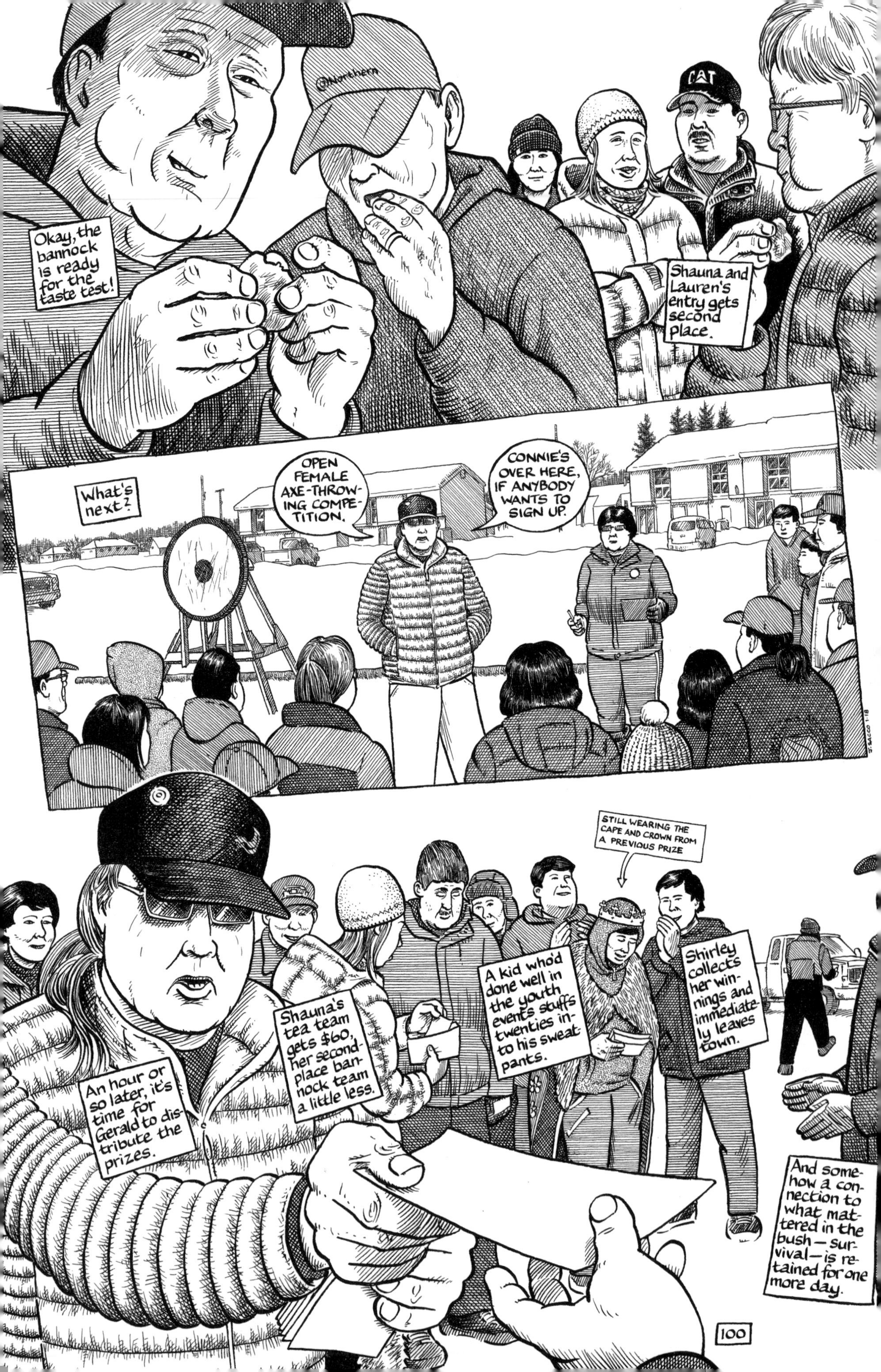

Okay, the bannock is ready for the taste test!
Shauna and Lauren's entry gets second place.
What's next?
OPEN FEMALE AXE-THROWING COMPETITION.
CONNIE'S OVER HERE, IF ANYBODY WANTS TO SIGN UP.
An hour or so later, it's time for Gerald to distribute the prizes.
Shauna's tea team gets $60, her second-place bannock team a little less.
A kid who'd done well in the youth events stuffs twenties into his sweatpants.
STILL WEARING THE CAPE AND CROWN FROM A PREVIOUS PRIZE
Shirley collects her winnings and immediately leaves town.
And somehow a connection to what mattered in the bush—survival—is retained for one more day.

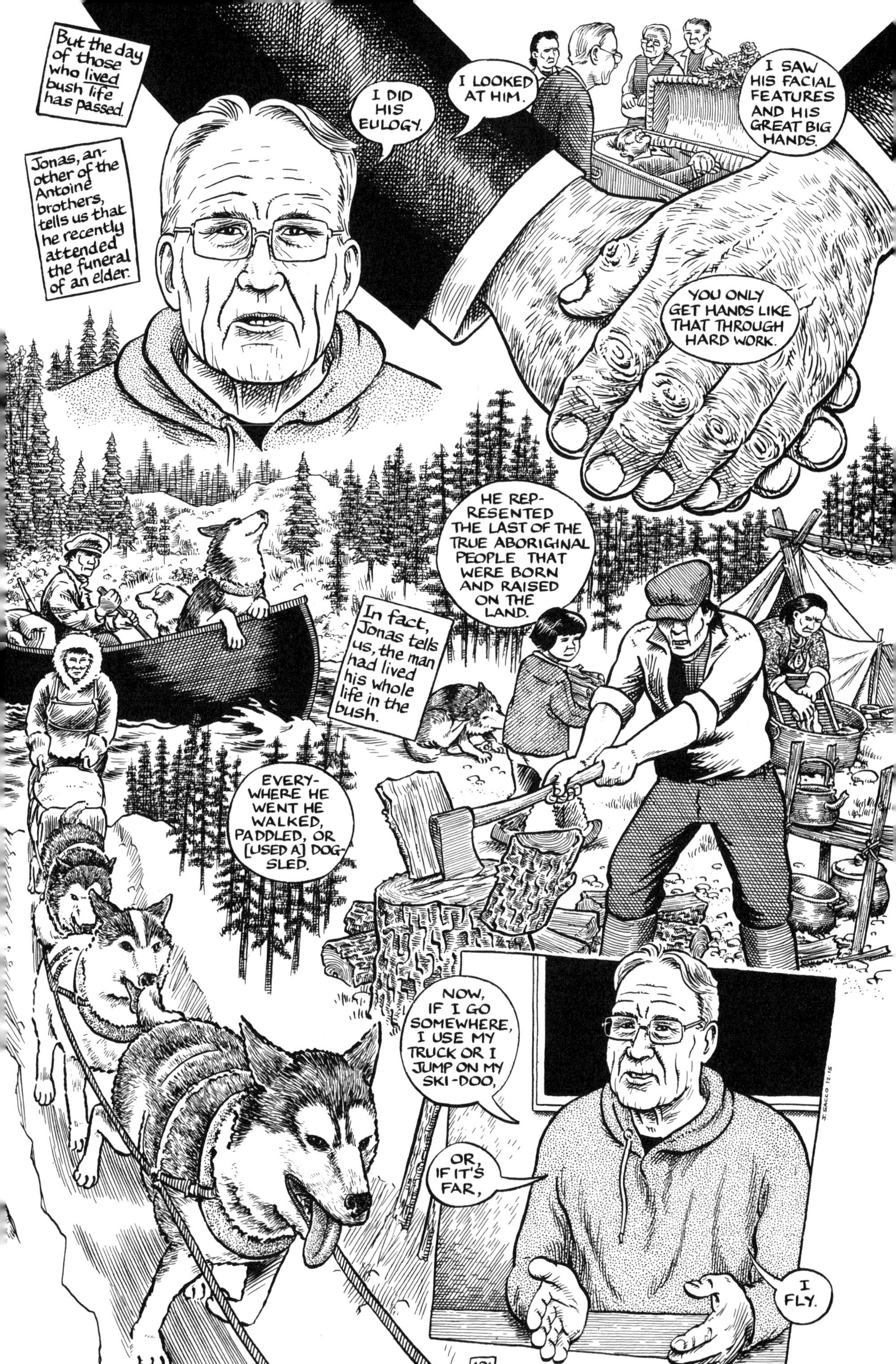

But the day of those who lived bush life has passed.
Jonas, another of the Antoine brothers, tells us that he recently attended the funeral of an elder.
I DID HIS EULOGY.
I LOOKED AT HIM.
I SAW HIS FACIAL FEATURES AND HIS GREAT BIG HANDS.
YOU ONLY GET HANDS LIKE THAT THROUGH HARD WORK.
HE REPRESENTED THE LAST OF THE TRUE ABORIGINAL PEOPLE THAT WERE BORN AND RAISED ON THE LAND.
In fact, Jonas tells us, the man had lived his whole life in the bush.
EVERYWHERE HE WENT HE WALKED, PADDLED, OR [USED A] DOG-SLED.
NOW, IF I GO SOMEWHERE, I USE MY TRUCK OR I JUMP ON MY SKI-DOO,
OR, IF IT'S FAR,
I FLY.

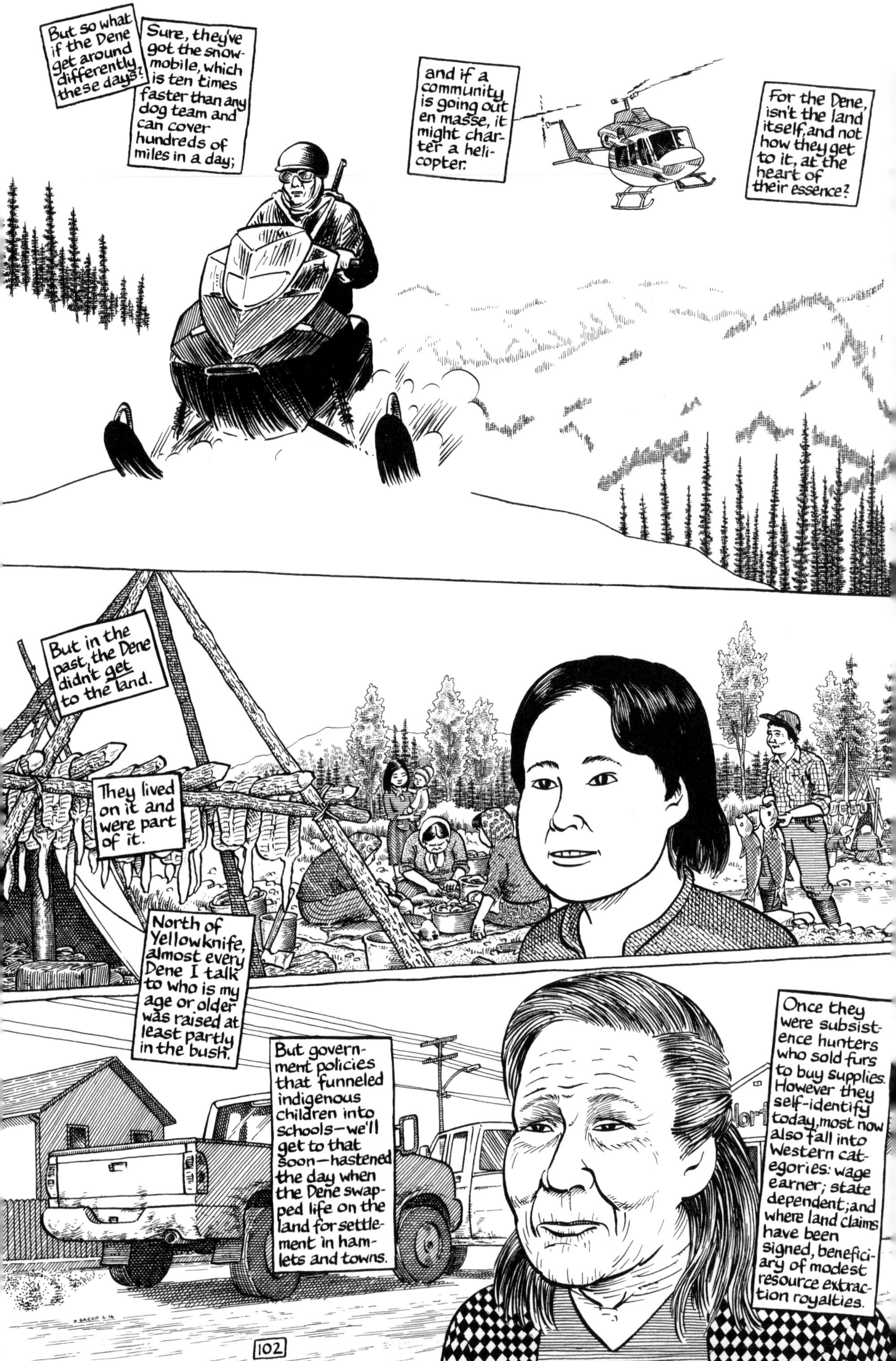
But so what if the Dene get around differently these days?
Sure, they've got the snowmobile, which is ten times faster than any dog team and can cover hundreds of miles in a day;
and if a community is going out en masse, it might charter a helicopter.
For the Dene, isn't the land itself, and not how they get to it, at the heart of their essence?
But in the past, the Dene didn't get to the land.
They lived on it and were part of it.
North of Yellowknife, almost every Dene I talk to who is my age or older was raised at least partly in the bush.
But government policies that funneled indigenous children into schools—we'll get to that soon—hastened the day when the Dene swapped life on the land for settlement in hamlets and towns.
Once they were subsistence hunters who sold furs to buy supplies. However they self-identify today, most now also fall into Western categories: wage earner; state dependent; and where land claims have been signed, beneficiary of modest resource extraction royalties.

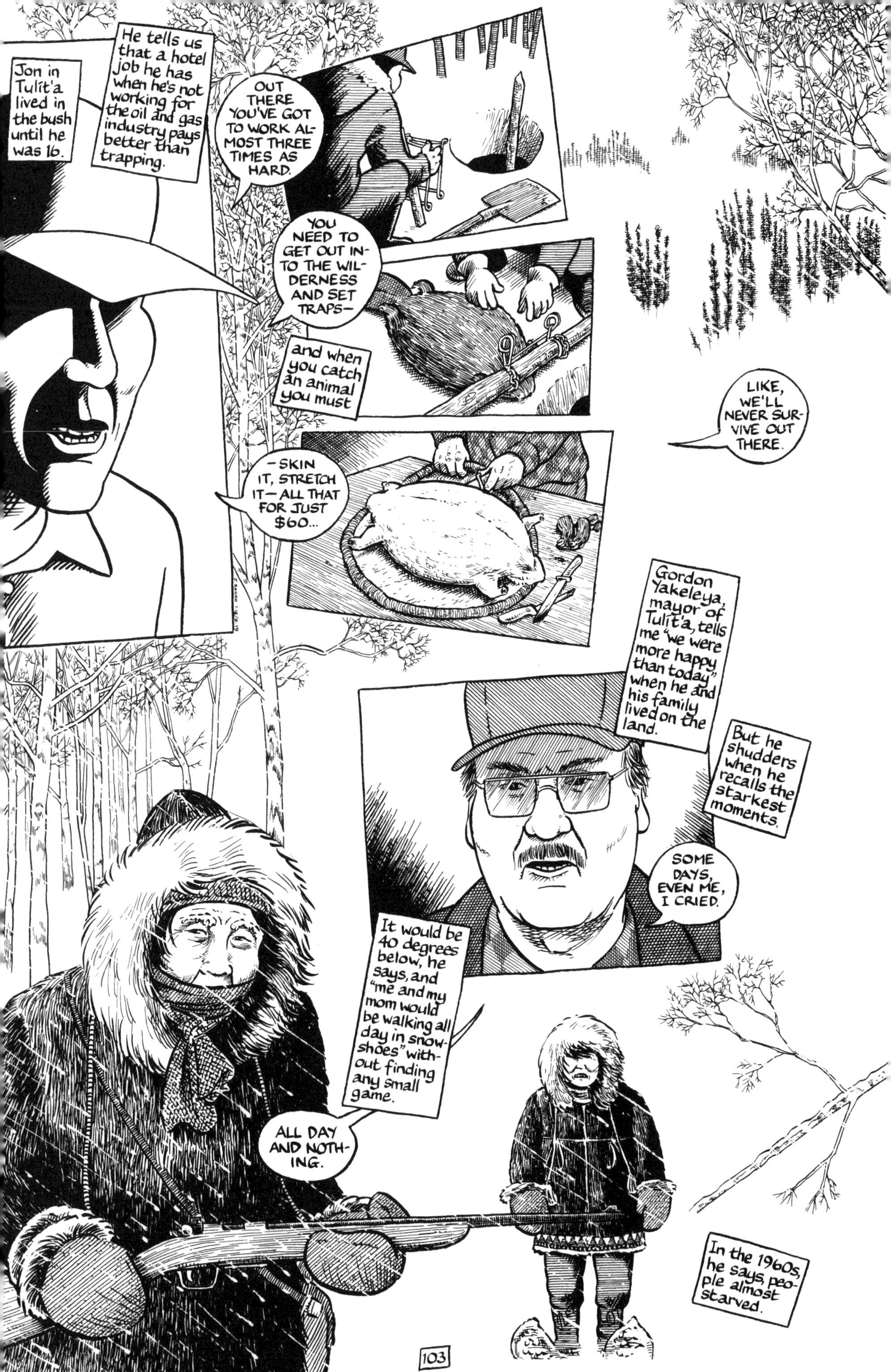

Jon in Tulít'a lived in the bush until he was 16.
He tells us that a hotel job he has when he's not working for the oil and gas industry pays better than trapping.
OUT THERE YOU'VE GOT TO WORK AL-MOST THREE TIMES AS HARD.
YOU NEED TO GET OUT IN-TO THE WIL-DERNESS AND SET TRAPS—
and when you catch an animal you must
—SKIN IT, STRETCH IT—ALL THAT FOR JUST $60...
LIKE, WE'LL NEVER SUR-VIVE OUT THERE.
Gordon Yakeleya, mayor of Tulít'a, tells me "we were more happy than today" when he and his family lived on the land.
But he shudders when he recalls the starkest moments.
SOME DAYS, EVEN ME, I CRIED.
It would be 40 degrees below, he says, and "me and my mom would be walking all day in snow-shoes" with-out finding any small game.
ALL DAY AND NOTH-ING.
In the 1960s, he says, peo-ple almost starved.

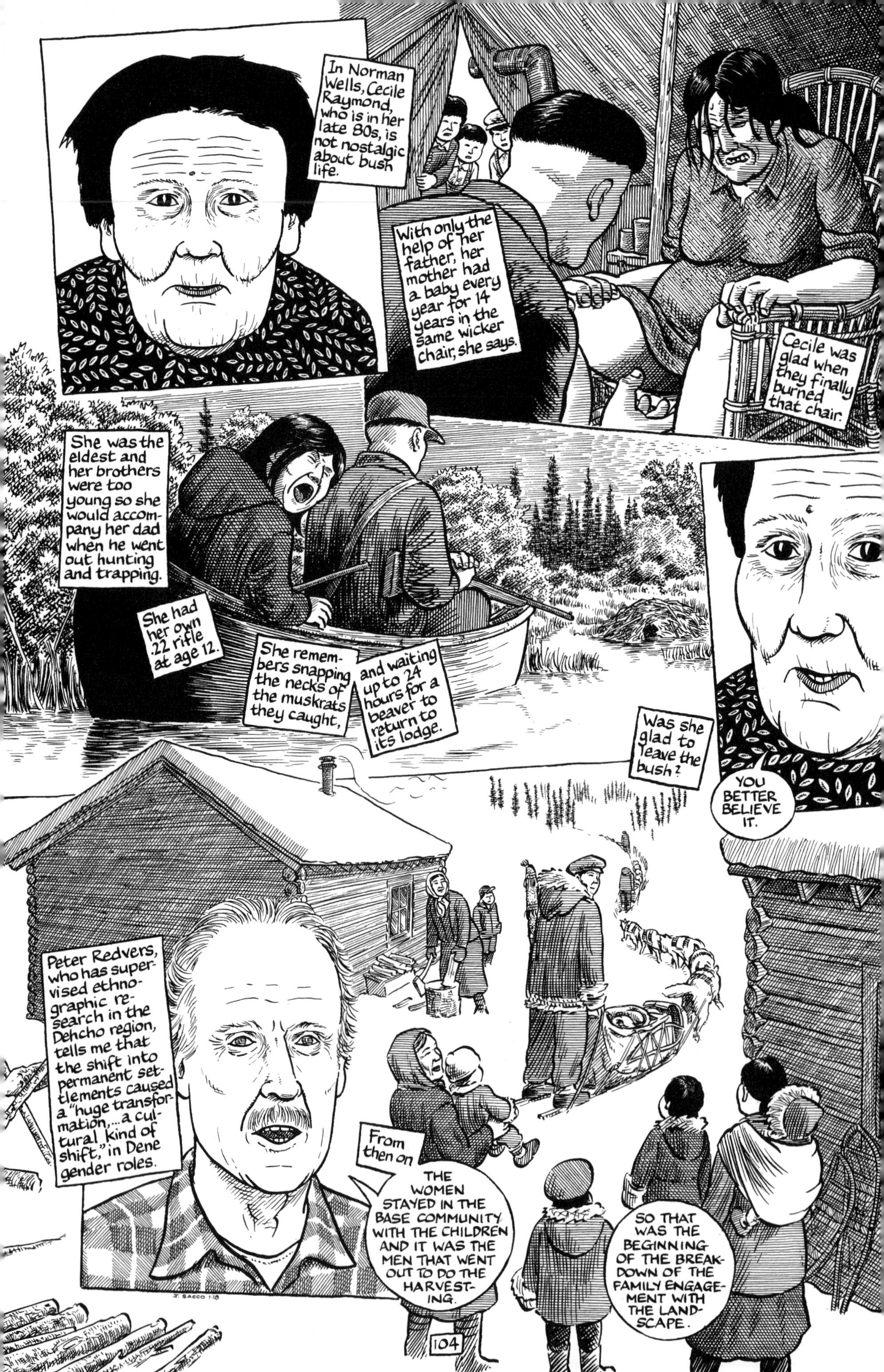
In Norman Wells, Cecile Raymond, who is in her late 80s, is not nostalgic about bush life.
With only the help of her father, her mother had a baby every year for 14 years in the same wicker chair, she says.
Cecile was glad when they finally burned that chair.
She was the eldest and her brothers were too young so she would accompany her dad when he went out hunting and trapping.
She had her own .22 rifle at age 12.
She remembers snapping the necks of the muskrats they caught,
and waiting up to 24 hours for a beaver to return to its lodge.
Was she glad to leave the bush?
YOU BETTER BELIEVE IT.
Peter Redvers, who has supervised ethnographic research in the Dehcho region, tells me that the shift into permanent settlements caused a "huge transformation,... a cultural kind of shift," in Dene gender roles.
From then on
THE WOMEN STAYED IN THE BASE COMMUNITY WITH THE CHILDREN AND IT WAS THE MEN THAT WENT OUT TO DO THE HARVESTING.
SO THAT WAS THE BEGINNING OF THE BREAKDOWN OF THE FAMILY ENGAGEMENT WITH THE LANDSCAPE.
J. SACCO 1.18

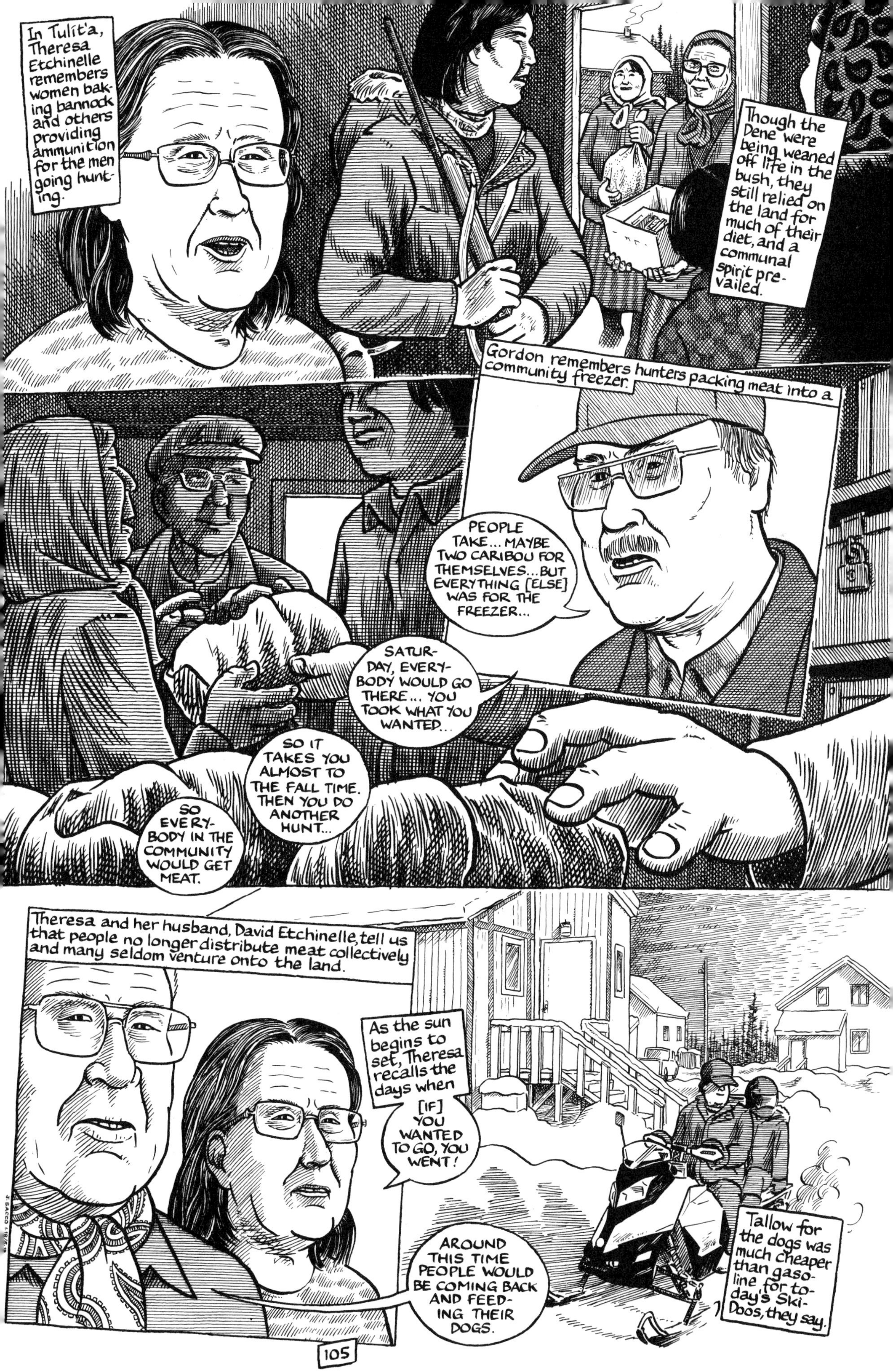
In Tulít'a, Theresa Etchinelle remembers women baking bannock and others providing ammunition for the men going hunting.
Though the Dene were being weaned off life in the bush, they still relied on the land for much of their diet, and a communal spirit prevailed.
Gordon remembers hunters packing meat into a community freezer.
PEOPLE TAKE... MAYBE TWO CARIBOU FOR THEMSELVES... BUT EVERYTHING [ELSE] WAS FOR THE FREEZER...
SATURDAY, EVERYBODY WOULD GO THERE... YOU TOOK WHAT YOU WANTED...
SO IT TAKES YOU ALMOST TO THE FALL TIME. THEN YOU DO ANOTHER HUNT...
SO EVERYBODY IN THE COMMUNITY WOULD GET MEAT.
Theresa and her husband, David Etchinelle, tell us that people no longer distribute meat collectively and many seldom venture onto the land.
As the sun begins to set, Theresa recalls the days when
[IF] YOU WANTED TO GO, YOU WENT!
AROUND THIS TIME PEOPLE WOULD BE COMING BACK AND FEEDING THEIR DOGS.
Tallow for the dogs was much cheaper than gasoline for today's Ski-Doos, they say.

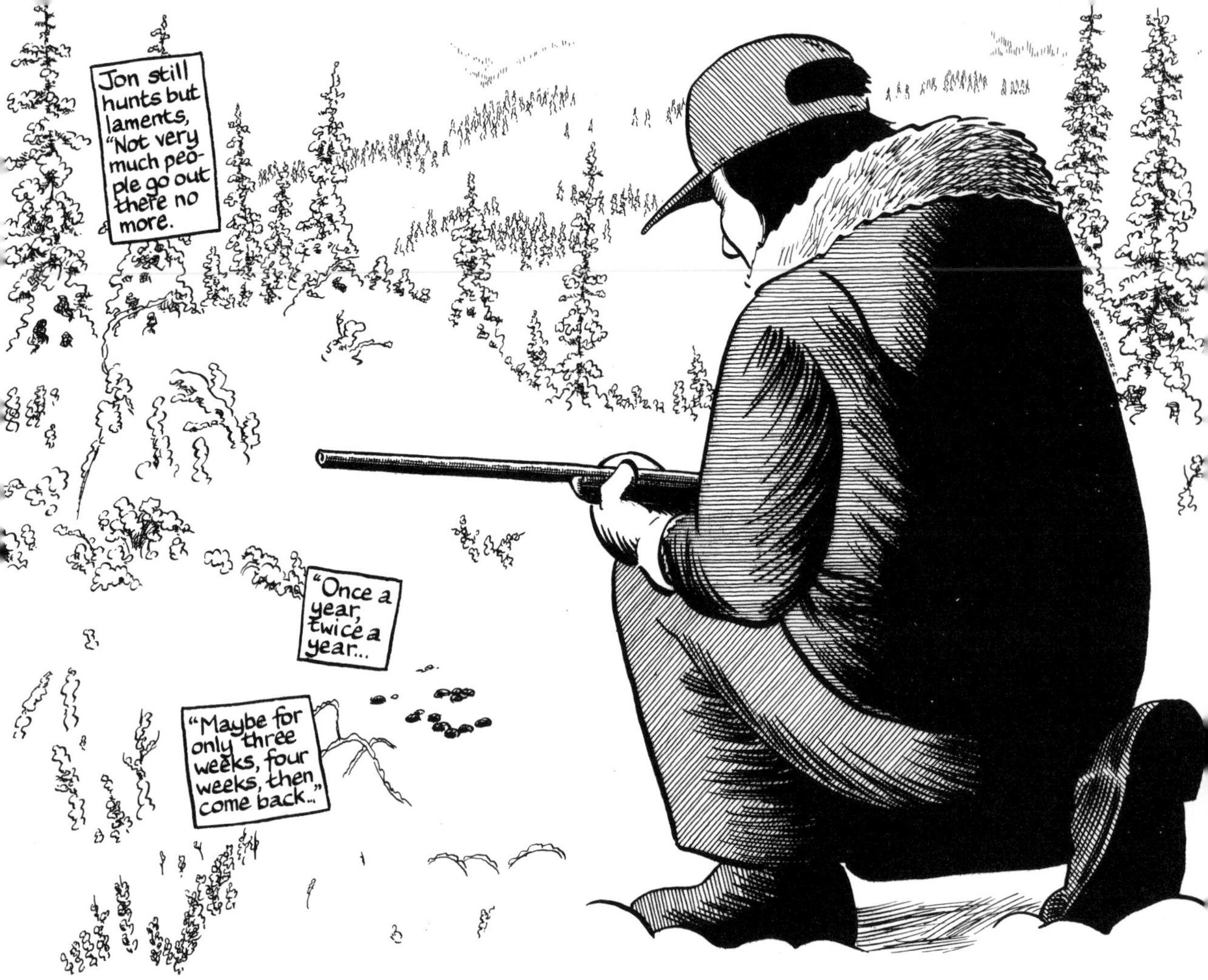
Jon still hunts but laments, "Not very much people go out there no more.
"Once a year, twice a year...
"Maybe for only three weeks, four weeks, then come back..."

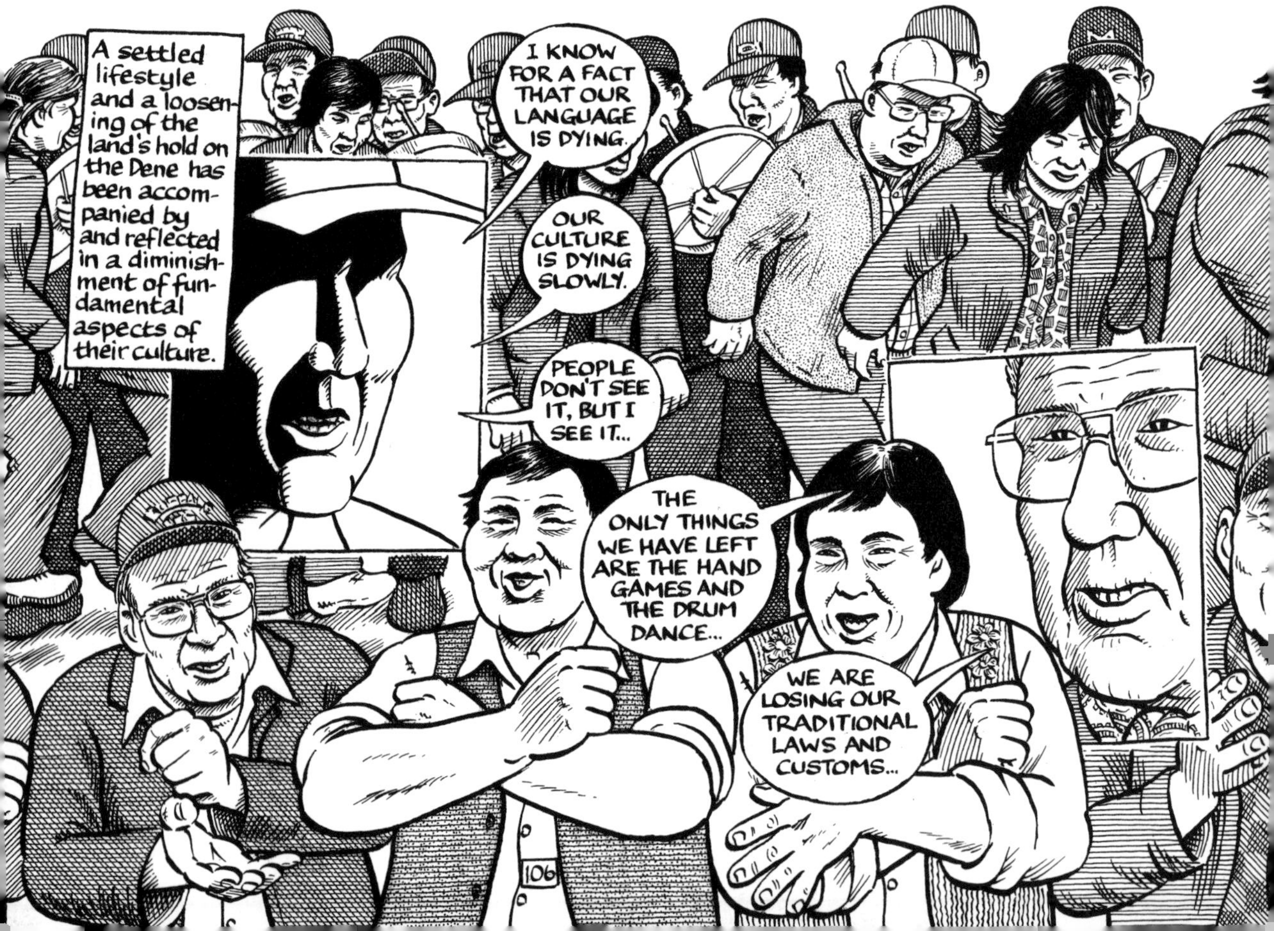
A settled lifestyle and a loosening of the land's hold on the Dene has been accompanied by and reflected in a diminishment of fundamental aspects of their culture.
I KNOW FOR A FACT THAT OUR LANGUAGE IS DYING.
OUR CULTURE IS DYING SLOWLY.
PEOPLE DON'T SEE IT, BUT I SEE IT...
THE ONLY THINGS WE HAVE LEFT ARE THE HAND GAMES AND THE DRUM DANCE...
WE ARE LOSING OUR TRADITIONAL LAWS AND CUSTOMS...

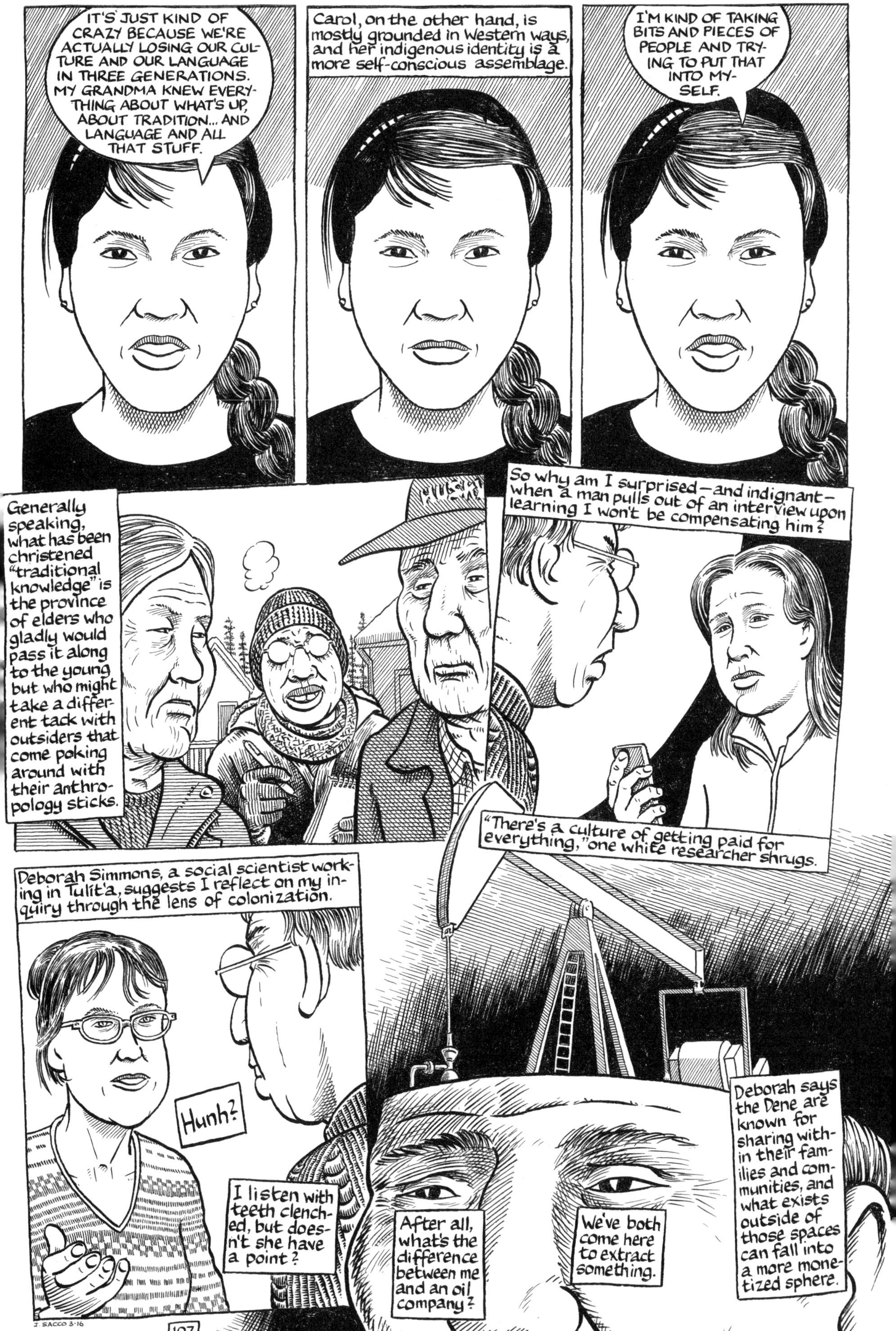
IT'S JUST KIND OF CRAZY BECAUSE WE'RE ACTUALLY LOSING OUR CULTURE AND OUR LANGUAGE IN THREE GENERATIONS. MY GRANDMA KNEW EVERYTHING ABOUT WHAT'S UP, ABOUT TRADITION... AND LANGUAGE AND ALL THAT STUFF.
Carol, on the other hand, is mostly grounded in Western ways, and her indigenous identity is a more self-conscious assemblage.
I'M KIND OF TAKING BITS AND PIECES OF PEOPLE AND TRYING TO PUT THAT INTO MYSELF.
Generally speaking, what has been christened "traditional knowledge" is the province of elders who gladly would pass it along to the young but who might take a different tack with outsiders that come poking around with their anthropology sticks.
So why am I surprised—and indignant—when a man pulls out of an interview upon learning I won't be compensating him?
"There's a culture of getting paid for everything," one white researcher shrugs.
Deborah Simmons, a social scientist working in Tulít'a, suggests I reflect on my inquiry through the lens of colonization.
Hunh?
I listen with teeth clenched, but doesn't she have a point?
After all, what's the difference between me and an oil company?
We've both come here to extract something.
Deborah says the Dene are known for sharing within their families and communities, and what exists outside of those spaces can fall into a more monetized sphere.
J. SACCO 3-16

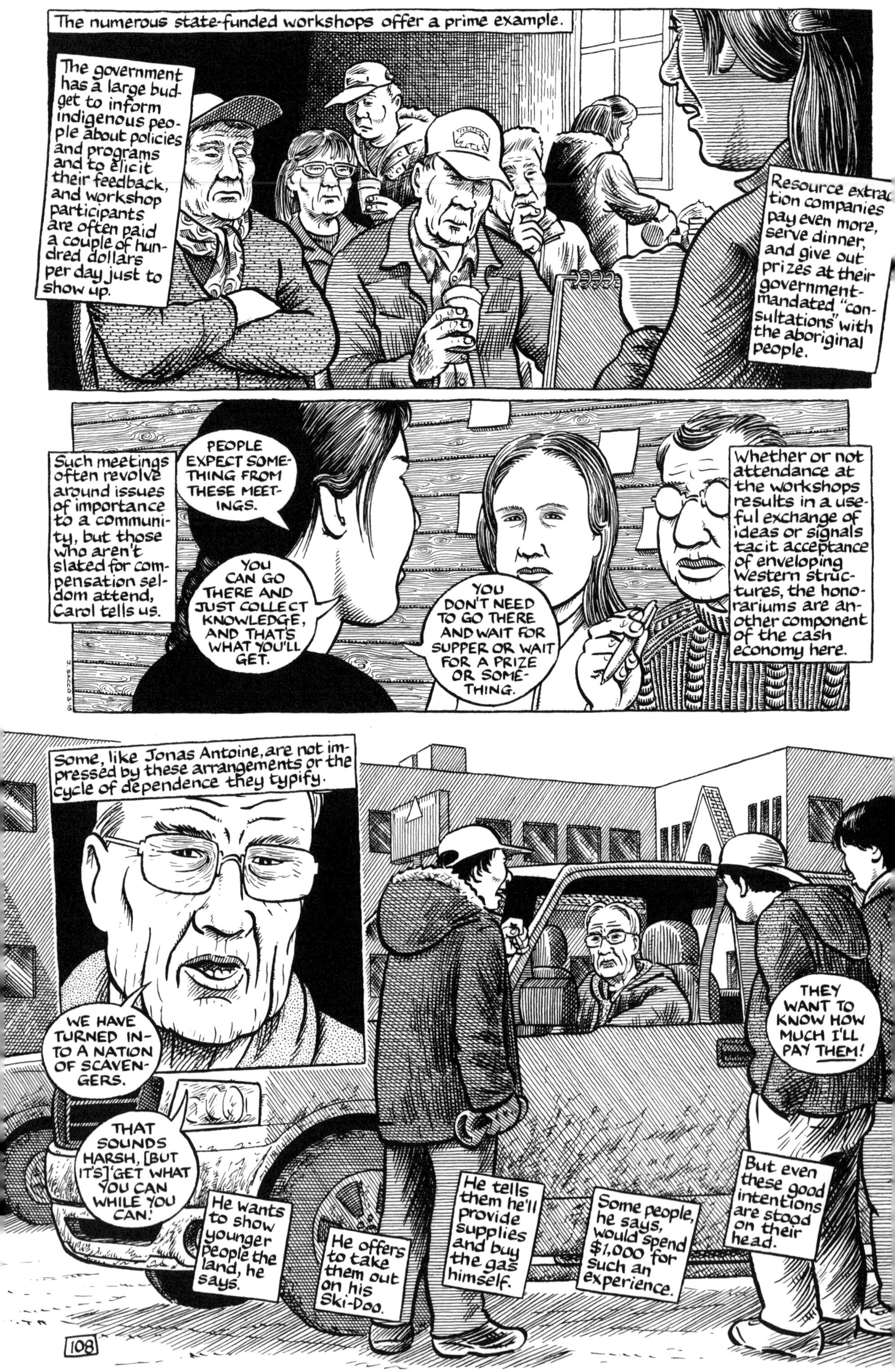

The numerous state-funded workshops offer a prime example.
The government has a large budget to inform indigenous people about policies and programs and to elicit their feedback, and workshop participants are often paid a couple of hundred dollars per day just to show up.
Resource extraction companies pay even more, serve dinner, and give out prizes at their government-mandated "consultations" with the aboriginal people.
Such meetings often revolve around issues of importance to a community, but those who aren't slated for compensation seldom attend, Carol tells us.
PEOPLE EXPECT SOMETHING FROM THESE MEETINGS.
YOU CAN GO THERE AND JUST COLLECT KNOWLEDGE, AND THAT'S WHAT YOU'LL GET.
YOU DON'T NEED TO GO THERE AND WAIT FOR SUPPER OR WAIT FOR A PRIZE OR SOMETHING.
Whether or not attendance at the workshops results in a useful exchange of ideas or signals tacit acceptance of enveloping Western structures, the honorariums are another component of the cash economy here.
Some, like Jonas Antoine, are not impressed by these arrangements or the cycle of dependence they typify.
WE HAVE TURNED INTO A NATION OF SCAVENGERS.
THAT SOUNDS HARSH, [BUT IT'S] 'GET WHAT YOU CAN WHILE YOU CAN.'
THEY WANT TO KNOW HOW MUCH I'LL PAY THEM!
He wants to show younger people the land, he says.
He offers to take them out on his Ski-Doo.
He tells them he'll provide supplies and buy the gas himself.
Some people, he says, would spend $1,000 for such an experience.
But even these good intentions are stood on their head.

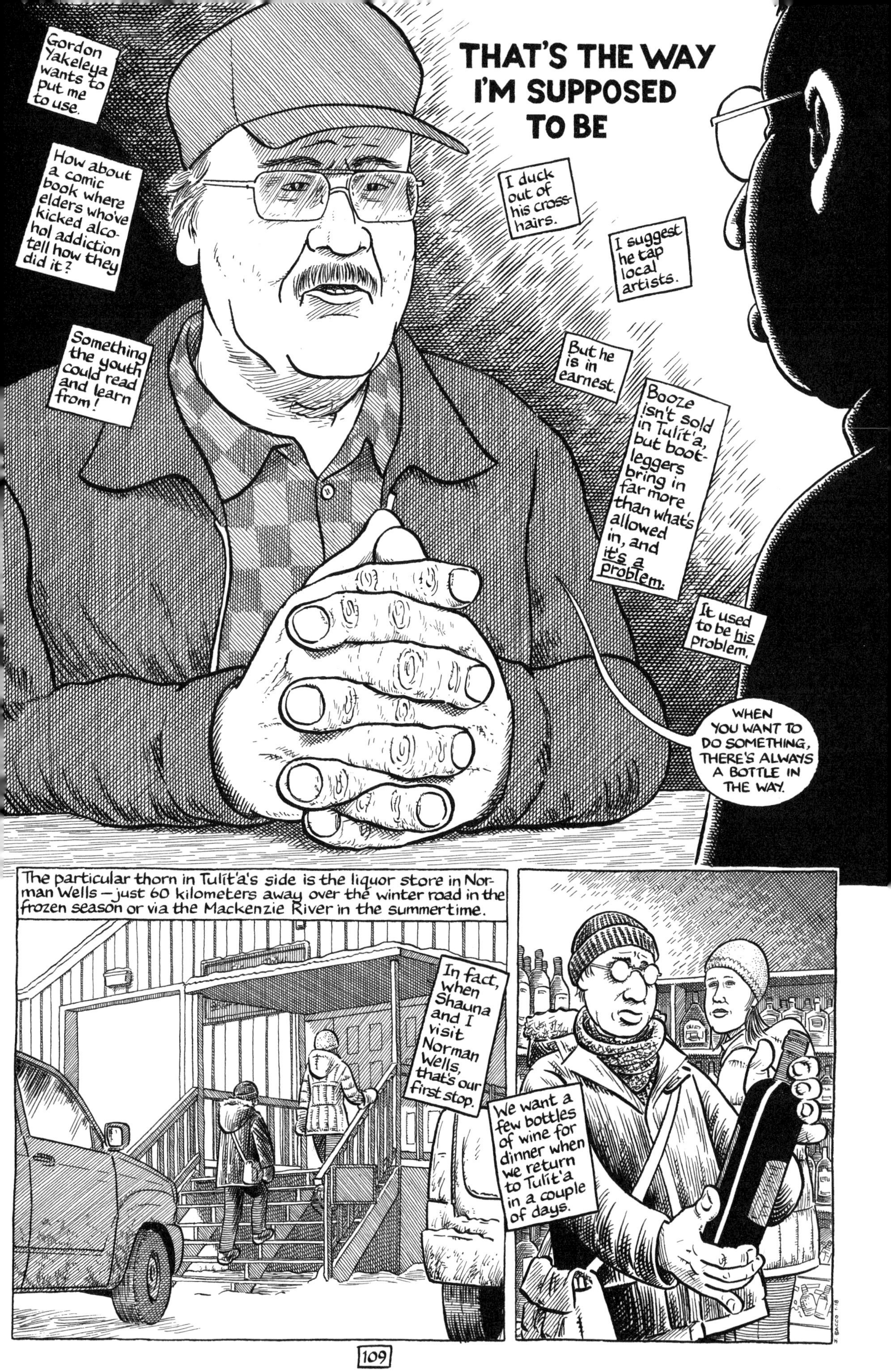
THAT'S THE WAY I'M SUPPOSED TO BE
Gordon Yakeleya wants to put me to use.
How about a comic book where elders who've kicked alcohol addiction tell how they did it?
Something the youth could read and learn from!
I duck out of his cross-hairs.
I suggest he tap local artists.
But he is in earnest.
Booze isn't sold in Tulít'a, but bootleggers bring in far more than what's allowed in, and it's a problem.
It used to be his problem.
WHEN YOU WANT TO DO SOMETHING, THERE'S ALWAYS A BOTTLE IN THE WAY.
The particular thorn in Tulít'a's side is the liquor store in Norman Wells — just 60 kilometers away over the winter road in the frozen season or via the Mackenzie River in the summertime.
In fact, when Shauna and I visit Norman Wells, that's our first stop.
We want a few bottles of wine for dinner when we return to Tulít'a in a couple of days.

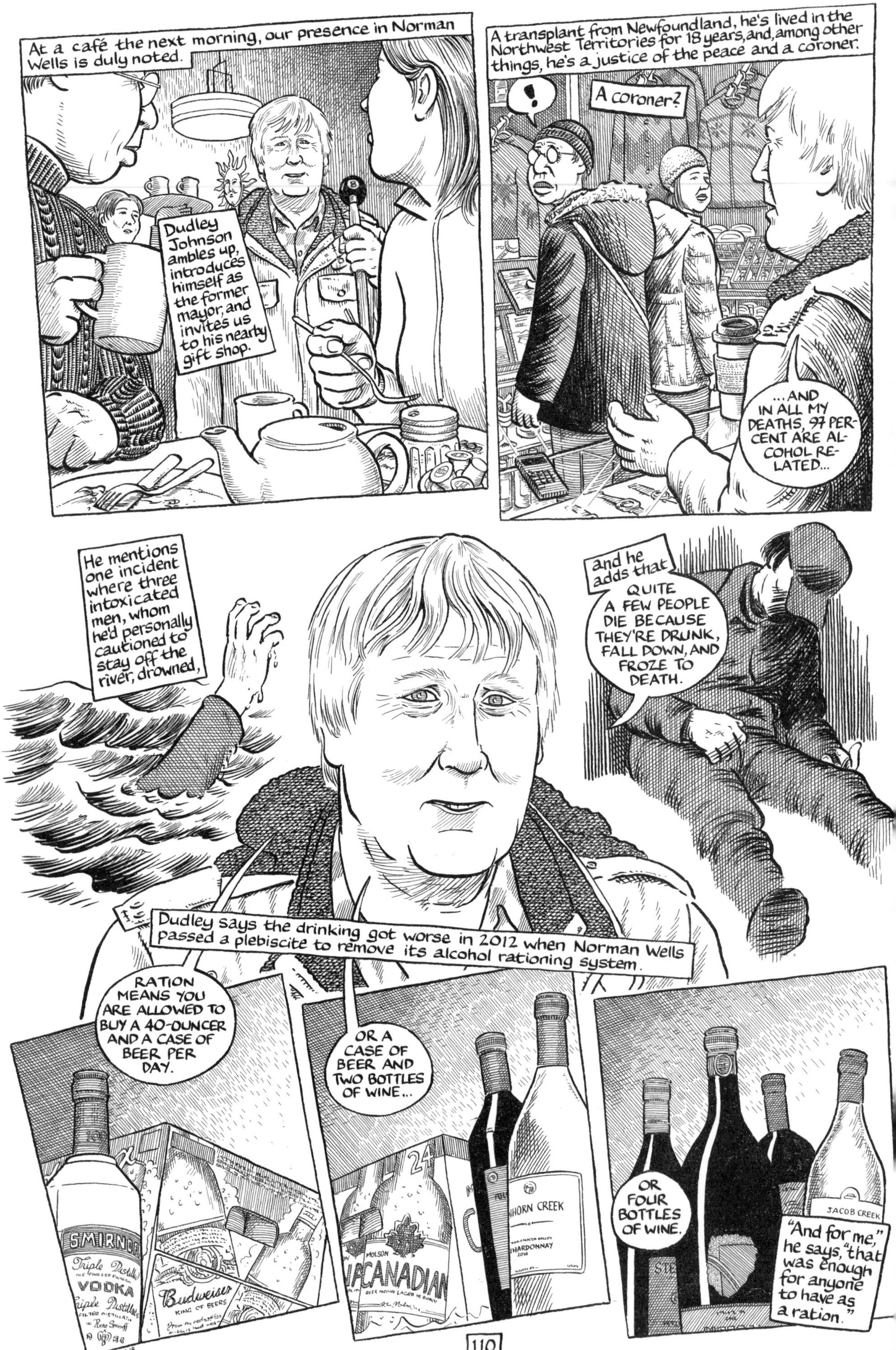
At a café the next morning, our presence in Norman Wells is duly noted.
Dudley Johnson ambles up, introduces himself as the former mayor, and invites us to his nearby gift shop.
A transplant from Newfoundland, he's lived in the Northwest Territories for 18 years, and, among other things, he's a justice of the peace and a coroner.
!
A coroner?
...AND IN ALL MY DEATHS, 97 PERCENT ARE ALCOHOL RELATED...
He mentions one incident where three intoxicated men, whom he'd personally cautioned to stay off the river, drowned,
and he adds that
QUITE A FEW PEOPLE DIE BECAUSE THEY'RE DRUNK, FALL DOWN, AND FROZE TO DEATH.
Dudley says the drinking got worse in 2012 when Norman Wells passed a plebiscite to remove its alcohol rationing system.
RATION MEANS YOU ARE ALLOWED TO BUY A 40-OUNCER AND A CASE OF BEER PER DAY.
OR A CASE OF BEER AND TWO BOTTLES OF WINE...
OR FOUR BOTTLES OF WINE.
"And for me," he says, "that was enough for anyone to have as a ration."
SMIRNOFF
Triple Distilled
VODKA
Budweiser
KING OF BEERS
MOLSON
CANADIAN
CHARDONNAY
JACOB CREEK
J. SACCO 1·18

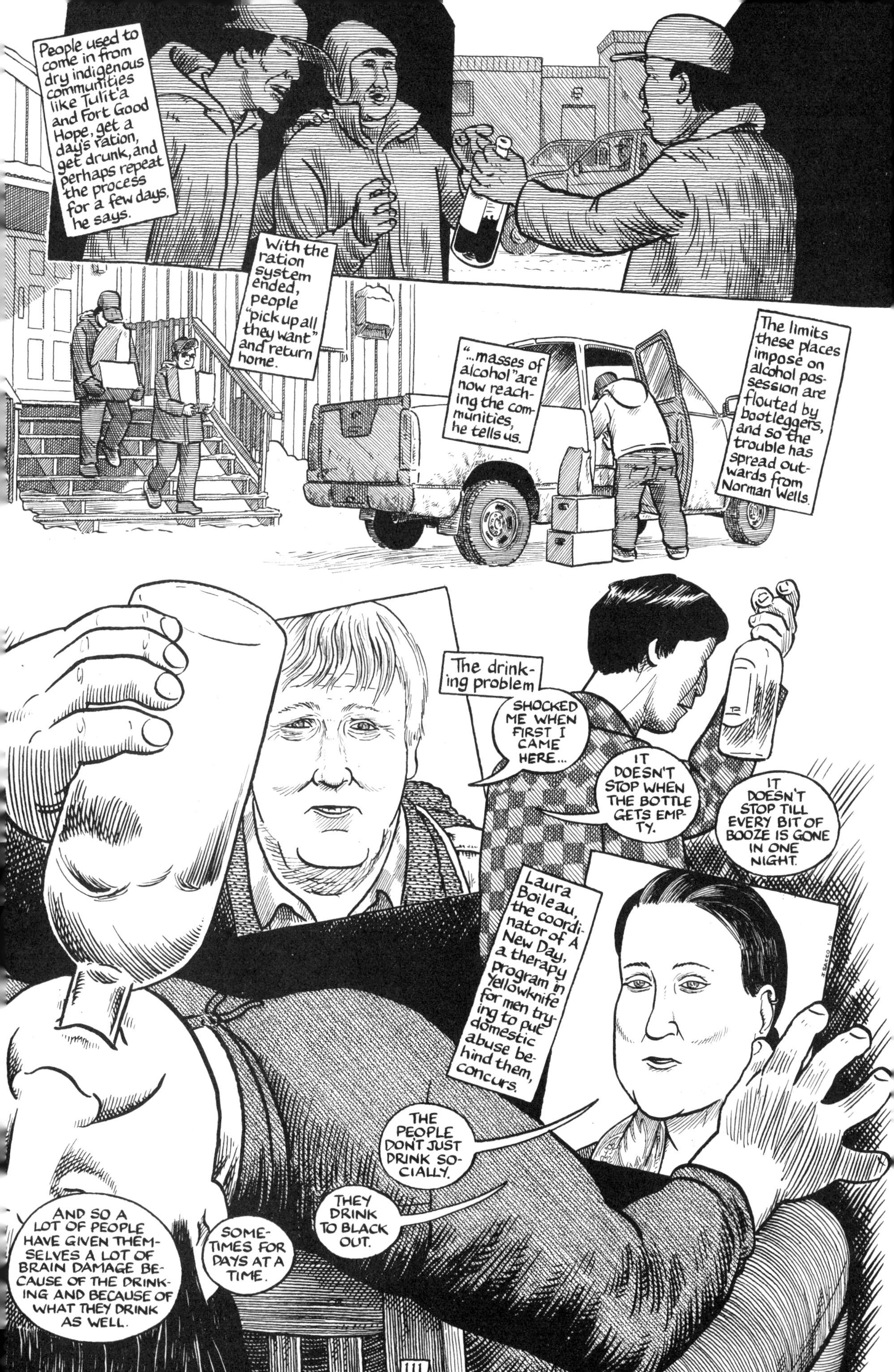
People used to come in from dry indigenous communities like Tulit'a and Fort Good Hope, get a day's ration, get drunk, and perhaps repeat the process for a few days, he says.
With the ration system ended, people "pick up all they want" and return home.
"...masses of alcohol" are now reaching the communities, he tells us.
The limits these places impose on alcohol possession are flouted by bootleggers, and so the trouble has spread outwards from Norman Wells.
The drinking problem
SHOCKED ME WHEN FIRST I CAME HERE...
IT DOESN'T STOP WHEN THE BOTTLE GETS EMPTY.
IT DOESN'T STOP TILL EVERY BIT OF BOOZE IS GONE IN ONE NIGHT.
Laura Boileau, the coordinator of A New Day, a therapy program in Yellowknife for men trying to put domestic abuse behind them, concurs.
THE PEOPLE DON'T JUST DRINK SOCIALLY.
THEY DRINK TO BLACK OUT.
SOMETIMES FOR DAYS AT A TIME.
AND SO A LOT OF PEOPLE HAVE GIVEN THEMSELVES A LOT OF BRAIN DAMAGE BECAUSE OF THE DRINKING AND BECAUSE OF WHAT THEY DRINK AS WELL.

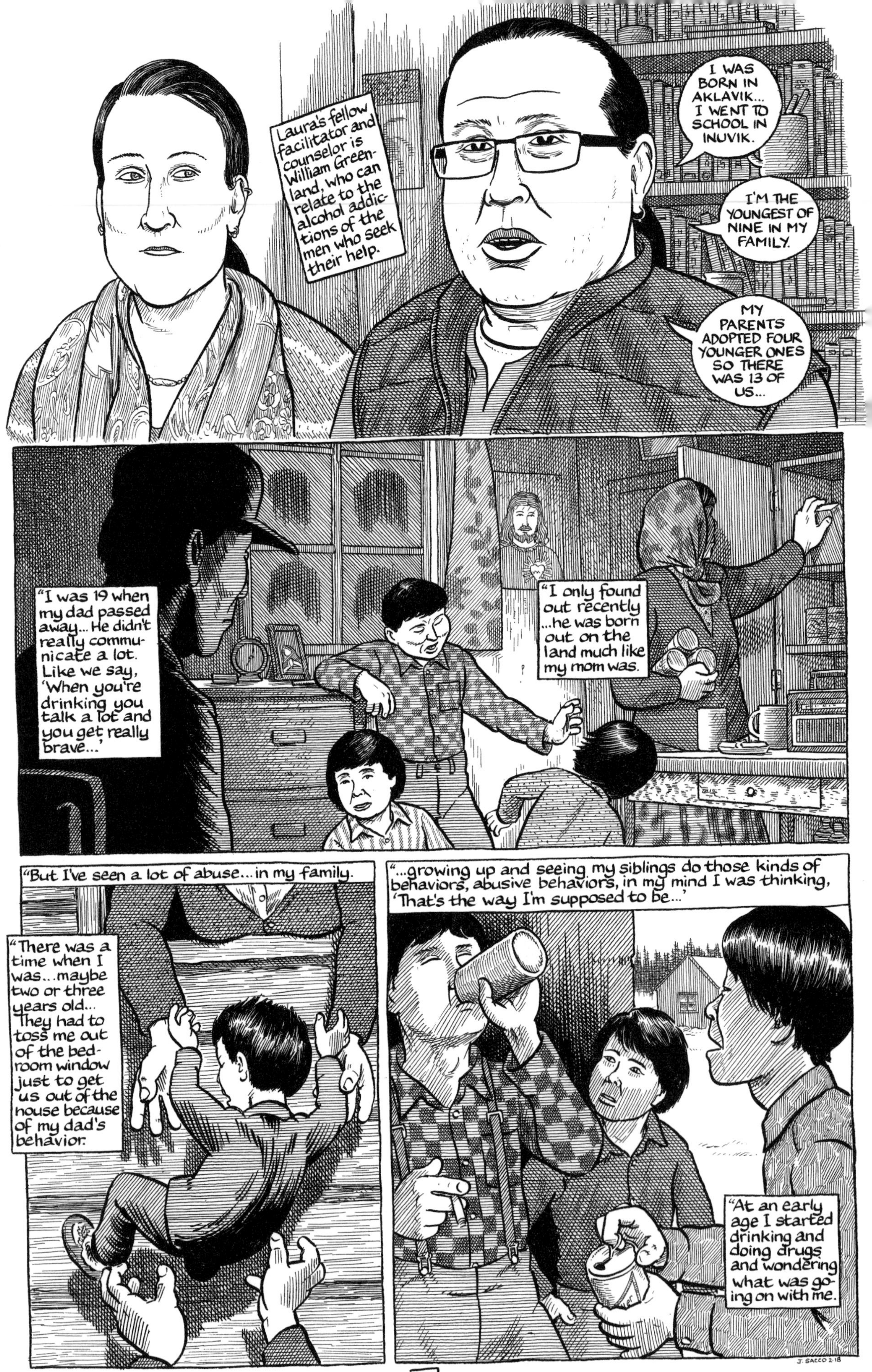
Laura's fellow facilitator and counselor is William Greenland, who can relate to the alcohol addictions of the men who seek their help.
I WAS BORN IN AKLAVIK... I WENT TO SCHOOL IN INUVIK.
I'M THE YOUNGEST OF NINE IN MY FAMILY.
MY PARENTS ADOPTED FOUR YOUNGER ONES SO THERE WAS 13 OF US...
"I was 19 when my dad passed away... He didn't really communicate a lot. Like we say, 'When you're drinking you talk a lot and you get really brave...'
"I only found out recently ...he was born out on the land much like my mom was.
"But I've seen a lot of abuse... in my family.
"There was a time when I was... maybe two or three years old... They had to toss me out of the bedroom window just to get us out of the house because of my dad's behavior.
"...growing up and seeing my siblings do those kinds of behaviors, abusive behaviors, in my mind I was thinking, 'That's the way I'm supposed to be...'
"At an early age I started drinking and doing drugs and wondering what was going on with me.
J. SACCO 2·18

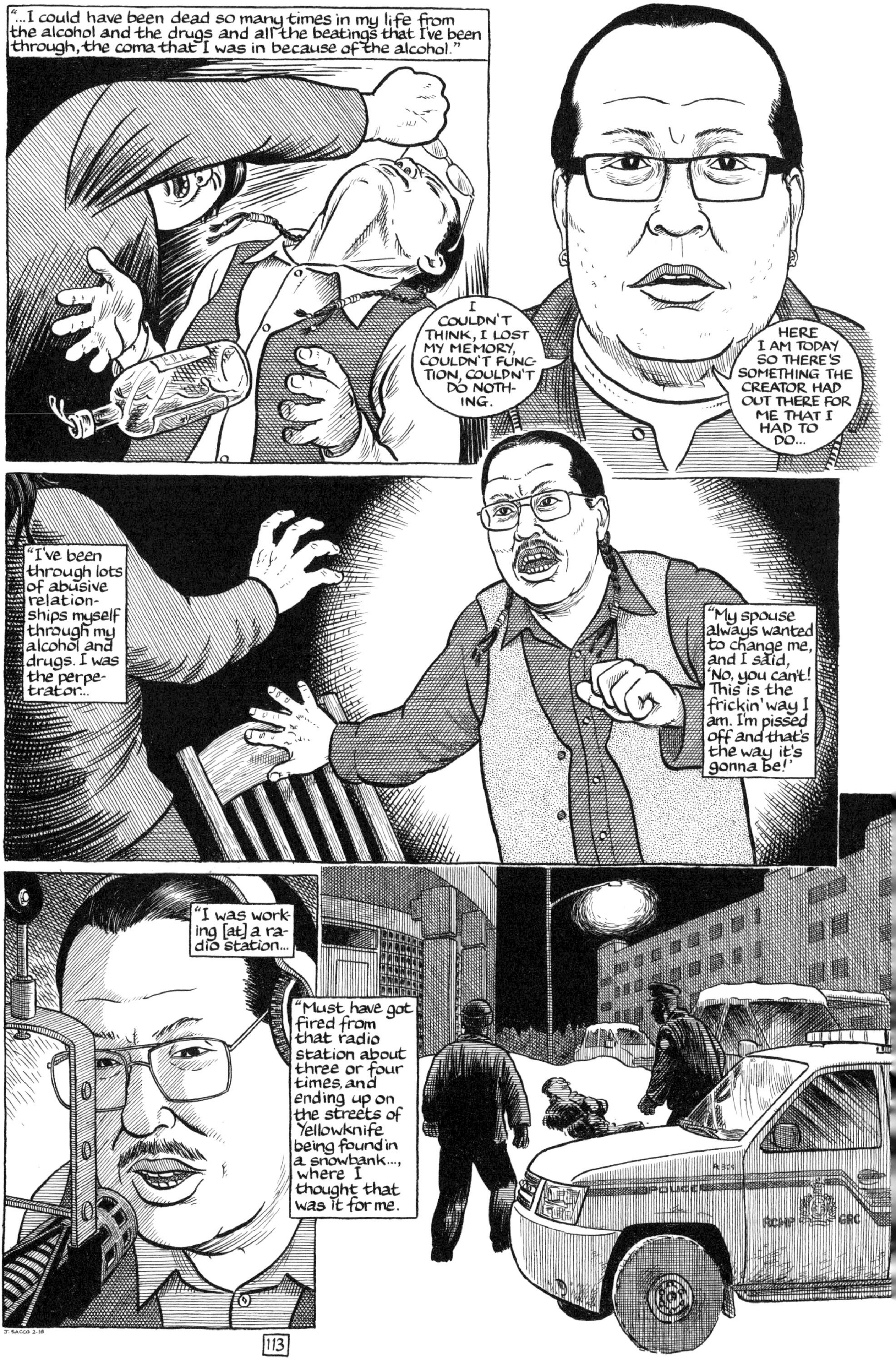
"...I could have been dead so many times in my life from the alcohol and the drugs and all the beatings that I've been through, the coma that I was in because of the alcohol."
I COULDN'T THINK, I LOST MY MEMORY, COULDN'T FUNCTION, COULDN'T DO NOTHING.
HERE I AM TODAY SO THERE'S SOMETHING THE CREATOR HAD OUT THERE FOR ME THAT I HAD TO DO...
"I've been through lots of abusive relationships myself through my alcohol and drugs. I was the perpetrator...
"My spouse always wanted to change me, and I said, 'No, you can't! This is the frickin' way I am. I'm pissed off and that's the way it's gonna be!'
"I was working [at] a radio station...
"Must have got fired from that radio station about three or four times, and ending up on the streets of Yellowknife being found in a snowbank..., where I thought that was it for me.
POLICE
RCMP GRC
J. SACCO 2-18

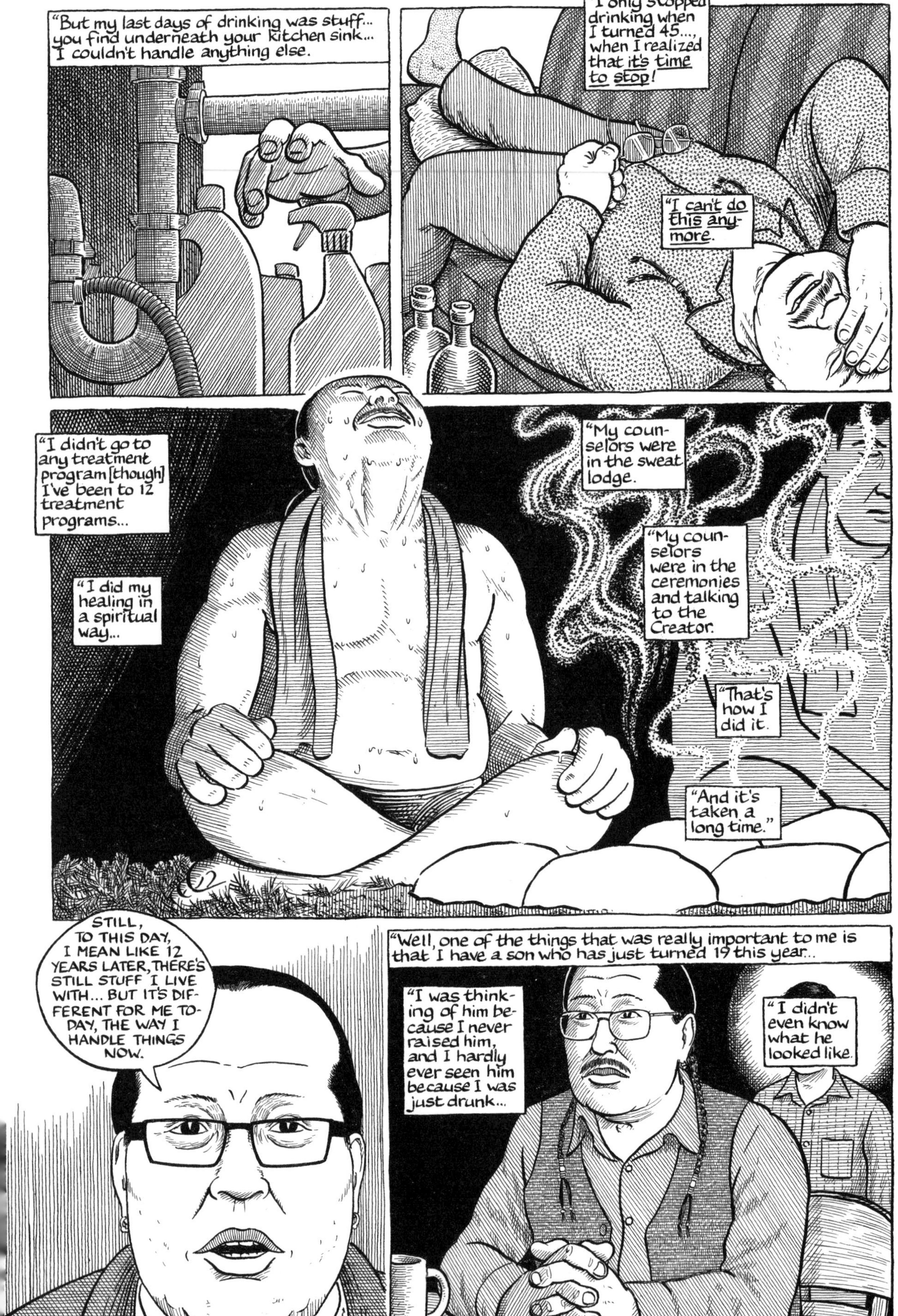
"But my last days of drinking was stuff... you find underneath your kitchen sink... I couldn't handle anything else.
"I only stopped drinking when I turned 45..., when I realized that it's time to stop!
"I can't do this anymore.
"I didn't go to any treatment program [though] I've been to 12 treatment programs...
"I did my healing in a spiritual way...
"My counselors were in the sweat lodge.
"My counselors were in the ceremonies and talking to the Creator.
"That's how I did it.
"And it's taken a long time."
STILL, TO THIS DAY, I MEAN LIKE 12 YEARS LATER, THERE'S STILL STUFF I LIVE WITH... BUT IT'S DIFFERENT FOR ME TODAY, THE WAY I HANDLE THINGS NOW.
"Well, one of the things that was really important to me is that I have a son who has just turned 19 this year...
"I was thinking of him because I never raised him, and I hardly ever seen him because I was just drunk...
"I didn't even know what he looked like.
J. SACCO 2-18

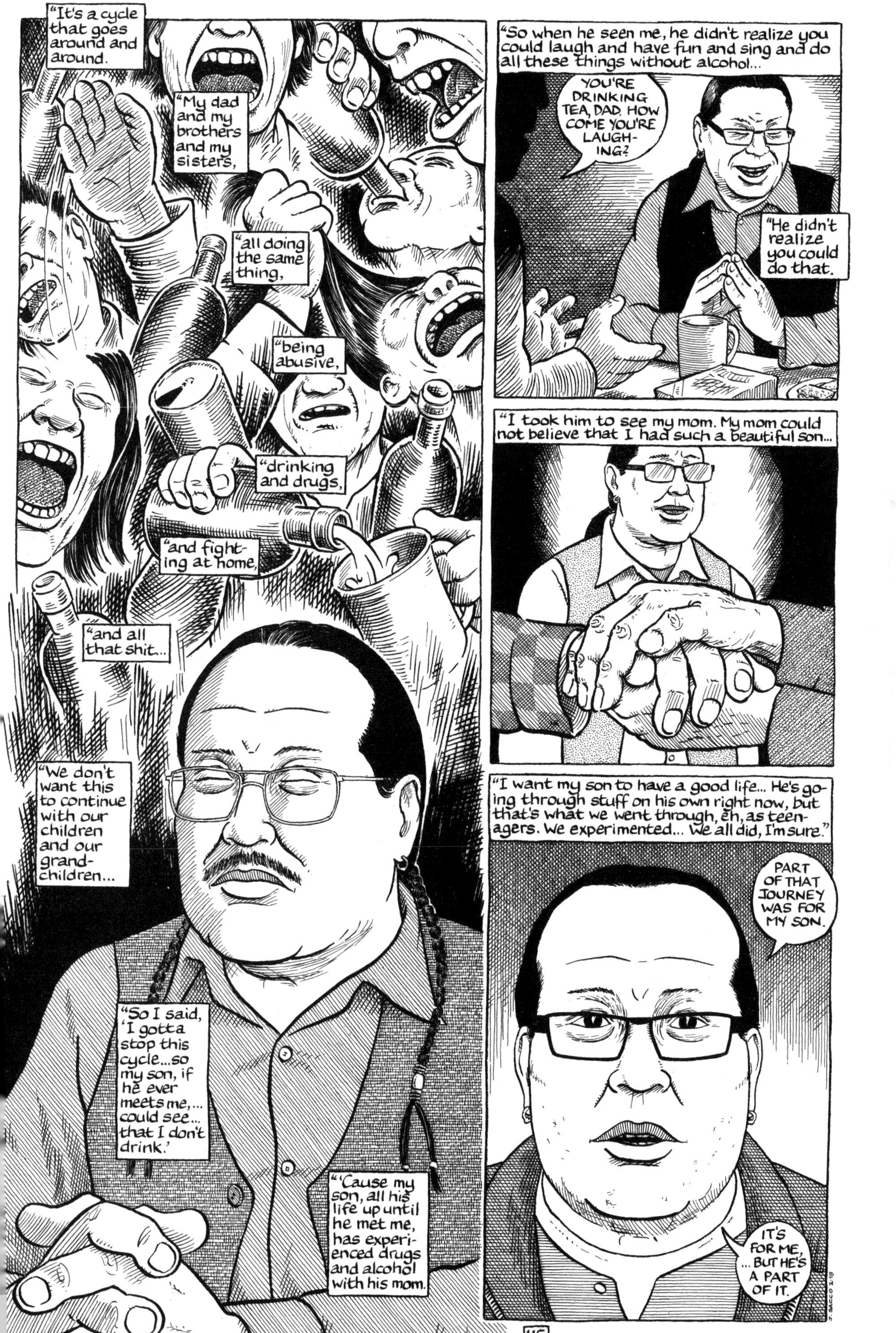
"It's a cycle that goes around and around.
"My dad and my brothers and my sisters,
"all doing the same thing,
"being abusive,
"drinking and drugs,
"and fighting at home,
"and all that shit...
"We don't want this to continue with our children and our grandchildren...
"So I said, 'I gotta stop this cycle...so my son, if he ever meets me,...could see...that I don't drink.'
"'Cause my son, all his life up until he met me, has experienced drugs and alcohol with his mom.
"So when he seen me, he didn't realize you could laugh and have fun and sing and do all these things without alcohol...
YOU'RE DRINKING TEA, DAD. HOW COME YOU'RE LAUGHING?
"He didn't realize you could do that.
"I took him to see my mom. My mom could not believe that I had such a beautiful son...
"I want my son to have a good life... He's going through stuff on his own right now, but that's what we went through, eh, as teenagers. We experimented... We all did, I'm sure."
PART OF THAT JOURNEY WAS FOR MY SON.
IT'S FOR ME, ...BUT HE'S A PART OF IT.

UNTIL I BLACK OUT

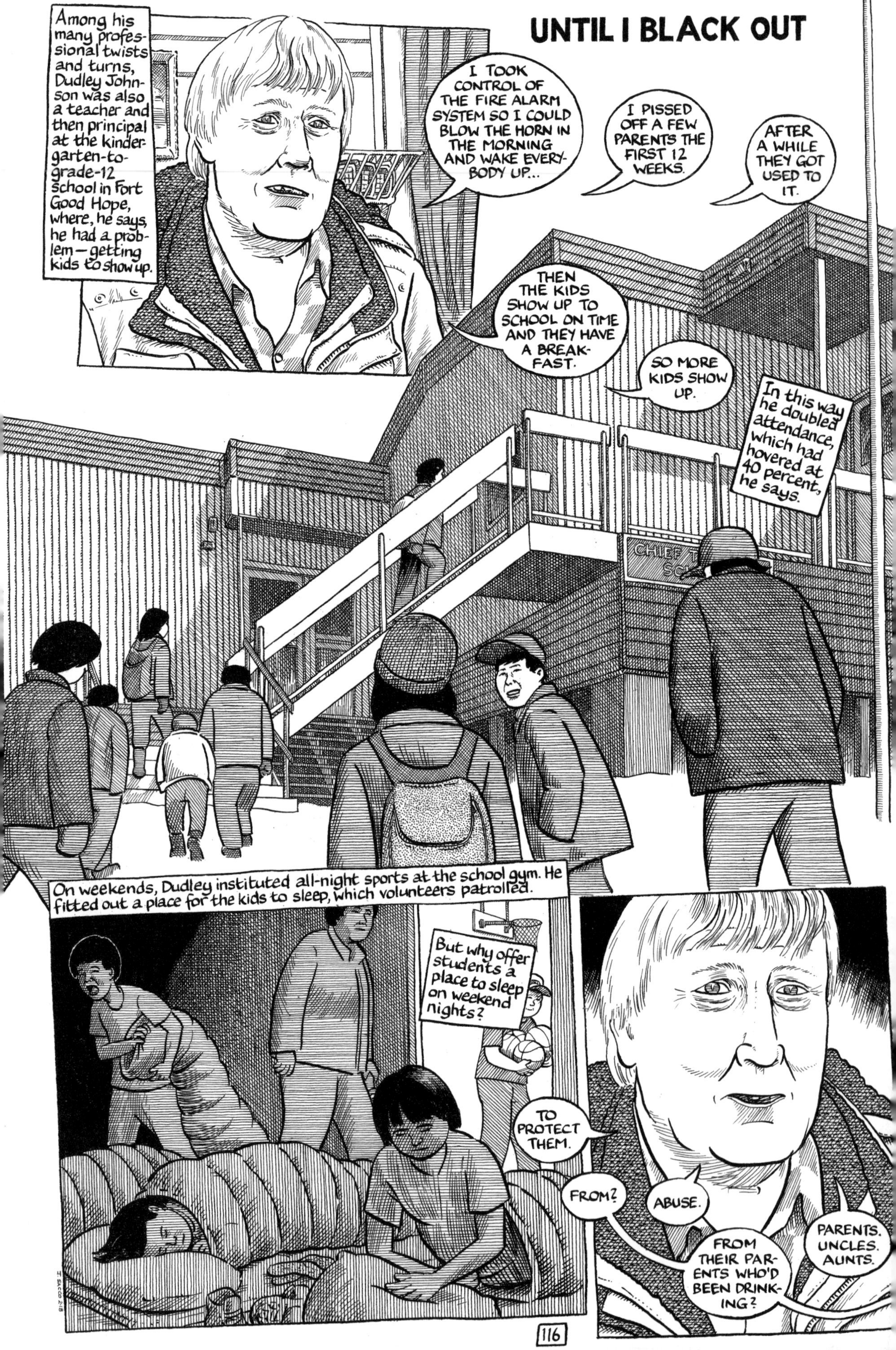

Among his many professional twists and turns, Dudley Johnson was also a teacher and then principal at the kindergarten-to-grade-12 school in Fort Good Hope, where, he says, he had a problem — getting kids to show up.
I TOOK CONTROL OF THE FIRE ALARM SYSTEM SO I COULD BLOW THE HORN IN THE MORNING AND WAKE EVERYBODY UP...
I PISSED OFF A FEW PARENTS THE FIRST 12 WEEKS.
AFTER A WHILE THEY GOT USED TO IT.
THEN THE KIDS SHOW UP TO SCHOOL ON TIME AND THEY HAVE A BREAKFAST.
SO MORE KIDS SHOW UP.
In this way he doubled attendance, which had hovered at 40 percent, he says.
On weekends, Dudley instituted all-night sports at the school gym. He fitted out a place for the kids to sleep, which volunteers patrolled.
But why offer students a place to sleep on weekend nights?
TO PROTECT THEM.
FROM?
ABUSE.
FROM THEIR PARENTS WHO'D BEEN DRINKING?
PARENTS. UNCLES. AUNTS.

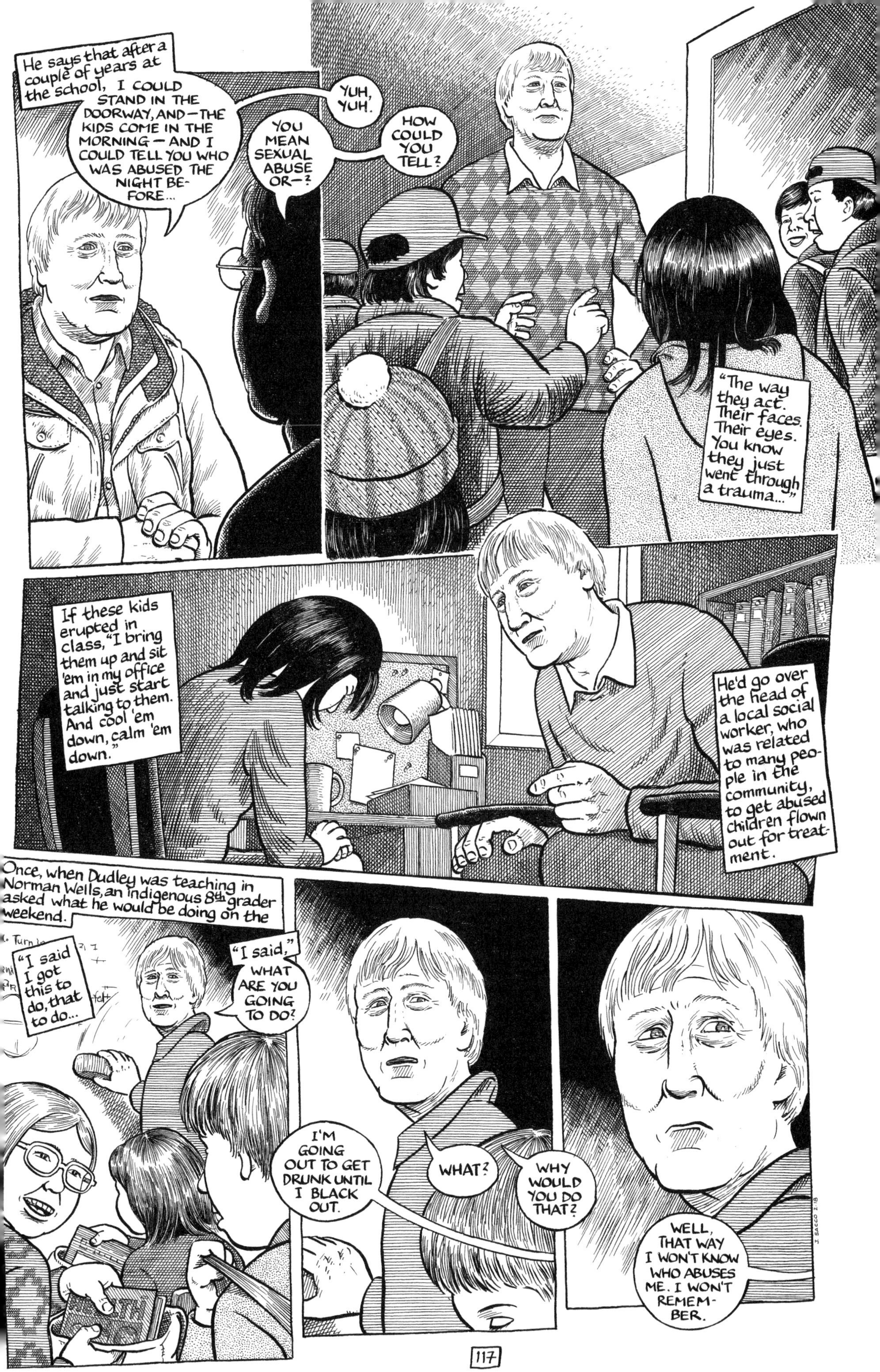
He says that after a couple of years at the school, I COULD STAND IN THE DOORWAY, AND—THE KIDS COME IN THE MORNING—AND I COULD TELL YOU WHO WAS ABUSED THE NIGHT BEFORE...
YUH, YUH.
YOU MEAN SEXUAL ABUSE OR—?
HOW COULD YOU TELL?
"The way they act. Their faces. Their eyes. You know they just went through a trauma..."
If these kids erupted in class, "I bring them up and sit 'em in my office and just start talking to them. And cool 'em down, calm 'em down."
He'd go over the head of a local social worker, who was related to many people in the community, to get abused children flown out for treatment.
Once, when Dudley was teaching in Norman Wells, an indigenous 8th grader asked what he would be doing on the weekend.
"I said I got this to do, that to do...
"I said," WHAT ARE YOU GOING TO DO?
I'M GOING OUT TO GET DRUNK UNTIL I BLACK OUT.
WHAT?
WHY WOULD YOU DO THAT?
WELL, THAT WAY I WON'T KNOW WHO ABUSES ME. I WON'T REMEMBER.
J. SACCO 2.18

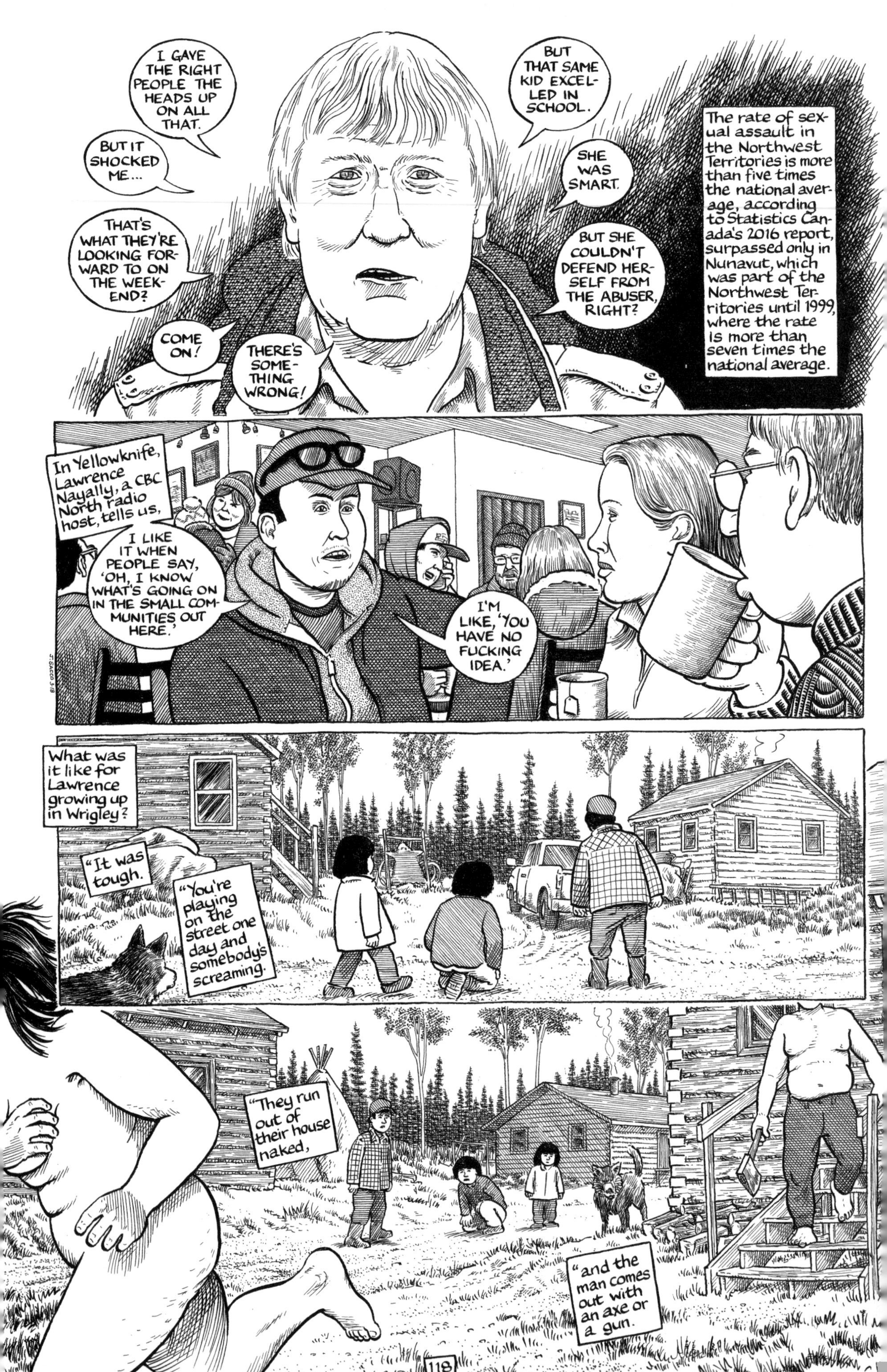

I GAVE THE RIGHT PEOPLE THE HEADS UP ON ALL THAT.
BUT IT SHOCKED ME...
THAT'S WHAT THEY'RE LOOKING FORWARD TO ON THE WEEKEND?
COME ON!
THERE'S SOMETHING WRONG!
BUT THAT SAME KID EXCELLED IN SCHOOL.
SHE WAS SMART.
BUT SHE COULDN'T DEFEND HERSELF FROM THE ABUSER, RIGHT?
The rate of sexual assault in the Northwest Territories is more than five times the national average, according to Statistics Canada's 2016 report, surpassed only in Nunavut, which was part of the Northwest Territories until 1999, where the rate is more than seven times the national average.
In Yellowknife, Lawrence Nayally, a CBC North radio host, tells us,
I LIKE IT WHEN PEOPLE SAY, 'OH, I KNOW WHAT'S GOING ON IN THE SMALL COMMUNITIES OUT HERE.'
I'M LIKE, 'YOU HAVE NO FUCKING IDEA.'
What was it like for Lawrence growing up in Wrigley?
"It was tough.
"You're playing on the street one day and somebody's screaming.
"They run out of their house naked,
"and the man comes out with an axe or a gun.

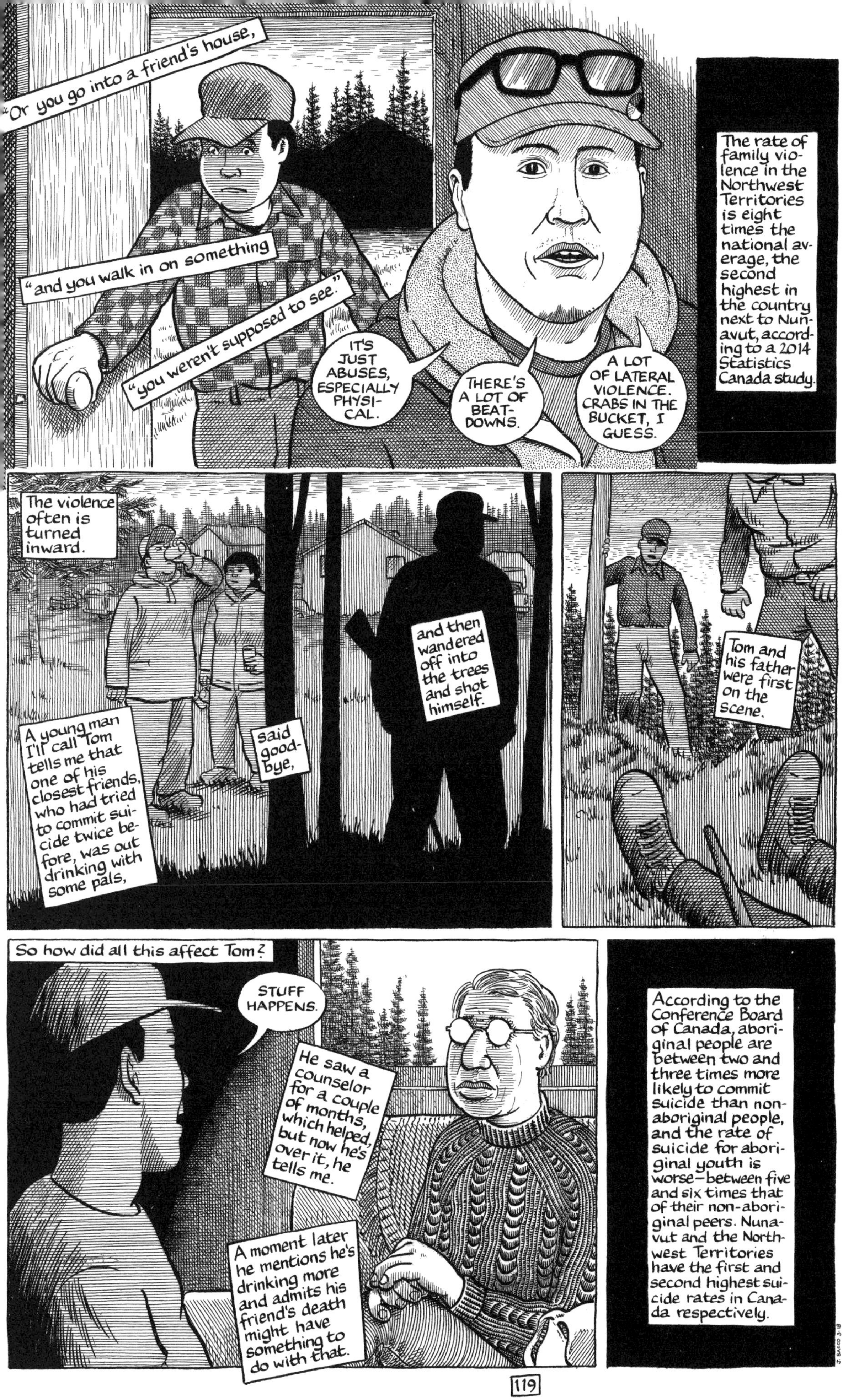
"Or you go into a friend's house,
"and you walk in on something
"you weren't supposed to see."
IT'S JUST ABUSES, ESPECIALLY PHYSI-CAL.
THERE'S A LOT OF BEAT-DOWNS.
A LOT OF LATERAL VIOLENCE. CRABS IN THE BUCKET, I GUESS.
The rate of family violence in the Northwest Territories is eight times the national average, the second highest in the country next to Nunavut, according to a 2014 Statistics Canada study.
The violence often is turned inward.
A young man I'll call Tom tells me that one of his closest friends, who had tried to commit suicide twice before, was out drinking with some pals,
said good-bye,
and then wandered off into the trees and shot himself.
Tom and his father were first on the scene.
So how did all this affect Tom?
STUFF HAPPENS.
He saw a counselor for a couple of months, which helped, but now he's over it, he tells me.
A moment later he mentions he's drinking more and admits his friend's death might have something to do with that.
According to the Conference Board of Canada, aboriginal people are between two and three times more likely to commit suicide than non-aboriginal people, and the rate of suicide for aboriginal youth is worse—between five and six times that of their non-aboriginal peers. Nunavut and the Northwest Territories have the first and second highest suicide rates in Canada respectively.
J. SACCO 3-18

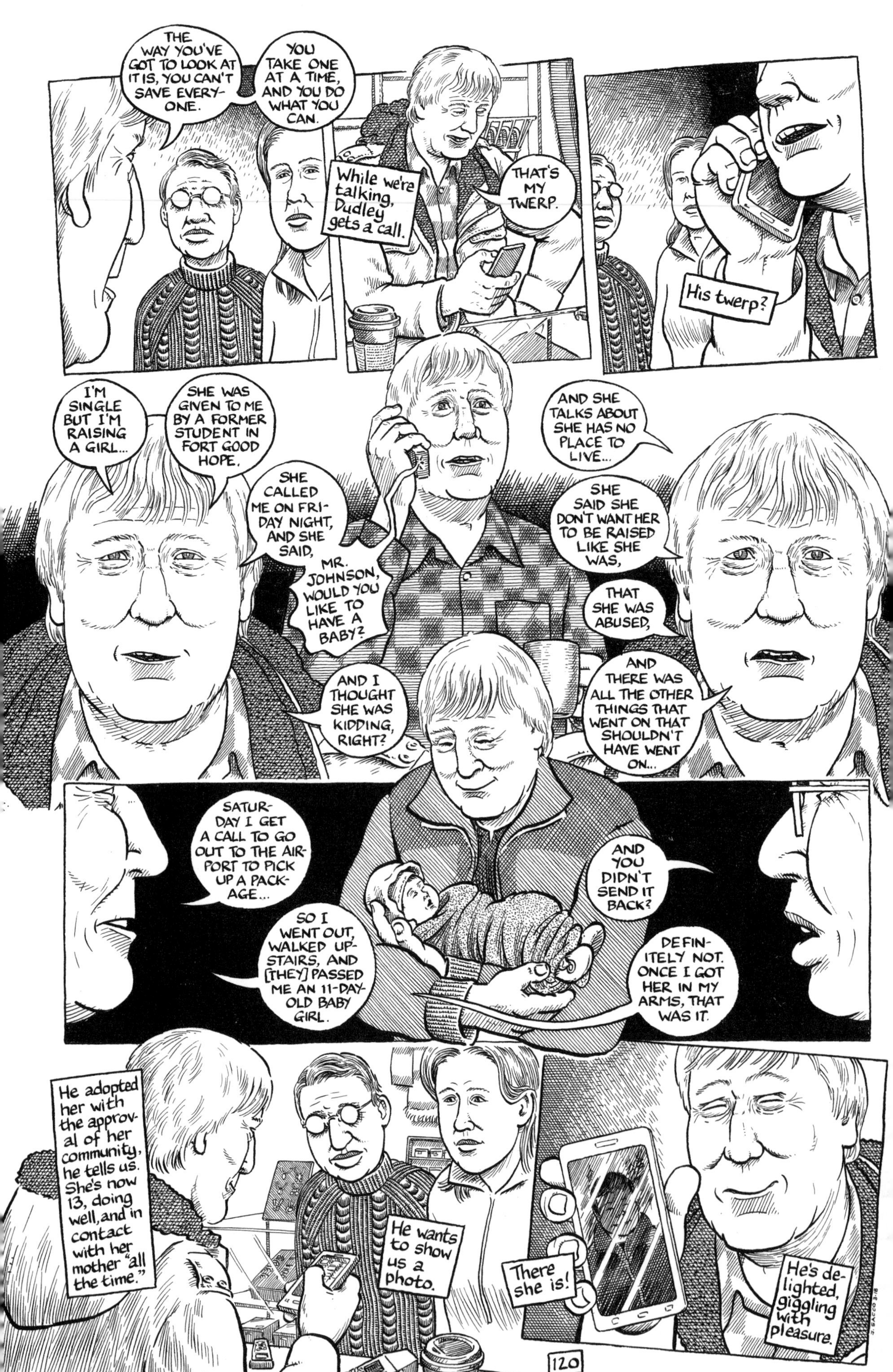
THE WAY YOU'VE GOT TO LOOK AT IT IS, YOU CAN'T SAVE EVERY-ONE.
YOU TAKE ONE AT A TIME, AND YOU DO WHAT YOU CAN.
While we're talking, Dudley gets a call.
THAT'S MY TWERP.
His twerp?
I'M SINGLE BUT I'M RAISING A GIRL...
SHE WAS GIVEN TO ME BY A FORMER STUDENT IN FORT GOOD HOPE.
SHE CALLED ME ON FRI-DAY NIGHT, AND SHE SAID,
MR. JOHNSON, WOULD YOU LIKE TO HAVE A BABY?
AND I THOUGHT SHE WAS KIDDING, RIGHT?
AND SHE TALKS ABOUT SHE HAS NO PLACE TO LIVE...
SHE SAID SHE DON'T WANT HER TO BE RAISED LIKE SHE WAS,
THAT SHE WAS ABUSED,
AND THERE WAS ALL THE OTHER THINGS THAT WENT ON THAT SHOULDN'T HAVE WENT ON...
SATUR-DAY I GET A CALL TO GO OUT TO THE AIR-PORT TO PICK UP A PACK-AGE...
SO I WENT OUT, WALKED UP-STAIRS, AND [THEY] PASSED ME AN 11-DAY-OLD BABY GIRL.
AND YOU DIDN'T SEND IT BACK?
DEFIN-ITELY NOT. ONCE I GOT HER IN MY ARMS, THAT WAS IT.
He adopted her with the approv-al of her community, he tells us. She's now 13, doing well, and in contact with her mother "all the time."
He wants to show us a photo.
There she is!
He's de-lighted, giggling with pleasure.
J. SACCO 3/18

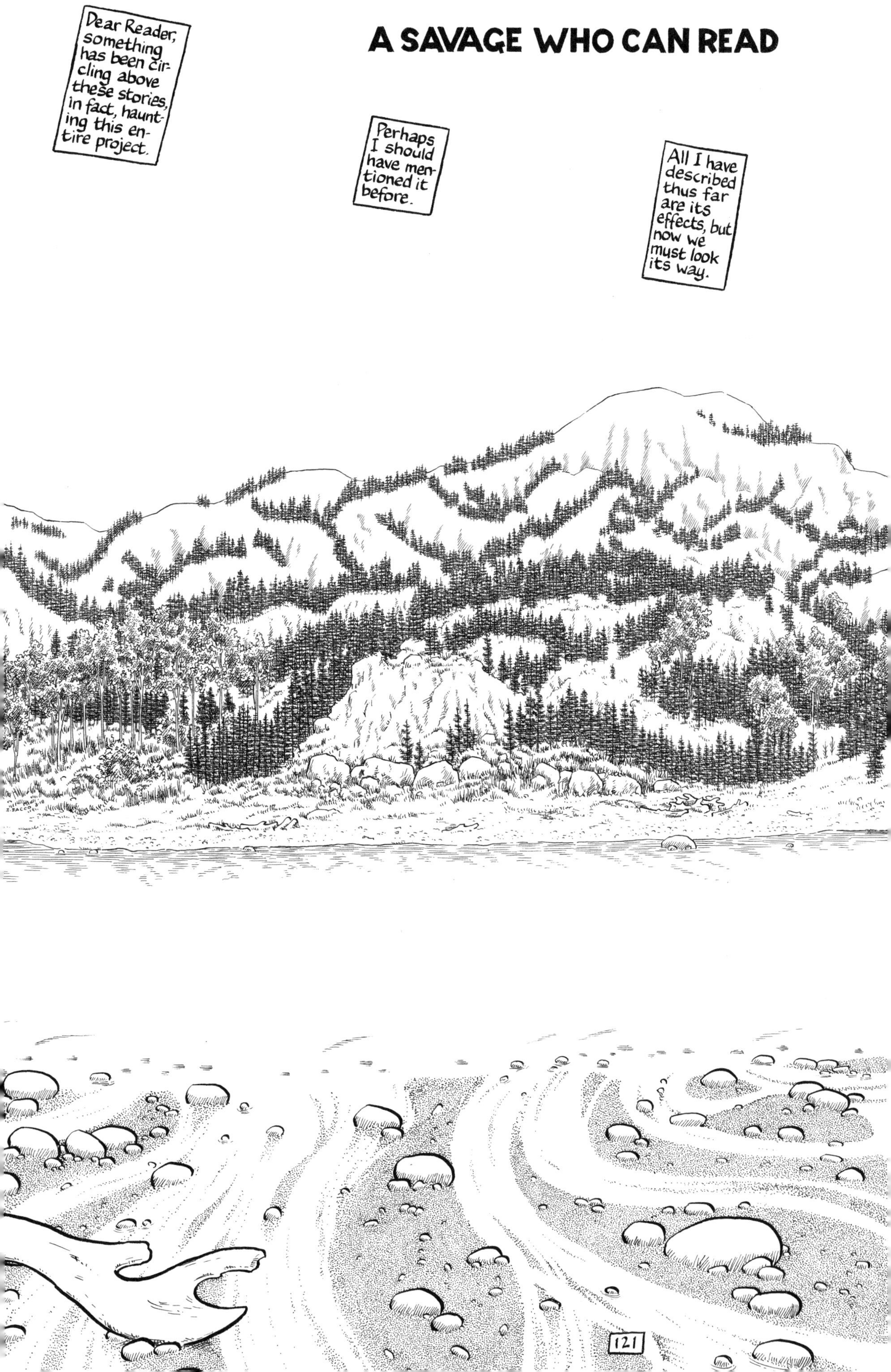
A SAVAGE WHO CAN READ
Dear Reader, something has been circling above these stories, in fact, haunting this entire project.
Perhaps I should have mentioned it before.
All I have described thus far are its effects, but now we must look its way.

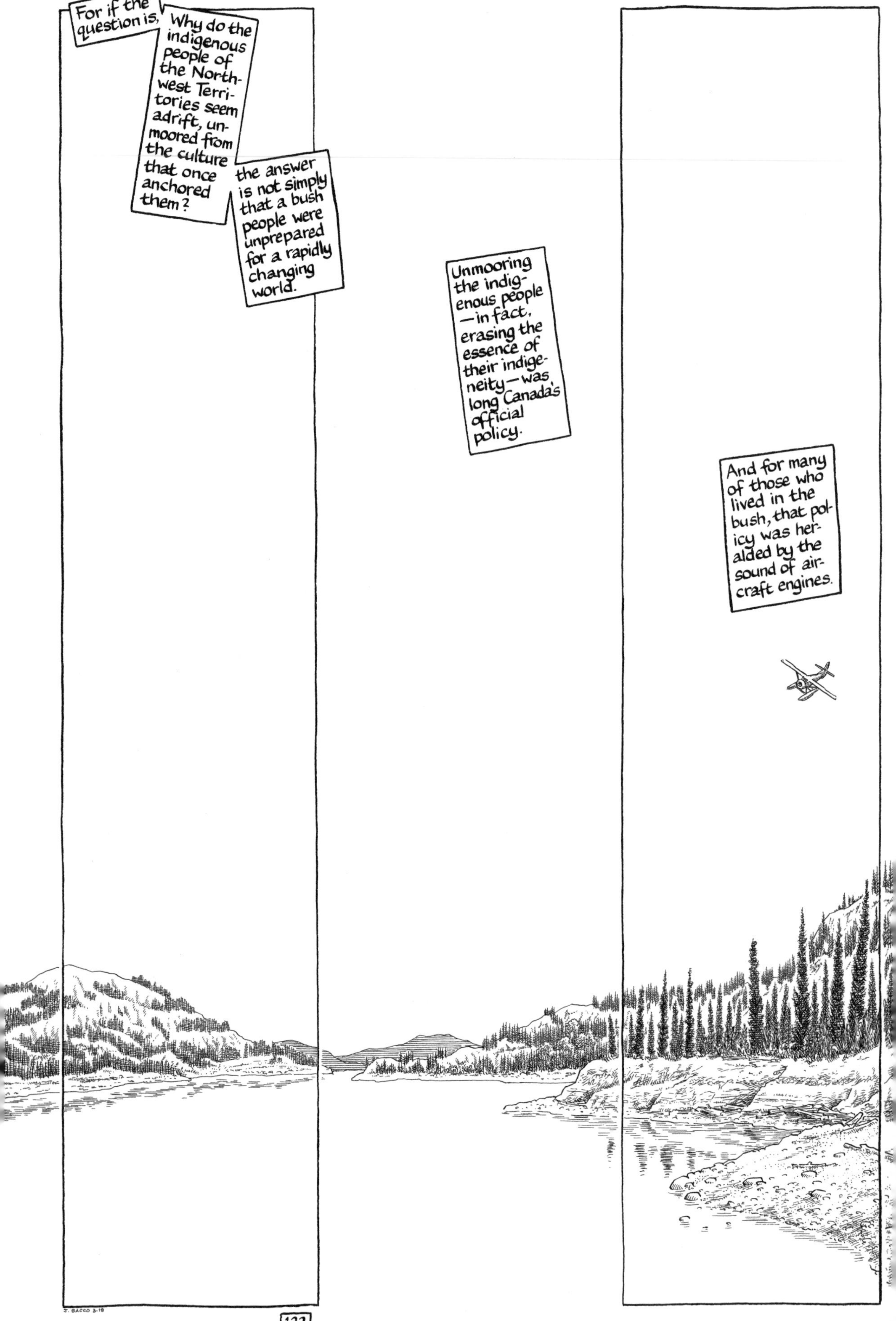
For if the question is,
Why do the indigenous people of the North-west Territories seem adrift, un-moored from the culture that once anchored them?
the answer is not simply that a bush people were unprepared for a rapidly changing world.
Unmooring the indig-enous people —in fact, erasing the essence of their indige-neity—was long Canada's official policy.
And for many of those who lived in the bush, that pol-icy was her-alded by the sound of air-craft engines.
J. SACCO 3.18

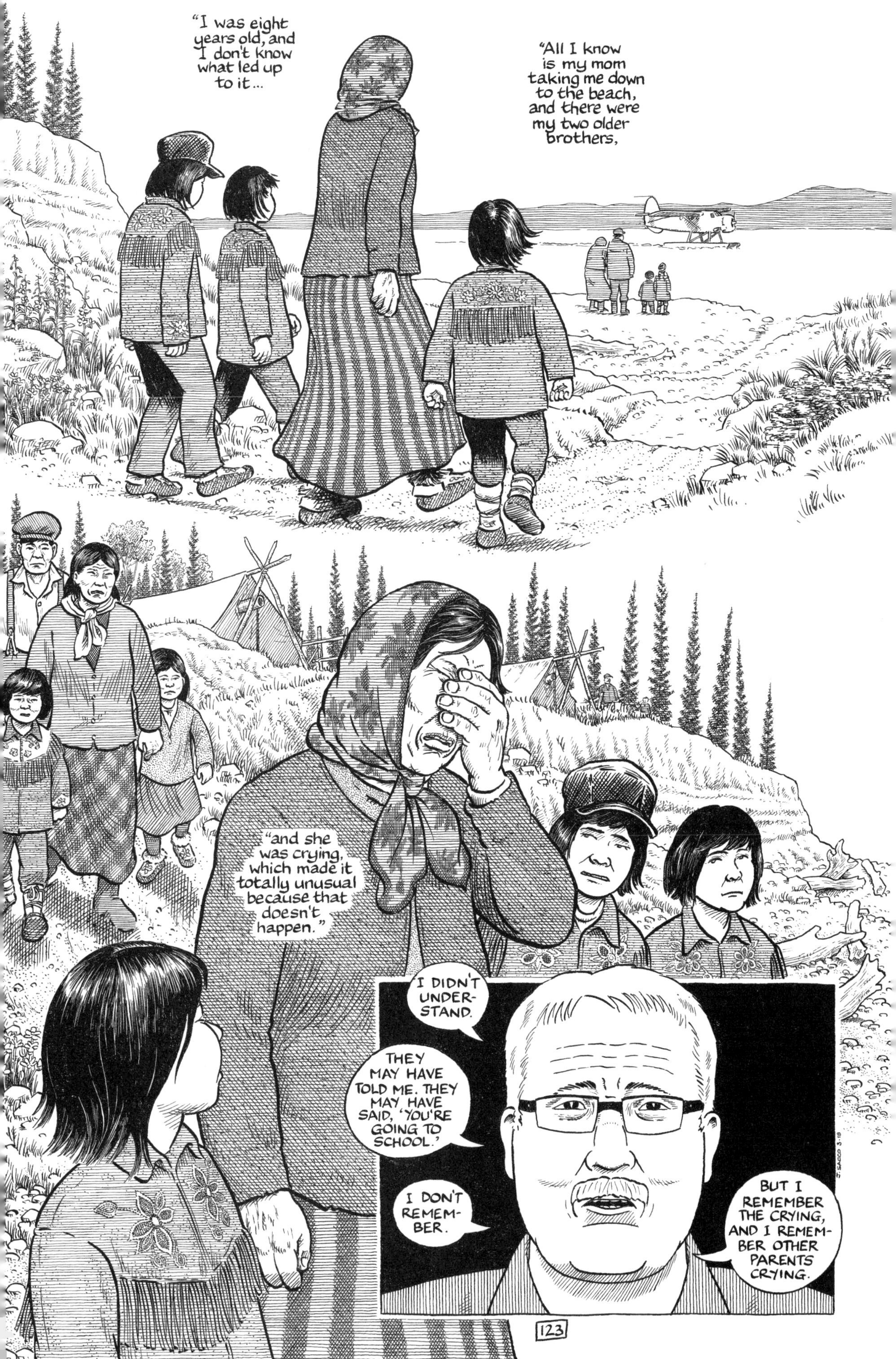
"I was eight years old, and I don't know what led up to it...
"All I know is my mom taking me down to the beach, and there were my two older brothers,
"and she was crying, which made it totally unusual because that doesn't happen."
I DIDN'T UNDER-STAND.
THEY MAY HAVE TOLD ME. THEY MAY HAVE SAID, 'YOU'RE GOING TO SCHOOL.'
I DON'T REMEM-BER.
BUT I REMEMBER THE CRYING, AND I REMEM-BER OTHER PARENTS CRYING.

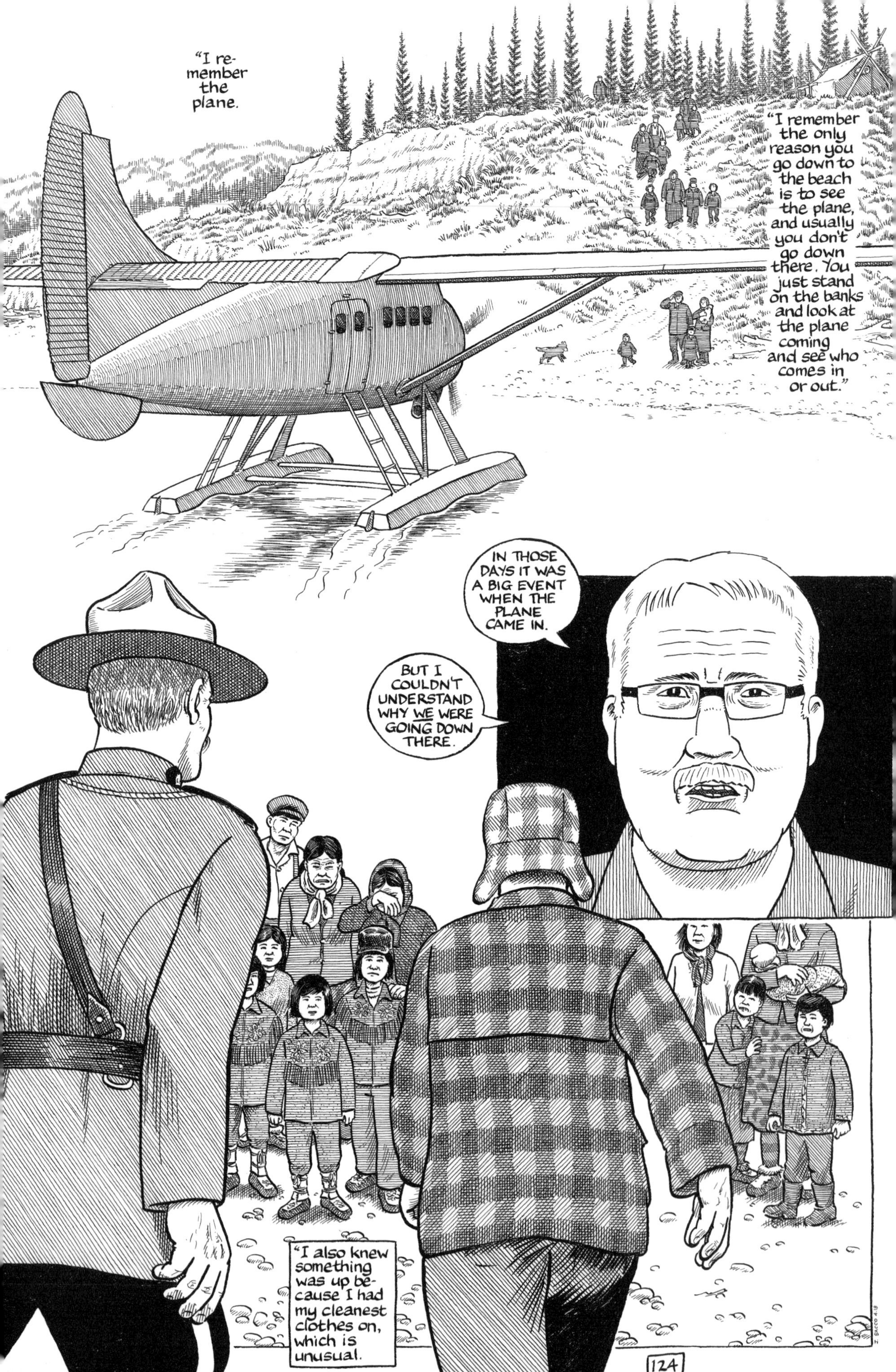

"I remember the plane.
"I remember the only reason you go down to the beach is to see the plane, and usually you don't go down there. You just stand on the banks and look at the plane coming and see who comes in or out."
IN THOSE DAYS IT WAS A BIG EVENT WHEN THE PLANE CAME IN.
BUT I COULDN'T UNDERSTAND WHY WE WERE GOING DOWN THERE.
"I also knew something was up because I had my cleanest clothes on, which is unusual.

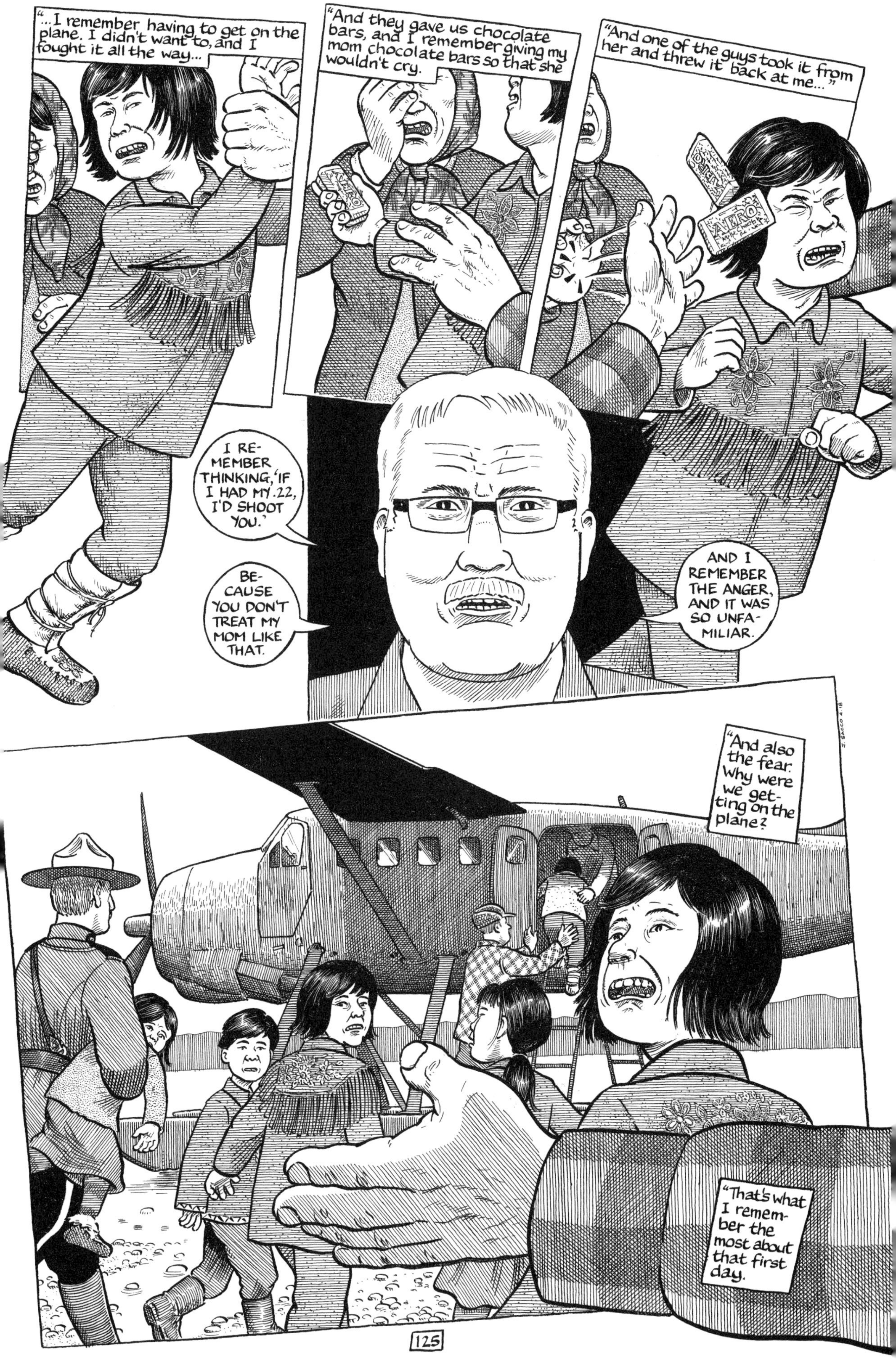
"...I remember having to get on the plane. I didn't want to, and I fought it all the way..."
"And they gave us chocolate bars, and I remember giving my mom chocolate bars so that she wouldn't cry.
"And one of the guys took it from her and threw it back at me..."
AERO
I REMEMBER THINKING, 'IF I HAD MY .22, I'D SHOOT YOU.'
BECAUSE YOU DON'T TREAT MY MOM LIKE THAT.
AND I REMEMBER THE ANGER, AND IT WAS SO UNFAMILIAR.
"And also the fear. Why were we getting on the plane?
"That's what I remember the most about that first day.

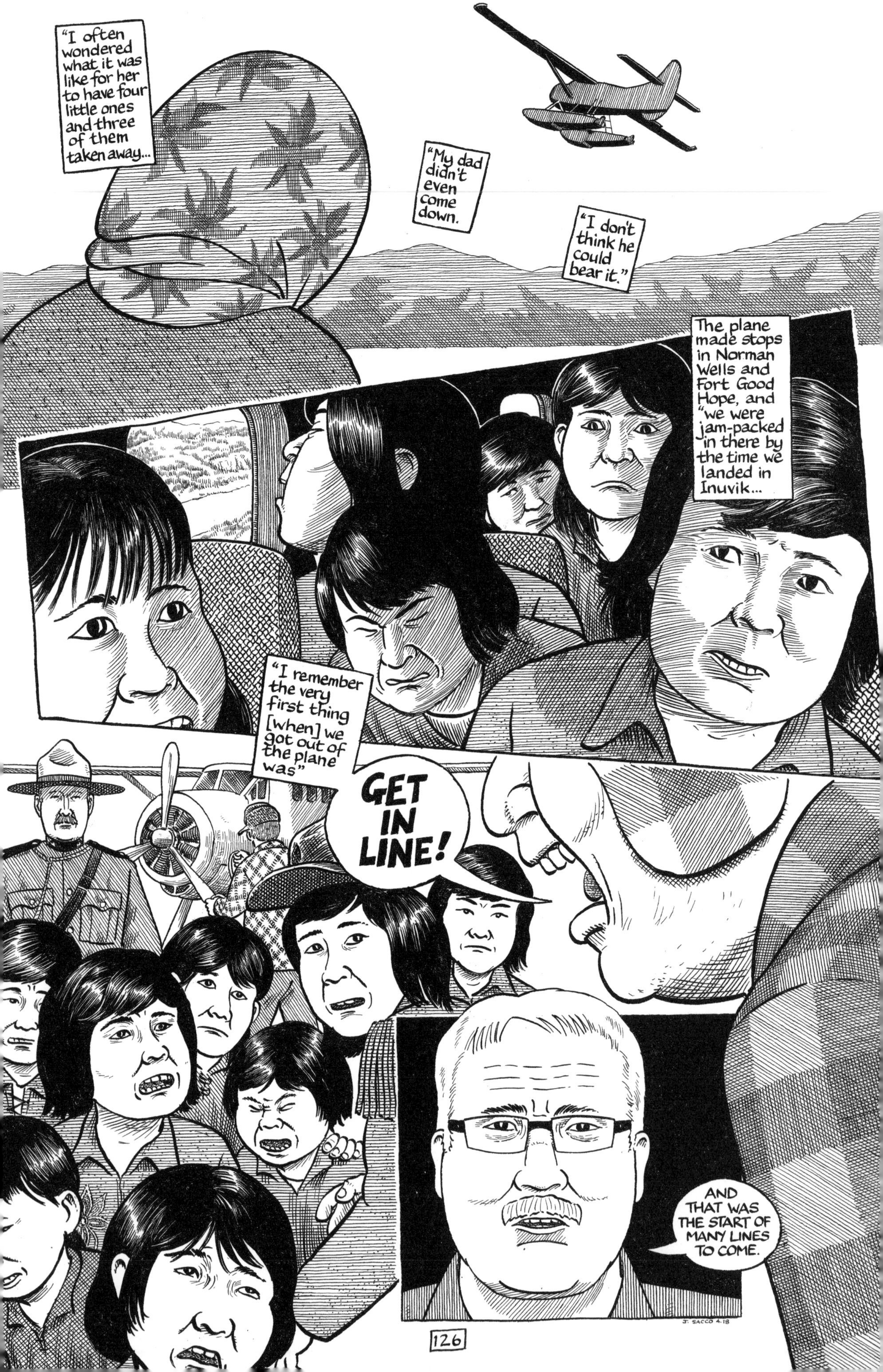
"I often wondered what it was like for her to have four little ones and three of them taken away...
"My dad didn't even come down.
"I don't think he could bear it."
The plane made stops in Norman Wells and Fort Good Hope, and "we were jam-packed in there by the time we landed in Inuvik...
"I remember the very first thing [when] we got out of the plane was"
GET IN LINE!
AND THAT WAS THE START OF MANY LINES TO COME.
J. SACCO 4.18

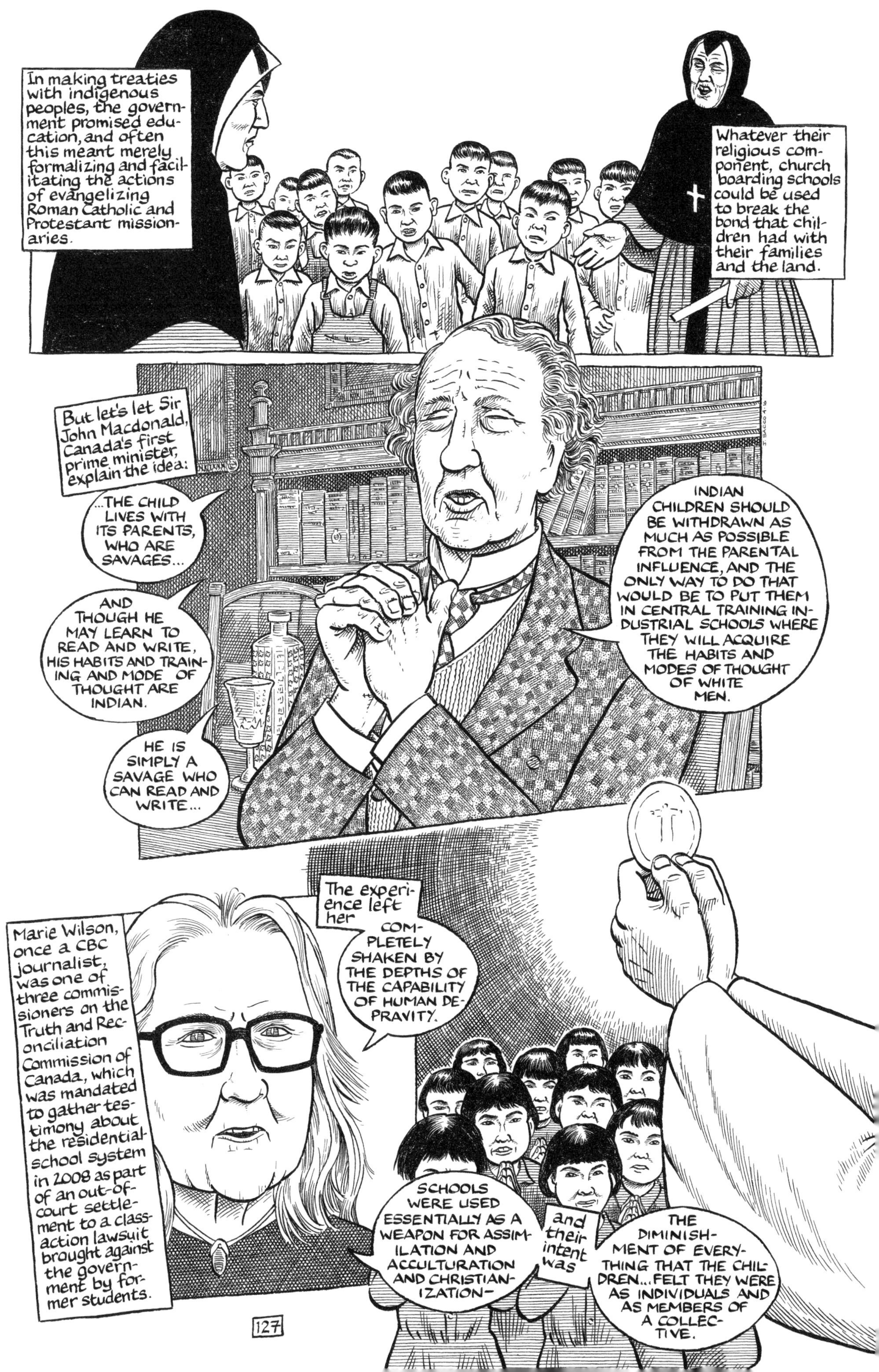

In making treaties with indigenous peoples, the government promised education, and often this meant merely formalizing and facilitating the actions of evangelizing Roman Catholic and Protestant missionaries.
Whatever their religious component, church boarding schools could be used to break the bond that children had with their families and the land.
But let's let Sir John Macdonald, Canada's first prime minister, explain the idea:
...THE CHILD LIVES WITH ITS PARENTS, WHO ARE SAVAGES...
AND THOUGH HE MAY LEARN TO READ AND WRITE, HIS HABITS AND TRAINING AND MODE OF THOUGHT ARE INDIAN.
HE IS SIMPLY A SAVAGE WHO CAN READ AND WRITE...
INDIAN CHILDREN SHOULD BE WITHDRAWN AS MUCH AS POSSIBLE FROM THE PARENTAL INFLUENCE, AND THE ONLY WAY TO DO THAT WOULD BE TO PUT THEM IN CENTRAL TRAINING INDUSTRIAL SCHOOLS WHERE THEY WILL ACQUIRE THE HABITS AND MODES OF THOUGHT OF WHITE MEN.
Marie Wilson, once a CBC journalist, was one of three commissioners on the Truth and Reconciliation Commission of Canada, which was mandated to gather testimony about the residential-school system in 2008 as part of an out-of-court settlement to a class-action lawsuit brought against the government by former students.
The experience left her
COMPLETELY SHAKEN BY THE DEPTHS OF THE CAPABILITY OF HUMAN DEPRAVITY.
SCHOOLS WERE USED ESSENTIALLY AS A WEAPON FOR ASSIMILATION AND ACCULTURATION AND CHRISTIANIZATION–
and their intent was
THE DIMINISHMENT OF EVERYTHING THAT THE CHILDREN...FELT THEY WERE AS INDIVIDUALS AND AS MEMBERS OF A COLLECTIVE.

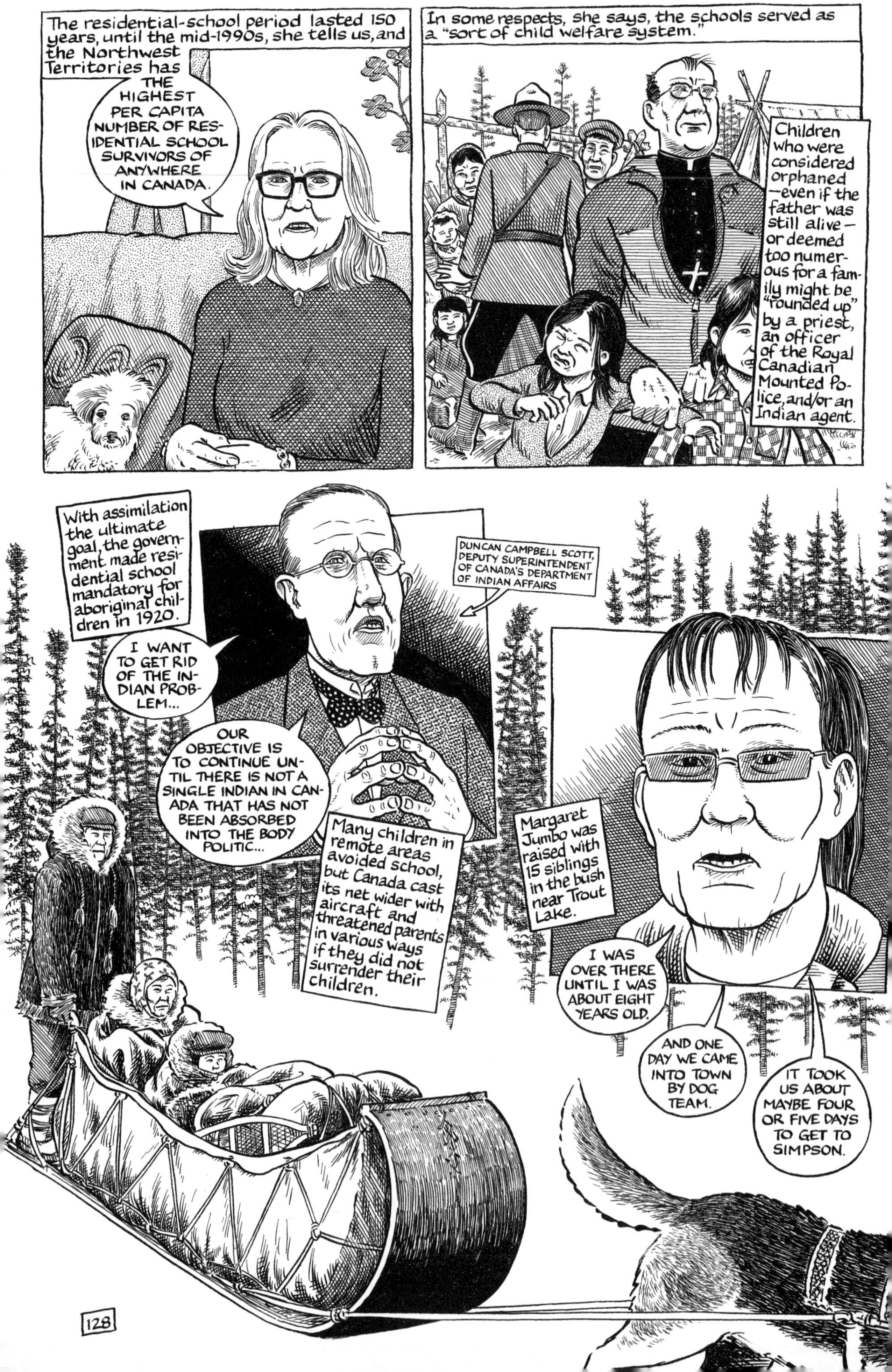

The residential-school period lasted 150 years, until the mid-1990s, she tells us, and the Northwest Territories has
THE HIGHEST PER CAPITA NUMBER OF RESIDENTIAL SCHOOL SURVIVORS OF ANYWHERE IN CANADA.
In some respects, she says, the schools served as a "sort of child welfare system."
Children who were considered orphaned—even if the father was still alive—or deemed too numerous for a family might be "rounded up" by a priest, an officer of the Royal Canadian Mounted Police, and/or an Indian agent.
With assimilation the ultimate goal, the government made residential school mandatory for aboriginal children in 1920.
DUNCAN CAMPBELL SCOTT, DEPUTY SUPERINTENDENT OF CANADA'S DEPARTMENT OF INDIAN AFFAIRS
I WANT TO GET RID OF THE INDIAN PROBLEM...
OUR OBJECTIVE IS TO CONTINUE UNTIL THERE IS NOT A SINGLE INDIAN IN CANADA THAT HAS NOT BEEN ABSORBED INTO THE BODY POLITIC...
Many children in remote areas avoided school, but Canada cast its net wider with aircraft and threatened parents in various ways if they did not surrender their children.
Margaret Jumbo was raised with 15 siblings in the bush near Trout Lake.
I WAS OVER THERE UNTIL I WAS ABOUT EIGHT YEARS OLD.
AND ONE DAY WE CAME INTO TOWN BY DOG TEAM.
IT TOOK US ABOUT MAYBE FOUR OR FIVE DAYS TO GET TO SIMPSON.

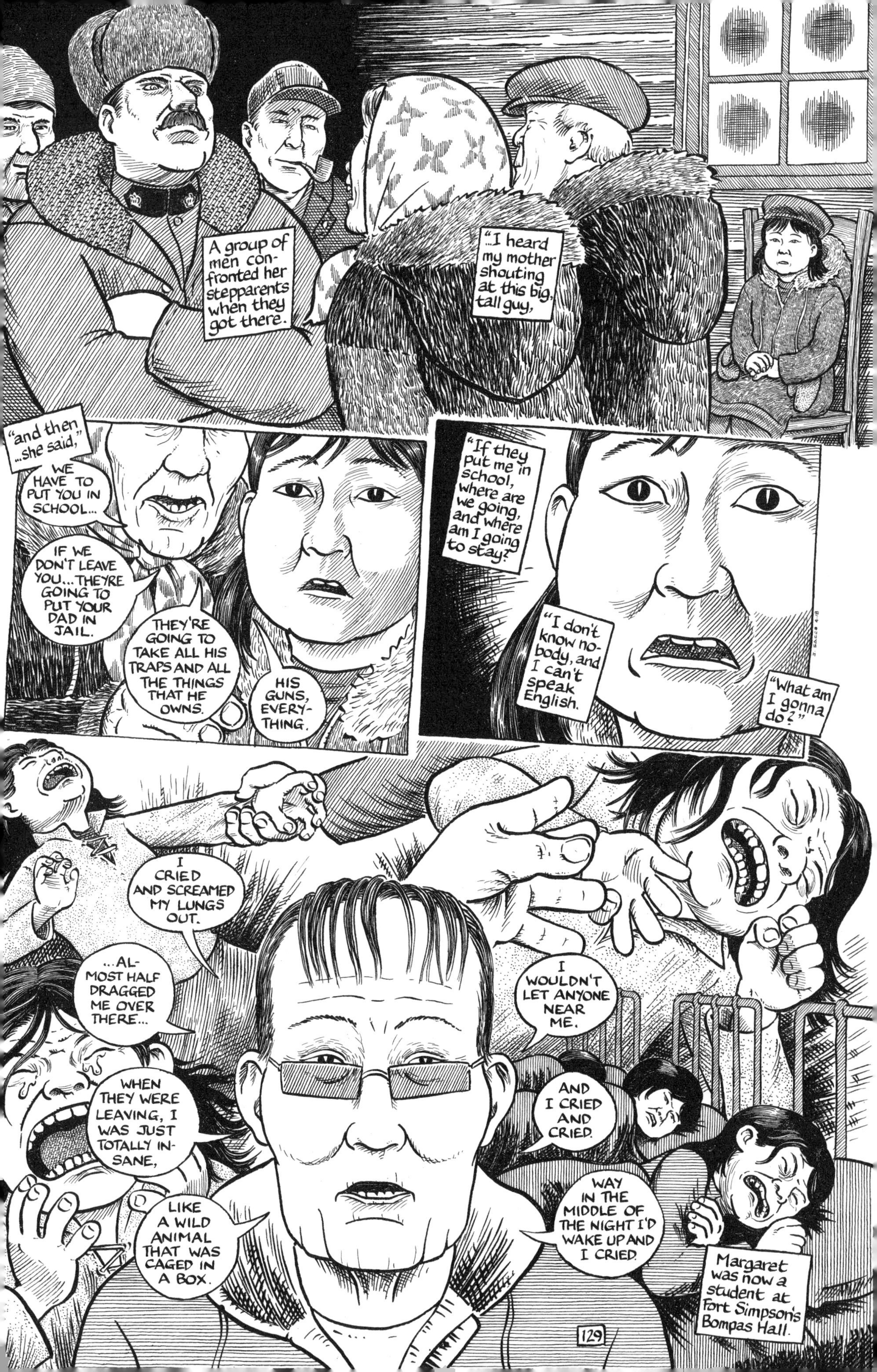
A group of men confronted her stepparents when they got there.
"...I heard my mother shouting at this big, tall guy,
"and then ...she said,"
WE HAVE TO PUT YOU IN SCHOOL...
IF WE DON'T LEAVE YOU... THEYRE GOING TO PUT YOUR DAD IN JAIL.
THEY'RE GOING TO TAKE ALL HIS TRAPS AND ALL THE THINGS THAT HE OWNS.
HIS GUNS, EVERYTHING.
"If they put me in school, where are we going, and where am I going to stay?
"I don't know nobody, and I can't speak English.
"What am I gonna do?"
I CRIED AND SCREAMED MY LUNGS OUT.
...ALMOST HALF DRAGGED ME OVER THERE...
I WOULDN'T LET ANYONE NEAR ME.
WHEN THEY WERE LEAVING, I WAS JUST TOTALLY INSANE,
LIKE A WILD ANIMAL THAT WAS CAGED IN A BOX.
AND I CRIED AND CRIED.
WAY IN THE MIDDLE OF THE NIGHT I'D WAKE UP AND I CRIED.
Margaret was now a student at Fort Simpson's Bompas Hall.

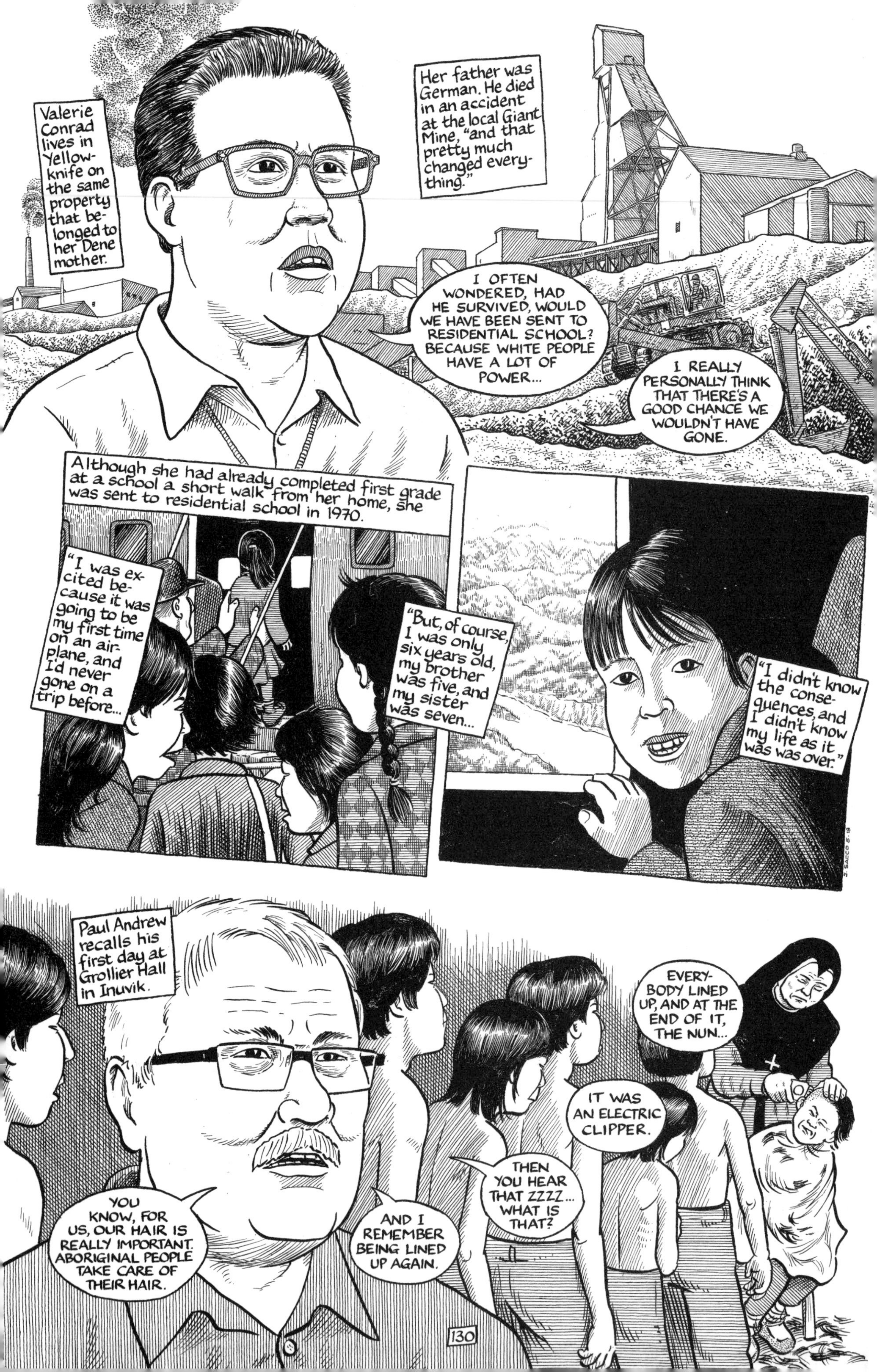
Valerie Conrad lives in Yellowknife on the same property that belonged to her Dene mother.
Her father was German. He died in an accident at the local Giant Mine, "and that pretty much changed everything."
I OFTEN WONDERED, HAD HE SURVIVED, WOULD WE HAVE BEEN SENT TO RESIDENTIAL SCHOOL? BECAUSE WHITE PEOPLE HAVE A LOT OF POWER...
I REALLY PERSONALLY THINK THAT THERE'S A GOOD CHANCE WE WOULDN'T HAVE GONE.
Although she had already completed first grade at a school a short walk from her home, she was sent to residential school in 1970.
"I was excited because it was going to be my first time on an airplane, and I'd never gone on a trip before...
"But, of course, I was only six years old, my brother was five, and my sister was seven...
"I didn't know the consequences, and I didn't know my life as it was was over."
J. SACCO 5.18
Paul Andrew recalls his first day at Grollier Hall in Inuvik.
YOU KNOW, FOR US, OUR HAIR IS REALLY IMPORTANT. ABORIGINAL PEOPLE TAKE CARE OF THEIR HAIR.
AND I REMEMBER BEING LINED UP AGAIN.
THEN YOU HEAR THAT ZZZZ... WHAT IS THAT?
IT WAS AN ELECTRIC CLIPPER.
EVERYBODY LINED UP, AND AT THE END OF IT, THE NUN...

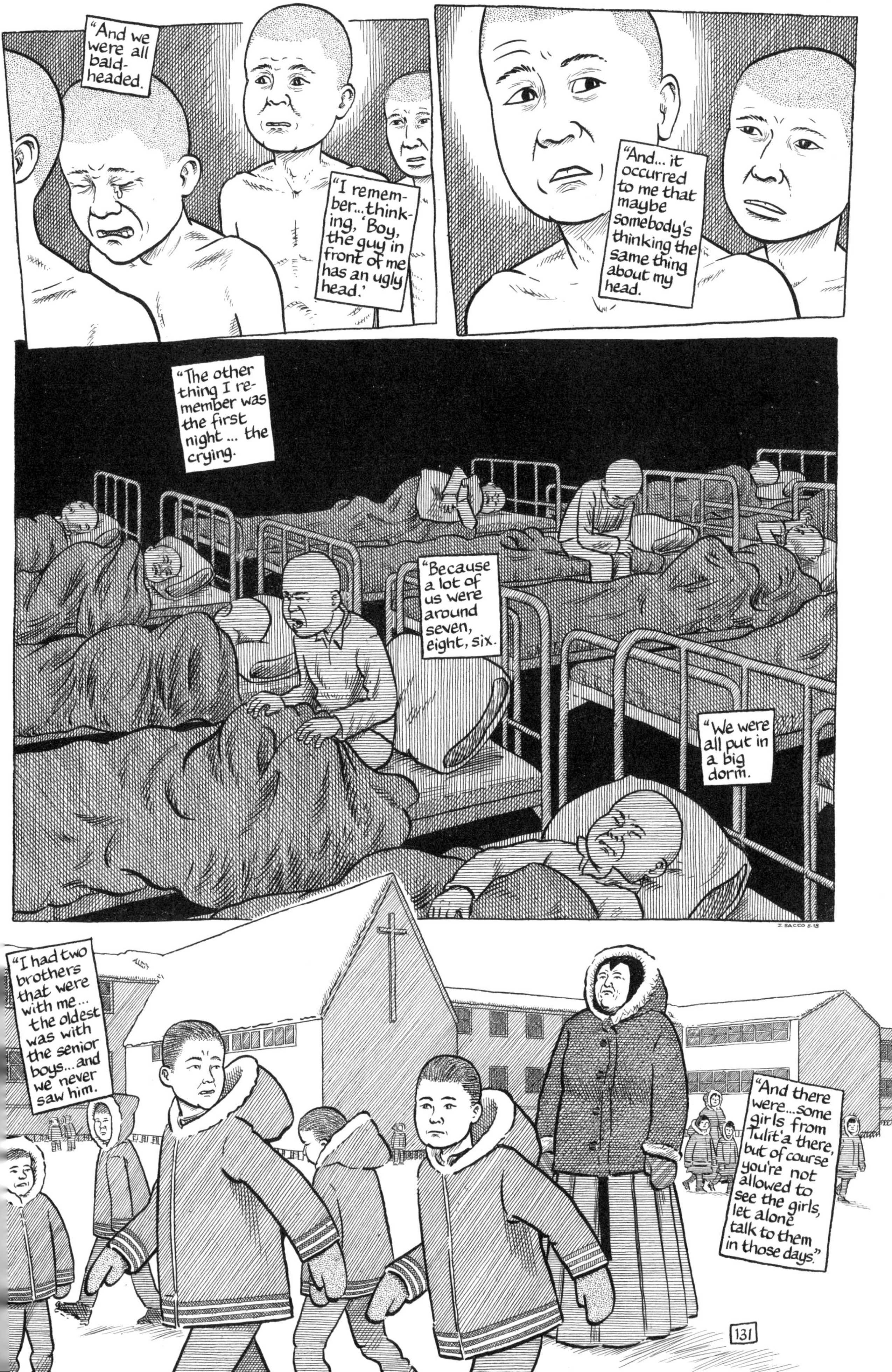
"And we were all bald-headed.
"I remember... thinking, 'Boy, the guy in front of me has an ugly head.'
"And... it occurred to me that maybe somebody's thinking the same thing about my head.
"The other thing I remember was the first night ... the crying.
"Because a lot of us were around seven, eight, six.
"We were all put in a big dorm.
J. SACCO 5.18
"I had two brothers that were with me... the oldest was with the senior boys... and we never saw him.
"And there were... some girls from Tulit'a there, but of course you're not allowed to see the girls, let alone talk to them in those days."
131

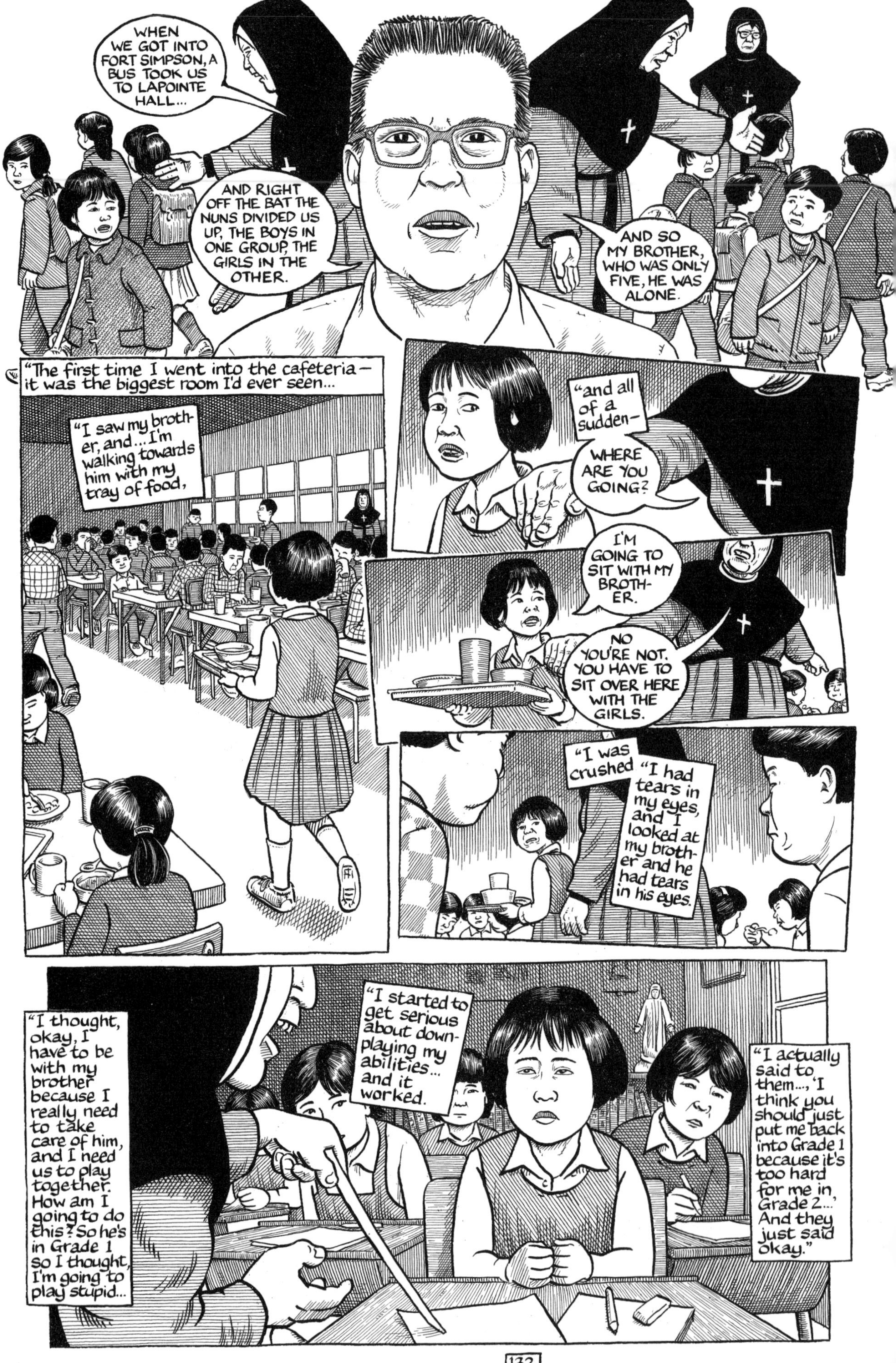
WHEN WE GOT INTO FORT SIMPSON, A BUS TOOK US TO LAPOINTE HALL...
AND RIGHT OFF THE BAT THE NUNS DIVIDED US UP, THE BOYS IN ONE GROUP, THE GIRLS IN THE OTHER.
AND SO MY BROTHER, WHO WAS ONLY FIVE, HE WAS ALONE.
"The first time I went into the cafeteria—it was the biggest room I'd ever seen...
"I saw my brother, and... I'm walking towards him with my tray of food,
"and all of a sudden—
WHERE ARE YOU GOING?
I'M GOING TO SIT WITH MY BROTHER.
NO YOU'RE NOT. YOU HAVE TO SIT OVER HERE WITH THE GIRLS.
"I was crushed
"I had tears in my eyes, and I looked at my brother and he had tears in his eyes.
"I thought, okay, I have to be with my brother because I really need to take care of him, and I need us to play together. How am I going to do this? So he's in Grade 1 so I thought, I'm going to play stupid...
"I started to get serious about downplaying my abilities... and it worked.
"I actually said to them..., 'I think you should just put me back into Grade 1 because it's too hard for me in Grade 2...' And they just said okay."

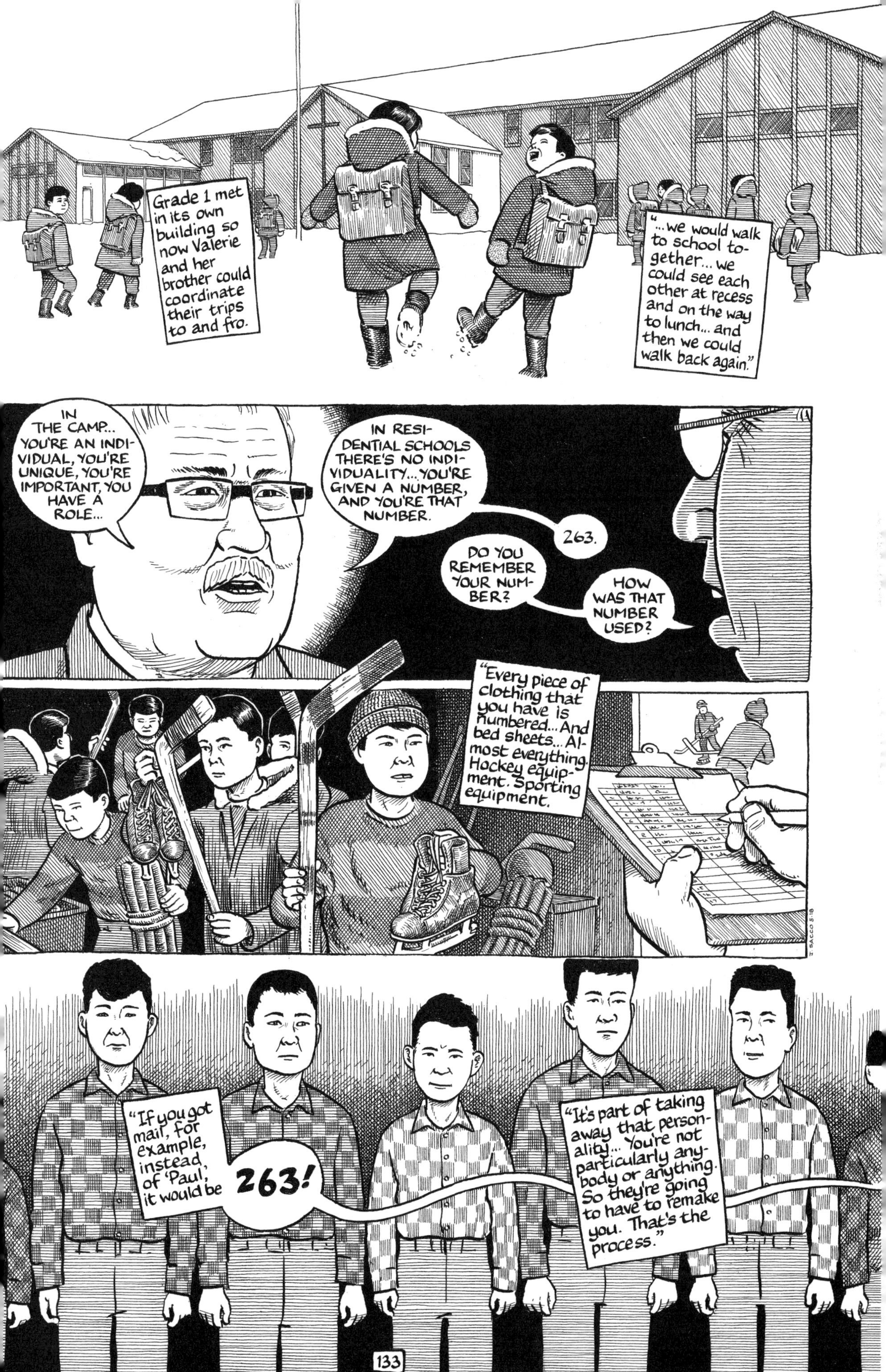
Grade 1 met in its own building so now Valerie and her brother could coordinate their trips to and fro.
"...we would walk to school together... we could see each other at recess and on the way to lunch... and then we could walk back again."
IN THE CAMP... YOU'RE AN INDIVIDUAL, YOU'RE UNIQUE, YOU'RE IMPORTANT, YOU HAVE A ROLE...
IN RESIDENTIAL SCHOOLS THERE'S NO INDIVIDUALITY... YOU'RE GIVEN A NUMBER, AND YOU'RE THAT NUMBER.
DO YOU REMEMBER YOUR NUMBER?
263.
HOW WAS THAT NUMBER USED?
"Every piece of clothing that you have is numbered... And bed sheets... Almost everything. Hockey equipment. Sporting equipment.
"If you got mail, for example, instead of 'Paul,' it would be
263!
"It's part of taking away that personality... You're not particularly anybody or anything. So they're going to have to remake you. That's the process."

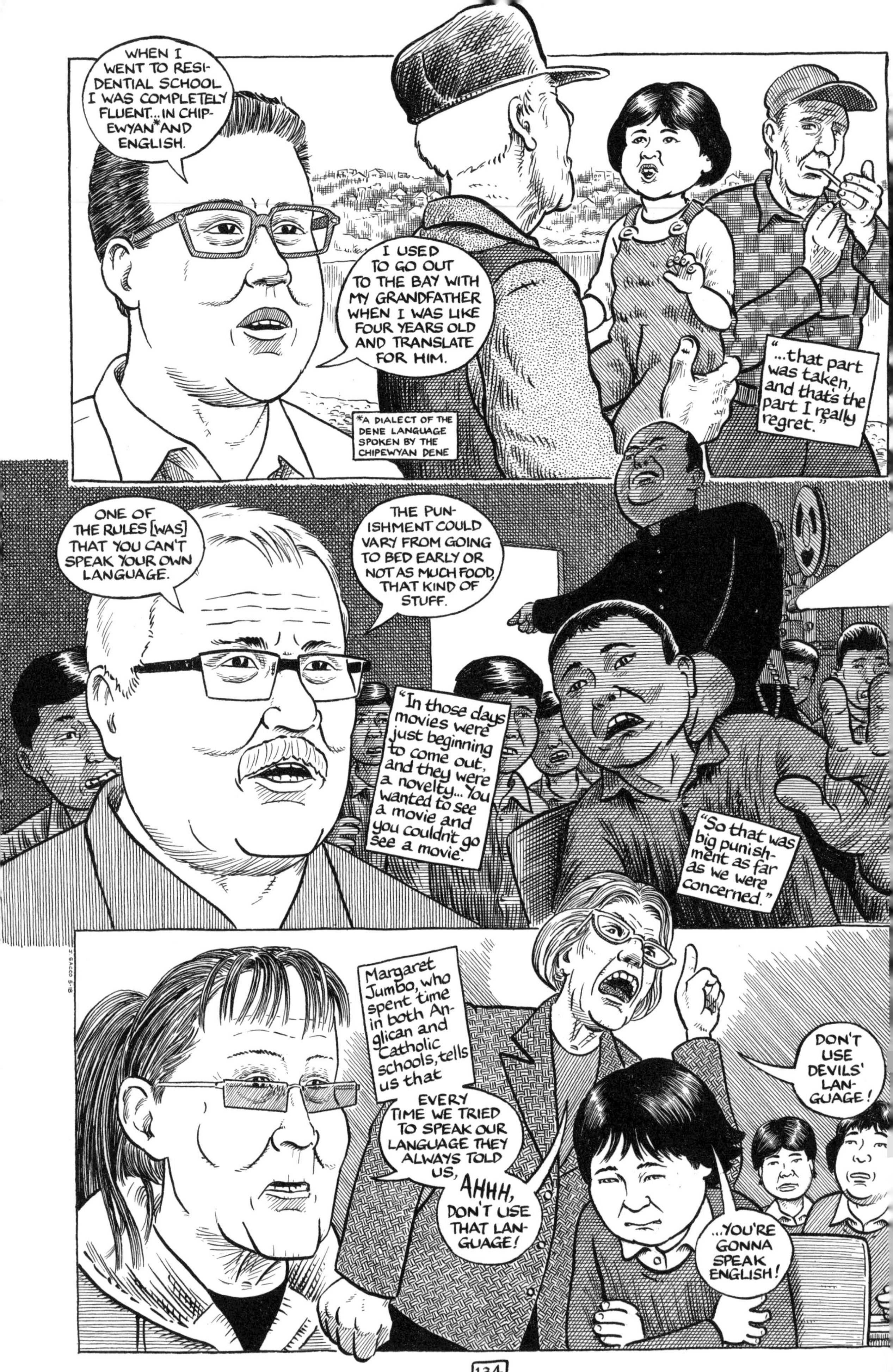
WHEN I WENT TO RESIDENTIAL SCHOOL I WAS COMPLETELY FLUENT... IN CHIPEWYAN* AND ENGLISH.
I USED TO GO OUT TO THE BAY WITH MY GRANDFATHER WHEN I WAS LIKE FOUR YEARS OLD AND TRANSLATE FOR HIM.
*A DIALECT OF THE DENE LANGUAGE SPOKEN BY THE CHIPEWYAN DENE
"...that part was taken, and that's the part I really regret."
ONE OF THE RULES [WAS] THAT YOU CAN'T SPEAK YOUR OWN LANGUAGE.
THE PUNISHMENT COULD VARY FROM GOING TO BED EARLY OR NOT AS MUCH FOOD, THAT KIND OF STUFF.
"In those days movies were just beginning to come out, and they were a novelty... You wanted to see a movie and you couldn't go see a movie.
"So that was big punishment as far as we were concerned."
Margaret Jumbo, who spent time in both Anglican and Catholic schools, tells us that
EVERY TIME WE TRIED TO SPEAK OUR LANGUAGE THEY ALWAYS TOLD US,
AHHH, DON'T USE THAT LANGUAGE!
DON'T USE DEVILS' LANGUAGE!
...YOU'RE GONNA SPEAK ENGLISH!

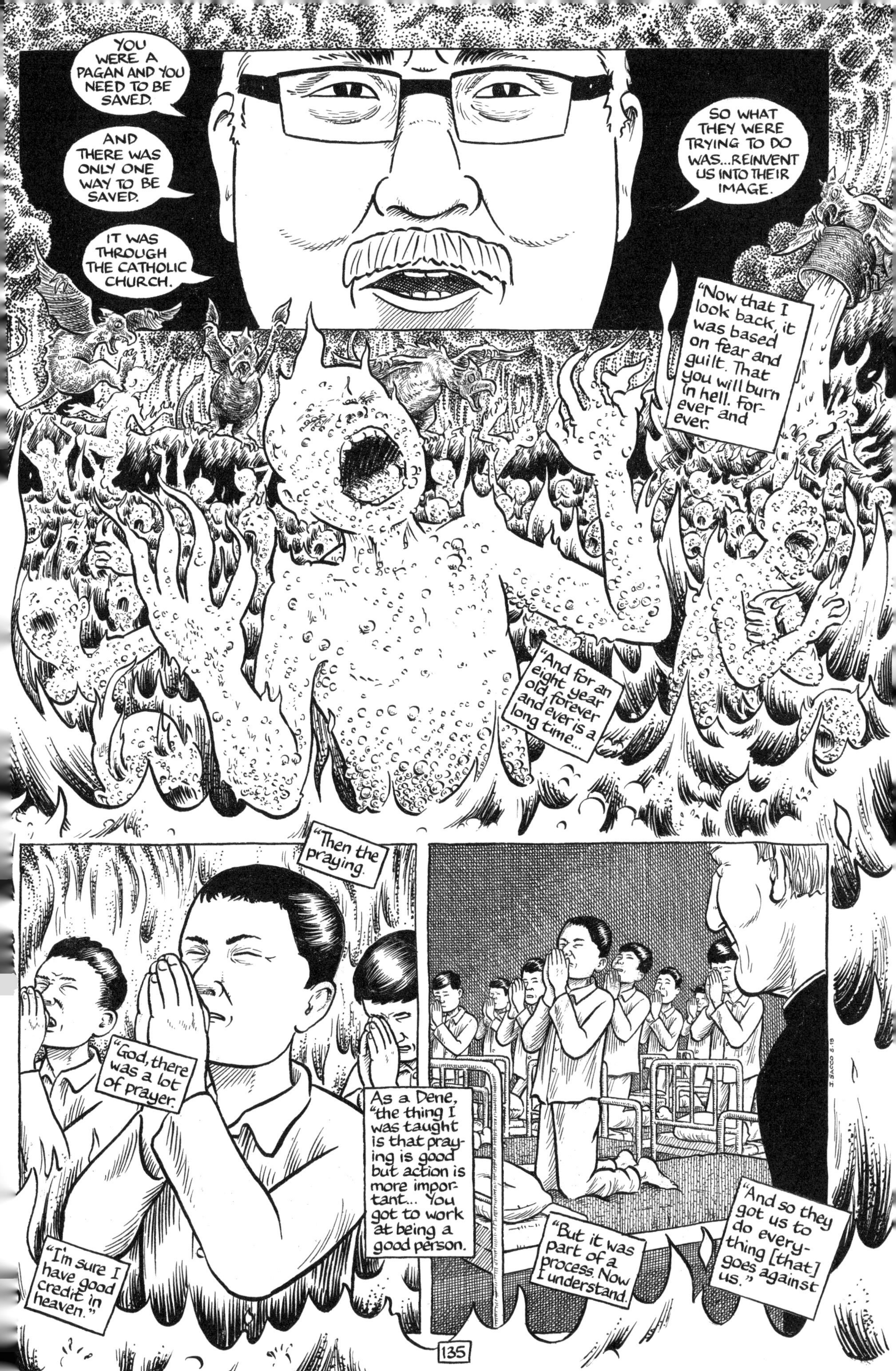
YOU WERE A PAGAN AND YOU NEED TO BE SAVED.
AND THERE WAS ONLY ONE WAY TO BE SAVED.
IT WAS THROUGH THE CATHOLIC CHURCH.
SO WHAT THEY WERE TRYING TO DO WAS...REINVENT US INTO THEIR IMAGE.
"Now that I look back, it was based on fear and guilt. That you will burn in hell. For-ever and ever.
"And for an eight year old, forever and ever is a long time...
"Then the praying.
"God, there was a lot of prayer.
As a Dene, "the thing I was taught is that pray-ing is good but action is more impor-tant... You got to work at being a good person.
"I'm sure I have good credit in heaven."
"But it was part of a process. Now I understand.
"And so they got us to do every-thing [that] goes against us."
J. SACCO 5.19

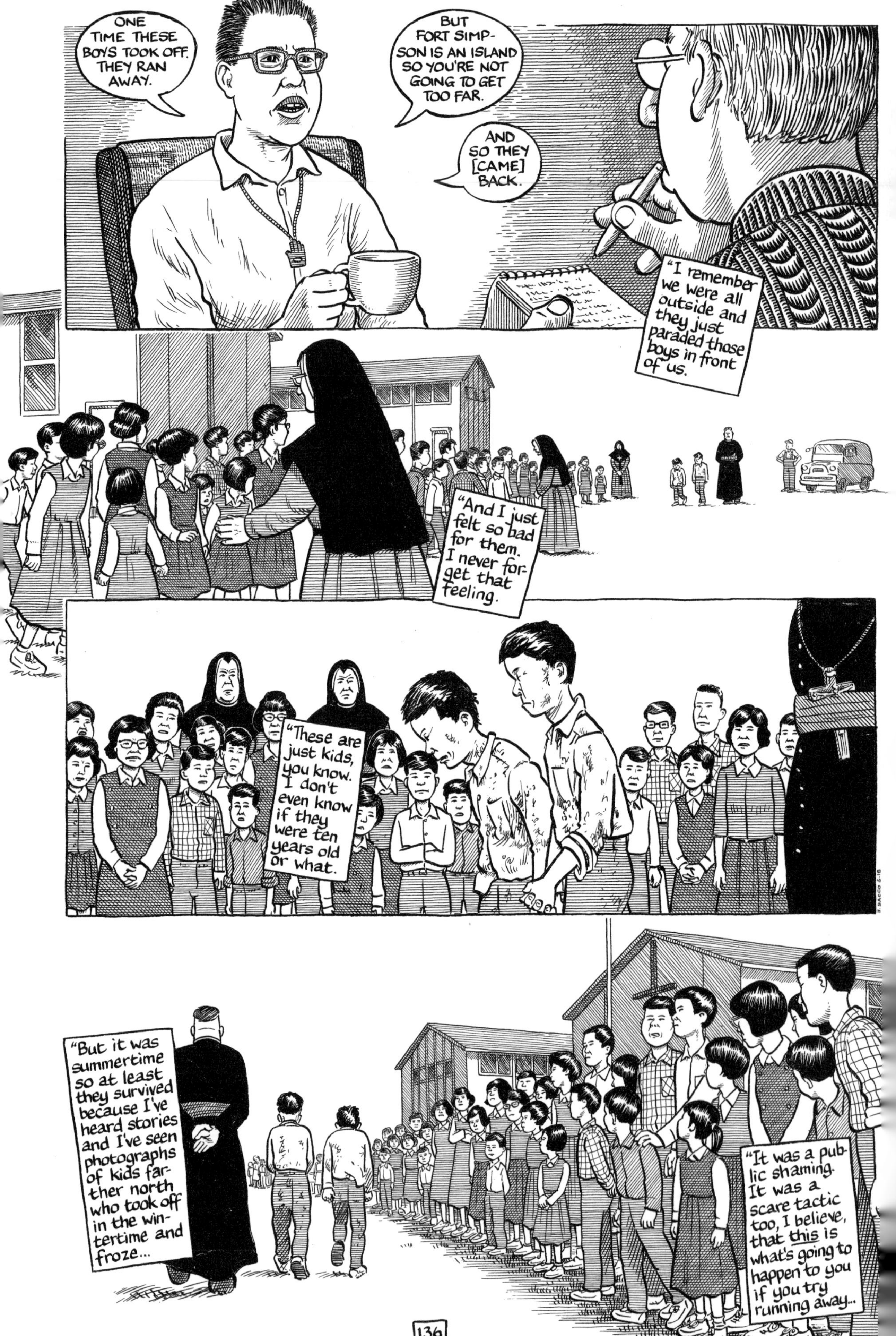
ONE TIME THESE BOYS TOOK OFF. THEY RAN AWAY.
BUT FORT SIMPSON IS AN ISLAND SO YOU'RE NOT GOING TO GET TOO FAR.
AND SO THEY [CAME] BACK.
"I remember we were all outside and they just paraded those boys in front of us.
"And I just felt so bad for them. I never forget that feeling.
"These are just kids, you know. I don't even know if they were ten years old or what.
"But it was summertime so at least they survived because I've heard stories and I've seen photographs of kids farther north who took off in the wintertime and froze...
"It was a public shaming. It was a scare tactic too, I believe, that this is what's going to happen to you if you try running away...

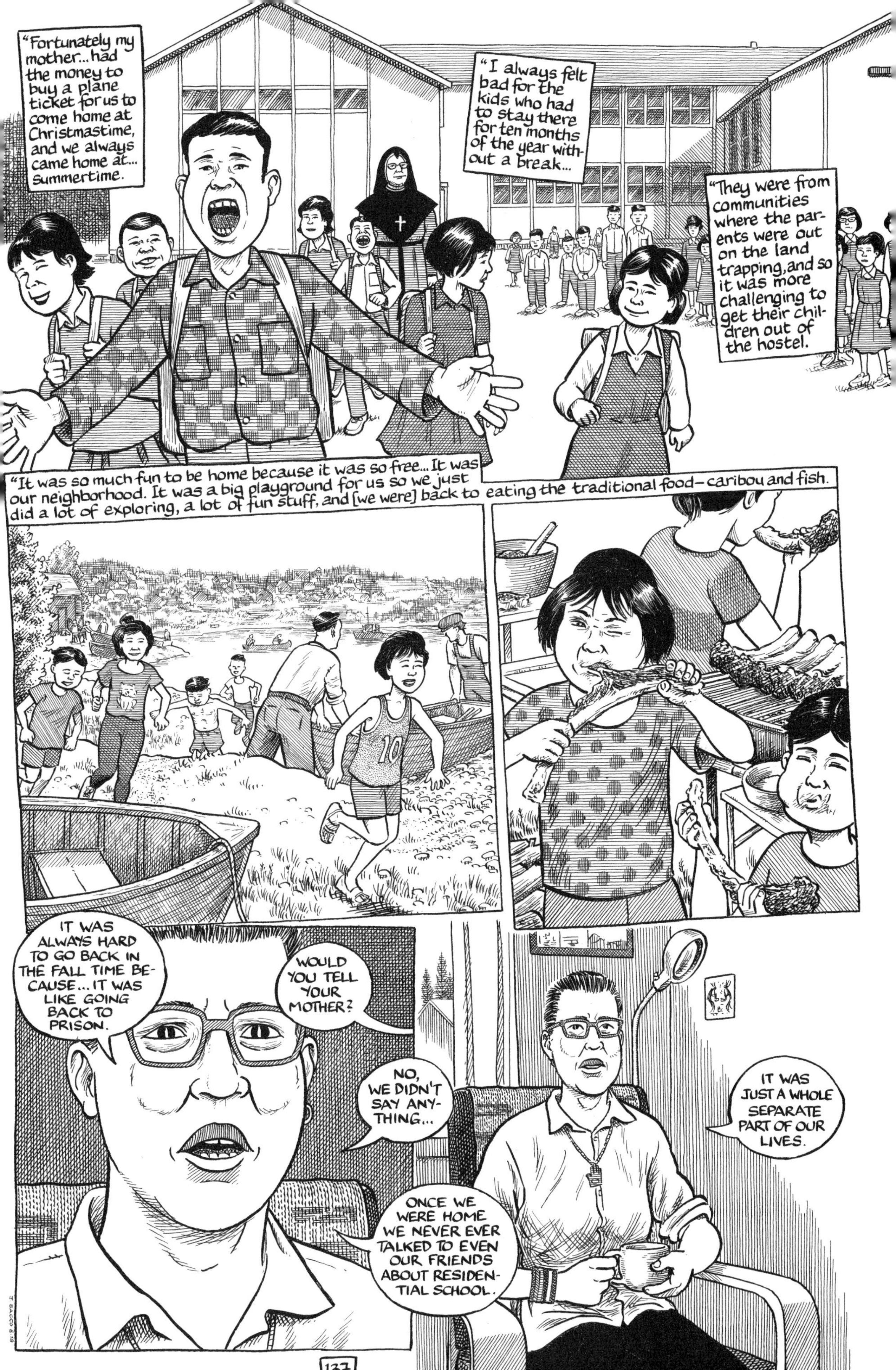
"Fortunately my mother...had the money to buy a plane ticket for us to come home at Christmastime, and we always came home at... summertime.
"I always felt bad for the kids who had to stay there for ten months of the year without a break...
"They were from communities where the parents were out on the land trapping, and so it was more challenging to get their children out of the hostel.
"It was so much fun to be home because it was so free... It was our neighborhood. It was a big playground for us so we just did a lot of exploring, a lot of fun stuff, and [we were] back to eating the traditional food—caribou and fish.
IT WAS ALWAYS HARD TO GO BACK IN THE FALL TIME BECAUSE... IT WAS LIKE GOING BACK TO PRISON.
WOULD YOU TELL YOUR MOTHER?
NO, WE DIDN'T SAY ANYTHING...
IT WAS JUST A WHOLE SEPARATE PART OF OUR LIVES.
ONCE WE WERE HOME WE NEVER EVER TALKED TO EVEN OUR FRIENDS ABOUT RESIDENTIAL SCHOOL.

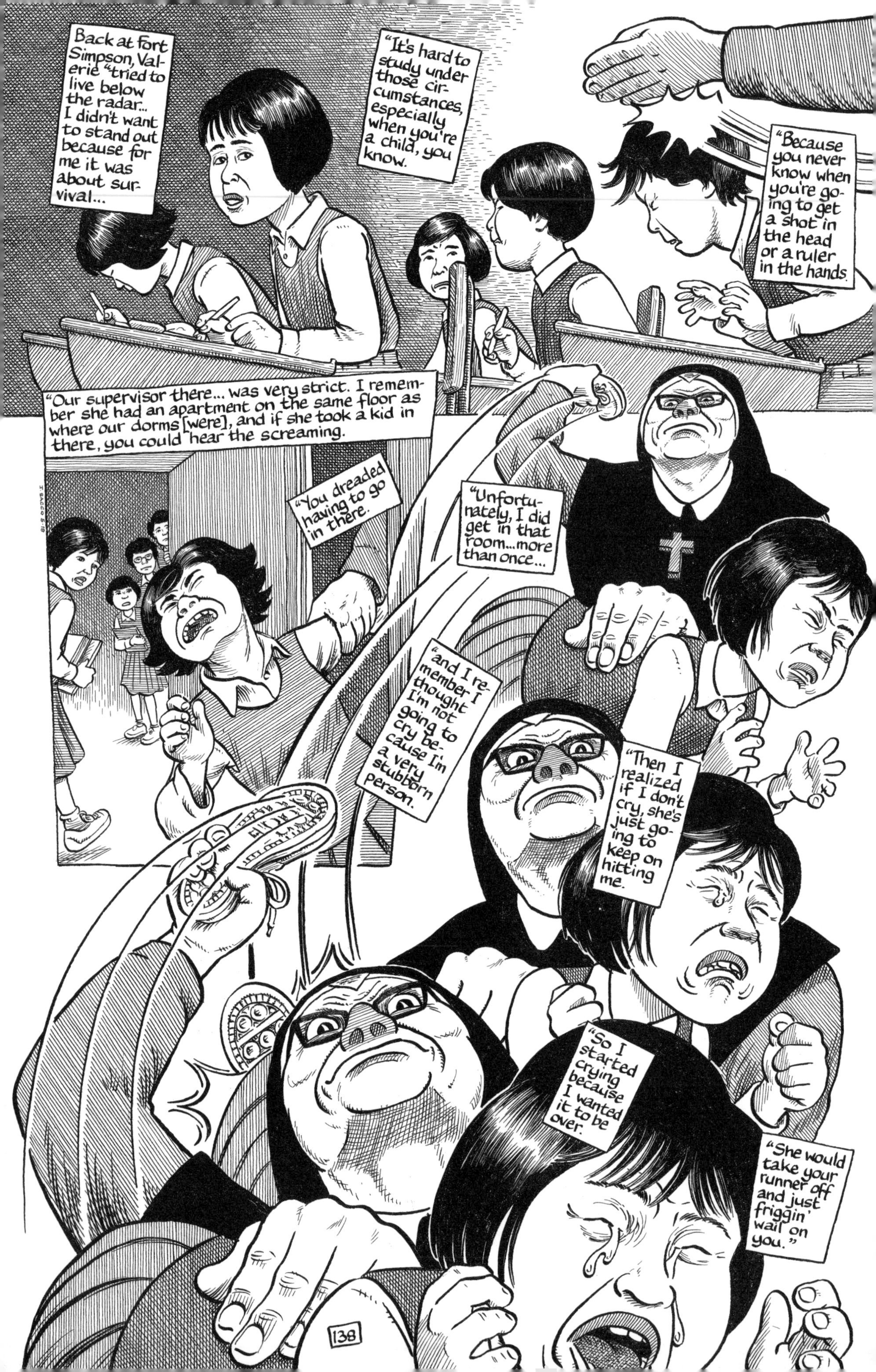
Back at Fort Simpson, Valerie "tried to live below the radar... I didn't want to stand out because for me it was about survival...
"It's hard to study under those circumstances, especially when you're a child, you know.
"Because you never know when you're going to get a shot in the head or a ruler in the hands.
"Our supervisor there... was very strict. I remember she had an apartment on the same floor as where our dorms [were], and if she took a kid in there, you could hear the screaming.
"You dreaded having to go in there.
"Unfortunately, I did get in that room...more than once...
"and I remember I thought I'm not going to cry because I'm a very stubborn person.
"Then I realized if I don't cry, she's just going to keep on hitting me.
"So I started crying because I wanted it to be over.
"She would take your runner off and just friggin' wail on you."

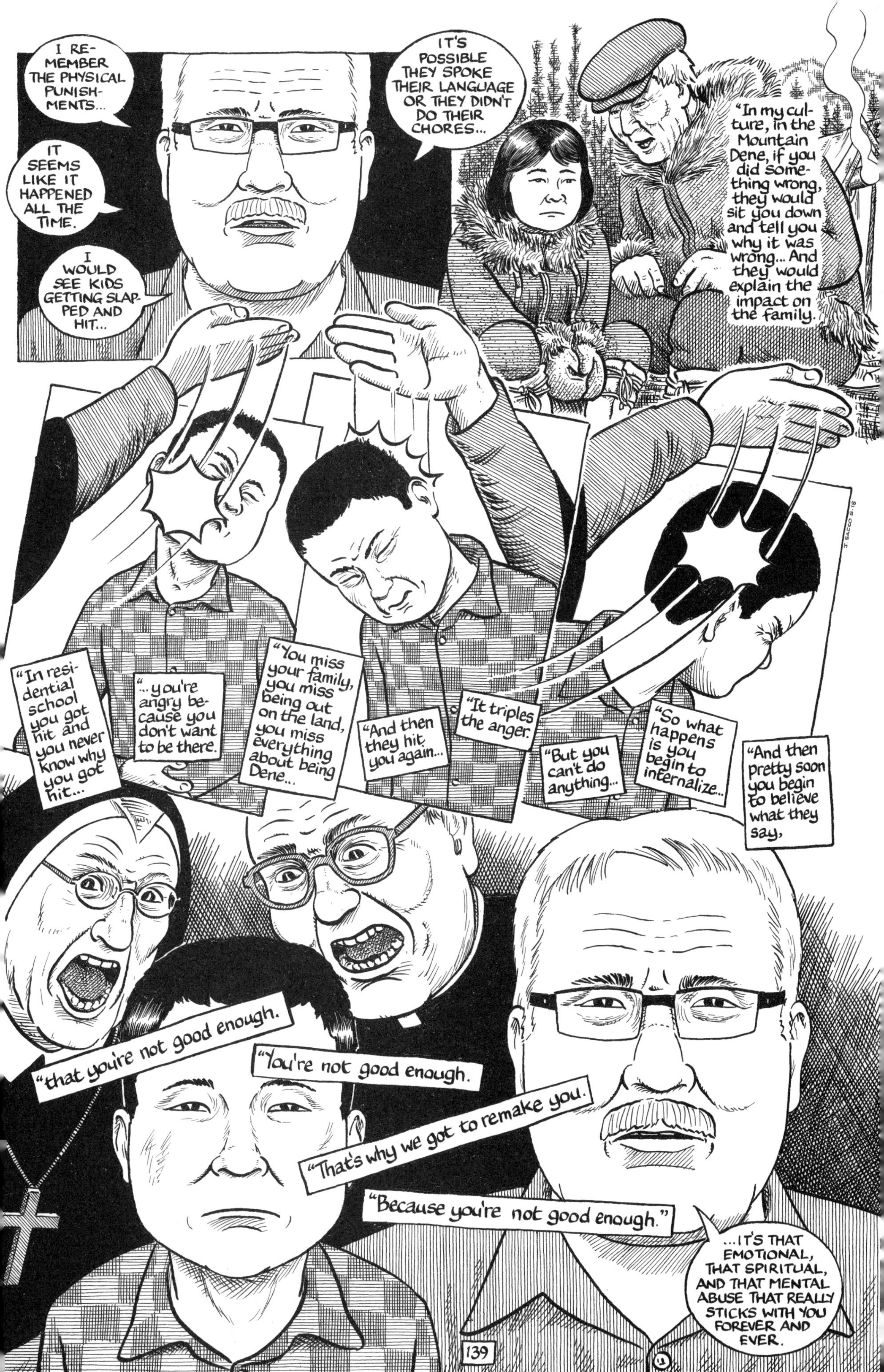

I RE-MEMBER THE PHYSICAL PUNISH-MENTS...
IT SEEMS LIKE IT HAPPENED ALL THE TIME.
I WOULD SEE KIDS GETTING SLAP-PED AND HIT...
IT'S POSSIBLE THEY SPOKE THEIR LANGUAGE OR THEY DIDN'T DO THEIR CHORES...
"In my culture, in the Mountain Dene, if you did something wrong, they would sit you down and tell you why it was wrong... And they would explain the impact on the family.
"In residential school you got hit and you never know why you got hit...
"...you're angry because you don't want to be there.
"You miss your family, you miss being out on the land, you miss everything about being Dene...
"And then they hit you again...
"It triples the anger.
"But you can't do anything...
"So what happens is you begin to internalize...
"And then pretty soon you begin to believe what they say,
"that you're not good enough.
"You're not good enough.
"That's why we got to remake you.
"Because you're not good enough."
...IT'S THAT EMOTIONAL, THAT SPIRITUAL, AND THAT MENTAL ABUSE THAT REALLY STICKS WITH YOU FOREVER AND EVER.
J. SACCO 6.18

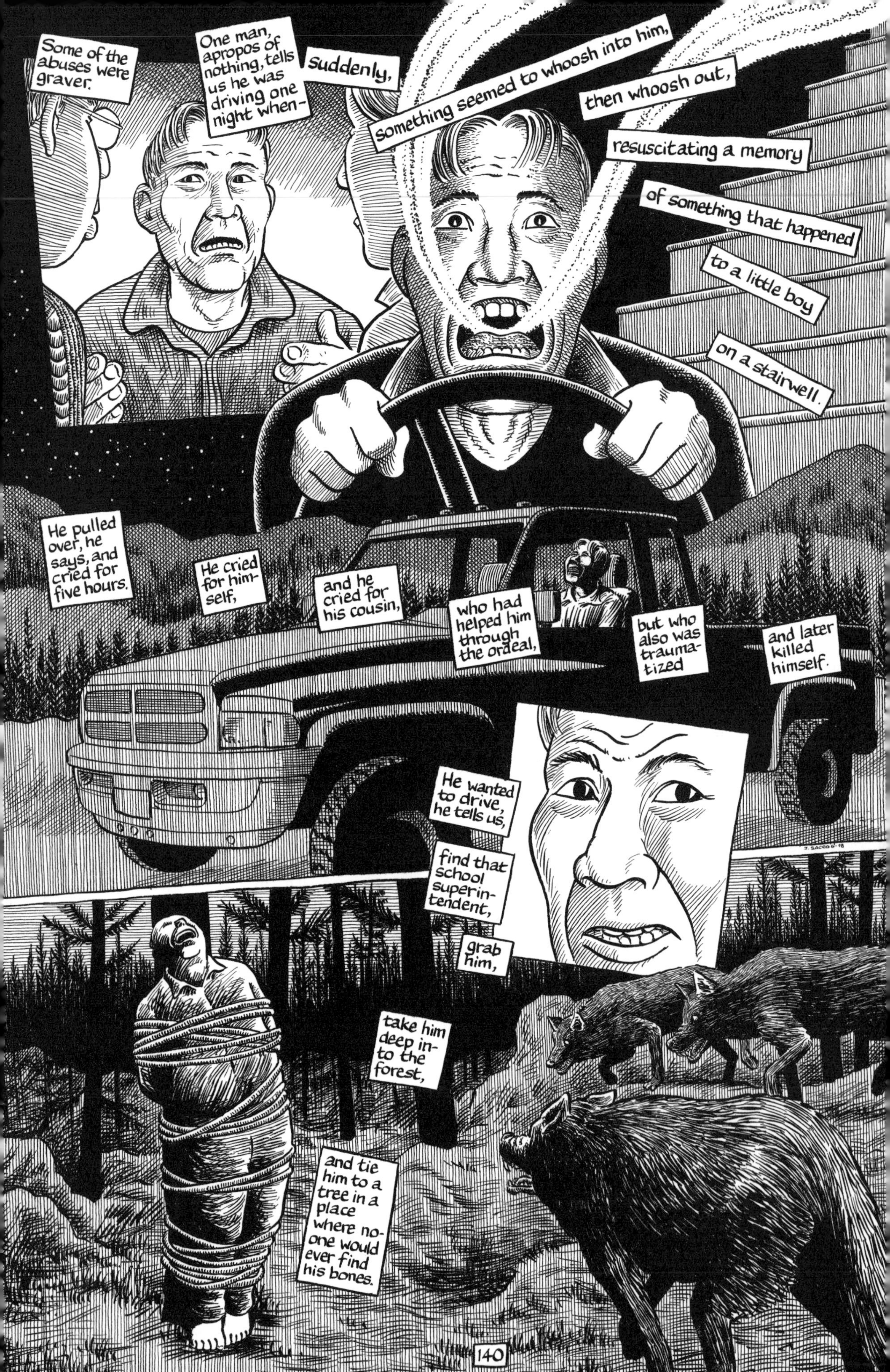
Some of the abuses were graver.
One man, apropos of nothing, tells us he was driving one night when-
suddenly,
something seemed to whoosh into him,
then whoosh out,
resuscitating a memory
of something that happened
to a little boy
on a stairwell.
He pulled over, he says, and cried for five hours.
He cried for him-self,
and he cried for his cousin,
who had helped him through the ordeal,
but who also was trauma-tized
and later killed himself.
He wanted to drive, he tells us,
find that school superin-tendent,
grab him,
take him deep in-to the forest,
and tie him to a tree in a place where no-one would ever find his bones.

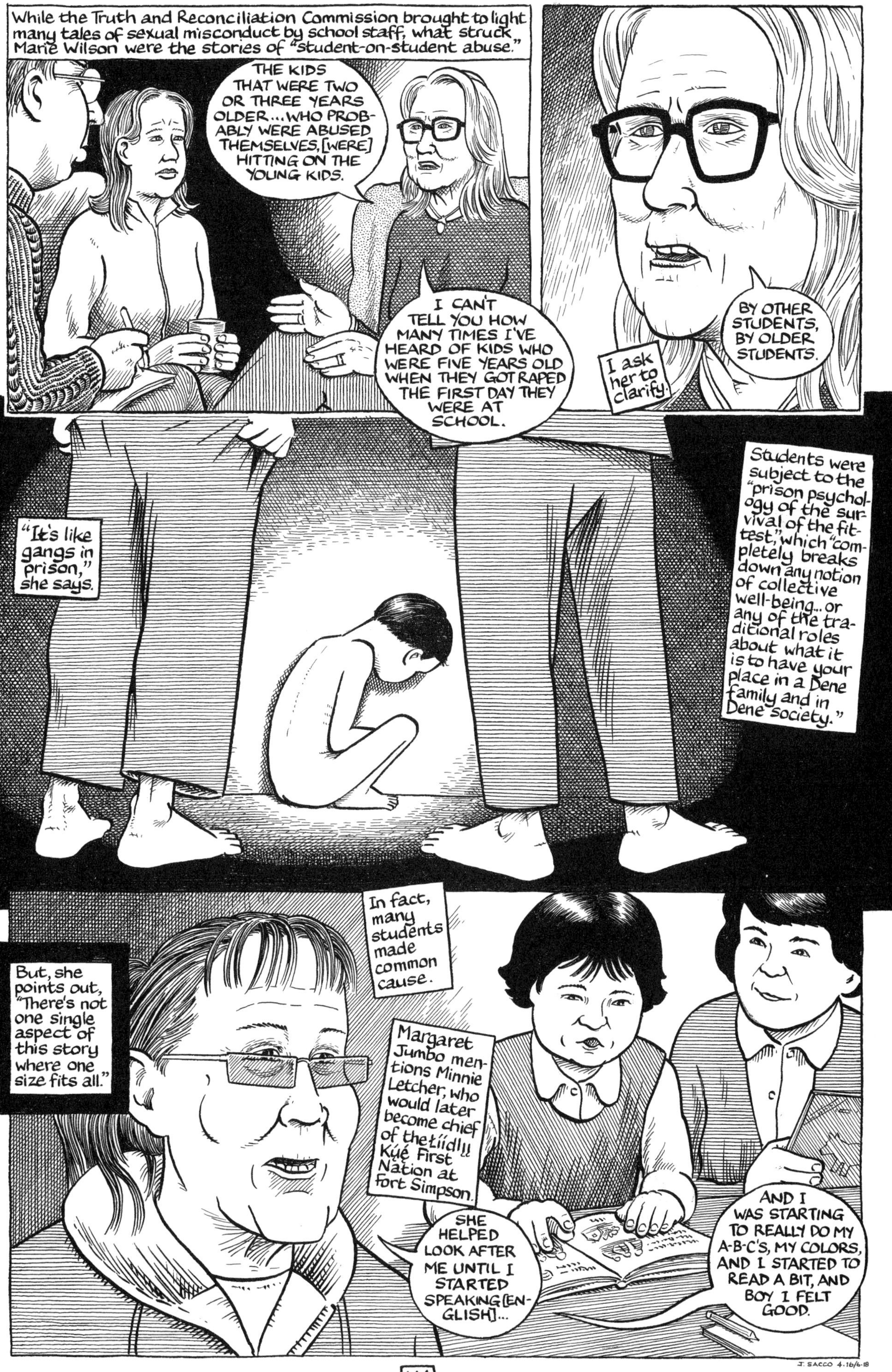

While the Truth and Reconciliation Commission brought to light many tales of sexual misconduct by school staff, what struck Marie Wilson were the stories of "student-on-student abuse."
THE KIDS THAT WERE TWO OR THREE YEARS OLDER... WHO PROBABLY WERE ABUSED THEMSELVES, [WERE] HITTING ON THE YOUNG KIDS.
I CAN'T TELL YOU HOW MANY TIMES I'VE HEARD OF KIDS WHO WERE FIVE YEARS OLD WHEN THEY GOT RAPED THE FIRST DAY THEY WERE AT SCHOOL.
I ask her to clarify.
BY OTHER STUDENTS, BY OLDER STUDENTS.
"It's like gangs in prison," she says.
Students were subject to the "prison psychology of the survival of the fittest," which "completely breaks down any notion of collective well-being... or any of the traditional roles about what it is to have your place in a Dene family and in Dene society."
But, she points out, "There's not one single aspect of this story where one size fits all."
In fact, many students made common cause.
Margaret Jumbo mentions Minnie Letcher, who would later become chief of the Łíídlı̨ Kų́ę́ First Nation at Fort Simpson.
SHE HELPED LOOK AFTER ME UNTIL I STARTED SPEAKING [ENGLISH]...
AND I WAS STARTING TO REALLY DO MY A-B-C'S, MY COLORS, AND I STARTED TO READ A BIT, AND BOY I FELT GOOD.
J. SACCO 4.16/6.18

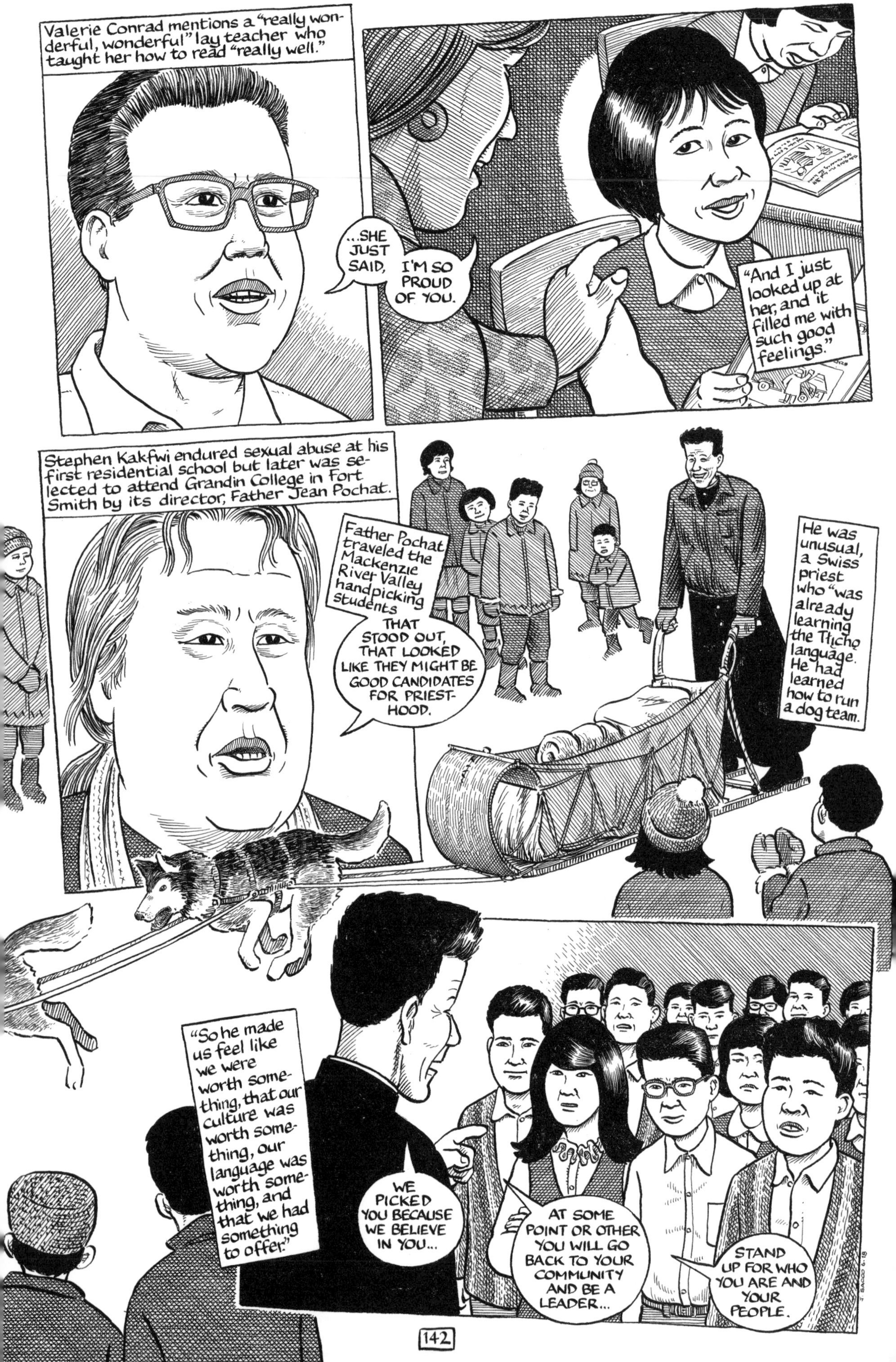

Valerie Conrad mentions a "really wonderful, wonderful" lay teacher who taught her how to read "really well."
...SHE JUST SAID,
I'M SO PROUD OF YOU.
"And I just looked up at her, and it filled me with such good feelings."
Stephen Kakfwi endured sexual abuse at his first residential school but later was selected to attend Grandin College in Fort Smith by its director, Father Jean Pochat.
Father Pochat traveled the Mackenzie River Valley handpicking students
THAT STOOD OUT, THAT LOOKED LIKE THEY MIGHT BE GOOD CANDIDATES FOR PRIESTHOOD.
He was unusual, a Swiss priest who "was already learning the Tłıchǫ language. He had learned how to run a dog team.
"So he made us feel like we were worth something, that our culture was worth something, our language was worth something, and that we had something to offer."
WE PICKED YOU BECAUSE WE BELIEVE IN YOU...
AT SOME POINT OR OTHER YOU WILL GO BACK TO YOUR COMMUNITY AND BE A LEADER...
STAND UP FOR WHO YOU ARE AND YOUR PEOPLE.

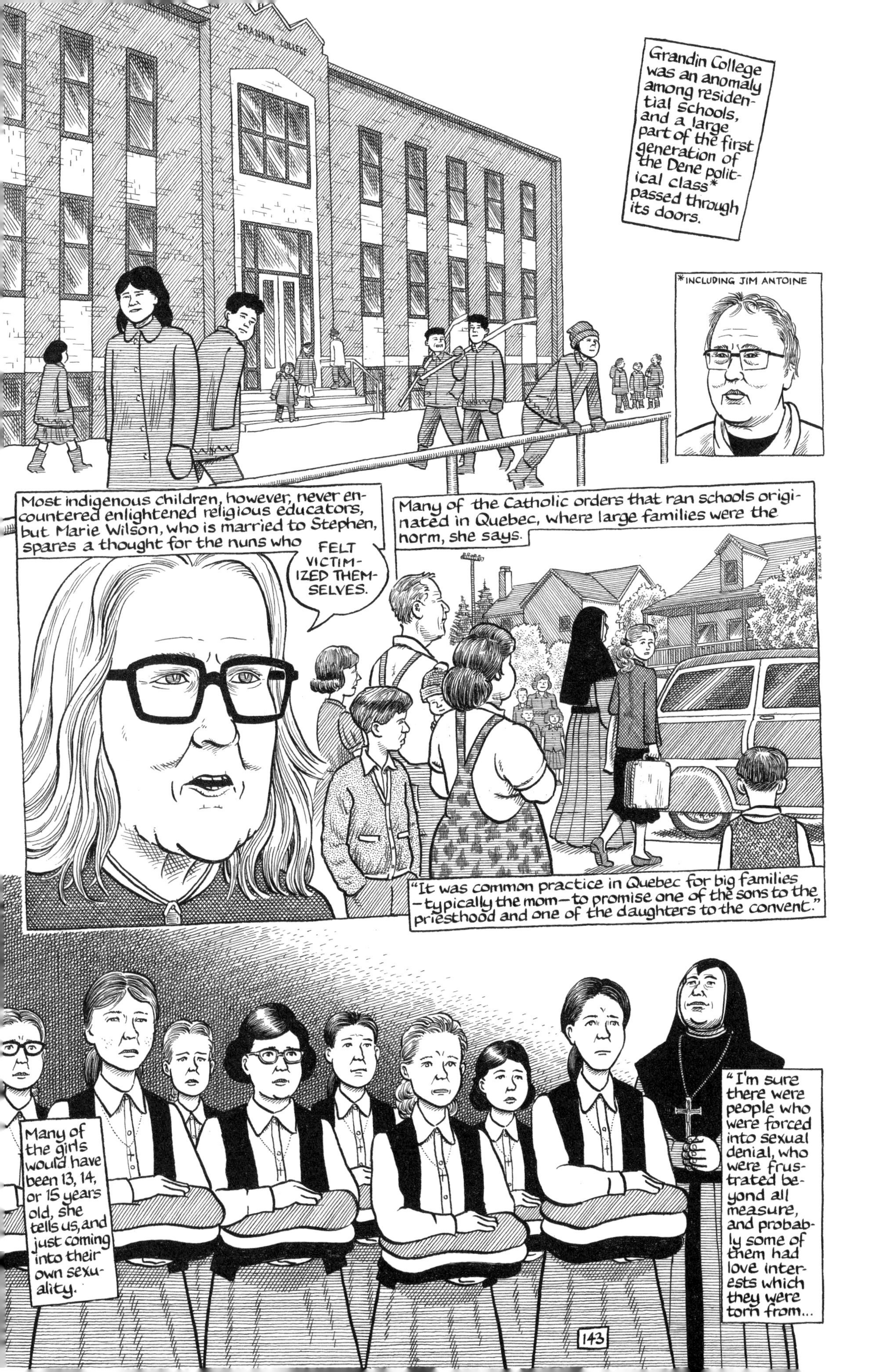
GRANDIN COLLEGE
Grandin College was an anomaly among residential schools, and a large part of the first generation of the Dene political class* passed through its doors.
*INCLUDING JIM ANTOINE
Most indigenous children, however, never encountered enlightened religious educators, but Marie Wilson, who is married to Stephen, spares a thought for the nuns who
FELT VICTIMIZED THEMSELVES.
Many of the Catholic orders that ran schools originated in Quebec, where large families were the norm, she says.
"It was common practice in Quebec for big families —typically the mom— to promise one of the sons to the priesthood and one of the daughters to the convent."
Many of the girls would have been 13, 14, or 15 years old, she tells us, and just coming into their own sexuality.
"I'm sure there were people who were forced into sexual denial, who were frustrated beyond all measure, and probably some of them had love interests which they were torn from...

"Imagine these nuns, these poor little nuns. Some of them would have been young, looking after class sizes, 50, 60 kids. You're on 24/7, 365 days a year in some isolated place.

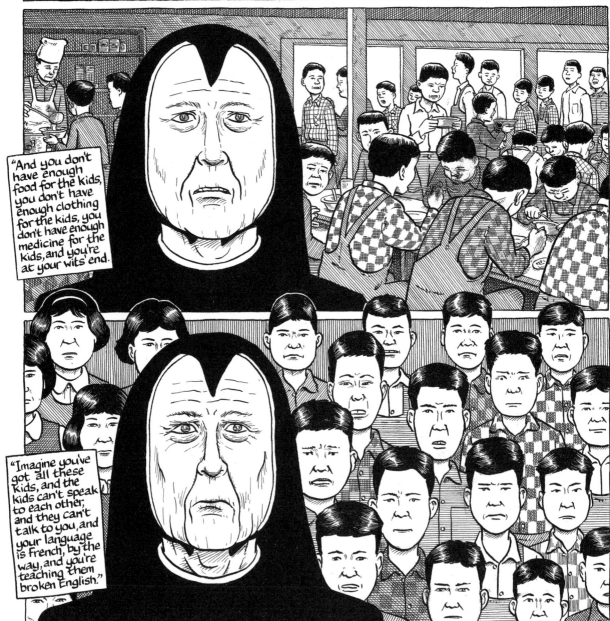

"And you don't have enough food for the kids, you don't have enough clothing for the kids, you don't have enough medicine for the kids, and you're at your wits' end.

"Imagine you've got all these kids, and the kids can't speak to each other, and they can't talk to you, and your language is French, by the way, and you're teaching them broken English."

J. SACCO 6-18

THERE'S A PART OF ME AS A GROWN WOMAN THAT HAS A HEART AS WELL FOR THOSE WOMEN WHO LOST IT...

THAT'S NOT TO SAY ANYTHING THAT HAPPENED WAS RIGHT, BUT I'M SAYING WRONG THINGS DON'T HAPPEN OUTSIDE A CONTEXT.

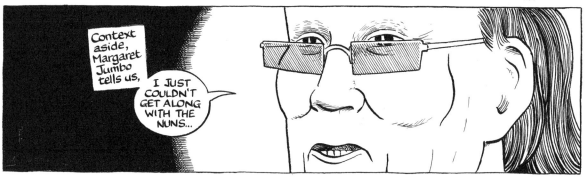

Context aside, Margaret Jumbo tells us,

I JUST COULDN'T GET ALONG WITH THE NUNS...

"I didn't like the way they treated other kids,... [saying] they're no good and that they're savage and stuff like that."

After several years, "I thought to myself, I'm not going to listen to this crap anymore.

YOU GET BACK IN HERE!

"I walked out. I didn't take nothing... I went back in the bush with my stepparents and that was it."

After their first year at school, Paul Andrew and his siblings joined their family for the summer break.

They retreated into the bush to avoid the plane when it flew in to return them to Inuvik.

145

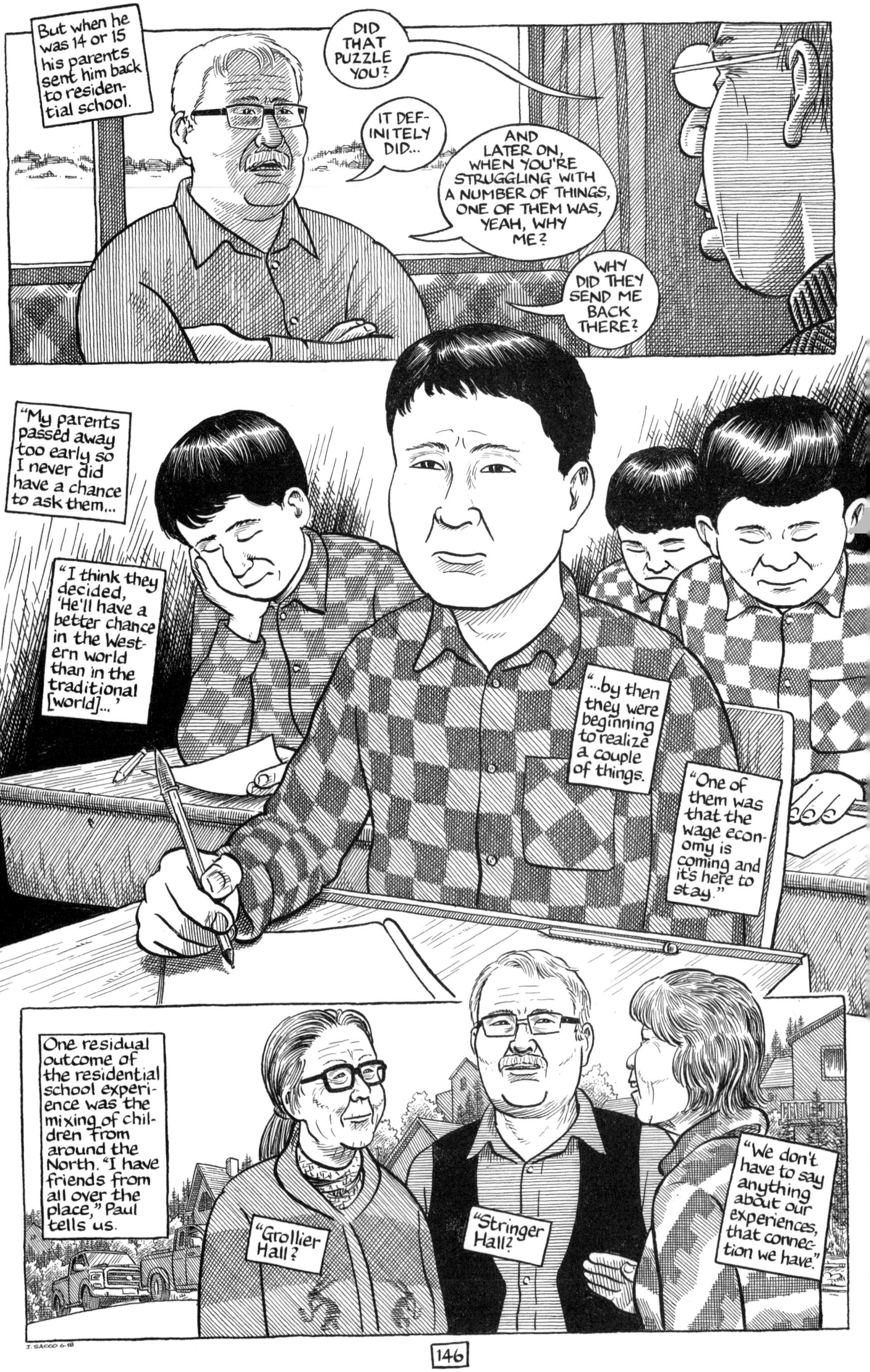

But when he was 14 or 15 his parents sent him back to residential school.
DID THAT PUZZLE YOU?
IT DEFINITELY DID...
AND LATER ON, WHEN YOU'RE STRUGGLING WITH A NUMBER OF THINGS, ONE OF THEM WAS, YEAH, WHY ME?
WHY DID THEY SEND ME BACK THERE?
"My parents passed away too early so I never did have a chance to ask them...
"I think they decided, 'He'll have a better chance in the Western world than in the traditional [world]...'
"...by then they were beginning to realize a couple of things.
"One of them was that the wage economy is coming and it's here to stay."
One residual outcome of the residential school experience was the mixing of children from around the North. "I have friends from all over the place," Paul tells us.
"Grollier Hall?
"Stringer Hall?
"We don't have to say anything about our experiences, that connection we have."
J. SACCO 6-18

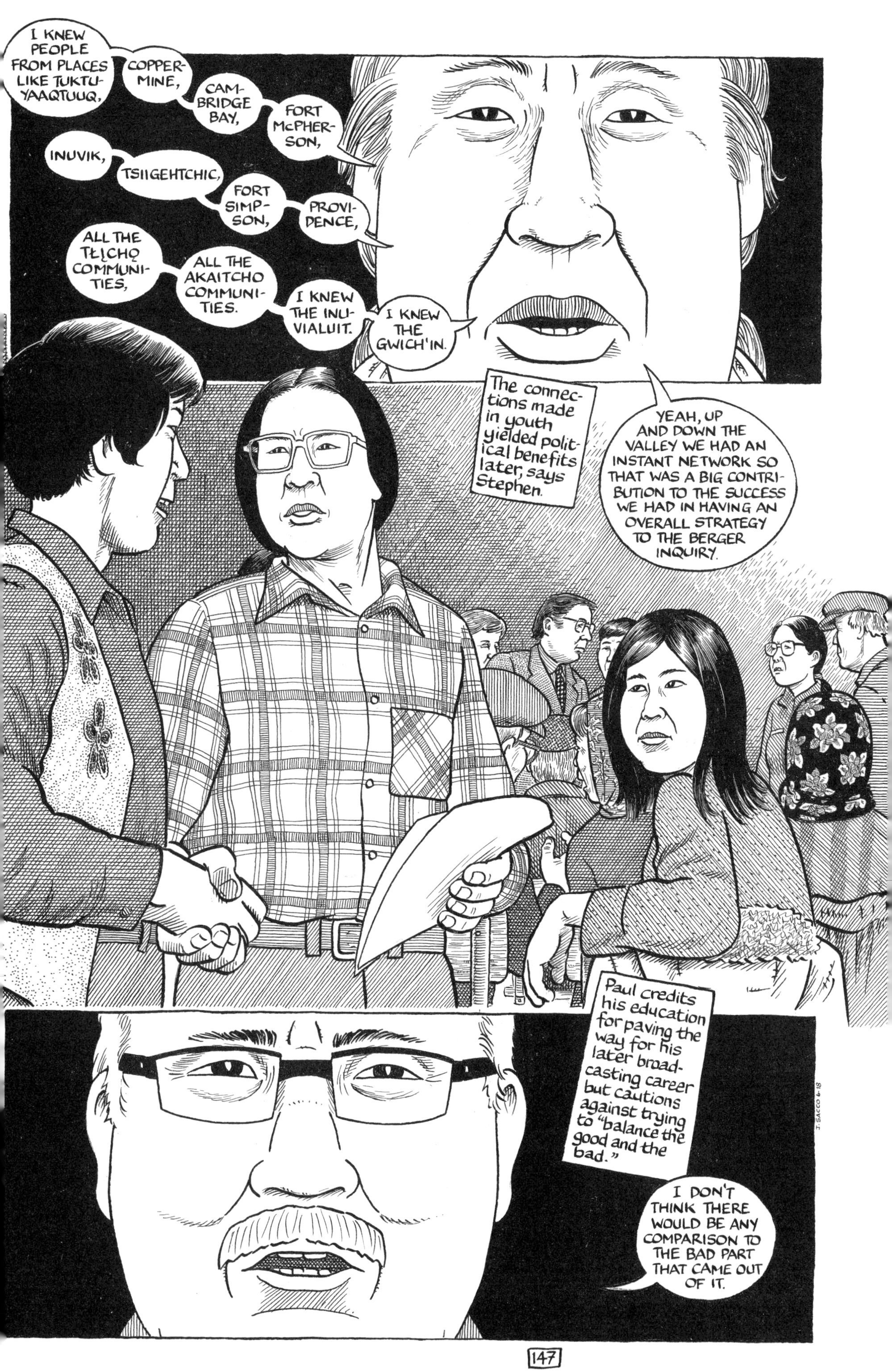
I KNEW PEOPLE FROM PLACES LIKE TUKTU-YAAQTUUQ,
COPPER-MINE,
CAM-BRIDGE BAY,
FORT McPHER-SON,
INUVIK,
TSIIGEHTCHIC,
FORT SIMP-SON,
PROVI-DENCE,
ALL THE TŁĮCHǪ COMMUNI-TIES,
ALL THE AKAITCHO COMMUNI-TIES.
I KNEW THE INU-VIALUIT.
I KNEW THE GWICH'IN.
The connec-tions made in youth yielded polit-ical benefits later, says Stephen.
YEAH, UP AND DOWN THE VALLEY WE HAD AN INSTANT NETWORK SO THAT WAS A BIG CONTRI-BUTION TO THE SUCCESS WE HAD IN HAVING AN OVERALL STRATEGY TO THE BERGER INQUIRY.
Paul credits his education for paving the way for his later broad-casting career but cautions against trying to "balance the good and the bad."
I DON'T THINK THERE WOULD BE ANY COMPARISON TO THE BAD PART THAT CAME OUT OF IT.
J. SACCO 6-18

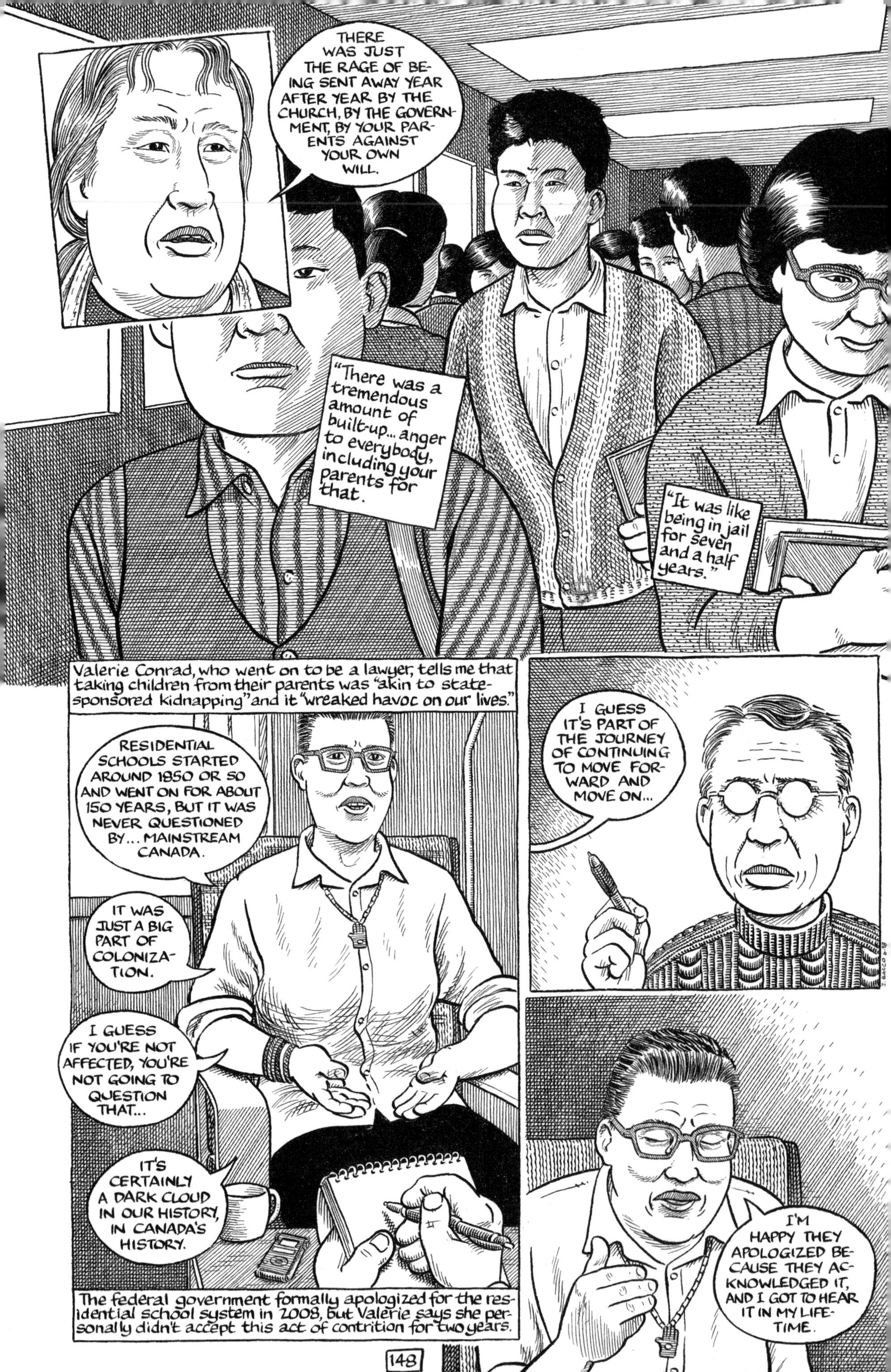
THERE WAS JUST THE RAGE OF BEING SENT AWAY YEAR AFTER YEAR BY THE CHURCH, BY THE GOVERNMENT, BY YOUR PARENTS AGAINST YOUR OWN WILL.
"There was a tremendous amount of built-up... anger to everybody, including your parents for that.
"It was like being in jail for seven and a half years."
Valerie Conrad, who went on to be a lawyer, tells me that taking children from their parents was "akin to state-sponsored kidnapping" and it "wreaked havoc on our lives."
RESIDENTIAL SCHOOLS STARTED AROUND 1850 OR SO AND WENT ON FOR ABOUT 150 YEARS, BUT IT WAS NEVER QUESTIONED BY... MAINSTREAM CANADA.
IT WAS JUST A BIG PART OF COLONIZATION.
I GUESS IF YOU'RE NOT AFFECTED, YOU'RE NOT GOING TO QUESTION THAT...
IT'S CERTAINLY A DARK CLOUD IN OUR HISTORY, IN CANADA'S HISTORY.
The federal government formally apologized for the residential school system in 2008, but Valerie says she personally didn't accept this act of contrition for two years.
I GUESS IT'S PART OF THE JOURNEY OF CONTINUING TO MOVE FORWARD AND MOVE ON...
I'M HAPPY THEY APOLOGIZED BECAUSE THEY ACKNOWLEDGED IT, AND I GOT TO HEAR IT IN MY LIFETIME.

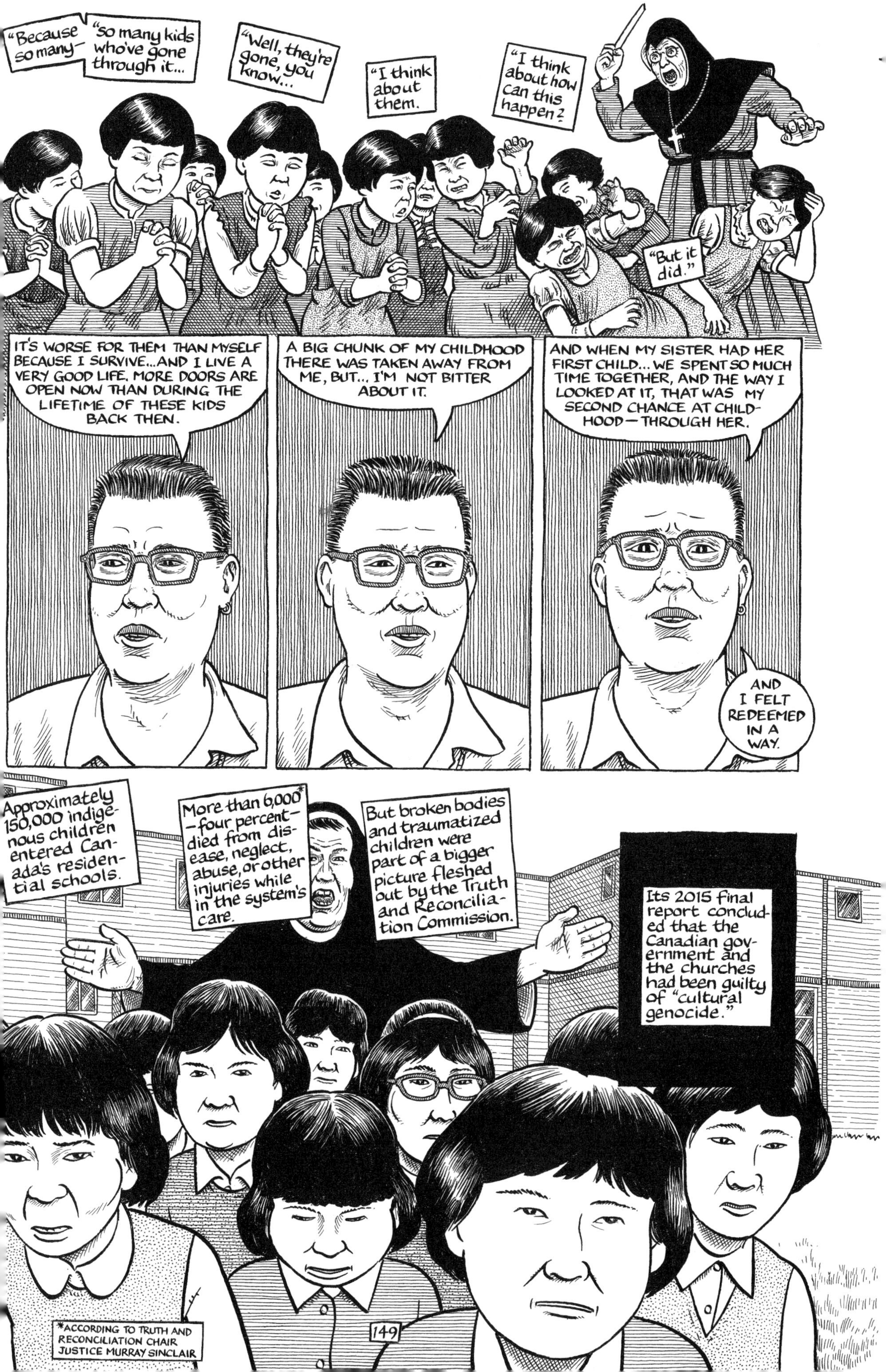
"Because so many-
"so many kids who've gone through it...
"Well, they're gone, you know...
"I think about them.
"I think about how can this happen?
"But it did."
IT'S WORSE FOR THEM THAN MYSELF BECAUSE I SURVIVE...AND I LIVE A VERY GOOD LIFE. MORE DOORS ARE OPEN NOW THAN DURING THE LIFETIME OF THESE KIDS BACK THEN.
A BIG CHUNK OF MY CHILDHOOD THERE WAS TAKEN AWAY FROM ME, BUT... I'M NOT BITTER ABOUT IT.
AND WHEN MY SISTER HAD HER FIRST CHILD... WE SPENT SO MUCH TIME TOGETHER, AND THE WAY I LOOKED AT IT, THAT WAS MY SECOND CHANCE AT CHILD-HOOD—THROUGH HER.
AND I FELT REDEEMED IN A WAY.
Approximately 150,000 indige-nous children entered Can-ada's residen-tial schools.
More than 6,000* -four percent-died from dis-ease, neglect, abuse, or other injuries while in the system's care.
But broken bodies and traumatized children were part of a bigger picture fleshed out by the Truth and Reconcilia-tion Commission.
Its 2015 final report conclud-ed that the Canadian gov-ernment and the churches had been guilty of "cultural genocide."
*ACCORDING TO TRUTH AND RECONCILIATION CHAIR JUSTICE MURRAY SINCLAIR

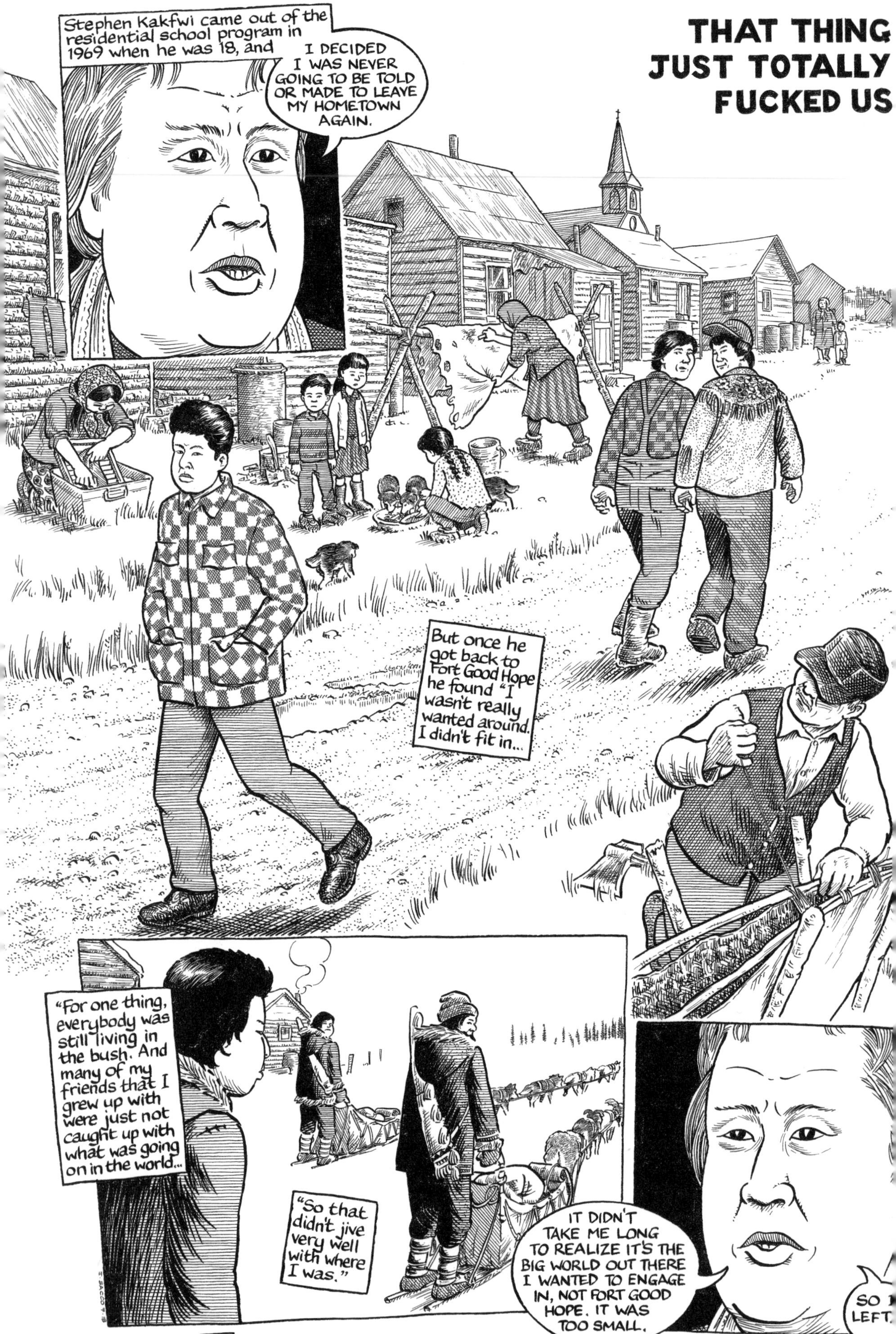
THAT THING JUST TOTALLY FUCKED US
Stephen Kakfwi came out of the residential school program in 1969 when he was 18, and
I DECIDED I WAS NEVER GOING TO BE TOLD OR MADE TO LEAVE MY HOMETOWN AGAIN.
But once he got back to Fort Good Hope he found "I wasn't really wanted around. I didn't fit in...
"For one thing, everybody was still living in the bush. And many of my friends that I grew up with were just not caught up with what was going on in the world...
"So that didn't jive very well with where I was."
IT DIDN'T TAKE ME LONG TO REALIZE IT'S THE BIG WORLD OUT THERE I WANTED TO ENGAGE IN, NOT FORT GOOD HOPE. IT WAS TOO SMALL.
SO I LEFT.

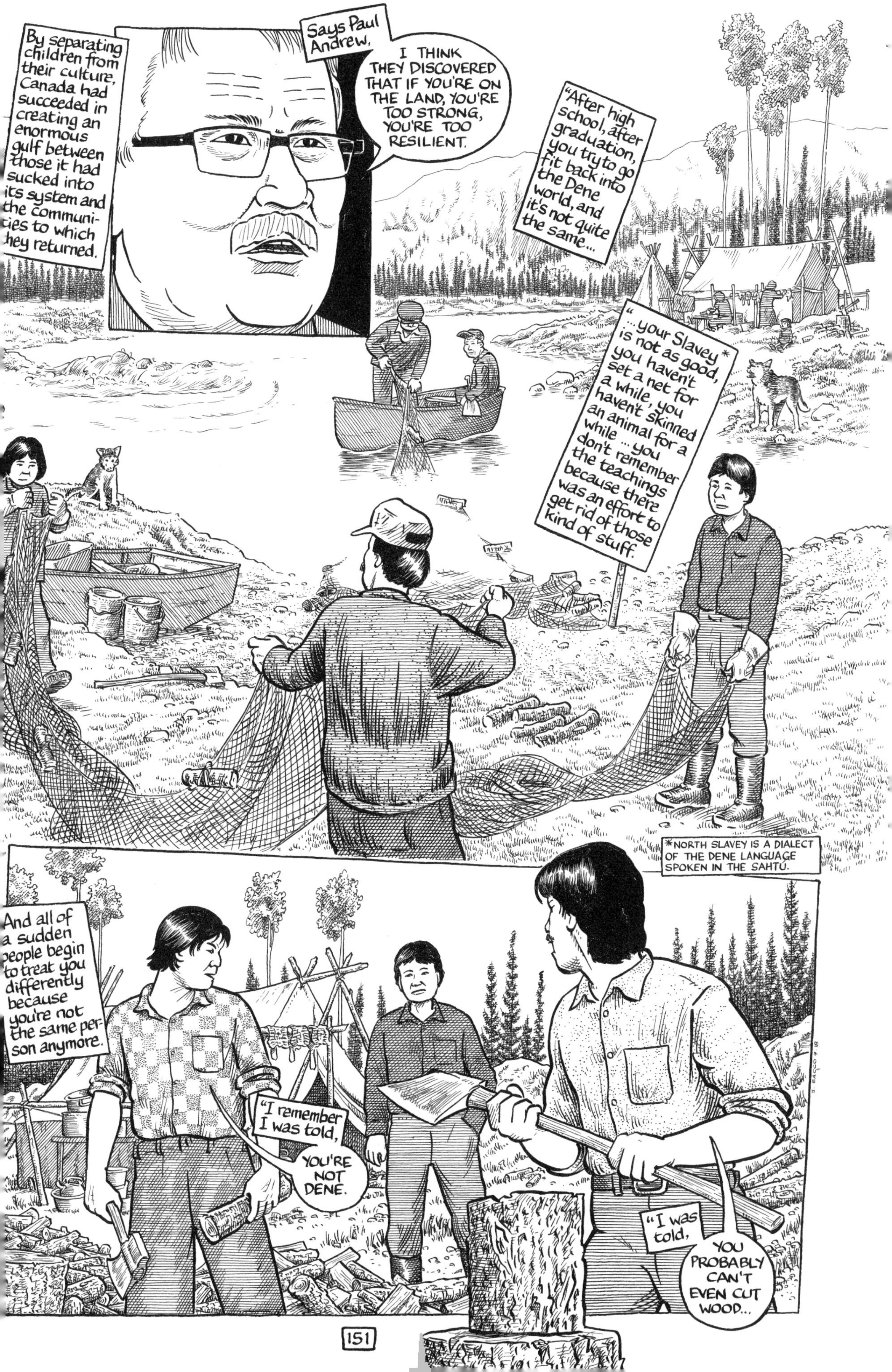

By separating children from their culture, Canada had succeeded in creating an enormous gulf between those it had sucked into its system and the communities to which they returned.
Says Paul Andrew,
I THINK THEY DISCOVERED THAT IF YOU'RE ON THE LAND, YOU'RE TOO STRONG, YOU'RE TOO RESILIENT.
"After high school, after graduation, you try to go fit back into the Dene world, and it's not quite the same...
...your Slavey* is not as good, you haven't set a net for a while, you haven't skinned an animal for a while ... you don't remember the teachings because there was an effort to get rid of those kind of stuff.
*NORTH SLAVEY IS A DIALECT OF THE DENE LANGUAGE SPOKEN IN THE SAHTÚ.
And all of a sudden people begin to treat you differently because you're not the same person anymore.
"I remember I was told,
YOU'RE NOT DENE.
"I was told,
YOU PROBABLY CAN'T EVEN CUT WOOD...

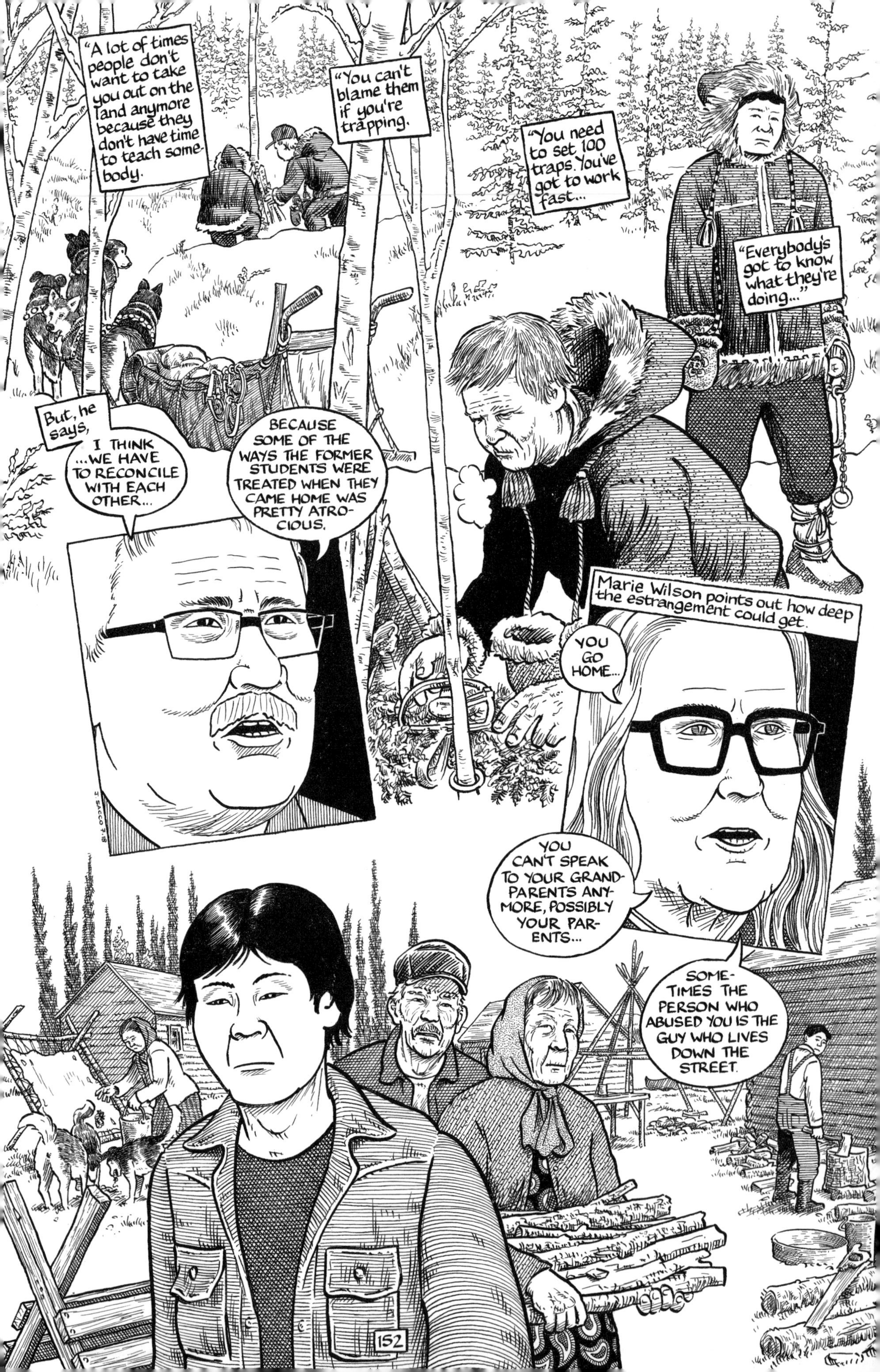
"A lot of times people don't want to take you out on the land anymore because they don't have time to teach somebody.
"You can't blame them if you're trapping.
"You need to set 100 traps. You've got to work fast...
"Everybody's got to know what they're doing..."
But, he says,
I THINK ...WE HAVE TO RECONCILE WITH EACH OTHER...
BECAUSE SOME OF THE WAYS THE FORMER STUDENTS WERE TREATED WHEN THEY CAME HOME WAS PRETTY ATROCIOUS.
Marie Wilson points out how deep the estrangement could get.
YOU GO HOME...
YOU CAN'T SPEAK TO YOUR GRANDPARENTS ANYMORE, POSSIBLY YOUR PARENTS...
SOMETIMES THE PERSON WHO ABUSED YOU IS THE GUY WHO LIVES DOWN THE STREET.

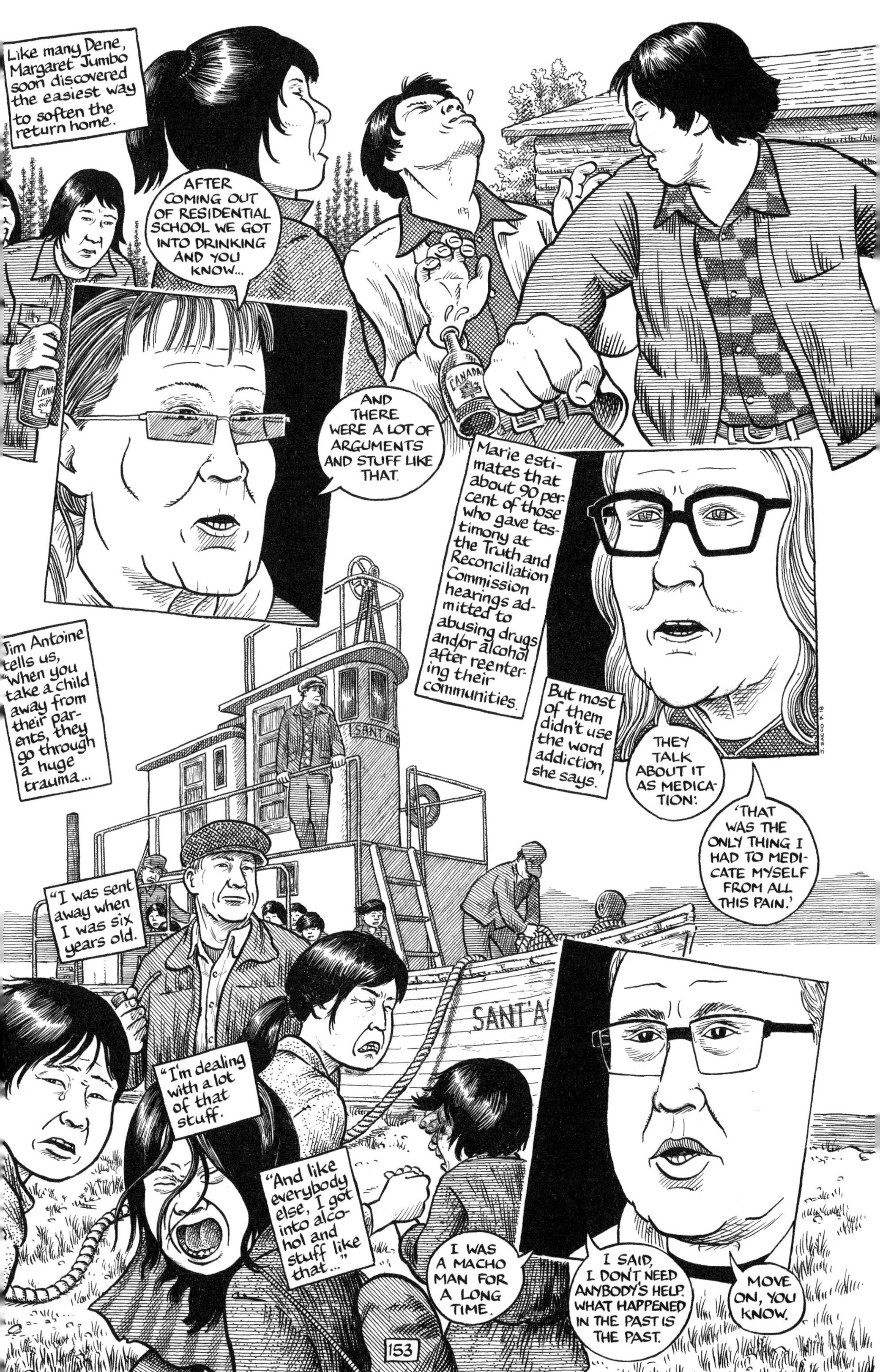
Like many Dene, Margaret Jumbo soon discovered the easiest way to soften the return home.
AFTER COMING OUT OF RESIDENTIAL SCHOOL WE GOT INTO DRINKING AND YOU KNOW...
AND THERE WERE A LOT OF ARGUMENTS AND STUFF LIKE THAT.
Marie estimates that about 90 percent of those who gave testimony at the Truth and Reconciliation Commission hearings admitted to abusing drugs and/or alcohol after reentering their communities.
But most of them didn't use the word addiction, she says.
THEY TALK ABOUT IT AS MEDICATION:
'THAT WAS THE ONLY THING I HAD TO MEDICATE MYSELF FROM ALL THIS PAIN.'
Jim Antoine tells us, "When you take a child away from their parents, they go through a huge trauma...
"I was sent away when I was six years old.
"I'm dealing with a lot of that stuff.
"And like everybody else, I got into alcohol and stuff like that..."
I WAS A MACHO MAN FOR A LONG TIME.
I SAID, I DON'T NEED ANYBODY'S HELP. WHAT HAPPENED IN THE PAST IS THE PAST.
MOVE ON, YOU KNOW.

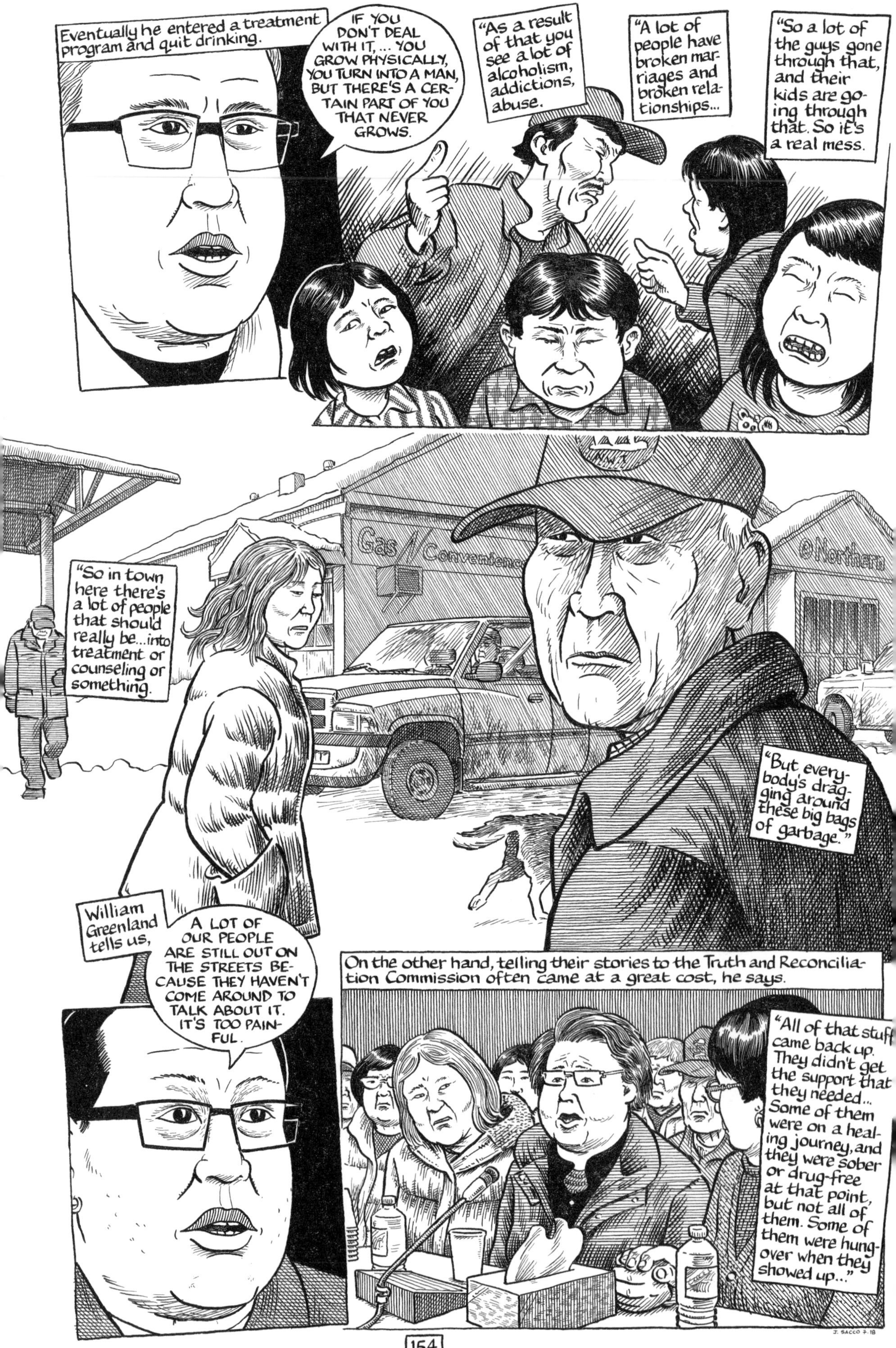
Eventually he entered a treatment program and quit drinking.
IF YOU DON'T DEAL WITH IT, ... YOU GROW PHYSICALLY, YOU TURN INTO A MAN, BUT THERE'S A CERTAIN PART OF YOU THAT NEVER GROWS.
"As a result of that you see a lot of alcoholism, addictions, abuse.
"A lot of people have broken marriages and broken relationships...
"So a lot of the guys gone through that, and their kids are going through that. So it's a real mess.
"So in town here there's a lot of people that should really be...into treatment or counseling or something.
Gas
Convenience
Northern
"But everybody's dragging around these big bags of garbage."
William Greenland tells us,
A LOT OF OUR PEOPLE ARE STILL OUT ON THE STREETS BECAUSE THEY HAVEN'T COME AROUND TO TALK ABOUT IT. IT'S TOO PAINFUL.
On the other hand, telling their stories to the Truth and Reconciliation Commission often came at a great cost, he says.
"All of that stuff came back up. They didn't get the support that they needed... Some of them were on a healing journey, and they were sober or drug-free at that point, but not all of them. Some of them were hungover when they showed up..."
J. SACCO 7.18

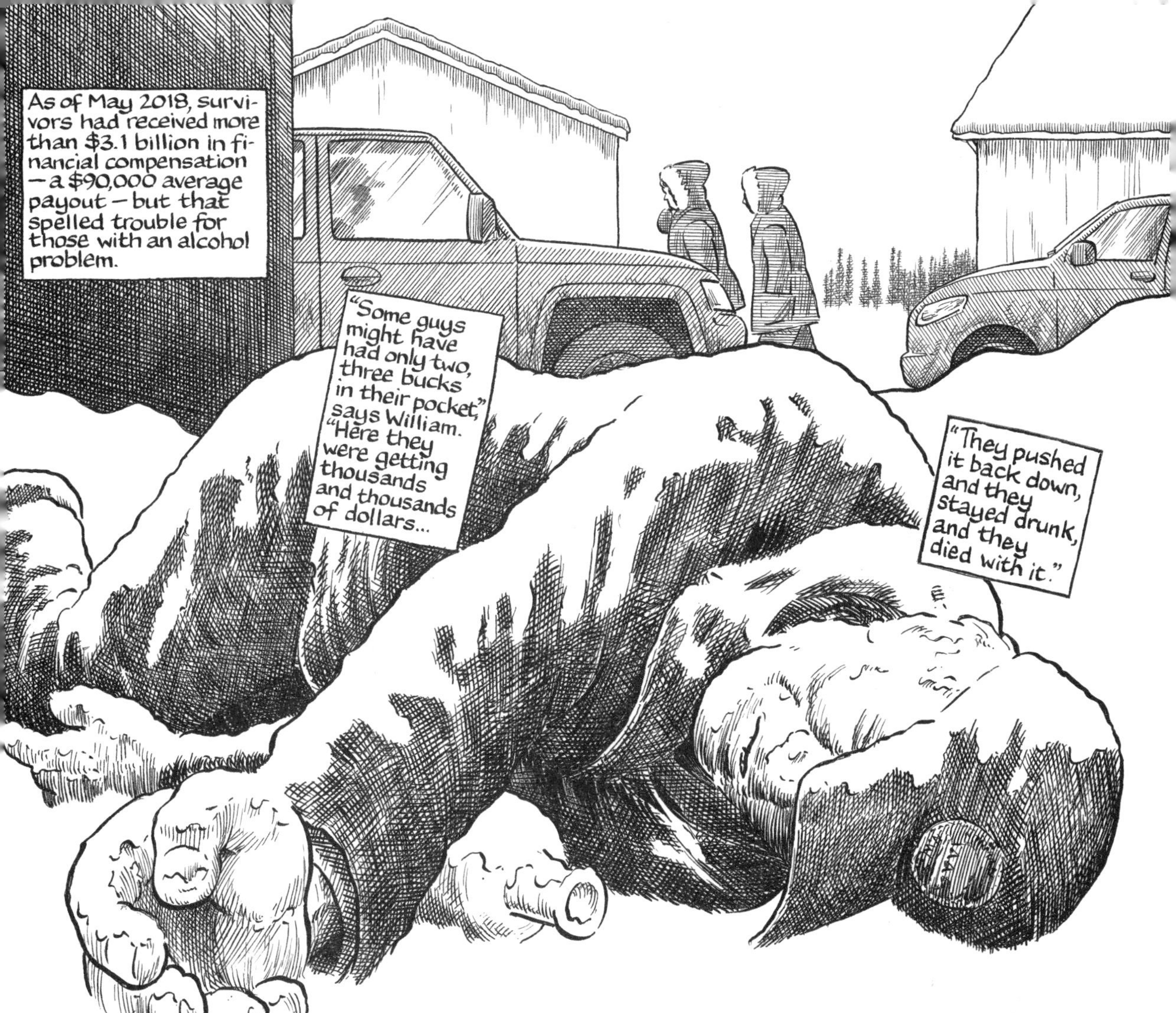

As of May 2018, survivors had received more than $3.1 billion in financial compensation—a $90,000 average payout—but that spelled trouble for those with an alcohol problem.
"Some guys might have had only two, three bucks in their pocket," says William. "Here they were getting thousands and thousands of dollars...
"They pushed it back down, and they stayed drunk, and they died with it."

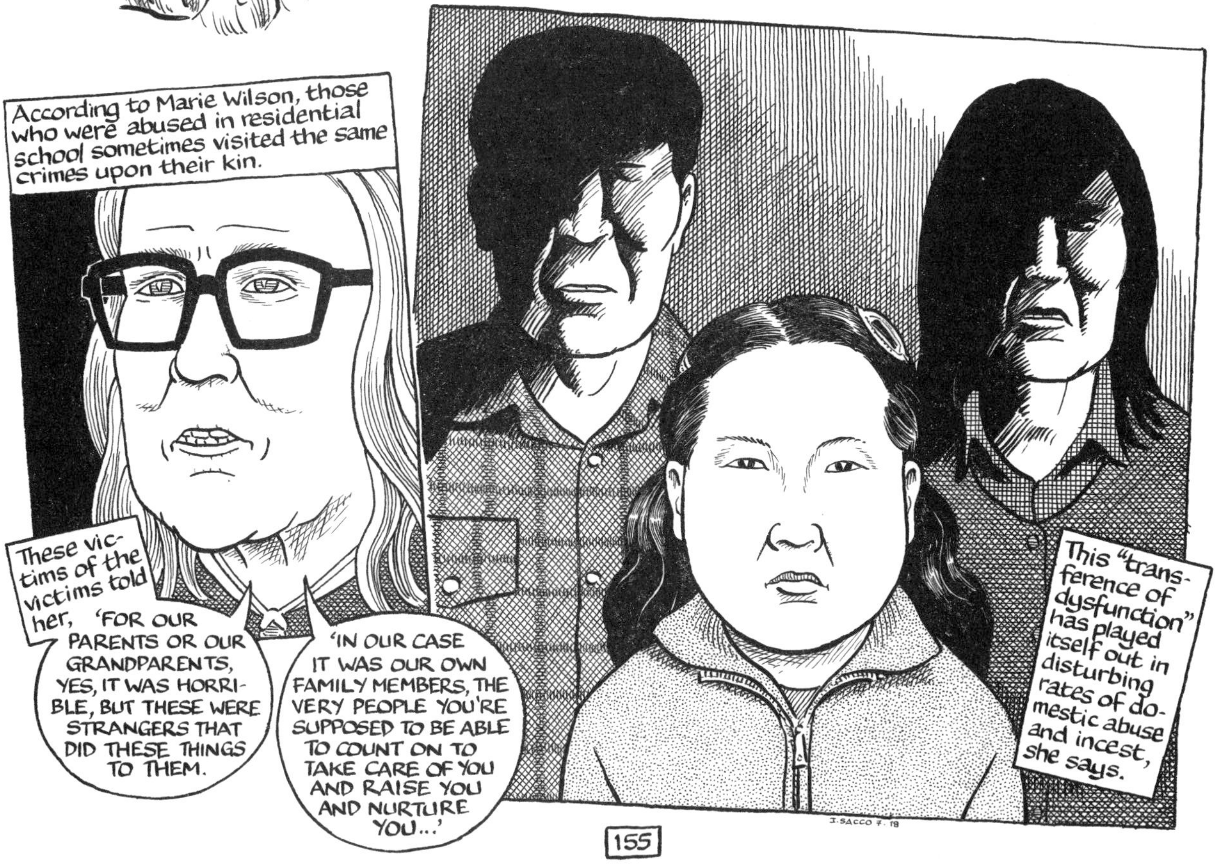

According to Marie Wilson, those who were abused in residential school sometimes visited the same crimes upon their kin.
These victims of the victims told her,
'FOR OUR PARENTS OR OUR GRANDPARENTS, YES, IT WAS HORRIBLE, BUT THESE WERE STRANGERS THAT DID THESE THINGS TO THEM.
'IN OUR CASE IT WAS OUR OWN FAMILY MEMBERS, THE VERY PEOPLE YOU'RE SUPPOSED TO BE ABLE TO COUNT ON TO TAKE CARE OF YOU AND RAISE YOU AND NURTURE YOU...'
This "transference of dysfunction" has played itself out in disturbing rates of domestic abuse and incest, she says.
J. SACCO 7.18

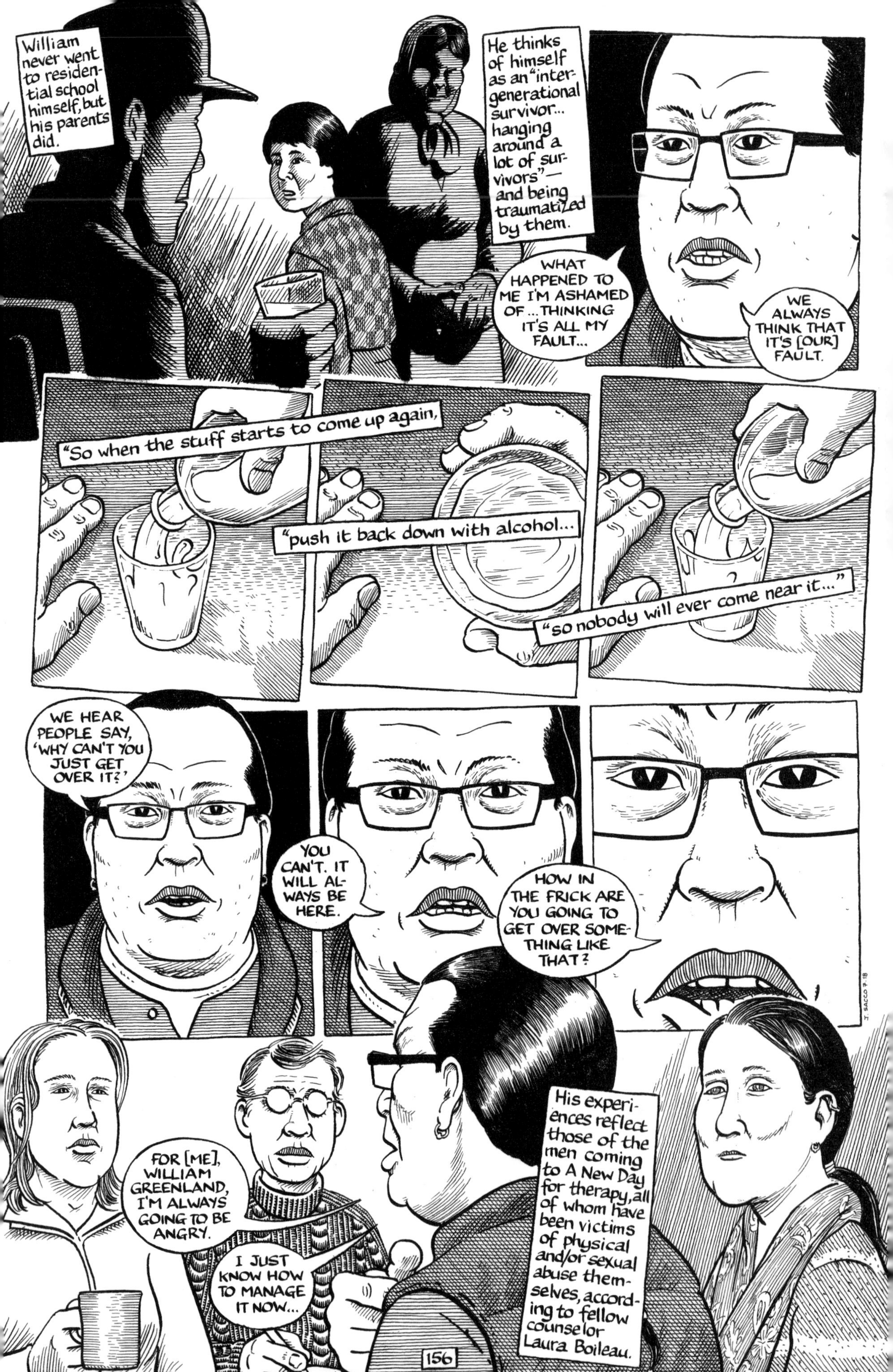
William never went to residential school himself, but his parents did.
He thinks of himself as an "intergenerational survivor... hanging around a lot of survivors"—and being traumatized by them.
WHAT HAPPENED TO ME I'M ASHAMED OF... THINKING IT'S ALL MY FAULT...
WE ALWAYS THINK THAT IT'S [OUR] FAULT.
"So when the stuff starts to come up again,
"push it back down with alcohol...
"so nobody will ever come near it..."
WE HEAR PEOPLE SAY, 'WHY CAN'T YOU JUST GET OVER IT?'
YOU CAN'T. IT WILL ALWAYS BE HERE.
HOW IN THE FRICK ARE YOU GOING TO GET OVER SOMETHING LIKE THAT?
FOR [ME], WILLIAM GREENLAND, I'M ALWAYS GOING TO BE ANGRY.
I JUST KNOW HOW TO MANAGE IT NOW...
His experiences reflect those of the men coming to A New Day for therapy, all of whom have been victims of physical and/or sexual abuse themselves, according to fellow counselor Laura Boileau.
J. SACCO 7.18

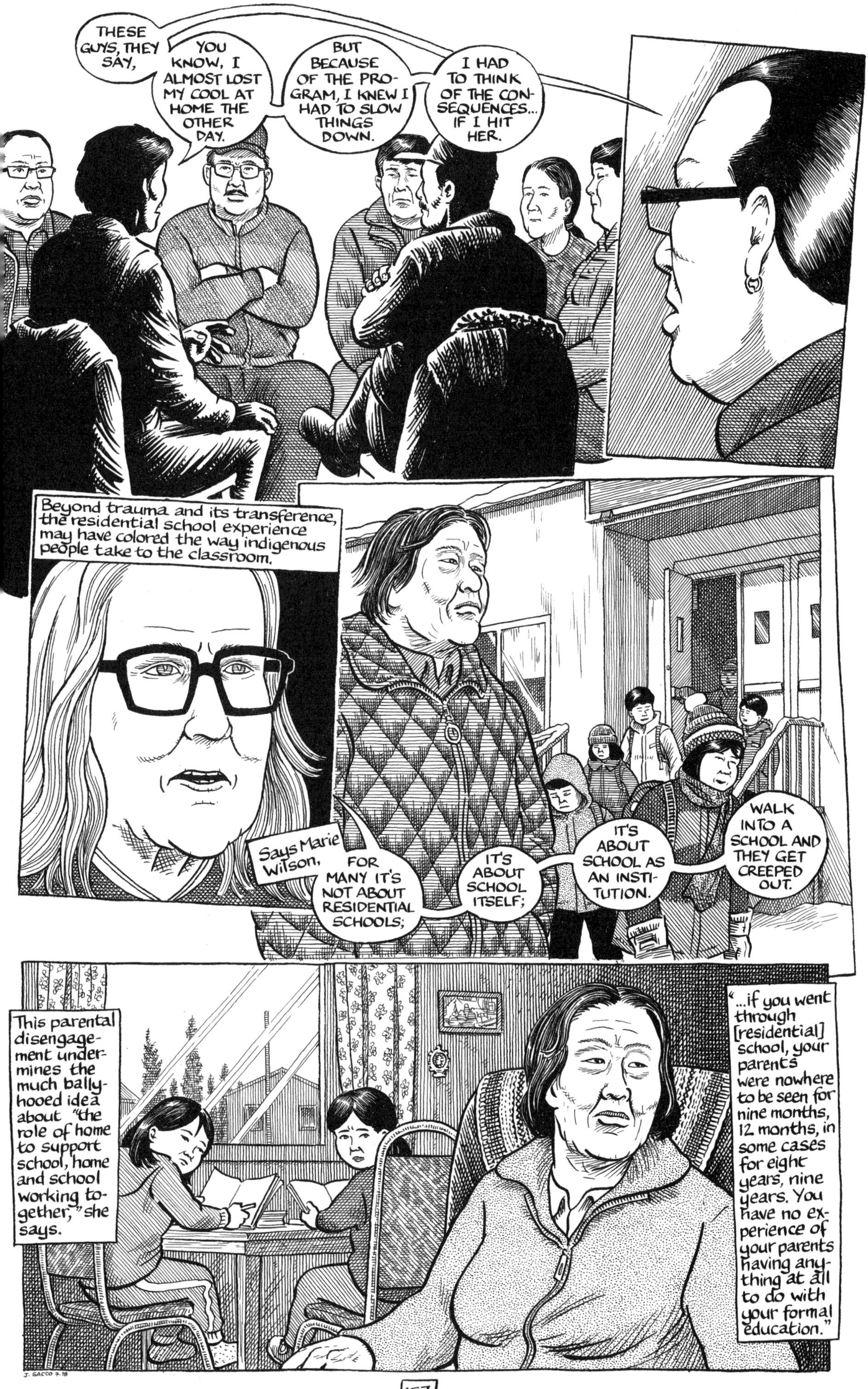
THESE GUYS, THEY SAY,
YOU KNOW, I ALMOST LOST MY COOL AT HOME THE OTHER DAY.
BUT BECAUSE OF THE PROGRAM, I KNEW I HAD TO SLOW THINGS DOWN.
I HAD TO THINK OF THE CONSEQUENCES... IF I HIT HER.
Beyond trauma and its transference, the residential school experience may have colored the way indigenous people take to the classroom.
Says Marie Wilson,
FOR MANY IT'S NOT ABOUT RESIDENTIAL SCHOOLS;
IT'S ABOUT SCHOOL ITSELF;
IT'S ABOUT SCHOOL AS AN INSTITUTION.
WALK INTO A SCHOOL AND THEY GET CREEPED OUT.
This parental disengagement undermines the much ballyhooed idea about "the role of home to support school, home and school working together," she says.
"...if you went through [residential] school, your parents were nowhere to be seen for nine months, 12 months, in some cases for eight years, nine years. You have no experience of your parents having anything at all to do with your formal education."
J. SACCO 7.18

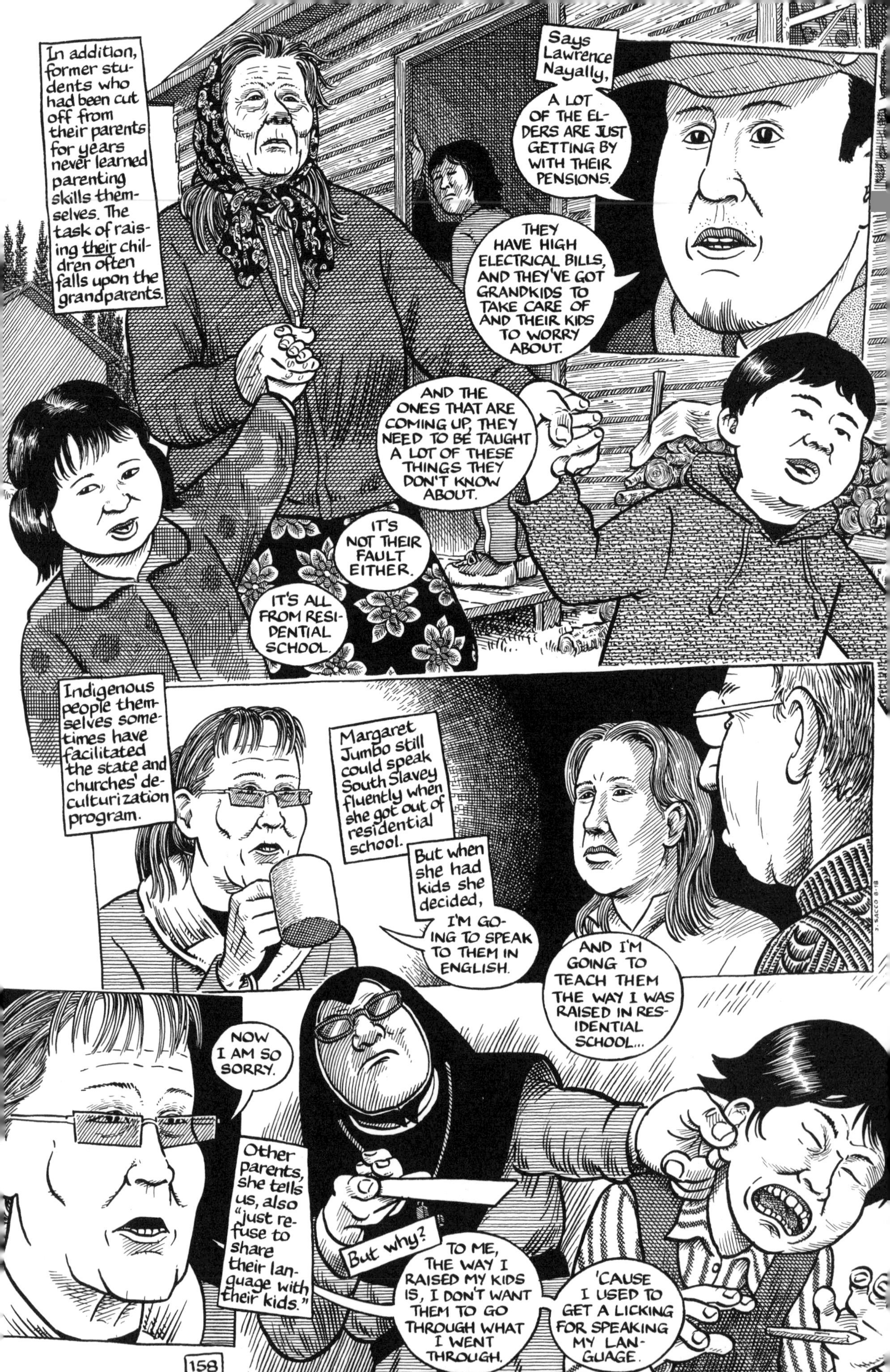

In addition, former students who had been cut off from their parents for years never learned parenting skills themselves. The task of raising their children often falls upon the grandparents.
Says Lawrence Nayally,
A LOT OF THE ELDERS ARE JUST GETTING BY WITH THEIR PENSIONS.
THEY HAVE HIGH ELECTRICAL BILLS, AND THEY'VE GOT GRANDKIDS TO TAKE CARE OF AND THEIR KIDS TO WORRY ABOUT.
AND THE ONES THAT ARE COMING UP, THEY NEED TO BE TAUGHT A LOT OF THESE THINGS THEY DON'T KNOW ABOUT.
IT'S NOT THEIR FAULT EITHER.
IT'S ALL FROM RESIDENTIAL SCHOOL.
Indigenous people themselves sometimes have facilitated the state and churches' deculturization program.
Margaret Jumbo still could speak South Slavey fluently when she got out of residential school.
But when she had kids she decided,
I'M GOING TO SPEAK TO THEM IN ENGLISH.
AND I'M GOING TO TEACH THEM THE WAY I WAS RAISED IN RESIDENTIAL SCHOOL...
NOW I AM SO SORRY.
Other parents, she tells us, also "just refuse to share their language with their kids."
But why?
TO ME, THE WAY I RAISED MY KIDS IS, I DON'T WANT THEM TO GO THROUGH WHAT I WENT THROUGH.
'CAUSE I USED TO GET A LICKING FOR SPEAKING MY LANGUAGE.

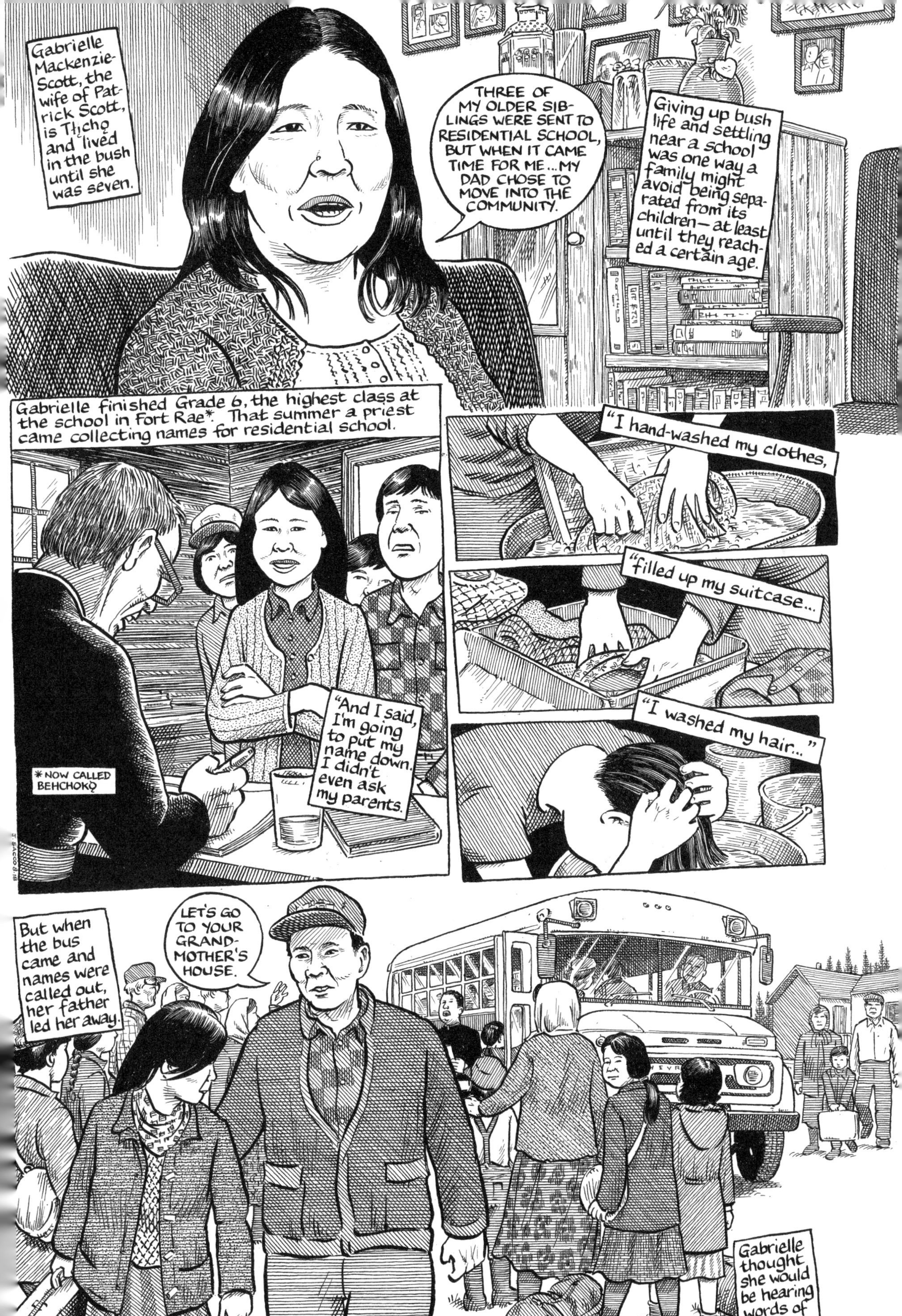
Gabrielle Mackenzie-Scott, the wife of Patrick Scott, is Tłįchǫ and lived in the bush until she was seven.
THREE OF MY OLDER SIBLINGS WERE SENT TO RESIDENTIAL SCHOOL, BUT WHEN IT CAME TIME FOR ME... MY DAD CHOSE TO MOVE INTO THE COMMUNITY.
Giving up bush life and settling near a school was one way a family might avoid being separated from its children—at least until they reached a certain age.
Gabrielle finished Grade 6, the highest class at the school in Fort Rae*. That summer a priest came collecting names for residential school.
"And I said, I'm going to put my name down. I didn't even ask my parents.
*NOW CALLED BEHCHOKǪ
"I hand-washed my clothes,
"filled up my suitcase...
"I washed my hair..."
But when the bus came and names were called out, her father led her away.
LET'S GO TO YOUR GRANDMOTHER'S HOUSE.
Gabrielle thought she would be hearing words of advice.

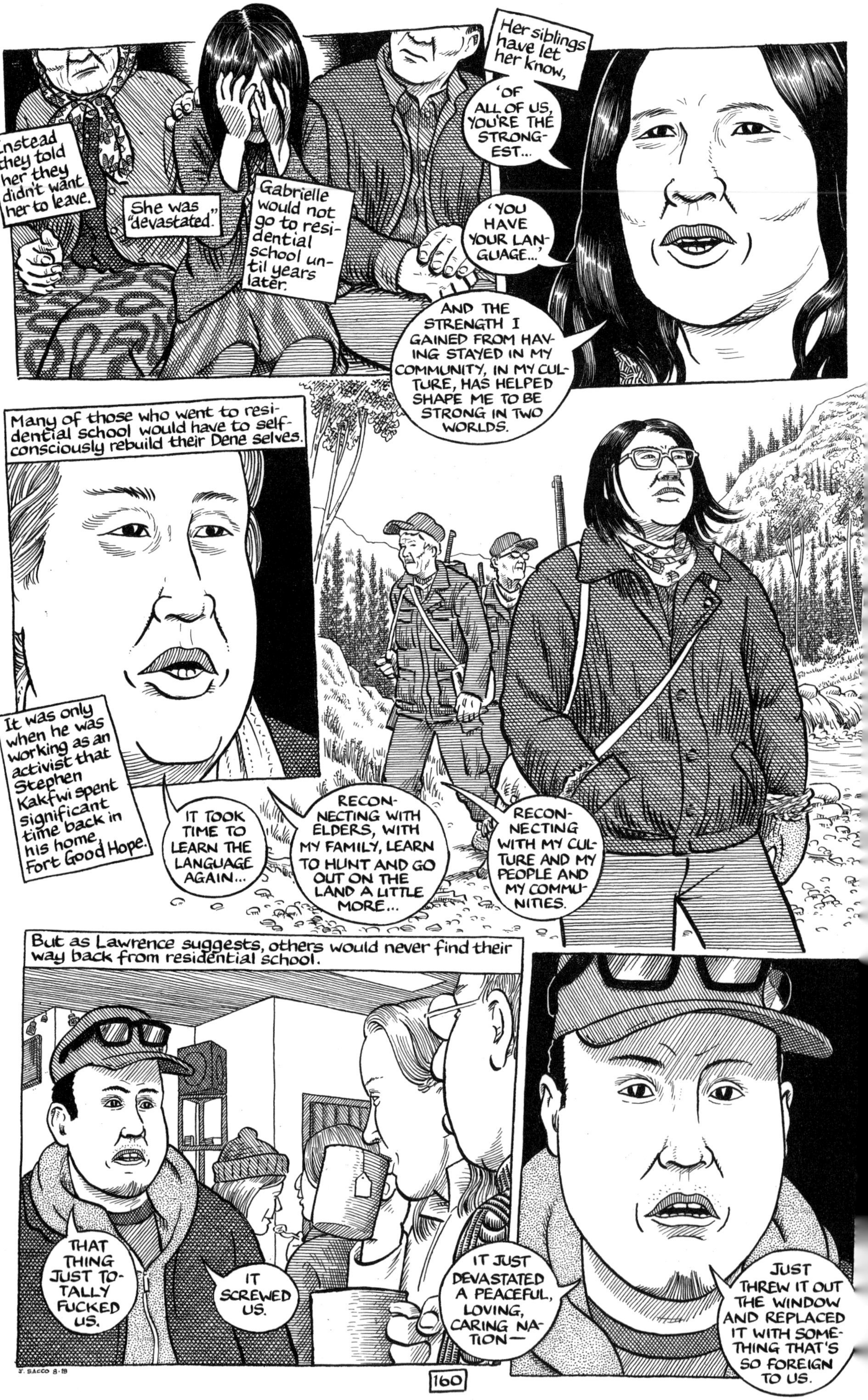
Instead they told her they didn't want her to leave.
She was "devastated."
Gabrielle would not go to residential school until years later.
Her siblings have let her know,
'OF ALL OF US, YOU'RE THE STRONGEST...
'YOU HAVE YOUR LANGUAGE...'
AND THE STRENGTH I GAINED FROM HAVING STAYED IN MY COMMUNITY, IN MY CULTURE, HAS HELPED SHAPE ME TO BE STRONG IN TWO WORLDS.
Many of those who went to residential school would have to self-consciously rebuild their Dene selves.
It was only when he was working as an activist that Stephen Kakfwi spent significant time back in his home, Fort Good Hope.
IT TOOK TIME TO LEARN THE LANGUAGE AGAIN...
RECONNECTING WITH ELDERS, WITH MY FAMILY, LEARN TO HUNT AND GO OUT ON THE LAND A LITTLE MORE...
RECONNECTING WITH MY CULTURE AND MY PEOPLE AND MY COMMUNITIES.
But as Lawrence suggests, others would never find their way back from residential school.
THAT THING JUST TOTALLY FUCKED US.
IT SCREWED US.
IT JUST DEVASTATED A PEACEFUL, LOVING, CARING NATION—
JUST THREW IT OUT THE WINDOW AND REPLACED IT WITH SOMETHING THAT'S SO FOREIGN TO US.
J. SACCO 8·18

V

NO ROAD TO ANYWHERE

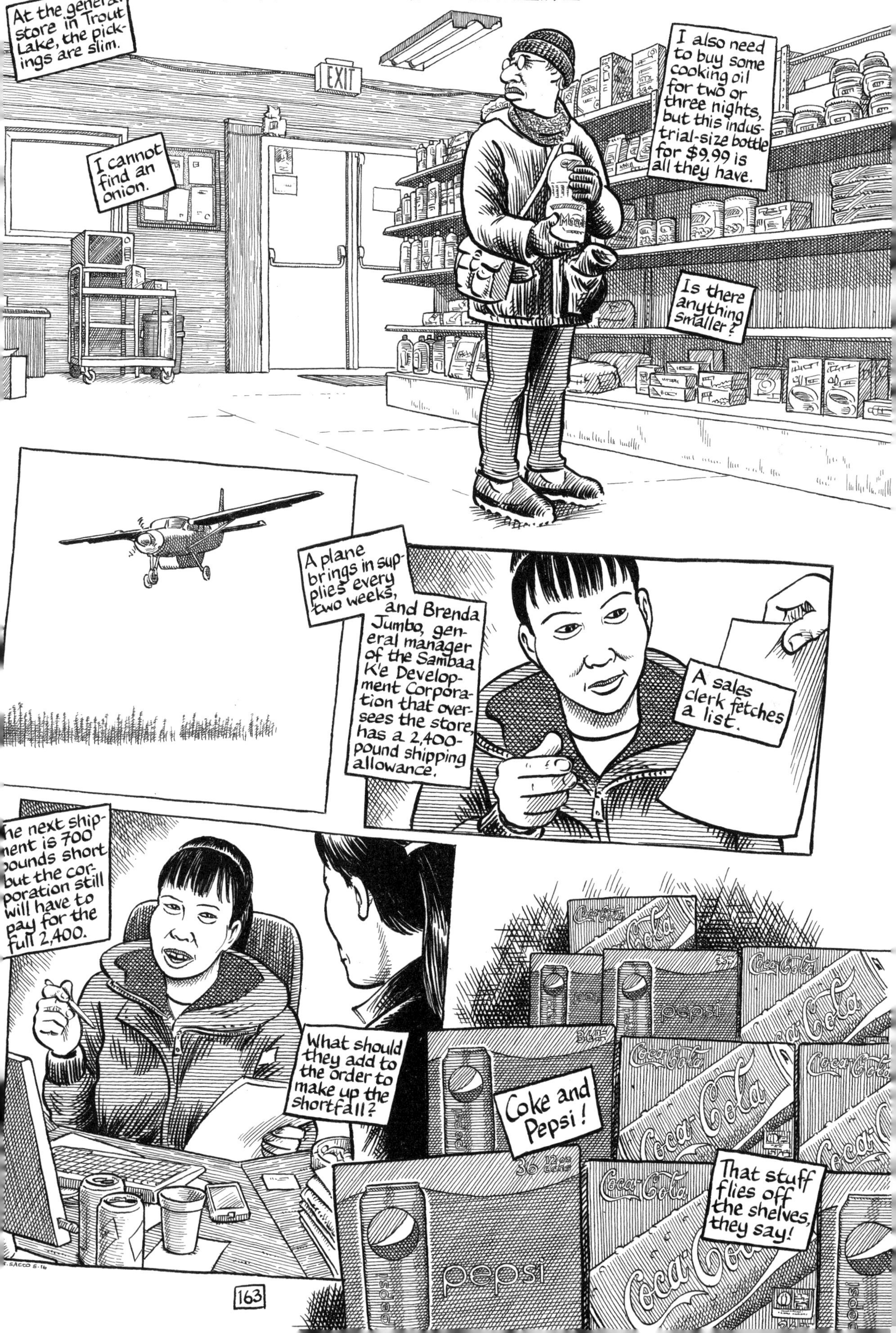

At the general store in Trout Lake, the pickings are slim.
EXIT
I cannot find an onion.
I also need to buy some cooking oil for two or three nights, but this industrial-size bottle for $9.99 is all they have.
Is there anything smaller?
A plane brings in supplies every two weeks,
and Brenda Jumbo, general manager of the Sambaa K'e Development Corporation that oversees the store, has a 2,400-pound shipping allowance.
A sales clerk fetches a list.
he next shipment is 700 ounds short but the corporation still will have to pay for the full 2,400.
What should they add to the order to make up the shortfall?
Coke and Pepsi!
That stuff flies off the shelves, they say!

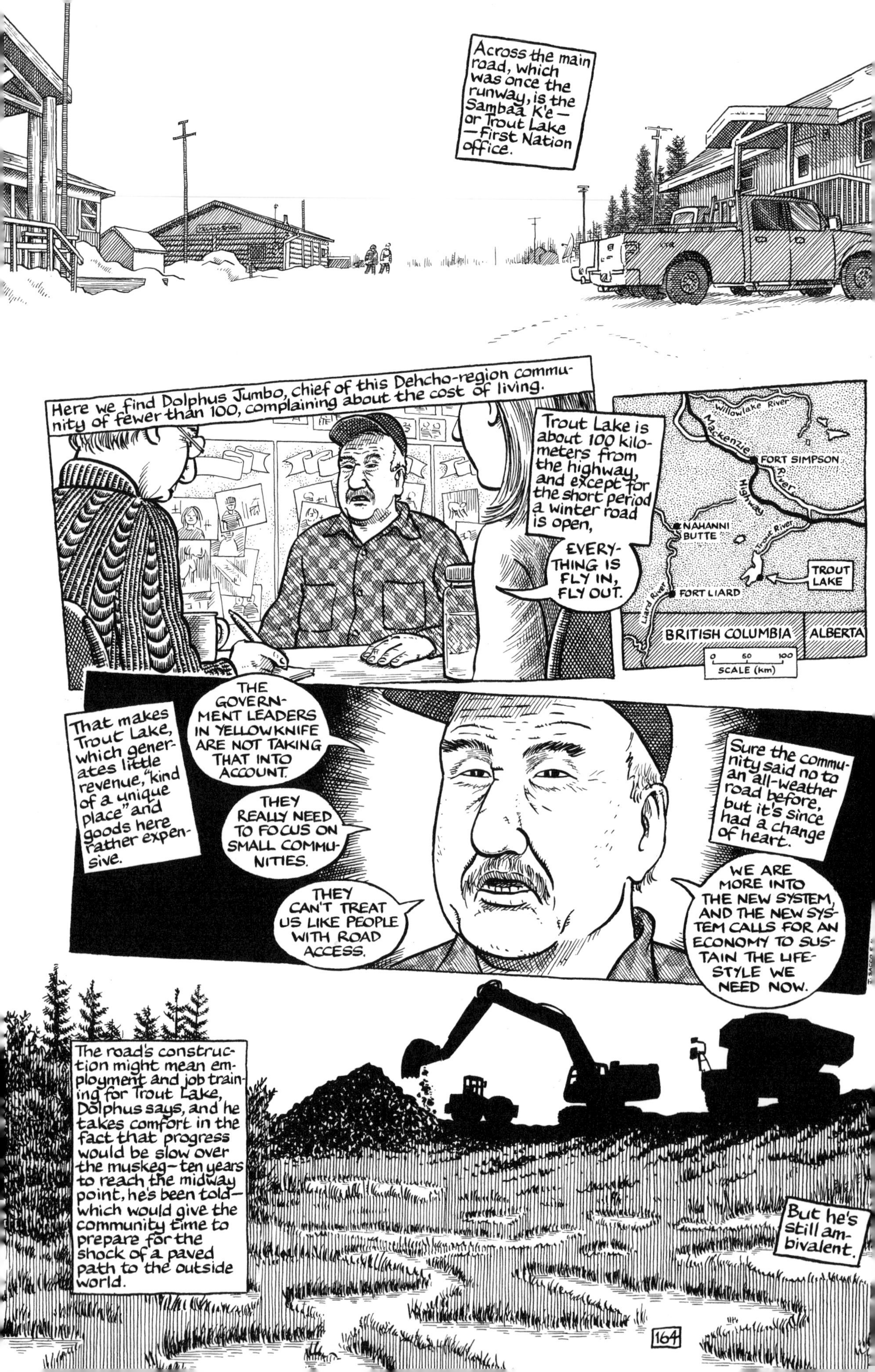
Across the main road, which was once the runway, is the Sambaa K'e — or Trout Lake — First Nation office.
Here we find Dolphus Jumbo, chief of this Dehcho-region community of fewer than 100, complaining about the cost of living.
Trout Lake is about 100 kilometers from the highway, and except for the short period a winter road is open,
EVERYTHING IS FLY IN, FLY OUT.
Willowlake River
Mackenzie River
FORT SIMPSON
Highway
NAHANNI BUTTE
Trout River
TROUT LAKE
Liard River
FORT LIARD
BRITISH COLUMBIA
ALBERTA
0 50 100
SCALE (km)
That makes Trout Lake, which generates little revenue, "kind of a unique place" and goods here rather expensive.
THE GOVERNMENT LEADERS IN YELLOWKNIFE ARE NOT TAKING THAT INTO ACCOUNT.
THEY REALLY NEED TO FOCUS ON SMALL COMMUNITIES.
THEY CAN'T TREAT US LIKE PEOPLE WITH ROAD ACCESS.
Sure the community said no to an all-weather road before, but it's since had a change of heart.
WE ARE MORE INTO THE NEW SYSTEM, AND THE NEW SYSTEM CALLS FOR AN ECONOMY TO SUSTAIN THE LIFESTYLE WE NEED NOW.
The road's construction might mean employment and job training for Trout Lake, Dolphus says, and he takes comfort in the fact that progress would be slow over the muskeg—ten years to reach the midway point, he's been told—which would give the community time to prepare for the shock of a paved path to the outside world.
But he's still ambivalent.

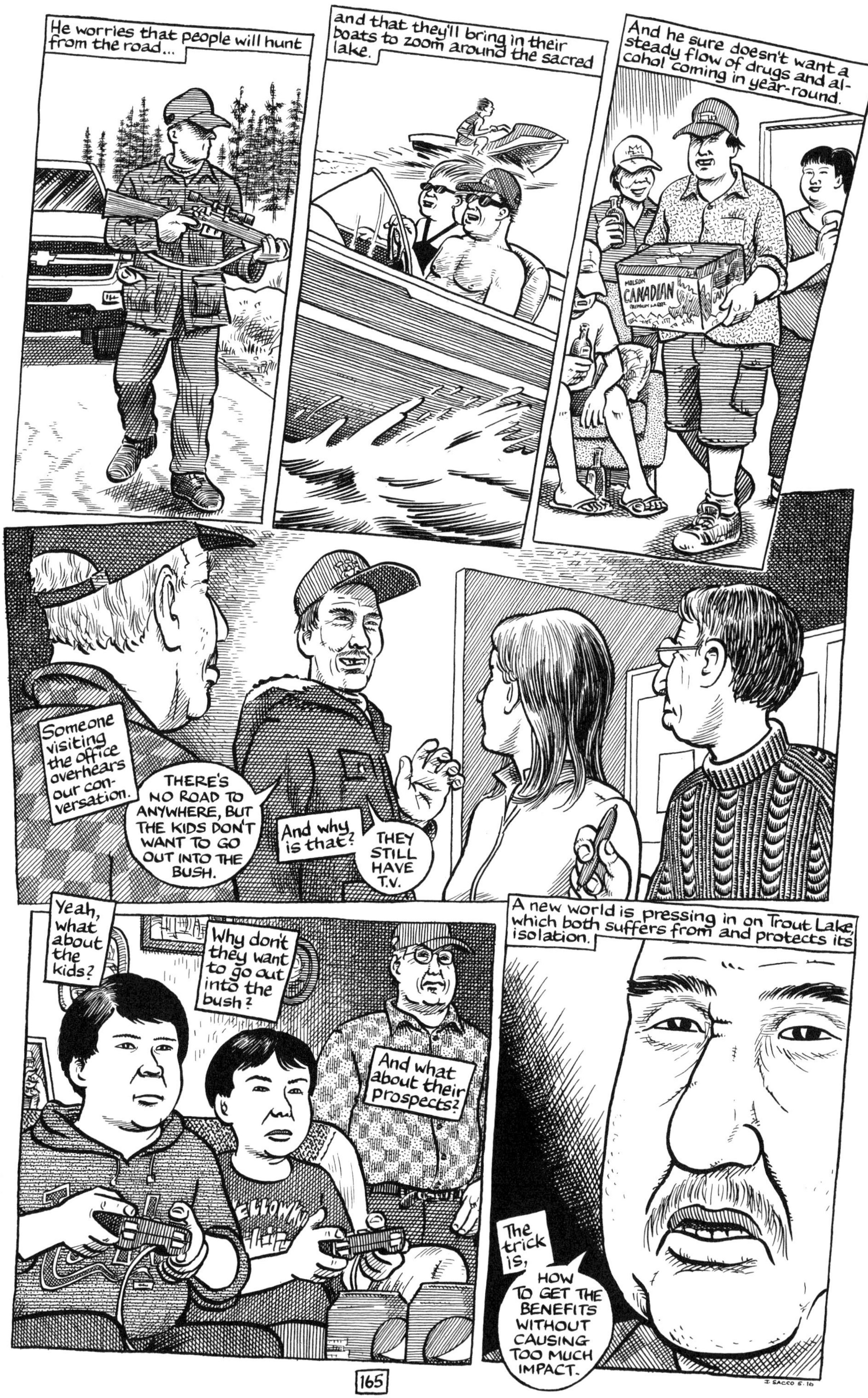
He worries that people will hunt from the road...
and that they'll bring in their boats to zoom around the sacred lake.
And he sure doesn't want a steady flow of drugs and alcohol coming in year-round.
MOLSON CANADIAN
Someone visiting the office overhears our conversation.
THERE'S NO ROAD TO ANYWHERE, BUT THE KIDS DON'T WANT TO GO OUT INTO THE BUSH.
And why is that?
THEY STILL HAVE T.V.
Yeah, what about the kids?
Why don't they want to go out into the bush?
And what about their prospects?
A new world is pressing in on Trout Lake which both suffers from and protects its isolation.
The trick is,
HOW TO GET THE BENEFITS WITHOUT CAUSING TOO MUCH IMPACT.
J. SACCO 5.16

OPPORTUNITY EVERYWHERE

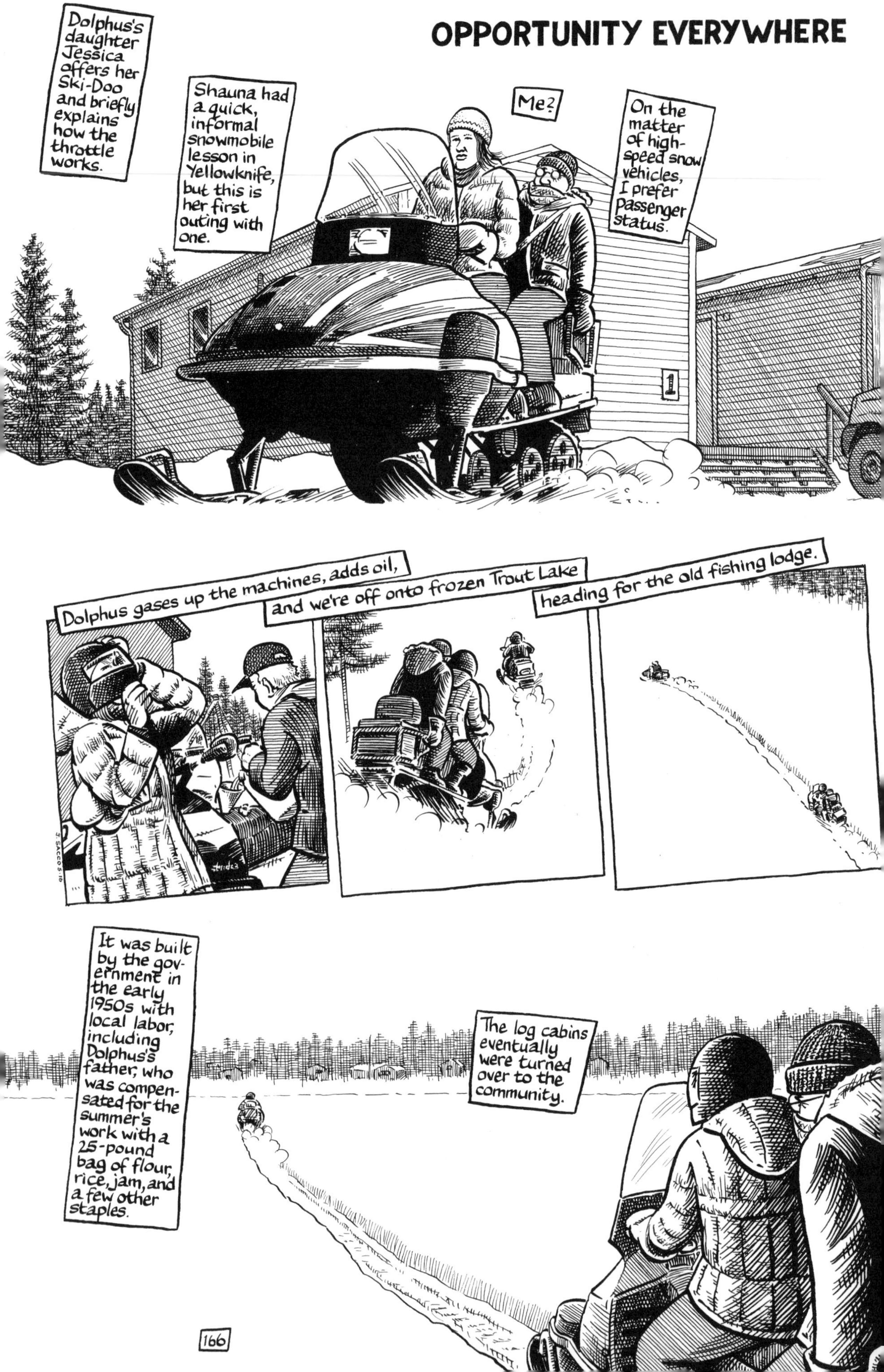

Dolphus's daughter Jessica offers her Ski-Doo and briefly explains how the throttle works.
Shauna had a quick, informal snowmobile lesson in Yellowknife, but this is her first outing with one.
Me?
On the matter of high-speed snow vehicles, I prefer passenger status.
Dolphus gases up the machines, adds oil,
and we're off onto frozen Trout Lake
heading for the old fishing lodge.
It was built by the government in the early 1950s with local labor, including Dolphus's father, who was compensated for the summer's work with a 25-pound bag of flour, rice, jam, and a few other staples.
The log cabins eventually were turned over to the community.

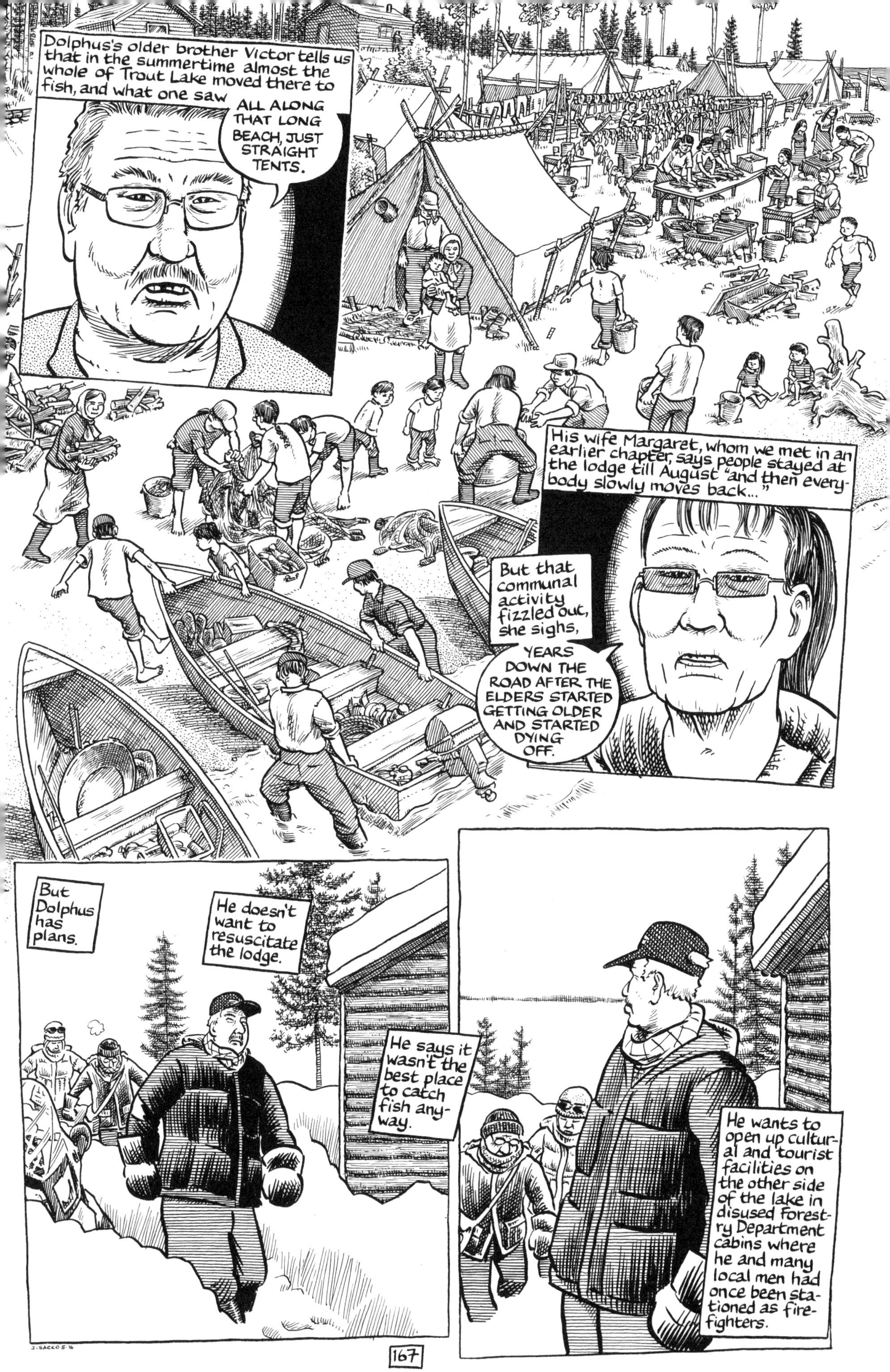
Dolphus's older brother Victor tells us that in the summertime almost the whole of Trout Lake moved there to fish, and what one saw
ALL ALONG THAT LONG BEACH, JUST STRAIGHT TENTS.
His wife Margaret, whom we met in an earlier chapter, says people stayed at the lodge till August "and then everybody slowly moves back..."
But that communal activity fizzled out, she sighs,
YEARS DOWN THE ROAD AFTER THE ELDERS STARTED GETTING OLDER AND STARTED DYING OFF.
But Dolphus has plans.
He doesn't want to resuscitate the lodge.
He says it wasn't the best place to catch fish anyway.
He wants to open up cultural and tourist facilities on the other side of the lake in disused Forestry Department cabins where he and many local men had once been stationed as firefighters.
J. SACCO 5.16

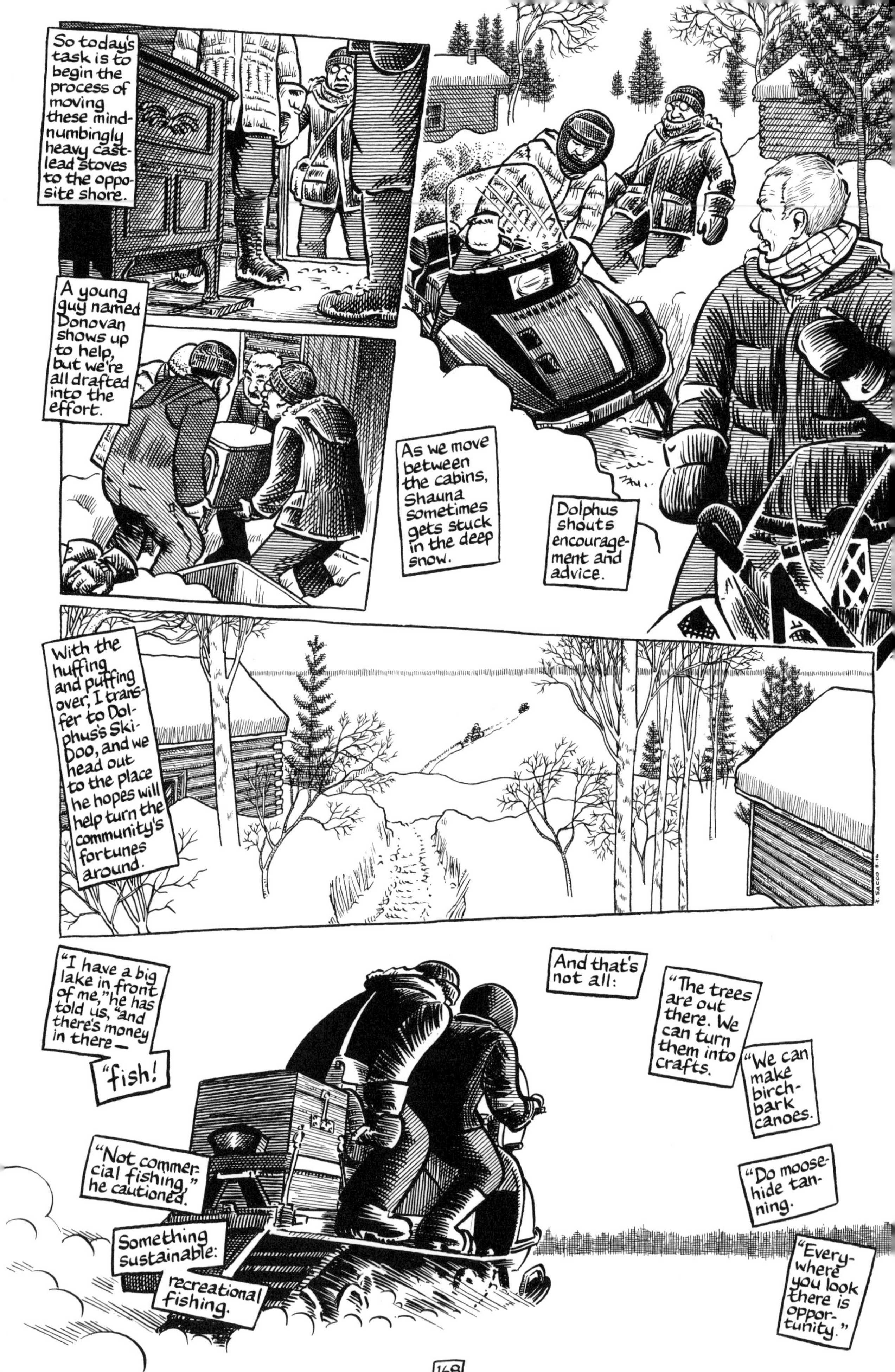
So today's task is to begin the process of moving these mind-numbingly heavy cast-lead stoves to the opposite shore.
A young guy named Donovan shows up to help, but we're all drafted into the effort.
As we move between the cabins, Shauna sometimes gets stuck in the deep snow.
Dolphus shouts encouragement and advice.
With the huffing and puffing over, I transfer to Dolphus's Ski-Doo, and we head out to the place he hopes will help turn the community's fortunes around.
"I have a big lake in front of me," he has told us, "and there's money in there—
"fish!
"Not commercial fishing," he cautioned.
Something sustainable:
recreational fishing.
And that's not all:
"The trees are out there. We can turn them into crafts.
"We can make birch-bark canoes.
"Do moose-hide tanning.
"Everywhere you look there is opportunity."

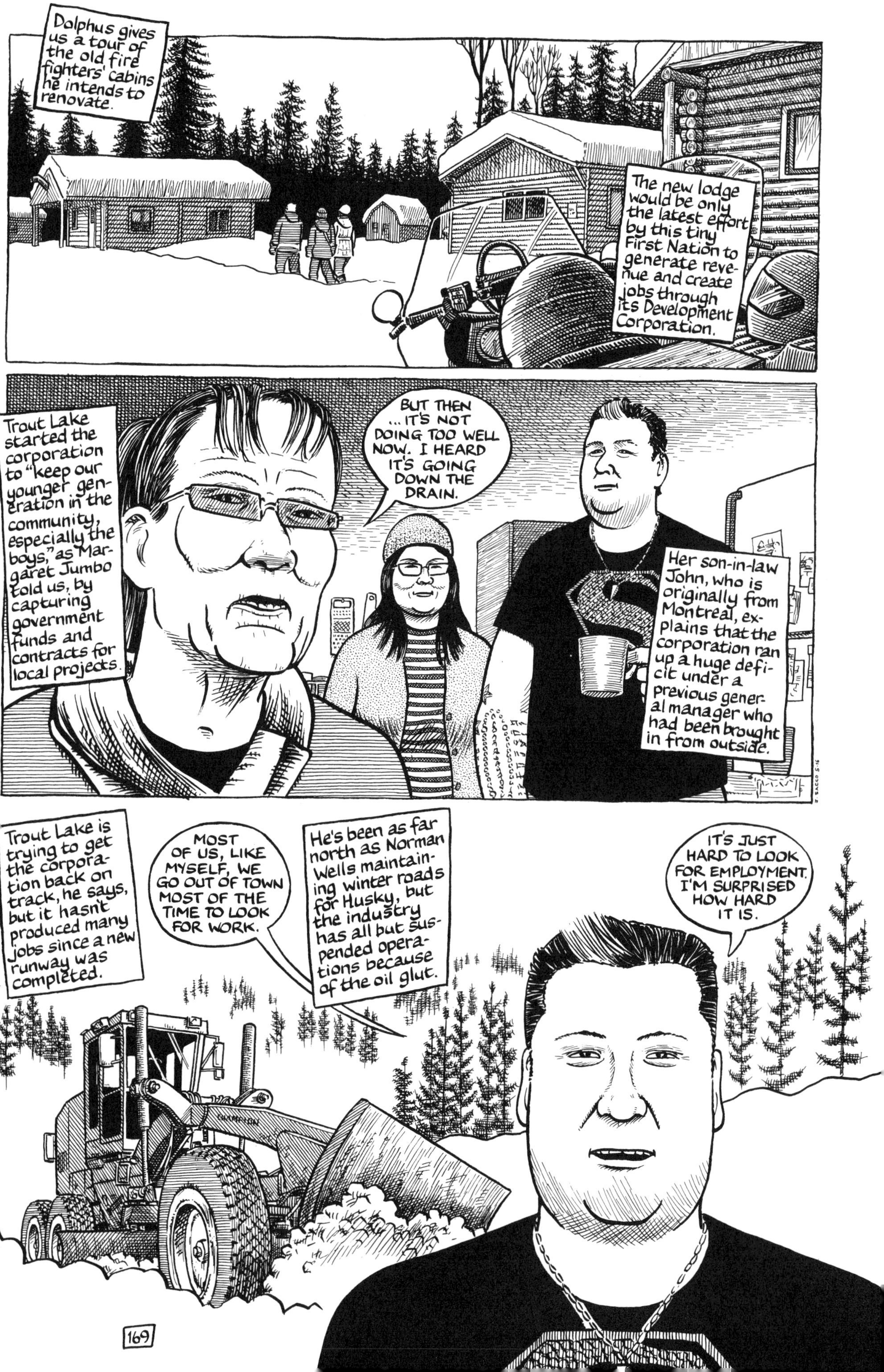
Dolphus gives us a tour of the old fire fighters' cabins he intends to renovate.
The new lodge would be only the latest effort by this tiny First Nation to generate revenue and create jobs through its Development Corporation.
Trout Lake started the corporation to "keep our younger generation in the community, especially the boys," as Margaret Jumbo told us, by capturing government funds and contracts for local projects.
BUT THEN ...IT'S NOT DOING TOO WELL NOW. I HEARD IT'S GOING DOWN THE DRAIN.
Her son-in-law John, who is originally from Montreal, explains that the corporation ran up a huge deficit under a previous general manager who had been brought in from outside.
Trout Lake is trying to get the corporation back on track, he says, but it hasn't produced many jobs since a new runway was completed.
MOST OF US, LIKE MYSELF, WE GO OUT OF TOWN MOST OF THE TIME TO LOOK FOR WORK.
He's been as far north as Norman Wells maintaining winter roads for Husky, but the industry has all but suspended operations because of the oil glut.
IT'S JUST HARD TO LOOK FOR EMPLOYMENT. I'M SURPRISED HOW HARD IT IS.

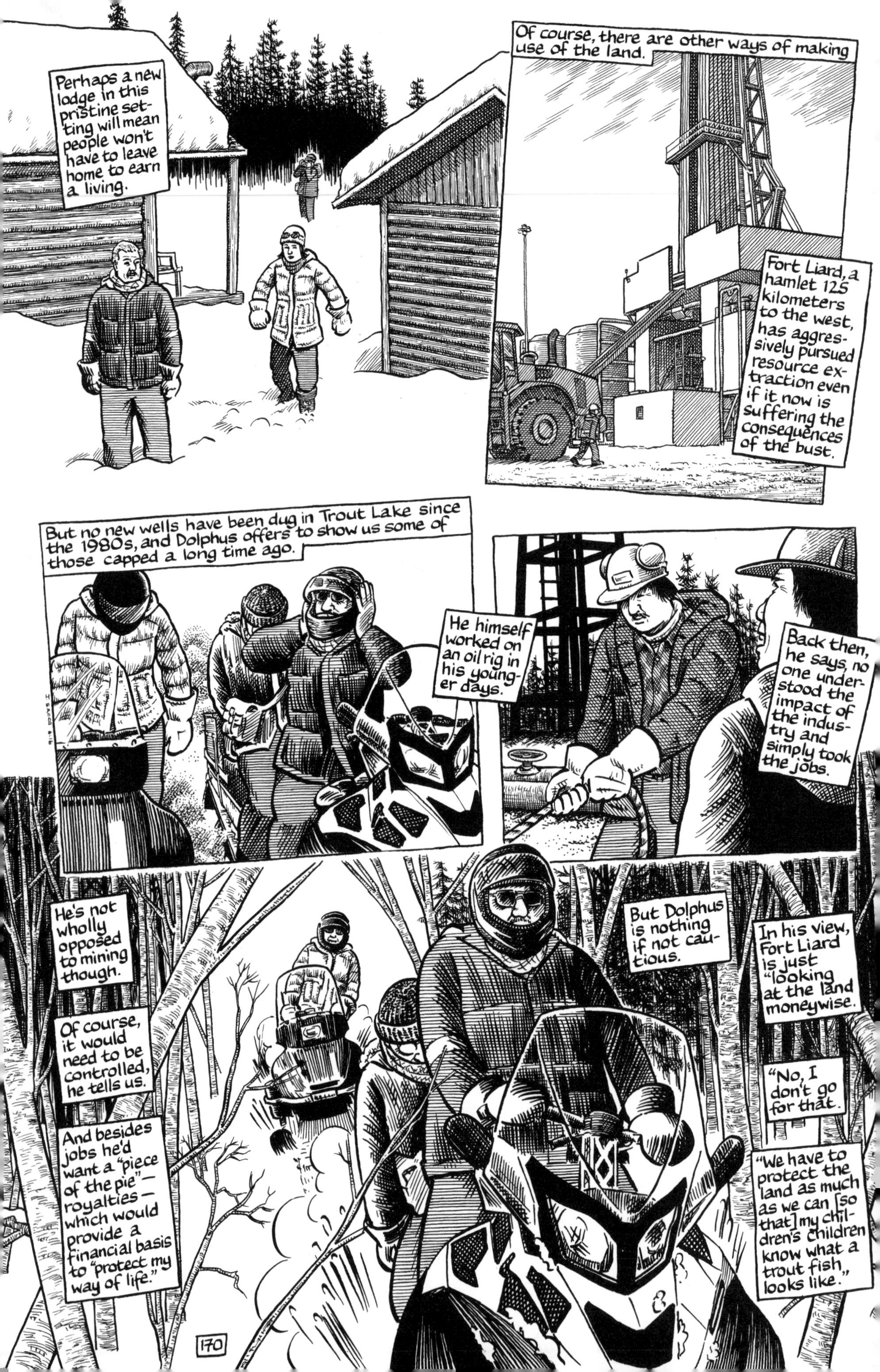

Perhaps a new lodge in this pristine setting will mean people won't have to leave home to earn a living.
Of course, there are other ways of making use of the land.
Fort Liard, a hamlet 125 kilometers to the west, has aggresively pursued resource extraction even if it now is suffering the consequences of the bust.
But no new wells have been dug in Trout Lake since the 1980s, and Dolphus offers to show us some of those capped a long time ago.
He himself worked on an oil rig in his younger days.
Back then, he says, no one understood the impact of the industry and simply took the jobs.
He's not wholly opposed to mining though.
Of course, it would need to be controlled, he tells us.
And besides jobs he'd want a "piece of the pie"—royalties—which would provide a financial basis to "protect my way of life."
But Dolphus is nothing if not cautious.
In his view, Fort Liard is just "looking at the land moneywise.
"No, I don't go for that.
"We have to protect the land as much as we can [so that] my children's children know what a trout fish looks like."

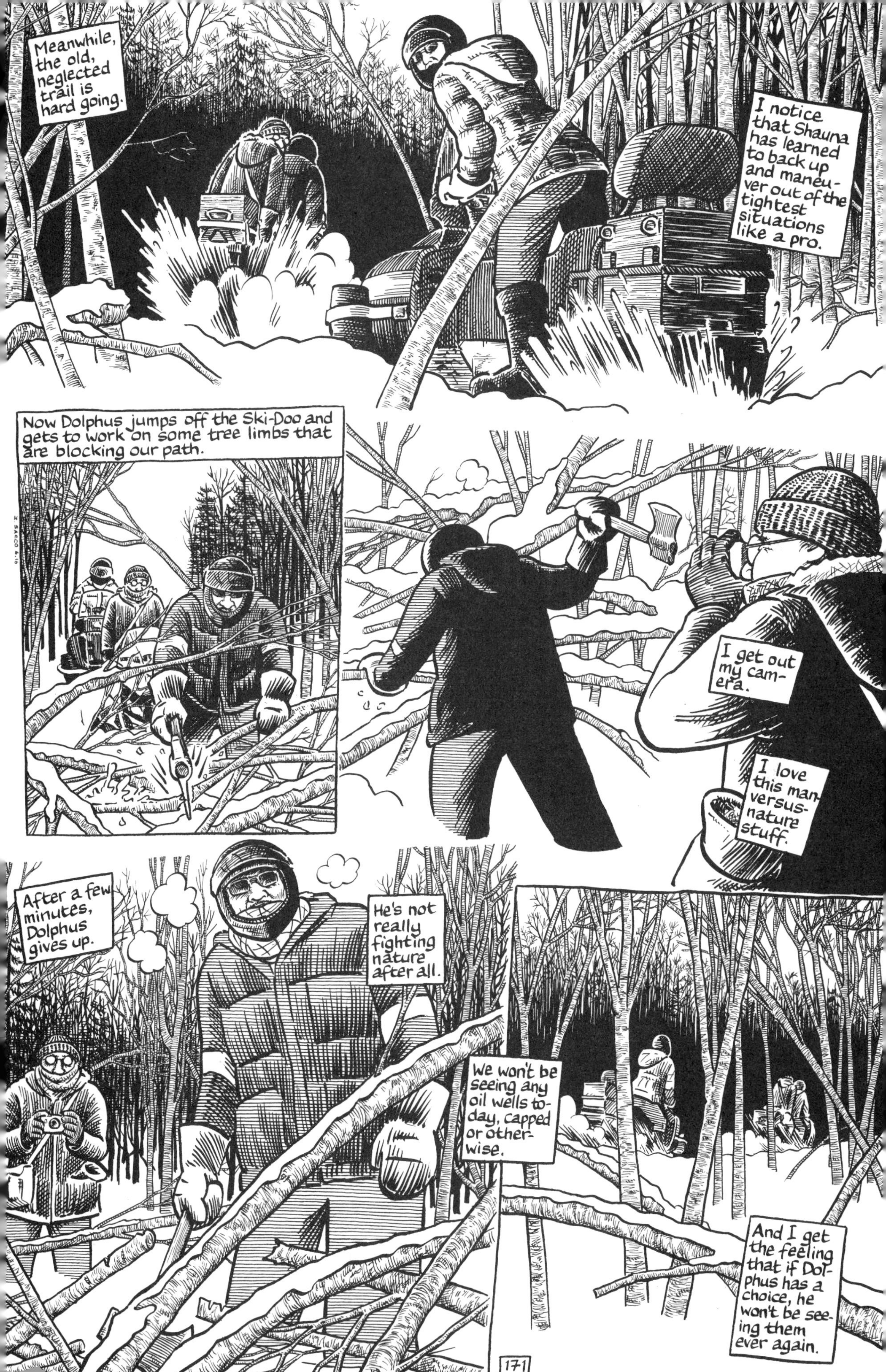
Meanwhile, the old, neglected trail is hard going.
I notice that Shauna has learned to back up and maneu-ver out of the tightest situations like a pro.
Now Dolphus jumps off the Ski-Doo and gets to work on some tree limbs that are blocking our path.
I get out my cam-era.
I love this man versus-nature stuff.
After a few minutes, Dolphus gives up.
He's not really fighting nature after all.
We won't be seeing any oil wells to-day, capped or other-wise.
And I get the feeling that if Dol-phus has a choice, he won't be see-ing them ever again.

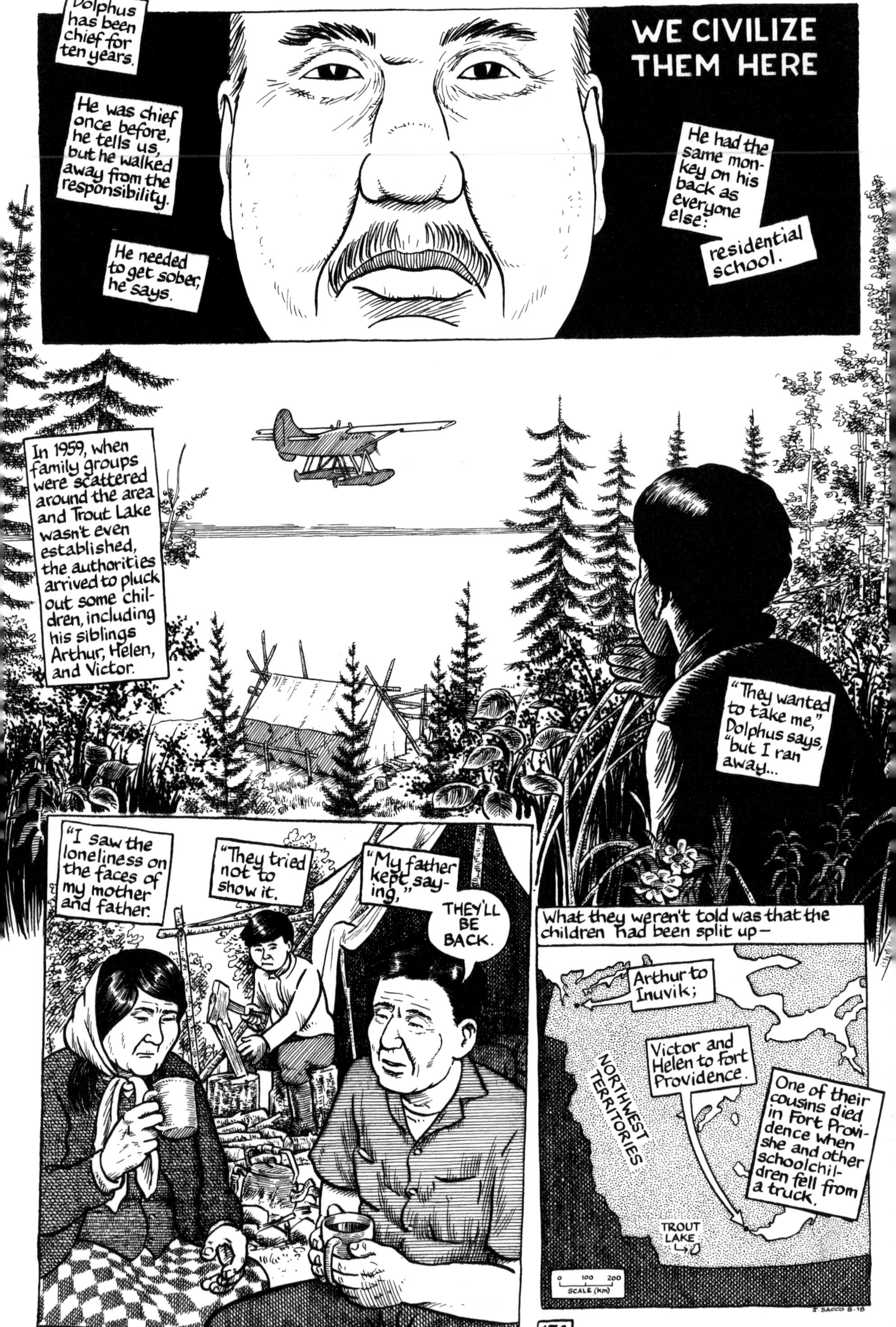
Dolphus has been chief for ten years.
WE CIVILIZE THEM HERE
He was chief once before, he tells us, but he walked away from the responsibility.
He needed to get sober, he says.
He had the same monkey on his back as everyone else:
residential school.
In 1959, when family groups were scattered around the area and Trout Lake wasn't even established, the authorities arrived to pluck out some children, including his siblings Arthur, Helen, and Victor.
"They wanted to take me," Dolphus says, "but I ran away...
"I saw the loneliness on the faces of my mother and father.
"They tried not to show it.
"My father kept saying,"
THEY'LL BE BACK.
What they weren't told was that the children had been split up—
Arthur to Inuvik;
Victor and Helen to Fort Providence.
NORTHWEST TERRITORIES
One of their cousins died in Fort Providence when she and other schoolchildren fell from a truck.
TROUT LAKE
0 100 200
SCALE (Km)
J. SACCO 8.18

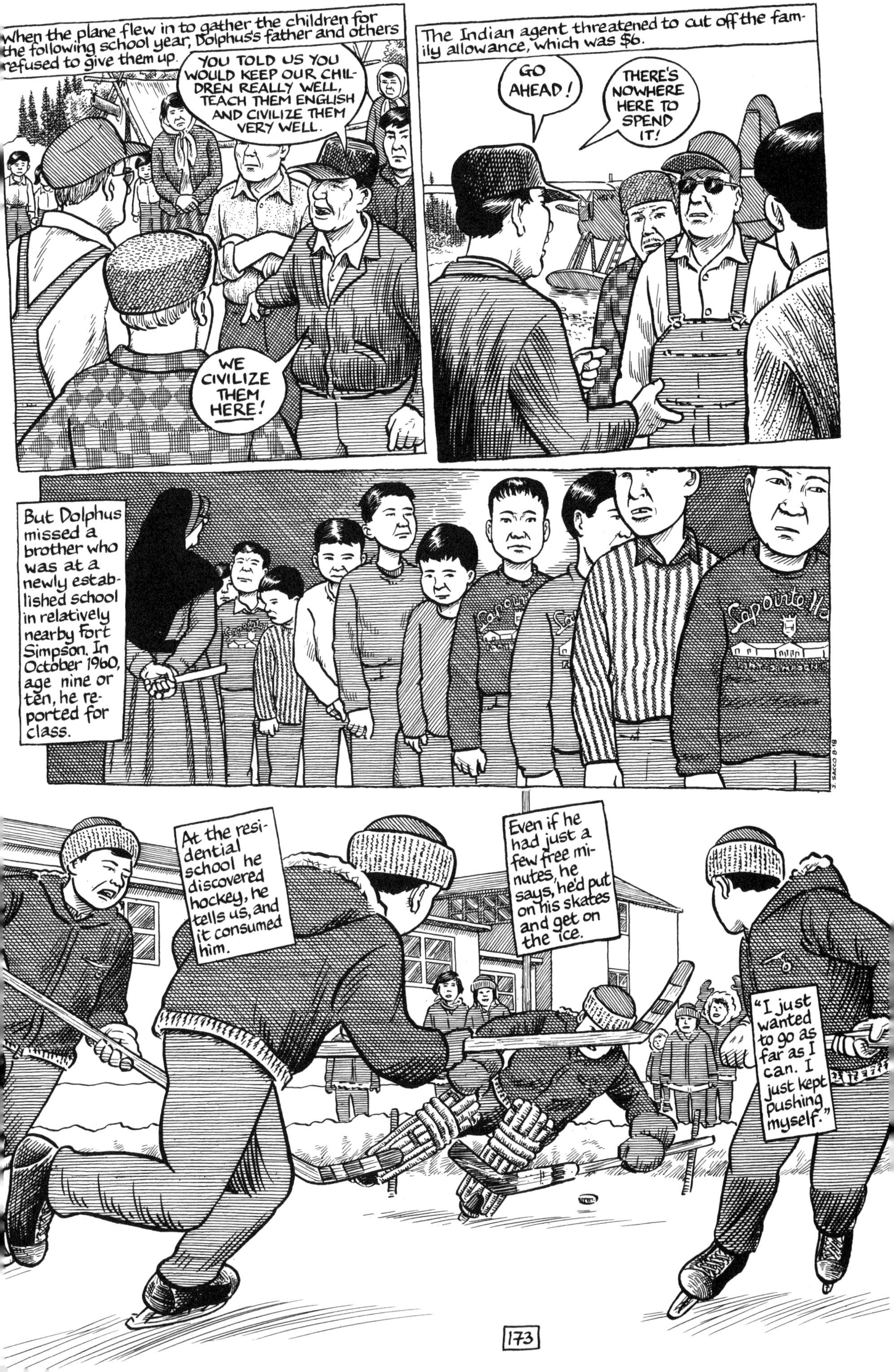
When the plane flew in to gather the children for the following school year, Dolphus's father and others refused to give them up.
YOU TOLD US YOU WOULD KEEP OUR CHILDREN REALLY WELL, TEACH THEM ENGLISH AND CIVILIZE THEM VERY WELL.
WE CIVILIZE THEM HERE!
The Indian agent threatened to cut off the family allowance, which was $6.
GO AHEAD!
THERE'S NOWHERE HERE TO SPEND IT!
But Dolphus missed a brother who was at a newly established school in relatively nearby Fort Simpson. In October 1960, age nine or ten, he reported for class.
J. SACCO 8.18
At the residential school he discovered hockey, he tells us, and it consumed him.
Even if he had just a few free minutes, he says, he'd put on his skates and get on the ice.
"I just wanted to go as far as I can. I just kept pushing myself."

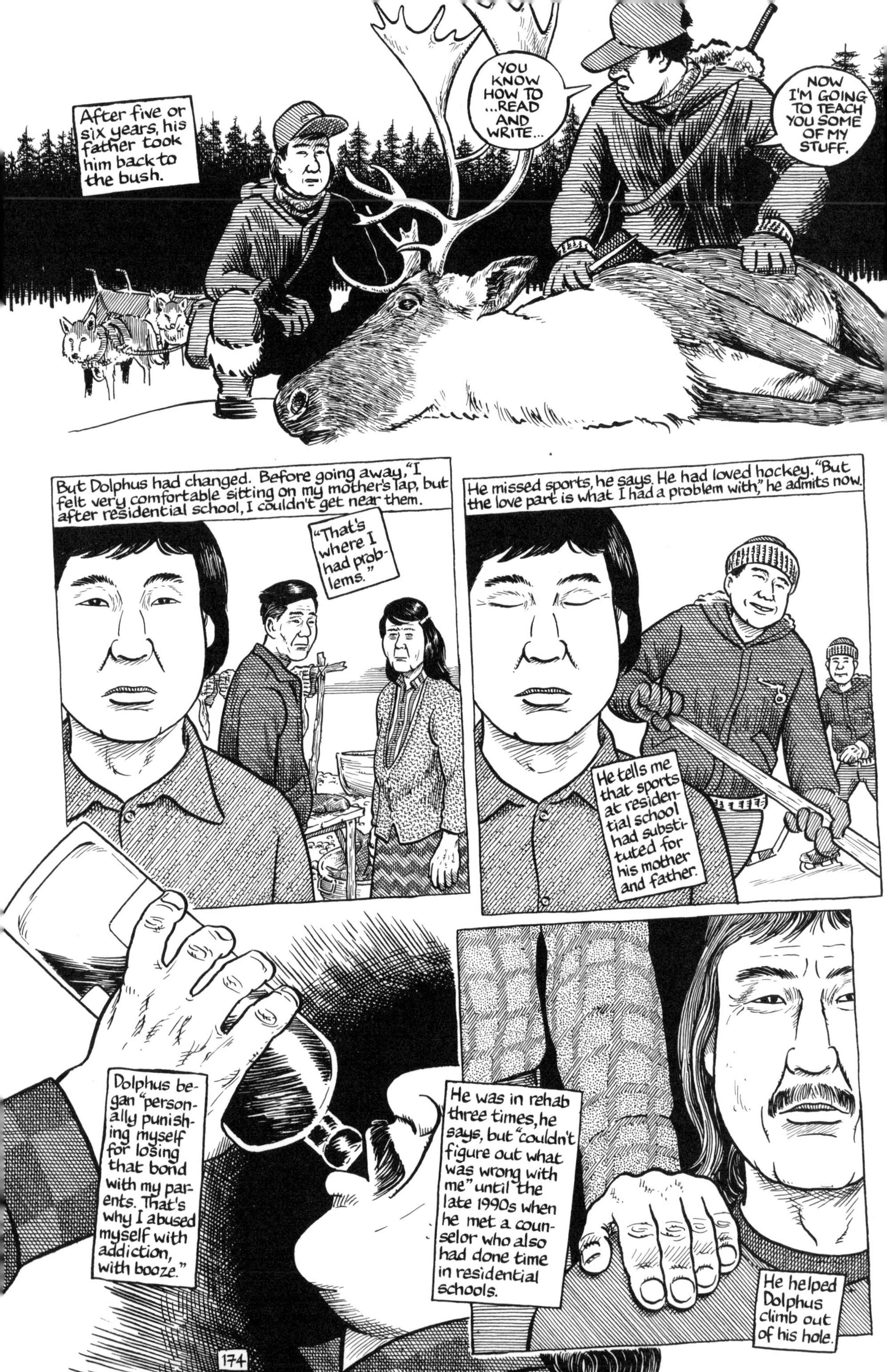

After five or six years, his father took him back to the bush.
YOU KNOW HOW TO ...READ AND WRITE...
NOW I'M GOING TO TEACH YOU SOME OF MY STUFF.
But Dolphus had changed. Before going away, "I felt very comfortable sitting on my mother's lap, but after residential school, I couldn't get near them.
"That's where I had problems."
He missed sports, he says. He had loved hockey. "But the love part is what I had a problem with," he admits now.
He tells me that sports at residential school had substituted for his mother and father.
Dolphus began "personally punishing myself for losing that bond with my parents. That's why I abused myself with addiction, with booze."
He was in rehab three times, he says, but "couldn't figure out what was wrong with me" until the late 1990s when he met a counselor who also had done time in residential schools.
He helped Dolphus climb out of his hole.

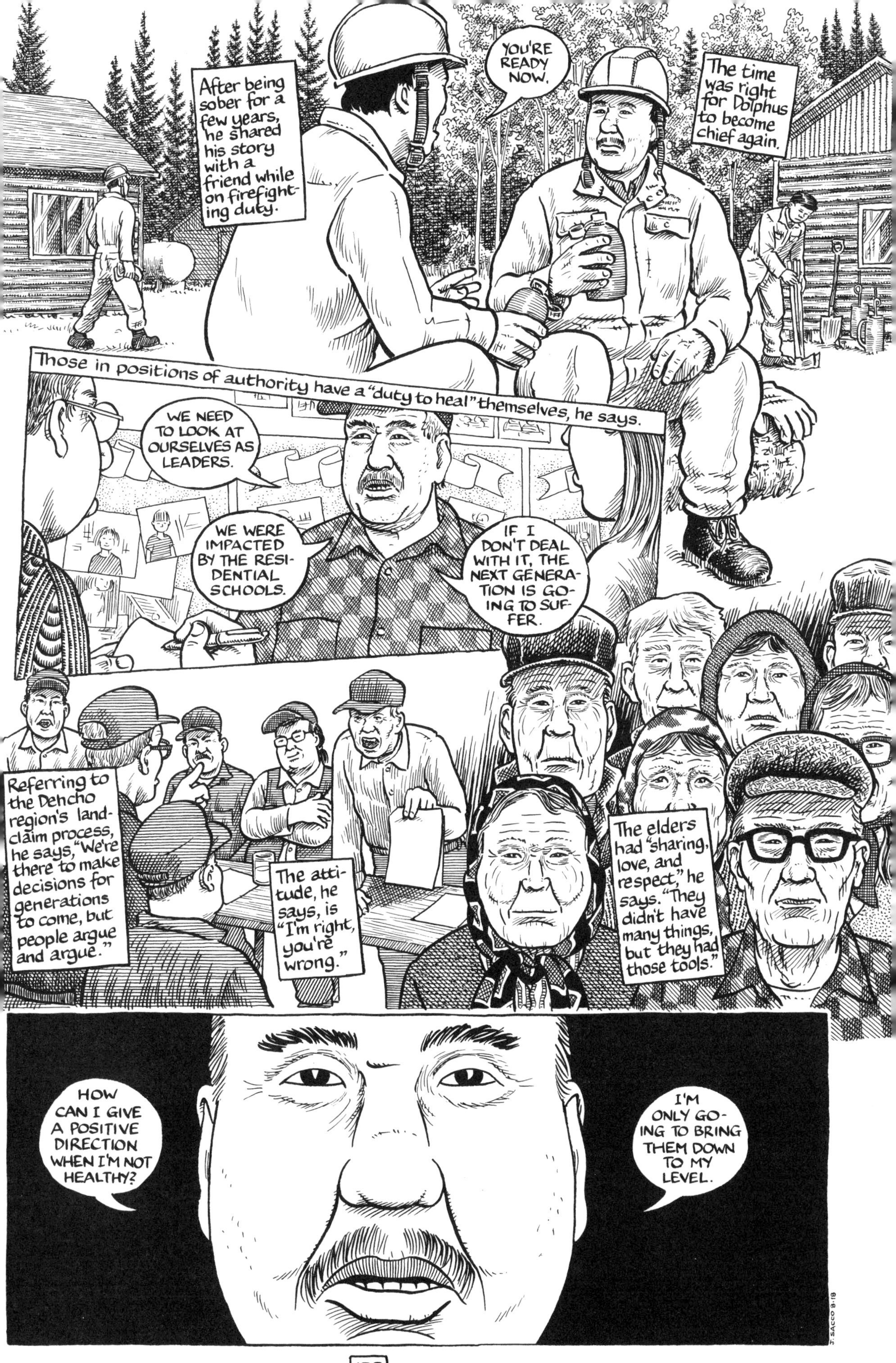
After being sober for a few years, he shared his story with a friend while on firefighting duty.
YOU'RE READY NOW.
The time was right for Dolphus to become chief again.
Those in positions of authority have a "duty to heal" themselves, he says.
WE NEED TO LOOK AT OURSELVES AS LEADERS.
WE WERE IMPACTED BY THE RESIDENTIAL SCHOOLS.
IF I DON'T DEAL WITH IT, THE NEXT GENERATION IS GOING TO SUFFER.
Referring to the Dehcho region's land-claim process, he says, "We're there to make decisions for generations to come, but people argue and argue."
The attitude, he says, is "I'm right, you're wrong."
The elders had "sharing, love, and respect," he says. "They didn't have many things, but they had those tools."
HOW CAN I GIVE A POSITIVE DIRECTION WHEN I'M NOT HEALTHY?
I'M ONLY GOING TO BRING THEM DOWN TO MY LEVEL.
J. SACCO 8.18

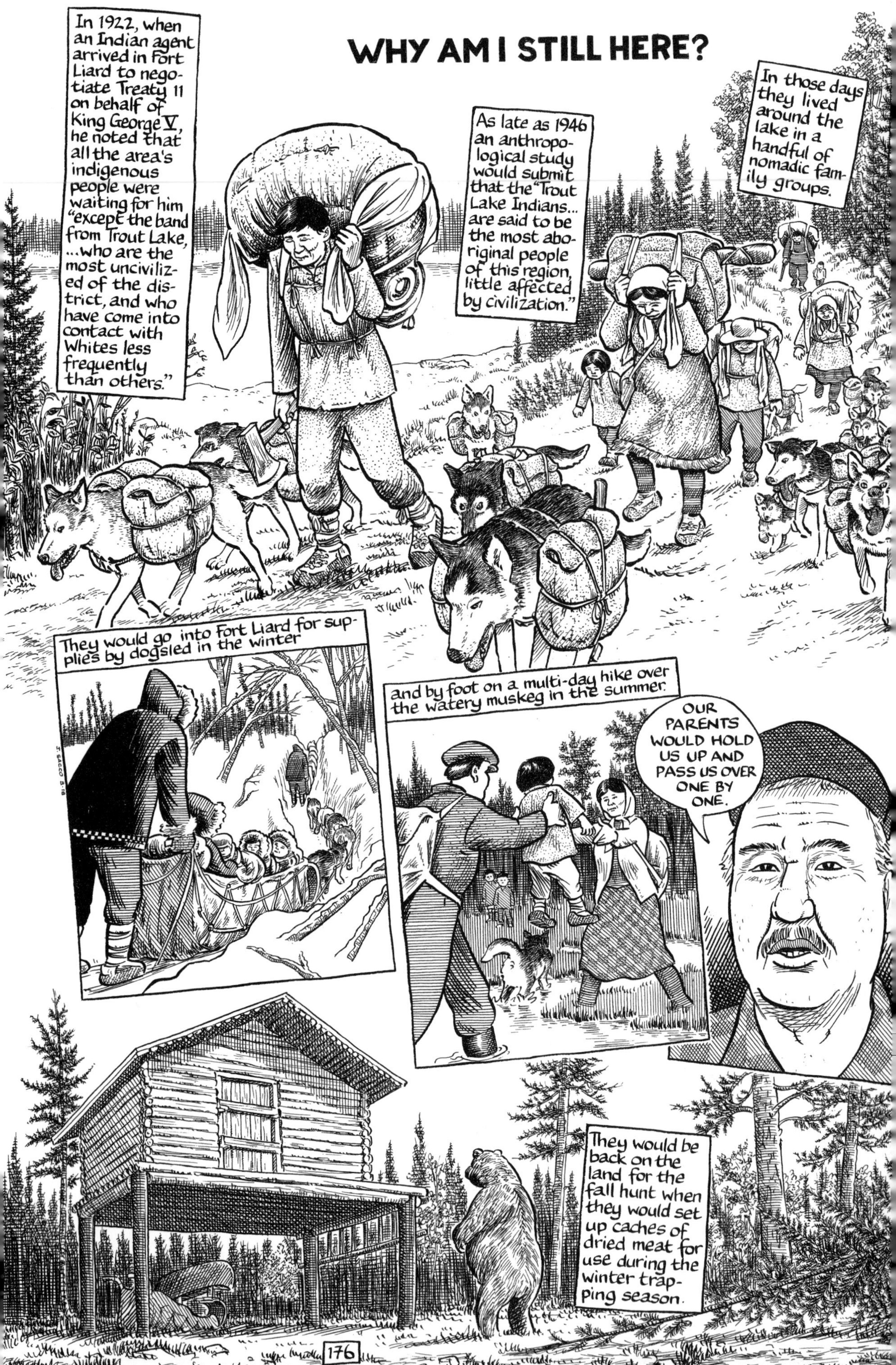

WHY AM I STILL HERE?
In 1922, when an Indian agent arrived in Fort Liard to negotiate Treaty 11 on behalf of King George V, he noted that all the area's indigenous people were waiting for him "except the band from Trout Lake, ...who are the most uncivilized of the district, and who have come into contact with Whites less frequently than others."
As late as 1946 an anthropological study would submit that the "Trout Lake Indians... are said to be the most aboriginal people of this region, little affected by civilization."
In those days they lived around the lake in a handful of nomadic family groups.
They would go into Fort Liard for supplies by dogsled in the winter
and by foot on a multi-day hike over the watery muskeg in the summer.
OUR PARENTS WOULD HOLD US UP AND PASS US OVER ONE BY ONE.
They would be back on the land for the fall hunt when they would set up caches of dried meat for use during the winter trapping season.

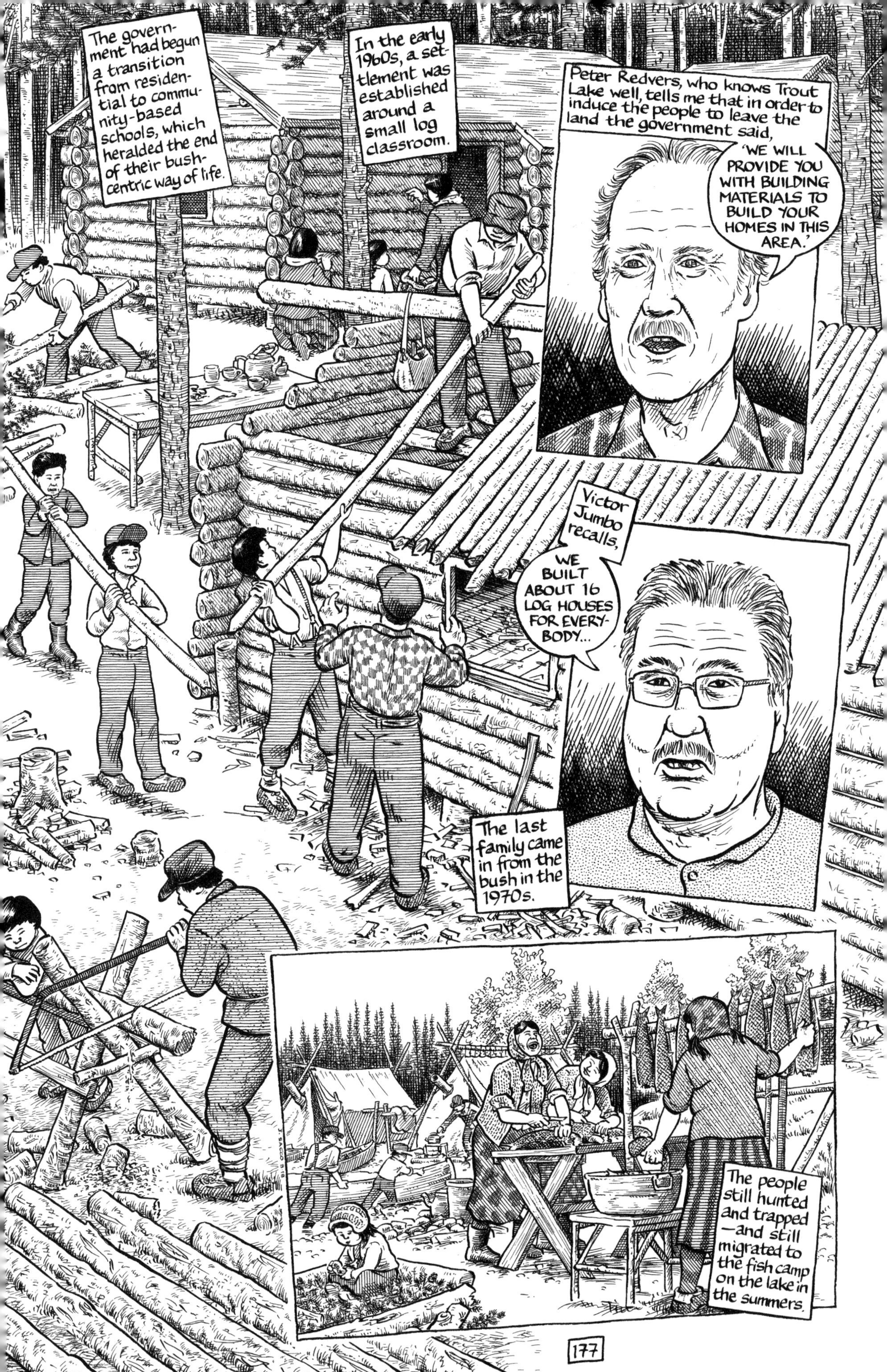
The government had begun a transition from residential to community-based schools, which heralded the end of their bush-centric way of life.
In the early 1960s, a settlement was established around a small log classroom.
Peter Redvers, who knows Trout Lake well, tells me that in order to induce the people to leave the land the government said,
'WE WILL PROVIDE YOU WITH BUILDING MATERIALS TO BUILD YOUR HOMES IN THIS AREA.'
Victor Jumbo recalls,
WE BUILT ABOUT 16 LOG HOUSES FOR EVERYBODY...
The last family came in from the bush in the 1970s.
The people still hunted and trapped—and still migrated to the fish camp on the lake in the summers.

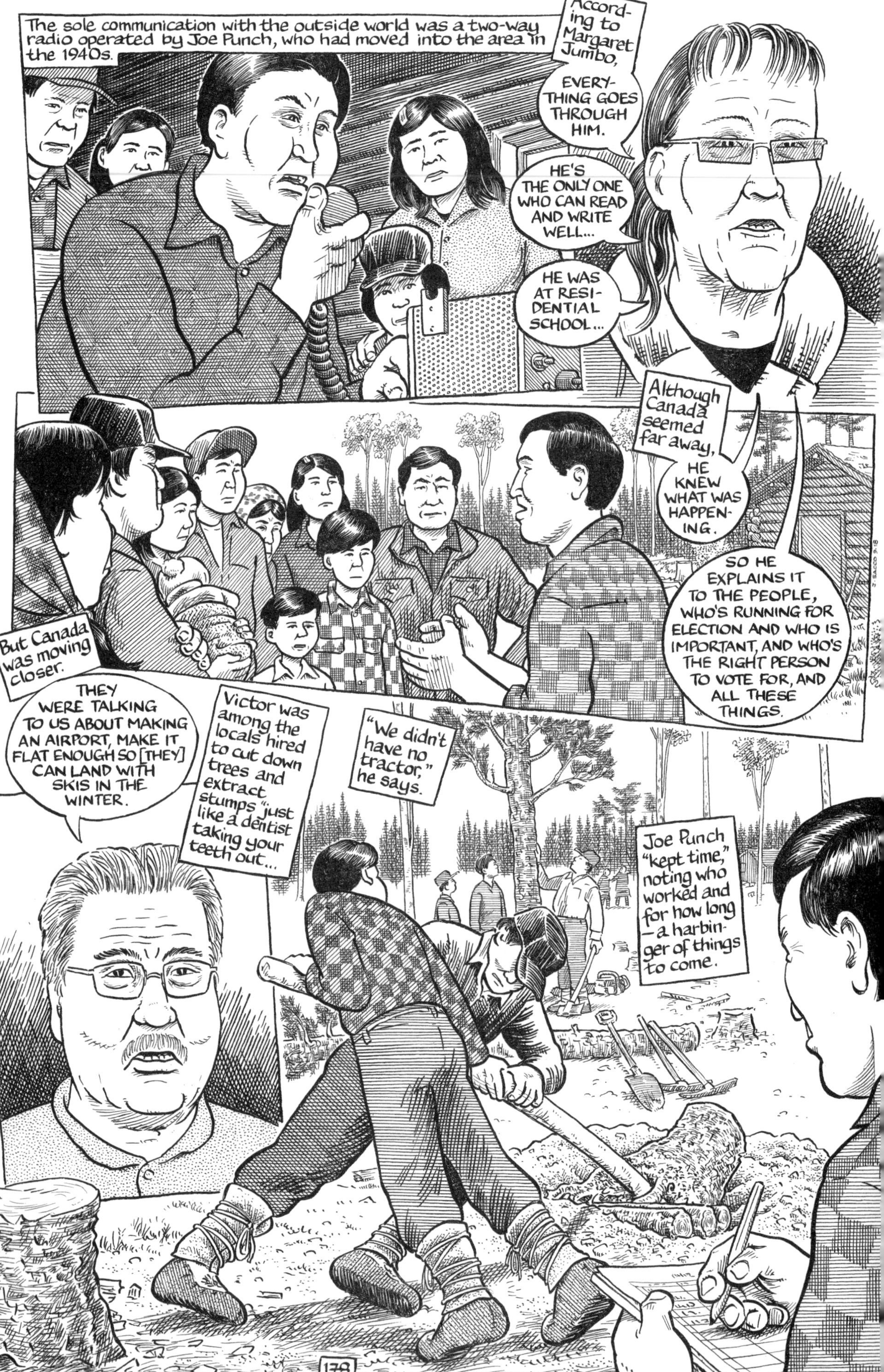

The sole communication with the outside world was a two-way radio operated by Joe Punch, who had moved into the area in the 1940s.
According to Margaret Jumbo,
EVERYTHING GOES THROUGH HIM.
HE'S THE ONLY ONE WHO CAN READ AND WRITE WELL...
HE WAS AT RESIDENTIAL SCHOOL...
Although Canada seemed far away,
HE KNEW WHAT WAS HAPPENING.
SO HE EXPLAINS IT TO THE PEOPLE, WHO'S RUNNING FOR ELECTION AND WHO IS IMPORTANT, AND WHO'S THE RIGHT PERSON TO VOTE FOR, AND ALL THESE THINGS.
But Canada was moving closer.
THEY WERE TALKING TO US ABOUT MAKING AN AIRPORT, MAKE IT FLAT ENOUGH SO [THEY] CAN LAND WITH SKIS IN THE WINTER.
Victor was among the locals hired to cut down trees and extract stumps "just like a dentist taking your teeth out...
"We didn't have no tractor," he says.
Joe Punch "kept time," noting who worked and for how long —a harbinger of things to come.

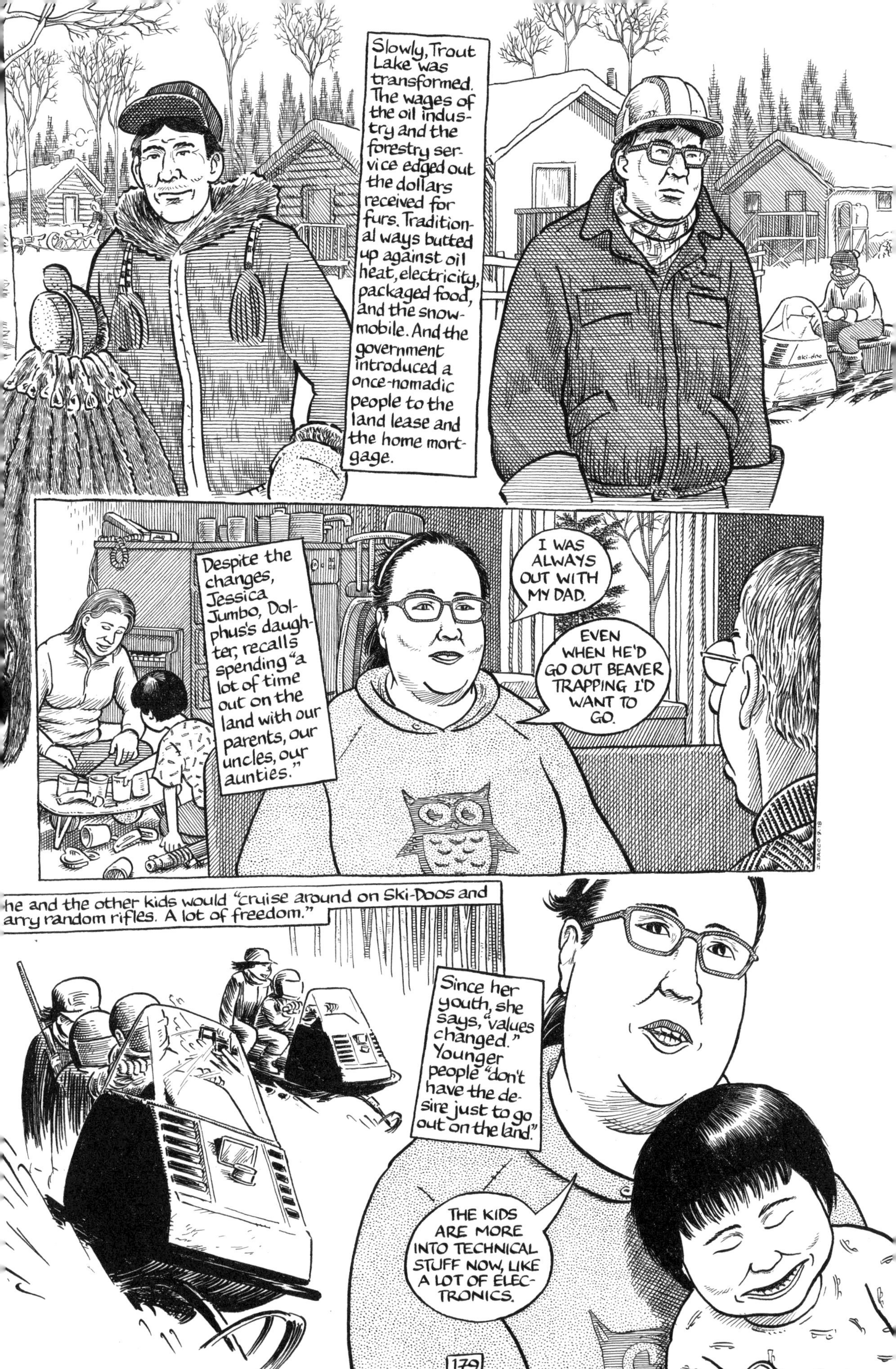
Slowly, Trout Lake was transformed. The wages of the oil industry and the forestry service edged out the dollars received for furs. Traditional ways butted up against oil heat, electricity, packaged food, and the snowmobile. And the government introduced a once-nomadic people to the land lease and the home mortgage.
ski-doo
Despite the changes, Jessica Jumbo, Dolphus's daughter, recalls spending "a lot of time out on the land with our parents, our uncles, our aunties."
I WAS ALWAYS OUT WITH MY DAD.
EVEN WHEN HE'D GO OUT BEAVER TRAPPING I'D WANT TO GO.
J. SACCO 9.18
he and the other kids would "cruise around on Ski-Doos and arry random rifles. A lot of freedom."
Since her youth, she says, "values changed." Younger people "don't have the desire just to go out on the land."
THE KIDS ARE MORE INTO TECHNICAL STUFF NOW, LIKE A LOT OF ELECTRONICS.

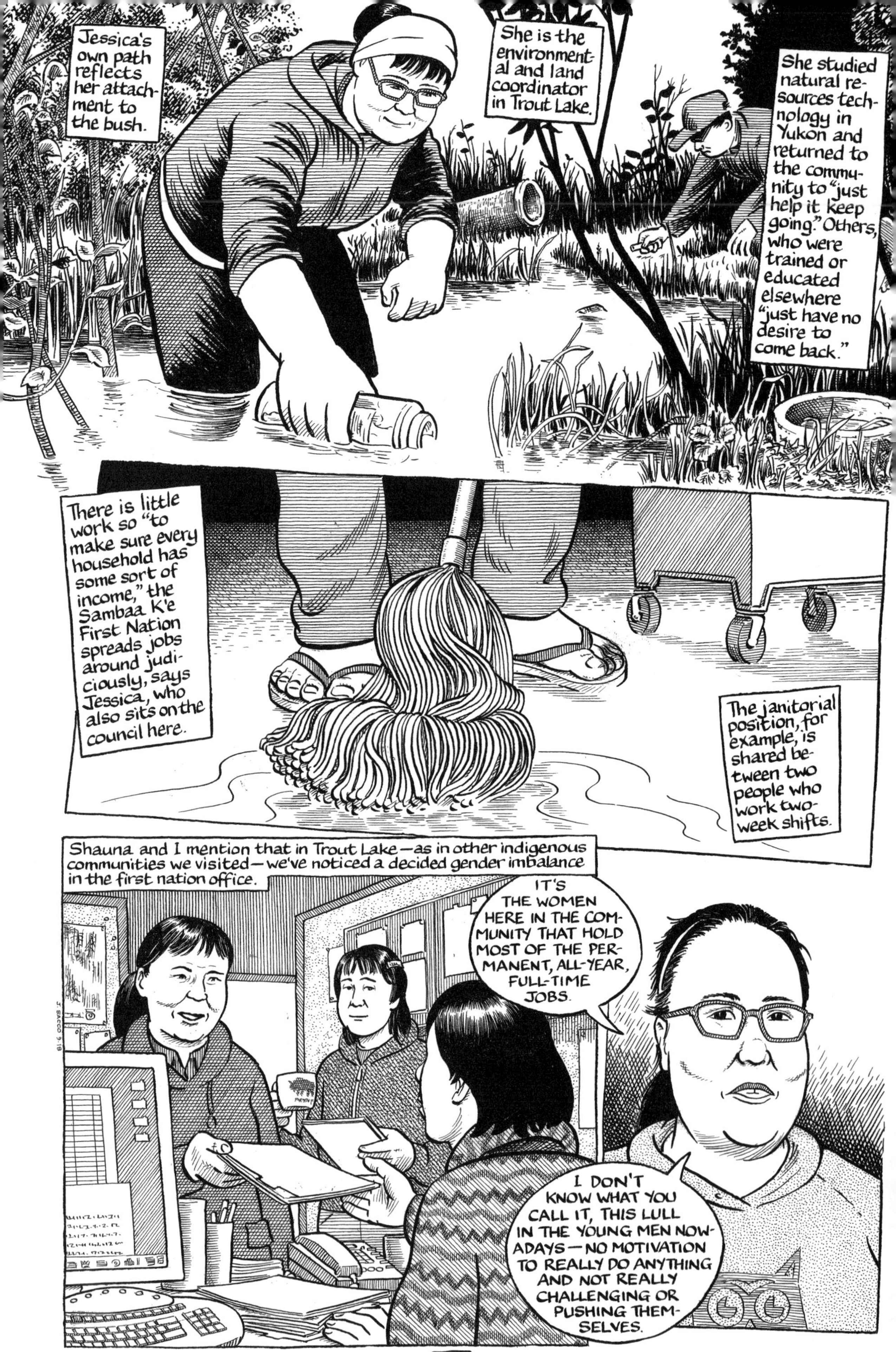
Jessica's own path reflects her attachment to the bush.
She is the environmental and land coordinator in Trout Lake.
She studied natural resources technology in Yukon and returned to the community to "just help it keep going." Others, who were trained or educated elsewhere "just have no desire to come back."
There is little work so "to make sure every household has some sort of income," the Sambaa K'e First Nation spreads jobs around judiciously, says Jessica, who also sits on the council here.
The janitorial position, for example, is shared between two people who work two-week shifts.
Shauna and I mention that in Trout Lake—as in other indigenous communities we visited—we've noticed a decided gender imbalance in the first nation office.
IT'S THE WOMEN HERE IN THE COMMUNITY THAT HOLD MOST OF THE PERMANENT, ALL-YEAR, FULL-TIME JOBS.
I DON'T KNOW WHAT YOU CALL IT, THIS LULL IN THE YOUNG MEN NOWADAYS—NO MOTIVATION TO REALLY DO ANYTHING AND NOT REALLY CHALLENGING OR PUSHING THEMSELVES.
J. SACCO 9.19

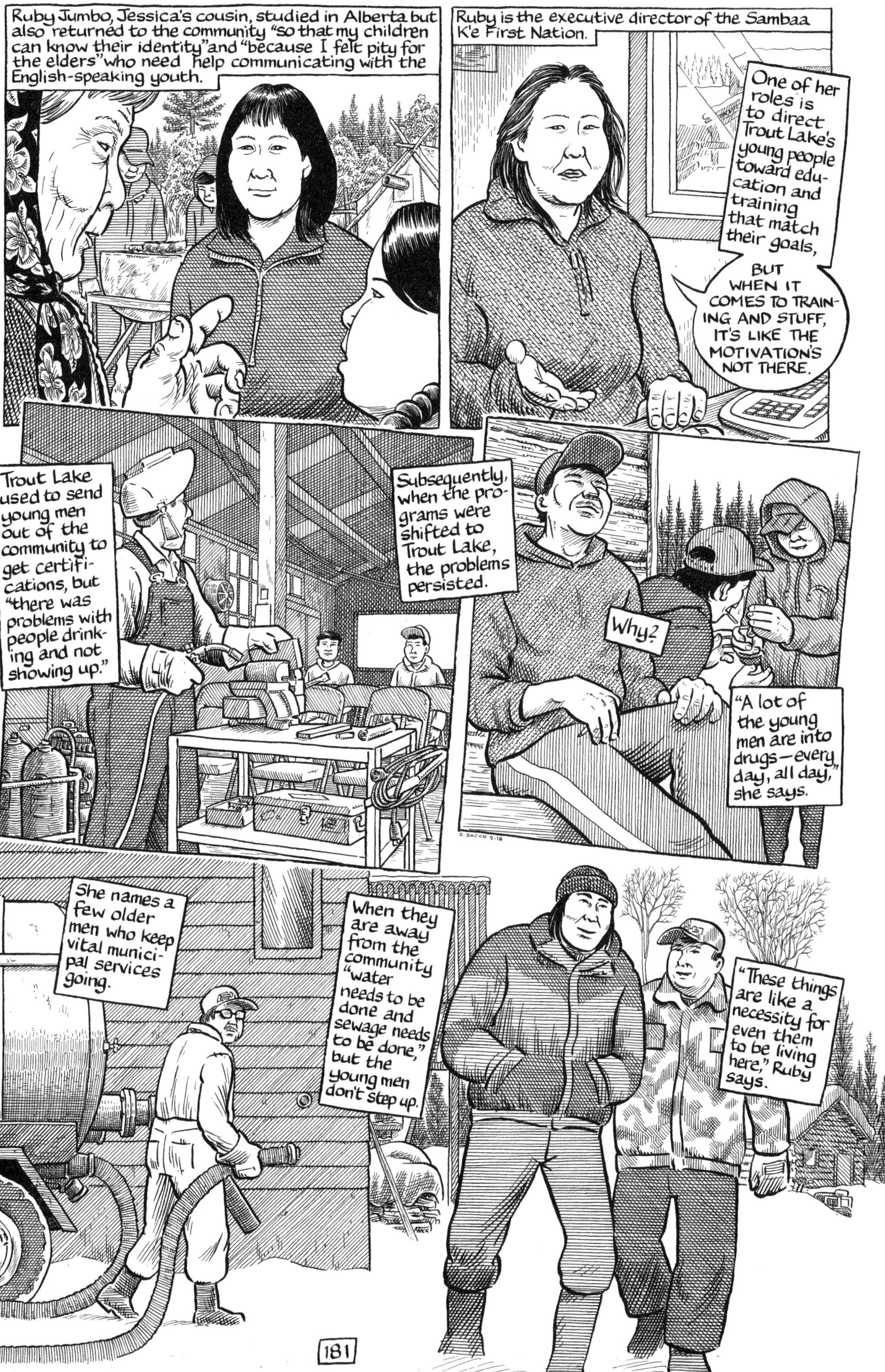
Ruby Jumbo, Jessica's cousin, studied in Alberta but also returned to the community "so that my children can know their identity" and "because I felt pity for the elders" who need help communicating with the English-speaking youth.
Ruby is the executive director of the Sambaa K'e First Nation.
One of her roles is to direct Trout Lake's young people toward education and training that match their goals,
BUT WHEN IT COMES TO TRAINING AND STUFF, IT'S LIKE THE MOTIVATION'S NOT THERE.
Trout Lake used to send young men out of the community to get certifications, but "there was problems with people drinking and not showing up."
Subsequently, when the programs were shifted to Trout Lake, the problems persisted.
Why?
"A lot of the young men are into drugs—every day, all day," she says.
J. SACCO 9.18
She names a few older men who keep vital municipal services going.
When they are away from the community "water needs to be done and sewage needs to be done," but the young men don't step up.
"These things are like a necessity for even them to be living here," Ruby says.

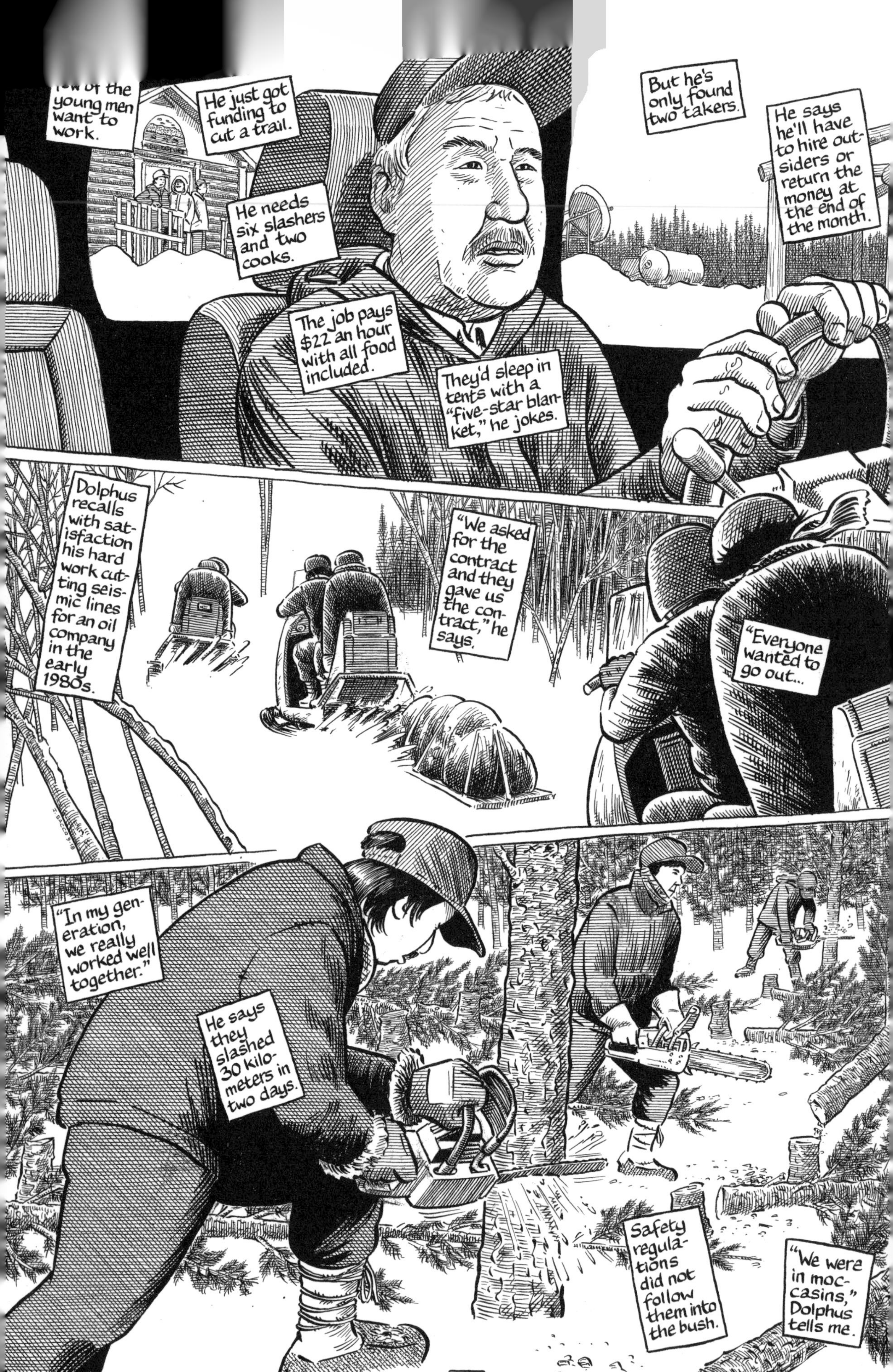
of the young men want to work.
He just got funding to cut a trail.
He needs six slashers and two cooks.
The job pays $22 an hour with all food included.
They'd sleep in tents with a "five-star blanket," he jokes.
But he's only found two takers.
He says he'll have to hire outsiders or return the money at the end of the month.
Dolphus recalls with satisfaction his hard work cutting seismic lines for an oil company in the early 1980s.
"We asked for the contract and they gave us the contract," he says.
"Everyone wanted to go out...
"In my generation, we really worked well together."
He says they slashed 30 kilometers in two days.
Safety regulations did not follow them into the bush.
"We were in moccasins," Dolphus tells me.

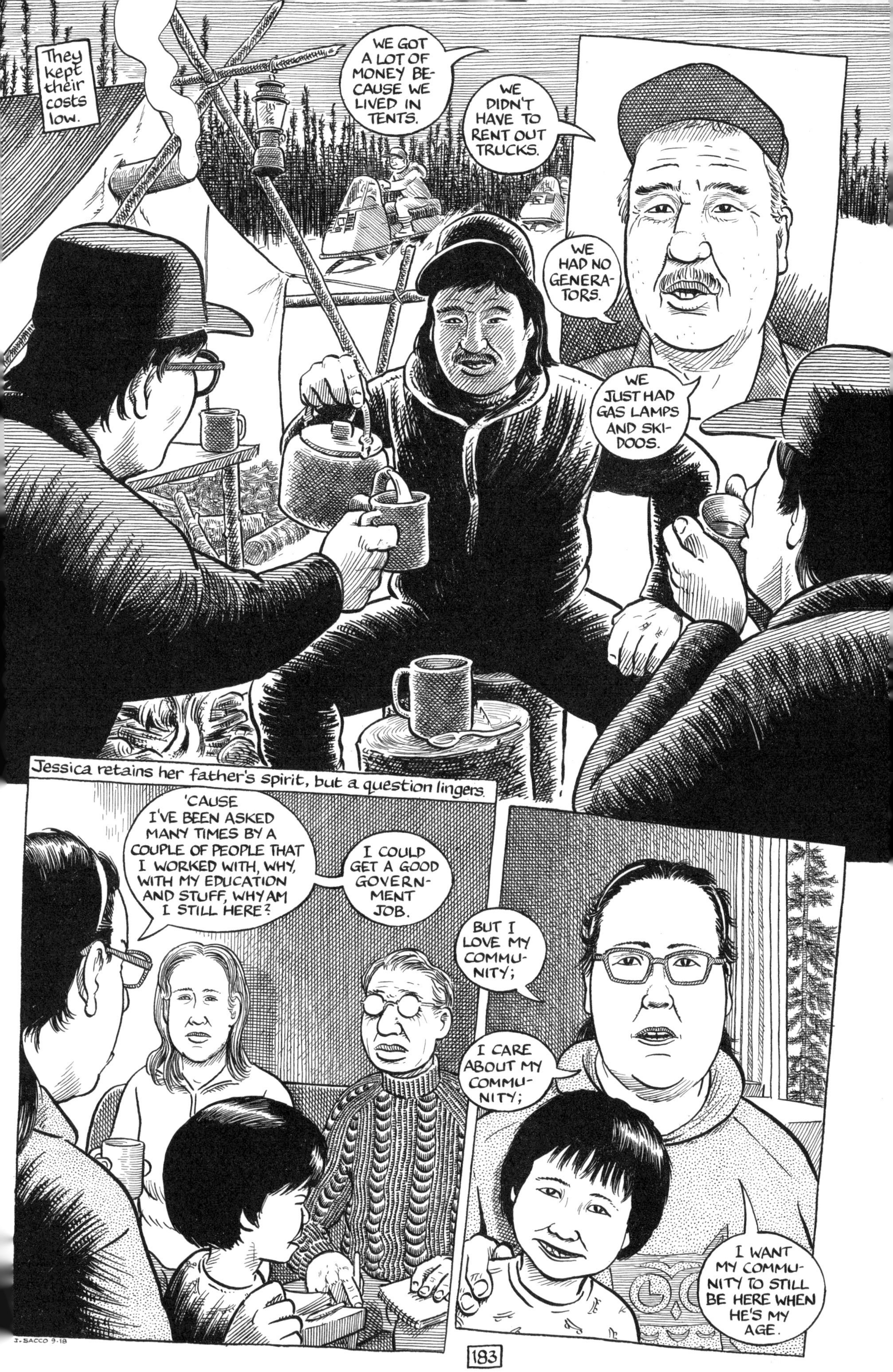
They kept their costs low.
WE GOT A LOT OF MONEY BECAUSE WE LIVED IN TENTS.
WE DIDN'T HAVE TO RENT OUT TRUCKS.
WE HAD NO GENERATORS.
WE JUST HAD GAS LAMPS AND SKI-DOOS.
Jessica retains her father's spirit, but a question lingers.
'CAUSE I'VE BEEN ASKED MANY TIMES BY A COUPLE OF PEOPLE THAT I WORKED WITH, WHY, WITH MY EDUCATION AND STUFF, WHY AM I STILL HERE?
I COULD GET A GOOD GOVERNMENT JOB.
BUT I LOVE MY COMMUNITY;
I CARE ABOUT MY COMMUNITY;
I WANT MY COMMUNITY TO STILL BE HERE WHEN HE'S MY AGE.
J. SACCO 9.18

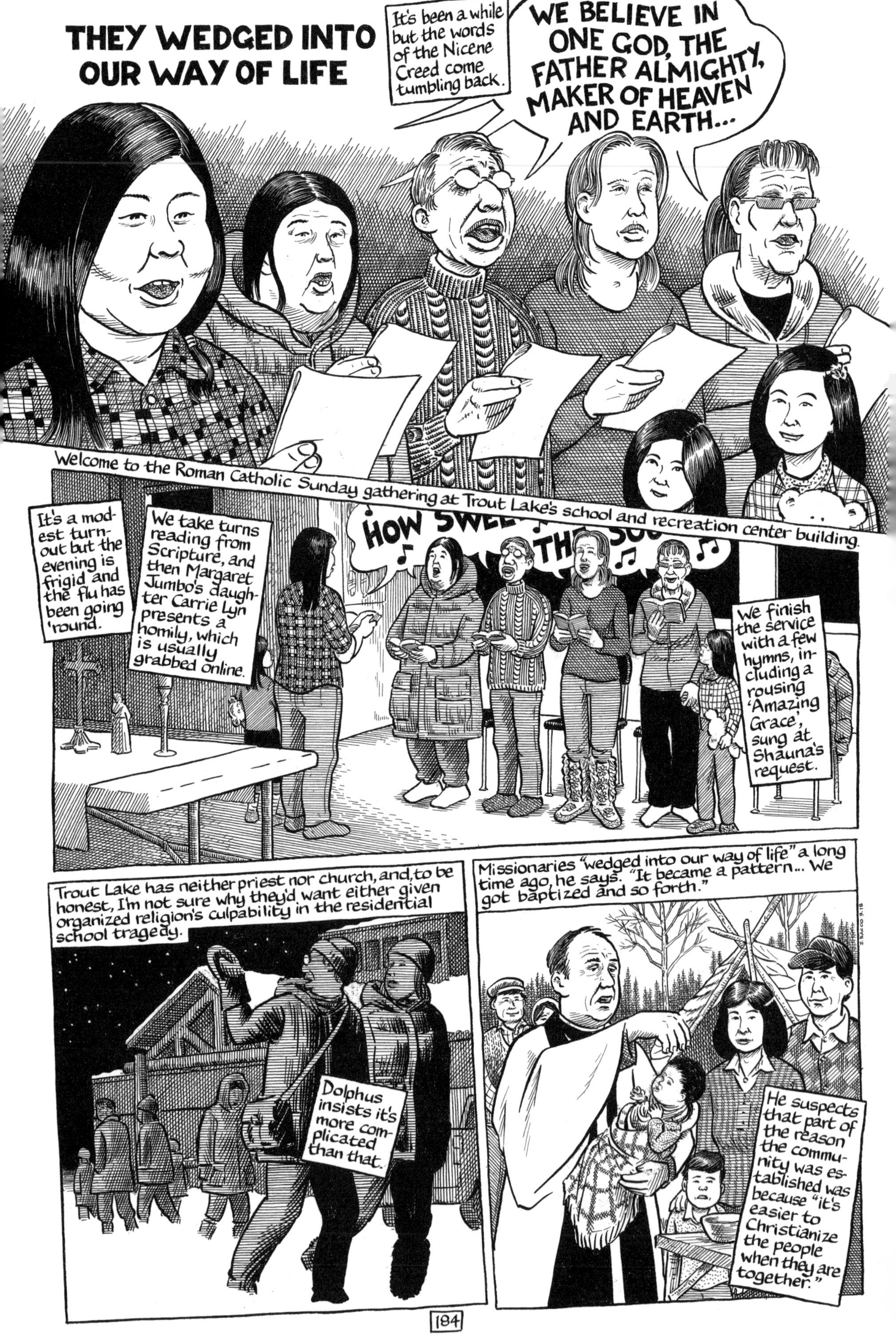

THEY WEDGED INTO OUR WAY OF LIFE
It's been a while but the words of the Nicene Creed come tumbling back.
WE BELIEVE IN ONE GOD, THE FATHER ALMIGHTY, MAKER OF HEAVEN AND EARTH...
Welcome to the Roman Catholic Sunday gathering at Trout Lake's school and recreation center building.
It's a modest turnout but the evening is frigid and the flu has been going 'round.
We take turns reading from Scripture, and then Margaret Jumbo's daughter Carrie Lyn presents a homily, which is usually grabbed online.
We finish the service with a few hymns, including a rousing 'Amazing Grace', sung at Shauna's request.
Trout Lake has neither priest nor church, and, to be honest, I'm not sure why they'd want either given organized religion's culpability in the residential school tragedy.
Dolphus insists it's more complicated than that.
Missionaries "wedged into our way of life" a long time ago, he says. "It became a pattern... We got baptized and so forth."
He suspects that part of the reason the community was established was because "it's easier to Christianize the people when they are together."

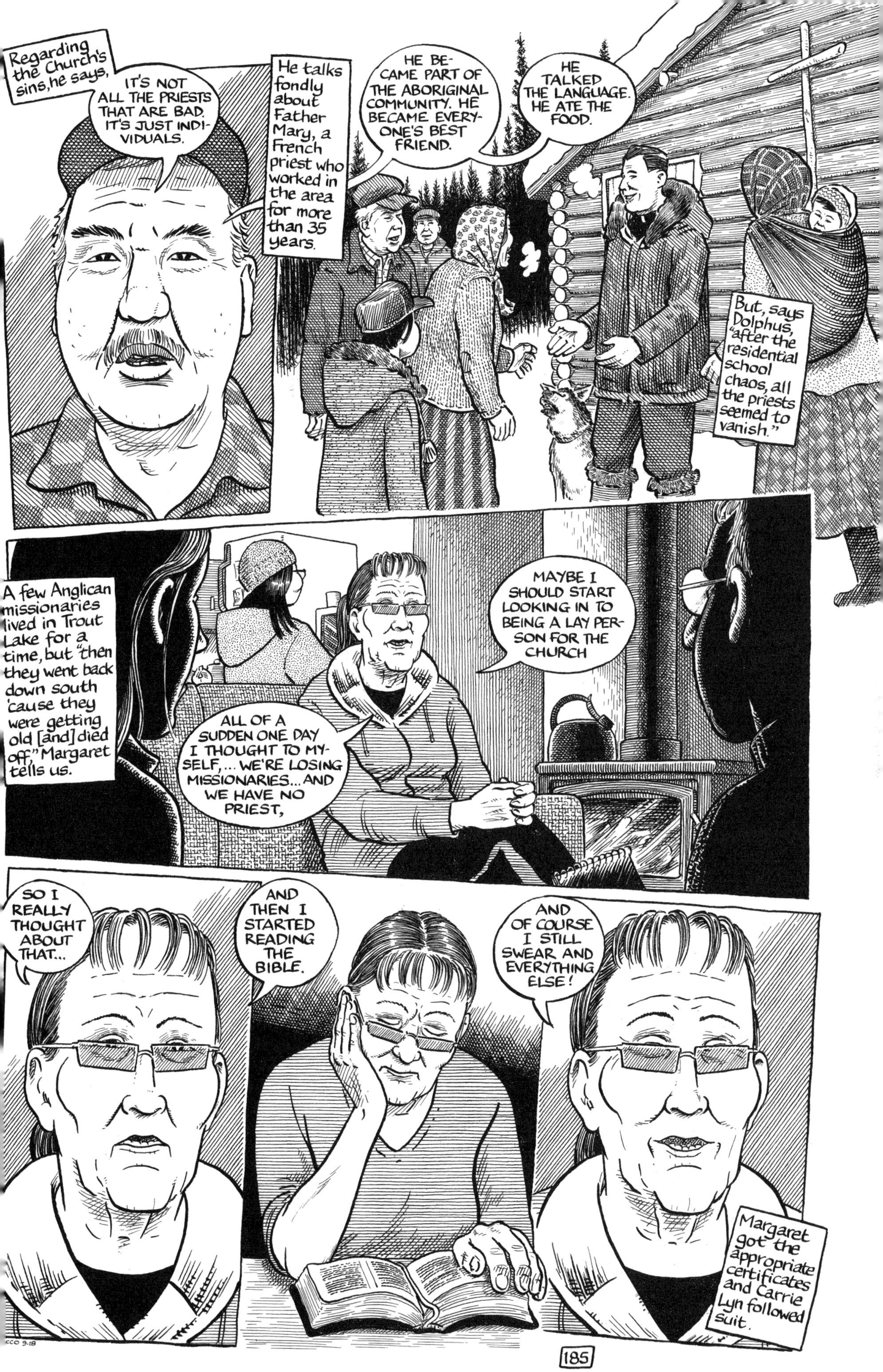

Regarding the Church's sins, he says,
IT'S NOT ALL THE PRIESTS THAT ARE BAD. IT'S JUST INDIVIDUALS.
He talks fondly about Father Mary, a French priest who worked in the area for more than 35 years.
HE BECAME PART OF THE ABORIGINAL COMMUNITY. HE BECAME EVERYONE'S BEST FRIEND.
HE TALKED THE LANGUAGE. HE ATE THE FOOD.
But, says Dolphus, "after the residential school chaos, all the priests seemed to vanish."
A few Anglican missionaries lived in Trout Lake for a time, but "then they went back down south 'cause they were getting old [and] died off," Margaret tells us.
ALL OF A SUDDEN ONE DAY I THOUGHT TO MYSELF, ... WE'RE LOSING MISSIONARIES... AND WE HAVE NO PRIEST,
MAYBE I SHOULD START LOOKING IN TO BEING A LAY PERSON FOR THE CHURCH
SO I REALLY THOUGHT ABOUT THAT...
AND THEN I STARTED READING THE BIBLE.
AND OF COURSE I STILL SWEAR AND EVERYTHING ELSE!
Margaret got the appropriate certificates and Carrie Lyn followed suit.
CCO 9.18

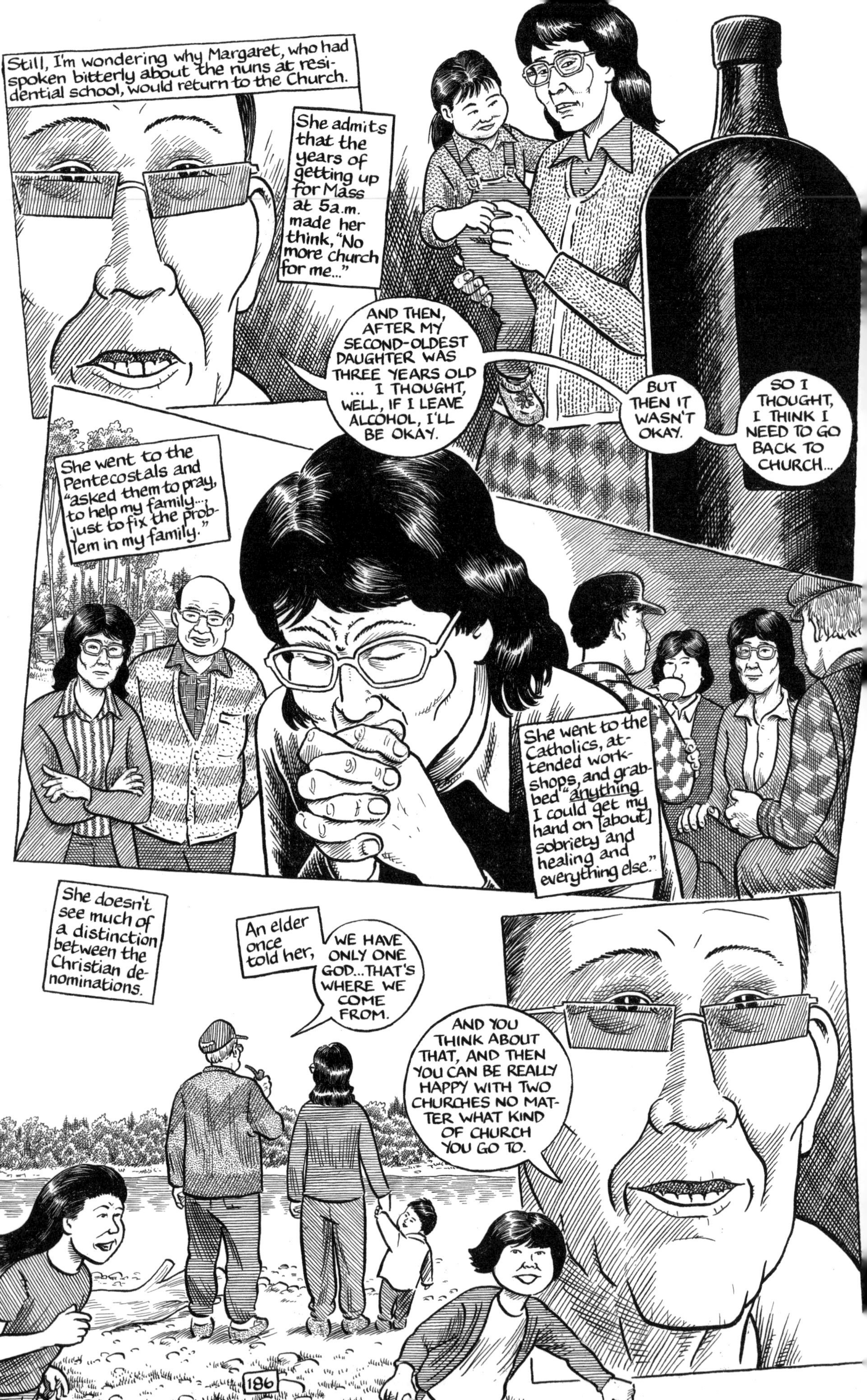
Still, I'm wondering why Margaret, who had spoken bitterly about the nuns at residential school, would return to the Church.
She admits that the years of getting up for Mass at 5a.m. made her think, "No more church for me..."
AND THEN, AFTER MY SECOND-OLDEST DAUGHTER WAS THREE YEARS OLD ... I THOUGHT, WELL, IF I LEAVE ALCOHOL, I'LL BE OKAY.
BUT THEN IT WASN'T OKAY.
SO I THOUGHT, I THINK I NEED TO GO BACK TO CHURCH...
She went to the Pentecostals and "asked them to pray, to help my family... just to fix the problem in my family."
She went to the Catholics, attended workshops, and grabbed "anything I could get my hand on [about] sobriety and healing and everything else."
She doesn't see much of a distinction between the Christian denominations.
An elder once told her,
WE HAVE ONLY ONE GOD...THAT'S WHERE WE COME FROM.
AND YOU THINK ABOUT THAT, AND THEN YOU CAN BE REALLY HAPPY WITH TWO CHURCHES NO MATTER WHAT KIND OF CHURCH YOU GO TO.

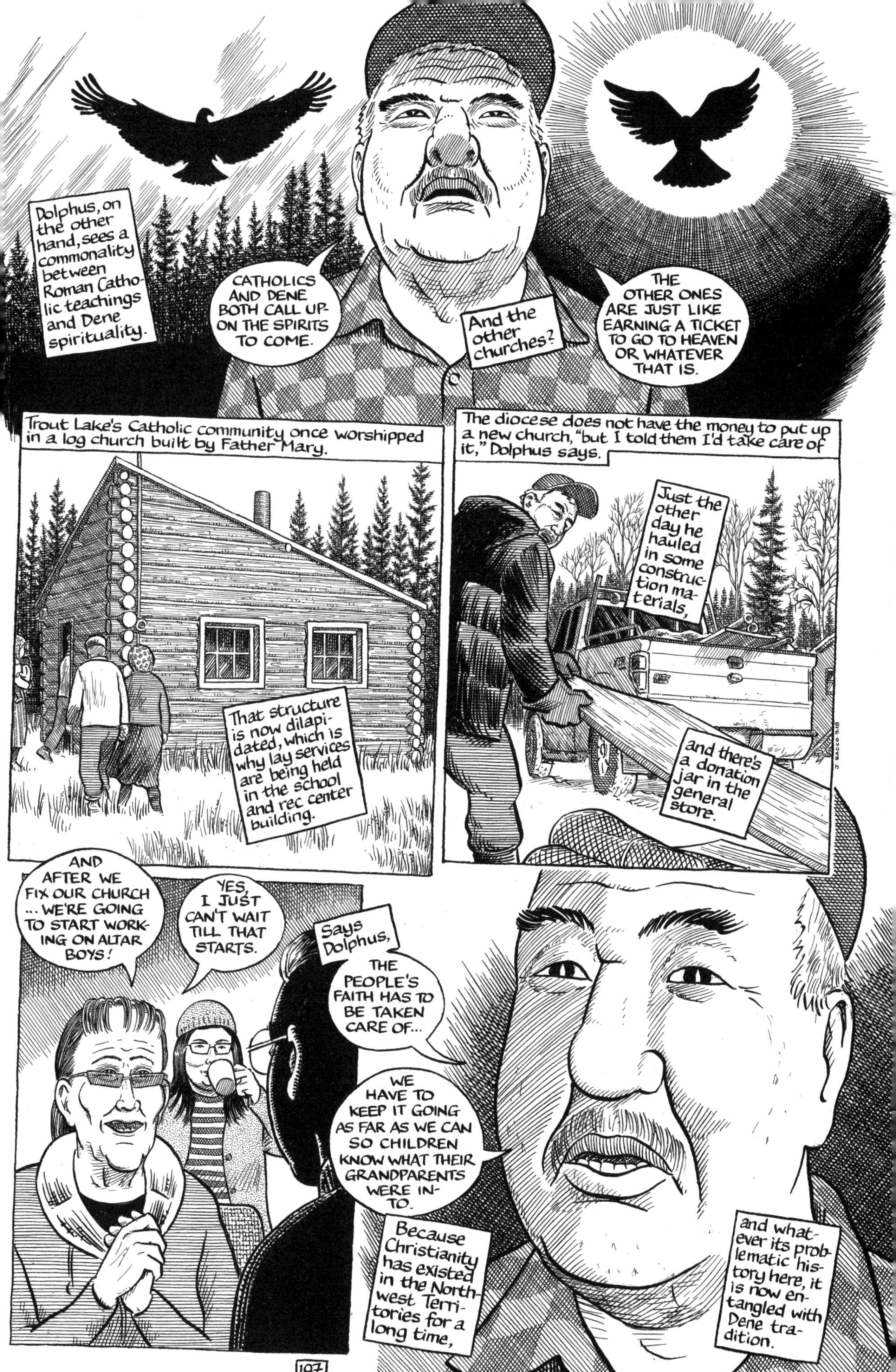

Dolphus, on the other hand, sees a commonality between Roman Catholic teachings and Dene spirituality.
CATHOLICS AND DENE BOTH CALL UPON THE SPIRITS TO COME.
And the other churches?
THE OTHER ONES ARE JUST LIKE EARNING A TICKET TO GO TO HEAVEN OR WHATEVER THAT IS.
Trout Lake's Catholic community once worshipped in a log church built by Father Mary.
That structure is now dilapidated, which is why lay services are being held in the school and rec center building.
The diocese does not have the money to put up a new church, "but I told them I'd take care of it," Dolphus says.
Just the other day he hauled in some construction materials,
and there's a donation jar in the general store.
J. SACCO 9.18
AND AFTER WE FIX OUR CHURCH ... WE'RE GOING TO START WORKING ON ALTAR BOYS!
YES, I JUST CAN'T WAIT TILL THAT STARTS.
Says Dolphus,
THE PEOPLE'S FAITH HAS TO BE TAKEN CARE OF...
WE HAVE TO KEEP IT GOING AS FAR AS WE CAN SO CHILDREN KNOW WHAT THEIR GRANDPARENTS WERE INTO.
Because Christianity has existed in the Northwest Territories for a long time,
and whatever its problematic history here, it is now entangled with Dene tradition.

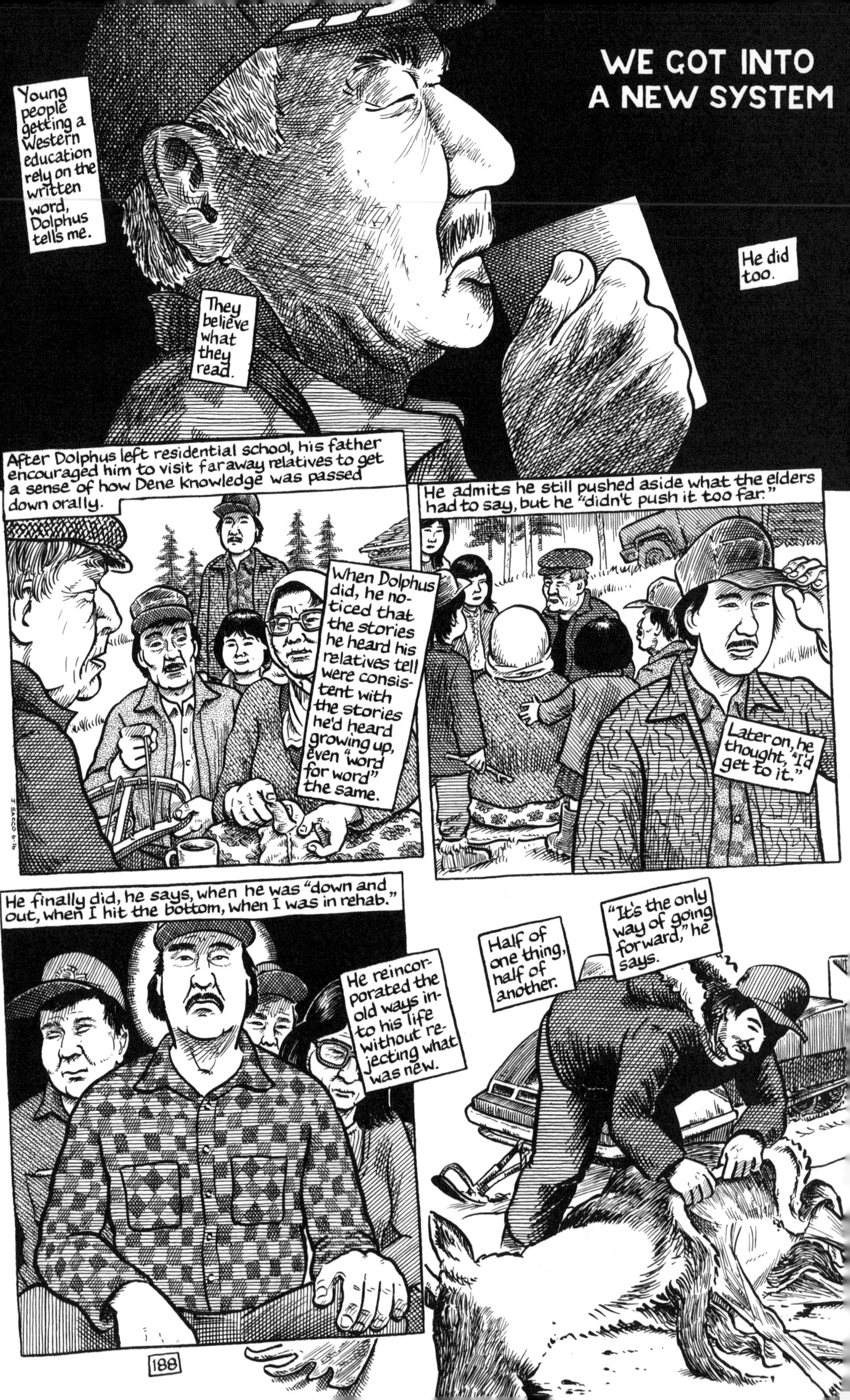
WE GOT INTO A NEW SYSTEM
Young people getting a Western education rely on the written word, Dolphus tells me.
They believe what they read.
He did too.
After Dolphus left residential school, his father encouraged him to visit faraway relatives to get a sense of how Dene knowledge was passed down orally.
When Dolphus did, he noticed that the stories he heard his relatives tell were consistent with the stories he'd heard growing up, even "word for word" the same.
J. SACCO 6·16
He admits he still pushed aside what the elders had to say, but he "didn't push it too far."
Later on, he thought, "I'd get to it."
He finally did, he says, when he was "down and out, when I hit the bottom, when I was in rehab."
He reincorporated the old ways into his life without rejecting what was new.
Half of one thing, half of another.
"It's the only way of going forward," he says.

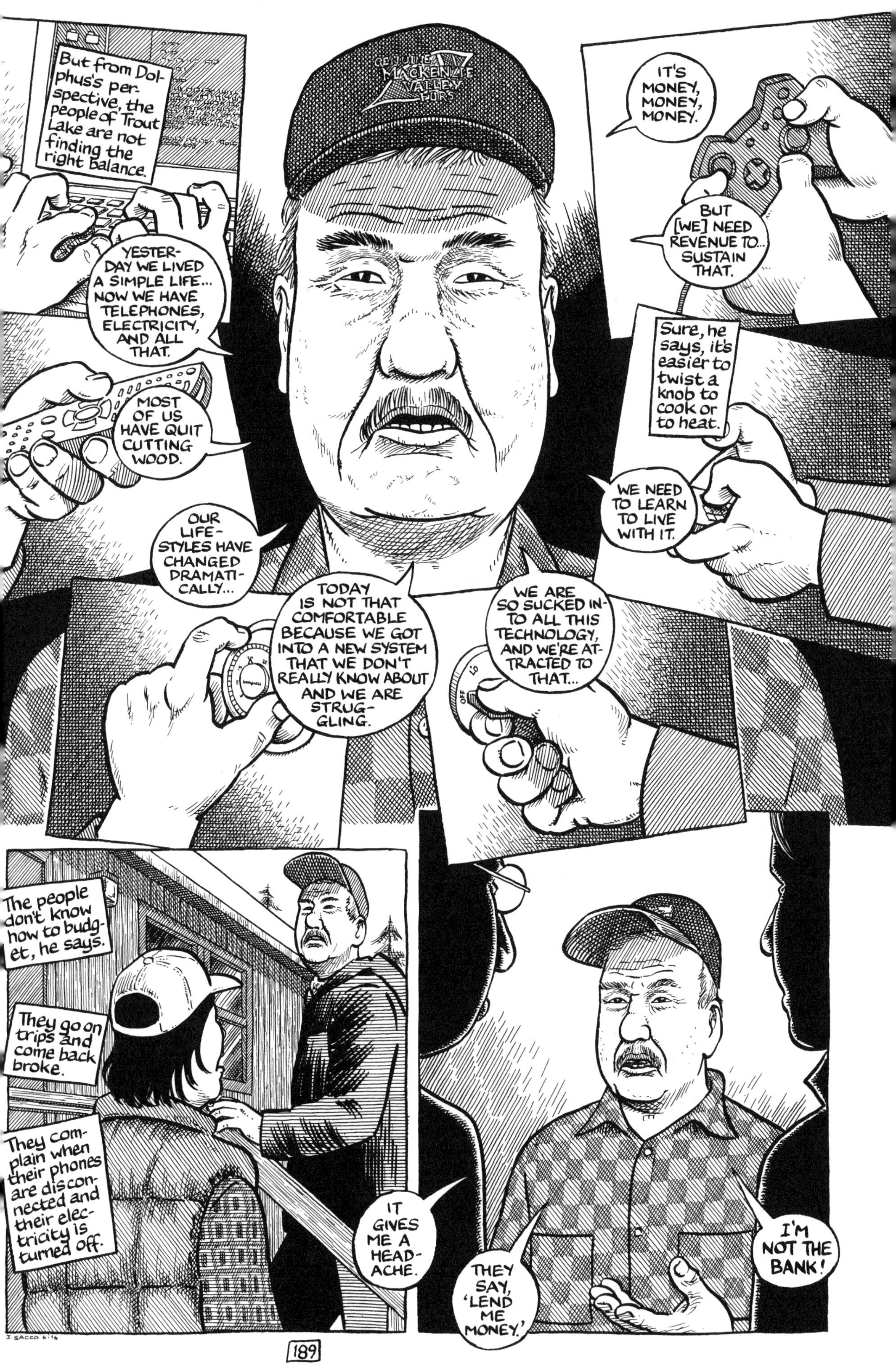

GENUINE MACKENZIE VALLEY FURS
But from Dolphus's perspective, the people of Trout Lake are not finding the right balance.
YESTERDAY WE LIVED A SIMPLE LIFE... NOW WE HAVE TELEPHONES, ELECTRICITY, AND ALL THAT.
MOST OF US HAVE QUIT CUTTING WOOD.
OUR LIFESTYLES HAVE CHANGED DRAMATICALLY...
TODAY IS NOT THAT COMFORTABLE BECAUSE WE GOT INTO A NEW SYSTEM THAT WE DON'T REALLY KNOW ABOUT AND WE ARE STRUGGLING.
WE ARE SO SUCKED INTO ALL THIS TECHNOLOGY, AND WE'RE ATTRACTED TO THAT...
IT'S MONEY, MONEY, MONEY.
BUT [WE] NEED REVENUE TO... SUSTAIN THAT.
Sure, he says, it's easier to twist a knob to cook or to heat.
WE NEED TO LEARN TO LIVE WITH IT.
The people don't know how to budget, he says.
They go on trips and come back broke.
They complain when their phones are disconnected and their electricity is turned off.
IT GIVES ME A HEADACHE.
THEY SAY, 'LEND ME MONEY.'
I'M NOT THE BANK!
J. SACCO 6.16

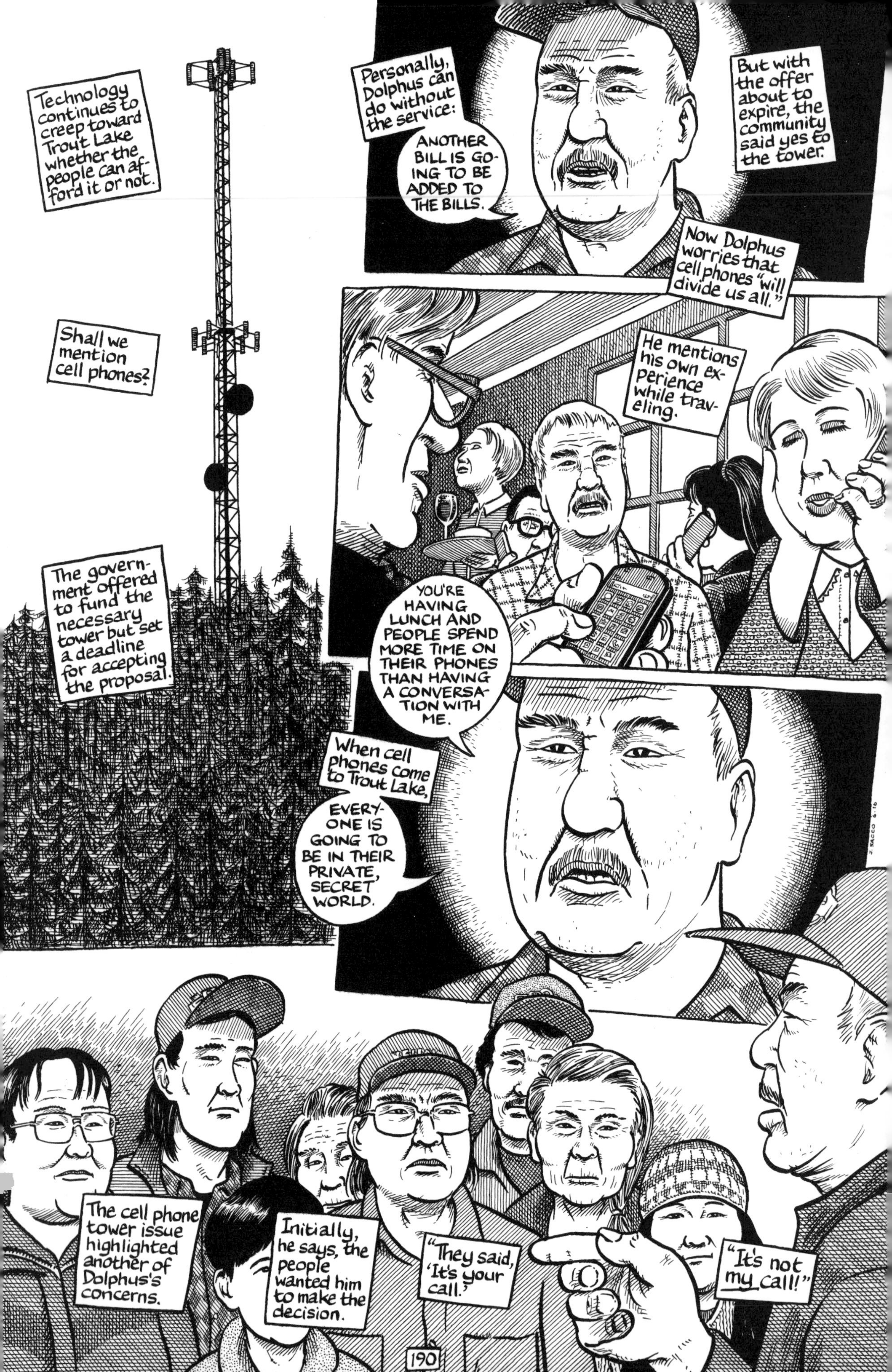

Technology continues to creep toward Trout Lake whether the people can afford it or not.
Personally, Dolphus can do without the service:
ANOTHER BILL IS GOING TO BE ADDED TO THE BILLS.
But with the offer about to expire, the community said yes to the tower.
Shall we mention cell phones?
Now Dolphus worries that cell phones "will divide us all."
He mentions his own experience while traveling.
The government offered to fund the necessary tower but set a deadline for accepting the proposal.
YOU'RE HAVING LUNCH AND PEOPLE SPEND MORE TIME ON THEIR PHONES THAN HAVING A CONVERSATION WITH ME.
When cell phones come to Trout Lake,
EVERYONE IS GOING TO BE IN THEIR PRIVATE, SECRET WORLD.
The cell phone tower issue highlighted another of Dolphus's concerns.
Initially, he says, the people wanted him to make the decision.
"They said, 'It's your call.'
"It's not my call!"

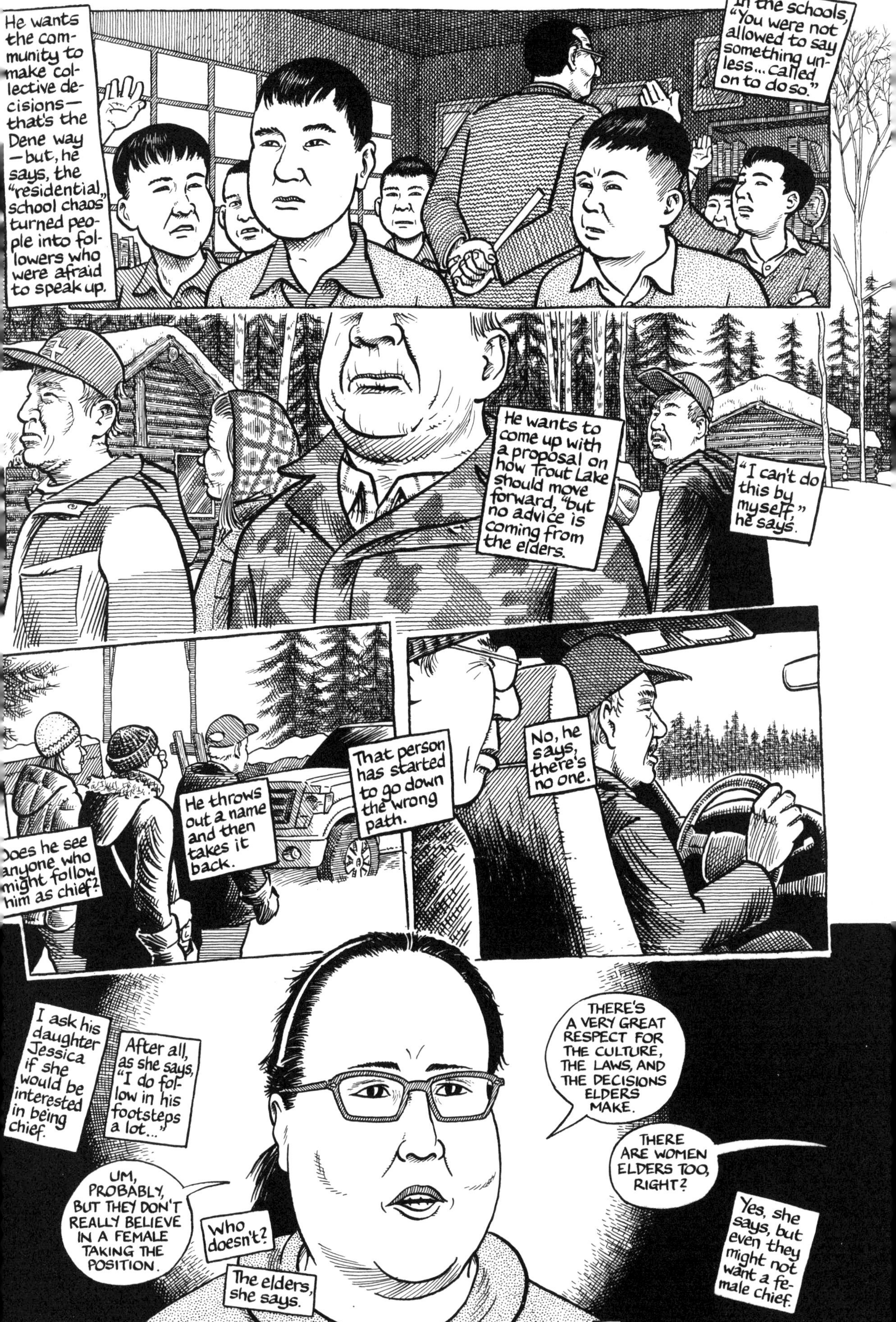
He wants the community to make collective decisions—that's the Dene way—but, he says, the "residential school chaos" turned people into followers who were afraid to speak up.
In the schools, "You were not allowed to say something unless... called on to do so."
He wants to come up with a proposal on how Trout Lake should move forward, "but no advice is coming from the elders.
"I can't do this by myself," he says.
Does he see anyone who might follow him as chief?
He throws out a name and then takes it back.
That person has started to go down the wrong path.
No, he says, there's no one.
I ask his daughter Jessica if she would be interested in being chief.
After all, as she says, "I do follow in his footsteps a lot..."
UM, PROBABLY, BUT THEY DON'T REALLY BELIEVE IN A FEMALE TAKING THE POSITION.
Who doesn't?
The elders, she says.
THERE'S A VERY GREAT RESPECT FOR THE CULTURE, THE LAWS, AND THE DECISIONS ELDERS MAKE.
THERE ARE WOMEN ELDERS TOO, RIGHT?
Yes, she says, but even they might not want a female chief.

She once asked her dad why women weren't right for the role.

I DON'T THINK HE KNEW HOW TO EXPLAIN IT TO ME, BUT HE JUST SAID, 'THEY THINK AND MAKE DECISIONS WITH THEIR EMOTIONS...'

She recalls her dad telling her how things used to be in the bush, how men cut down trees and hunted, how they walked through beaver ponds in the night. They did the dangerous work.

Women and children stayed in the camps for protection because "back then you really had to make sure...life kept going."

She could point out a recent female chief in Fort Simpson and the current one in Jean Marie River, a community in said to have been founded by three sisters.

But Jessica approaches the issue gently.

I DON'T KNOW IF MY DAD WOULD EVER LET ME BE CHIEF.

IT WOULD SURE BE INTERESTING, I THINK.

Meanwhile, Dolphus is tired of the job. "You get stuck in there," he says.

I JUST WANT TO GO IN THE BUSH.

I'M HUNGRY FOR THAT PART OF MY OWN LIFE.

192

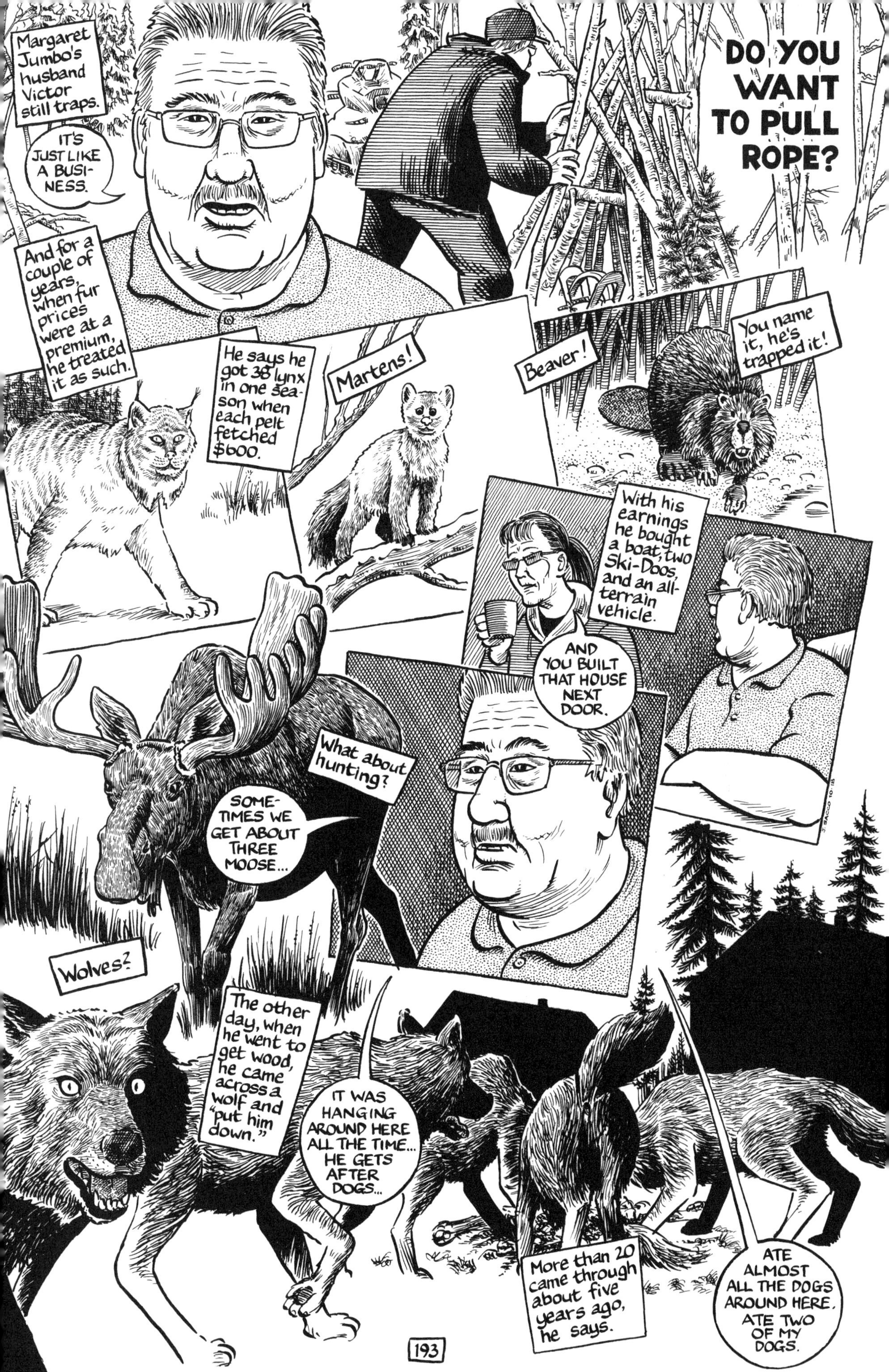

Margaret Jumbo's husband Victor still traps.
IT'S JUST LIKE A BUSINESS.
DO YOU WANT TO PULL ROPE?
And for a couple of years, when fur prices were at a premium, he treated it as such.
He says he got 38 lynx in one season when each pelt fetched $600.
Martens!
Beaver!
You name it, he's trapped it!
With his earnings he bought a boat, two Ski-Doos, and an all-terrain vehicle.
AND YOU BUILT THAT HOUSE NEXT DOOR.
What about hunting?
SOMETIMES WE GET ABOUT THREE MOOSE...
Wolves?
The other day, when he went to get wood, he came across a wolf and "put him down."
IT WAS HANGING AROUND HERE ALL THE TIME... HE GETS AFTER DOGS...
More than 20 came through about five years ago, he says.
ATE ALMOST ALL THE DOGS AROUND HERE. ATE TWO OF MY DOGS.

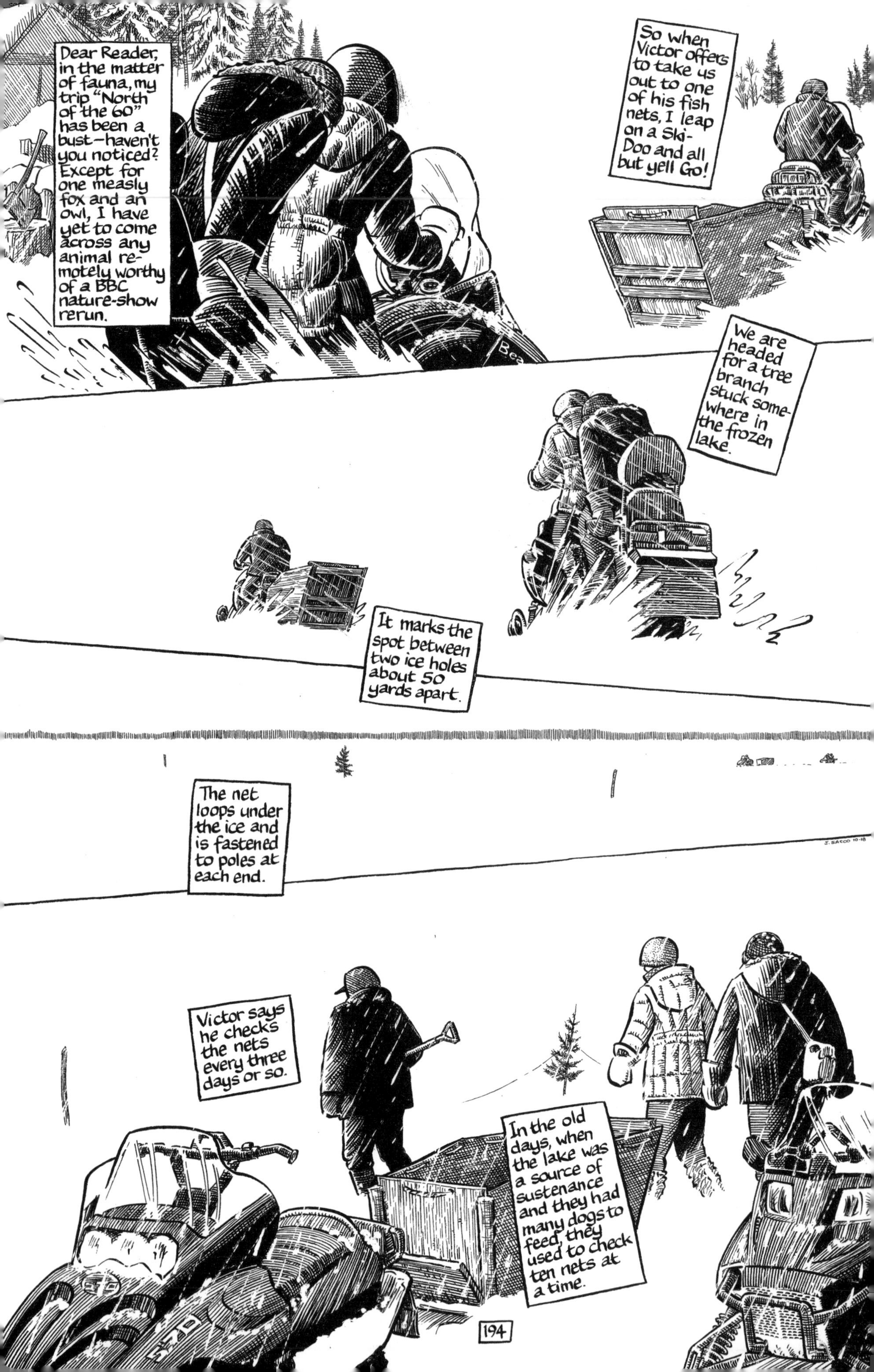

Dear Reader, in the matter of fauna, my trip "North of the 60" has been a bust—haven't you noticed? Except for one measly fox and an owl, I have yet to come across any animal remotely worthy of a BBC nature-show rerun.
So when Victor offers to take us out to one of his fish nets, I leap on a Ski-Doo and all but yell Go!
We are headed for a tree branch stuck somewhere in the frozen lake.
It marks the spot between two ice holes about 50 yards apart.
The net loops under the ice and is fastened to poles at each end.
J. SACCO 10-18
Victor says he checks the nets every three days or so.
In the old days, when the lake was a source of sustenance and they had many dogs to feed, they used to check ten nets at a time.

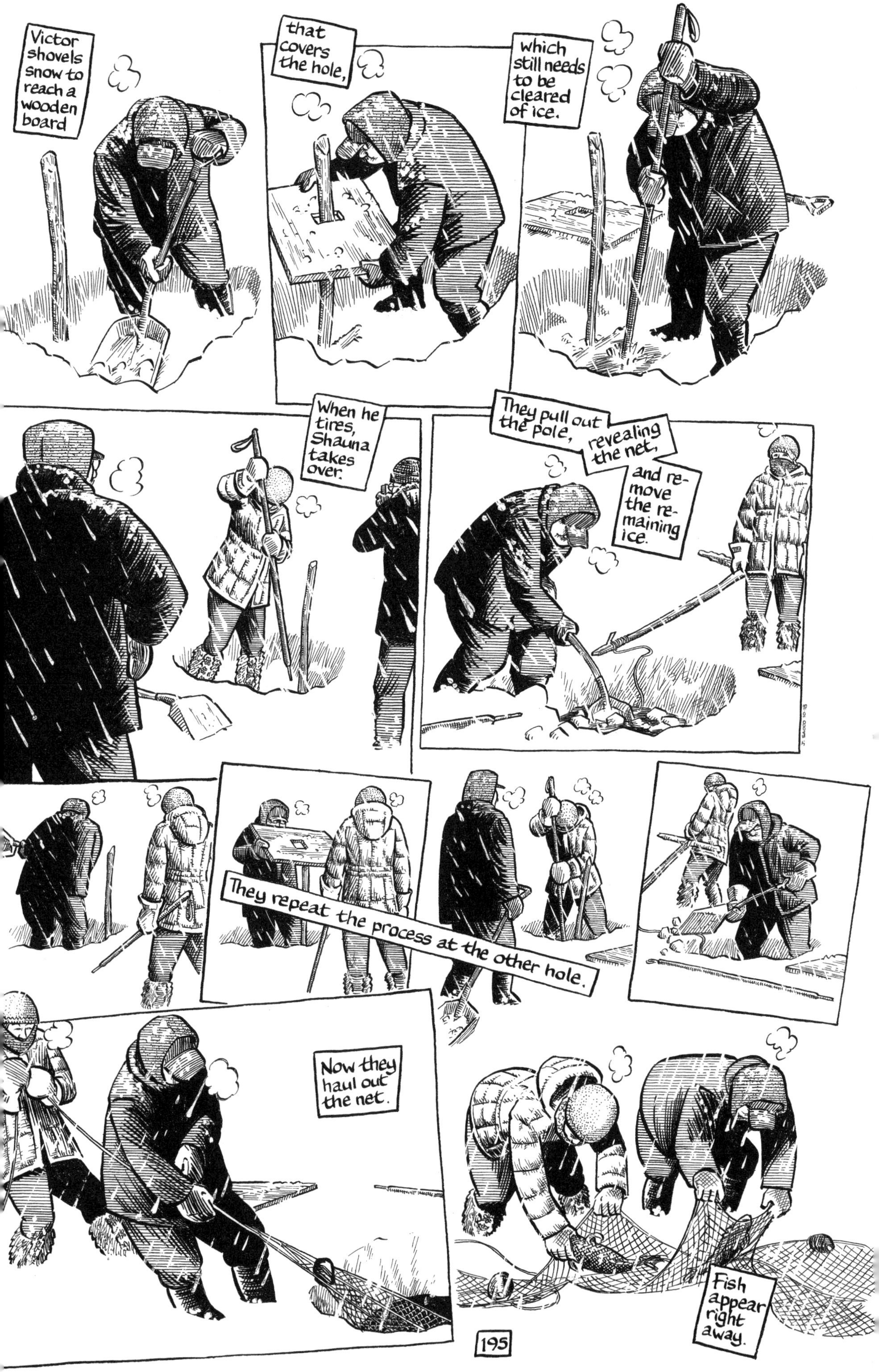
Victor shovels snow to reach a wooden board
that covers the hole,
which still needs to be cleared of ice.
When he tires, Shauna takes over.
They pull out the pole,
revealing the net,
and remove the remaining ice.
J. SACCO 10-18
They repeat the process at the other hole.
Now they haul out the net.
Fish appear right away.

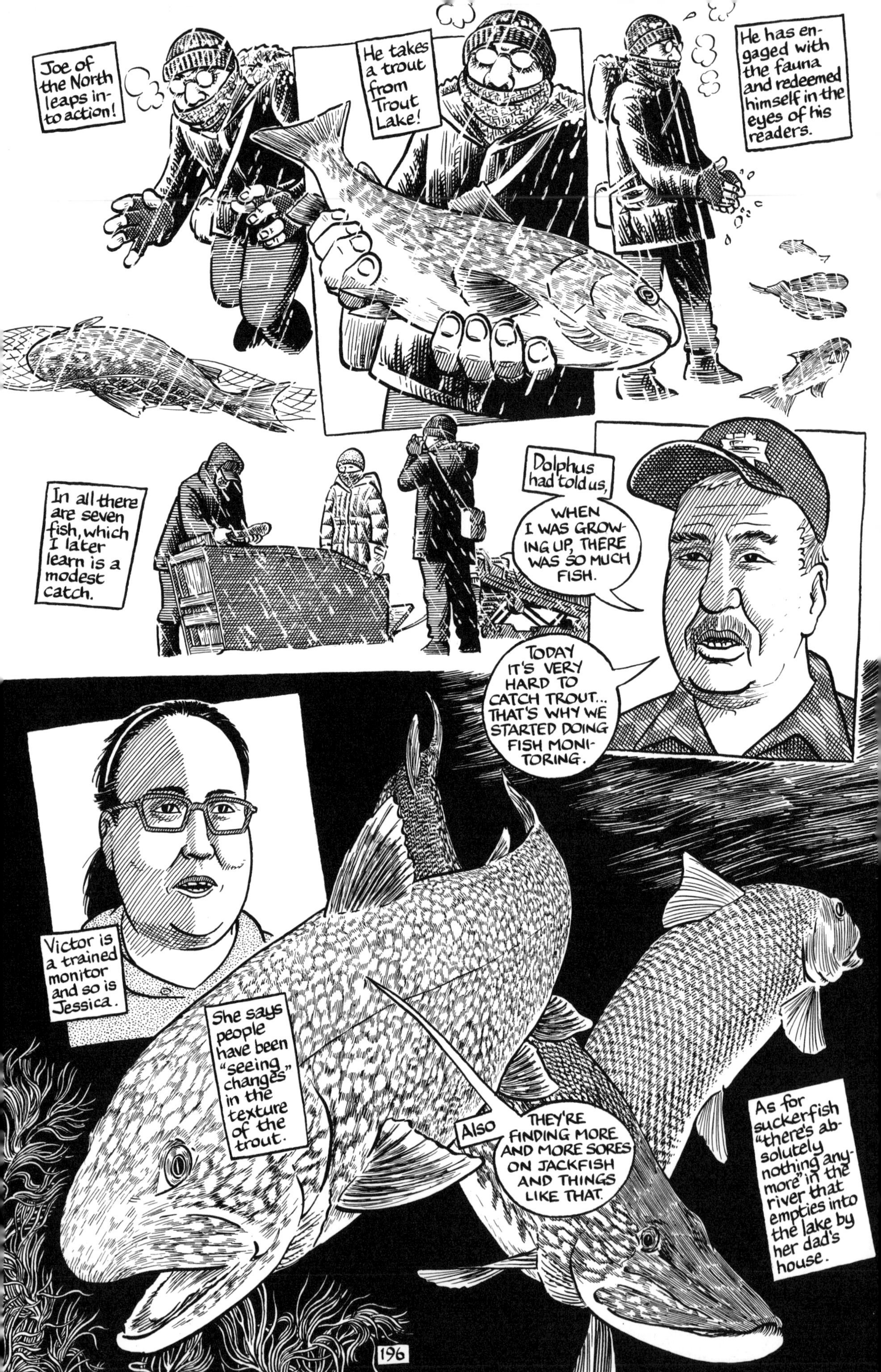
Joe of the North leaps into action!
He takes a trout from Trout Lake!
He has engaged with the fauna and redeemed himself in the eyes of his readers.
In all there are seven fish, which I later learn is a modest catch.
Dolphus had told us,
WHEN I WAS GROWING UP, THERE WAS SO MUCH FISH.
TODAY IT'S VERY HARD TO CATCH TROUT... THAT'S WHY WE STARTED DOING FISH MONITORING.
Victor is a trained monitor and so is Jessica.
She says people have been "seeing changes" in the texture of the trout.
Also
THEY'RE FINDING MORE AND MORE SORES ON JACKFISH AND THINGS LIKE THAT.
As for suckerfish "there's absolutely nothing anymore" in the river that empties into the lake by her dad's house.

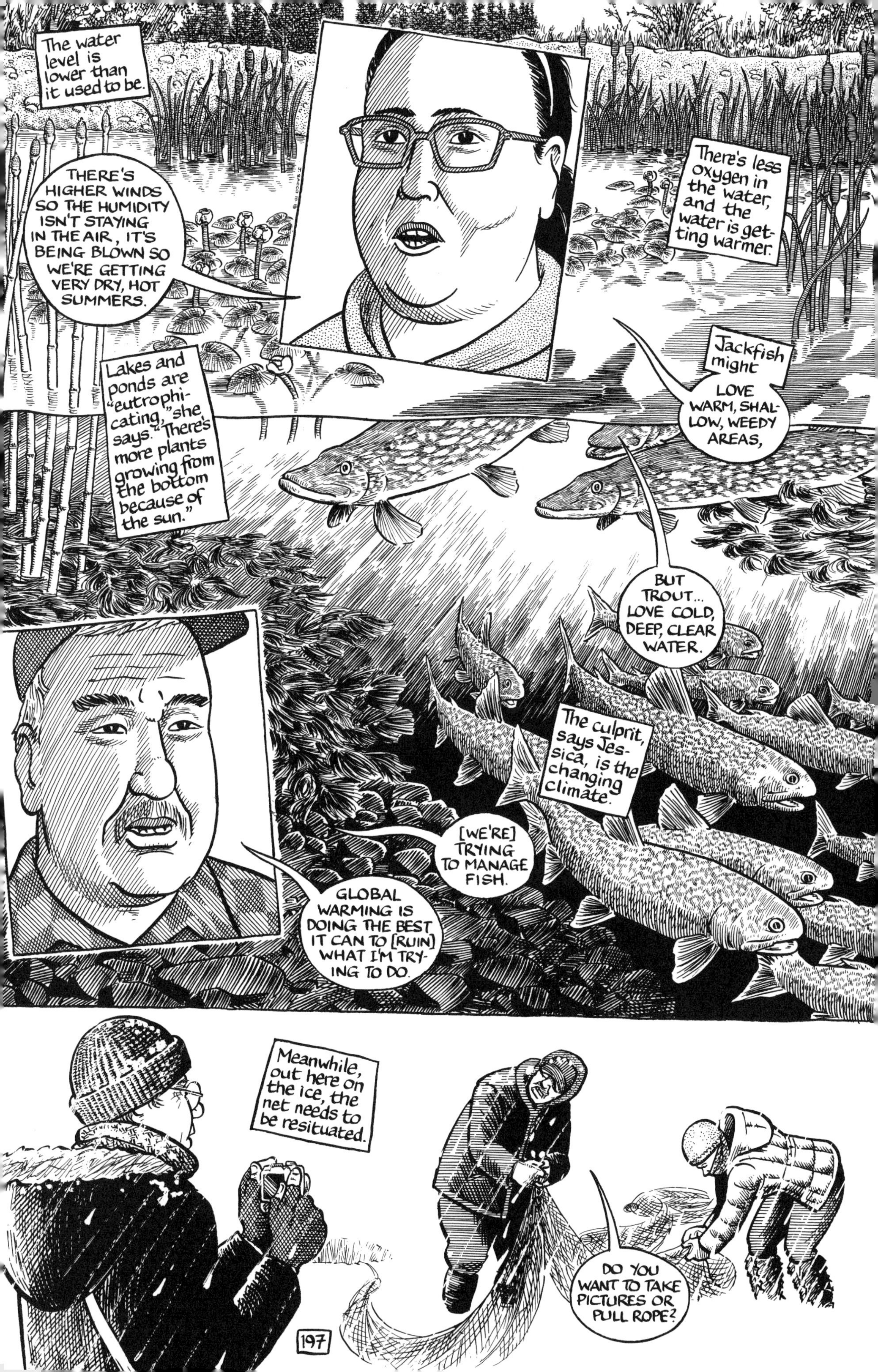

The water level is lower than it used to be.
THERE'S HIGHER WINDS SO THE HUMIDITY ISN'T STAYING IN THE AIR, IT'S BEING BLOWN SO WE'RE GETTING VERY DRY, HOT SUMMERS.
There's less oxygen in the water, and the water is getting warmer.
Lakes and ponds are "eutrophicating," she says. "There's more plants growing from the bottom because of the sun."
Jackfish might
LOVE WARM, SHALLOW, WEEDY AREAS,
BUT TROUT... LOVE COLD, DEEP, CLEAR WATER.
The culprit, says Jessica, is the changing climate.
[WE'RE] TRYING TO MANAGE FISH.
GLOBAL WARMING IS DOING THE BEST IT CAN TO [RUIN] WHAT I'M TRYING TO DO.
Meanwhile, out here on the ice, the net needs to be resituated.
DO YOU WANT TO TAKE PICTURES OR PULL ROPE?

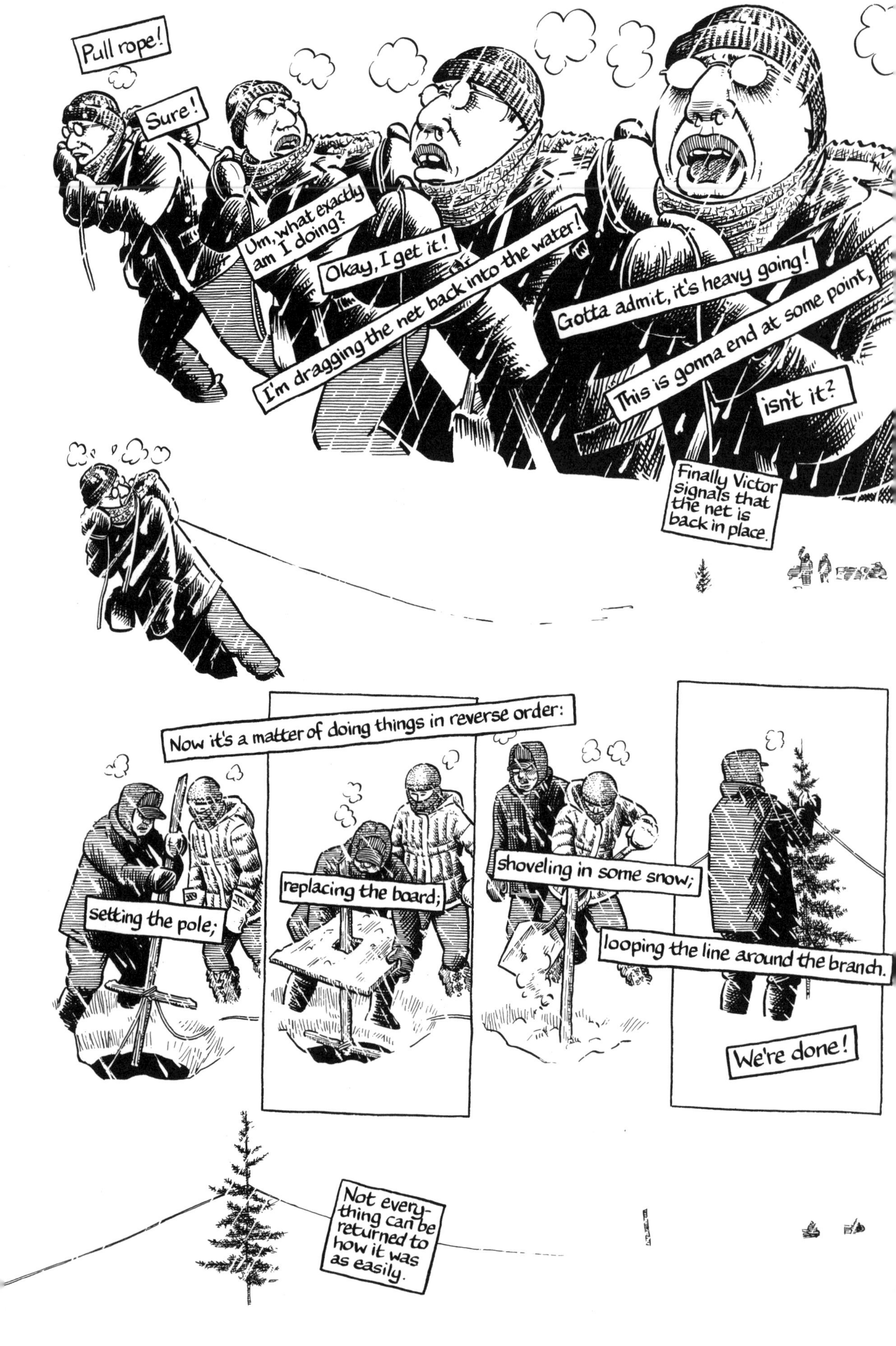
Pull rope!
Sure!
Um, what exactly am I doing?
Okay, I get it!
I'm dragging the net back into the water!
Gotta admit, it's heavy going!
This is gonna end at some point,
isn't it?
Finally Victor signals that the net is back in place.
Now it's a matter of doing things in reverse order:
setting the pole;
replacing the board;
shoveling in some snow;
looping the line around the branch.
We're done!
Not everything can be returned to how it was as easily.

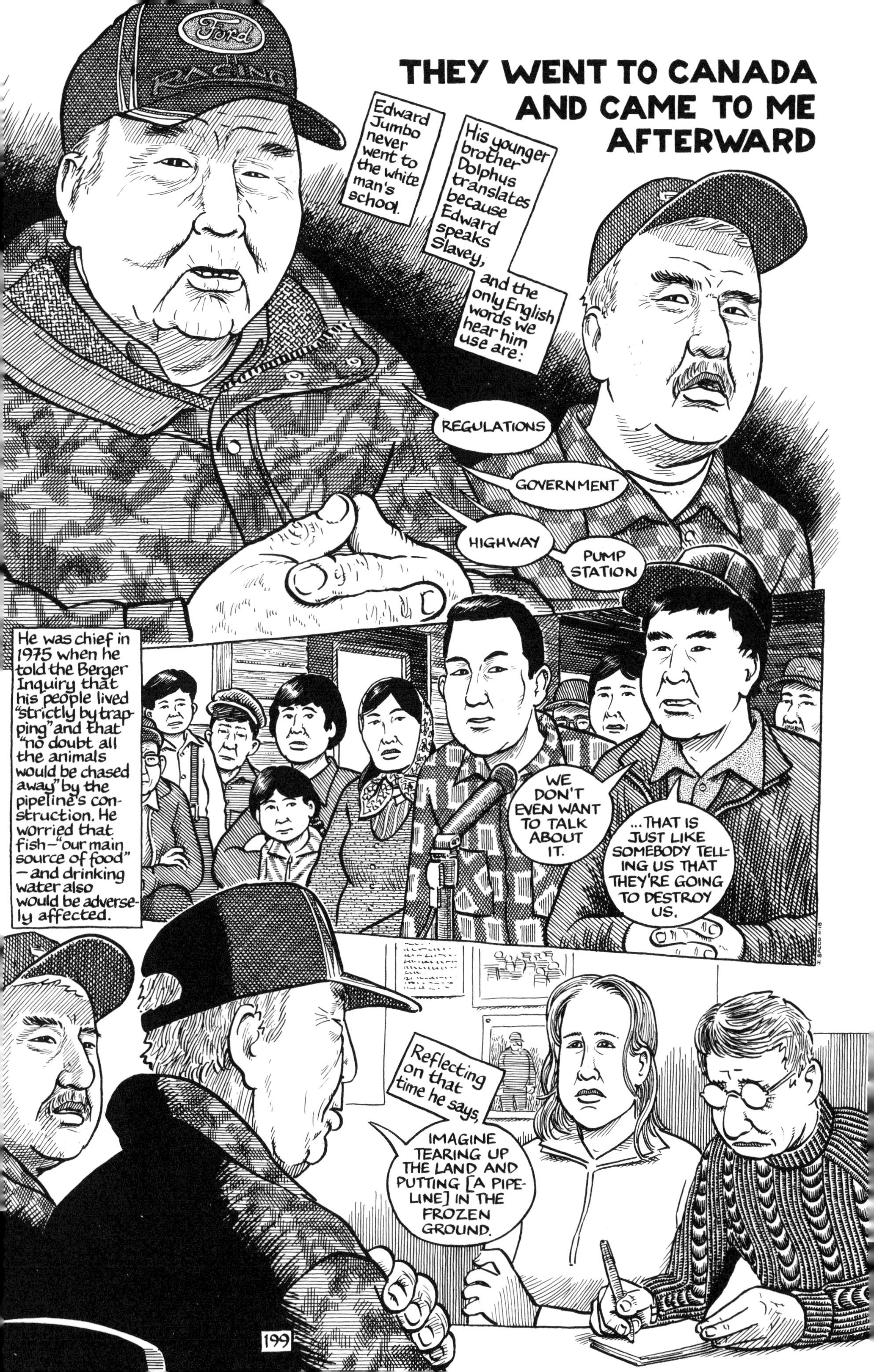

THEY WENT TO CANADA AND CAME TO ME AFTERWARD
Ford RACING
Edward Jumbo never went to the white man's school.
His younger brother Dolphus translates because Edward speaks Slavey,
and the only English words we hear him use are:
REGULATIONS
GOVERNMENT
HIGHWAY
PUMP STATION
He was chief in 1975 when he told the Berger Inquiry that his people lived "strictly by trapping" and that "no doubt all the animals would be chased away" by the pipeline's construction. He worried that fish—"our main source of food"—and drinking water also would be adversely affected.
WE DON'T EVEN WANT TO TALK ABOUT IT.
...THAT IS JUST LIKE SOMEBODY TELLING US THAT THEY'RE GOING TO DESTROY US.
Reflecting on that time he says,
IMAGINE TEARING UP THE LAND AND PUTTING [A PIPELINE] IN THE FROZEN GROUND.

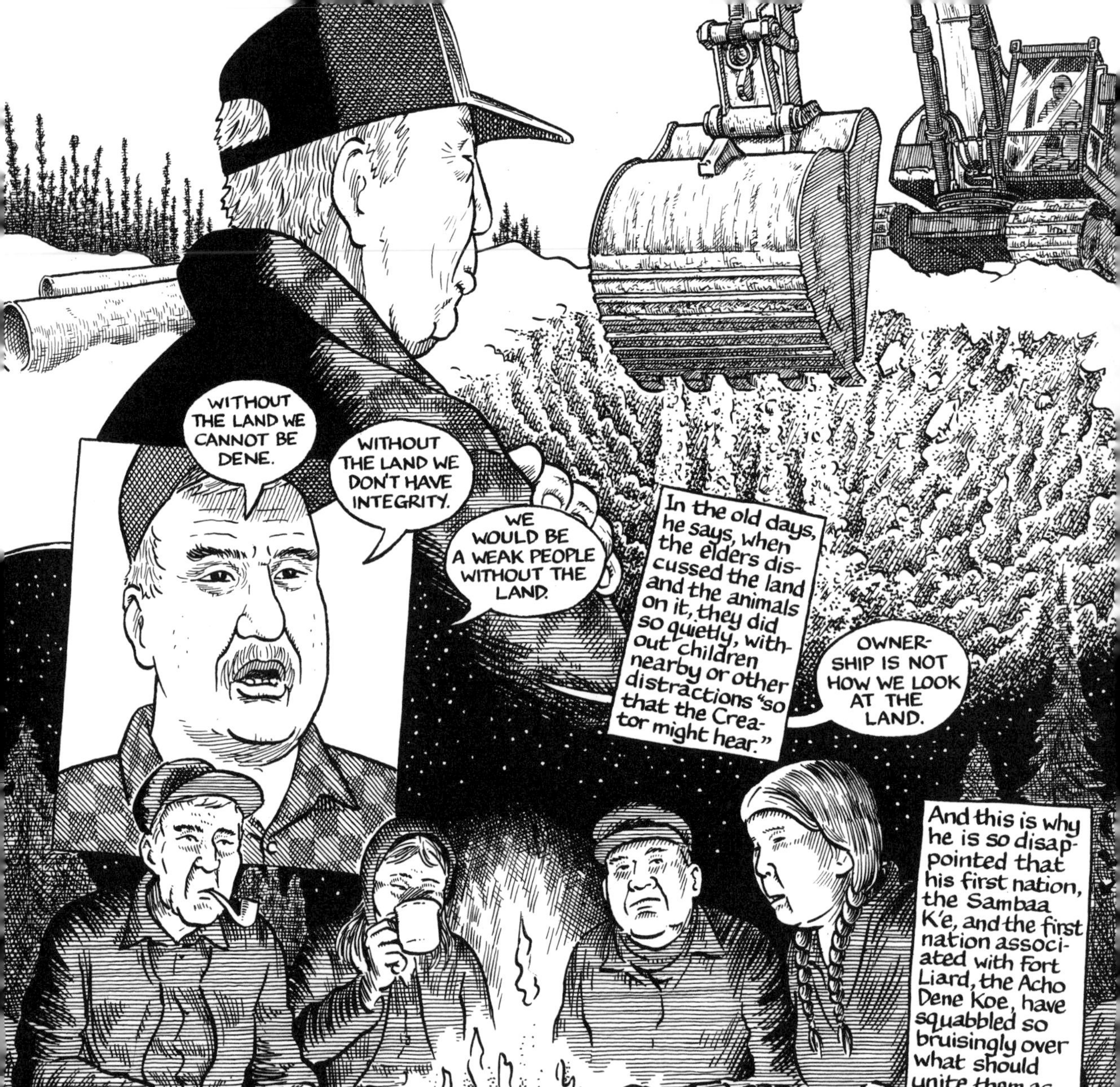
WITHOUT THE LAND WE CANNOT BE DENE.
WITHOUT THE LAND WE DON'T HAVE INTEGRITY.
WE WOULD BE A WEAK PEOPLE WITHOUT THE LAND.
In the old days, he says, when the elders discussed the land and the animals on it, they did so quietly, without children nearby or other distractions "so that the Creator might hear."
OWNERSHIP IS NOT HOW WE LOOK AT THE LAND.
And this is why he is so disappointed that his first nation, the Sambaa K'e, and the first nation associated with Fort Liard, the Acho Dene Koe, have squabbled so bruisingly over what should unite them as Dene.

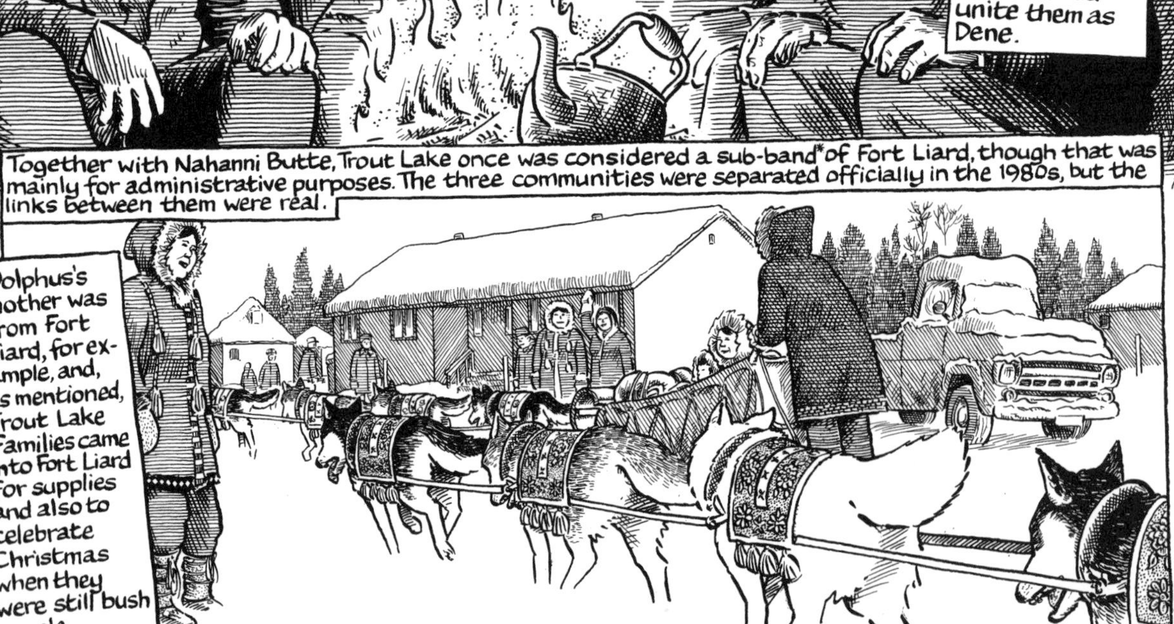
Together with Nahanni Butte, Trout Lake once was considered a sub-band* of Fort Liard, though that was mainly for administrative purposes. The three communities were separated officially in the 1980s, but the links between them were real.
Dolphus's mother was from Fort Liard, for example, and, as mentioned, Trout Lake families came into Fort Liard for supplies and also to celebrate Christmas when they were still bush people.

*IN THIS CONTEXT, A BAND IS A LOCAL, OFFICIALLY RECOGNIZED INDIGENOUS UNIT.

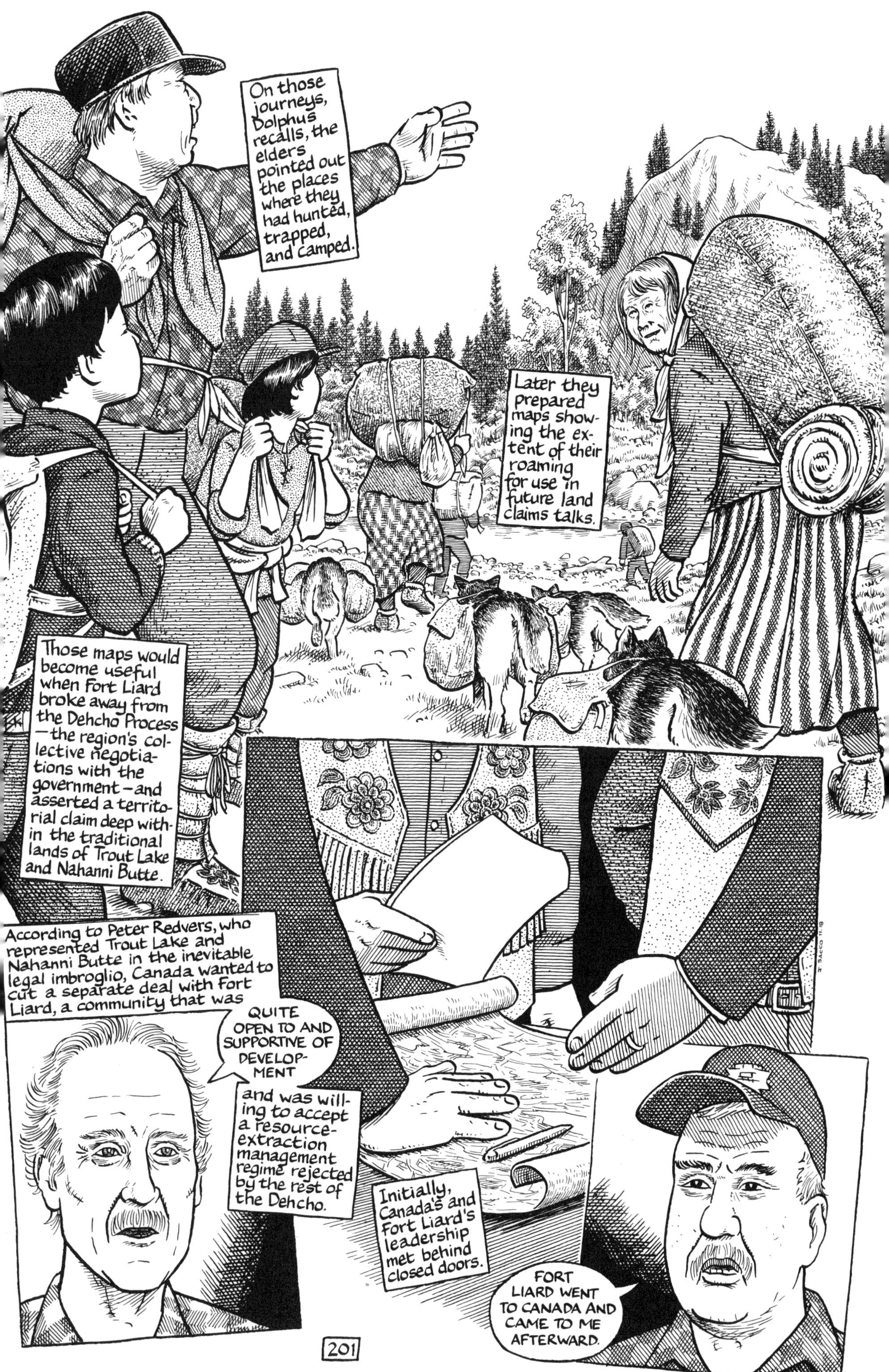
On those journeys, Dolphus recalls, the elders pointed out the places where they had hunted, trapped, and camped.
Later they prepared maps showing the extent of their roaming for use in future land claims talks.
Those maps would become useful when Fort Liard broke away from the Dehcho Process—the region's collective negotiations with the government—and asserted a territorial claim deep within the traditional lands of Trout Lake and Nahanni Butte.
According to Peter Redvers, who represented Trout Lake and Nahanni Butte in the inevitable legal imbroglio, Canada wanted to cut a separate deal with Fort Liard, a community that was
QUITE OPEN TO AND SUPPORTIVE OF DEVELOPMENT
and was willing to accept a resource-extraction management regime rejected by the rest of the Dehcho.
Initially, Canada's and Fort Liard's leadership met behind closed doors.
FORT LIARD WENT TO CANADA AND CAME TO ME AFTERWARD.

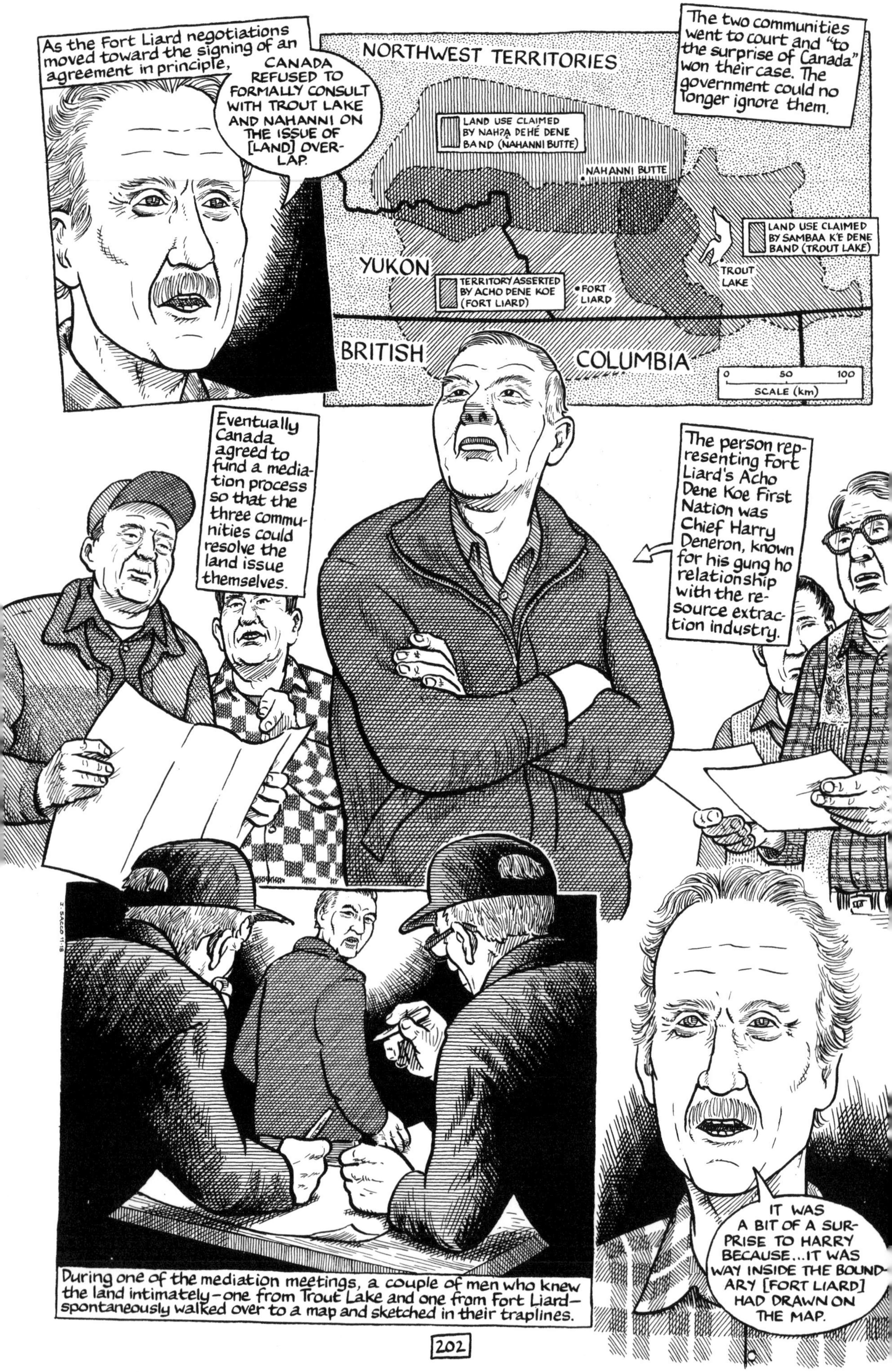
As the Fort Liard negotiations moved toward the signing of an agreement in principle,
CANADA REFUSED TO FORMALLY CONSULT WITH TROUT LAKE AND NAHANNI ON THE ISSUE OF [LAND] OVER-LAP.
NORTHWEST TERRITORIES
LAND USE CLAIMED BY NAHʔĄ DEHÉ DENE BAND (NAHANNI BUTTE)
NAHANNI BUTTE
LAND USE CLAIMED BY SAMBAA K'E DENE BAND (TROUT LAKE)
TROUT LAKE
YUKON
TERRITORY ASSERTED BY ACHO DENE KOE (FORT LIARD)
FORT LIARD
BRITISH COLUMBIA
0 50 100
SCALE (km)
The two communities went to court and "to the surprise of Canada" won their case. The government could no longer ignore them.
Eventually Canada agreed to fund a mediation process so that the three communities could resolve the land issue themselves.
The person representing Fort Liard's Acho Dene Koe First Nation was Chief Harry Deneron, known for his gung ho relationship with the resource extraction industry.
During one of the mediation meetings, a couple of men who knew the land intimately—one from Trout Lake and one from Fort Liard—spontaneously walked over to a map and sketched in their traplines.
IT WAS A BIT OF A SURPRISE TO HARRY BECAUSE...IT WAS WAY INSIDE THE BOUNDARY [FORT LIARD] HAD DRAWN ON THE MAP.

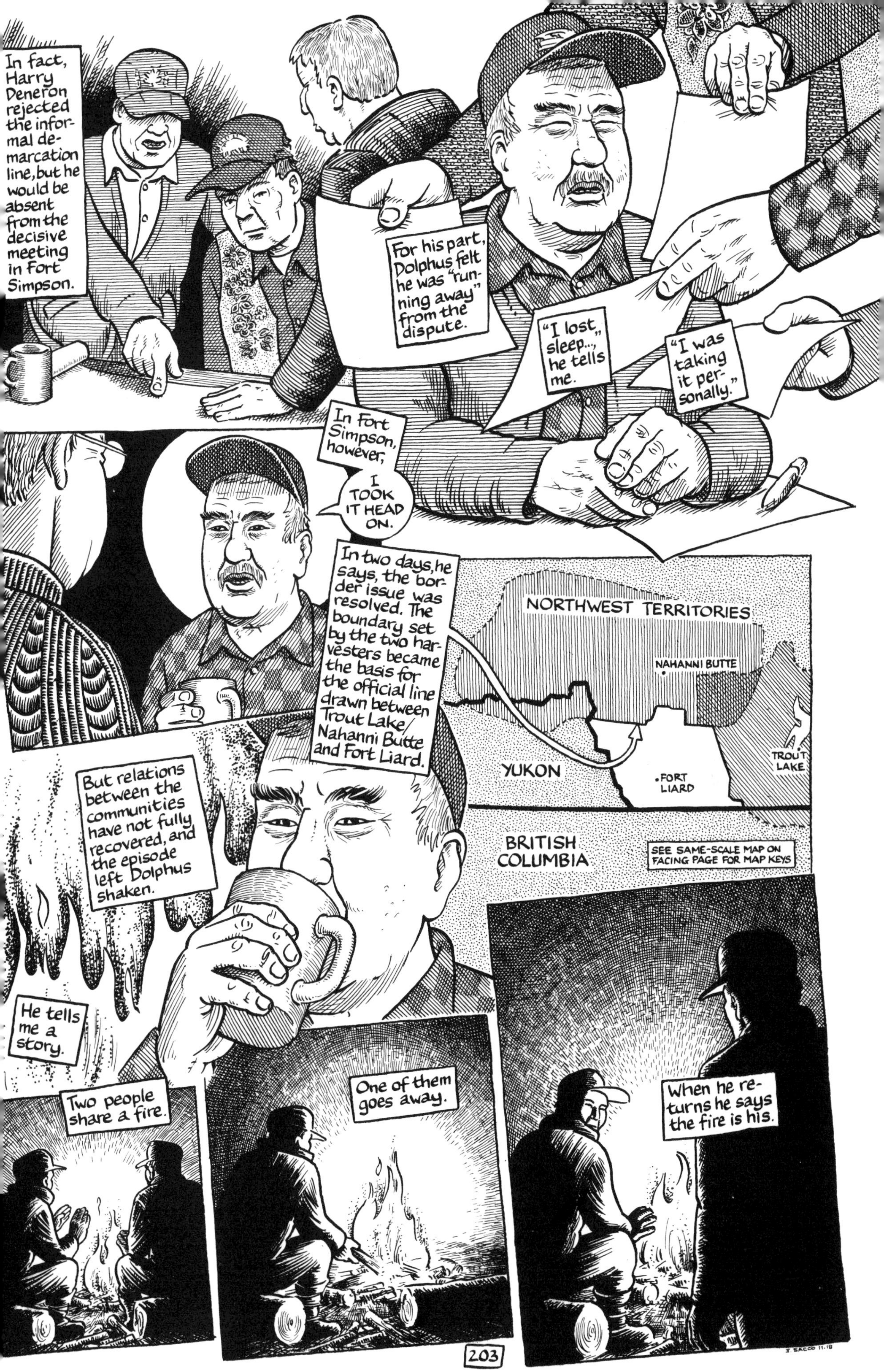

In fact, Harry Deneron rejected the informal demarcation line, but he would be absent from the decisive meeting in Fort Simpson.
For his part, Dolphus felt he was "running away" from the dispute.
"I lost sleep...," he tells me.
"I was taking it personally."
In Fort Simpson, however,
I TOOK IT HEAD ON.
In two days, he says, the border issue was resolved. The boundary set by the two harvesters became the basis for the official line drawn between Trout Lake/Nahanni Butte and Fort Liard.
NORTHWEST TERRITORIES
NAHANNI BUTTE
YUKON
FORT LIARD
TROUT LAKE
BRITISH COLUMBIA
SEE SAME-SCALE MAP ON FACING PAGE FOR MAP KEYS
But relations between the communities have not fully recovered, and the episode left Dolphus shaken.
He tells me a story.
Two people share a fire.
One of them goes away.
When he returns he says the fire is his.
J. SACCO 11.18

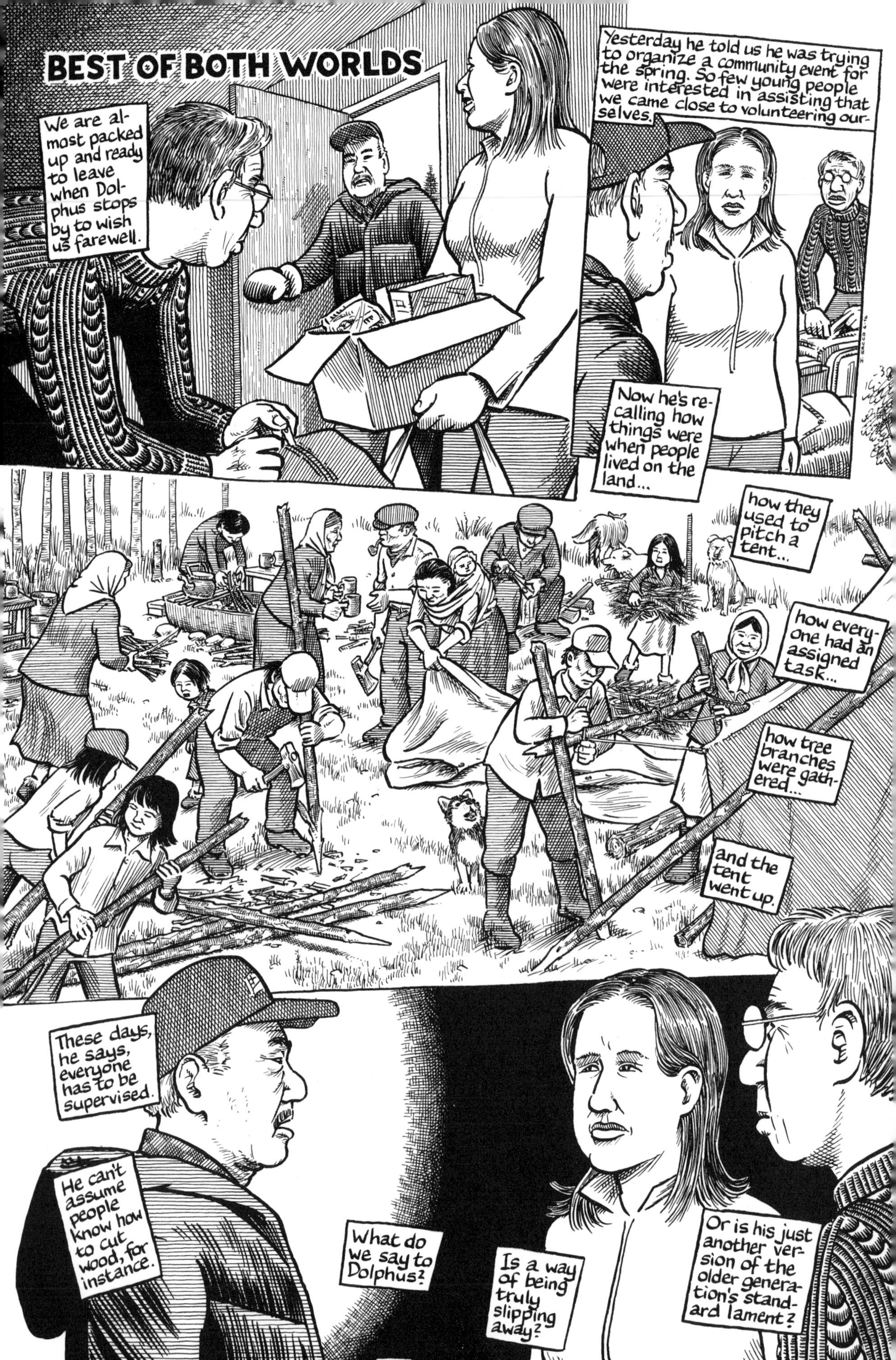
BEST OF BOTH WORLDS
We are almost packed up and ready to leave when Dolphus stops by to wish us farewell.
Yesterday he told us he was trying to organize a community event for the spring. So few young people were interested in assisting that we came close to volunteering ourselves.
Now he's recalling how things were when people lived on the land...
how they used to pitch a tent...
how everyone had an assigned task...
how tree branches were gathered...
and the tent went up.
These days, he says, everyone has to be supervised.
He can't assume people know how to cut wood, for instance.
What do we say to Dolphus?
Is a way of being truly slipping away?
Or is his just another version of the older generation's standard lament?

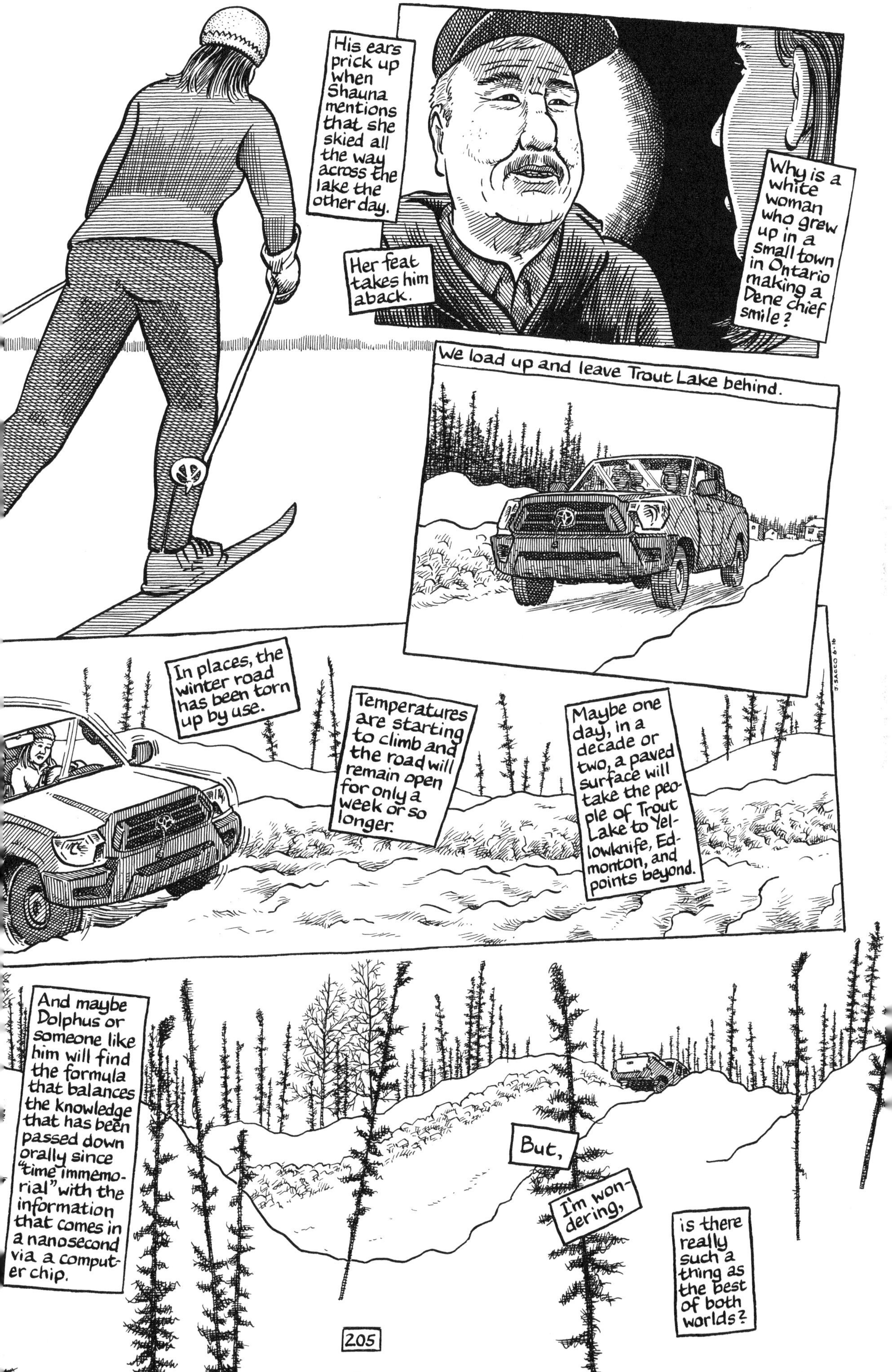

His ears prick up when Shauna mentions that she skied all the way across the lake the other day.
Her feat takes him aback.
Why is a white woman who grew up in a small town in Ontario making a Dene chief smile?
We load up and leave Trout Lake behind.
In places, the winter road has been torn up by use.
Temperatures are starting to climb and the road will remain open for only a week or so longer.
Maybe one day, in a decade or two, a paved surface will take the people of Trout Lake to Yellowknife, Edmonton, and points beyond.
And maybe Dolphus or someone like him will find the formula that balances the knowledge that has been passed down orally since "time immemorial" with the information that comes in a nanosecond via a computer chip.
But,
I'm wondering,
is there really such a thing as the best of both worlds?

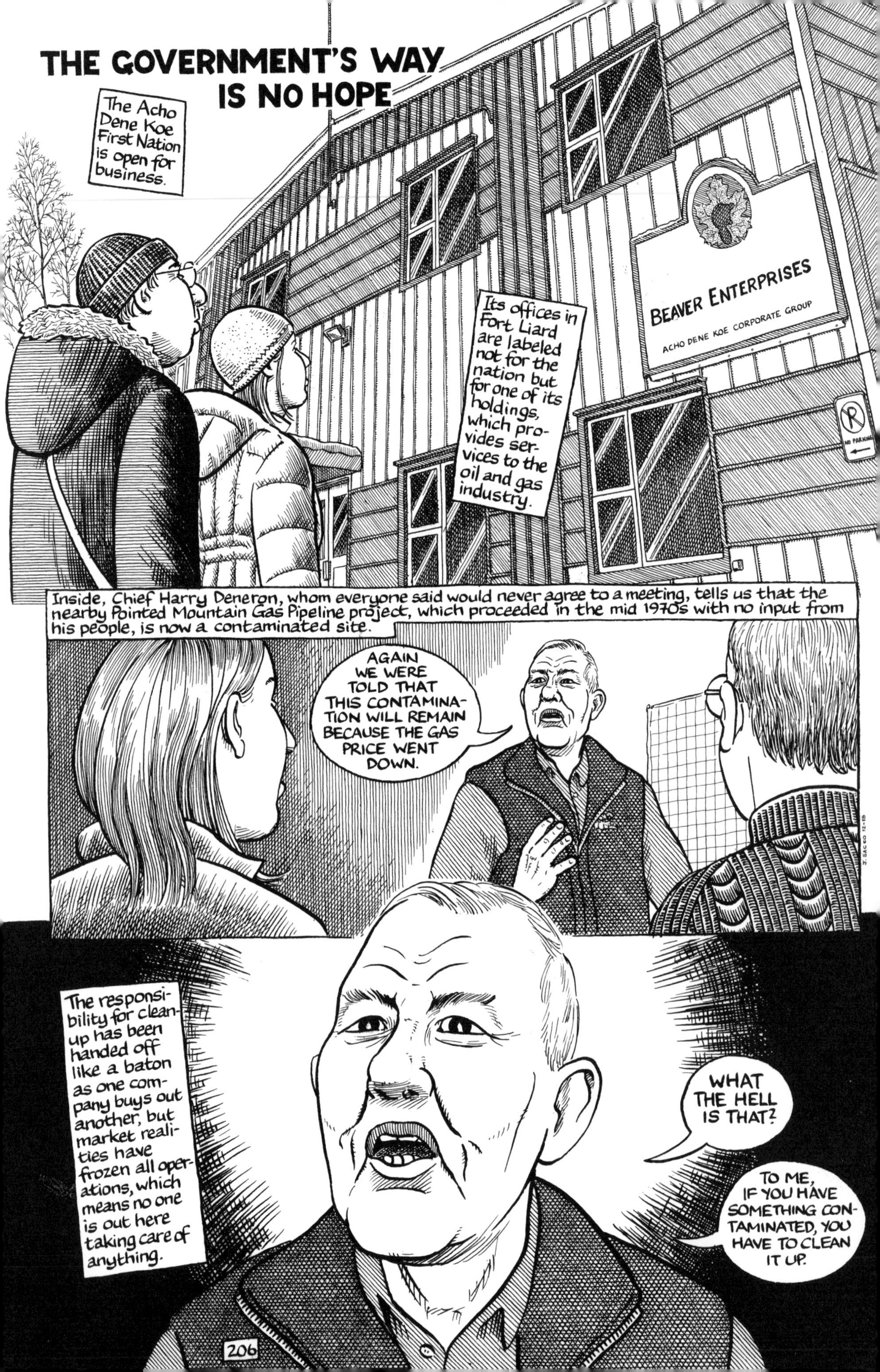
THE GOVERNMENT'S WAY IS NO HOPE
The Acho Dene Koe First Nation is open for business.
BEAVER ENTERPRISES
ACHO DENE KOE CORPORATE GROUP
NO PARKING
Its offices in Fort Liard are labeled not for the nation but for one of its holdings, which provides services to the oil and gas industry.
Inside, Chief Harry Deneron, whom everyone said would never agree to a meeting, tells us that the nearby Pointed Mountain Gas Pipeline project, which proceeded in the mid 1970s with no input from his people, is now a contaminated site.
AGAIN WE WERE TOLD THAT THIS CONTAMINATION WILL REMAIN BECAUSE THE GAS PRICE WENT DOWN.
The responsibility for clean-up has been handed off like a baton as one company buys out another, but market realities have frozen all operations, which means no one is out here taking care of anything.
WHAT THE HELL IS THAT?
TO ME, IF YOU HAVE SOMETHING CONTAMINATED, YOU HAVE TO CLEAN IT UP.

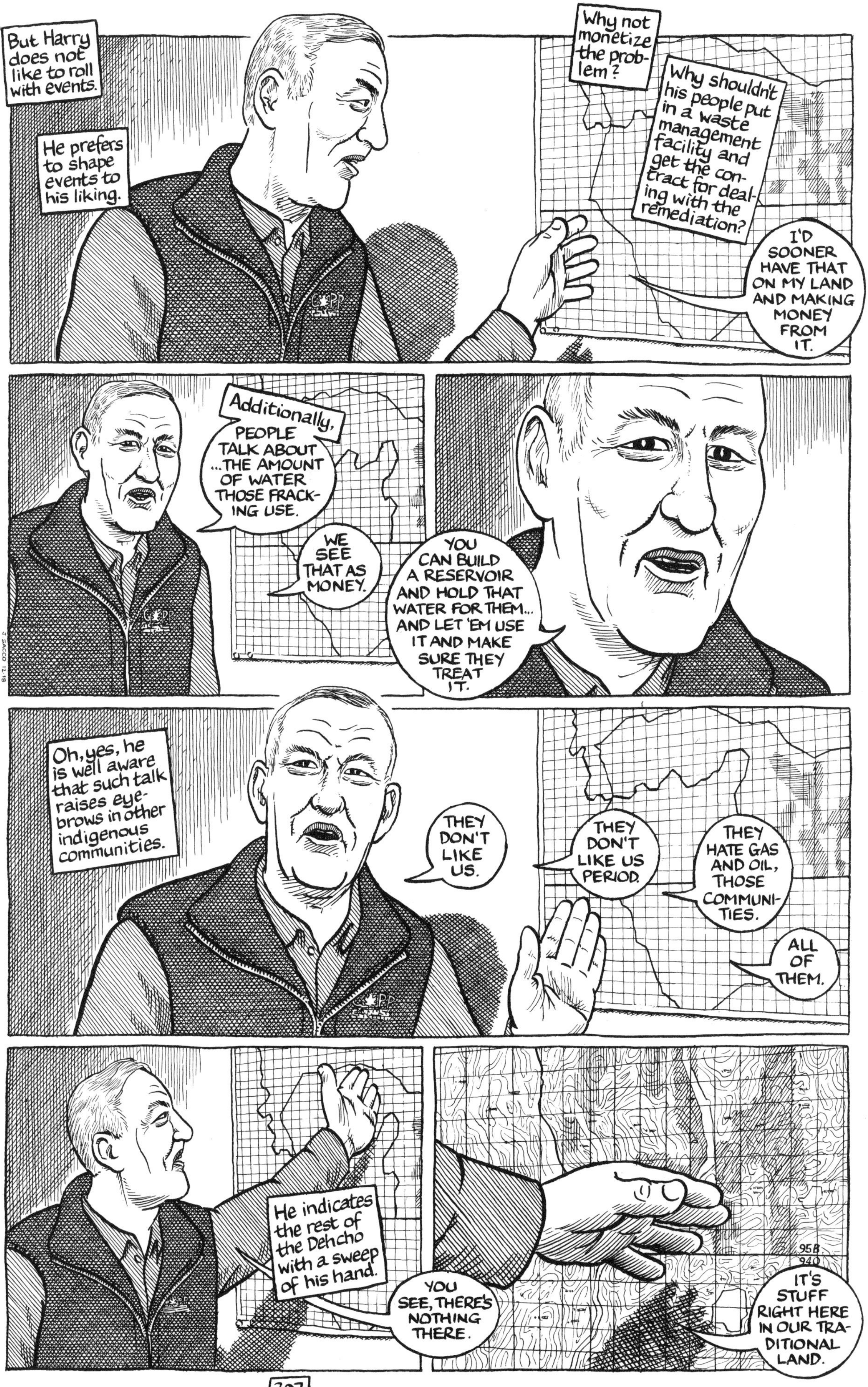

But Harry does not like to roll with events.
He prefers to shape events to his liking.
Why not monetize the problem?
Why shouldn't his people put in a waste management facility and get the contract for dealing with the remediation?
I'D SOONER HAVE THAT ON MY LAND AND MAKING MONEY FROM IT.
Additionally,
PEOPLE TALK ABOUT ...THE AMOUNT OF WATER THOSE FRACKING USE.
WE SEE THAT AS MONEY.
YOU CAN BUILD A RESERVOIR AND HOLD THAT WATER FOR THEM... AND LET 'EM USE IT AND MAKE SURE THEY TREAT IT.
Oh, yes, he is well aware that such talk raises eyebrows in other indigenous communities.
THEY DON'T LIKE US.
THEY DON'T LIKE US PERIOD.
THEY HATE GAS AND OIL, THOSE COMMUNITIES.
ALL OF THEM.
He indicates the rest of the Dehcho with a sweep of his hand.
YOU SEE, THERE'S NOTHING THERE.
IT'S STUFF RIGHT HERE IN OUR TRADITIONAL LAND.

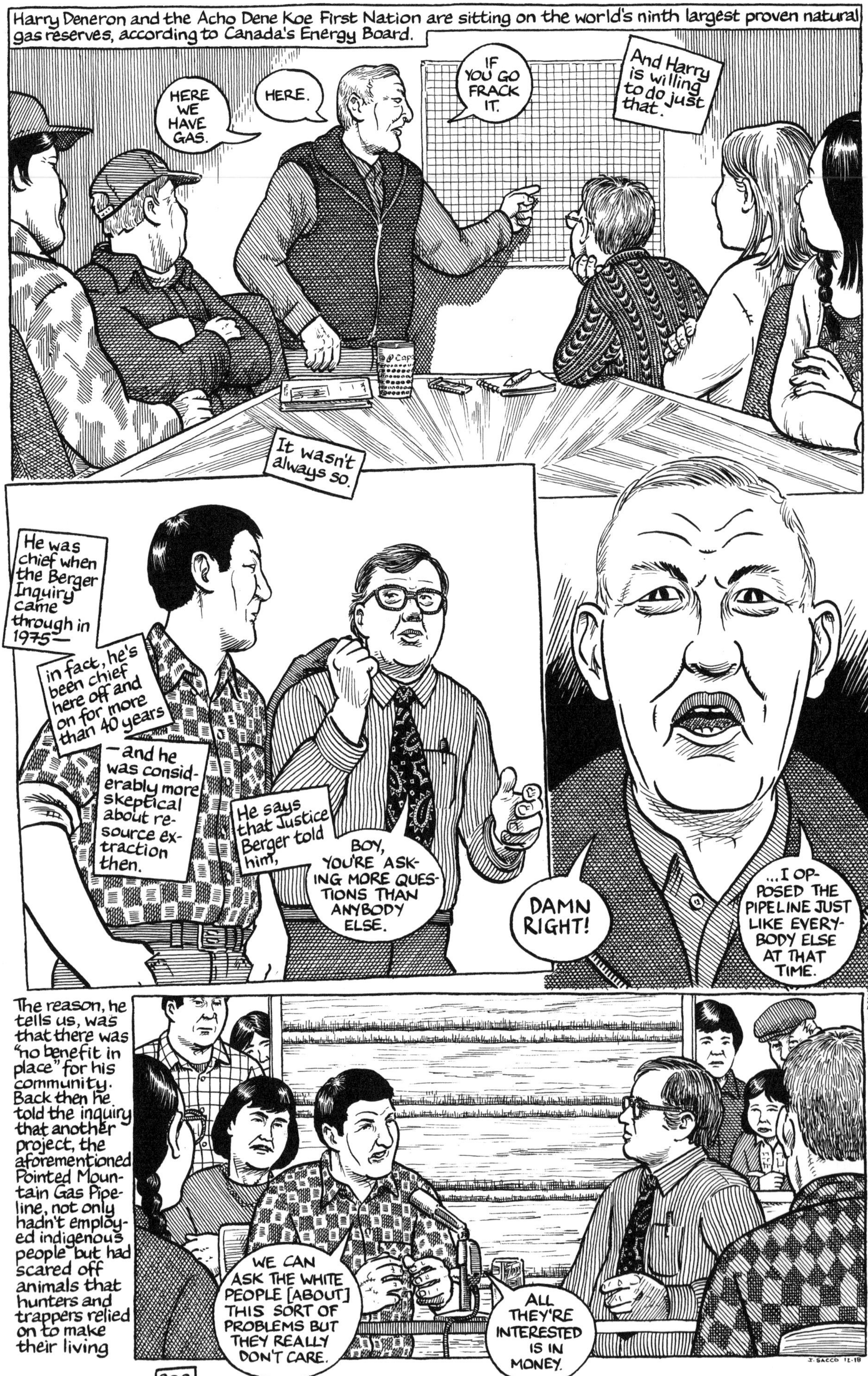

Harry Deneron and the Acho Dene Koe First Nation are sitting on the world's ninth largest proven natural gas reserves, according to Canada's Energy Board.
HERE WE HAVE GAS.
HERE.
IF YOU GO FRACK IT.
And Harry is willing to do just that.
It wasn't always so.
He was chief when the Berger Inquiry came through in 1975—
in fact, he's been chief here off and on for more than 40 years
—and he was considerably more skeptical about resource extraction then.
He says that Justice Berger told him,
BOY, YOU'RE ASKING MORE QUESTIONS THAN ANYBODY ELSE.
DAMN RIGHT!
...I OPPOSED THE PIPELINE JUST LIKE EVERYBODY ELSE AT THAT TIME.
The reason, he tells us, was that there was "no benefit in place" for his community. Back then he told the inquiry that another project, the aforementioned Pointed Mountain Gas Pipeline, not only hadn't employed indigenous people but had scared off animals that hunters and trappers relied on to make their living
WE CAN ASK THE WHITE PEOPLE [ABOUT] THIS SORT OF PROBLEMS BUT THEY REALLY DON'T CARE.
ALL THEY'RE INTERESTED IS IN MONEY.
J. SACCO 12-18

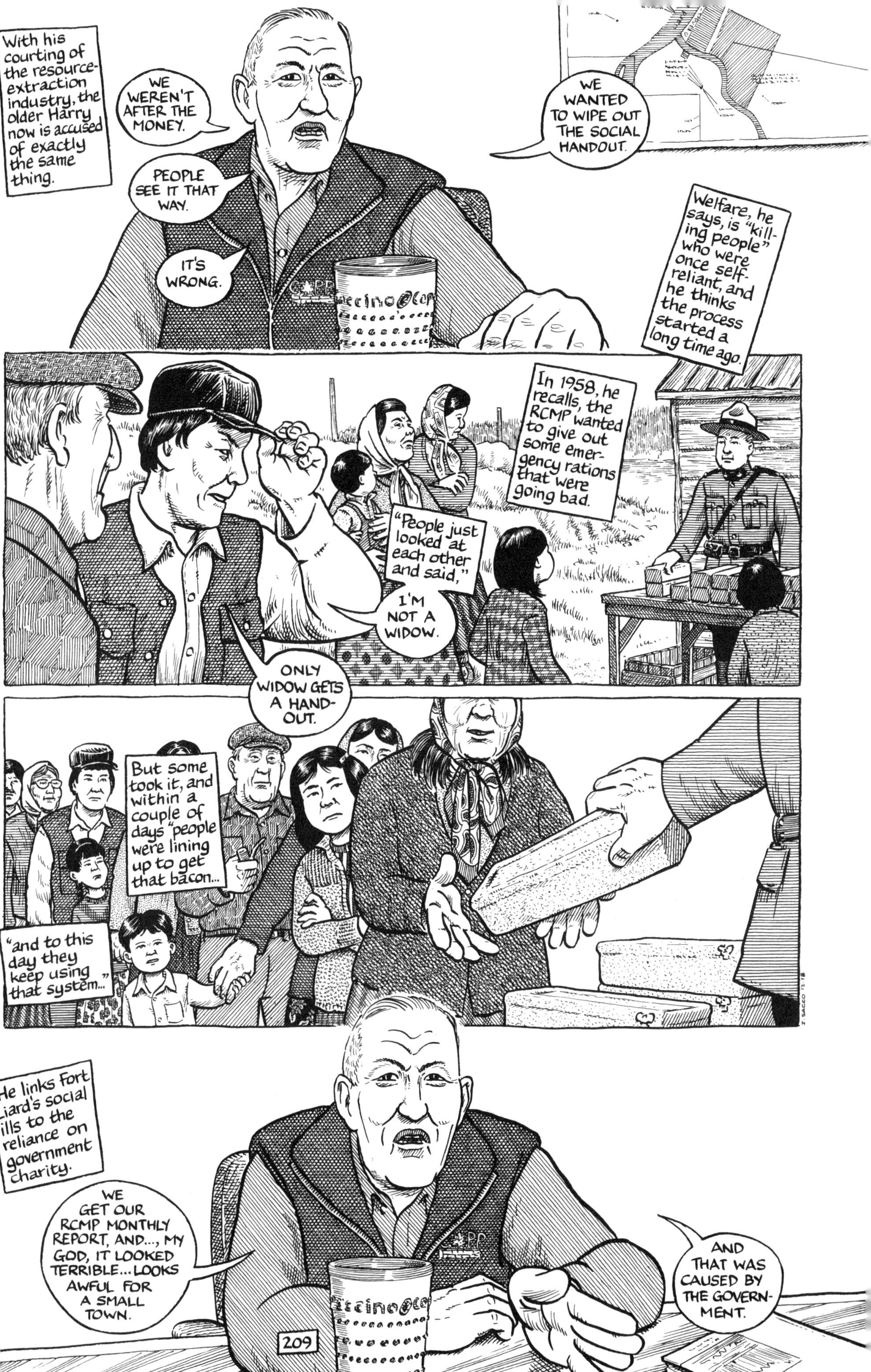
With his courting of the resource-extraction industry, the older Harry now is accused of exactly the same thing.
WE WEREN'T AFTER THE MONEY.
PEOPLE SEE IT THAT WAY.
IT'S WRONG.
WE WANTED TO WIPE OUT THE SOCIAL HANDOUT.
Welfare, he says, is "killing people" who were once self-reliant, and he thinks the process started a long time ago.
In 1958, he recalls, the RCMP wanted to give out some emergency rations that were going bad.
"People just looked at each other and said,"
I'M NOT A WIDOW.
ONLY WIDOW GETS A HAND-OUT.
But some took it, and within a couple of days "people were lining up to get that bacon...
"and to this day they keep using that system..."
He links Fort Liard's social ills to the reliance on government charity.
WE GET OUR RCMP MONTHLY REPORT, AND..., MY GOD, IT LOOKED TERRIBLE... LOOKS AWFUL FOR A SMALL TOWN.
AND THAT WAS CAUSED BY THE GOVERNMENT.

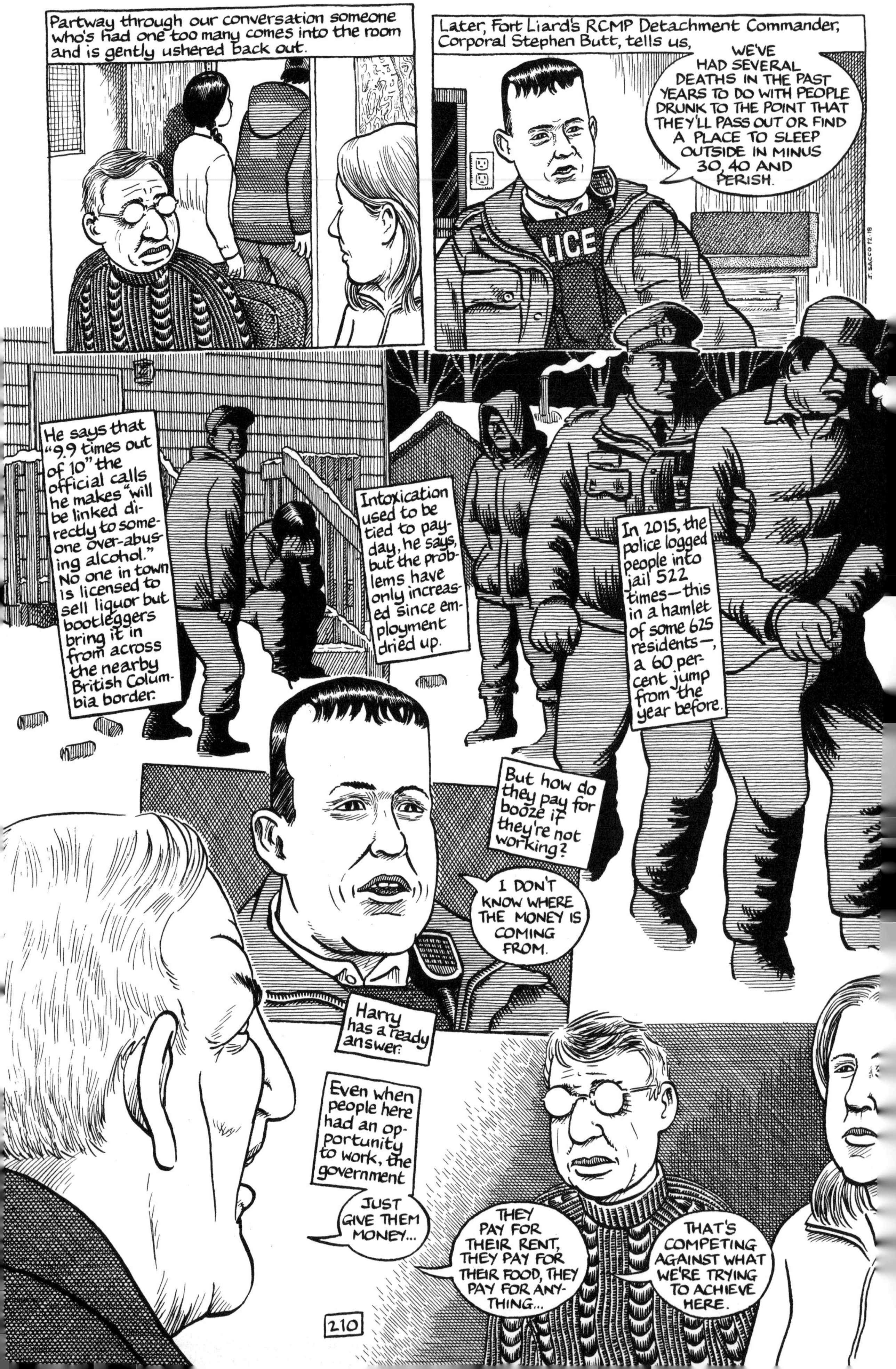

Partway through our conversation someone who's had one too many comes into the room and is gently ushered back out.
Later, Fort Liard's RCMP Detachment Commander, Corporal Stephen Butt, tells us,
WE'VE HAD SEVERAL DEATHS IN THE PAST YEARS TO DO WITH PEOPLE DRUNK TO THE POINT THAT THEY'LL PASS OUT OR FIND A PLACE TO SLEEP OUTSIDE IN MINUS 30, 40 AND PERISH.
LICE
He says that "9.9 times out of 10" the official calls he makes "will be linked directly to someone over-abusing alcohol." No one in town is licensed to sell liquor but bootleggers bring it in from across the nearby British Columbia border.
Intoxication used to be tied to payday, he says, but the problems have only increased since employment dried up.
In 2015, the police logged people into jail 522 times—this in a hamlet of some 625 residents—, a 60 percent jump from the year before.
But how do they pay for booze if they're not working?
I DON'T KNOW WHERE THE MONEY IS COMING FROM.
Harry has a ready answer:
Even when people here had an opportunity to work, the government
JUST GIVE THEM MONEY...
THEY PAY FOR THEIR RENT, THEY PAY FOR THEIR FOOD, THEY PAY FOR ANYTHING...
THAT'S COMPETING AGAINST WHAT WE'RE TRYING TO ACHIEVE HERE.

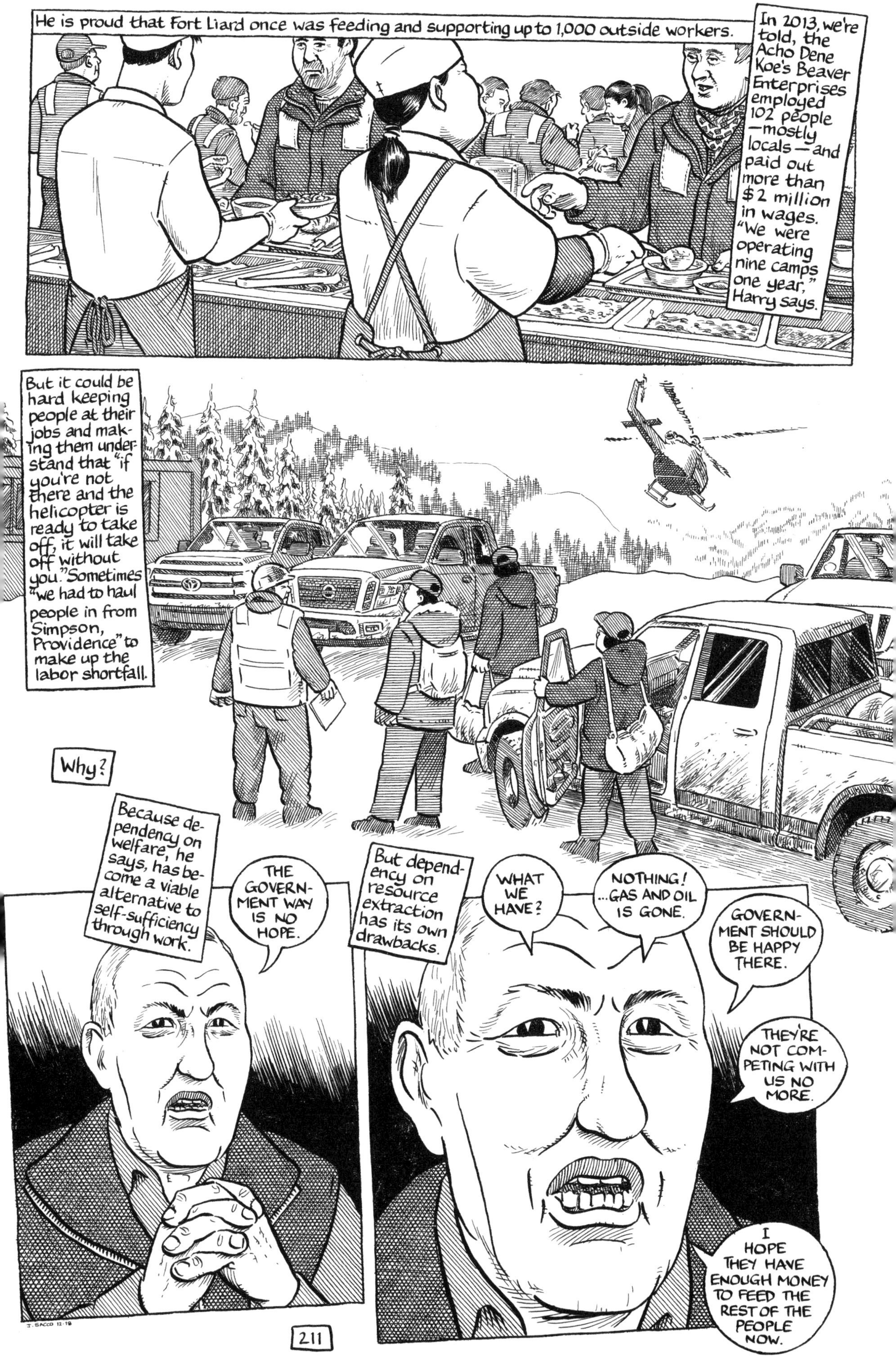
He is proud that Fort Liard once was feeding and supporting up to 1,000 outside workers.
In 2013, we're told, the Acho Dene Koe's Beaver Enterprises employed 102 people—mostly locals—and paid out more than $2 million in wages. "We were operating nine camps one year," Harry says.
But it could be hard keeping people at their jobs and making them understand that "if you're not there and the helicopter is ready to take off, it will take off without you." Sometimes "we had to haul people in from Simpson, Providence" to make up the labor shortfall.
Why?
Because dependency on welfare, he says, has become a viable alternative to self-sufficiency through work.
THE GOVERNMENT WAY IS NO HOPE.
But dependency on resource extraction has its own drawbacks.
WHAT WE HAVE?
NOTHING! ...GAS AND OIL IS GONE.
GOVERNMENT SHOULD BE HAPPY THERE.
THEY'RE NOT COMPETING WITH US NO MORE.
I HOPE THEY HAVE ENOUGH MONEY TO FEED THE REST OF THE PEOPLE NOW.
J. SACCO 12·18

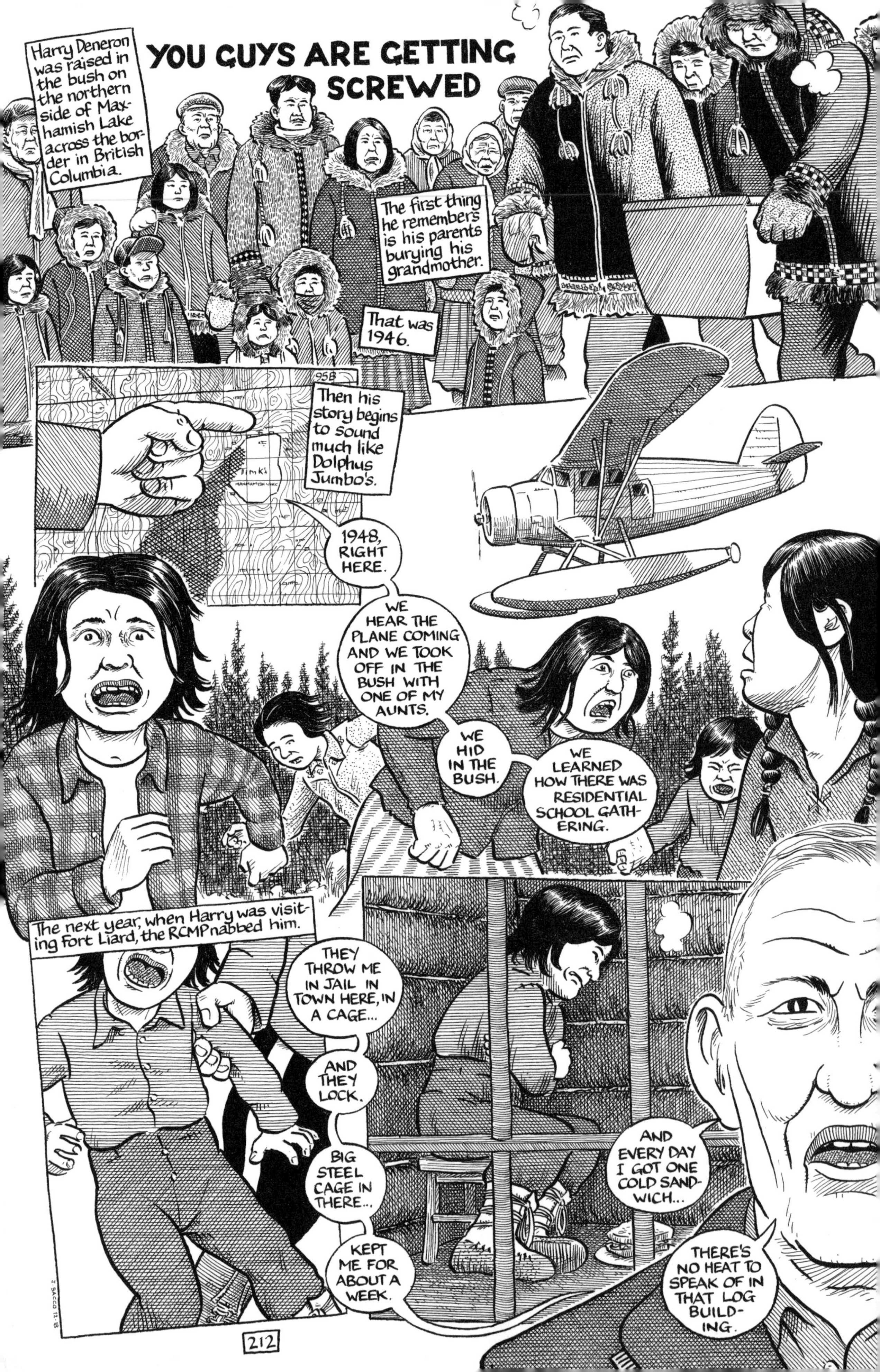
YOU GUYS ARE GETTING SCREWED
Harry Deneron was raised in the bush on the northern side of Maxhamish Lake across the border in British Columbia.
The first thing he remembers is his parents burying his grandmother.
That was 1946.
Then his story begins to sound much like Dolphus Jumbo's.
1948, RIGHT HERE.
WE HEAR THE PLANE COMING AND WE TOOK OFF IN THE BUSH WITH ONE OF MY AUNTS.
WE HID IN THE BUSH.
WE LEARNED HOW THERE WAS RESIDENTIAL SCHOOL GATHERING.
The next year, when Harry was visiting Fort Liard, the RCMP nabbed him.
THEY THROW ME IN JAIL IN TOWN HERE, IN A CAGE...
AND THEY LOCK.
BIG STEEL CAGE IN THERE...
KEPT ME FOR ABOUT A WEEK.
AND EVERY DAY I GOT ONE COLD SANDWICH...
THERE'S NO HEAT TO SPEAK OF IN THAT LOG BUILDING.
J. SACCO 12.18

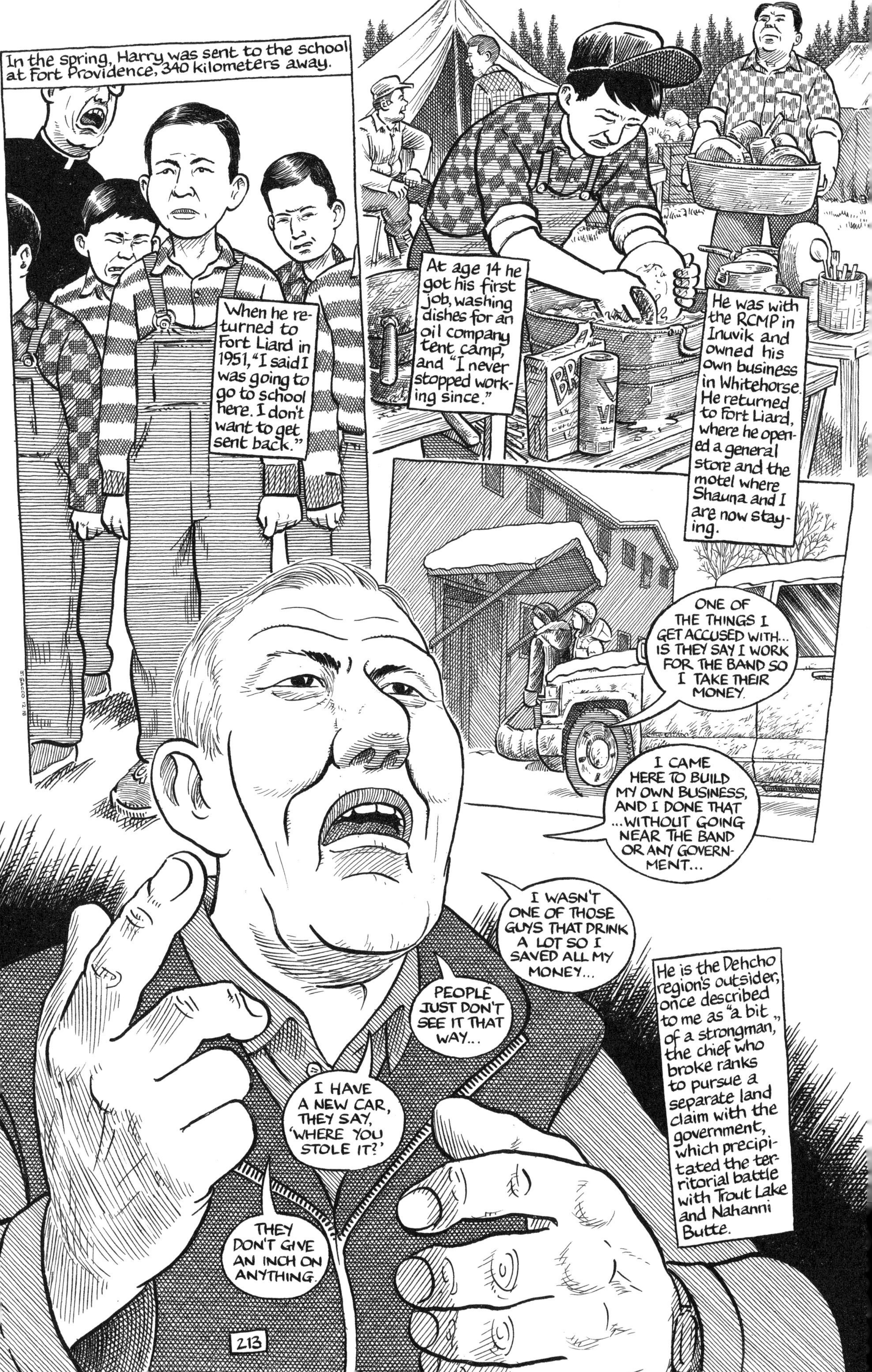
In the spring, Harry was sent to the school at Fort Providence, 340 kilometers away.
When he returned to Fort Liard in 1951, "I said I was going to go to school here. I don't want to get sent back."
At age 14 he got his first job, washing dishes for an oil company tent camp, and "I never stopped working since."
He was with the RCMP in Inuvik and owned his own business in Whitehorse. He returned to Fort Liard, where he opened a general store and the motel where Shauna and I are now staying.
ONE OF THE THINGS I GET ACCUSED WITH... IS THEY SAY I WORK FOR THE BAND SO I TAKE THEIR MONEY.
I CAME HERE TO BUILD MY OWN BUSINESS, AND I DONE THAT ...WITHOUT GOING NEAR THE BAND OR ANY GOVERNMENT...
I WASN'T ONE OF THOSE GUYS THAT DRINK A LOT SO I SAVED ALL MY MONEY...
PEOPLE JUST DON'T SEE IT THAT WAY...
I HAVE A NEW CAR, THEY SAY, 'WHERE YOU STOLE IT?'
THEY DON'T GIVE AN INCH ON ANYTHING.
He is the Dehcho region's outsider, once described to me as "a bit of a strongman," the chief who broke ranks to pursue a separate land claim with the government, which precipitated the territorial battle with Trout Lake and Nahanni Butte.

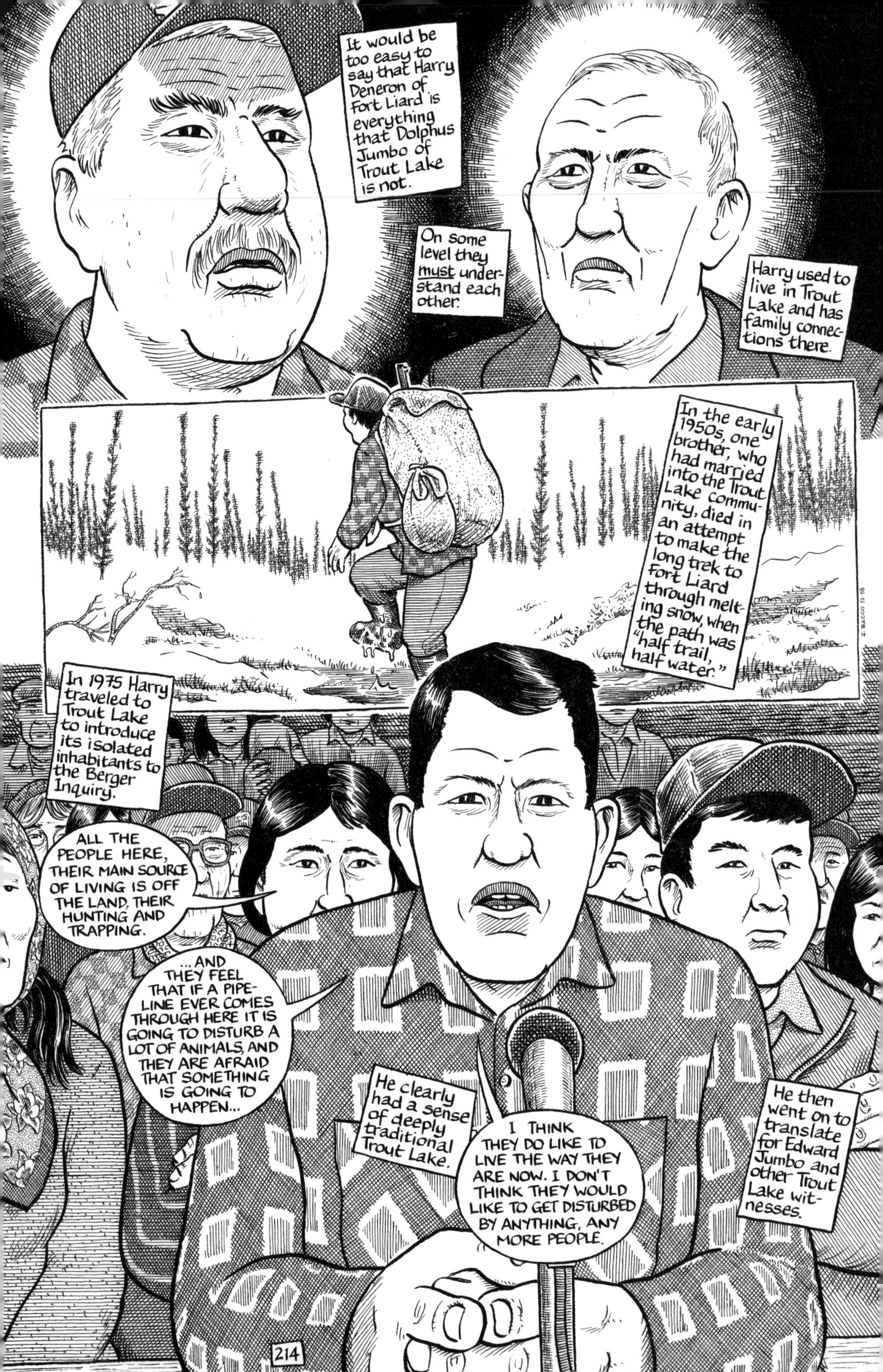
It would be too easy to say that Harry Deneron of Fort Liard is everything that Dolphus Jumbo of Trout Lake is not.
On some level they must understand each other.
Harry used to live in Trout Lake and has family connections there.
In the early 1950s, one brother, who had married into the Trout Lake community, died in an attempt to make the long trek to Fort Liard through melting snow, when the path was "half trail, half water."
J. SACCO 12-18
In 1975 Harry traveled to Trout Lake to introduce its isolated inhabitants to the Berger Inquiry.
ALL THE PEOPLE HERE, THEIR MAIN SOURCE OF LIVING IS OFF THE LAND, THEIR HUNTING AND TRAPPING.
...AND THEY FEEL THAT IF A PIPELINE EVER COMES THROUGH HERE IT IS GOING TO DISTURB A LOT OF ANIMALS, AND THEY ARE AFRAID THAT SOMETHING IS GOING TO HAPPEN...
He clearly had a sense of deeply traditional Trout Lake.
I THINK THEY DO LIKE TO LIVE THE WAY THEY ARE NOW. I DON'T THINK THEY WOULD LIKE TO GET DISTURBED BY ANYTHING, ANY MORE PEOPLE.
He then went on to translate for Edward Jumbo and other Trout Lake witnesses.

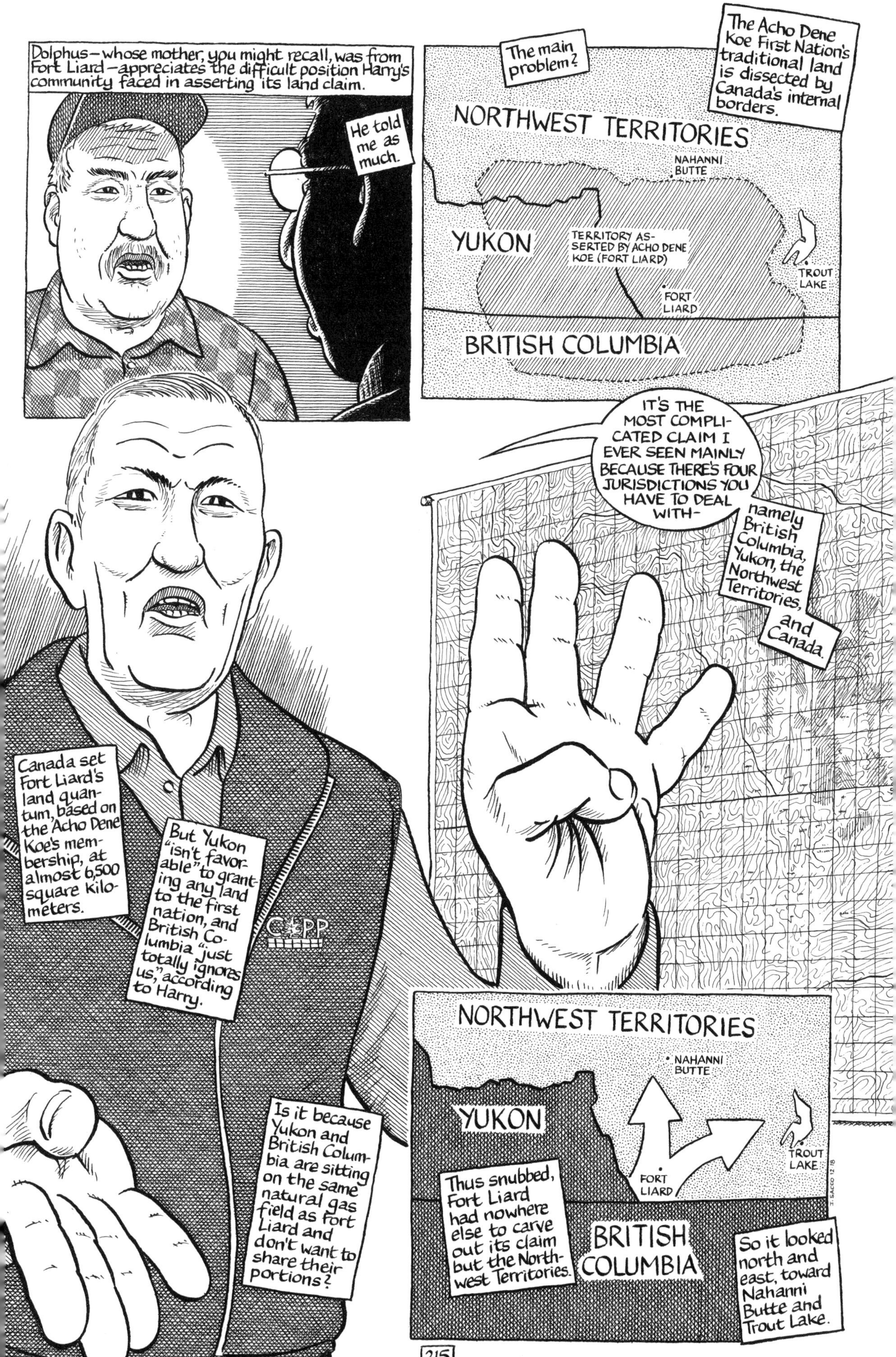

Dolphus—whose mother, you might recall, was from Fort Liard—appreciates the difficult position Harry's community faced in asserting its land claim.
He told me as much.
The main problem?
The Acho Dene Koe First Nation's traditional land is dissected by Canada's internal borders.
NORTHWEST TERRITORIES
NAHANNI BUTTE
YUKON
TERRITORY ASSERTED BY ACHO DENE KOE (FORT LIARD)
TROUT LAKE
FORT LIARD
BRITISH COLUMBIA
IT'S THE MOST COMPLICATED CLAIM I EVER SEEN MAINLY BECAUSE THERE'S FOUR JURISDICTIONS YOU HAVE TO DEAL WITH-
namely British Columbia, Yukon, the Northwest Territories, and Canada.
Canada set Fort Liard's land quantum, based on the Acho Dene Koe's membership, at almost 6,500 square kilometers.
But Yukon "isn't favorable" to granting any land to the first nation, and British Columbia "just totally ignores us," according to Harry.
Is it because Yukon and British Columbia are sitting on the same natural gas field as Fort Liard and don't want to share their portions?
NORTHWEST TERRITORIES
NAHANNI BUTTE
YUKON
TROUT LAKE
FORT LIARD
BRITISH COLUMBIA
Thus snubbed, Fort Liard had nowhere else to carve out its claim but the Northwest Territories.
So it looked north and east, toward Nahanni Butte and Trout Lake.

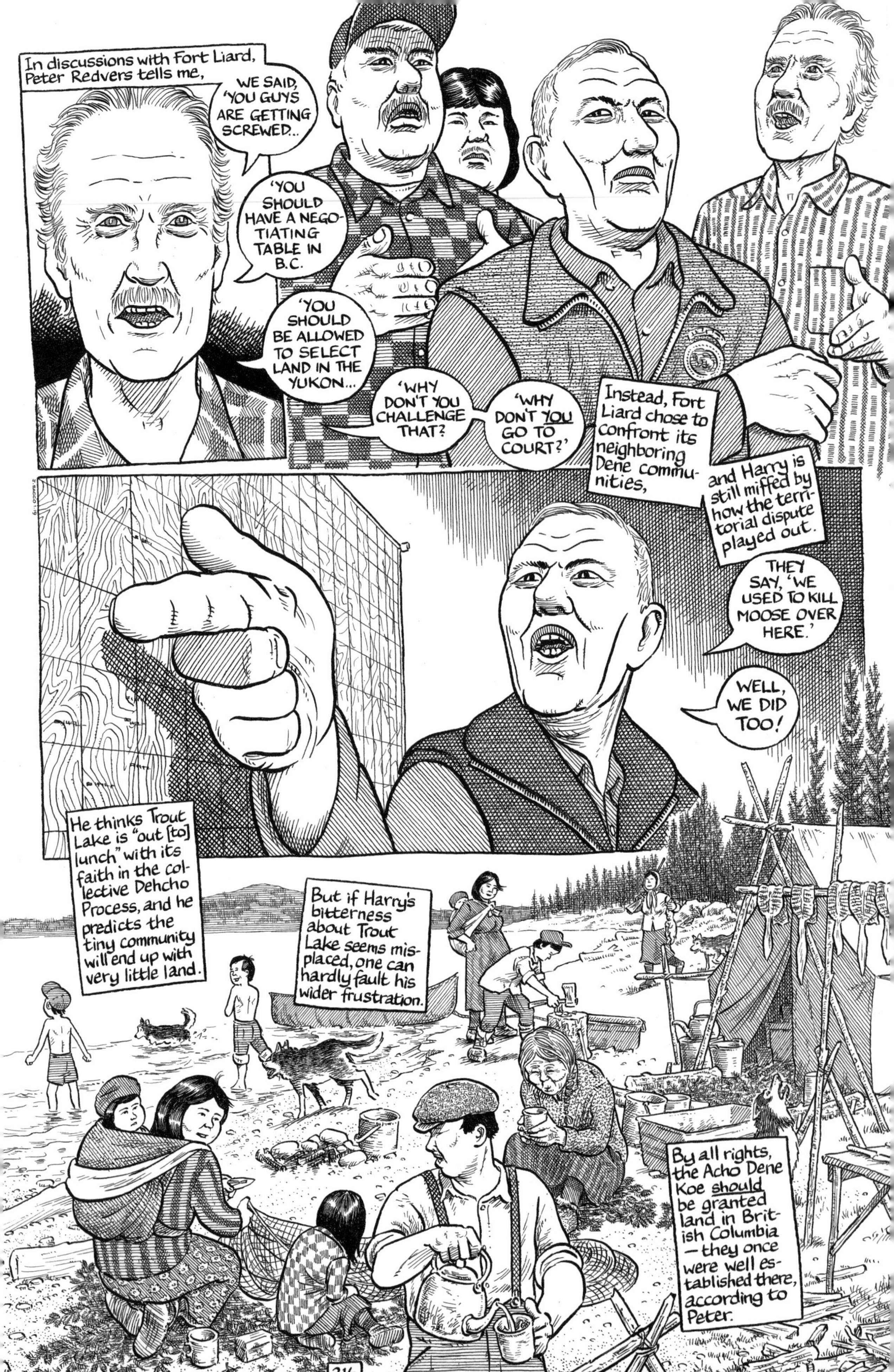
In discussions with Fort Liard, Peter Redvers tells me,
WE SAID, 'YOU GUYS ARE GETTING SCREWED...
'YOU SHOULD HAVE A NEGOTIATING TABLE IN B.C.
'YOU SHOULD BE ALLOWED TO SELECT LAND IN THE YUKON...
'WHY DON'T YOU CHALLENGE THAT?
'WHY DON'T YOU GO TO COURT?'
Instead, Fort Liard chose to confront its neighboring Dene communities,
and Harry is still miffed by how the territorial dispute played out.
THEY SAY, 'WE USED TO KILL MOOSE OVER HERE.'
WELL, WE DID TOO!
He thinks Trout Lake is "out [to] lunch" with its faith in the collective Dehcho Process, and he predicts the tiny community will end up with very little land.
But if Harry's bitterness about Trout Lake seems misplaced, one can hardly fault his wider frustration.
By all rights, the Acho Dene Koe should be granted land in British Columbia — they once were well established there, according to Peter.

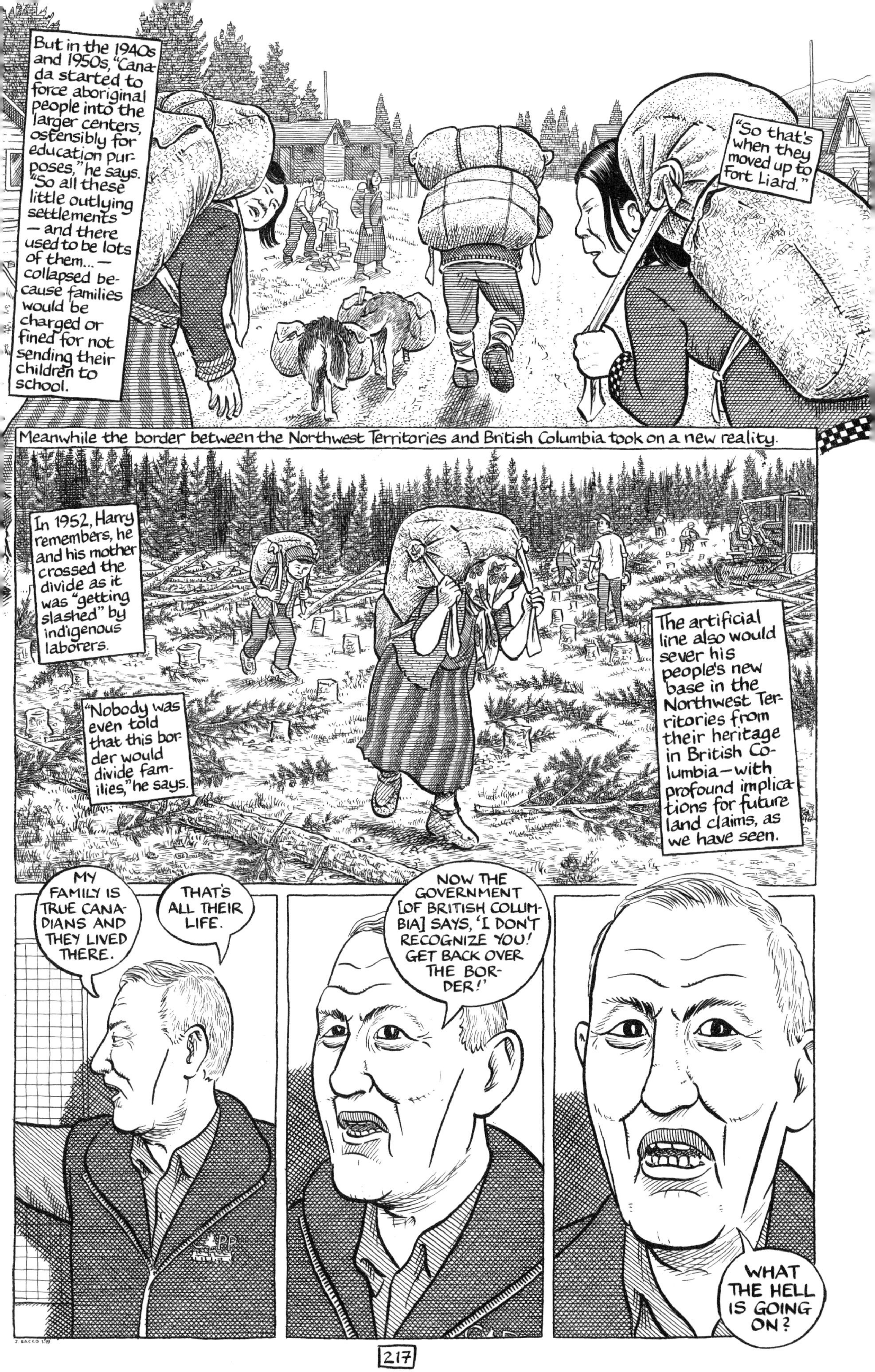

But in the 1940s and 1950s, "Canada started to force aboriginal people into the larger centers, ostensibly for education purposes," he says. "So all these little outlying settlements — and there used to be lots of them... — collapsed because families would be charged or fined for not sending their children to school.
"So that's when they moved up to Fort Liard."
Meanwhile the border between the Northwest Territories and British Columbia took on a new reality.
In 1952, Harry remembers, he and his mother crossed the divide as it was "getting slashed" by indigenous laborers.
"Nobody was even told that this border would divide families," he says.
The artificial line also would sever his people's new base in the Northwest Territories from their heritage in British Columbia—with profound implications for future land claims, as we have seen.
MY FAMILY IS TRUE CANADIANS AND THEY LIVED THERE.
THAT'S ALL THEIR LIFE.
NOW THE GOVERNMENT [OF BRITISH COLUMBIA] SAYS, 'I DON'T RECOGNIZE YOU! GET BACK OVER THE BORDER!'
WHAT THE HELL IS GOING ON?

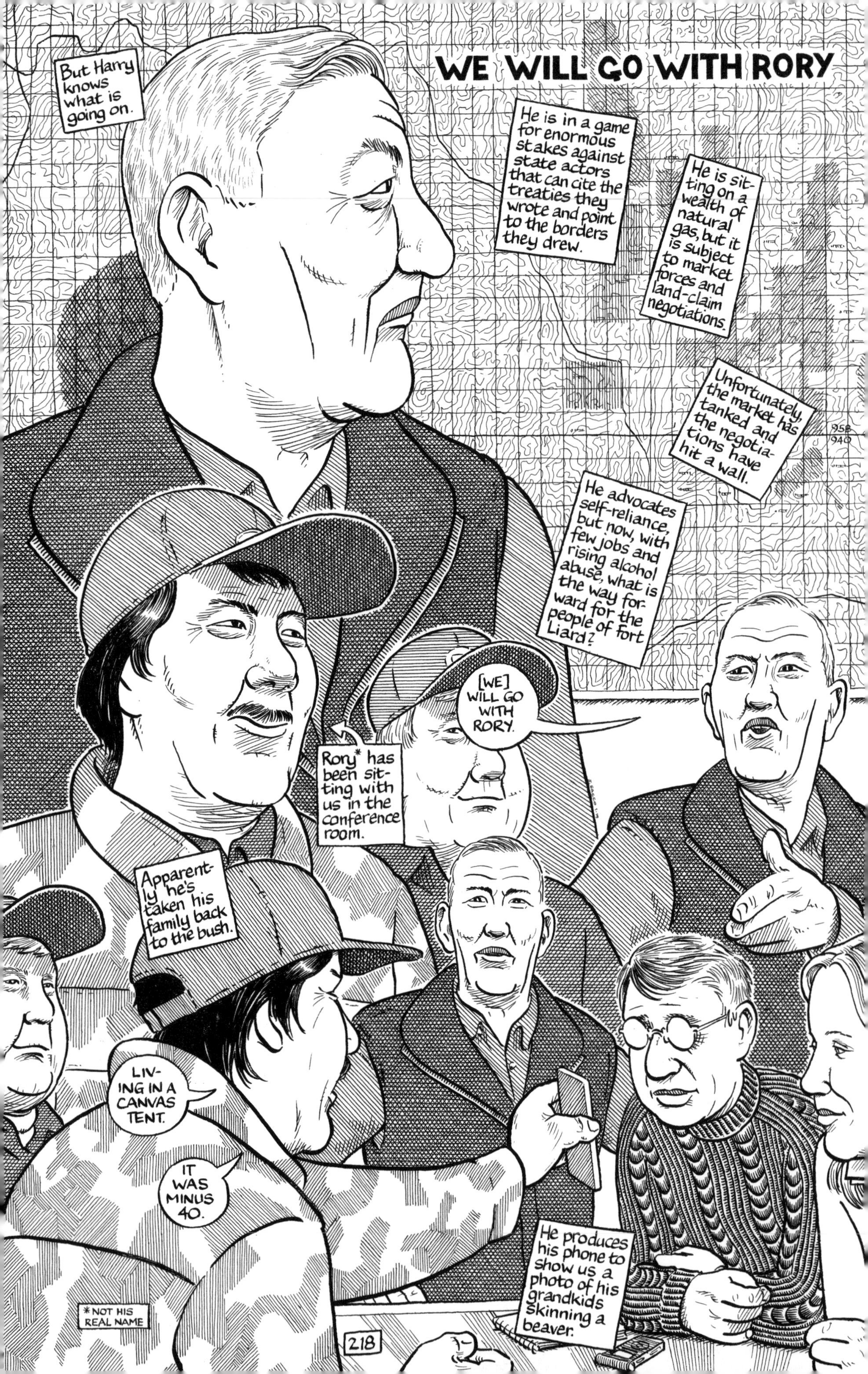

WE WILL GO WITH RORY
But Harry knows what is going on.
He is in a game for enormous stakes against state actors that can cite the treaties they wrote and point to the borders they drew.
He is sitting on a wealth of natural gas, but it is subject to market forces and land-claim negotiations.
Unfortunately, the market has tanked and the negotiations have hit a wall.
He advocates self-reliance, but now, with few jobs and rising alcohol abuse, what is the way forward for the people of Fort Liard?
[WE] WILL GO WITH RORY.
Rory* has been sitting with us in the conference room.
Apparently he's taken his family back to the bush.
LIVING IN A CANVAS TENT.
IT WAS MINUS 40.
He produces his phone to show us a photo of his grandkids skinning a beaver.
*NOT HIS REAL NAME

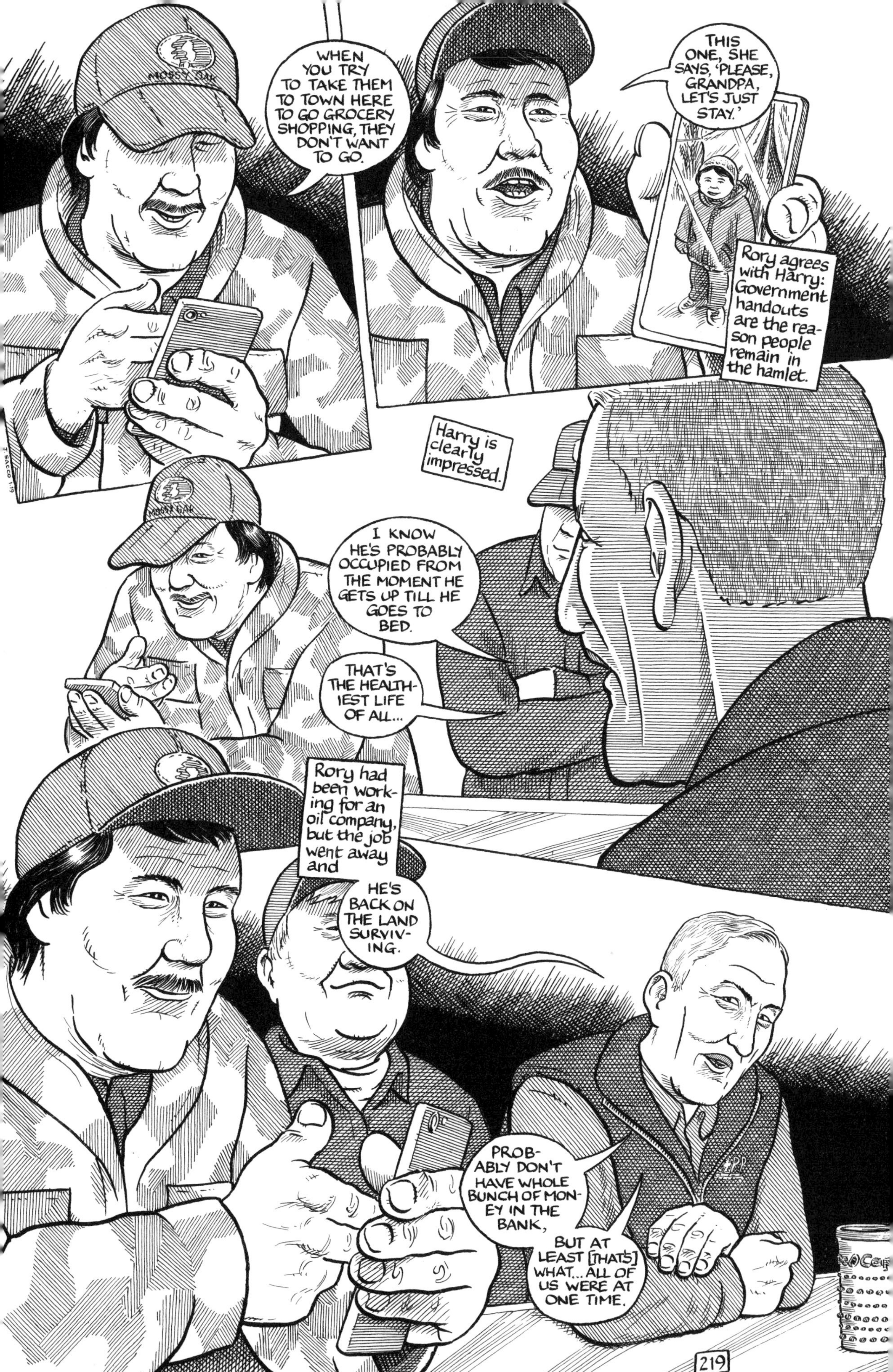

MOSSY OAK
WHEN YOU TRY TO TAKE THEM TO TOWN HERE TO GO GROCERY SHOPPING, THEY DON'T WANT TO GO.
THIS ONE, SHE SAYS, 'PLEASE, GRANDPA, LET'S JUST STAY.'
Rory agrees with Harry: Government handouts are the reason people remain in the hamlet.
Harry is clearly impressed.
I KNOW HE'S PROBABLY OCCUPIED FROM THE MOMENT HE GETS UP TILL HE GOES TO BED.
THAT'S THE HEALTHIEST LIFE OF ALL...
Rory had been working for an oil company, but the job went away and
HE'S BACK ON THE LAND SURVIVING.
PROBABLY DON'T HAVE WHOLE BUNCH OF MONEY IN THE BANK,
BUT AT LEAST [THAT'S] WHAT... ALL OF US WERE AT ONE TIME.

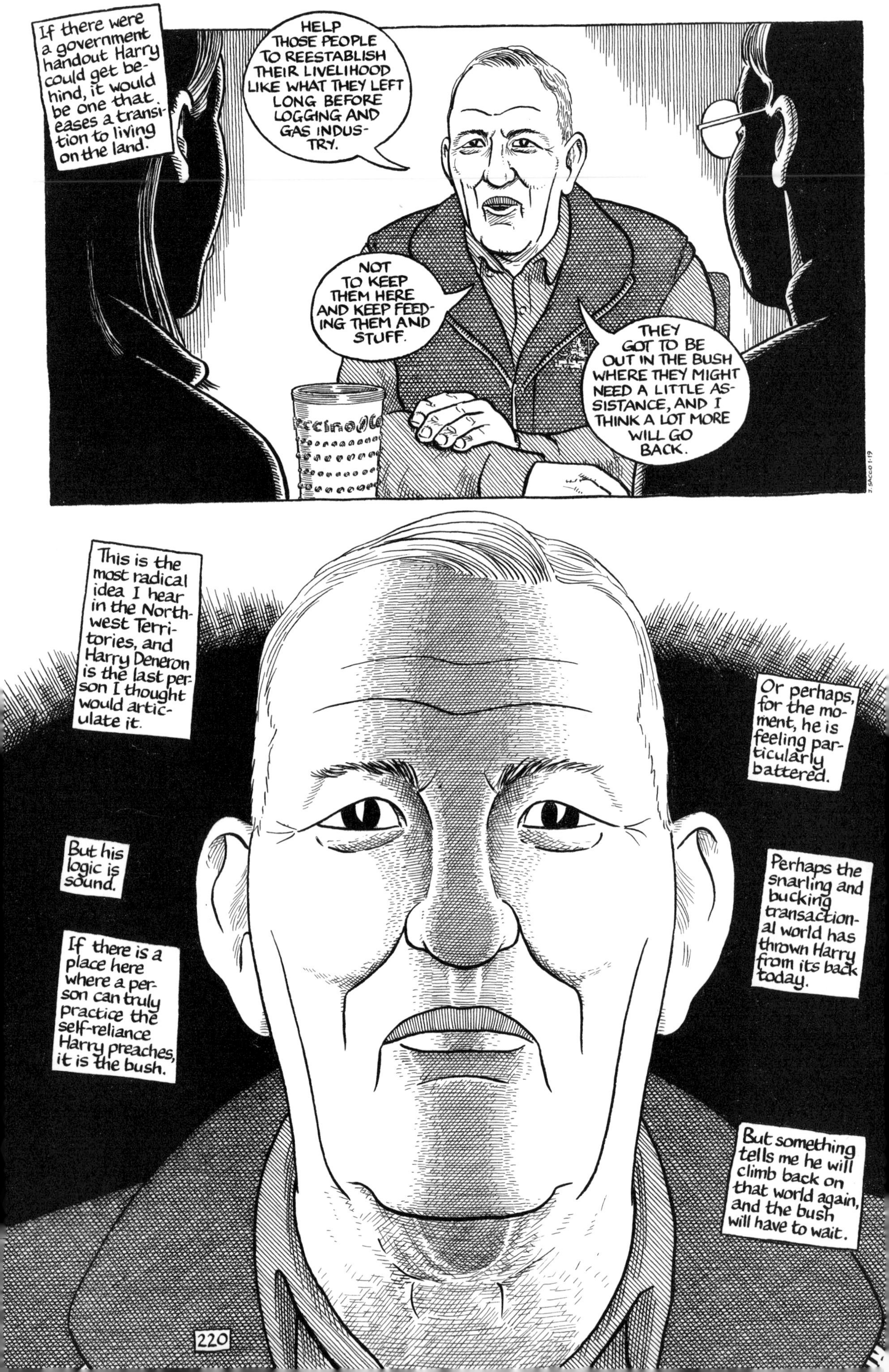
If there were a government handout Harry could get behind, it would be one that eases a transition to living on the land.
HELP THOSE PEOPLE TO REESTABLISH THEIR LIVELIHOOD LIKE WHAT THEY LEFT LONG BEFORE LOGGING AND GAS INDUSTRY.
NOT TO KEEP THEM HERE AND KEEP FEEDING THEM AND STUFF.
THEY GOT TO BE OUT IN THE BUSH WHERE THEY MIGHT NEED A LITTLE ASSISTANCE, AND I THINK A LOT MORE WILL GO BACK.
This is the most radical idea I hear in the Northwest Territories, and Harry Deneron is the last person I thought would articulate it.
But his logic is sound.
If there is a place here where a person can truly practice the self-reliance Harry preaches, it is the bush.
Or perhaps, for the moment, he is feeling particularly battered.
Perhaps the snarling and bucking transactional world has thrown Harry from its back today.
But something tells me he will climb back on that world again, and the bush will have to wait.

VI

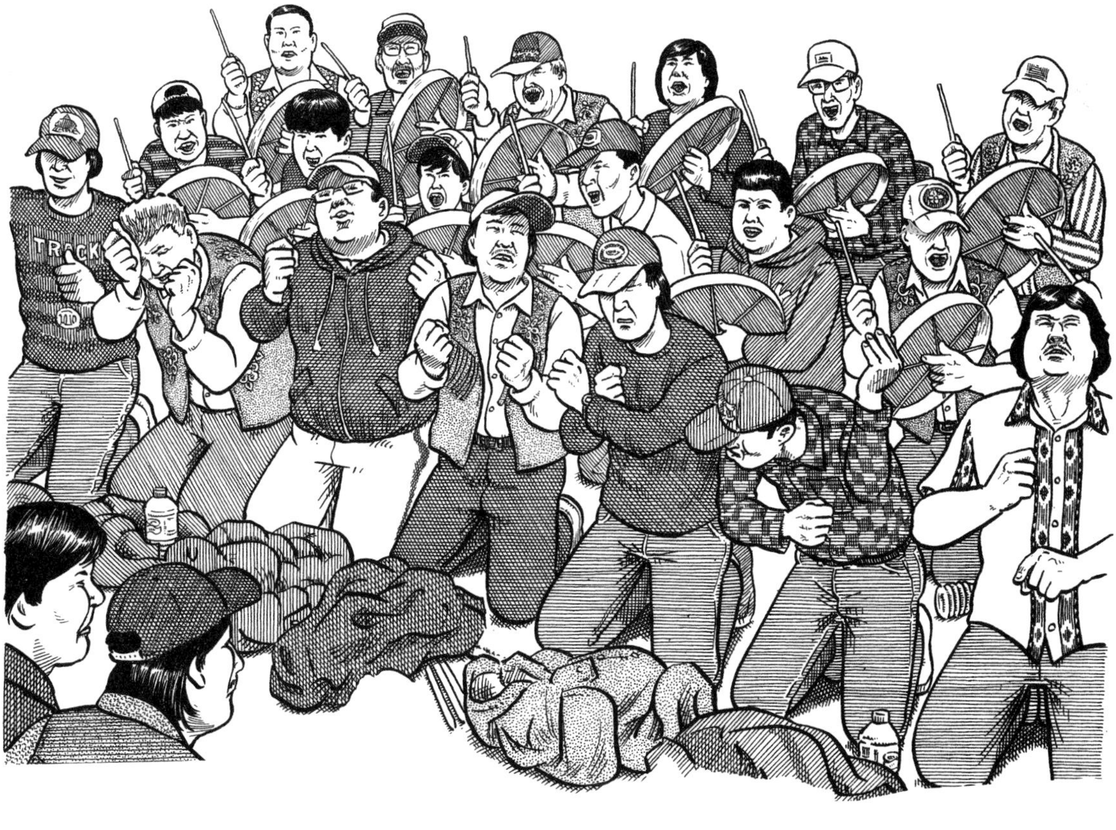
TRACK

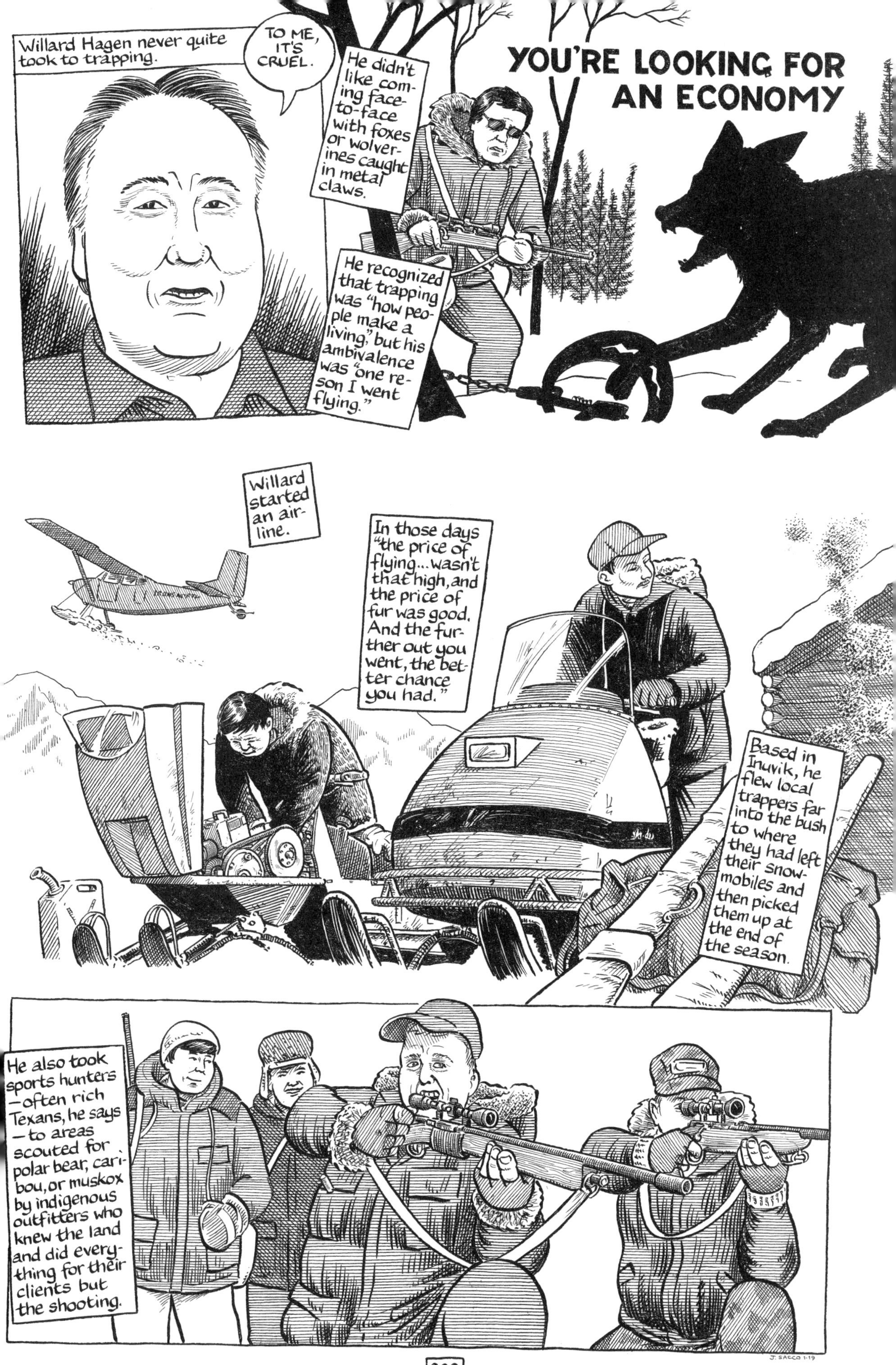
YOU'RE LOOKING FOR AN ECONOMY
Willard Hagen never quite took to trapping.
TO ME, IT'S CRUEL.
He didn't like coming face-to-face with foxes or wolverines caught in metal claws.
He recognized that trapping was "how people make a living," but his ambivalence was "one reson I went flying."
Willard started an airline.
In those days "the price of flying... wasn't that high, and the price of fur was good. And the further out you went, the better chance you had."
Based in Inuvik, he flew local trappers far into the bush to where they had left their snowmobiles and then picked them up at the end of the season.
He also took sports hunters —often rich Texans, he says —to areas scouted for polar bear, caribou, or muskox by indigenous outfitters who knew the land and did everything for their clients but the shooting.
J. SACCO 1-19

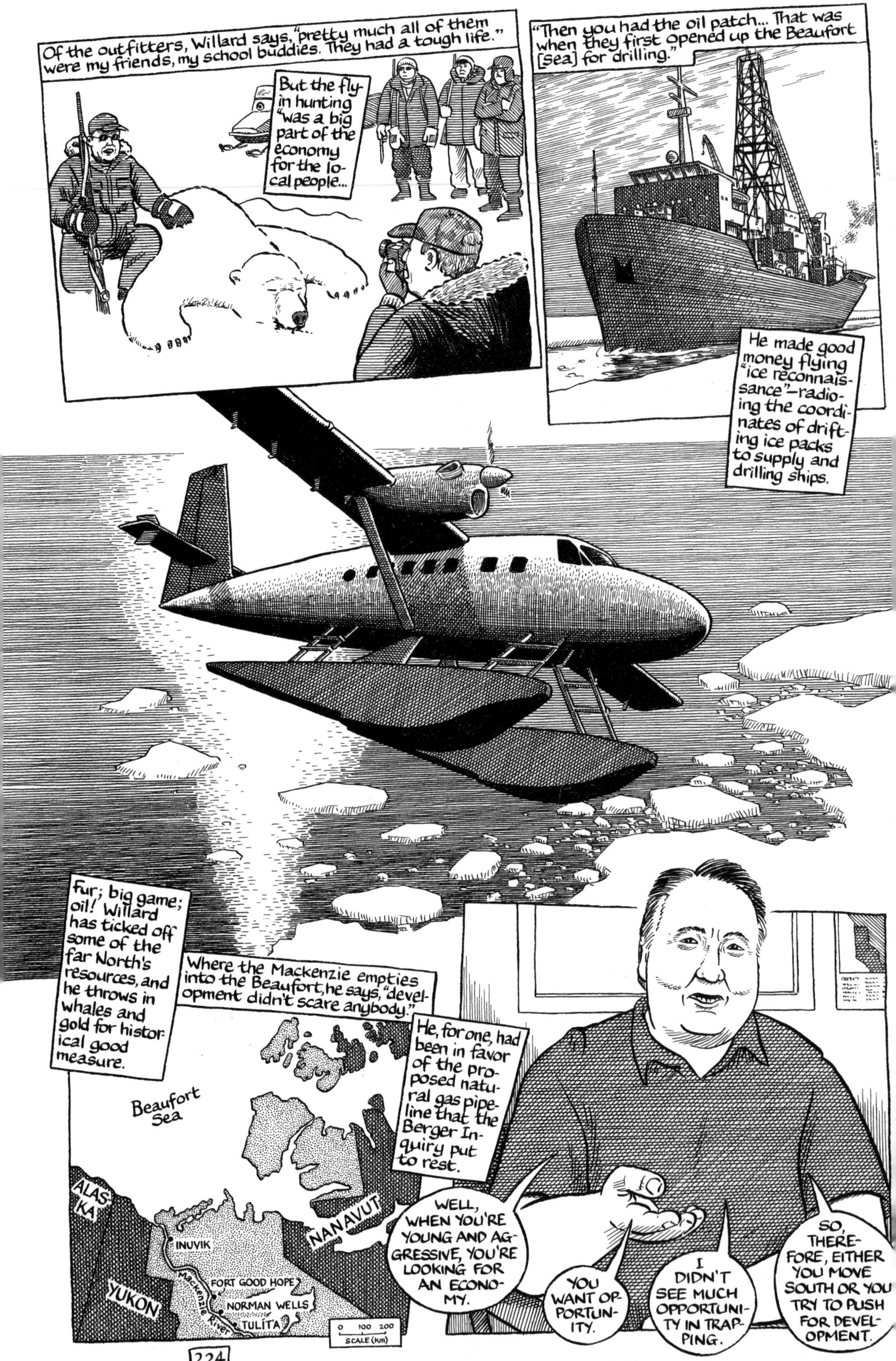

Of the outfitters, Willard says, "pretty much all of them were my friends, my school buddies. They had a tough life."
But the fly-in hunting "was a big part of the economy for the local people...
"Then you had the oil patch... That was when they first opened up the Beaufort [Sea] for drilling."
He made good money flying "ice reconnaissance"—radioing the coordinates of drifting ice packs to supply and drilling ships.
Fur; big game; oil! Willard has ticked off some of the far North's resources, and he throws in whales and gold for historical good measure.
Where the Mackenzie empties into the Beaufort, he says, "development didn't scare anybody."
He, for one, had been in favor of the proposed natural gas pipeline that the Berger Inquiry put to rest.
Beaufort Sea
ALASKA
YUKON
NANAVUT
INUVIK
Mackenzie River
FORT GOOD HOPE
NORMAN WELLS
TULITA
0 100 200
SCALE (Km)
WELL, WHEN YOU'RE YOUNG AND AGGRESSIVE, YOU'RE LOOKING FOR AN ECONOMY.
YOU WANT OPPORTUNITY.
I DIDN'T SEE MUCH OPPORTUNITY IN TRAPPING.
SO, THEREFORE, EITHER YOU MOVE SOUTH OR YOU TRY TO PUSH FOR DEVELOPMENT.

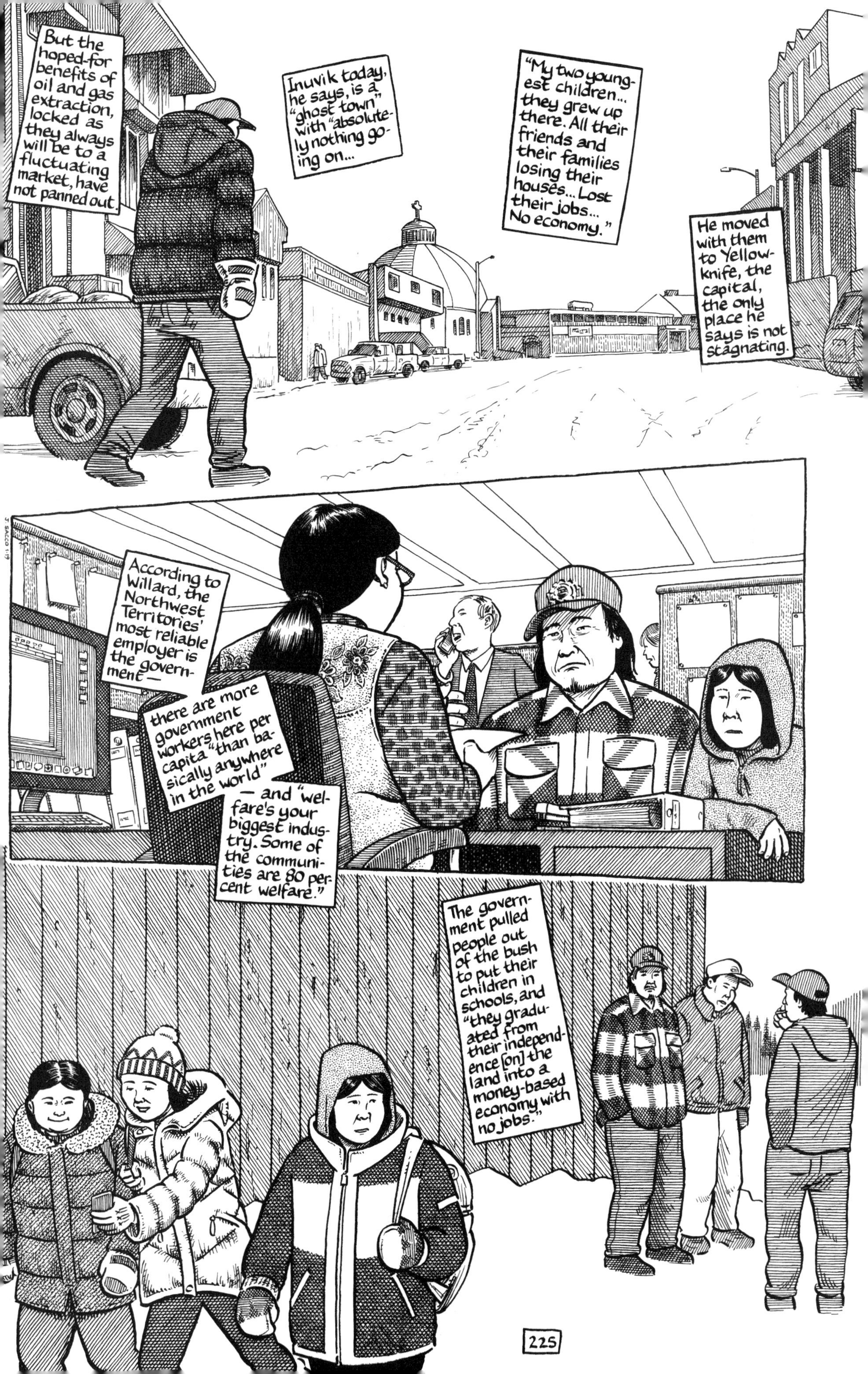

But the hoped-for benefits of oil and gas extraction, locked as they always will be to a fluctuating market, have not panned out.
Inuvik today, he says, is a "ghost town" with "absolutely nothing going on...
"My two youngest children... they grew up there. All their friends and their families losing their houses... Lost their jobs... No economy."
He moved with them to Yellowknife, the capital, the only place he says is not stagnating.
According to Willard, the Northwest Territories' most reliable employer is the government—
there are more government workers here per capita "than basically anywhere in the world"
— and "welfare's your biggest industry. Some of the communities are 80 percent welfare."
The government pulled people out of the bush to put their children in schools, and "they graduated from their independence [on] the land into a money-based economy with no jobs."
J. SACCO 1.19

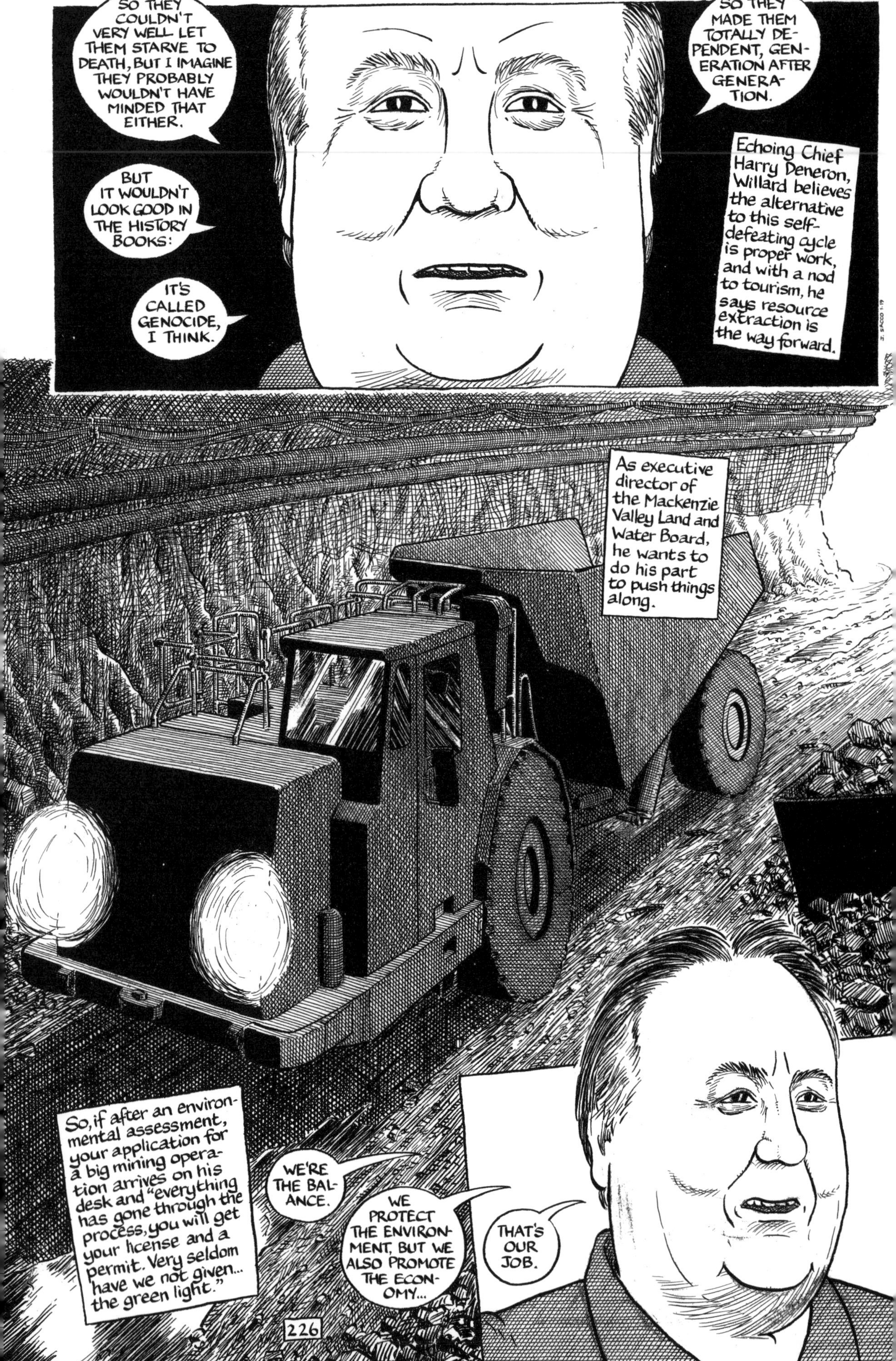
SO THEY COULDN'T VERY WELL LET THEM STARVE TO DEATH, BUT I IMAGINE THEY PROBABLY WOULDN'T HAVE MINDED THAT EITHER.
SO THEY MADE THEM TOTALLY DEPENDENT, GENERATION AFTER GENERATION.
BUT IT WOULDN'T LOOK GOOD IN THE HISTORY BOOKS:
IT'S CALLED GENOCIDE, I THINK.
Echoing Chief Harry Deneron, Willard believes the alternative to this self-defeating cycle is proper work, and with a nod to tourism, he says resource extraction is the way forward.
As executive director of the Mackenzie Valley Land and Water Board, he wants to do his part to push things along.
So, if after an environmental assessment, your application for a big mining operation arrives on his desk and "everything has gone through the process, you will get your license and a permit. Very seldom have we not given... the green light."
WE'RE THE BALANCE.
WE PROTECT THE ENVIRONMENT, BUT WE ALSO PROMOTE THE ECONOMY...
THAT'S OUR JOB.

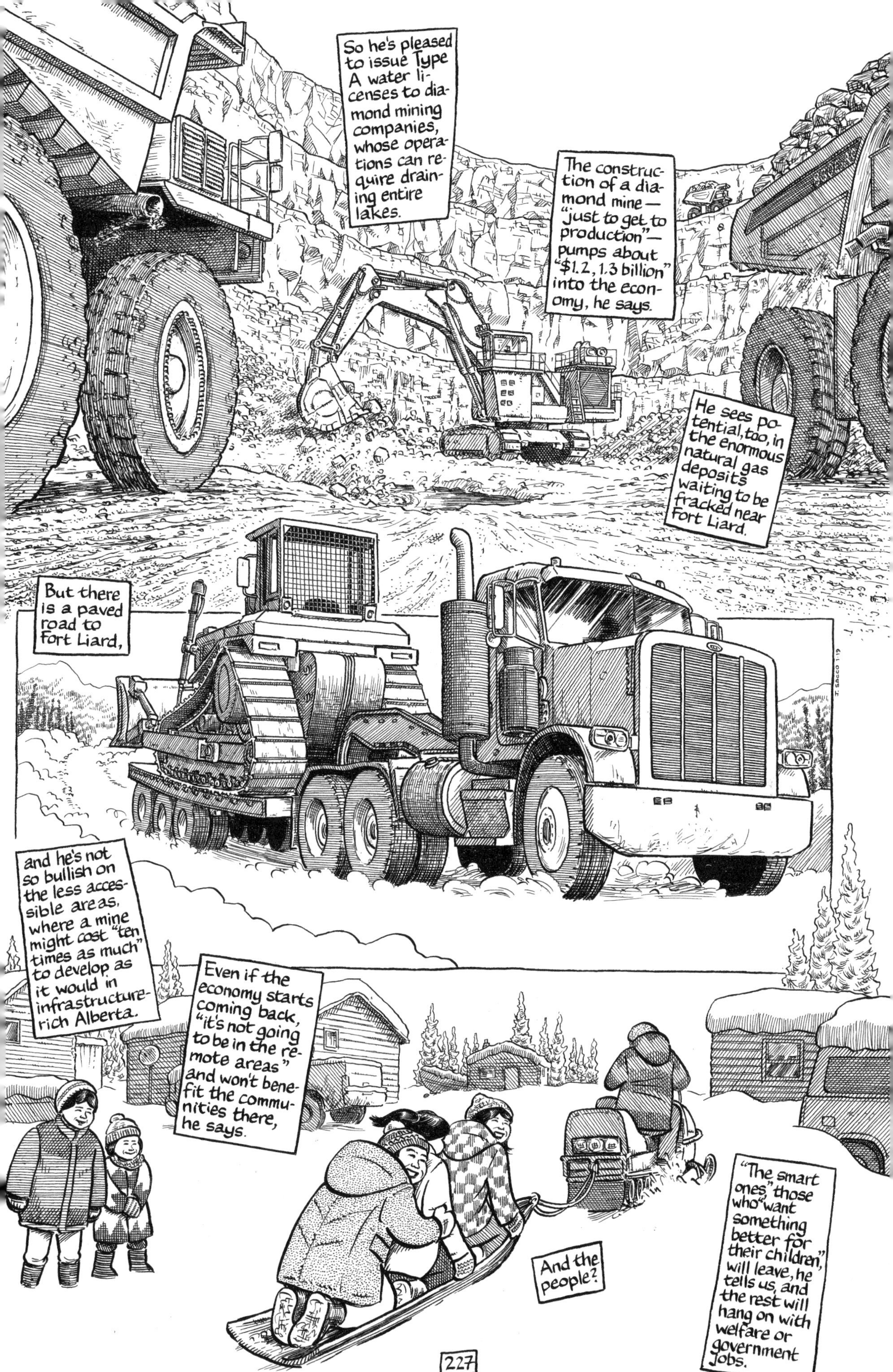
So he's pleased to issue Type A water licenses to diamond mining companies, whose operations can require draining entire lakes.
The construction of a diamond mine—"just to get to production"—pumps about "$1.2, 1.3 billion" into the economy, he says.
He sees potential, too, in the enormous natural gas deposits waiting to be fracked near Fort Liard.
But there is a paved road to Fort Liard,
and he's not so bullish on the less accessible areas, where a mine might cost "ten times as much" to develop as it would in infrastructure-rich Alberta.
Even if the economy starts coming back, "it's not going to be in the remote areas" and won't benefit the communities there, he says.
And the people?
"The smart ones," those who "want something better for their children," will leave, he tells us, and the rest will hang on with welfare or government jobs.

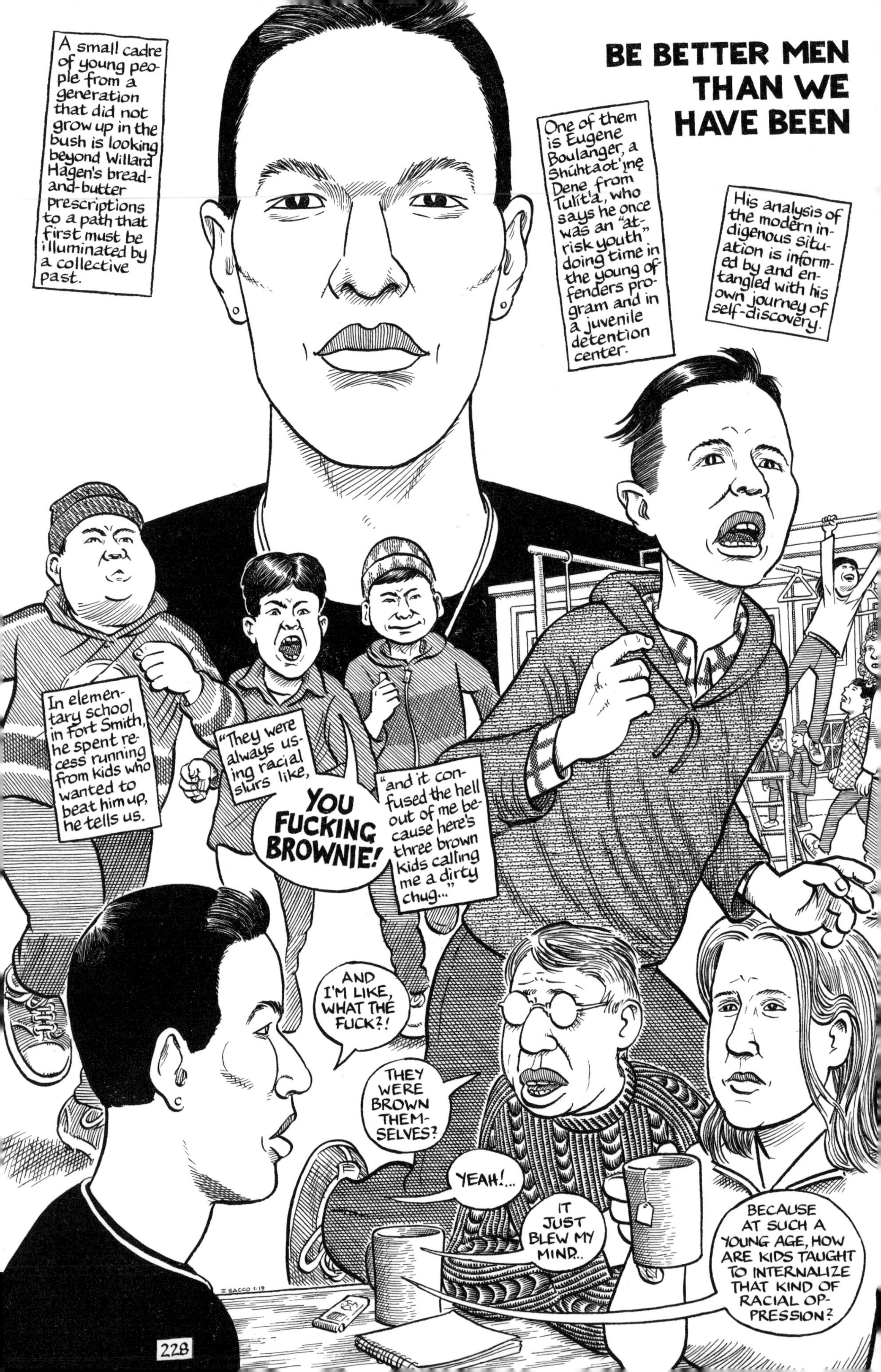
BE BETTER MEN THAN WE HAVE BEEN
A small cadre of young people from a generation that did not grow up in the bush is looking beyond Willard Hagen's bread-and-butter prescriptions to a path that first must be illuminated by a collective past.
One of them is Eugene Boulanger, a Shúhtaot'įnę Dene from Tulít'a, who says he once was an "at-risk youth" doing time in the young offenders program and in a juvenile detention center.
His analysis of the modern indigenous situation is informed by and entangled with his own journey of self-discovery.
In elementary school in Fort Smith, he spent recess running from kids who wanted to beat him up, he tells us.
"They were always using racial slurs like,
YOU FUCKING BROWNIE!
"and it confused the hell out of me because here's three brown kids calling me a dirty chug..."
AND I'M LIKE, WHAT THE FUCK?!
THEY WERE BROWN THEMSELVES?
YEAH!...
IT JUST BLEW MY MIND...
BECAUSE AT SUCH A YOUNG AGE, HOW ARE KIDS TAUGHT TO INTERNALIZE THAT KIND OF RACIAL OPPRESSION?
J. SACCO 1-19

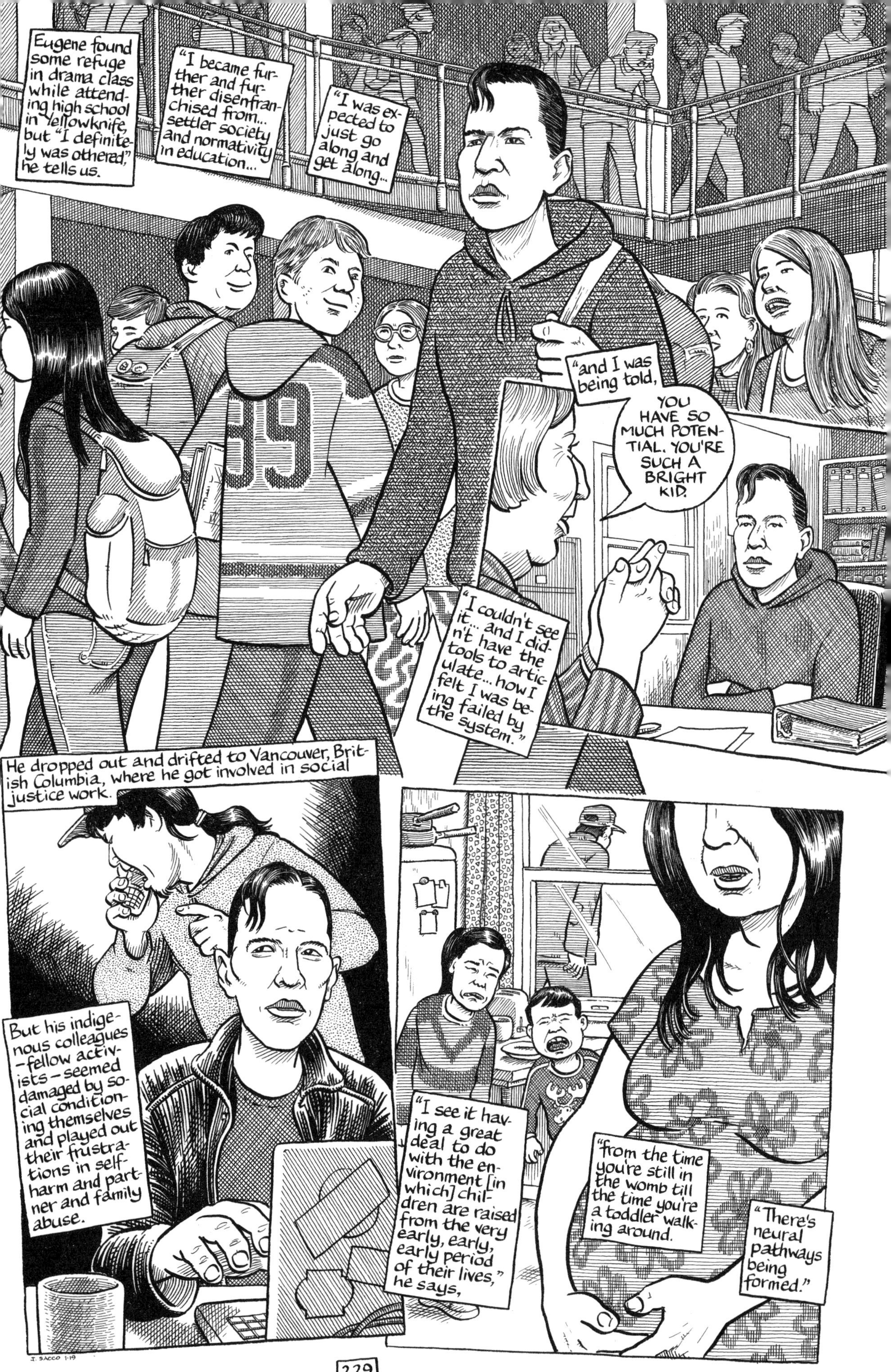
Eugene found some refuge in drama class while attending high school in Yellowknife, but "I definitely was othered," he tells us.
"I became further and further disenfranchised from... settler society and normativity in education...
"I was expected to just go along and get along...
"and I was being told,
YOU HAVE SO MUCH POTENTIAL. YOU'RE SUCH A BRIGHT KID.
"I couldn't see it... and I didn't have the tools to articulate... how I felt I was being failed by the system."
He dropped out and drifted to Vancouver, British Columbia, where he got involved in social justice work.
But his indigenous colleagues—fellow activists—seemed damaged by social conditioning themselves and played out their frustrations in self-harm and partner and family abuse.
"I see it having a great deal to do with the environment [in which] children are raised from the very early, early, early period of their lives," he says,
"from the time you're still in the womb till the time you're a toddler walking around.
"There's neural pathways being formed."
J. SACCO 1-19

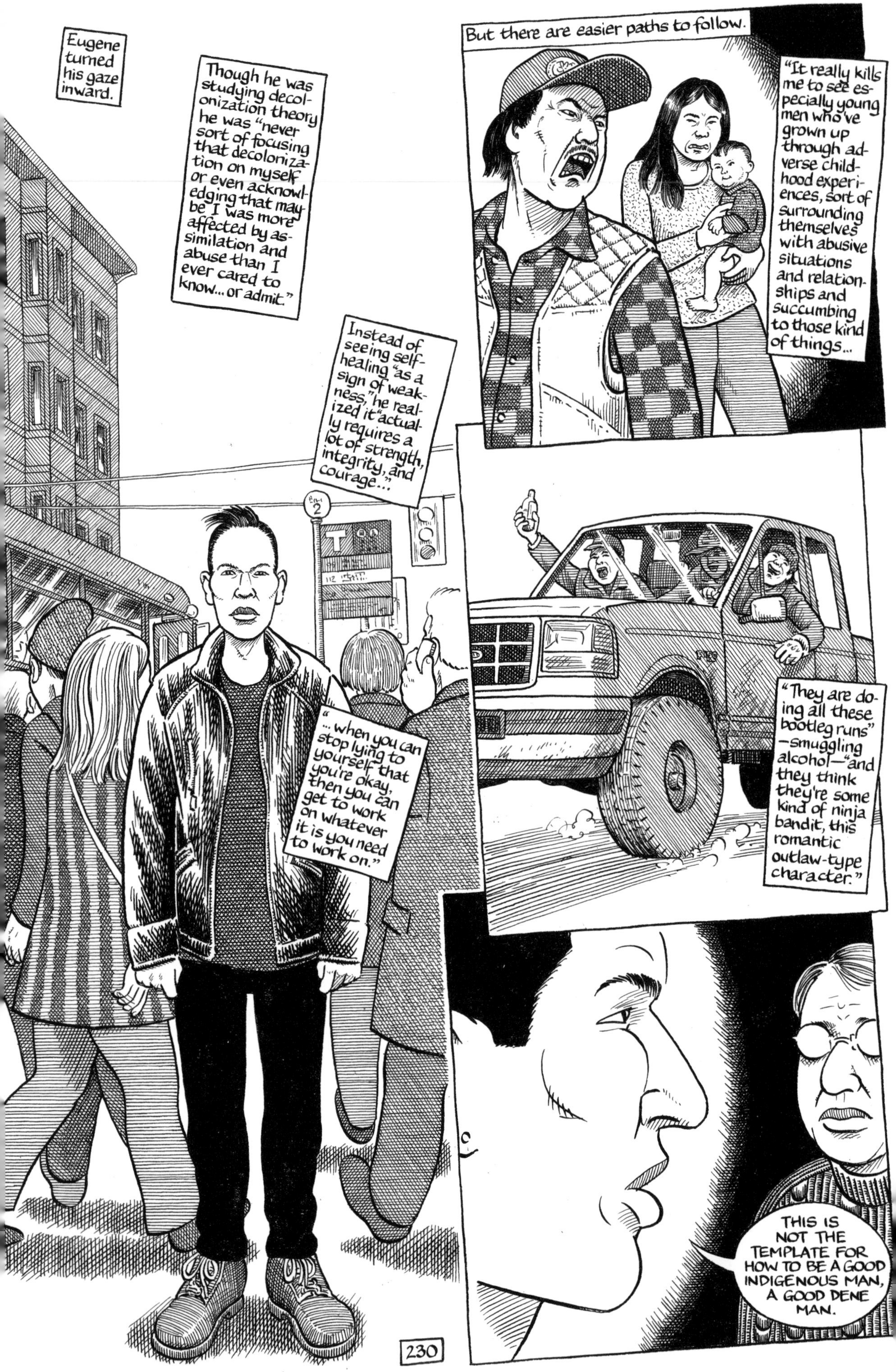
Eugene turned his gaze inward.
Though he was studying decolonization theory he was "never sort of focusing that decolonization on myself or even acknowledging that maybe I was more affected by assimilation and abuse than I ever cared to know... or admit."
Instead of seeing self-healing "as a sign of weakness," he realized it "actually requires a lot of strength, integrity, and courage..."
"... when you can stop lying to yourself that you're okay, then you can get to work on whatever it is you need to work on."
But there are easier paths to follow.
"It really kills me to see especially young men who've grown up through adverse childhood experiences, sort of surrounding themselves with abusive situations and relationships and succumbing to those kind of things...
"They are doing all these bootleg runs" —smuggling alcohol—"and they think they're some kind of ninja bandit, this romantic outlaw-type character."
THIS IS NOT THE TEMPLATE FOR HOW TO BE A GOOD INDIGENOUS MAN, A GOOD DENE MAN.

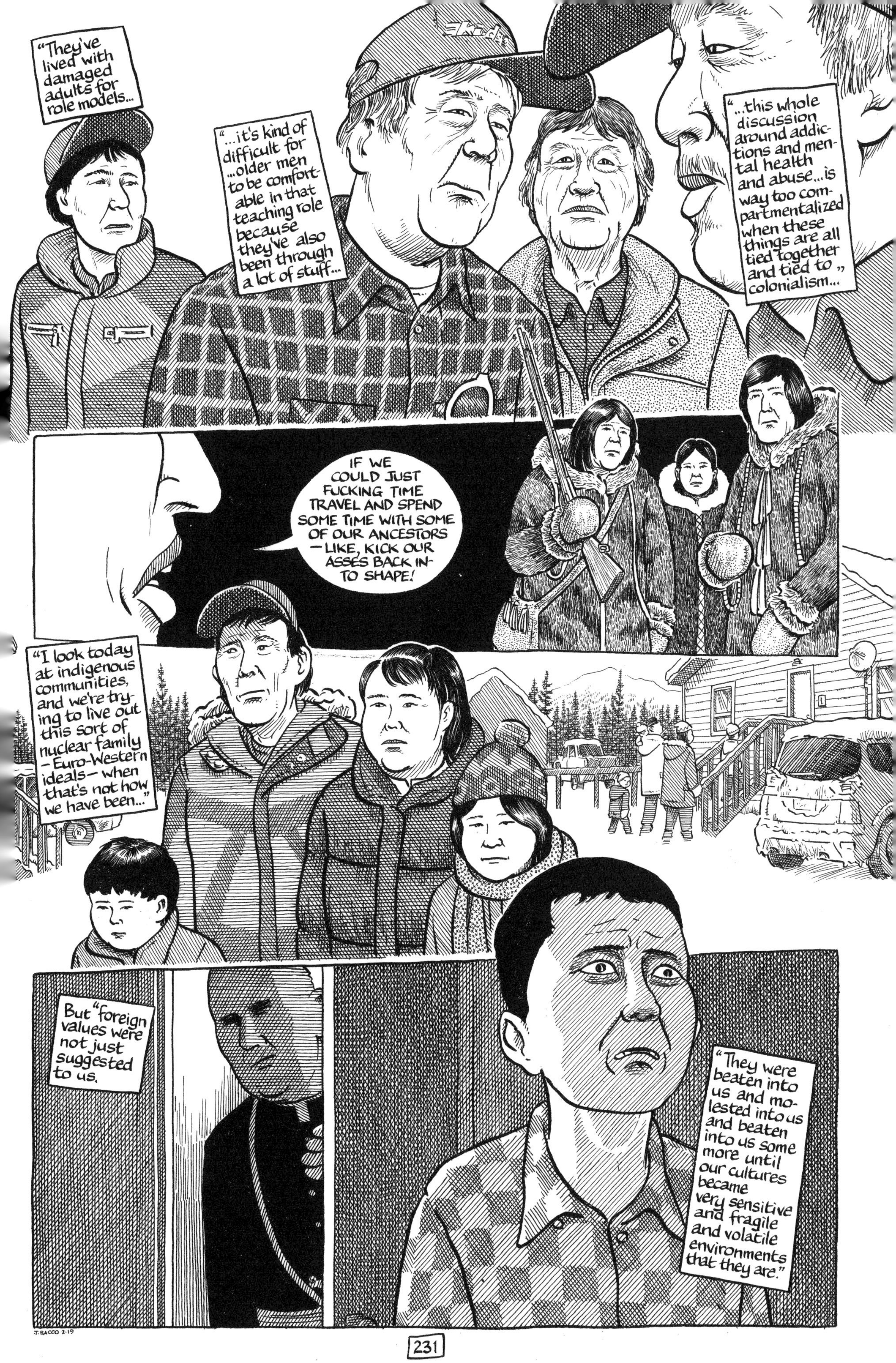
"They've lived with damaged adults for role models...
"...it's kind of difficult for ...older men to be comfortable in that teaching role because they've also been through a lot of stuff...
"...this whole discussion around addictions and mental health and abuse...is way too compartmentalized when these things are all tied together and tied to colonialism...
IF WE COULD JUST FUCKING TIME TRAVEL AND SPEND SOME TIME WITH SOME OF OUR ANCESTORS —LIKE, KICK OUR ASSES BACK INTO SHAPE!
"I look today at indigenous communities, and we're trying to live out this sort of nuclear family —Euro-Western ideals— when that's not how we have been..."
But "foreign values were not just suggested to us.
"They were beaten into us and molested into us and beaten into us some more until our cultures became very sensitive and fragile and volatile environments that they are."
J. SACCO 2·19

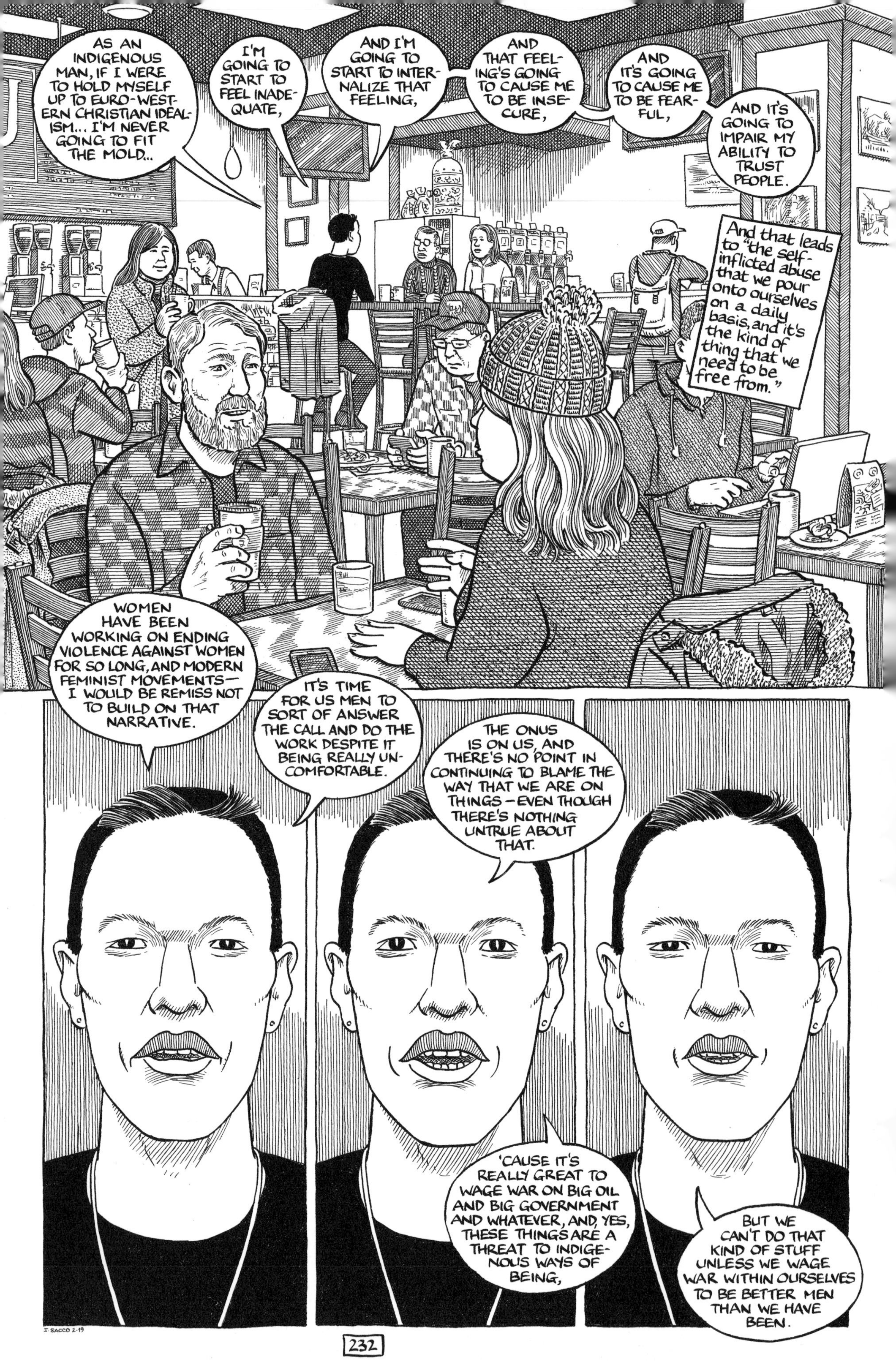
AS AN INDIGENOUS MAN, IF I WERE TO HOLD MYSELF UP TO EURO-WESTERN CHRISTIAN IDEALISM... I'M NEVER GOING TO FIT THE MOLD...
I'M GOING TO START TO FEEL INADEQUATE,
AND I'M GOING TO START TO INTERNALIZE THAT FEELING,
AND THAT FEELING'S GOING TO CAUSE ME TO BE INSECURE,
AND IT'S GOING TO CAUSE ME TO BE FEARFUL,
AND IT'S GOING TO IMPAIR MY ABILITY TO TRUST PEOPLE.
And that leads to "the self-inflicted abuse that we pour onto ourselves on a daily basis, and it's the kind of thing that we need to be free from."
WOMEN HAVE BEEN WORKING ON ENDING VIOLENCE AGAINST WOMEN FOR SO LONG, AND MODERN FEMINIST MOVEMENTS— I WOULD BE REMISS NOT TO BUILD ON THAT NARRATIVE.
IT'S TIME FOR US MEN TO SORT OF ANSWER THE CALL AND DO THE WORK DESPITE IT BEING REALLY UNCOMFORTABLE.
THE ONUS IS ON US, AND THERE'S NO POINT IN CONTINUING TO BLAME THE WAY THAT WE ARE ON THINGS—EVEN THOUGH THERE'S NOTHING UNTRUE ABOUT THAT.
'CAUSE IT'S REALLY GREAT TO WAGE WAR ON BIG OIL AND BIG GOVERNMENT AND WHATEVER, AND, YES, THESE THINGS ARE A THREAT TO INDIGENOUS WAYS OF BEING,
BUT WE CAN'T DO THAT KIND OF STUFF UNLESS WE WAGE WAR WITHIN OURSELVES TO BE BETTER MEN THAN WE HAVE BEEN.
J. SACCO 2-19

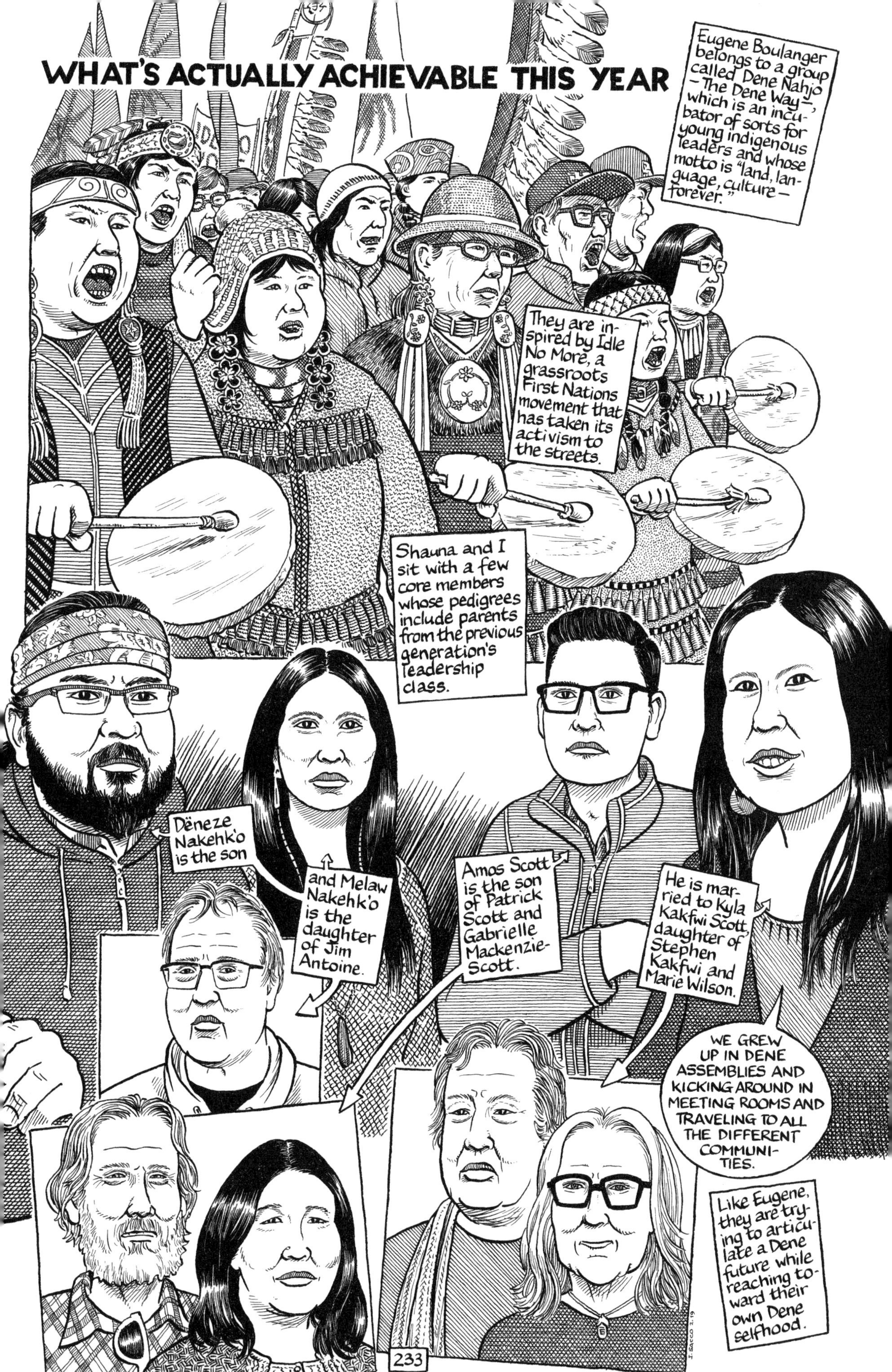
WHAT'S ACTUALLY ACHIEVABLE THIS YEAR
Eugene Boulanger belongs to a group called Dene Nahjo —The Dene Way—, which is an incubator of sorts for young indigenous leaders and whose motto is "land, language, culture—forever."
They are inspired by Idle No More, a grassroots First Nations movement that has taken its activism to the streets.
Shauna and I sit with a few core members whose pedigrees include parents from the previous generation's leadership class.
Dëneze Nakehk'o is the son
and Melaw Nakehk'o is the daughter of Jim Antoine.
Amos Scott is the son of Patrick Scott and Gabrielle Mackenzie-Scott.
He is married to Kyla Kakfwi Scott, daughter of Stephen Kakfwi and Marie Wilson.
WE GREW UP IN DENE ASSEMBLIES AND KICKING AROUND IN MEETING ROOMS AND TRAVELING TO ALL THE DIFFERENT COMMUNITIES.
Like Eugene, they are trying to articulate a Dene future while reaching toward their own Dene selfhood.

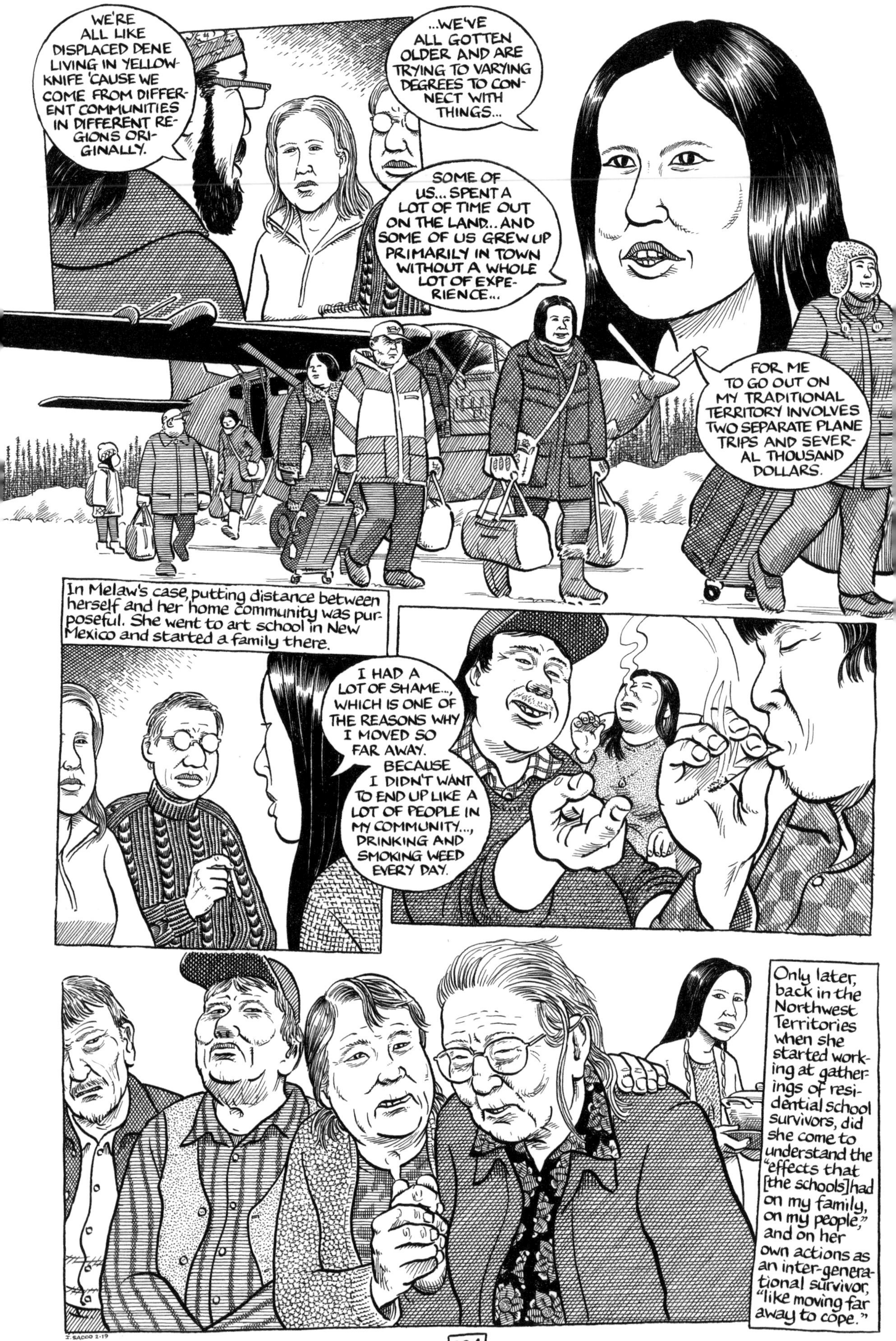
WE'RE ALL LIKE DISPLACED DENE LIVING IN YELLOWKNIFE 'CAUSE WE COME FROM DIFFERENT COMMUNITIES IN DIFFERENT REGIONS ORIGINALLY.
...WE'VE ALL GOTTEN OLDER AND ARE TRYING TO VARYING DEGREES TO CONNECT WITH THINGS...
SOME OF US... SPENT A LOT OF TIME OUT ON THE LAND... AND SOME OF US GREW UP PRIMARILY IN TOWN WITHOUT A WHOLE LOT OF EXPERIENCE...
FOR ME TO GO OUT ON MY TRADITIONAL TERRITORY INVOLVES TWO SEPARATE PLANE TRIPS AND SEVERAL THOUSAND DOLLARS.
In Melaw's case, putting distance between herself and her home community was purposeful. She went to art school in New Mexico and started a family there.
I HAD A LOT OF SHAME..., WHICH IS ONE OF THE REASONS WHY I MOVED SO FAR AWAY.
BECAUSE I DIDN'T WANT TO END UP LIKE A LOT OF PEOPLE IN MY COMMUNITY..., DRINKING AND SMOKING WEED EVERY DAY.
Only later, back in the Northwest Territories when she started working at gatherings of residential school survivors, did she come to understand the "effects that [the schools] had on my family, on my people," and on her own actions as an inter-generational survivor, "like moving far away to cope."
J. SACCO 2-19

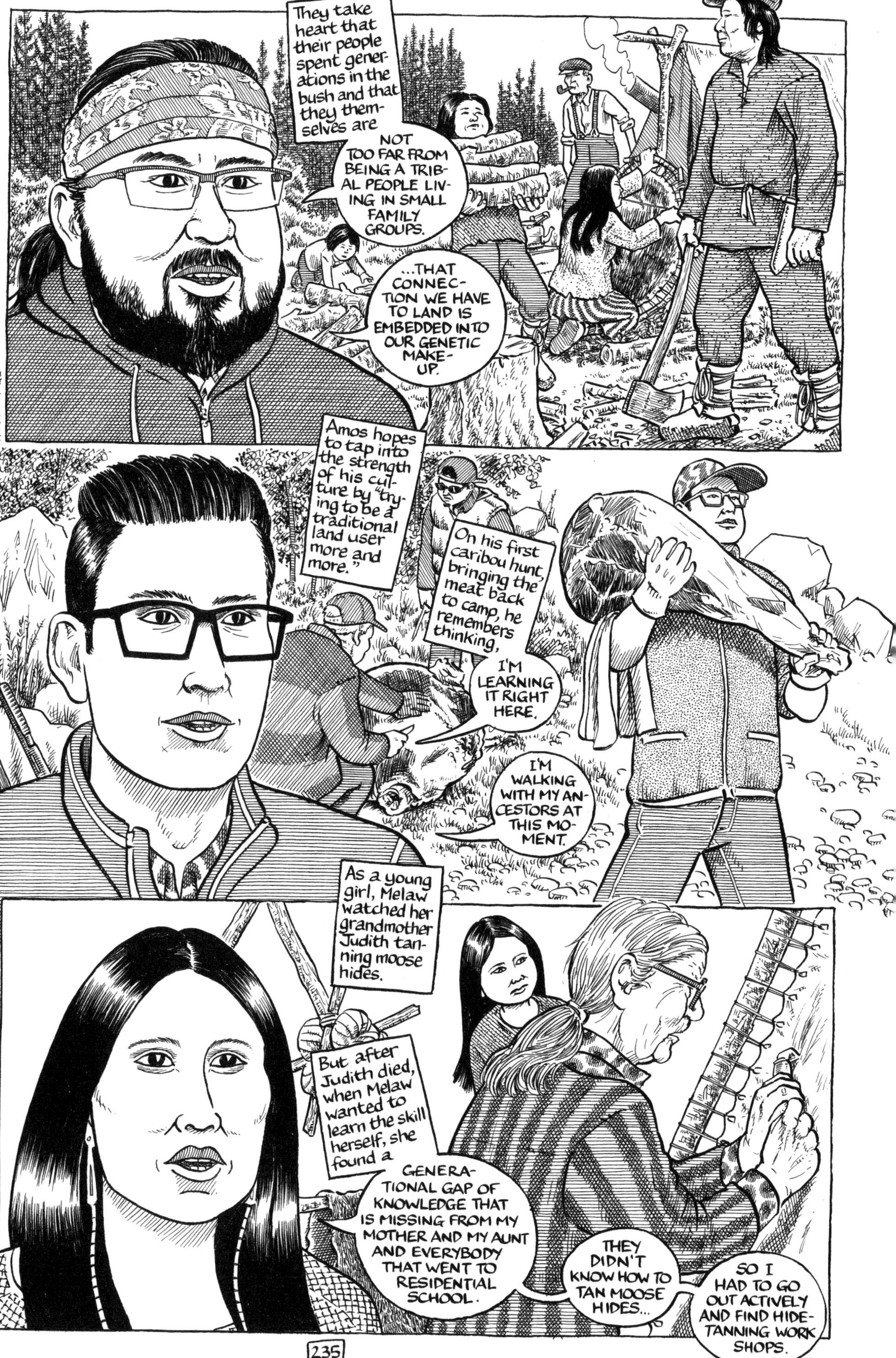
They take heart that their people spent generations in the bush and that they themselves are
NOT TOO FAR FROM BEING A TRIBAL PEOPLE LIVING IN SMALL FAMILY GROUPS.
...THAT CONNECTION WE HAVE TO LAND IS EMBEDDED INTO OUR GENETIC MAKE-UP.
Amos hopes to tap into the strength of his culture by "trying to be a traditional land user more and more."
On his first caribou hunt, bringing the meat back to camp, he remembers thinking,
I'M LEARNING IT RIGHT HERE.
I'M WALKING WITH MY ANCESTORS AT THIS MOMENT.
As a young girl, Melaw watched her grandmother Judith tanning moose hides.
But after Judith died, when Melaw wanted to learn the skill herself, she found a
GENERATIONAL GAP OF KNOWLEDGE THAT IS MISSING FROM MY MOTHER AND MY AUNT AND EVERYBODY THAT WENT TO RESIDENTIAL SCHOOL.
THEY DIDN'T KNOW HOW TO TAN MOOSE HIDES...
SO I HAD TO GO OUT ACTIVELY AND FIND HIDE-TANNING WORKSHOPS.

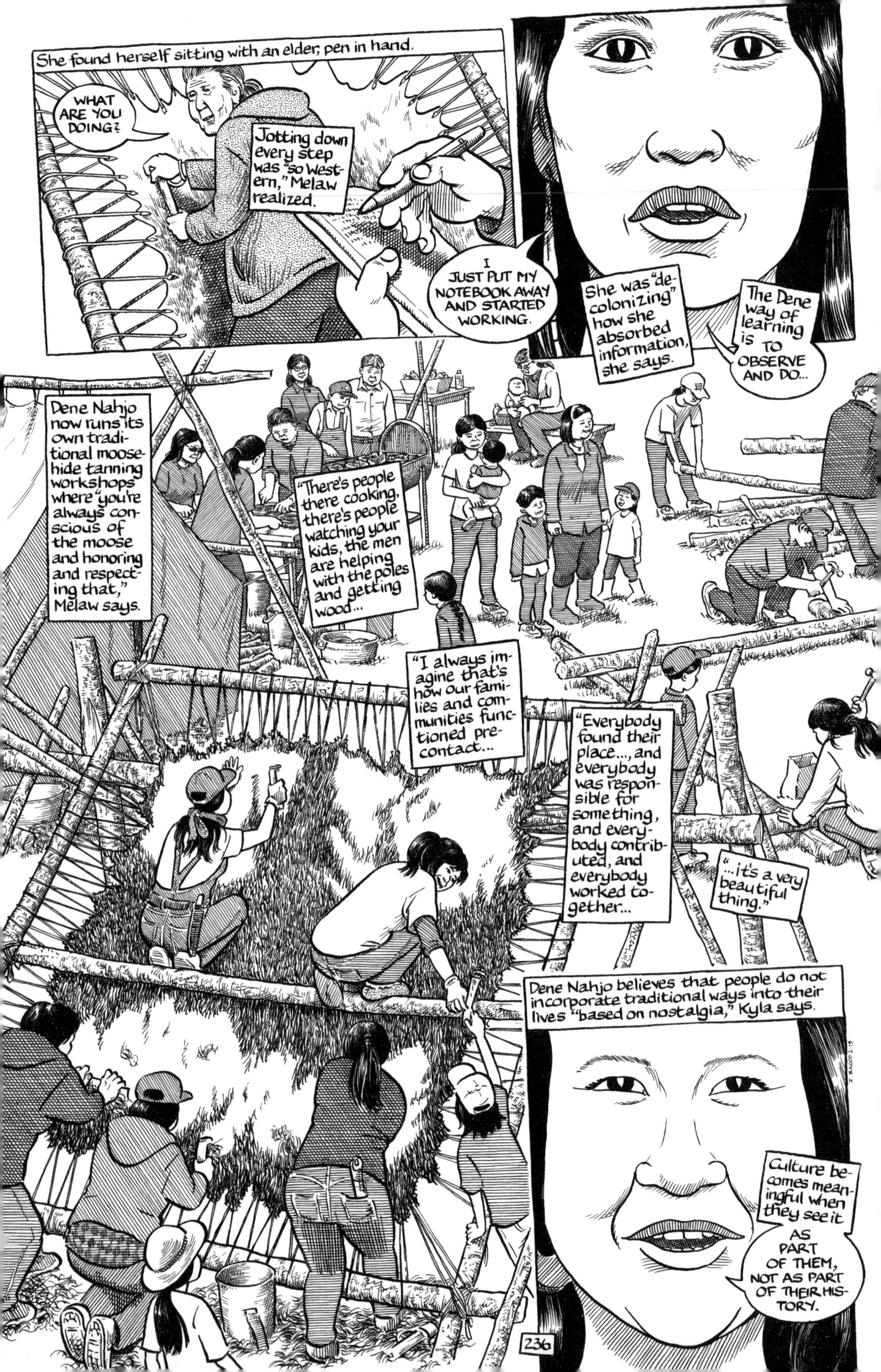
She found herself sitting with an elder, pen in hand.
WHAT ARE YOU DOING?
Jotting down every step was "so Western," Melaw realized.
I JUST PUT MY NOTEBOOK AWAY AND STARTED WORKING.
She was "de-colonizing" how she absorbed information, she says.
The Dene way of learning is TO OBSERVE AND DO...
Dene Nahjo now runs its own traditional moose-hide tanning workshops where "you're always conscious of the moose and honoring and respecting that," Melaw says.
"There's people there cooking, there's people watching your kids, the men are helping with the poles and getting wood...
"I always imagine that's how our families and communities functioned pre-contact...
"Everybody found their place..., and everybody was responsible for something, and everybody contributed, and everybody worked together...
"...it's a very beautiful thing."
Dene Nahjo believes that people do not incorporate traditional ways into their lives "based on nostalgia," Kyla says.
Culture becomes meaningful when they see it
AS PART OF THEM, NOT AS PART OF THEIR HISTORY.

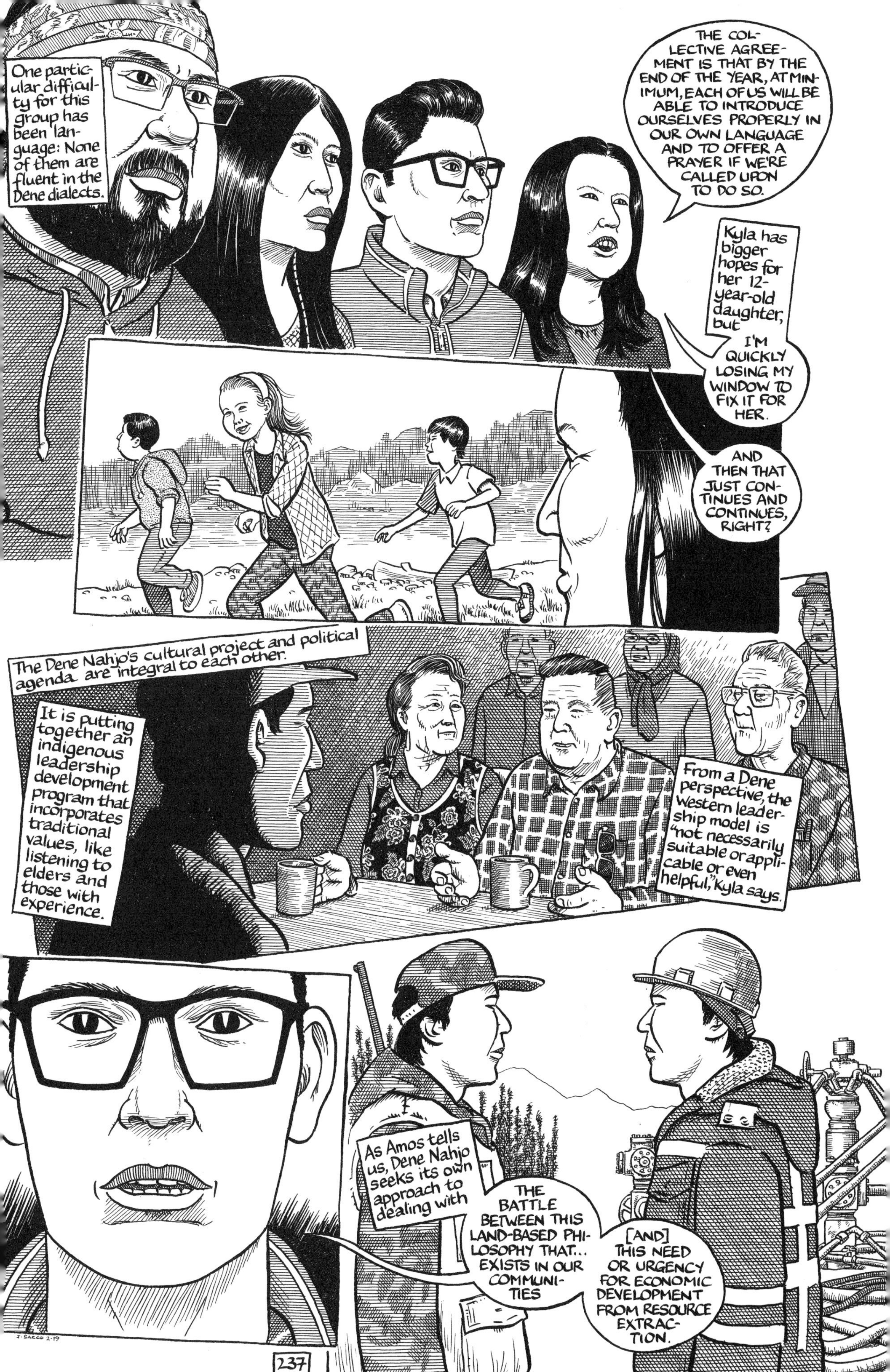

One particular difficulty for this group has been language: None of them are fluent in the Dene dialects.
THE COLLECTIVE AGREEMENT IS THAT BY THE END OF THE YEAR, AT MINIMUM, EACH OF US WILL BE ABLE TO INTRODUCE OURSELVES PROPERLY IN OUR OWN LANGUAGE AND TO OFFER A PRAYER IF WE'RE CALLED UPON TO DO SO.
Kyla has bigger hopes for her 12-year-old daughter, but
I'M QUICKLY LOSING MY WINDOW TO FIX IT FOR HER.
AND THEN THAT JUST CONTINUES AND CONTINUES, RIGHT?
The Dene Nahjo's cultural project and political agenda are integral to each other.
It is putting together an indigenous leadership development program that incorporates traditional values, like listening to elders and those with experience.
From a Dene perspective, the Western leadership model is "not necessarily suitable or applicable or even helpful," Kyla says.
As Amos tells us, Dene Nahjo seeks its own approach to dealing with
THE BATTLE BETWEEN THIS LAND-BASED PHILOSOPHY THAT... EXISTS IN OUR COMMUNITIES
[AND] THIS NEED OR URGENCY FOR ECONOMIC DEVELOPMENT FROM RESOURCE EXTRACTION.
J. SACCO 2-19

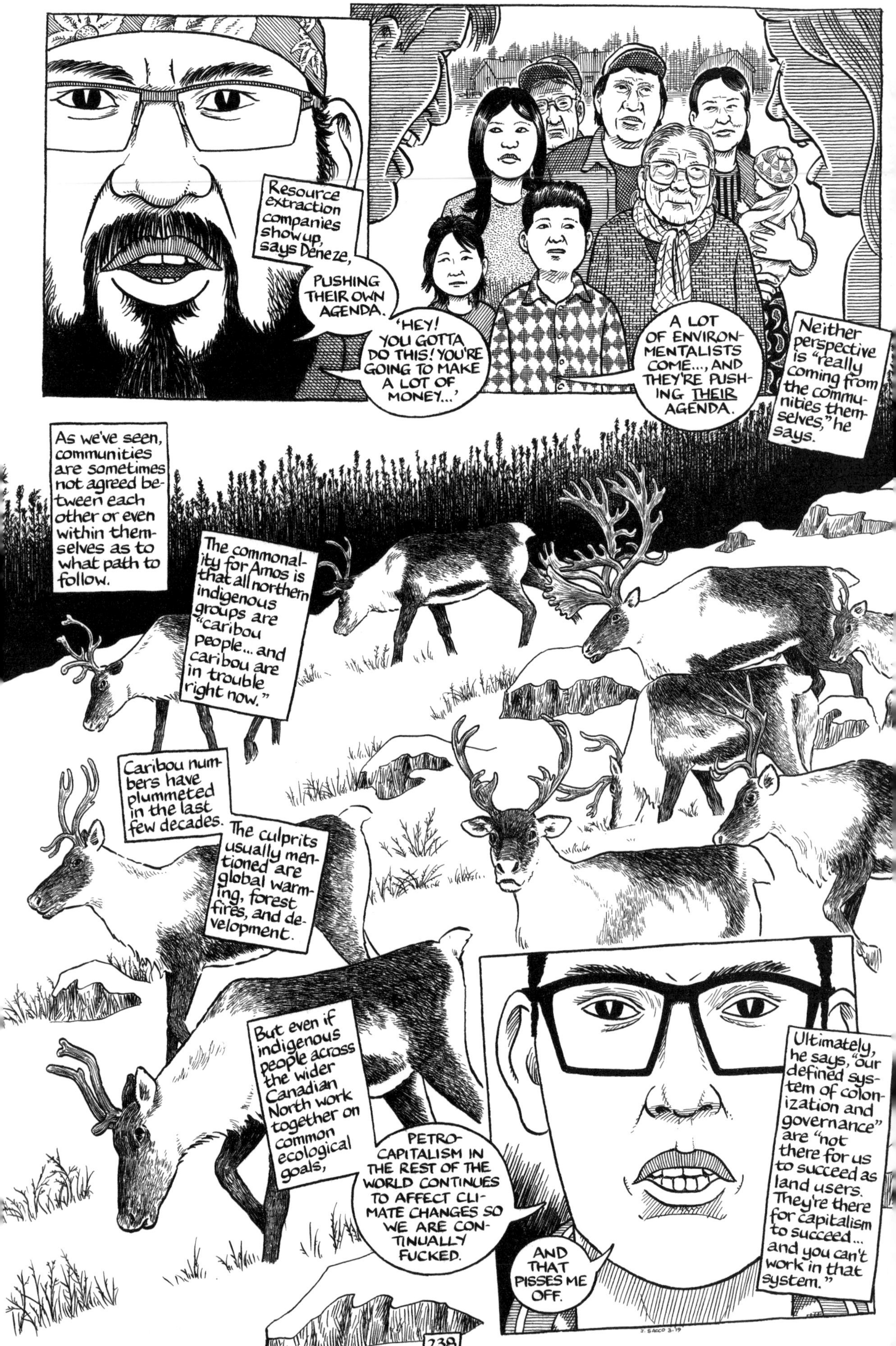
Resource extraction companies show up, says Deneze,
PUSHING THEIR OWN AGENDA.
'HEY! YOU GOTTA DO THIS! YOU'RE GOING TO MAKE A LOT OF MONEY...'
A LOT OF ENVIRONMENTALISTS COME..., AND THEY'RE PUSHING THEIR AGENDA.
Neither perspective is "really coming from the communities themselves," he says.
As we've seen, communities are sometimes not agreed between each other or even within themselves as to what path to follow.
The commonality for Amos is that all northern indigenous groups are "caribou people... and caribou are in trouble right now."
Caribou numbers have plummeted in the last few decades.
The culprits usually mentioned are global warming, forest fires, and development.
But even if indigenous people across the wider Canadian North work together on common ecological goals,
PETRO-CAPITALISM IN THE REST OF THE WORLD CONTINUES TO AFFECT CLIMATE CHANGES SO WE ARE CONTINUALLY FUCKED.
AND THAT PISSES ME OFF.
Ultimately, he says, "our defined system of colonization and governance" are "not there for us to succeed as land users. They're there for capitalism to succeed... and you can't work in that system."
J. SACCO 3.19

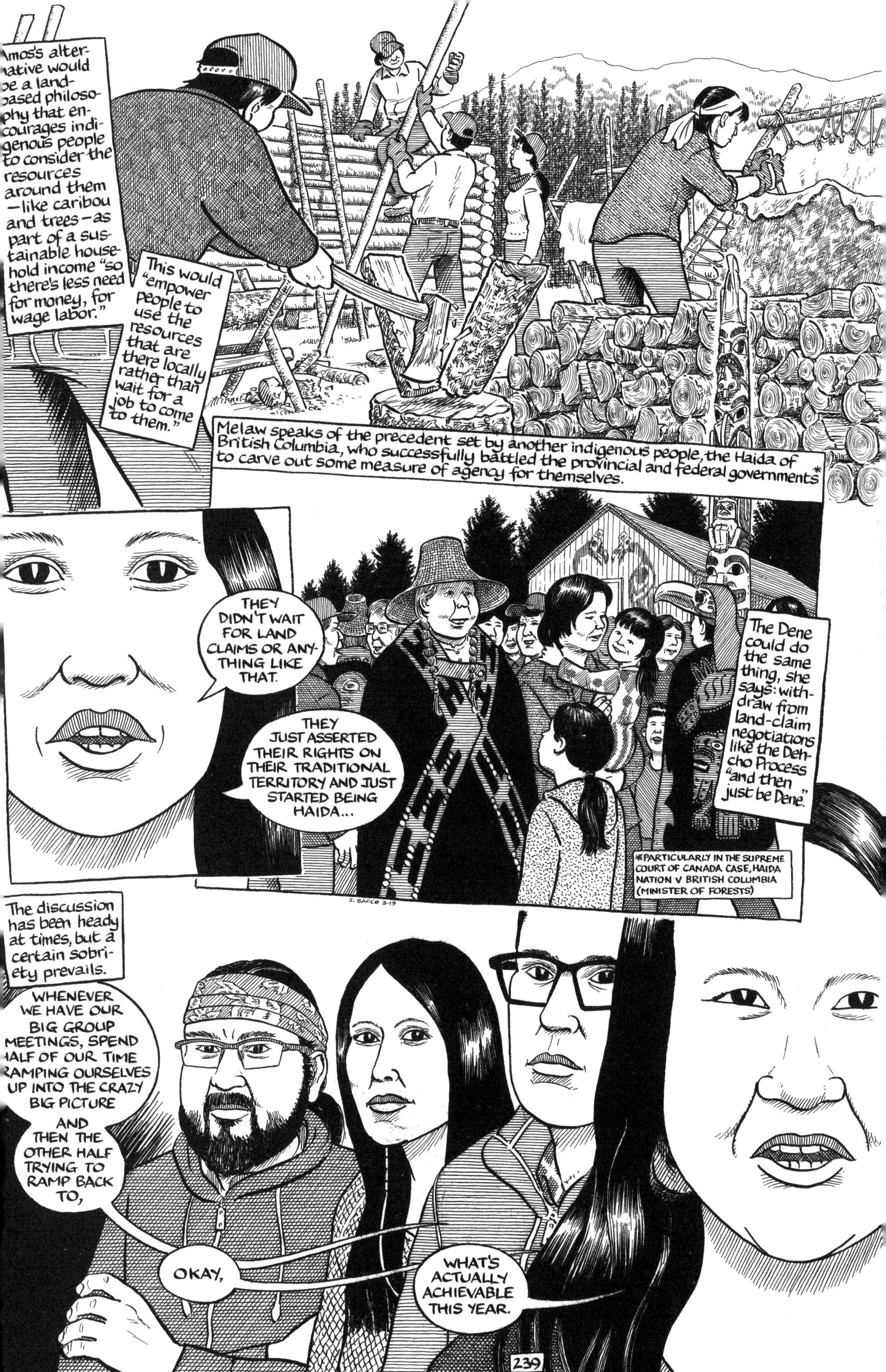
Amos's alternative would be a land-based philosophy that encourages indigenous people to consider the resources around them —like caribou and trees—as part of a sustainable household income "so there's less need for money, for wage labor."
This would "empower people to use the resources that are there locally rather than wait for a job to come to them."
Melaw speaks of the precedent set by another indigenous people, the Haida of British Columbia, who successfully battled the provincial and federal governments* to carve out some measure of agency for themselves.
THEY DIDN'T WAIT FOR LAND CLAIMS OR ANYTHING LIKE THAT.
THEY JUST ASSERTED THEIR RIGHTS ON THEIR TRADITIONAL TERRITORY AND JUST STARTED BEING HAIDA...
The Dene could do the same thing, she says: withdraw from land-claim negotiations like the Dehcho Process "and then just be Dene."
*PARTICULARLY IN THE SUPREME COURT OF CANADA CASE, HAIDA NATION V BRITISH COLUMBIA (MINISTER OF FORESTS)
J. SACCO 3-19
The discussion has been heady at times, but a certain sobriety prevails.
WHENEVER WE HAVE OUR BIG GROUP MEETINGS, SPEND HALF OF OUR TIME RAMPING OURSELVES UP INTO THE CRAZY BIG PICTURE
AND THEN THE OTHER HALF TRYING TO RAMP BACK TO,
OKAY,
WHAT'S ACTUALLY ACHIEVABLE THIS YEAR.

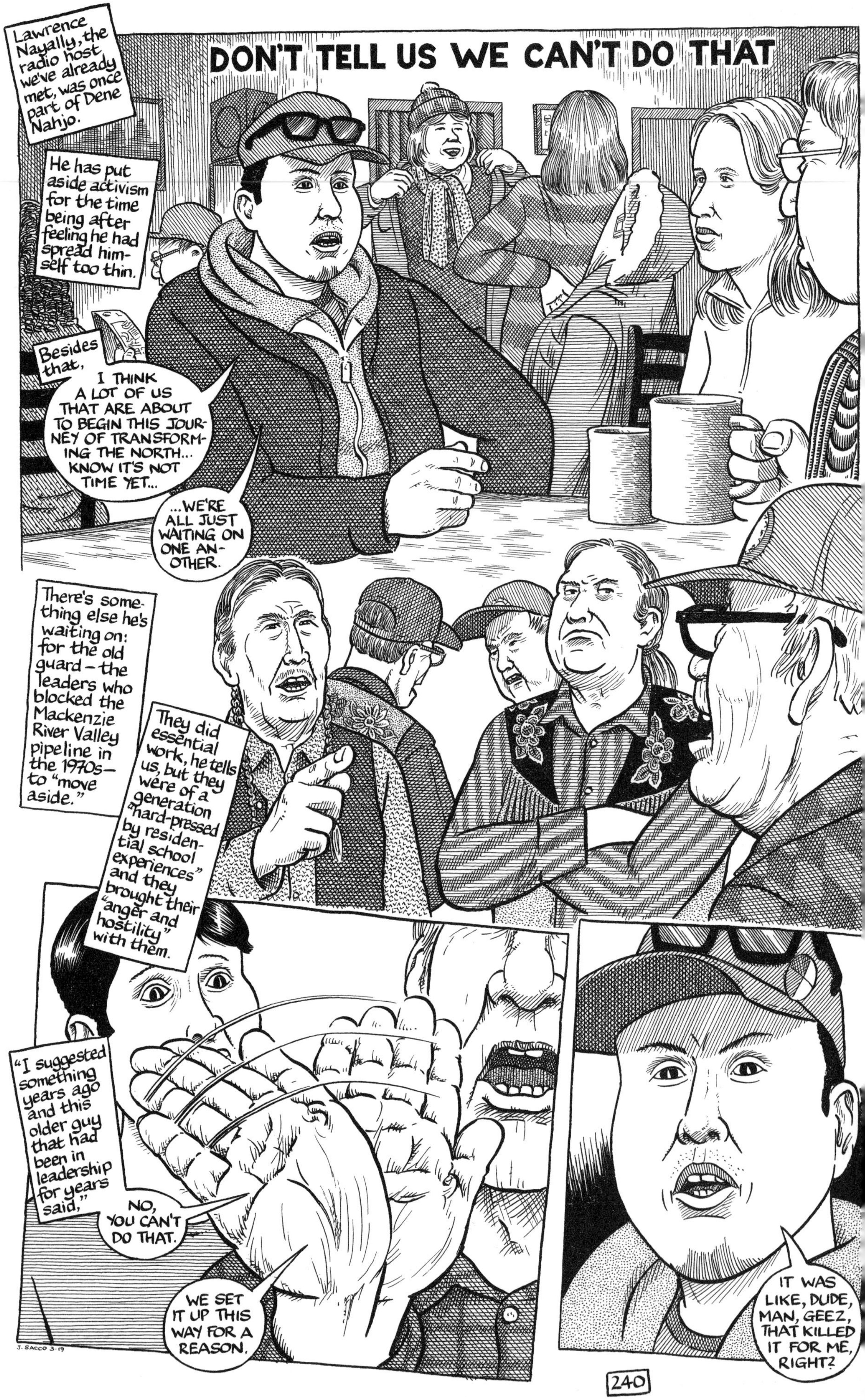
DON'T TELL US WE CAN'T DO THAT
Lawrence Nayally, the radio host we've already met, was once part of Dene Nahjo.
He has put aside activism for the time being after feeling he had spread himself too thin.
Besides that,
I THINK A LOT OF US THAT ARE ABOUT TO BEGIN THIS JOURNEY OF TRANSFORMING THE NORTH... KNOW IT'S NOT TIME YET...
...WE'RE ALL JUST WAITING ON ONE ANOTHER.
There's something else he's waiting on: for the old guard – the leaders who blocked the Mackenzie River Valley pipeline in the 1970s – to "move aside."
They did essential work, he tells us, but they were of a generation "hard-pressed by residential school experiences" and they brought their "anger and hostility" with them.
"I suggested something years ago and this older guy that had been in leadership for years said,"
NO, YOU CAN'T DO THAT.
WE SET IT UP THIS WAY FOR A REASON.
IT WAS LIKE, DUDE, MAN, GEEZ, THAT KILLED IT FOR ME, RIGHT?
J. SACCO 3.19

PUSH US.

GUIDE US A LITTLE BIT.

BUT DON'T TELL US WE CAN'T DO THAT BECAUSE YOU TOLD YOURSELF YOU CAN'T DO THAT.

I COME FROM A DIFFERENT GENERATION THAT IS ABLE TO SEE BEYOND WHAT THOSE LIMITS ARE, RIGHT?

AND WE WANT TO PUSH THE BOUNDARIES.

Lawrence's own background is steeped in both Dene traditions and Dene realities.

I DON'T NEED TO BE REVITALIZED.

I STILL KNOW MY LANGUAGE.

I KNOW MY CULTURE.

I KNOW MY IDENTITY.

I COMMUNICATE WITH ELDERS PRETTY FREQUENTLY.

As a youth he was the beneficiary of a cultural push, in particular a spiritually and land-based curriculum called Dene Kede, which was formulated by a group of elders and endorsed by the territorial government.

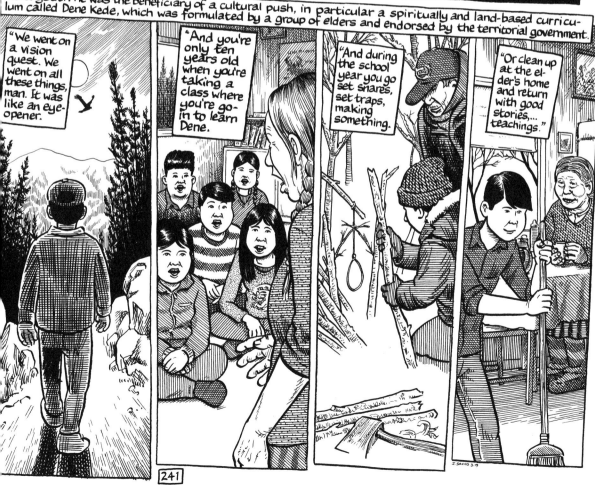

"We went on a vision quest. We went on all these things, man. It was like an eye-opener.

"And you're only ten years old when you're taking a class where you're goin to learn Dene.

"And during the school year you go set snares, set traps, making something.

"Or clean up at the elder's home and return with good stories,... teachings."

J. SACCO 3.19

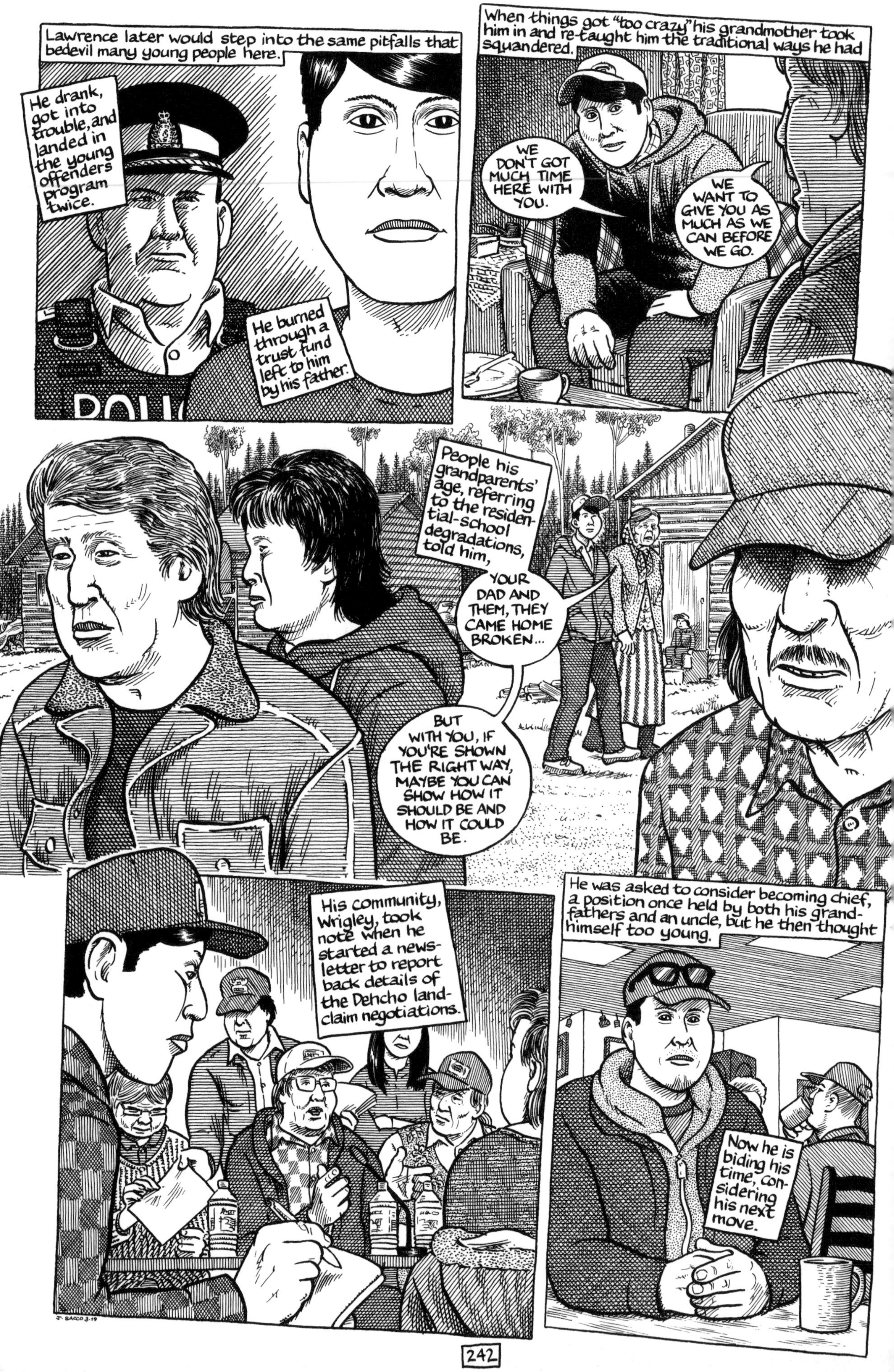

Lawrence later would step into the same pitfalls that bedevil many young people here.
He drank, got into trouble, and landed in the young offenders program twice.
POLI
He burned through a trust fund left to him by his father.
When things got "too crazy" his grandmother took him in and re-taught him the traditional ways he had squandered.
WE DON'T GOT MUCH TIME HERE WITH YOU.
WE WANT TO GIVE YOU AS MUCH AS WE CAN BEFORE WE GO.
People his grandparents' age, referring to the residential-school degradations, told him,
YOUR DAD AND THEM, THEY CAME HOME BROKEN...
BUT WITH YOU, IF YOU'RE SHOWN THE RIGHT WAY, MAYBE YOU CAN SHOW HOW IT SHOULD BE AND HOW IT COULD BE.
His community, Wrigley, took note when he started a newsletter to report back details of the Dehcho land-claim negotiations.
J. SACCO 3.19
He was asked to consider becoming chief, a position once held by both his grandfathers and an uncle, but he then thought himself too young.
Now he is biding his time, considering his next move.

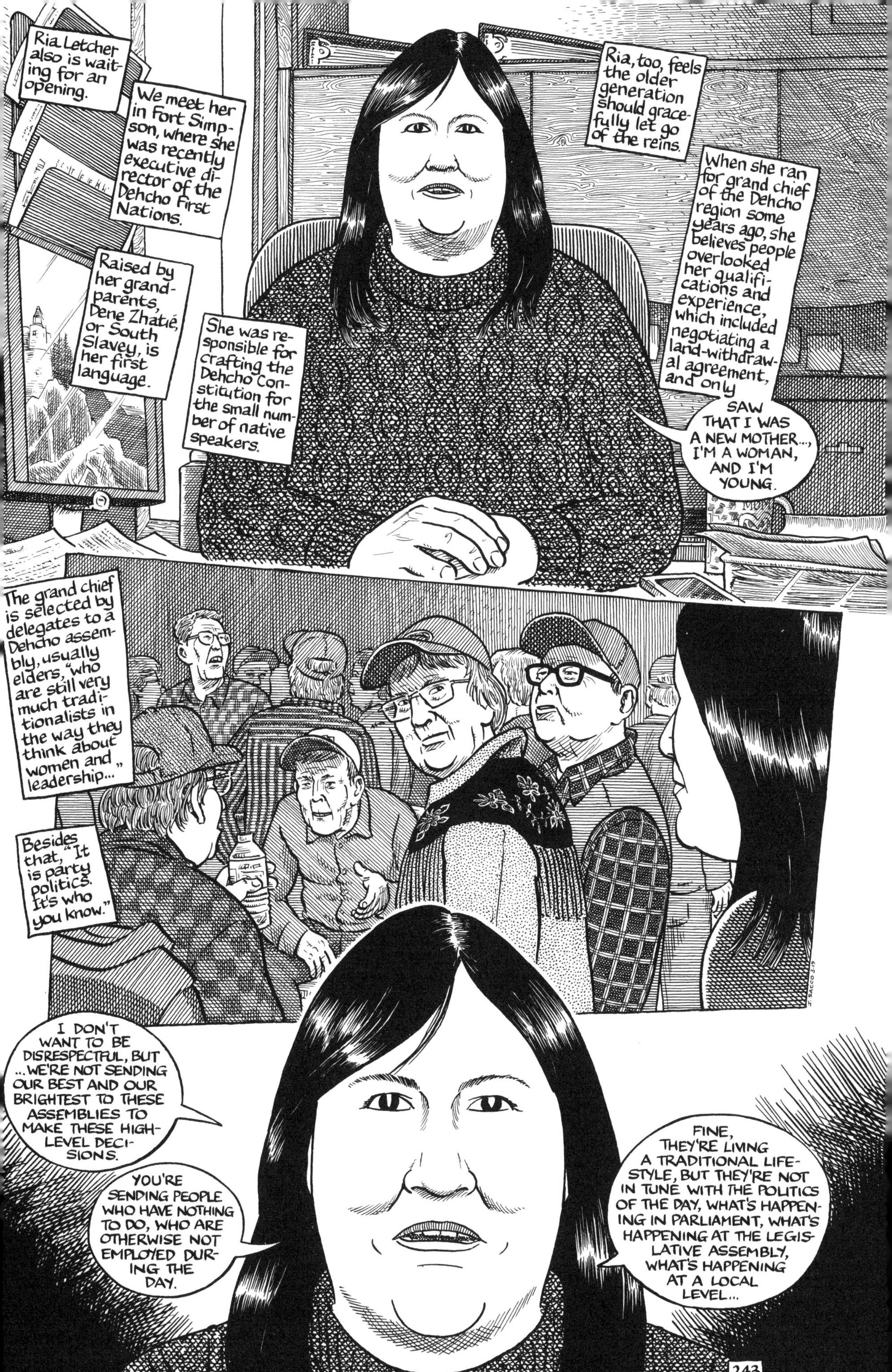
Ria Letcher also is waiting for an opening.
We meet her in Fort Simpson, where she was recently executive director of the Dehcho First Nations.
Raised by her grandparents, Dene Zhatié, or South Slavey, is her first language.
She was responsible for crafting the Dehcho Constitution for the small number of native speakers.
Ria, too, feels the older generation should gracefully let go of the reins.
When she ran for grand chief of the Dehcho region some years ago, she believes people overlooked her qualifications and experience, which included negotiating a land-withdrawal agreement, and only
SAW THAT I WAS A NEW MOTHER..., I'M A WOMAN, AND I'M YOUNG.
The grand chief is selected by delegates to a Dehcho assembly, usually elders, "who are still very much traditionalists in the way they think about women and leadership..."
Besides that, "It is party politics. It's who you know."
I DON'T WANT TO BE DISRESPECTFUL, BUT ...WE'RE NOT SENDING OUR BEST AND OUR BRIGHTEST TO THESE ASSEMBLIES TO MAKE THESE HIGH-LEVEL DECISIONS.
YOU'RE SENDING PEOPLE WHO HAVE NOTHING TO DO, WHO ARE OTHERWISE NOT EMPLOYED DURING THE DAY.
FINE, THEY'RE LIVING A TRADITIONAL LIFESTYLE, BUT THEY'RE NOT IN TUNE WITH THE POLITICS OF THE DAY, WHAT'S HAPPENING IN PARLIAMENT, WHAT'S HAPPENING AT THE LEGISLATIVE ASSEMBLY, WHAT'S HAPPENING AT A LOCAL LEVEL...

"I don't like fighting my own people, right? I'm into fighting [the federal] government and territorial government," she says.

But Ria admits it's hard to keep everyone on the same page.

Dependency on government employment stymies a united indigenous front, she tells us.

The majority OF OUR TALENTED PEOPLE HAVE JOBS WITH EITHER THE FEDERAL GOVERNMENT OR THE TERRITORIAL GOVERNMENT...

AND THEN WITHIN [THE] TERRITORIAL GOVERNMENT THEY HAVE... POLICIES THAT PREVENT [EMPLOYEES] FROM... PARTICIPATING IN POLITICAL ARENAS.

THEY CAN'T EFFECTIVELY NEGOTIATE AGAINST THEIR EMPLOYER.

Ria was politicized in her early 20s when she and her husband wanted to build a lodge and were informed that they would have to lease the land from the federal government.

"I was like, WHAT? THIS IS OUR LAND...

"My husband had to explain it to me because I was raised by my grandparents who believed and who taught me that this is our land.

"This is nobody else's land. This is ours."

Ria isn't convinced that someone putting an X on a piece of paper in 1921 "behind the people's back" transferred anything to anyone.

Signed... Day 10... 1921 Majesty King... ...ul lut, nation of aboriginal honour named titan and... Witnesses

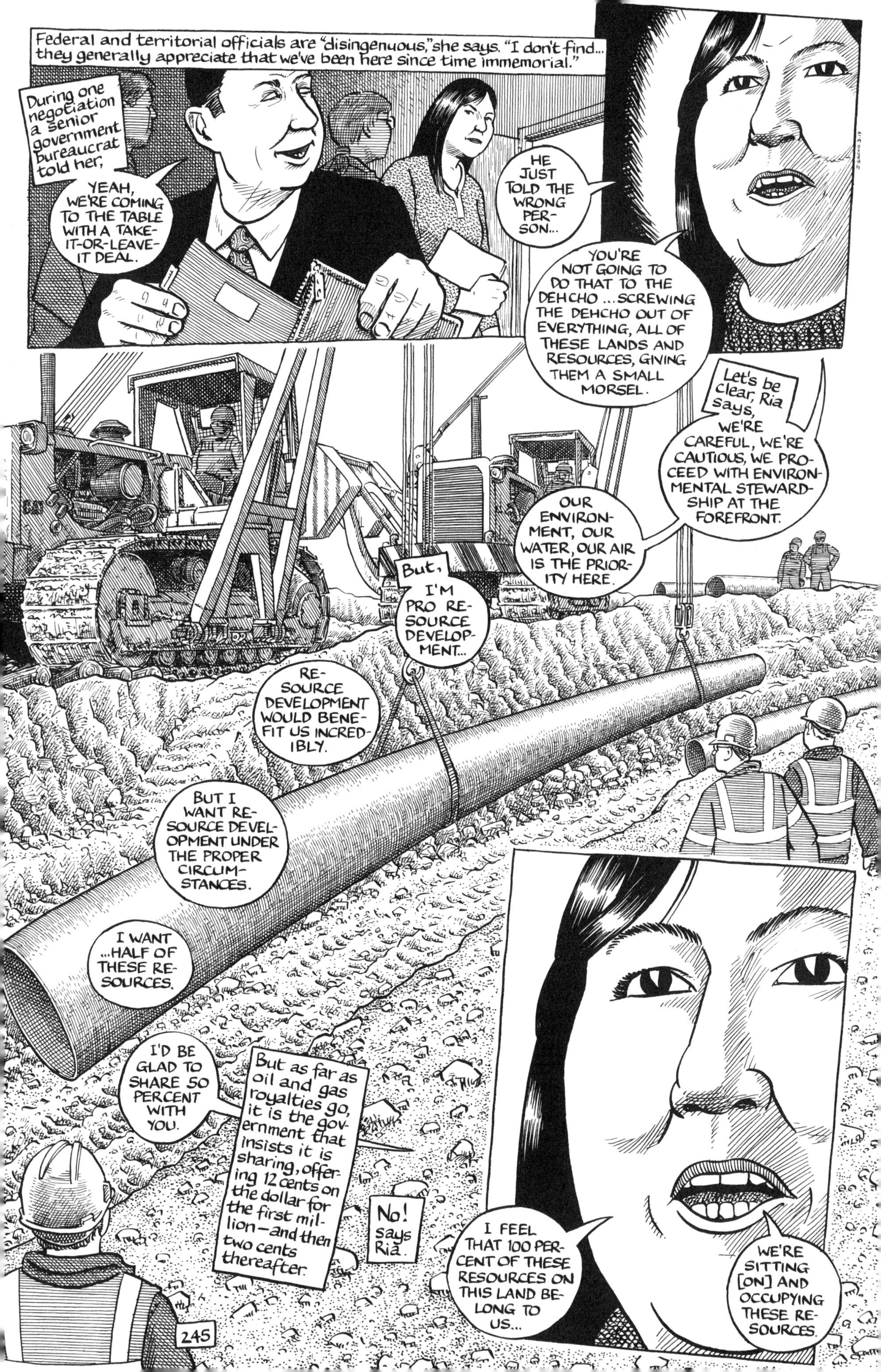

Federal and territorial officials are "disingenuous," she says. "I don't find... they generally appreciate that we've been here since time immemorial."
During one negotiation a senior government bureaucrat told her,
YEAH, WE'RE COMING TO THE TABLE WITH A TAKE-IT-OR-LEAVE-IT DEAL.
HE JUST TOLD THE WRONG PERSON...
YOU'RE NOT GOING TO DO THAT TO THE DEHCHO ... SCREWING THE DEHCHO OUT OF EVERYTHING, ALL OF THESE LANDS AND RESOURCES, GIVING THEM A SMALL MORSEL.
Let's be clear, Ria says,
WE'RE CAREFUL, WE'RE CAUTIOUS, WE PROCEED WITH ENVIRONMENTAL STEWARDSHIP AT THE FOREFRONT.
OUR ENVIRONMENT, OUR WATER, OUR AIR IS THE PRIORITY HERE.
But,
I'M PRO RESOURCE DEVELOPMENT...
RESOURCE DEVELOPMENT WOULD BENEFIT US INCREDIBLY.
BUT I WANT RESOURCE DEVELOPMENT UNDER THE PROPER CIRCUMSTANCES.
I WANT ...HALF OF THESE RESOURCES.
I'D BE GLAD TO SHARE 50 PERCENT WITH YOU.
But as far as oil and gas royalties go, it is the government that insists it is sharing, offering 12 cents on the dollar for the first million—and then two cents thereafter.
No! says Ria.
I FEEL THAT 100 PERCENT OF THESE RESOURCES ON THIS LAND BELONG TO US...
WE'RE SITTING [ON] AND OCCUPYING THESE RESOURCES.

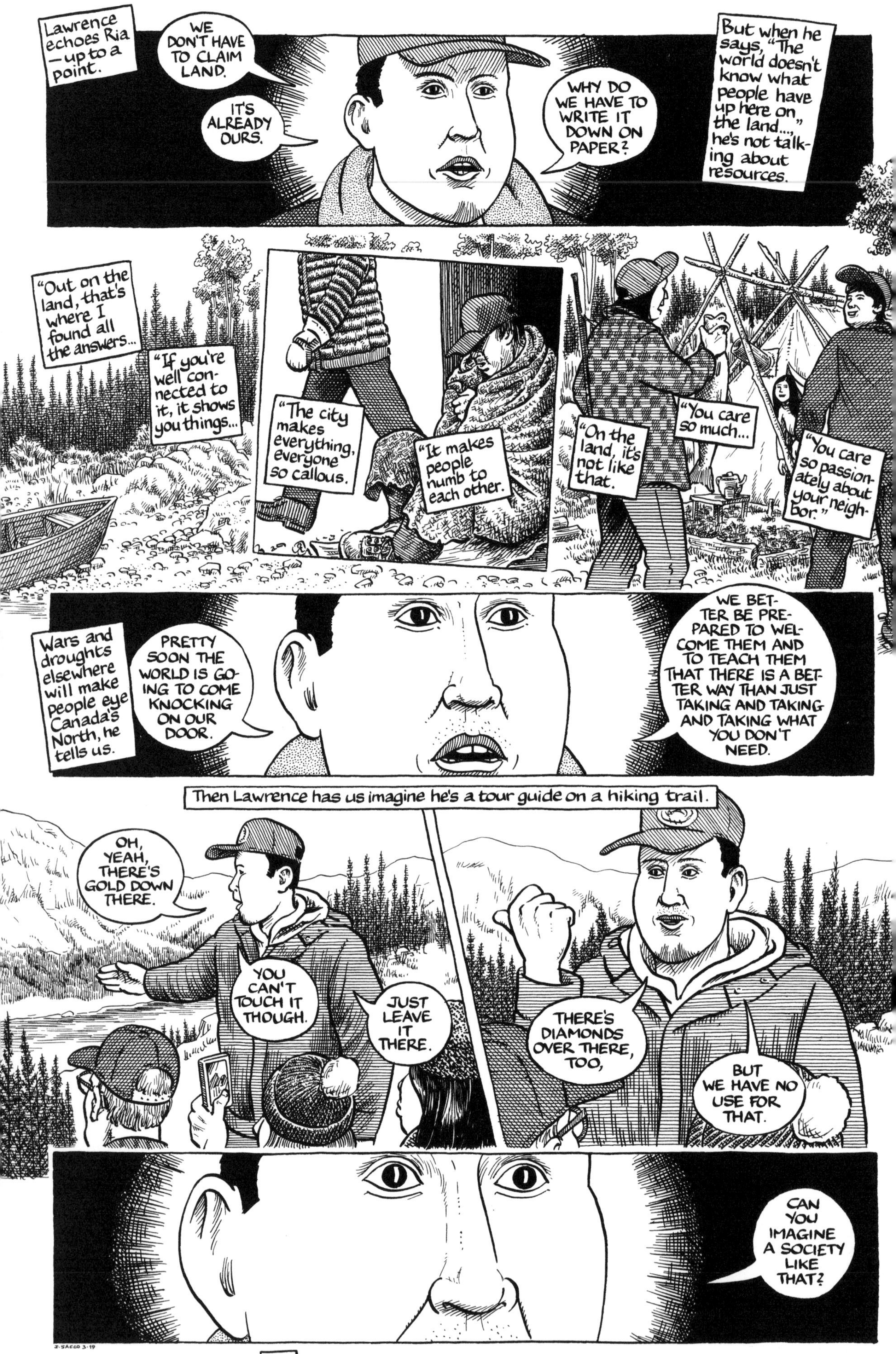
Lawrence echoes Ria—up to a point.
WE DON'T HAVE TO CLAIM LAND.
IT'S ALREADY OURS.
WHY DO WE HAVE TO WRITE IT DOWN ON PAPER?
But when he says, "The world doesn't know what people have up here on the land...," he's not talking about resources.
"Out on the land, that's where I found all the answers...
"If you're well connected to it, it shows you things...
"The city makes everything, everyone so callous.
"It makes people numb to each other.
"On the land, it's not like that.
"You care so much...
"You care so passionately about your neighbor."
Wars and droughts elsewhere will make people eye Canada's North, he tells us.
PRETTY SOON THE WORLD IS GOING TO COME KNOCKING ON OUR DOOR.
WE BETTER BE PREPARED TO WELCOME THEM AND TO TEACH THEM THAT THERE IS A BETTER WAY THAN JUST TAKING AND TAKING AND TAKING WHAT YOU DON'T NEED.
Then Lawrence has us imagine he's a tour guide on a hiking trail.
OH, YEAH, THERE'S GOLD DOWN THERE.
YOU CAN'T TOUCH IT THOUGH.
JUST LEAVE IT THERE.
THERE'S DIAMONDS OVER THERE, TOO,
BUT WE HAVE NO USE FOR THAT.
CAN YOU IMAGINE A SOCIETY LIKE THAT?
J. SACCO 3.19

THE CIRCLE IS CLOSED

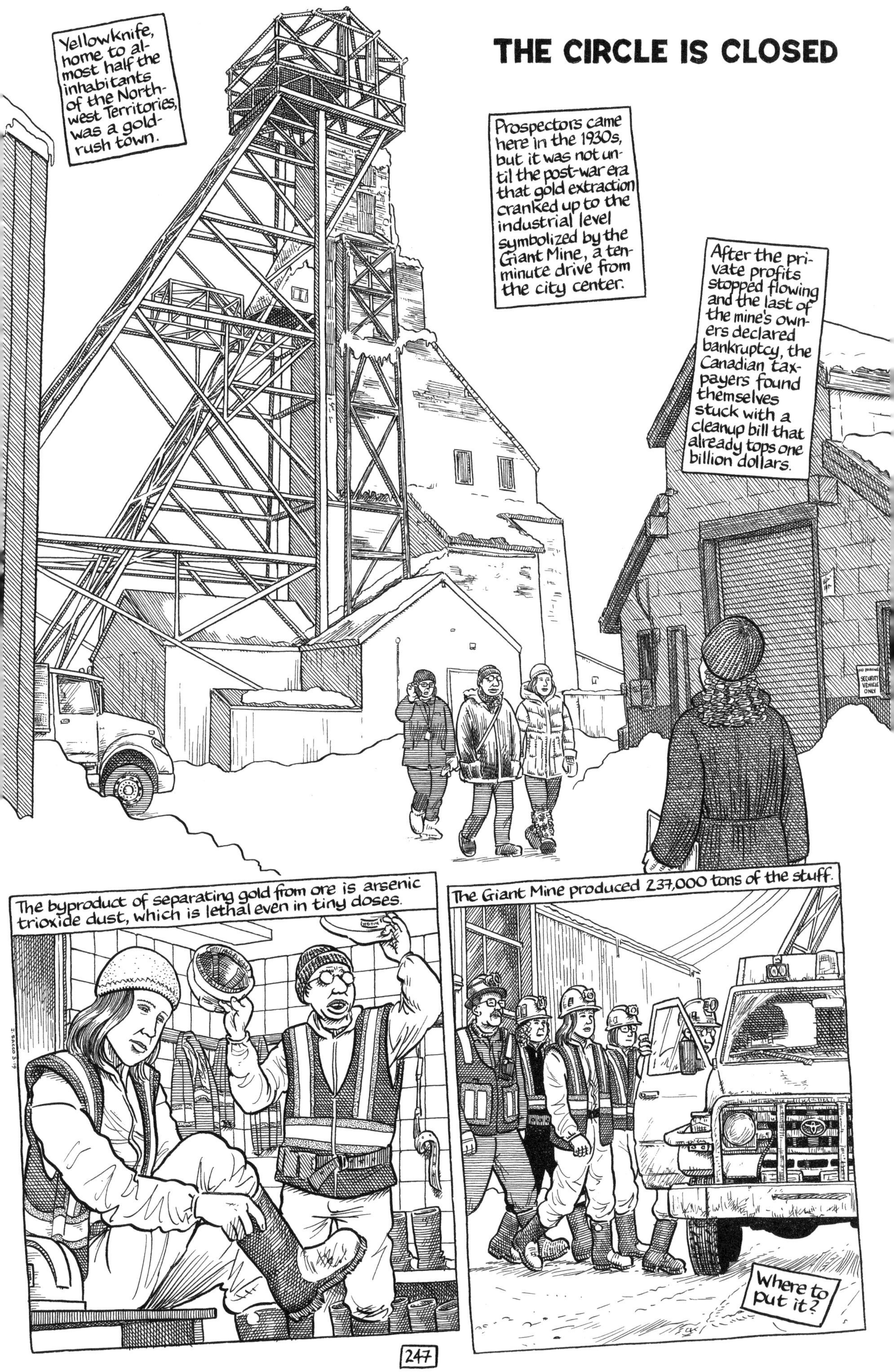

Yellowknife, home to almost half the inhabitants of the Northwest Territories, was a gold-rush town.
Prospectors came here in the 1930s, but it was not until the post-war era that gold extraction cranked up to the industrial level symbolized by the Giant Mine, a ten-minute drive from the city center.
After the private profits stopped flowing and the last of the mine's owners declared bankruptcy, the Canadian taxpayers found themselves stuck with a cleanup bill that already tops one billion dollars.
NO PARKING
SECURITY VEHICLE ONLY
The byproduct of separating gold from ore is arsenic trioxide dust, which is lethal even in tiny doses.
The Giant Mine produced 237,000 tons of the stuff.
Where to put it?

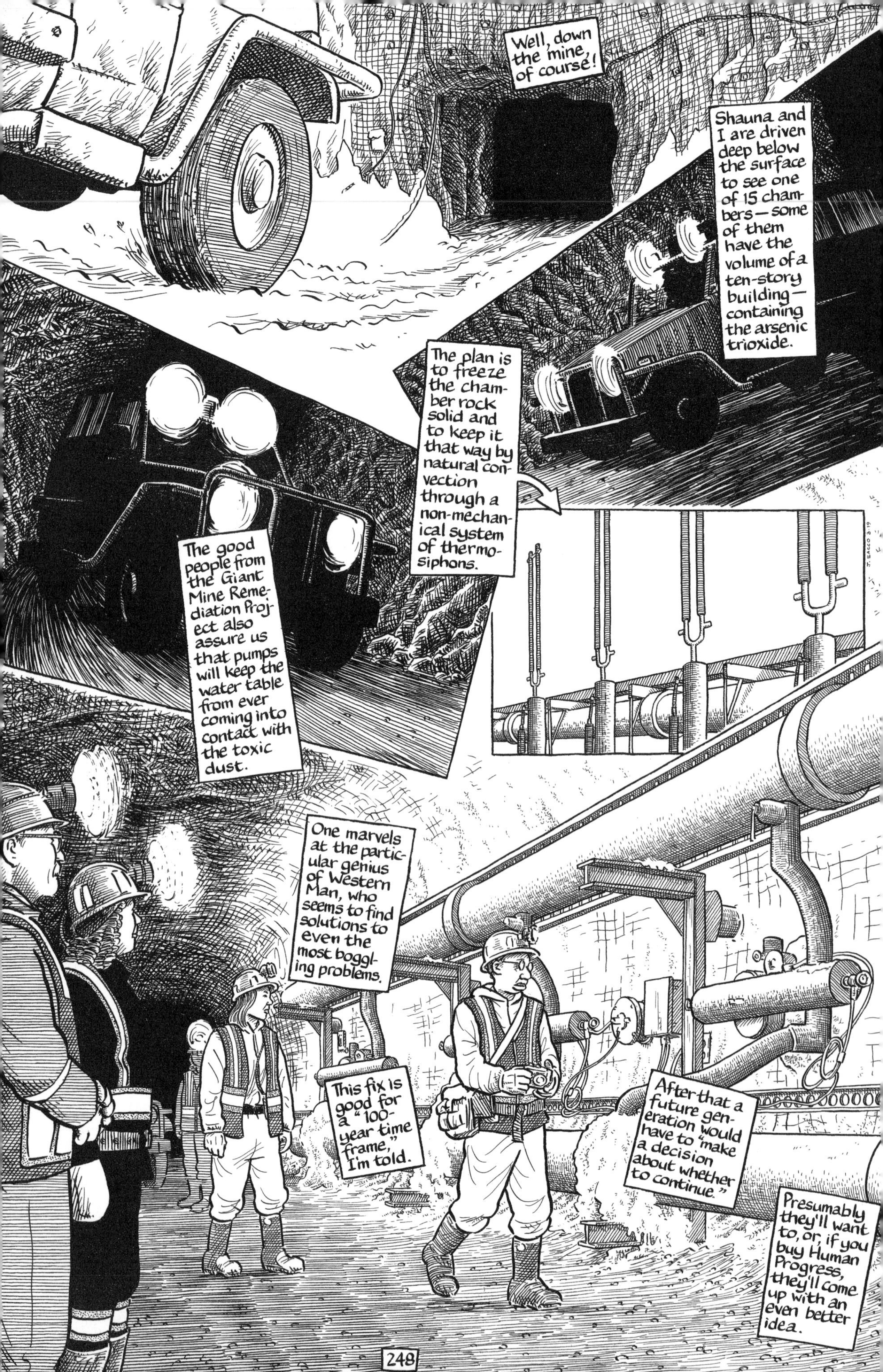
Well, down the mine, of course!
Shauna and I are driven deep below the surface to see one of 15 cham-bers—some of them have the volume of a ten-story building—containing the arsenic trioxide.
The plan is to freeze the cham-ber rock solid and to keep it that way by natural con-vection through a non-mechan-ical system of thermo-siphons.
The good people from the Giant Mine Reme-diation Proj-ect also assure us that pumps will keep the water table from ever coming into contact with the toxic dust.
J. SACCO 3.19
One marvels at the partic-ular genius of Western Man, who seems to find solutions to even the most boggl-ing problems.
This fix is good for a "100-year time frame," I'm told.
After that a future gen-eration would have to "make a decision about whether to continue."
Presumably they'll want to, or, if you buy Human Progress, they'll come up with an even better idea.

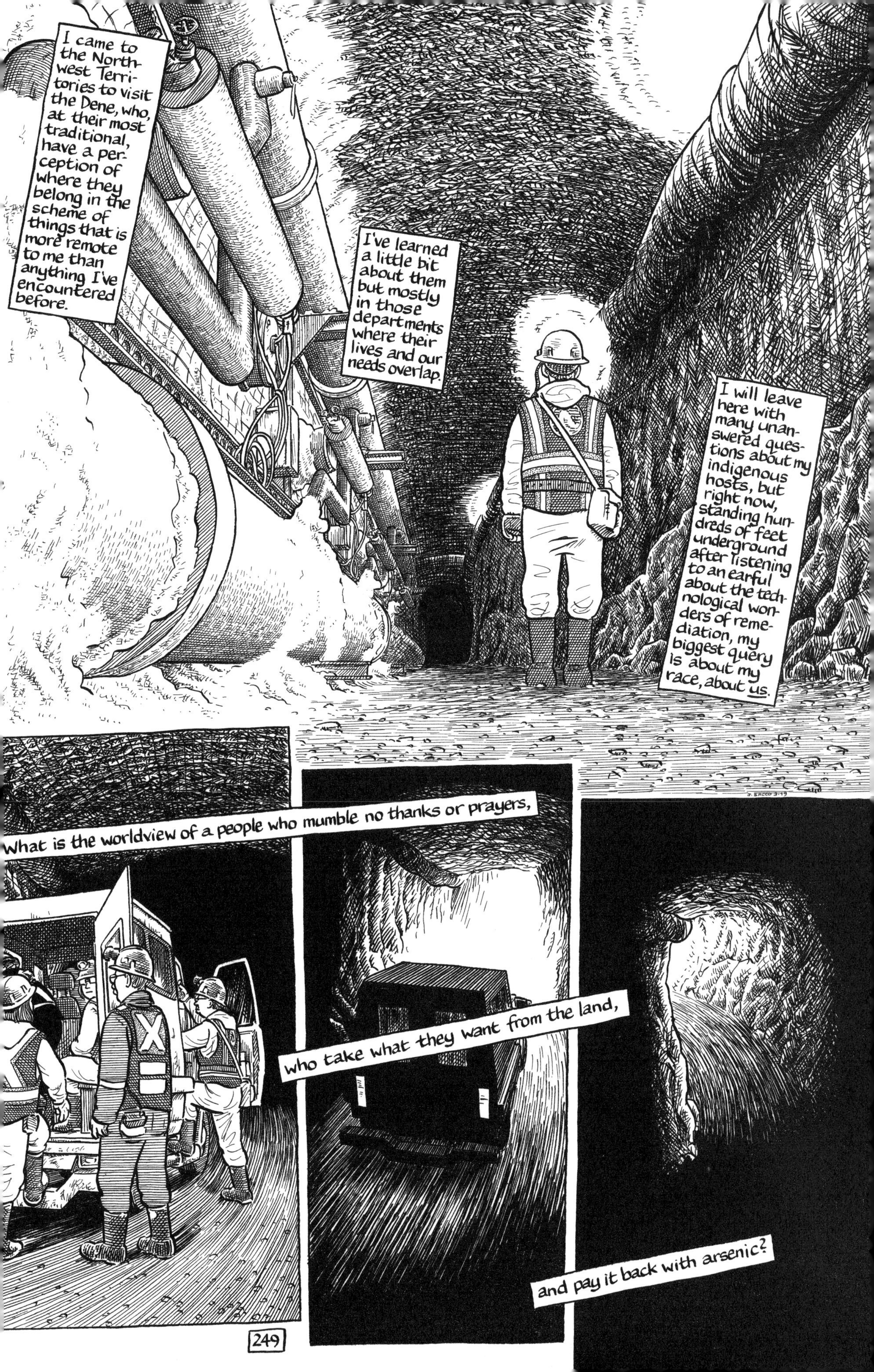
I came to the Northwest Territories to visit the Dene, who, at their most traditional, have a perception of where they belong in the scheme of things that is more remote to me than anything I've encountered before.
I've learned a little bit about them but mostly in those departments where their lives and our needs overlap.
I will leave here with many unanswered questions about my indigenous hosts, but right now, standing hundreds of feet underground after listening to an earful about the technological wonders of remediation, my biggest query is about my race, about us.
What is the worldview of a people who mumble no thanks or prayers,
who take what they want from the land,
and pay it back with arsenic?

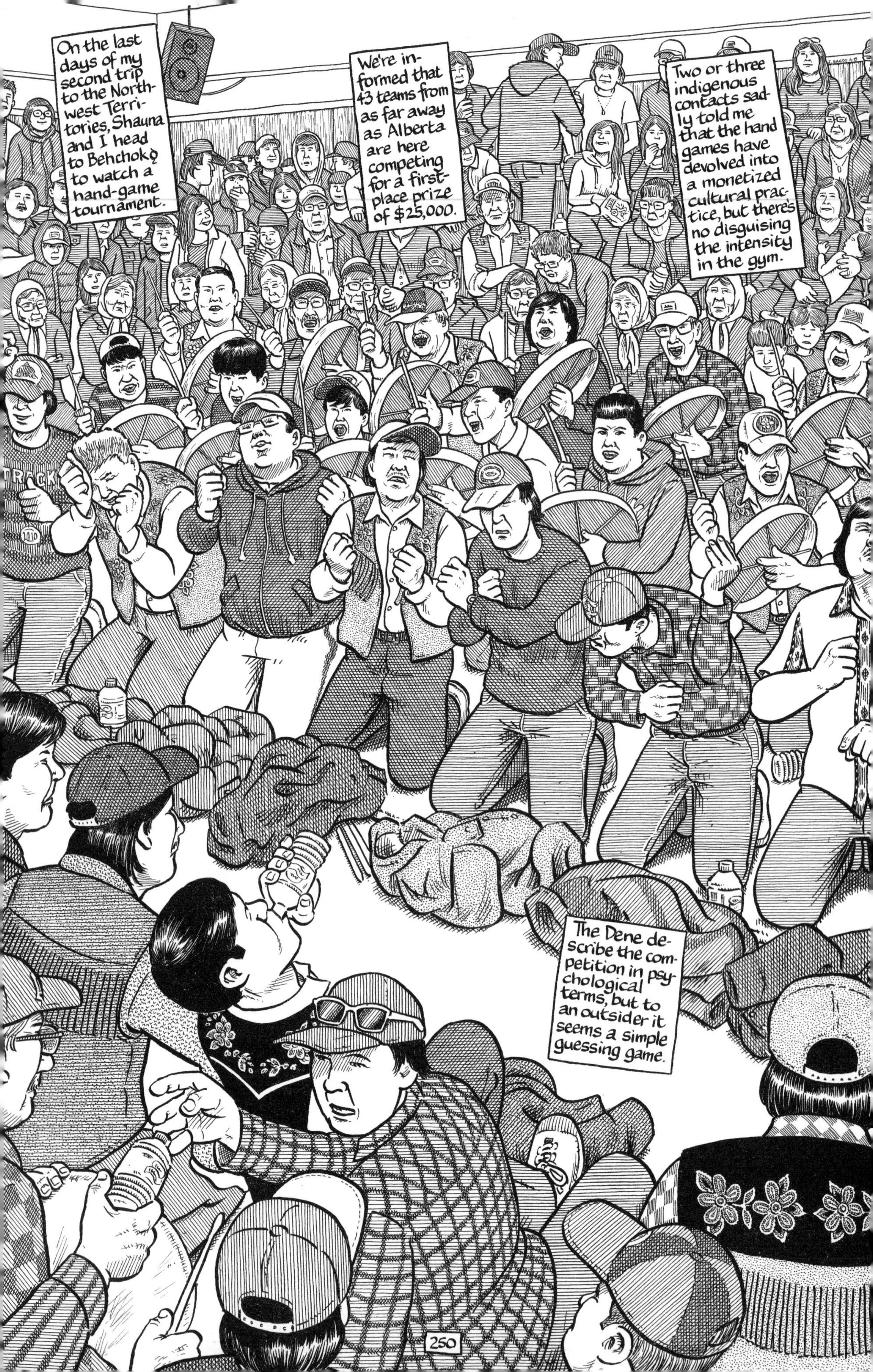
On the last days of my second trip to the Northwest Territories, Shauna and I head to Behchokǫ̀ to watch a hand-game tournament.
We're informed that 43 teams from as far away as Alberta are here competing for a first-place prize of $25,000.
Two or three indigenous contacts sadly told me that the hand games have devolved into a monetized cultural practice, but there's no disguising the intensity in the gym.
The Dene describe the competition in psychological terms, but to an outsider it seems a simple guessing game.

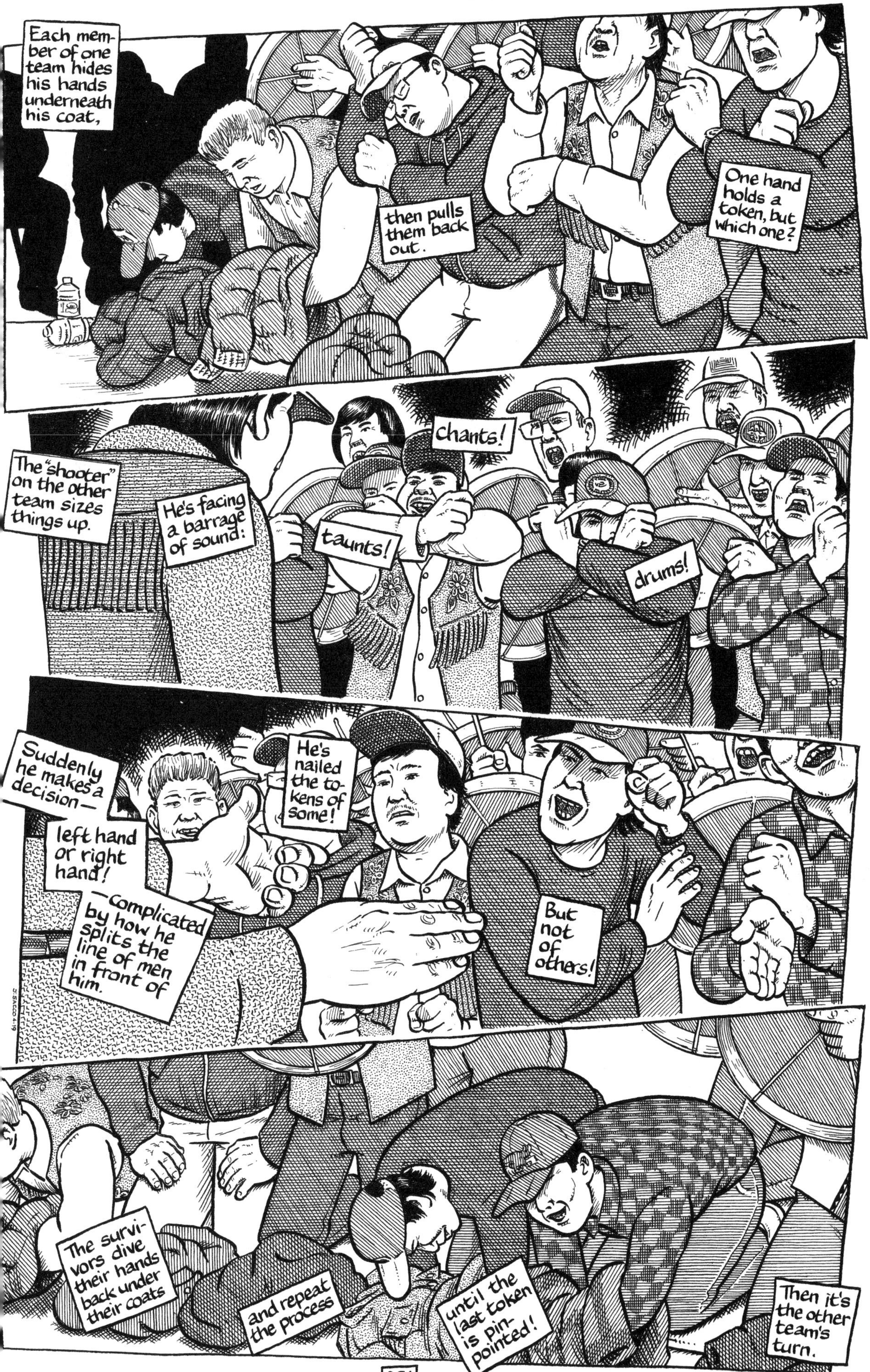
Each member of one team hides his hands underneath his coat,
then pulls them back out.
One hand holds a token, but which one?
The "shooter" on the other team sizes things up.
He's facing a barrage of sound:
chants!
taunts!
drums!
Suddenly he makes a decision—
left hand or right hand!
—Complicated by how he splits the line of men in front of him.
He's nailed the tokens of some!
But not of others!
The survivors dive their hands back under their coats
and repeat the process
until the last token is pinpointed!
Then it's the other team's turn.

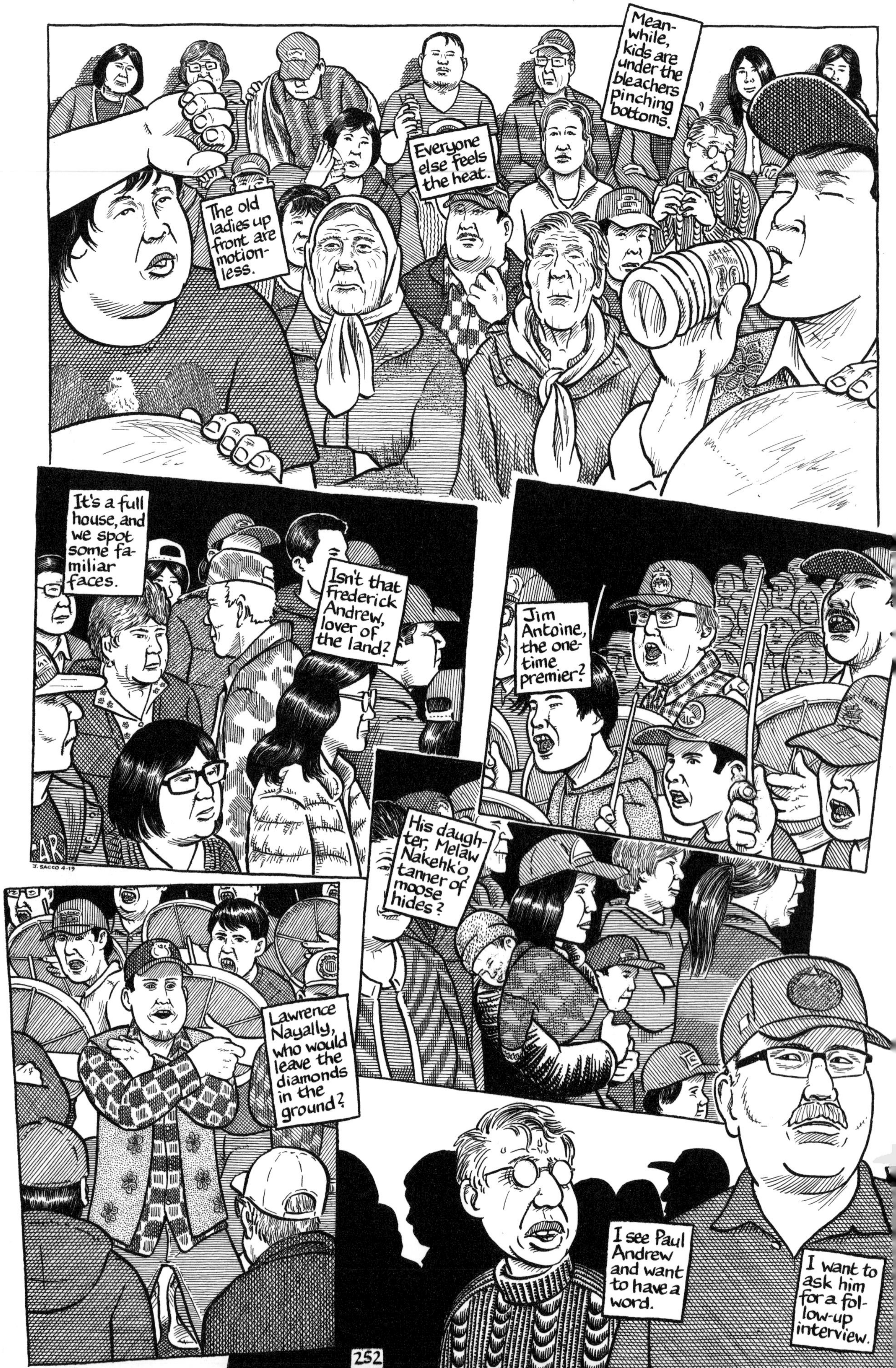

The old ladies up front are motion-less.
Everyone else feels the heat.
Mean-while, kids are under the bleachers pinching bottoms.
It's a full house, and we spot some fa-miliar faces.
Isn't that Frederick Andrew, lover of the land?
Jim Antoine, the one-time premier?
His daugh-ter, Melaw Nakehk'o tanner of moose hides?
Lawrence Nayally, who would leave the diamonds in the ground?
I see Paul Andrew and want to have a word.
I want to ask him for a fol-low-up interview.
J. SACCO 4-19

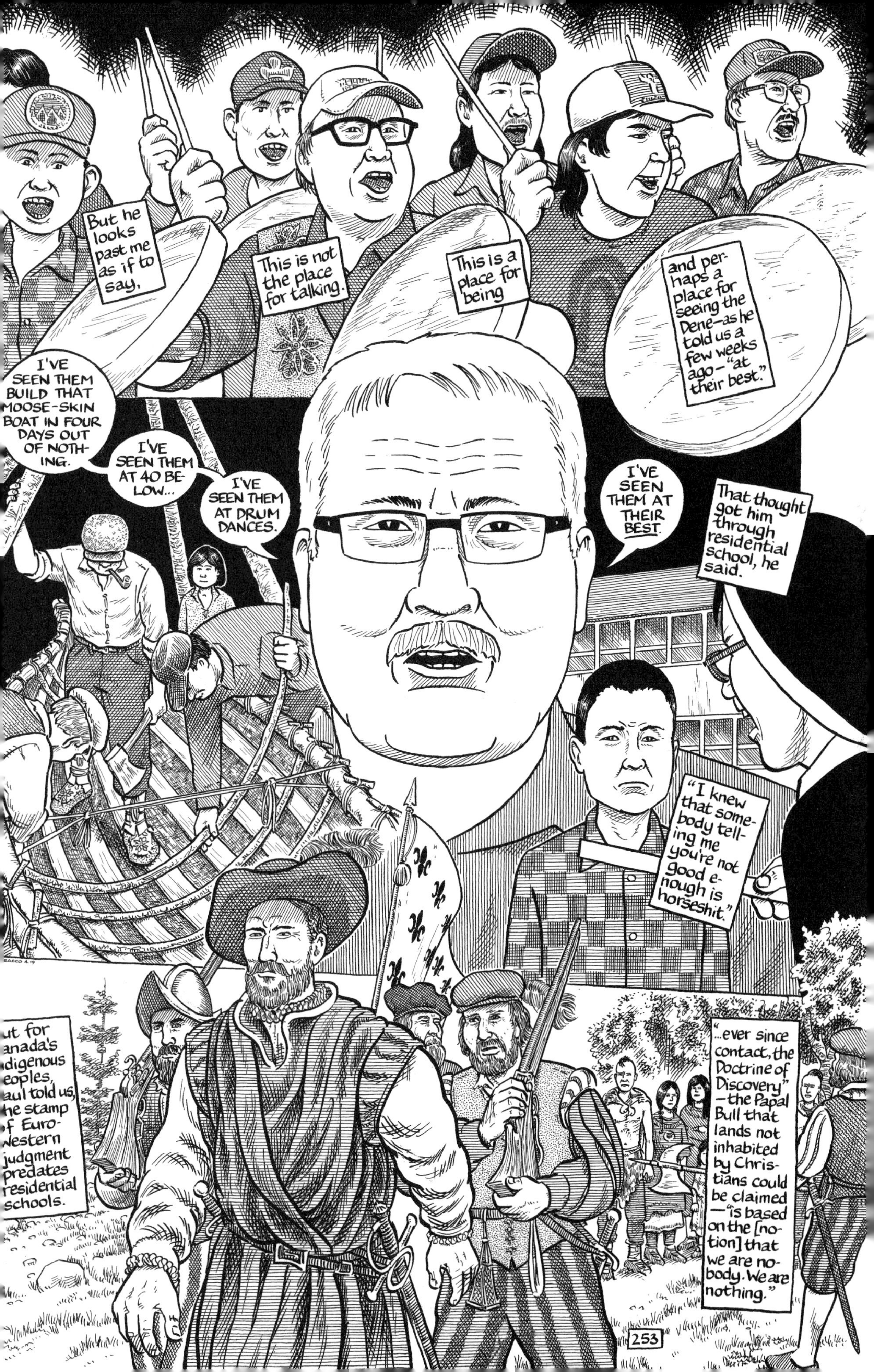
But he looks past me as if to say,
This is not the place for talking.
This is a place for being
and perhaps a place for seeing the Dene—as he told us a few weeks ago—"at their best."
I'VE SEEN THEM BUILD THAT MOOSE-SKIN BOAT IN FOUR DAYS OUT OF NOTHING.
I'VE SEEN THEM AT 40 BELOW...
I'VE SEEN THEM AT DRUM DANCES.
I'VE SEEN THEM AT THEIR BEST.
That thought got him through residential school, he said.
"I knew that somebody telling me you're not good enough is horseshit."
SACCO 4.19
ut for anada's ndigenous eoples, aul told us, he stamp f Euro-Western judgment predates residential schools.
"...ever since contact, the Doctrine of Discovery"—the Papal Bull that lands not inhabited by Christians could be claimed—"is based on the [notion] that we are nobody. We are nothing."

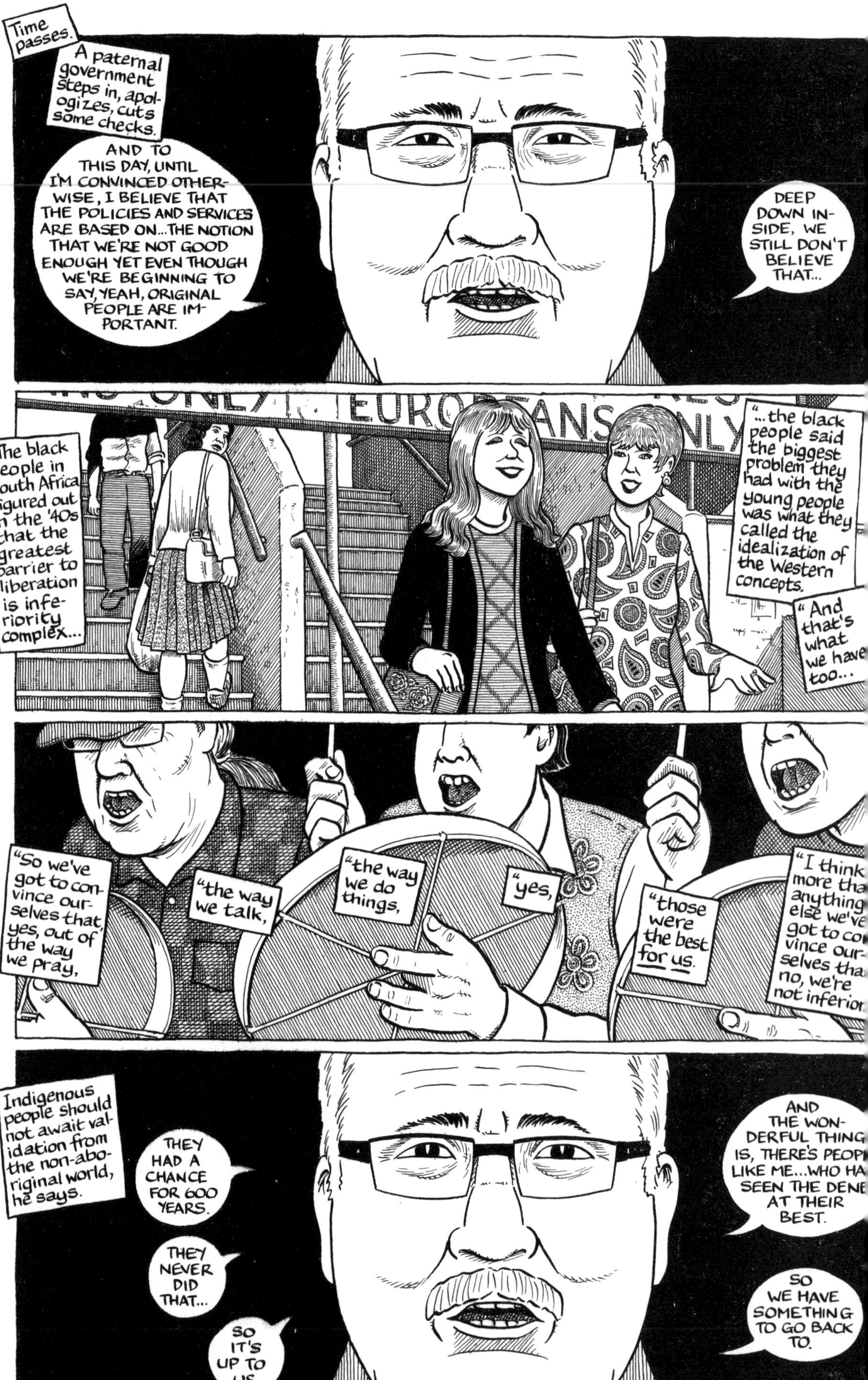

Time passes.
A paternal government steps in, apologizes, cuts some checks.
AND TO THIS DAY, UNTIL I'M CONVINCED OTHERWISE, I BELIEVE THAT THE POLICIES AND SERVICES ARE BASED ON...THE NOTION THAT WE'RE NOT GOOD ENOUGH YET EVEN THOUGH WE'RE BEGINNING TO SAY, YEAH, ORIGINAL PEOPLE ARE IMPORTANT.
DEEP DOWN INSIDE, WE STILL DON'T BELIEVE THAT...
EUROPEANS ONLY
"The black people in South Africa figured out in the '40s that the greatest barrier to liberation is inferiority complex...
"...the black people said the biggest problem they had with the young people was what they called the idealization of the Western concepts.
"And that's what we have too...
"So we've got to convince ourselves that yes, out of the way we pray,
"the way we talk,
"the way we do things,
"yes,
"those were the best for us.
"I think more tha anything else we've got to co vince ourselves tha no, we're not inferior
Indigenous people should not await validation from the non-aboriginal world, he says.
THEY HAD A CHANCE FOR 600 YEARS.
THEY NEVER DID THAT...
SO IT'S UP TO US.
AND THE WONDERFUL THING IS, THERE'S PEOP LIKE ME...WHO HA SEEN THE DENE AT THEIR BEST.
SO WE HAVE SOMETHING TO GO BACK TO.
J. SACCO 4·19

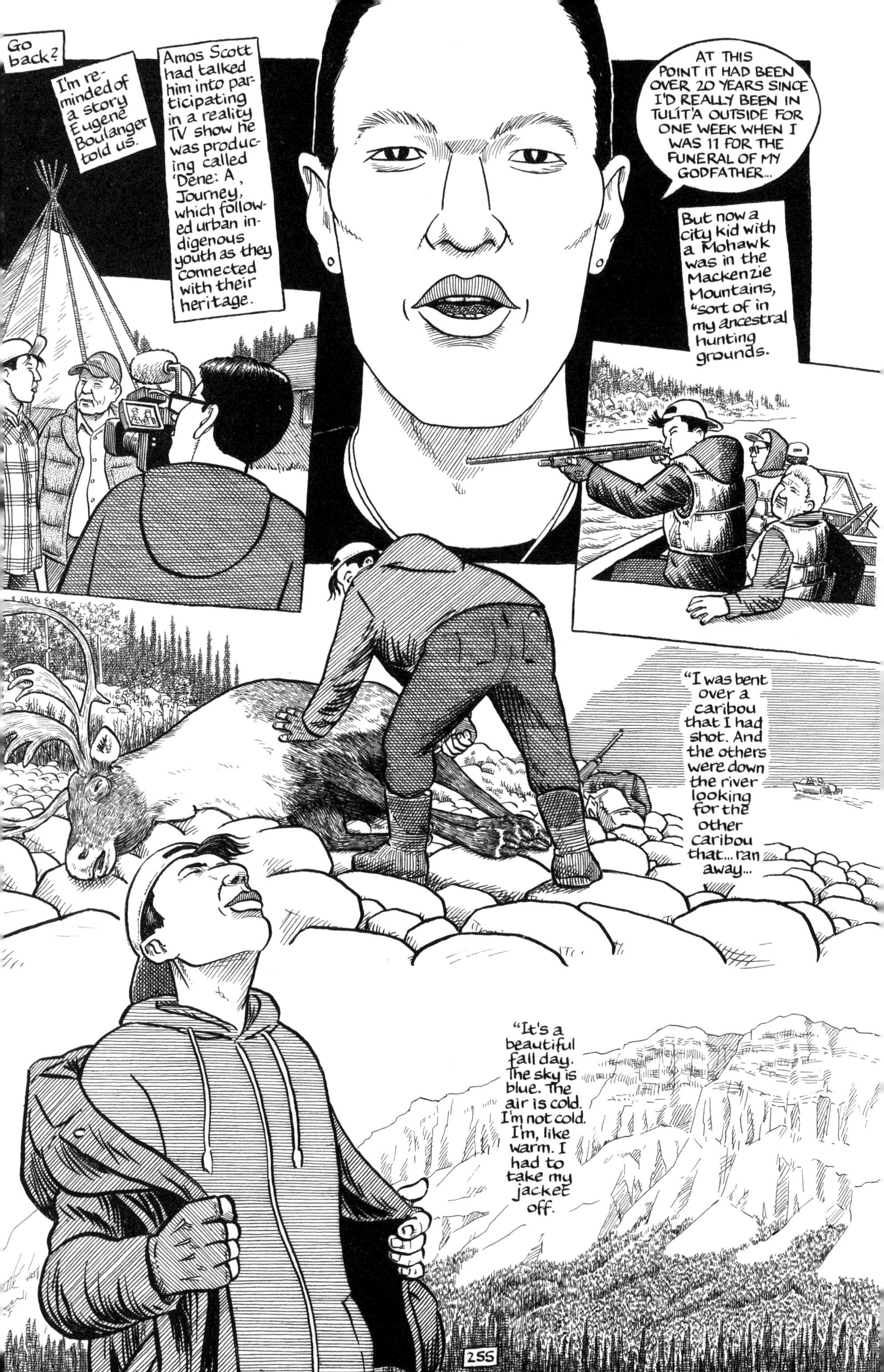
Go back?
I'm reminded of a story Eugene Boulanger told us.
Amos Scott had talked him into participating in a reality TV show he was producing called 'Dene: A Journey,' which followed urban indigenous youth as they connected with their heritage.
AT THIS POINT IT HAD BEEN OVER 20 YEARS SINCE I'D REALLY BEEN IN TULÍT'A OUTSIDE FOR ONE WEEK WHEN I WAS 11 FOR THE FUNERAL OF MY GODFATHER...
But now a city kid with a Mohawk was in the Mackenzie Mountains, "sort of in my ancestral hunting grounds.
"I was bent over a caribou that I had shot. And the others were down the river looking for the other caribou that... ran away...
"It's a beautiful fall day. The sky is blue. The air is cold. I'm not cold. I'm, like warm. I had to take my jacket off.

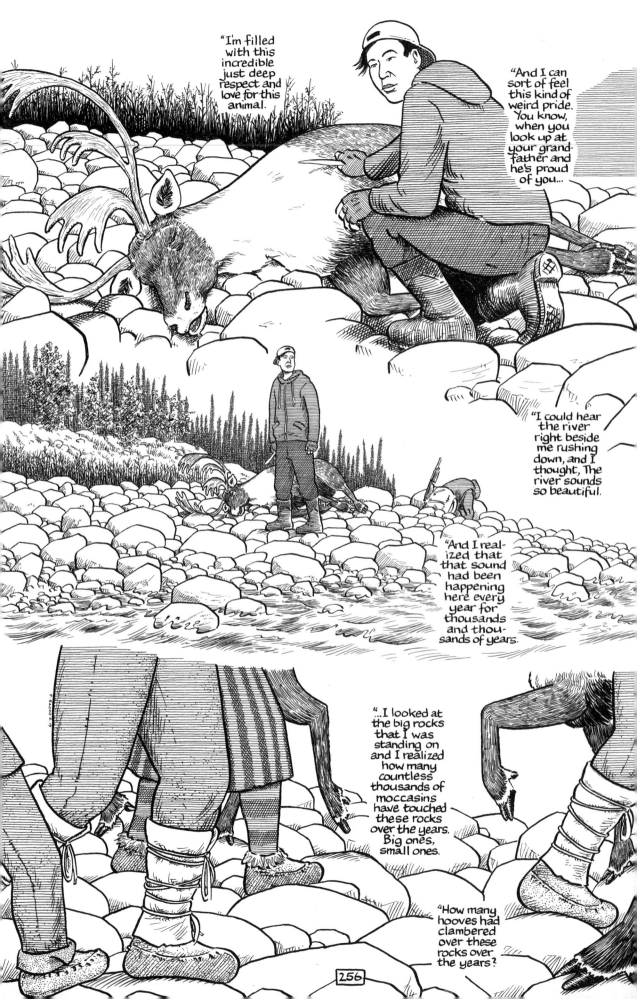

"I'm filled with this incredible just deep respect and love for this animal.

"And I can sort of feel this kind of weird pride. You know, when you look up at your grandfather and he's proud of you...

"I could hear the river right beside me rushing down, and I thought, The river sounds so beautiful.

"And I realized that that sound had been happening here every year for thousands and thousands of years.

"...I looked at the big rocks that I was standing on and I realized how many countless thousands of moccasins have touched these rocks over the years. Big ones, small ones.

"How many hooves had clambered over these rocks over the years?

256

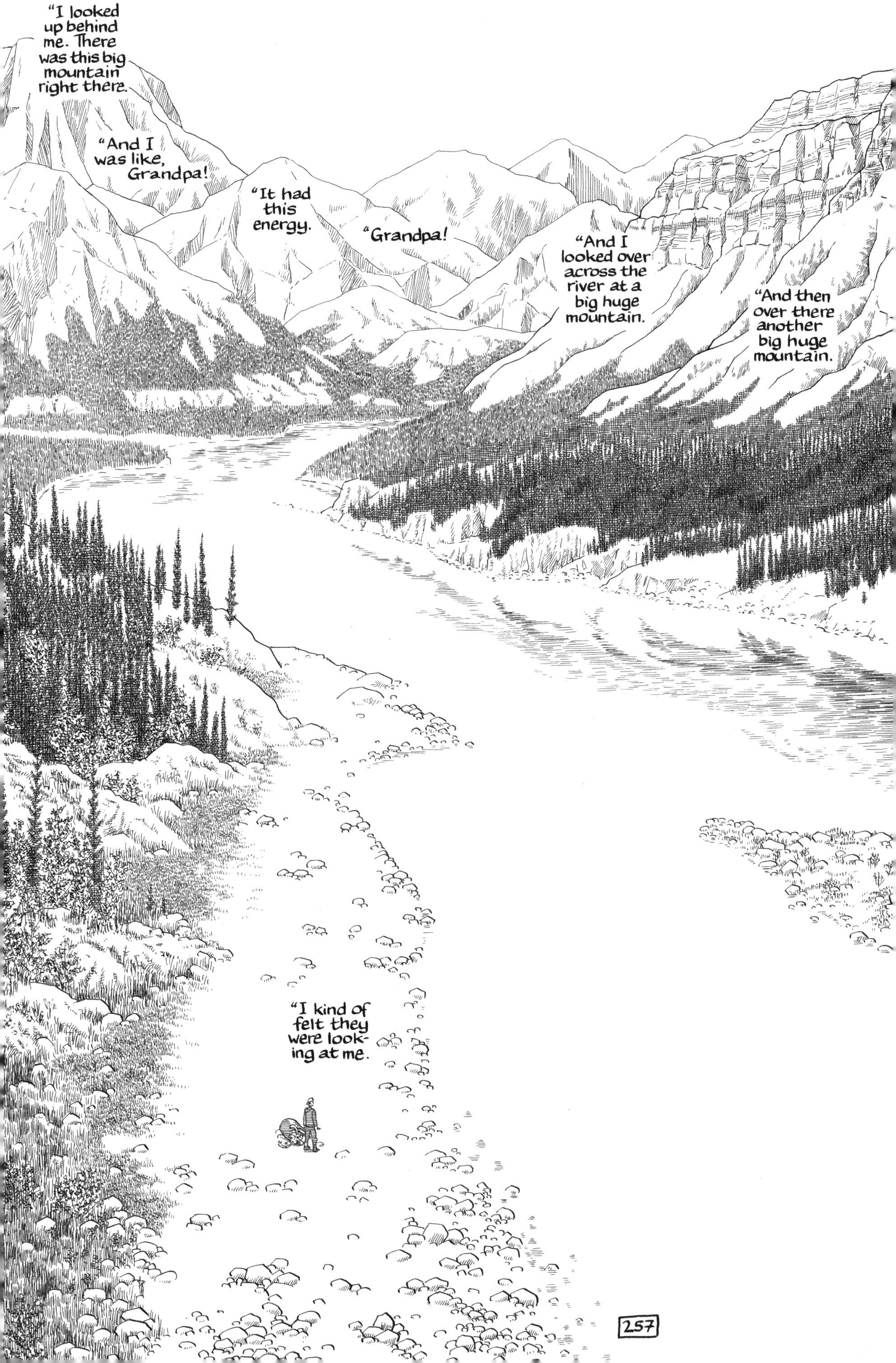
"I looked up behind me. There was this big mountain right there.
"And I was like, Grandpa!
"It had this energy.
"Grandpa!
"And I looked over across the river at a big huge mountain.
"And then over there another big huge mountain.
"I kind of felt they were looking at me.

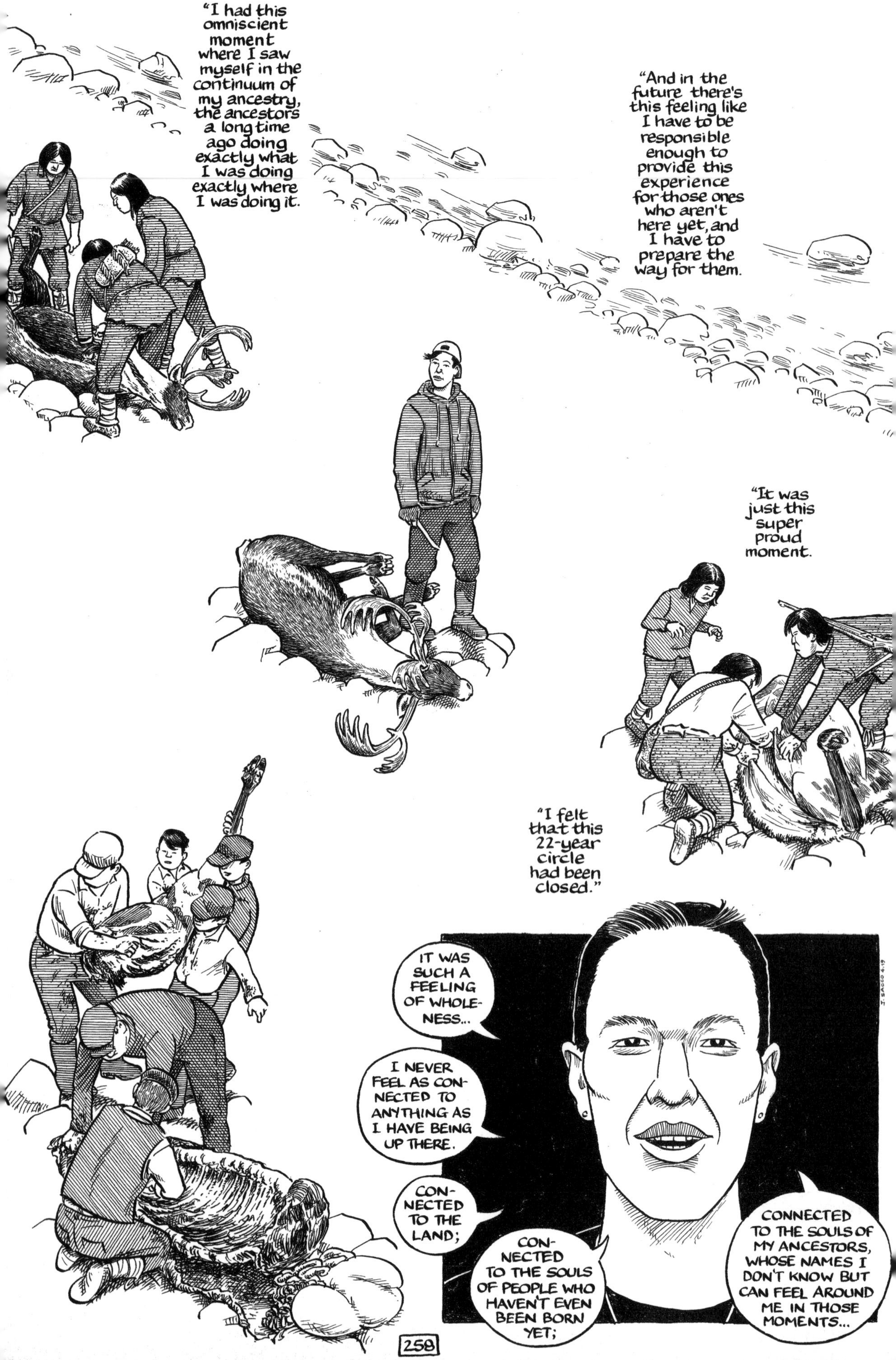
"I had this omniscient moment where I saw myself in the continuum of my ancestry, the ancestors a long time ago doing exactly what I was doing exactly where I was doing it.
"And in the future there's this feeling like I have to be responsible enough to provide this experience for those ones who aren't here yet, and I have to prepare the way for them.
"It was just this super proud moment.
"I felt that this 22-year circle had been closed."
IT WAS SUCH A FEELING OF WHOLENESS...
I NEVER FEEL AS CONNECTED TO ANYTHING AS I HAVE BEING UP THERE.
CONNECTED TO THE LAND;
CONNECTED TO THE SOULS OF PEOPLE WHO HAVEN'T EVEN BEEN BORN YET;
CONNECTED TO THE SOULS OF MY ANCESTORS, WHOSE NAMES I DON'T KNOW BUT CAN FEEL AROUND ME IN THOSE MOMENTS...

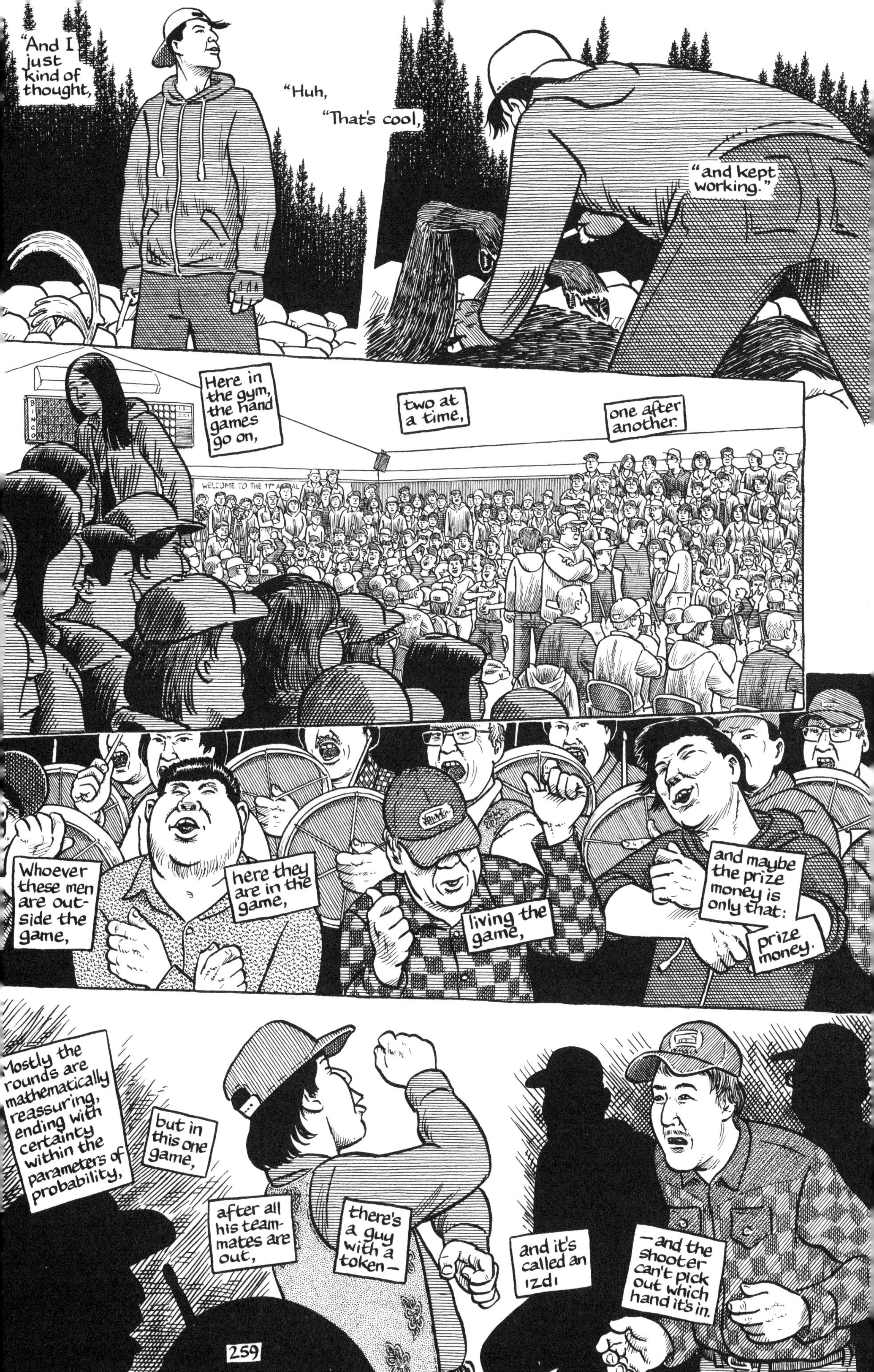
"And I just kind of thought,
"Huh,
"That's cool,
"and kept working."
Here in the gym, the hand games go on,
two at a time,
one after another.
WELCOME TO THE 11TH ANNUAL
Whoever these men are outside the game,
here they are in the game,
living the game,
and maybe the prize money is only that:
prize money.
Mostly the rounds are mathematically reassuring, ending with certainty within the parameters of probability,
but in this one game,
after all his teammates are out,
there's a guy with a token—
and it's called an izdi
—and the shooter can't pick out which hand it's in.

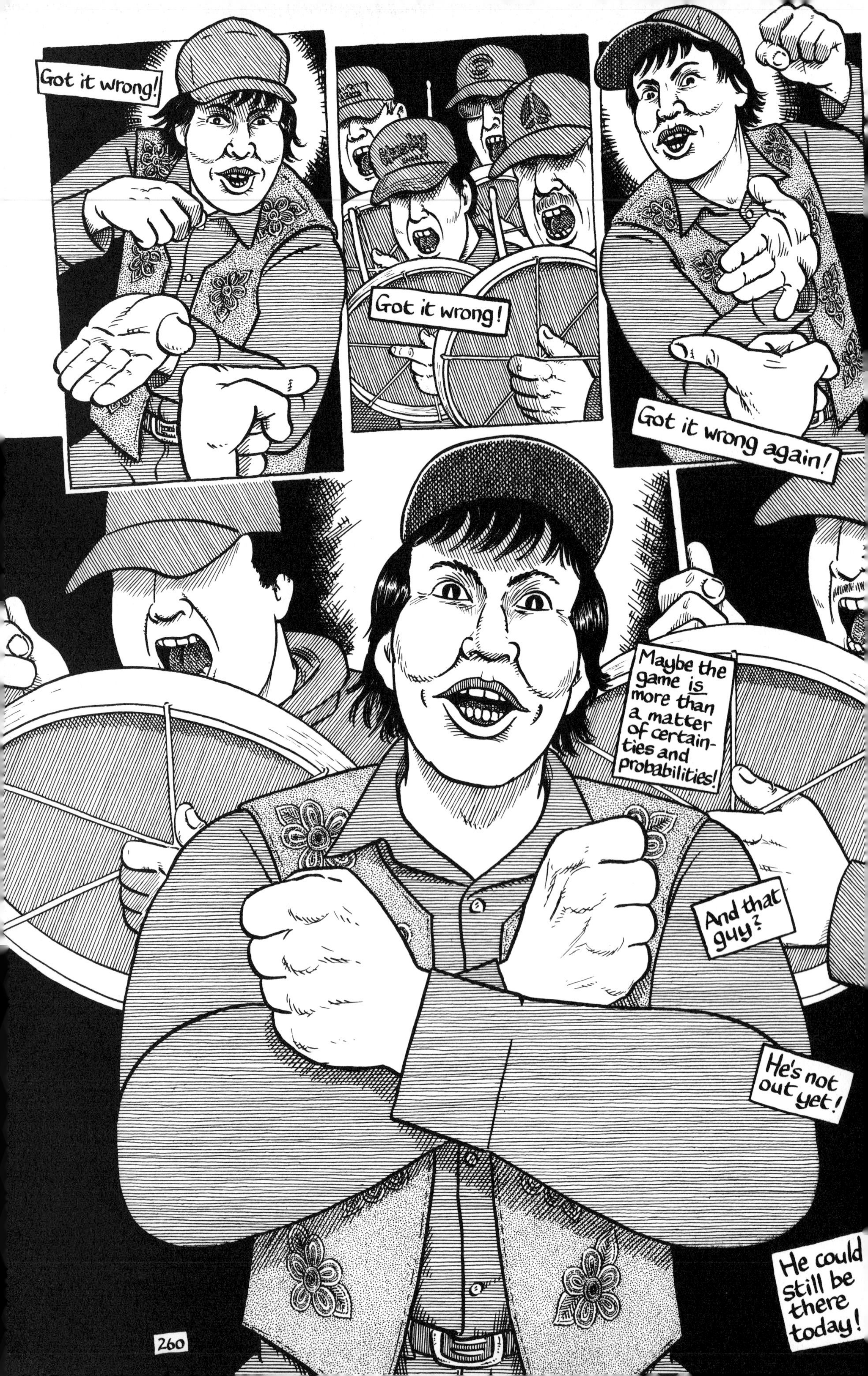
Got it wrong!
Got it wrong!
Got it wrong again!
Maybe the game is more than a matter of certainties and probabilities!
And that guy?
He's not out yet!
He could still be there today!

NOTES ON DENE LANGUAGES

The Dene languages of the Northwest Territories are part of a larger language family called Athabascan which extends down to northern Mexico. I have endeavored to use Dene place names whenever possible and these and a few Dene-language words are sprinkled throughout the text. The written Dene languages are still evolving. In the absence of standard/universal/regularized spellings, Dene words are rendered in the International Phonetic Alphabet and with the most up-to-date spelling.

The main Dene languages referenced are listed below, along with websites that provide more information for those who are interested.

The Shúhtaot'įnę (Mountain Dene) of Tulít'a speak a dialect of the Sahtú region's Dene language, known to linguists as North Slavey. Three North Slavey dialect dictionaries, including one for Tulít'a, can be found at:

http://www.sahtudec.ca/view.php?action=documents&id=63.

The Dene language of the Dehcho region, known by linguists as South Slavey, is used in Trout Lake (now called Sambaa K'e), Fort Liard, and Fort Simpson. A dictionary for one of its dialects, Katłodeeche Dene Zhatıe, can be found at:

http://www.ssdec.nt.ca/Dictionary/.

The Dene language in the Tłįchǫ region, known by linguists as Dogrib, is used in Behchokǫ̀. A dictionary for one of the Tłįchǫ dialects, Tłįchǫ Yatıì, can be found at:

http://tlicho.ling.uvic.ca/default.aspx?AspxAutoDetectCookieSupport=1.

More information about the Dene language of the Gwich'in, including audio samples, can be found at:

https://www.gwichin.ca/how-we-speak.

NOTE ON TROUT LAKE

I have used the name Trout Lake as that is how the settlement was referred to in conversation at the time of my visit. In June 2016, the place name was officially changed to Sambaa K'e, which means "place of trout" in South Slavey.

ACKNOWLEDGMENTS

As always, a project like this, with one person's name on it, has a long list of behind-the-scenes contributors and participants who deserve thanks and credit.

Shauna Morgan is responsible for this book happening, though not for any mistakes, which are mine alone. She had tried to organize a talk by me in Yellowknife and told me that if I visited she would introduce me to some of the local issues related to the Dene and their environment. I couldn't make it, but about three years later, when I first began thinking of exploring how resource extraction intersects with indigenous people, I looked her up, we wrote back and forth, and quite quickly the framework of a visit to the Northwest Territories began to take shape. She planned our trips according to my interests, set up numerous interviews, and acted as my guide and driver. More than that, she was a good-humored comrade, someone with whom I could bounce off ideas on the long drives between communities. She is currently on the Yellowknife City Council, and if you live in Yellowknife and ever have a chance to vote for her, please do!

While I was in Yellowknife, Kris Schlagintweit and Helen Bowen kindly let me stay at their warm and lovely home. I very much enjoyed their dinners and our many relaxed conversations.

In Tulít'a, Shauna and I stayed with Deborah Simmons and her roommates at the time, Jean Polfus and Joe Hanlon, who, too, were wonderful hosts. Deborah was very helpful introducing me to decolonization theory, answering my questions about Dene languages, and passing along my images to indigenous people to check on details. Jean shared many of her splendid photos that helped me understand some of the finer aspects of caribou hunting.

Patrick Scott, whose knowledge of the politics of the Northwest Territories is enormous, very kindly helped me fine-tune the intricate passages about the complicated land-claims debates. He was a great and good-humored resource over the years, and he was never anything but generous with his time and knowledge.

Peter Redvers looked over the passages related to the land dispute between Trout Lake (with Nahanni Butte) and Fort Liard to make sure nothing essential was lost as I tried to boil down the episode.

Terry Woolf gave me a ride with his dog team, which was one of the most delightful experiences I had in the Northwest Territories.

Jim Antoine, besides sitting down with me twice for extensive interviews about his experiences with the Indian Brotherhood, the Dene Nation, the Berger Inquiry, and his tenure in the legislative assembly and as premier of the Northwest Territories, made an herbal tea from scratch for me to alleviate a very bad cold I suffered.

This book wouldn't be half of what it is without the kindness, help, and patience of Dolphus Jumbo, chief of Trout Lake (now Sambaa K'e), who gave his time to Shauna and me when we visited his lovely community. Meeting Dolphus is what made me decide to turn what was ostensibly a two-part magazine piece into a book. On our second trip, Dolphus opened up his house and gave us a place to sleep.

Paul Andrew, Valerie Conrad, Willard Hagen, David and Theresa Etchinelle, Frederick Andrew, and Stephen Kakfwi all answered additional questions over the years. Morris Modeste looked over the pages on bush life and helped me correct some of my drawn mistakes.

I thank all my interview subjects in general. People told me difficult stories about difficult times or intimate stories about their connection to the land, and they simply trusted that I would use what they said in the right way, mostly so others might learn from their experiences and knowledge. It was a privilege to be let into the lives of the Dene even in a small way. As they say there, Mahsi.

Thanks to my chiropractor, Dr. Heidi, without whom I don't think I could have sat at a desk these last four years.

Thanks to Patrick de Saint-Exupéry, who commissioned me to do a sixty-page comic about the Northwest Territories for the French long-form narrative magazine *XXI* and encouraged me along the way.

Thanks as always to my incomparable agent, Nicole Aragi, and my amazing editor, Riva Hocherman, who hammered this book into a better shape than it was when I first turned it in.

And thanks to Amalie for everything else and for all the things that don't have words.